Seventh Edition

BUSINESS FINANCE
Theory and Practice

Eddie McLaney

University of Plymouth Business School

FT Prentice Hall

FINANCIAL TIMES

An imprint of **Pearson Education**

Harlow, England • London • New York • Boston • San Francisco • Toronto • Sydney • Singapore • Hong Kong
Tokyo • Seoul • Taipei • New Delhi • Cape Town • Madrid • Mexico City • Amsterdam • Munich • Paris • Milan

Pearson Education Limited

Edinburgh Gate
Harlow
Essex CM20 2JE
England

and Associated Companies throughout the world

Visit us on the World Wide Web at:
www.pearsoned.co.uk

First published 1986	Macdonald & Evans Limited
Second edition published 1991	Published as *Business Finance for Decision Makers*
	by Pitman Publishing, a division of Longman Group UK Ltd
Third edition published 1994	Published as *Business Finance for Decision Makers*
	by Pitman Publishing, a division of Longman Group UK Ltd
Fourth edition published 1997	Pitman Publishing, a division of Pearson Professional Limited
Fifth edition published 2000	Pearson Education Ltd
Sixth edition published 2003	Pearson Education Ltd
Seventh edition published 2006	**Pearson Education Limited**

ISBN-10 0-273-70262-9
ISBN-13 978-0-273-70262-7

British Library Cataloguing-in-Publication Data
A catalogue record for this book is available from the British Library

Library of Congress Cataloging-in-Publication Data
A catalog record for this book is available from the Library of Congress

10 9 8 7 6 5 4 3 2 1
08 07 06

Typeset in 9.5/13pt Palatino by 35
Printed and bound by Mateu-Cromo Artes Graficas, Madrid, Spain

The publisher's policy is to use paper manufactured from sustainable forests.

BUSINESS FINANCE
Theory and Practice

Visit the *Business Finance*, seventh edition, Companion Website at
www.pearsoned.co.uk/atrillmclaney to find valuable **student** learning
material including:

→ **Learning outcomes** for each chapter.

→ **Multiple choice questions** to test your learning.

→ **Extensive links** to valuable resources on the web.

→ An **online glossary** to explain key terms.

PEARSON
Education

We work with leading authors to develop the strongest
educational materials in business and finance, bringing
cutting-edge thinking and best learning practice to a
global market.

Under a range of well-known imprints, including
Financial Times Prentice Hall, we craft high quality print
and electronic publications which help readers to
understand and apply their content, whether studying
or at work.

To find out more about the complete range of our
publishing, please visit us on the World Wide Web at:
www.pearsoned.co.uk

Contents

Part 1 The business finance environment

1 Introduction   3

2 A framework for financial decision making   17

Part 3 Financing decisions

Part 4 Integrated decisions

Objectives Bullet points at the start of each chapter show what you can expect to learn from that chapter, and highlight the core coverage.

Key terms The key concepts and techniques in each chapter are highlighted in colour where they are first introduced, with an adjacent icon in the margin to help you refer back to the most important points.

Bullet point chapter summary Each chapter ends with a 'bullet point' summary. This highlights the material covered in the chapter and can be used as a quick reminder of the main issues.

Examples At frequent intervals throughout most chapters, there are examples that pose a problem and provide step-by-step workings to follow through to the solution.

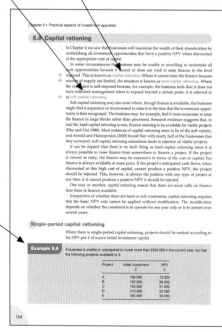

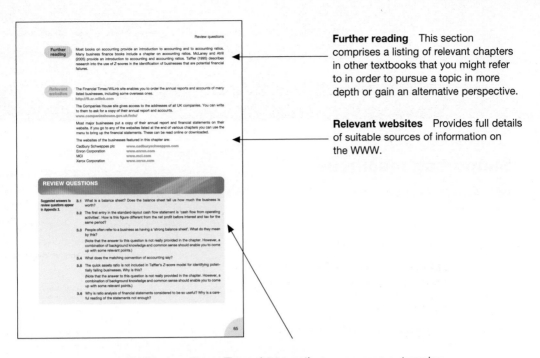

Further reading This section comprises a listing of relevant chapters in other textbooks that you might refer to in order to pursue a topic in more depth or gain an alternative perspective.

Relevant websites Provides full details of suitable sources of information on the WWW.

Review questions These short questions encourage you to review and/or critically discuss your understanding of the main topics covered in each chapter, either individually or in a group. Solutions to these questions can be found on the Companion Website at **www.pearsoned.co.uk/atrillmclaney**

Problems Towards the end of most chapters you will encounter these questions, allowing you to check your understanding and progress. Solutions are provided in Appendix 4.

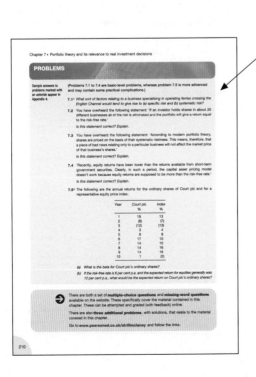

Supporting resources

Visit **www.pearsoned.co.uk/atrillmclaney** to find valuable online resources:

Companion Website for students

→ Learning outcomes for each chapter.

→ Multiple choice questions to test your learning.

→ Extensive links to valuable resources on the web.

→ An online glossary to explain key terms.

For instructors

→ Complete, downloadable Instructor's Manual.

→ PowerPoint slides that can be downloaded and used as OHTs.

→ Tutorial/seminar questions and solutions.

→ Additional Case studies and suggested solutions.

Also: The Companion Website provides the following features:

→ Search tool to help locate specific items of content.

→ E-mail results and profile tools to send results of quizzes to instructors.

→ Online help and support to assist with website usage and trouble-shooting.

For more information please contact your local Pearson Education sales representative or visit **www.pearsoned.co.uk/atrillmclaney**

This book attempts to deal with financing and investment decision making, with particular focus on the private sector of the UK economy. Its approach is to set out the theories that surround each area of financial decision making and relate these to what appears to happen in practice. Where theory and practice diverge, the book tries to reconcile and explain the differences. It also attempts to assess the practical usefulness of some of the theories that do not seem to be applied widely in practice.

Although the focus of the book is on the UK private sector, the theories and practices examined are, for the main part, equally valid in the context of the private sector of all the world's countries. Also, much of the content of the book is relevant to many parts of the public sector, both in the UK and overseas.

Most of the organisations to which the subject matter of this book relates will be limited companies or groups of companies, though some may be partnerships, cooperatives or other forms. For simplicity, the word 'business' has been used as a general term for a business entity, referring to specific legal forms only where the issue under discussion relates specifically to a particular form.

The book attempts to make the subject as accessible as possible to readers coming to business finance for the first time. In doing this, unnecessarily technical language has been avoided as much as possible, and the issues are described in a narrative form as well as in more formal statements. The more technical terms are highlighted in blue when they are first mentioned and these are included in the glossary at the end of the book. Detailed proofs of theoretical propositions have generally been placed in appendices to the relevant chapters. Readers should not take this to mean that these proofs are particularly difficult to follow. The objective was to make the book as readable as possible, and it was felt that sometimes formal proofs can disturb the flow if they are included in the main body of the text.

Although the topics in the book are interrelated, the book has been divided into sections. Chapters 1 to 3 are concerned with setting the scene, Chapters 4 to 7 with investment decisions, and Chapters 8 to 12 with financing decision areas, leaving Chapters 13 to 16 to deal with hybrid matters.

Some reviewers have made the point that the subject of the existing Chapter 9 (capital market efficiency) pervades all aspects of business finance and should, therefore, be dealt with in an introductory chapter. After some consideration it was decided to retain the same chapter order as in the previous editions. The logic for this is that a complete understanding of capital market efficiency requires knowledge that does not appear until Chapter 8. A very brief introduction to capital market efficiency appears at the beginning of Chapter 7, which is the first chapter in which capital market efficiency needs to be specifically referred to. It is felt that the chapter ordering provides a reasonable compromise and one that makes life as straightforward as possible for the reader.

In making revisions for this seventh edition, the opportunity has been taken to make the book more readable and understandable. Most of the practical examples have been updated and expanded. Where possible, examples of practice in particular businesses are given. This should make the book more focused on the real business world. More recent research evidence has been included. The opportunity has also been taken to include an introduction to the subjects of corporate governance, creative accounting and bond rating.

Nothing in this book requires any great mathematical ability on the part of the reader. Although not essential, some basic understanding of correlation, statistical probabilities and differential calculus would be helpful. Any reader who feels that it might be necessary to brush up on these topics could refer to Bancroft and O'Sullivan (2000). This reference and each of the others given in the chapters are listed alphabetically towards the end of the book.

At the end of each chapter there are six review questions. These are designed to enable readers to assess how well they can recall key points from the chapter. Suggested answers to these are contained in Appendix 3, at the end of the book. Also at the end of most chapters are up to nine problems. These are questions designed to test readers' understanding of the contents of the chapters and to give some practice in working through questions. The problems are graded either as 'basic', that is, fairly straightforward questions, or as 'more advanced', that is, they may contain a few practical complications. Those problems marked with an asterisk (about half of the total) have suggested answers in Appendix 4 at the end of the book. Suggested answers to the remaining problems are contained in the Instructor's Manual, which is available as an accompaniment to this text.

The book is directed at those who are studying business finance as part of an undergraduate course, for example a degree or Higher National Diploma in business studies. It is also directed at postgraduate, post-experience students who are either following a university course or seeking a qualification such as the Certified Diploma in Accounting and Finance. It should also prove useful to those studying for the professional examinations of the accounting bodies.

Eddie McLaney
September 2005

Plan of the book

Part 1 The business finance environment

Chapter 1 Introduction	**Chapter 2** A framework for financial decision making	**Chapter 3** Financial (accounting) statements and their interpretation

Part 2 Investment decisions

Chapter 4 Investment appraisal methods	**Chapter 5** Practical aspects of investment appraisal	**Chapter 6** Risk in investment appraisal	**Chapter 7** Portfolio theory and its relevance to real investment decisions

Part 3 Financing decisions

Chapter 8 Sources of long-term finance	**Chapter 9** The secondary capital market (the stock exchange) and its efficiency	**Chapter 10** Cost of capital estimations and the discount rate	**Chapter 11** Gearing, the cost of capital and shareholders' wealth	**Chapter 12** The dividend decision

Part 4 Integrated decisions

Chapter 13 Management of working capital	**Chapter 14** Corporate restructuring (including takeovers and divestments)	**Chapter 15** International aspects of business finance	**Chapter 16** Small businesses

References	Appendices	Glossary	Index

PART 1

The business finance environment

Business finance is concerned with making decisions about which investments the business should make and how best to finance those investments. This part of the book attempts to explain the context in which those decisions are made. This is important in its own right, not just as an introduction to later parts of the book.

Chapter 1 explains the nature of business finance. It continues with some discussion of the framework of regulations in which most private sector businesses operate. Chapter 2 considers the decision-making process, with particular emphasis on the objectives pursued by businesses. It also considers the problem faced by managers where people, affected by a decision, have conflicting objectives. Chapter 3 provides an overview of the sources and nature of the information provided to financial decision makers by financial (accounting) statements prepared by businesses on a regular (annual/six-monthly) basis. As is explained in Chapter 1, business finance and accounting are distinctly different areas. Financial statements are, however, a very important source of information upon which to base financial decisions.

Chapter 1

Introduction

1.1 The role of business finance

Businesses may fairly be regarded as investment agencies or intermediaries. This is to say that their role is to raise money from members of the public, and from other investors, and to invest it. Usually, money will be obtained from the owners of the business (the shareholders) and from long-term lenders, with some short-term finance being provided by banks (perhaps in the form of overdrafts), other financial institutions and trade creditors.

Businesses typically invest in real assets such as land, buildings, plant and trading stocks, though they may also invest in financial assets, including making loans to, and buying shares in, other businesses. People are employed to manage the investments, that is, to do all those things necessary to create and sell the goods and services in the provision of which the business is engaged. Surpluses remaining after meeting the costs of operating the business – wages, raw material costs, and so forth – accrue to the investors.

Of crucial importance to the business will be decisions about the types and quantity of finance to raise, and the choice of investments to be made. Business finance is the study of how these financing and investment decisions should be made in theory, and how they are made in practice.

A practical subject

Business finance is a relatively new subject. Until the 1960s it consisted mostly of narrative accounts of decisions that had been made and how, if identifiable, those decisions had been reached. More recently, theories of business finance have emerged and been tested so that the subject now has a firmly based theoretical framework – a framework that stands up pretty well to testing with real-life events. In other words, the accepted theories that attempt to explain and predict actual outcomes in business finance broadly succeed in their aim.

Business finance draws from many disciplines. Financing and investment decision making relates closely to certain aspects of economics, accounting, law, quantitative methods and the behavioural sciences. Despite the fact that business finance draws what it finds most useful from other disciplines, it is nonetheless a subject in its own right. Business finance is vital to the business.

Decisions on financing and investment go right to the heart of the business and its success or failure. This is because:

- such decisions often involve financial amounts that are very significant to the business concerned;

- once made, such decisions are not easy to reverse, so the business is typically committed in the long term to a particular type of finance or to a particular investment.

Although modern business finance practice relies heavily on sound theory, we must be very clear that business finance is an intensely practical subject, which is concerned with real-world, practical, decision making.

1.2 Risk and business finance

All decision making involves the future. We can only make decisions about the future; no matter how much we may regret it, we cannot alter the past. Financial decision making is no exception to this general rule.

There is only one thing certain about the future, which is that we cannot be sure what is going to happen. Sometimes we may be able to predict with confidence that what will occur will be one of a limited range of possibilities. We may even feel able to ascribe statistical probabilities to the likelihood of occurrence of each possible

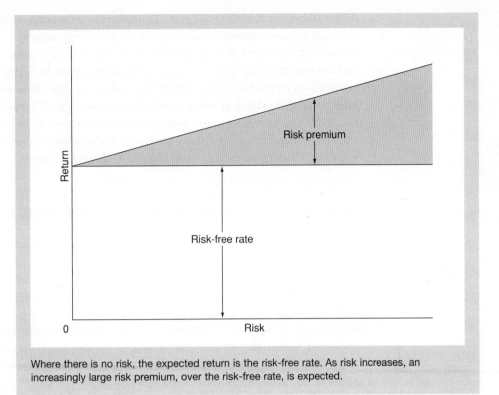

Figure 1.1
Relationship
between risk
and return

Where there is no risk, the expected return is the risk-free rate. As risk increases, an increasingly large risk premium, over the risk-free rate, is expected.

outcome; but we can never be completely certain of the future. **Risk** is therefore an important factor in all financial decision making, and one that must be considered explicitly in all cases.

In business finance, as in other aspects of life, risk and return tend to be related. Intuitively we expect returns to relate to risk in something like the way shown in Figure 1.1.

In investment, for example, people require a minimum rate to induce them to invest at all, but they require an increased rate of return – the addition of a risk premium – to compensate them for taking risk. We shall see in Chapter 7 that, when considering marketable stocks and shares, there does actually appear to be the linear relationship that Figure 1.1 suggests between levels of risk perceived and the returns that investors expect to receive. Much of business finance is concerned with striking the appropriate balance between risk and return.

1.3 The relationship between business finance and accounting

Business finance and accounting are not the same thing. Accounting is concerned with financial record keeping, the production of periodic reports, statements and analyses, and the dissemination of information to managers and, to some extent, to investors and the world outside the business. It is also much involved with the quality, relevance and timeliness of its information output. Obviously, financial decision makers will rely heavily on accounting reports and the accounting database generally. Knowledge of past events may well be a good pointer to the future, so reliable information on the past is invaluable. However, the role of the financial manager is not to provide financial information but to make decisions involving finance.

In smaller businesses, with narrow portfolios of management skills, the accountant and the financial manager may well be the same person. In a large business, the roles are likely to be discharged by different people or groups of people. Not surprisingly, many financial managers are accountants by training and background, but some are not. With the increasing importance of business finance in the curricula of business schools and in higher education generally, the tendency is probably towards more specialist financial managers, with their own career structure.

1.4 The organisation of businesses – the limited company

This book is primarily concerned with business finance as it affects businesses in the private sector of the UK economy. Most of our discussion will centre on larger businesses, that is, those that are listed on the secondary capital market (for example, the London Stock Exchange) and where there is fairly widespread ownership of the business among individual members of the public and the investing institutions (insurance companies, pension funds, unit trusts and so forth). Towards the end of the book (in Chapter 16), we shall take a look at the smaller, owner-managed businesses to see how the issues, discussed up to that point in the context of large businesses, apply to this important sector of the economy.

Irrespective of whether we are considering large or small businesses, virtually all of them will be limited companies. There are businesses in the UK – indeed, many of them – that are not limited companies. Most of these, however, are very small (one- or two-person enterprises), or are highly specialised professional service providers such as solicitors and accountants.

Since the limited company predominates in the UK private sector, we shall discuss business finance in this context. The principles of business finance that will emerge apply equally, however, irrespective of the precise legal status of the business concerned. The private sectors of virtually all of the countries in the world are dominated by businesses that are similar in nature to UK limited companies.

We now consider briefly the legal and administrative environment in which limited companies operate. The objective here is by no means to provide a detailed examination of the limited company; it is simply to outline its more significant features. More particularly, the aim is to explain in broad terms those aspects that impinge on business finance. A lack of a broad understanding of these aspects may make life difficult for us in later chapters.

What is a limited company?

A limited company is an artificially created legal person. It is an entity that is legally separate from all other persons including those who own and manage it. It is quite possible for a limited company to take legal action, say for breach of contract, against any other legal persons, including those who own and manage it. Actions between limited companies and their owners or managers do occur from time to time.

Obviously, an artificial person can only function through the intervention of human beings. Those who ultimately control the company are the owners who each hold one or more shares in the ownership or equity of it.

Limited liability

One of the results of the peculiar position of the company having its own separate legal identity is that the financial liability of the owners (shareholders) is limited to the amount that they have paid (or have pledged to pay) for their shares. If the company becomes insolvent (financial obligations exceed value of assets), its liability is, like that of any human legal person, limited only by the amount of its assets. It can be forced to pay over all of its assets to try to meet its liabilities, but no more. Since the company and the owners are legally separate, owners cannot be compelled to introduce further finance. An example of the effect of limited liability occurred in 2002 with the collapse of **ITV Digital plc**. This company was established as a joint venture by **Carlton** and **Granada**, two media businesses. ITV Digital failed as a result of the reluctance on the part of the public to subscribe for its broadcasts. When this happened, its shareholders, Carlton and Granada, were able to ignore the claims of the company's creditors, principally the Nationwide Football League clubs (members of the three divisions below the Premiership) with whom ITV Digital had a contract. This was because of the separate entity status of ITV Digital.

The position of a shareholder in this regard does not depend upon whether the shares were acquired by taking up an issue from the company or as a result of buying the shares from an existing shareholder.

Transferability

As a separate legal entity, the company does not depend on the identity of its shareholders for its existence. Transfer of shares by buying and selling or by gift is therefore possible. Thus a part, even all, of the company's ownership or equity can change hands without it necessarily having any effect on the business activity of the company.

Since the company can continue irrespective of precisely who the shareholders happen to be at any given moment, the company can in theory have a perpetual lifespan, unlike its human counterparts.

Formation of a limited company

Creating a new company is a very simple operation which can be carried out cheaply (from about £100) and with little effort on the part of the promoters.

Formation basically requires the promoters to make an application to a UK government official, the Registrar of Companies (Department of Trade and Industry). The application must be accompanied by several documents, the most important of which is a proposed set of rules or constitution for the company defining how it will be administered. These rules are contained in two documents known as the Memorandum of Association and the Articles of Association.

All of the documentation becomes public once the company has been formally registered. A file is opened at Companies House in Cardiff, on which are placed the various documents; the file is constantly available for examination by any member of the public who wishes to see it.

Recognition of companies

Limited companies are required to use the words 'Limited' (Ltd) or 'Public Limited Company' (plc) after their name in all formal documentation to warn those dealing with the company that its members' liability is limited.

'Limited' is used by private limited companies. These are basically the smaller, family-type companies, which have certain rights on the restriction of transfer of their shares. Public companies are typically the larger companies with more widespread share ownership.

Shareholders and directors

The shareholders (or members, as they are often known) are the owners of the company: profits and gains accrue to them, and losses are borne by them up to a maximum of the amount of their investment in the company. The shareholders, at any particular time, need not be the original shareholders, that is, those who first owned the shares. Transfers by sale or gift (including legacy on death) lead to shares changing hands.

For a variety of sound practical reasons, the day-to-day management of the company is delegated by the shareholders to directors. The directors may or may not themselves own some shares in the company. Shareholders elect directors in much the same way as citizens elect Members of Parliament in a parliamentary democracy. They also fail to re-elect them if the directors' performance is judged by shareholders to be unsatisfactory. Usually, one-third of the directors retire from office each year, frequently offering themselves for re-election. Typically, each shareholder has one vote for each share owned. Where a company has a large number of shareholders, a particular individual holding a large number of shares, even though not a majority of them, can wield tremendous power. The board of directors is the company's top level of management, therefore owning enough shares to control the board's composition is substantially to control the company.

Accountability of directors

The law imposes a duty on directors to report annually, both to the shareholders and, to some extent, to the world at large, on the performance of the company's trading and on its financial position.

Each year, directors are required to prepare (or to have prepared on their behalf) a report for the shareholders. The minimum contents of the report are prescribed by International Accounting Standards, which have the weight of UK law. In practice this minimum content is often exceeded. The report consists principally of a profit and loss account, a balance sheet and a cash flow statement. These financial statements are subject to audit by an independent firm of accountants, whose main role is to express an opinion on the truth and fairness of the view shown by the financial statements. The auditor's expression of opinion is attached to the annual report.

A copy of the report (containing the financial statements) must be sent to each shareholder. A copy must also be sent to the Registrar of Companies for insertion on the company's file in Cardiff. This file must be available for inspection by anyone wishing to do so. In practice, large companies also send copies of the report to financial analysts and journalists. They will usually comply with a request from any private individual for a copy. Virtually all major companies place a copy of their annual report on their website.

The annual report is a major, but not the only, source of information for interested parties, including existing and prospective shareholders, on the progress of the company. Companies whose shares are listed (that is, eligible to be bought and sold) on the Stock Exchange are required by its rules to publish summarised accounting statements each half-year (also usually available on the companies' websites). In practice, most large companies, from time to time, issue information over and above that which is contained in the annual and half-yearly reports.

The nature of the financial statements and how those statements can be interpreted are discussed in Chapter 3.

1.5 Corporate governance and the role of directors

In recent years, the issue of corporate governance has generated much debate. The term is used to describe the ways that companies are directed and controlled. The issue of corporate governance is important because, with companies of any size, those who own the company (the shareholders) are usually divorced from the day-to-day control of the business. The shareholders employ the directors to manage the company for them. Given this position, it may seem reasonable to assume that the best interests of shareholders will guide the directors' decisions. However, in practice this does not always occur. The directors may be more concerned with pursuing their own interests, such as increasing their pay and 'perks' (such as expensive motor cars, overseas visits and so on) and improving their job security and status. As a result, a conflict can occur between the interests of shareholders and the interests of directors.

Where directors pursue their own interests at the expense of the shareholders, it is clearly a problem for the shareholders. It may also be a problem for society as a whole, however. If shareholders feel that their funds are likely to be mismanaged, they will be reluctant to invest. A shortage of funds will mean fewer investments can be made and the cost of funds will increase as businesses compete for what funds are available. Thus, a lack of concern for shareholders can have a profound effect on the performance of the economy. To avoid these problems, most competitive market economies have a framework of rules to help monitor and control the behaviour of directors.

These rules are usually based around three guiding principles:

- *Disclosure*. This lies at the heart of good corporate governance. A report from the Organisation for Economic Co-operation and Development (OECD 1998) summed up the benefits of disclosure as follows:

  > Adequate and timely information about corporate performance enables investors to make informed buy-and-sell decisions and thereby helps the market reflect the value of a corporation under present management. If the market determines that present management is not performing, a decrease in stock (share) price will sanction management's failure and open the way to management change.

- *Accountability*. This involves defining the roles and duties of the directors and establishing an adequate monitoring process. In the UK, company law requires that directors of a business act in the best interests of shareholders. This means, among other things, that they must not try to use their position and knowledge to make gains at the expense of the shareholders. The law also requires larger companies to have their annual financial statements independently audited. The purpose of an independent audit is to lend credibility to the financial statements prepared by the directors.

- *Fairness*. Directors should not be able to benefit from access to 'inside' information that is not available to shareholders. As a result, both the law and the Stock Exchange place restrictions on the ability of directors to deal in the shares of the business. One example of these restrictions is that the directors cannot buy or sell shares immediately before the announcement of the final results of the business each year or before the announcement of a significant event such as a planned merger or the loss of the chief executive.

Strengthening the framework of rules

The number of rules designed to safeguard shareholders has increased considerably over the years. This has been in response to weaknesses in corporate governance procedures, which have been exposed through well-publicised business failures and frauds, excessive pay increases to directors and evidence that some financial reports were being 'massaged' so as to mislead shareholders. However, some believe that the shareholders must shoulder some of the blame for any weaknesses. Not all shareholders in large companies are private individuals owning just a few shares each. In fact, 80 per cent, by market value, of the shares listed on the London Stock Exchange are owned by the investing 'institutions', including insurance businesses and pension funds. These are often massive operations, owning large quantities of the shares of the companies in which they invest. The institutional investors employ specialist staff to manage their portfolios of shares. It is often argued that these large institutional shareholders, despite their size and relative expertise, are not very active in corporate governance matters, and that consequently there has been little monitoring of directors. However, things are changing.

The codes of practice

During the 1990s there was a real effort by the accountancy profession and the London Stock Exchange to address the problems mentioned above. A code of best practice on corporate governance emerged in 1992. This was concerned with accountability and financial reporting. In 1995, a separate code of practice emerged. This dealt with directors' pay and conditions. These two codes were revised, fine tuned and amalgamated to produce the Combined Code, which was issued in 1998.

The Combined Code was revised in 2003, following the recommendations of the Higgs Report. These recommendations were mainly concerned with the roles of the company chairman (senior director) and the other directors. It was particularly concerned with the role of 'non-executive' directors. These are directors who do not work full time in the company, but act solely in the role of director. This contrasts with 'executive' directors who are salaried employees. For example, the finance director of most large companies is a full-time employee. This person is a member of the board of directors and, as such, takes part in the key decision making at board level. At the same time, s/he is also responsible for managing the departments of the company that act on those board decisions as far as finance is concerned.

The view reflected in the 2003 Combined Code is that executive directors can become too embroiled in the day-to-day management of the company to be able to take the broad view. It also reflects the view that, for executive directors, conflicts can arise between their own interests and those of the shareholders. The advantage of non-executive directors can be that they are much more independent of the company than their executive colleagues. Non-executive directors are remunerated by the company for their work, but this would normally form only a small proportion of their total income. This gives them an independence that the executive directors may not have. Non-executive directors are often senior managers in other businesses or people who have had good experience of such roles.

Both the 1998 and 2003 Combined Codes received the backing of the London Stock Exchange. This means that companies listed on the London Stock Exchange are expected to comply with the requirements of the Code or must give their shareholders good reason why they do not. Failure to do one or other of these can lead to the company's shares being suspended from listing. This is an important sanction against wayward directors.

An example of an improvement in corporate governance

English football clubs have been criticised for weaknesses in corporate governance surrounding transfers of players involving a transfer fee. Generally it has been felt that there has been a lack of transparency in this area, perhaps particularly with the payment of fees to the agents of the players concerned.

In its 2004 annual report, under the heading 'Corporate governance – player transactions', **Manchester United plc** reported: 'During the year the Board reviewed its processes surrounding transfers and wage negotiations.' It went on to say: 'we have increased our disclosures on player transfers and seek to set out new standards for the industry on transparency over these costs'.

Liquidation

A limited company, because it has separate existence from its shareholders, does not die when they do. The only way in which the company's demise can be brought about is by following the statutorily defined steps to liquidate (or wind up) the company. Liquidation involves appointing a liquidator to realise the company's assets, to pay the claimants and formally to lay the company to rest.

The initiative to liquidate the company usually comes from either:

- the shareholders, perhaps because the purpose for which the company was formed has been served; or
- the company's creditors (including loan creditors), where the company is failing to pay its debts. In these circumstances the objective is to stop the company from trading and to ensure that non-cash assets are sold, the proceeds being used to meet (perhaps only partially) the claims of the creditors. This type of liquidation is sometimes referred to colloquially as bankruptcy.

Order of paying claimants

Irrespective of which type of liquidation is involved, the liquidator, having realised all of the non-cash assets, must take great care as to the order in which the claimants are paid. Broadly speaking, the order is:

1 *Secured creditors.* Where the security is on a specified asset or group of assets, the proceeds of disposal of the asset are to be applied to meeting the specific claim. If the proceeds are insufficient, the secured creditors must stand with the unsecured creditors for the shortfall. If the proceeds exceed the amount of the claim, the excess goes into the fund available to unsecured creditors.

2 *Unsecured creditors.* This would usually include most trade creditors. It would also include any unsecured loan creditors.

In fact, ranking even before the secured creditors come claimants who have preferential rights. These include the Inland Revenue for the company's corporation tax liability (if any), and the employees for their wages or salary arrears.

Only after the creditors have been paid in full will the balance of the funds be paid out to the shareholders, each ordinary share commanding an equal slice of the funds remaining after the creditors and preference shareholders have had their entitlement.

The order of payment of creditors will be of little consequence except where there are insufficient funds to meet all claims. Where this is the case, each class of claim must be met in full before the next class may participate.

Although this summary of company regulation is set in a UK context, as was mentioned earlier, virtually all of the world's free enterprise economies have similar laws surrounding the way in which most businesses are organised.

1.6 Long-term financing of companies

Much of the semi-permanent finance of companies – in some cases (for example, **Next plc**, the retailer) all of it – is provided by shareholders. Many companies have different classes of shares. Most companies also borrow money on a long-term basis. (Many borrow finance on a short-term basis as well.) In later chapters we shall examine how and why companies issue more than one class of share and borrow money; here we confine ourselves to a brief overview of long-term corporate finance.

Ordinary shares

Ordinary shares are issued by the company to investors who are prepared to expose themselves to risk in order also to expose themselves to the expectation of high investment returns, which both intuition and the evidence, which we shall come across later in the book, tell us is associated with risk. Ordinary shares are frequently referred to as 'equities'. It is normal for companies to pay part of their realised profits, after tax, to the shareholders in the form of a cash dividend. The amount that each shareholder receives is linked directly to the number of shares he or she owns. The amount of each year's dividend is at the discretion of the directors.

Dividends are often portrayed as being the reward of the shareholders, in much the same way as a payment of interest is the reward of the loan creditor. This is, however, a dubious interpretation of the nature of dividends. All profits, whether paid as dividends or reinvested by the directors, belong to the shareholders. If funds generated from past profits are reinvested, they should have the effect of causing an increase in the value of the shares. This increase should be capable of being realised by shareholders who sell their shares. It remains the subject of vigorous debate as to whether reinvesting profits is as beneficial to the shareholders as paying them a dividend from the funds concerned. This debate is examined in Chapter 12.

As we have seen, if the company were to be closed down and liquidated (wound up), each equity holder would receive an appropriate share of the funds left after all other legitimate claimants had been satisfied in full.

Where shares are traded between investors, there is no reason why they should be priced according to their original issue price or according to their face value (nominal or par value). Perceptions of the value of a share in any particular company will change with varying expectations of economic circumstances, so that share prices will shift over time.

It should be noted that a shareholder selling shares in a particular company for some particular price has no direct financial effect on that company. The company will simply pay future dividends and give future voting rights to the new shareholder.

It is the ordinary shareholders who have the voting power within the company. Thus it is the equity holders who control the company.

Each ordinary share confers equal rights on its owner in terms of dividend entitlement, repayment on liquidation and voting power. Two shares carry exactly twice as much of these rights as does one share. The law forbids the directors from discriminating between the rights of different shareholders other than on the basis of the number of shares owned (assuming that the shares owned are of the same class). Ms X owning 100 shares in Z plc should have equal rights in respect of her shareholding to those of Mr Y who owns a similar number of shares in the same company. The Stock Exchange and other non-statutory agencies also seek to promote this equality.

Preference shares

→ **Preference shares** represent part of the risk-bearing ownership of the company, although they usually confer on their holders a right to receive the first slice of any dividend that is paid. There is an upper limit on the preference share dividend per share, which is usually defined as a percentage of the nominal value of the share. Preference share dividends are usually paid in full. Preference shares give more sure returns than equities, though they by no means provide certain returns. Preference shares do not usually confer voting rights nor do they usually give the same preference in repayment in a liquidation as they do in payment of dividends, though in some companies they do.

Preference shares of many companies are traded in the capital market. As with equities, prices of preference shares will vary with investors' perceptions of future prospects. Generally, preference share prices are less volatile than those of equities, as dividends tend to be fairly stable and usually have an upper limit.

For most companies, preference shares do not represent a major source of finance.

Loans

Most companies borrow funds on a long-term, occasionally on a perpetual, basis. Lenders enter into a contractual relationship with the company, with the rate of interest, its date of payment, the redemption date and amount all being terms of the contract. Many long-term lenders require rather more by way of security for their loan than the rights conferred on any lender under the law of contract. Typically they insist that the principal and sometimes the interest are secured on some specific asset of the borrowing company, frequently land. Such security might confer on lenders a right to seize the asset and sell it to satisfy their claims where repayment of principal or interest payment is overdue. Loan stocks (debentures) are, in the case of many companies, traded in the capital market. It is thus possible for someone owed £100 by X plc to sell this debt to another investor who, from the date of the sale, will become entitled to receive interest, and repayment of the principal in due course. Such payment amounts and dates are contractual obligations, so there is less doubt surrounding them than applies to dividends from shares, more particularly where the loan is secured. For this reason the market values of loan stocks tend to fluctuate even less than those of preference shares.

The relationship between the fixed return elements (preference shares and loan stocks), in the long-term financial structure, and the equity is usually referred to as capital or financial gearing ('leverage' in the USA). We shall consider in Chapter 11 the reasons why companies have capital gearing.

Broadly speaking, companies have a fair amount of power to issue and redeem ordinary shares, preference shares and loan stocks. Where redemption of shares is to be undertaken, the directors have a duty to take certain steps to safeguard the position of creditors, which might be threatened by significant amounts of assets being transferred to shareholders.

1.7 Derivatives

A striking development of business finance, and of other areas of commercial management, since around 1980 is the use of derivatives. Derivatives are assets or obligations whose value is dependent on some asset from which they are derived. In principle, any asset could be the subject of a derivative. In practice, assets such as *commodities* (for example, coffee, grain, copper) and *financial instruments* (for example, shares in companies, loans, foreign currency) are the ones that we tend to encounter as the basis of a derivative.

A straightforward example of a derivative is an option to buy or sell a specified asset, on a specified date or within a specified range of dates (the exercise date), for a specified price (the exercise price). For example, a UK exporter who has made a sale in euros and expects the cash to be received in two months' time, may buy the option to sell the euros for sterling at a price set now, but where delivery of the euros would not take place until receipt from the customer in two months' time. Note that this is a right to sell but not an obligation. Thus if the sterling value of a euro in two months' time is above the exercise price specified in the option contract, the exporter will ignore the option contract and sell the euros for sterling in the open market. Here the option will be worth nothing. On the other hand, if the sterling value of a euro in two month's time is below the option contract exercise price, the exporter will exercise its option and sell the euros to the seller of the option contract according to the terms of that contract. In this case the option will be worth, at the exercise date, the difference between what the exporter would receive under the option contract and the current market sterling value of those euros.

Why should the exporter want to enter into such an option contract? Who would sell the exporter such a contract and why? A UK business with a debt in a currency other than sterling is exposed to risk. The value of one currency, relative to that of another, tends to fluctuate according to supply and demand. Entering into the option contract eliminates risk as far as the exporter is concerned. In fact the risk is transferred to the other party (the 'counterparty') in the option contract. This is exactly the same principle as insurance. When we pay a premium to insure one of our possessions against theft, we are paying a counterparty (the insurance business) to bear the risk. If the object is not stolen we do not claim; if the sterling value of the euro turns out to be above the option contract exercise price, the exporter does not exercise the option. In both cases a sum has been paid to transfer the risk.

The exporter is under no obligation to transfer the risk; it can bear the risk itself and save the cost of buying the option. This is a commercial judgement.

The seller of the currency option (the counterparty) might well be a foreign exchange dealer or simply a business that grants currency options. This business enters into the option contract because it makes the commercial judgement, taking account of possible movements in the sterling/euro rate between the contract date and the exercise date, that the price it charges for the option is capable of yielding a reasonable profit. This is rather like the attitude taken by an insurance business when setting premiums.

Many types of derivative are concerned with transferring risk, but not all. Derivatives pervade many areas of business finance and we shall consider various derivatives, in context, at various stages in the book.

According to a 1997 survey of large UK businesses, 60 per cent of them use derivatives to some extent (Mallin, Ow-yong and Reynolds 2001). Smaller businesses tend to use derivatives less than larger ones.

Summary

Business finance

- Investment decisions.
- Financing decisions.
- Usually involving significant amounts.
- Risk always a major factor.
- Not the same as accounting.

Organisation of businesses

- Most UK businesses are limited companies.
- Artificial person, with separate legal personality.
- Enables investors to limit their losses on equity investments.
- Shares in the ownership of companies can be transferred.
- Cheap and easy to form a limited company.
- Managed by directors on behalf of shareholders.
- Duty of directors to account for their management of the shareholders' assets.
- Corporate governance has become a major issue; scandals have led to the emergence of the Combined Code.
- Limited companies can only come to an end through a formal liquidation (winding up).

Long-term financing

- Business are financed by:
  - ordinary shares;
  - preference shares; and
  - loans.

Derivatives

- Assets or obligations whose existence and value depends on some other asset or obligation from which they 'derive'.
- Usually concerned with risk management.
- Financial derivatives widely used in business.

Further reading

The role of business finance is discussed by Brealey and Myers (2002) and by Atrill (2006). Numerous books deal with the provisions of UK company law. Keenan and Riches (2004) outline the more important aspects.

Relevant websites

The Financial Times website gives access to current financial information and articles on various aspects of business and finance.
http://news.ft.com/home/uk

The Economist website gives access to current financial information and articles on various aspects of business and finance.
www.economist.com

The websites of the businesses featured in this chapter are:

Granada Media plc   www.granadamedia.com
Manchester United plc   www.manutd.com
Next plc   www.next.co.uk

The websites of businesses tend to be menu driven. They typically have a lot of information on the business's products as well as sections dealing with finance and accounting issues relevant to themselves, such as their annual financial statements. The sites often refer to the latter as 'shareholder' or 'corporate' information.

REVIEW QUESTIONS

Suggested answers to review questions appear in Appendix 3.

1.1 What factors seem likely to explain the popularity of the limited liability company as the legal form of so many UK businesses?

1.2 How does the position of a limited company compare with that of a human person regarding liability for commercial debts?

1.3 How does the position of a shareholder in a limited company differ from that of a sole trader?

1.4 'Preference shares and loan stocks are much the same.' Is this statement correct?

1.5 Why are many investment and financing decisions of particular importance to the business?

1.6 How are risk and return related, both in theory and in practice?

There are both a set of **multiple-choice questions** and **missing-word questions** available on the website. These specifically cover the material contained in this chapter. These can be attempted and graded (with feedback) online.

Go to **www.pearsoned.co.uk/atrillmclaney** and follow the links.

Chapter 2

A framework for financial decision making

Objectives

In this chapter we shall deal with the following:

→ the steps in financial decision making

→ the various objectives that, it has been suggested, might be followed by businesses

→ some evidence on objectives that UK businesses actually follow

→ some theoretical rules for financial decision making; the separation theorem

2.1 Financial decision making

Like any other decision-making area, financial decisions involve choices between two or more possible courses of action. If there is only one possible course of action, no decision is needed. Often, continuing with a situation that has existed until the time of the decision is one option open to the decision maker. All decision making should involve the following six steps.

Step 1: Define objectives

The decision maker should be clear what the outcome of the decision is intended to achieve. A person leaving home in the morning needs to make a decision on which way to turn into the road. To do this, it is necessary to know what the immediate objective is. If the objective is to get to work, it might require a decision to turn to the right; if it is a visit to the local shop, the decision might be to turn left. If our decision maker does not know the desired destination, it is impossible to make a sensible decision on which way to turn. Likely objectives of businesses will be considered later in this chapter.

Step 2: Identify possible courses of action

The available courses of action should be recognised. In doing this, consideration should be given to any restrictions on freedom of action imposed by law or other forces not within the control of the decision maker.

Good decision making requires that the horizon should constantly be surveyed for opportunities that will better enable the objectives to be achieved. In the business finance context, this includes spotting new investment opportunities and the means to finance them. Such opportunities will not often make themselves obvious, and businesses need to be searching for them constantly. A business failing to do so will almost certainly be heading into decline, and opportunities will be lost to its more innovative competitors.

Step 3: Assemble data relevant to the decision

Each possible course of action must be reviewed and the relevant data identified. Not all data on a particular course of action are relevant. Suppose that a person wishes to buy a car of a particular engine size, the only objective being to get the one with the best trade-off between reliability and cost. Only data related to reliability and cost of the cars available will be of any interest to that person. Other information, such as colour, design or country of manufacture, is irrelevant. That is not to say that a car buyer's objectives should be restricted to considerations of cost and reliability, simply that, if they are in a particular case, then other factors become irrelevant.

Even some data that bear directly on running cost, such as road tax, should be ignored if they are common to all cars of the engine size concerned. As decisions involve selecting from options, it is on the basis of differences between options that the decision can sensibly be made. If the decision were between owning or not owning a car, then road tax would become relevant as it is one of the costs of car ownership. It will not be incurred if the car is not bought. If common factors are irrelevant to decision making, then past costs must be irrelevant, since they must be the same for all possible courses of action.

Example 2.1	**Relevant and irrelevant costs**

Tariq Ltd is a business that owns a machine that cost £5000 when it was bought new a year ago. Now the business finds that it has no further use for the machine. Enquiries reveal that it could be sold in its present state for £2000, or it could be modified at a cost of £500 and sold for £3000.

Assuming that the objective of the business is to make as much money as possible, what should it do, sell the machine modified or unmodified?

Solution	

If the machine is modified, there will be a net cash receipt of £2500 (that is, £3000 less £500). If the machine is not modified there will be a cash receipt of £2000. Clearly, given that the business's aim is to make as much money as possible, it will modify and sell the machine as this will make the business richer than the alternative.

Note that the original cost of the machine is irrelevant to this decision. This is because it is a past cost and one that cannot now be undone. As a past cost it is common to both possible future courses of action. The machine originally cost £5000 irrespective of what is now to happen.

It is important therefore to recognise what information is relevant to the decision and what is not. Often, gathering the information can be costly and time consuming, and so restricting it to the relevant may well lead to considerable savings in the costs of making the decision. Also, the presence of irrelevant information can confuse decision makers, leading to sub-optimal decisions.

Step 4: Assess the data and reach a decision

This involves comparing the options by using the relevant data in such a way as to identify those courses of action that will best work towards the achievement of the objectives. Much of this book will be concerned with the ways in which assessment of data relating to financial decisions should be carried out.

Step 5: Implement the decision

It is pointless taking time and trouble to make good decisions if no attempt is to be made to ensure that action follows the decision. Such action is not restricted to what is necessary to set the selected option into motion, but includes controlling it through its life. Steps should be taken to ensure, or to try to ensure, that what was planned actually happens.

Step 6: Monitor the effects of decisions

Good decision making requires that the effects of previous decisions are closely monitored. There are broadly two reasons for this:

- It is valuable to assess the reliability of forecasts on which the decision was based. If forecasts prove to be poor, then decision makers must ask themselves whether reliability could be improved by using different techniques and bases. It is obviously too late to improve the decision already made and acted upon, but this practice could improve the quality of future decisions.

- If a decision is proving to be a bad one for any reason, including unforeseeable changes in the commercial environment, monitoring should reveal this so that some modification might be considered that could improve matters. This is not to say that the original decision can be reversed. Unfortunately we cannot alter the past, but we can often take steps to limit the bad effects of a poor decision. For example, suppose that a business makes a decision to buy a machine to manufacture plastic ducks as wall decorations, for which it sees a profitable market for five years. One year after buying the machine and launching the product, it is obvious that there is little demand for plastic ducks. At that point it is not possible to decide not to enter into the project a year earlier, but it is possible and may very well be desirable to abandon production immediately to avoid throwing good money after bad.

In practice most of the monitoring of financial decisions is through the accounting system, particularly the budgetary control routines.

2.2 Business objectives

What businesses are seeking to achieve, and therefore what investment and financing decisions should try to promote, is a question central to business finance, and one that has attracted considerable discussion as the subject has developed. We now review some of the more obvious and popular suggestions and try to assess how well each of them stands up to scrutiny.

Maximisation of profit

Profit here would normally be interpreted as accounting profit, which is discussed at some length in Chapter 3. This objective arises from the fact that the shareholders are the owners of the business and, as such, both the exercisers of ultimate control and the beneficiaries of profits. It is therefore argued that the shareholders will cause managers to pursue policies that would be expected to result in the maximum possible profit. This analysis is acceptable up to a point, but maximising profit could easily be sub-optimal to the shareholders. Profit may be able to be increased by expanding the business's scale of operations. If the increase merely results from the raising of additional external finance, it might mean that profit per share could actually decrease, leaving the shareholders worse off.

Pharmaceutical products manufacturers typically spend vast amounts of money on developing and testing new products. It is in the nature of the industry that the time taken to bring a new drug to the market can easily be ten years. A particular business that stopped spending money on research and development would enhance current profit because costs would be cut but revenues arising from development costs in past years would continue for the time being. Thus current profits would be buoyant but the business would face a bleak future since there would be no new drugs to replace the old ones.

It is probably open to most businesses to increase their profits without additional investment if they are prepared to take additional risks. For example, cost cutting on the control of the quality of the business's output could lead to increased profits, at least in the short term. In the longer term, placing substandard products on the market could lead to the loss of future sales and profits.

Clearly, increasing profitability through greater efficiency is a desirable goal from the shareholders' point of view. However, maximisation of profit is far too broad a definition of what is likely to be beneficial to shareholders.

Maximisation of the return on capital employed

This objective is probably an improvement on profit maximisation since it relates profit to the size of the business. However, as with profit maximisation, no account is taken of risk and long-term stability.

Survival

Undoubtedly most businesses would see survival as a necessary, but insufficient, objective to pursue. Investors would be unlikely to be attracted to become shareholders in a business that had no other long-term ambition than merely to survive. In times of economic recession and other hardship, many businesses will see survival as their short-term objective, but in the longer term they would almost certainly set their sights somewhat higher.

Long-term stability

This is similar to survival and is similarly unrealistic in its lack of ambition as a long-term target.

Growth

Growth of profits and/or assets does seem a more realistic goal and appears to reflect the attitude of managers. Growth implies that short-term profit will not be pursued at the cost of long-term stability or survival. Growth is not really a precise enough statement of an objective. This is because growth (as we have seen) can be achieved merely by raising new finance. It is doubtful whether any businesses would state their objective as being to issue as many new shares as possible.

Satisficing

Many see objectives that relate only to the welfare of shareholders as unrealistic at the start of the third millennium. They see the business as a coalition of suppliers of capital, suppliers of managerial skills, suppliers of labour, suppliers of goods and services, and customers. None of the participants in the coalition is viewed as having pre-eminence over any of the others. This coalition is not seen as a self-contained entity but viewed in a wider societal context. Cyert and March (1963) were amongst the first to mention this view.

The objectives, it is argued, should reflect this coalition so that the business should seek to give all participants satisfactory return for their inputs, rather than seek to maximise the return to any one of them. This is known as satisficing.

Maximisation of shareholders' wealth

This is probably a more credible goal than those concerned with either return/growth or stability/survival as single objectives, since wealth maximisation takes account of both return and risk simultaneously. Rational investors will value Business A more highly than Business B if the returns expected from each business are equal but those from Business B are considered more risky (less likely that expectations will be fulfilled). Wealth maximisation also balances short- and long-term benefits in a way that profit-maximising goals cannot.

A wealth maximisation objective should cause financial managers to take decisions that balance returns and risk in such a way as to maximise the benefits, through dividends and enhancement of share price, to the shareholders.

Despite its credibility, wealth maximisation seems in conflict with the perhaps still more credible objective of satisficing. Wealth maximising seems to imply the pursuit of the interests of only one member of the coalition, perhaps at the expense of the others. To the extent that this implication is justified, the shareholder wealth maximisation criterion provides a basis for financial decisions that must then be balanced against those derived from objectives directed more towards the other members of the coalition.

It could, however, be argued that satisficing and shareholder wealth maximisation are not as much in conflict as they might at first appear to be. This is to say that wealth maximisation might best be promoted by other members of the coalition receiving satisfactory returns. Consider one of the members of the coalition, say the employees. What will be the effect on share prices and dividend prospects if employees do not receive satisfactory treatment? Unsatisfactory treatment is likely to lead to high rates of staff turnover, lack of commitment by staff, the possibility of strikes – in short, an unprofitable and uncertain future for the business. Clearly this is not likely to be viewed with enthusiasm by the investing public. This in turn would be expected to lead to a low share price. Conversely, a satisfied workforce is likely to be perceived favourably by investors. It is reasonable to believe that a broadly similar conclusion will be reached if other members of the coalition are considered in the same light.

Maximisation of shareholders' wealth may not be a perfect summary of the typical business's financial objective. It does, however, provide a reasonable working basis for financial decision making. What must be true is that businesses cannot continually make decisions that reduce their shareholders' wealth since this would imply that the worth of the business would constantly be diminishing. Each business has only a finite amount of wealth, so sooner or later it would be forced out of business by the results of such decisions.

Jensen (2001) makes the point that it is impractical to expect managers to pursue more than one goal. This is partly because it is difficult to know how to strike the balance between the interests of the various members of the coalition that make up the business. Jensen also argues that trying to pursue more than one goal makes it impossible for managers to make purposeful decisions. Without a way to assess their success, managers in effect become less accountable. Whatever may be said against maximisation of shareholders' wealth as the business objective, it has the great merit that management's achievement is relatively easily assessed, certainly for businesses whose shares are traded in an open market, where their value can be observed.

Evidence on objectives

Survey evidence

Several studies have been conducted in the UK, most of which have involved questioning senior managers of large businesses by interview or postal questionnaire.

Pike and Ooi (1988) conducted a postal questionnaire at two points in time, 1980 and 1986. The 1980 questionnaire was sent to 208 large UK businesses. The 1986 questionnaire was sent to the businesses that had responded in 1980, provided that they had not disappeared as a result of amalgamations, takeovers and the like. In both surveys, the usable response rate exceeded 70 per cent. In both surveys, senior finance executives were asked to indicate on a five-point scale the importance to their businesses of five financial objectives, two of which were short term and three of which were long term.

The mean rankings for the objectives were as shown in Table 2.1. Note that a ranking of 5 implies that the objective is very important and a ranking of 1 implies an unimportant objective.

Table 2.1 **The importance of financial objectives (1980–86)**

Objective	1980	1986
Short-term (1 to 3 years):		
Profitability (e.g. percentage rate of return on investment)	4.28	4.61
Profits or earnings (i.e. a profit target)	4.01	4.41
Long-term (over 3 years):		
Growth in sales	3.18	2.97
Growth in earnings per share	2.83	4.38
Growth in shareholders' wealth	3.07	4.06

Source: Adapted from Pike and Ooi (1988).

These results indicate a number of goals, important to the business, being simultaneously pursued. They also imply an increasing importance of four of them (sales growth being the exception) over time. It appears that, in 1980, shorter-term objectives were more important to the respondents than were the longer-term ones. However, by 1986, EPS (earnings per share) and growth in shareholders' wealth had become nearly as important as the shorter-term goals.

The Pike and Ooi results show some consistency with evidence from other surveys conducted both in the UK and in the USA over recent years.

It should be noted that profit or earnings are properly defined as the net increase in a business's wealth as a result of its commercial activities. Thus goals that emphasise profits or EPS are not necessarily in conflict with those that emphasise growth in shareholders' wealth. It is only where the longer-term benefit is being jeopardised in favour of short-term profitability that there is conflict. Thus when Pike and Ooi's respondents identified short-term profitability as a goal they were presumably not identifying it at the expense of longer-term goals. In fact the importance placed on EPS and growth in shareholders' wealth by the same respondents emphasises this point.

Evidence from annual reports

UK companies are legally required to report their accounting results and other information about themselves in an annual report. Many businesses take the opportunity to include information about themselves, including their business philosophy and an outline of their objectives. Some businesses are fairly unequivocal that increasing, if not maximising, shareholder wealth is their goal. **British Sky Broadcasting Group plc ('BSkyB')**, the satellite broadcasting business stated in its 2004 annual report that its objective is 'to maximise value for shareholders by focussing on profitable growth in subscribers to its digital pay television services in the UK and Ireland'. In its 2003 annual report, **Balfour Beatty plc**, the building and civil engineering business, said: 'Our aim is to create long-term shareholder value by providing engineering, construction and service skills to customers for whom infrastructure quality, efficiency and reliability are critical. We seek to operate safely and sustainably.' **Severn Trent plc**, the water supplier and waste disposal business, said: 'We aim to increase shareholder value by providing integrated solutions to environmental problems; and by grasping the growth opportunities created by new legislation and new requirements in the private and public sectors' (annual report 2004). **Reckitt Benckiser plc**, the household products manufacturer (for example, Dettol, Harpic and Vanish), said: 'Our ultimate purpose is to create shareholder value' (annual report 2003).

Some businesses relate the benefits to shareholders in a way that seems to support the point made on page 21 that maximisation of shareholder value is linked to *satisficing*. **Prudential plc**, the insurance business, says: 'Our commitment to the shareholders who own Prudential is to maximise the value over time of their investment. We do this by investing for the long term to develop and bring out the best in our people and our businesses to produce superior products and services, and hence superior financial returns' (annual report 2003). Prudential goes on to say: 'our aim is lasting relationships with our customers and policyholders, through products and services that offer value for money and security'.

Probably a majority of businesses do not state their objective as being enhancement of shareholder wealth quite as clearly as BSkyB, Balfour Beatty, Severn Trent and Prudential. Despite this, the message implied by their annual reports is that they are pursuing shareholder wealth. For example, **Tesco plc**, the supermarket business, states its objective as, 'to create value for customers to earn their lifetime loyalty' (annual report 2004) – no mention of shareholders at all. However, Tesco, typical of most businesses, paid very substantial bonuses to directors, based on the level of returns to shareholders – an indication that directors' attention was being focused clearly on the welfare of shareholders.

Many businesses report a measure known as the 'total shareholder return'. This is the sum of benefits to shareholders: dividends plus increase in share price for a period. Some of these compare their own performance with that of a peer group of similar businesses. Some, **Boots Group plc** (the chemist) for example, use this measure as the basis of bonuses to managers.

Many businesses, nearly all larger ones, grant 'share options' to their directors and senior managers. This is an arrangement where shares offered at the current market price can be taken up and paid for at some future time. This means that the directors can benefit directly, and without risk, from any increases in the business's share price. If the share price goes up, they exercise their option and can immediately sell the shares at the higher price. If the price does not go up, the directors are not required to take up the shares.

We can probably summarise the evidence provided by looking at what individual businesses say and do, as follows. Most businesses do not state their objective to be shareholder wealth maximisation, though some do. Nearly all larger UK businesses pay sizeable bonuses to their directors. These bonuses are almost always linked closely to returns to shareholders. On top of this, most larger businesses grant substantial share options to directors. So directors have a strong incentive to benefit the shareholders. Bonuses and share option benefits can easily exceed basic salaries of many directors. So, while most businesses do not state shareholder wealth maximisation as their goal, their actions, including the incentives given to senior managers, strongly imply that the economic welfare of shareholders is a major issue.

2.3 Conflicts of interests: shareholders versus managers – the 'agency' problem

The problem

Although the shareholders control the business in theory, in practice the managers control it on a day-to-day basis. It has been suggested that some businesses might pursue policies that are likely to maximise the welfare of their managers, at the same time giving the shareholders sufficient rewards to stop them from becoming too dissatisfied and causing discomfort to the managers, rather than maximising shareholders' wealth. The ways in which managers might seek to maximise their welfare include:

● paying themselves good levels of salary and 'perks', but not too much to alert shareholders to whom, by law, directors' salaries must be disclosed;

● providing themselves with larger empires, through merger and internal expansion, thus increasing their opportunities for promotion and social status; and

● reducing risk through diversification, which, as we shall see in Chapter 7, may not benefit the shareholders, but may well improve the managers' security.

We saw in Chapter 1 that the Combined Code on corporate governance seeks to avoid the more extravagant divergences between the welfare of the shareholders and that of the directors. No amount of regulation is likely to avoid this problem completely, however.

There is no reason to believe that managers consider only their own interests at the expense of the shareholders. However, it is likely that some, possibly most, managers would consider their own welfare when making decisions about the business. This, no doubt, can cause decisions to be made that are sub-optimal from the shareholders' viewpoint. Unfortunately, the costs of undertaking some sort of management audit to monitor managers' decisions are likely to be considerable, making it unreasonable to attempt.

The costs to the shareholders of managers making decisions that are not in the shareholders' best interests and/or of the shareholders monitoring the managers, are known as agency costs. This is because managers act as agents of the shareholders in the management of the assets of the business. Agency cost is a factor that arises in several areas of business finance. Of course, bonuses linked to shareholder returns and directors' share options, which we discussed on page 23, are examples of agency costs incurred to encourage the managers to run the business in a shareholder-wealth-enhancing manner. We shall look at other areas where agency is a potential problem, in various contexts, later in the book.

There is, however, a strong sanction against managers who continually make sub-optimal decisions, and that is the possibility of takeover. A business whose share price reflects underutilisation of assets is likely to become a prime target for a takeover, which might well leave the delinquent managers without jobs. Buoyant share prices make businesses unattractive as takeover targets, so that managers have a vested interest in promoting buoyancy, if not maximisation, of share prices. We shall look at takeovers in Chapter 14.

Short termism

The existence of the takeover sanction may not be sufficient to cause management to be completely selfless in its conduct of the business's affairs, however.

One area where the takeover sanction may not be effective is where managers take too short term a view. Although the best interests of the shareholders may be served by an emphasis on long-term profitability, the best interests of managers could be served by so-called short termism. Managers may see their careers as lasting only two or three years with a particular business before they move on to other employment. Their reputations may therefore depend on what happens whilst they are still with the business rather than on the ultimate effect of their actions. Perhaps more importantly, management remuneration may well be based on immediate profit flows. Both of these factors could promote a tendency to concentrate on the short term.

Another factor that might encourage managerial short termism is where managers perceive that investors are interested only in the short term. If such a perception were correct, it would mean that businesses whose managements failed to take decisions that would enhance short-term profits, would experience a fall in their share price. Thus managers might promote short-term profits for one or both of two reasons:

- It is quite common, as we have seen, for managerial remuneration to be linked to the business's share price: the higher the share price, the larger the bonus.

- A weak share price might encourage a takeover of the business.

Demirag (1998) found evidence that businesses' managers *believe* investors to be short termists. This supported an earlier study by the same researcher. Marston and Craven (1998) found that there is no strong evidence that investors are *in fact* short termist. These researchers also found that, nevertheless, managers believe investors to be so. In view of these findings, it could be the case that managers may have a tendency to favour short-term investments, in the mistaken belief that this is what shareholders want. There is no strong evidence to support this conjecture, however.

For the remainder of this book we shall assume that shareholder wealth maximisation is the major financial goal of the business. However, we should continually bear in mind that, in reality, decisions reached on the basis of this objective might be in conflict with a business's non-financial goals. If this is the case, the final decision may need to be a compromise.

2.4 Financing, investment and separation

If we accept that businesses should seek to maximise the wealth of the shareholders in making their financial decisions, we can now turn our attention to how, in theory at least, managers should approach their decision making so as to promote this objective. Let us do this by consideration of an example.

Example 2.2 **Project X – to invest or to spend**

Industries Ltd is a business owned by a number of independently minded shareholders. Three of these, Eager, Patient and Steady, own 20 000 each of the business's total of 200 000 ordinary shares. At present, Industries Ltd has only one asset, namely £100 000 in cash. Management is undecided whether to pay this cash to the shareholders as a dividend, which would amount to £10 000 (one-tenth of £100 000) in the case of each of the above trio, or to invest it in Project X. This investment project requires an initial cash investment of the whole of the £100 000 payable now, and will produce a cash receipt of £120 000 in a year's time, and then come to a close. If the project is undertaken the whole of the cash proceeds will be paid as a dividend next year (£12 000 each for Eager, Patient and Steady). For the time being, let us assume that there is no alternative investment project available to the business, nor any shareholdings in other businesses available to investors, also that it is not possible to borrow or lend money.

Suspecting that there might be disagreement between shareholders on Project X, the management decided to call a shareholders' meeting to sound out opinion. During the meeting the following three comments were made.

- Eager said that she thought Industries Ltd should not make the investment but should pay the dividend immediately because, while she does not necessarily want to spend the money now, it would be nice to have it available should some need arise. She does not consider the additional £2000 of dividend will compensate her for delaying.

- Patient said that he would prefer Project X to be undertaken because he would not, in any case, spend his dividend before next year and would prefer to have £12 000 than £10 000 when he does come to spend it.

- Steady said that she would be in favour of Project X but that, since she needs the cash in six months' time to pay for a new extension to her house, she would reluctantly have to vote for the immediate dividend.

Similarly diverse views were expressed by the business's other shareholders.

Clearly, management has a problem. If it were trying to maximise the wealth of the shareholders then perhaps a decision to undertake Project X would be the correct one. This would not be acceptable to at least two shareholders: Eager would rather have her money now and Steady must have it in six months at the latest. Clearly, £12 000 is more wealth than £10 000, but if it is not to be available to spend when it is wanted or needed, the £10 000 may be preferred. It seems impossible to maximise the satisfaction that each shareholder gets from the business: satisfying some dissatisfies others because timing of spending matters to people, but not to each person in the same way.

Borrowing and lending

If we introduce a bit more realism into the example by assuming that both Industries Ltd and its shareholders can borrow and lend money, management's dilemma disappears. To illustrate this, let us assume that the interest rate is 10 per cent p.a. and see how the introduction of borrowing and lending affects the position of the trio if Project X is undertaken.

- Eager, who wants her money now, could borrow from the bank such an amount that would, with interest, grow to £12 000 by next year. The borrowings could then be discharged using the cash from the dividend to be received in a year's time.

  The borrowed amount would be £10 909, that is, £12 000 × 100/(100 + 10) [check: £10 909 + (10% × £10 909) = £12 000]. Thus she could immediately have £909 more to spend than if Project X were to be rejected by the business. Of course, she would still owe the bank £12 000 by the end of the year, but she would use her dividend to pay this.

- Patient, who prefers to wait the year, will receive and spend his £12 000 in a year's time. If Project X were to be rejected, the best that he could do would be to lend the £10 000 dividend to the bank, which, with interest at 10 per cent, would grow to £11 000 over the year.

- Steady, who needs her money in six months' time, could at that time borrow such an amount as will grow with interest to £12 000 by the end of the year. Since she does not need the money during the first six months she will only need to borrow for the second half of the year. The borrowed amount would be £11 429 [that is, £12 000 × 100/(100 + 5)]. If Project X were rejected by the business and Steady lent her £10 000 to the bank for six months, it would grow to only £10 500 [that is, £10 000 + (£10 000 × $\frac{1}{2}$ × 10%)].

It seems clear that all three investors will have more to spend if Project X is undertaken than if it is not, irrespective of when they wish to spend. This will also be true for each of the business's other shareholders. The shareholders will be unanimous that Project X should go ahead.

Project Y

Now let us suppose that Project X is not available but that the choice is either pay the dividend now or undertake Project Y. This project also requires an immediate cash investment of £100 000, but will produce only £109 000 next year when it will cease.

Let us consider how accepting Project Y will affect Eager, who wants her money now. Again she could borrow against next year's dividend (£10 900); the amount that she could borrow will be £9909 [that is, £10 900 × 100/(100 + 10)]. On the other hand, if Project Y is rejected she would have £10 000 to spend. Clearly she would prefer rejection of the project. We could easily illustrate, using the same logic as that which we applied to Project X, that Patient and Steady would agree with her, as indeed would all of the other shareholders. Project X and Project Y suggest what is obviously true: that where the business undertakes projects whose rates of return are greater than the interest rate at which shareholders can borrow or lend, their wealth will be increased. Projects that yield a lower rate than the shareholders' interest rate will have the effect of reducing the wealth of the shareholders. Project X produces a return of 20 per cent p.a., that is, (£120 000 – £100 000)/£100 000, Project Y makes a 9 per cent return; the interest rate is 10 per cent. It is obvious that a project yielding 10 per cent would not alter the wealth of shareholders.

Opportunity cost of finance

→ The borrowing/lending interest rate represents the opportunity cost to the shareholder of making investments in the projects. The existence of the facility to borrow or to lend means that those who have the cash but do not want to spend, have the opportunity to lend at the interest rate as an alternative to investing. Any investments in projects must therefore compete with that opportunity and, to be desirable, produce returns in excess of the interest rate.

Borrowing by the business

Suppose that Industries Ltd's management decided to undertake Project X, but for some reason or another, it also decided to pay an immediate dividend of £50 000, making up the shortfall of the cash needed for the investment by borrowing at 10 per cent p.a. for the duration of the project. This would mean that the £50 000 borrowed with interest, a total of £55 000, would have to be repaid from the £120 000 proceeds from the investment, leaving £65 000 of the £120 000 proceeds from Project X to be paid as a dividend next year.

For Eager this would mean a dividend of £5000 now and another one of £6500 next year. What effect will this have on her present wealth? She can borrow the amount that will, with interest, grow to £6500; this will be £5909 [that is, £6500 × 100/(100 + 10)], which together with the £5000 dividend will give her £10 909, an increase in wealth of £909. Note that this is identical to the increase in her current wealth that we found when we assessed Project X assuming that it was to be financed entirely by the shareholders. Not surprisingly, it could equally well be shown that this would also be true for the other shareholders, and no matter what proportion of the £100 000 the business borrows, Project X will remain equally attractive.

Therefore, it seems not to matter where the cash comes from: if the investment will increase shareholders' wealth under one financing scheme, it will increase it by the same amount under some other scheme.

The theoretical implications of Projects X and Y

Example 2.2 illustrates three important propositions of business finance:

1 *Businesses should invest in projects that make them wealthier.* By doing this the wealth of the shareholders will be increased. By investing in as many such projects as are available, shareholders' wealth will be maximised.

> 2 *Personal consumption/investment preferences of individual shareholders are irrelevant in making corporate investment decisions.* Irrespective of when and how much individuals wish to spend, there will be more available to them (their wealth will be maximised) provided that the investment policy outlined in Proposition 1 (above) is followed. This is because individual shareholders can use borrowing or lending to adjust the dividends from the business to match their personal tastes. Put another way, the pattern of dividends does not affect the wealth of the shareholders.

> 3 *The financing method does not affect the shareholders' wealth.* Provided that the investment policy outlined in Proposition 1 (above) is followed, it does not matter whether the investment is financed by the shareholders or by borrowing.

These may be summarised as the separation theorem, which says that *investment decisions* and *financing decisions* should be made independently of one another. This proposition was first identified by Irving Fisher in the 1930s and was formally set out by Hirshleifer (1958).

These propositions may seem like not-too-subtle glimpses of the obvious, yet when they were first formally propounded they met with quite a lot of scepticism, not entirely because of the lack of reality of some of the assumptions that we have made. Much of the scepticism was due to the fact that the propositions were in conflict with widely held views on these aspects of business finance.

The assumptions

Our consideration of Projects X and Y, and indeed of the separation theorem generally, is based on four major assumptions:

1 Investments last for only one year.

2 Returns from investments are known with certainty: for example, there is no doubt that if Project X is undertaken, £120 000 will flow in next year.

3 All individuals prefer more wealth to less.

4 Borrowing and lending rates are equal as between one another, and as between individuals and businesses.

Clearly, some of these assumptions are unrealistic, particularly the first two. Whether this seriously weakens the separation theorem and its implications is probably impossible to assess directly. Even if the theorem does not strictly hold true in practice, it does give some insights into the relationship between shareholders and managers in the context of real investment decisions. The theorem certainly provides a foundation for several major financial theories that we shall encounter later in this book.

The formal derivation of the separation theorem by Hirshleifer is reviewed in the appendix to this chapter.

2.5 Theory and practice

We have discussed what business finance is about and what financial decisions are intended to achieve. We have also considered some theoretical propositions of how we should make financing and investment decisions. In the remainder of this book we shall explore how such decisions should be made in theory, and how they appear to be made in practice, and we shall try to reconcile the differences between theory and practice where they occur.

Summary

Financial decision making has six steps

1 Define objective(s).
2 Identify possible courses of action.
3 Assemble data relevant to the decision.
4 Assess the data and reach a decision.
5 Implement the decision.
6 Monitor the effects of the decision.

Business objectives

- Various possibilities suggested: for example, maximisation of profit.
- Maximisation of shareholders' wealth is generally accepted as the key objective because it takes account of returns and risk, and provides a practical measure.

Agency problems

- Conflicts of interest between shareholders and directors.
- The agency problem can lead to costs for shareholders.
- Arises in various contexts in business finance.

Financing, investment and separation

- If there is the opportunity to borrow and lend money, investment and financing decisions can be separated.
- Businesses should invest in all opportunities that have a rate of return higher than the borrowing/lending rate in order to maximise shareholders' wealth.
- Personal preferences of individual shareholders are irrelevant to directors because shareholders can maximise these for themselves.
- The financing method does not affect shareholders' wealth.
- These assertions are based on simplifying assumptions.

Further reading

The subject of corporate objectives has been widely dealt with in the literature. Cyert and March (1963), to which reference was made in the chapter, discuss it at length. Most finance texts devote some space to it, as do most business economics texts. The article by Pike and Ooi (1988) to which reference was made in the chapter, is worth reading, as is the original article by Hirshleifer (1958), also referred to in the chapter and reviewed in the appendix. Lumby and Jones (2003) clearly explain the separation theorem and its formal derivation. A more extensive treatment of relevant costs is provided in McLaney and Atrill (2005), Chapter 8.

This site allows you to access the contents pages of most of the leading business finance journals in the English-speaking world.
http://fisher.osu.edu/fin/journal/jofsites.htm

The websites of the businesses featured in this chapter are:

Balfour Beatty plc	www.balfourbeatty.com
Boots Group plc	www.boots-plc.com
British Sky Broadcasting Group plc	www.sky.com
Prudential plc	www.prudential.co.uk/plc
Reckitt Benckiser plc	www.reckittbenckiser.com
Severn Trent plc	www.severntrent.com
Tesco plc	www.tesco.com

REVIEW QUESTIONS

Suggested answers to review questions appear in Appendix 3.

2.1 When making a decision, an item of information needs to satisfy two criteria in order to be relevant and worthy of taking into account. What are these two criteria?

2.2 Why is profit maximisation considered incomplete as the definition of what most businesses seek to achieve?

2.3 Is exploitation of customers by a monopoly supplier, who charges very high prices, consistent with the objective of maximising shareholders' wealth? Explain your response.

2.4 A business has £1 million at its disposal and managers feel that this could either be invested in new production facilities or be paid to shareholders as a dividend. What does the separation theorem suggest that the business should do? Can the business both pay the dividend and make the investment? Explain.

2.5 Explain why, according to the separation theorem, the financing method (equity or loan) does not affect shareholders' wealth.

2.6 Why, in practice, would borrowing by the business to raise cash to pay a dividend not be economically equivalent to borrowing by the individual shareholders to provide themselves with cash?
(Note that the answer to this question is not really provided in the chapter. A combination of background knowledge and common sense should enable you to come up with some relevant points, however.)

PROBLEM

A sample answer to this problem appears in Appendix 4.

(This problem is a basic-level one.)

2.1 Talco Ltd undertakes research work. It also manufactures engineering products. It is currently engaged on a research project which, when completed, will be sold for £250 000. So far, costs totalling £200 000 have been incurred by Talco on the project. This is more than was budgeted to bring the project to the present stage and, as a result, the question arises as to whether it would be better to complete the project or abandon it immediately.

It is estimated that the following will be necessary to complete the project:

1 Material, already bought at a cost of £40 000 (not included in the £200 000 mentioned above) and currently held in stock. This is toxic material for which Talco has no other use. It has no market value, but it will, if the project is abandoned, have to be disposed of at a cost of £8000.

2 Labour, which will cost a further £25 000. This labour is skilled and in demand elsewhere in the business. Were the project to be abandoned, the labour will be used to make and sell 2000 units of a standard product. This product will be sold for £25 each with a material cost of £12 each.

3 Project management, which will cost a further £10 000. If the project is abandoned the manager concerned will be made redundant at a cost of £8000. Under the terms of the manager's contract, no redundancy pay is due if the project goes on to completion.

Show figures and explanations that indicate whether, assuming a wealth maximisation objective, the project should be continued or abandoned.

There are both a set of **multiple-choice questions** and **missing-word questions** available on the website. These specifically cover the material contained in this chapter. These can be attempted and graded (with feedback) online.

There are also **two additional problems**, with solutions, that relate to the material covered in this chapter.

Go to **www.pearsoned.co.uk/atrillmclaney** and follow the links.

APPENDIX Formal derivation of the separation theorem

The nature of investment

Investment is in essence laying out cash in order to give rise to future cash receipts. Usually most or all of the outlay occurs before the inflows. Thus investment has a time dimension.

Let us now consider the position of an investor who has an amount of wealth which may either be spent (consumed) or be invested in productive assets (plant, machinery, trading stocks and so forth). At this stage, let us restrict ourselves to considering only investment horizons of one period (say a year). Thus the individual may invest part or all of the current wealth for one year and consume the proceeds of the investment next year, or consume it all immediately.

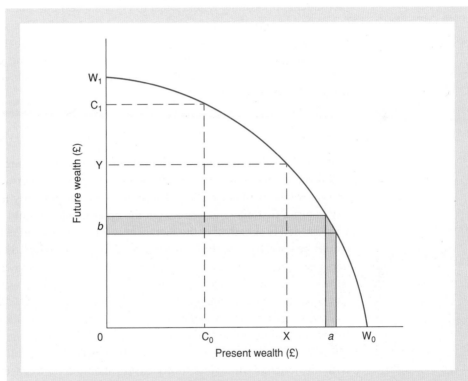

Figure 2.1
The productive investment opportunities available to an individual whose wealth totals W_0

W_0 could all be invested, in which case it would yield wealth totalling W_1, after one year. These investment opportunities consist of a number of individual opportunities, like the shaded one. Here an investment of amount a made immediately would generate amount b after one year.

In Figure 2.1, $0W_0$ represents the total amount of wealth available for present consumption and/or investment by an individual. The curved line W_0W_1 represents the investments available to our investor. All of the present wealth ($0W_0$) may be invested, thus yielding $0W_1$ after a year, or all of the present wealth ($0W_0$) could be consumed, leaving no wealth at the end of the year. A third (and perhaps more likely) possibility is that the investor might choose to consume part of the present wealth and invest part – after all, there is a need to eat, both now and next year. If our investor decided to invest C_0W_0 of the present wealth (and consume $0C_0$), this investment would result in $0C_1$ at the year end.

Note, incidentally, that the investment opportunities become less and less attractive as the amount invested by the individual increases, that is, the line W_0W_1 becomes less steep as it rises – meaning that increasing amounts of present wealth will need to be invested to yield an extra £1 of wealth after one year. An investment XW_0 will yield wealth of $0Y$ after one year, but a similar-size investment C_0X will increase next year's wealth by only YC_1.

Line W_0W_1 does not represent a single investment opportunity but a large number of them – in fact all of the opportunities available to the investor at the time. The shaded space between the two sets of unbroken parallel lines in Figure 2.1 represents just one of that large number of hypothetical investments available. This particular one involves an investment now (reduction in current consumption) of amount £a, which will yield (increase future consumption by) £b in a year's time. Since the line W_0W_1 flattens towards the horizontal as it goes from right to left, the better investment prospects (greater return per £1 invested) lie to the right, the worse ones to the left. The investment opportunity lying closest to W_0 is the best one, and opportunities decrease in desirability as the curve moves from right to left. This reflects reality in that investors, particularly those who invest in real assets, find that as they take on more and more investments the yield from each subsequent one becomes less. This is because they will tend to undertake the most advantageous investments first, leaving the less desirable ones.

Investment and utility

The investor whose wealth and investment opportunities are shown in Figure 2.1 will want to know how much to invest, but will probably not want to invest all of the present wealth because this leaves nothing with which to buy food, shelter or indeed any luxuries that may be desired. On the other hand, it would be an unusual person who decided to spend all of the money now and face starvation next year. How much would be invested and how much would be spent, which is clearly a question of personal taste, could be represented by the utility curves shown in Figure 2.2. These curves depict this individual's attitude to the trade-off between consumption now and consumption after one year.

Each point on any particular curve represents some combination of present and future consumption that will render this individual similar amounts of satisfaction or utility: the higher the curve, the greater the satisfaction. (Readers who are unfamiliar with the notion of utility and utility curves should refer to page 162.)

The curves in Figure 2.2 indicate that the investor is very reluctant to forgo consumption completely, either now or next year. The fact that the curves are moving towards the vertical at the top left and towards the horizontal at the bottom right shows this. For example, at the lower levels of present consumption (that is, reduction in present wealth, where the curves are steepest), any further lowering of consumption will only be undertaken if large increases in future consumption will follow. This tendency increases as the level of present consumption is reduced, until we reach a point where no amount of future consumption would justify further reductions in present consumption. The converse applies at low levels of future consumption. The curves depicted in Figure 2.2 do, of course, represent the present/future consumption preferences of an individual. Other individuals might well have different attitudes. It is not likely, though, that their attitudes would be fundamentally different since they too would need to eat, both now and next year. The consumption/investment utility

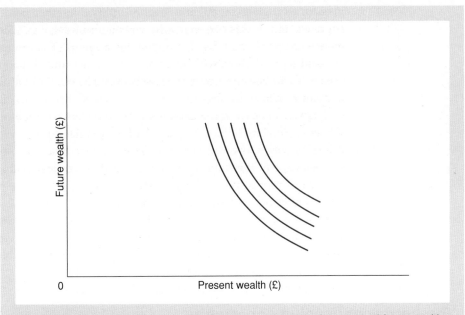

Figure 2.2
Utility of present/
future consumption
for some individual

Each point along any particular curve represents a combination of present and future wealth that a particular individual would find equally satisfactory: the higher the line the greater the satisfaction which the combinations would give.

curves of all rational individuals would therefore be broadly similar to those shown in Figure 2.2.

If we combine Figures 2.1 and 2.2, the result of which is shown in Figure 2.3, we can see that point P is the best combination of investment/consumption for our particular

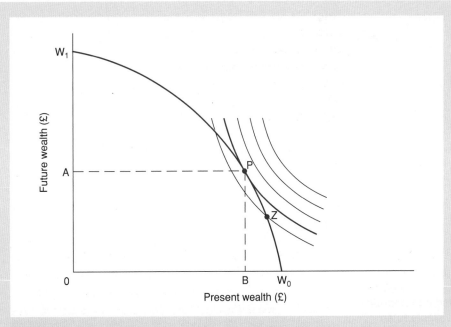

Figure 2.3
Utility of
consumption/
investment for
some individual

This person would invest along curve W_0W_1 to the point where maximum utility would be achieved. This would be at point P.

investor as it gives the highest level of utility. No other point along the production curve will enable this person to achieve as high a level of satisfaction as will the investment/consumption decision implied by point P. Therefore the amount invested should be BW_0 (which will yield $0A$ after a year), and $0B$ should be consumed now, giving $0A$ to consume next year. Suppose that our individual in fact only invests to point Z, which is a feasible possibility. Whilst this would give some consumption, both now and next year, it does not give what this person would regard as the most satisfying combination of present and future consumption. We know this because Z coincides with a lower utility curve. Given our individual's preferences (represented by the shape of the utility curve) and the state of the world as far as investment is concerned (represented by the investment line W_0W_1), P is clearly the most satisfying level of investment for our individual.

This is not necessarily the same as would be chosen by other individuals because they are unlikely to have the same views on the trade-off between present and future consumption. So there would be *no unanimity* as to the desirable level of investment – it would vary from person to person.

The borrowing/lending opportunity

At this point let us introduce a further factor into the analysis and so make it more realistic. That factor is the opportunity available to individuals for borrowing and lending through banks and other financial institutions (the financial market).

Figure 2.4 shows another possibility, which could be used alone or in conjunction with the production opportunities. If the investor were to lend all of the wealth (W_0)

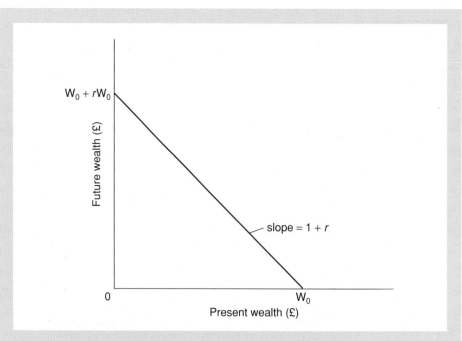

Figure 2.4
The borrowing/lending opportunity available to an individual with an amount of wealth (W_0)

This amount could be lent at an interest rate r so that it would grow to $W_0 + rW_0$ after one time period. Alternatively, an amount W_0 borrowed at an interest rate r would lead to $W_0 + rW_0$ being owed after one time period.

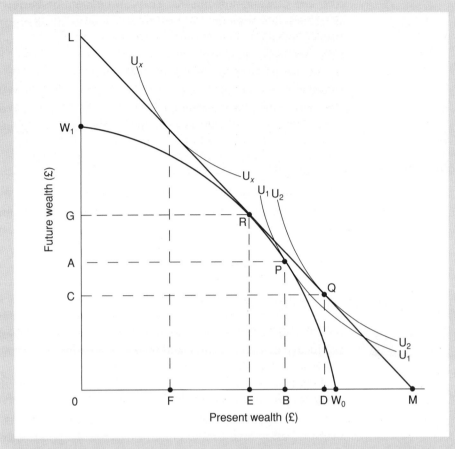

Figure 2.5
Utility of
consumption/
investment of some
individual with the
borrowing/lending
opportunity

This indicates that most individuals can reach a greater level of utility through a combination of productive investment *and* borrowing or lending than could be achieved without the borrowing/lending option. It also shows that individuals will be unanimous about the level of productive investment that will maximise their utility, despite having widely differing attitudes to present and future consumption.

now, it would, with interest at rate r, become $W_0 + rW_0$ after a year. Thus the slope of the borrowing/lending line is $(W_0 + rW_0)/W_0 = 1 + r$.

The existence of borrowing/lending opportunities enables levels of investment to be undertaken in excess of the amount of wealth left after a desired level of consumption has been undertaken. This is achieved by borrowing the required amount now and repaying it (with interest) next year. Similarly, not all of the present wealth left after consuming the desired amount need be invested in production; some of it can be lent, to be received back (again with interest) next year. This broadening of the possibilities may well enable the investor to achieve higher levels of satisfaction (utility).

Figure 2.5 combines Figures 2.3 and 2.4, that is, it introduces the borrowing/lending line into the investment/consumption configuration. Figure 2.5 does look rather complicated, but it is basically only what we have already met.

Without the borrowing/lending opportunity, point P represented the optimum consumption/investment combination for our investor, achieving utility curve U_1U_1. With the introduction of borrowing/lending, a higher level of satisfaction can be achieved, moving up to utility curve U_2U_2. Our individual can now invest amount

EW_0 and consume amount 0D. This can be done by borrowing the shortfall (ED). Obviously this amount will have to be repaid (with interest) next year, but, nonetheless, consumption of 0D now and 0C next year represents a more attractive (higher utility) prospect than consuming 0B now and 0A next year. Thus the introduction of borrowing/lending has increased utility. Note that GC (the amount that must be repaid next year out of 0G to leave the individual with 0C) is equal to ED (the amount borrowed now) plus interest on ED, that is, ED $(1 + r)$. This is evident from Figure 2.5 if we bear in mind that the slope of the borrowing/lending line is $(1 + r)$.

The separation theorem

An examination of Figure 2.5 reveals an important point. Irrespective of the individual's time preferences (shape of utility curve), all investors faced with the productive investment opportunities depicted in Figure 2.5 would invest up to point R and then achieve their personal highest level of utility by use of the borrowing/lending opportunity. Those investors whose highest utility curve would be tangential to the borrowing/lending line above R would invest up to R and lend that part of the remainder of their wealth that they wish not to consume. In Figure 2.5, U_xU_x is a utility curve of a different investor from the one whose preferences are represented by U_1U_1, U_2U_2. This second individual would choose to invest up to point R on the productive investment curve and then lend amount FE, leaving 0F for consumption.

An individual whose highest utility curve coincides with point R will obviously wish to invest up to that point but will not need to use the borrowing/lending opportunity.

Irrespective of the personal preferences of various investors, all the investors agree that it is best to invest up to point R, which is the point where the slope of the production curve W_0W_1 is equal to that of the borrowing/lending line. This unanimity among investors as to the optimum level of productive investment is quite interesting in the context of individuals. In the context of businesses where managers should try to make investments that most benefit all their shareholders, the unanimity becomes of major importance.

The assumptions on which the above is based and their implications were each discussed in the main body of this chapter.

Chapter 3

Financial (accounting) statements and their interpretation

Objectives   In this chapter we shall deal with the following:

→ the financial statements published by companies

→ the accounting conventions that underpin those statements

→ creative accounting

→ interpretation of financial statements

→ the use of accounting ratios

→ accounting ratios in detail

3.1 Introduction

Most UK businesses that trade as limited companies are required to publish three financial statements each year. These are:

● the profit and loss account (or income statement);

● the balance sheet (or position statement); and

● the cash flow statement.

These statements provide a very valuable source of information for financial managers who work within the business, and for investors, potential investors and their advisers. They also provide helpful insights for others who have a relationship with the business, including customers, employees, suppliers and the community in general. It is likely that managers will have access to information beyond that which is made public. The nature of the additional information and the way in which it is derived, however, are probably very similar to the nature and derivation of published information. In this chapter we shall consider the nature of the three accounting statements, the rules that are followed in preparing them, and the way they may be interpreted so that the user is able to draw conclusions about the business that go beyond the obvious.

It should be said that the approach to accounting that is taken in the UK is, in principle, very much the same as is taken throughout the world. Larger UK companies must comply with International Accounting Standards, set up by the International Accounting Standards Board. This is also true of larger businesses throughout the European Union and in an increasing number of other countries. The objective is that all of the world's larger businesses should adopt a common set of accounting rules. There is a tendency for smaller businesses to follow the accounting practices of their larger counterparts.

The intention of this chapter is not to provide a detailed course in accounting, but to give a broad overview of the subject. This should be useful in later chapters because reference will be made to the value of accounting information and the use of accounting ratios. If you feel that you would like to look at the subject in greater detail you could take up the suggestions for further reading that are given at the end of this chapter.

3.2 The financial statements

We shall now take a look at the financial statements. These will be explained in the broadest way. Some of the points that will be made about the statements will be qualified in the next section when we consider the rules that underpin the statements.

Businesses that trade as companies are required to produce the financial statements annually. Most businesses actually produce these statements much more frequently for their own internal purposes. The statements are often used by managers as aids to financial planning in that the data that they contain will be based on plans and forecasts. The published statements are, of course, based on past events.

The profit and loss account

→ The **profit and loss account (income statement)** is a statement that sets out a summary of the trading events that will have affected the wealth of the business over a particular period, the amount by which each type of event has affected wealth, and the resulting net effect on wealth. The statement also goes on to show how any net increase in the business's wealth over the period has been deployed.

Wealth in this context is not restricted to cash. It is all the things that have economic value to the business, net of such obligations that the business may have to outsiders in respect of any part of its wealth. Things that have economic value to the business (assets) include, for example, an office building owned by the business and the money owed to it by a customer who has bought some of the business's output on credit. Outside obligations would include an amount owed to a loan stockholder.

We shall now look at an example of a profit and loss account. Jackson plc is an imaginary manufacturing business. The nature of the business's marketing strategy is that goods are made to order so there are never any stocks (inventories) of finished goods. The form of financial statements varies from one business to the next. The layout that is shown here is broadly in line with that which most UK businesses use for the annual published financial statements. Individual businesses can and do use different layouts for financial statements.

Jackson plc's profit and loss account for the year 2006 shows that the business generated wealth (earned revenues) of £837 000 by making sales to external customers. This led directly to the wealth being reduced (expenses incurred) in respect of meeting the cost of making those sales revenues; also in distributing the goods sold and meeting the administrative costs of running the business. This left the business with a net increase in wealth, as a result of operating for the year, of £135 000. The interest that the business was under a contractual obligation to pay accounted for a further £30 000.

The last part of the statement looks at how the business deployed the wealth that it had generated. This includes profit of the current year, from which £27 000 will be paid to the Inland Revenue for corporation tax, leaving an after-tax profit of £78 000. It also includes those profits from previous years (£151 000) that had not been specifically allocated. From this total of £229 000, £20 000 has been paid to the shareholders as a dividend. You should be clear that the £209 000 of unappropriated profit at the end of the year is that part of the business's end-of-year wealth that has arisen from profits generated over the years up to 31 December 2006, to the extent that it had not been:

- extinguished by trading losses;
- paid to the Inland Revenue; or
- paid to the shareholders as dividends.

The £209 000 is unlikely to be in the form of cash. As has already been pointed out, wealth does not just mean cash. In practice the retained profit is probably in various forms – plant, stocks etc.

Jackson plc
Profit and loss account for the year ended 31 December 2006

	£000	£000	£000
Revenue			837
Cost of sales (including depreciation £28 000			
and raw materials stock usage £253 000			
Raw material purchases totalled £255 000)			(478)
Gross profit			359
Distribution costs			
Salaries and wages	(37)		
Motor expenses	(43)		
Depreciation of motor vehicles	(16)		
Sundry distribution expenses	(15)	(111)	
Administrative expenses			
Salaries and wages	(58)		
Motor expenses	(22)		
Depreciation of motor vehicles	(19)		
Sundry administrative expenses	(14)	(113)	(224)
Operating profit for the year			135
Interest payable			(30)
Profit on ordinary activities before taxation			105
Tax on ordinary activities			(27)
Profit on ordinary activities after taxation			78
Retained profit brought forward from last year			151
			229
Dividend paid on ordinary shares			(20)
Retained profit carried forward to next year			209

The balance sheet

→ The balance sheet is a statement of the manner in which the business holds its wealth, how much of its wealth it has in each category, how much of the wealth that the business controls is committed to outsiders, and the net wealth of the business.

This net wealth belongs to the shareholders. Unlike the profit and loss account, which summarises the effects of various trading events on the wealth of the business over a period, the balance sheet shows the position at a specified point in time.

The balance sheet of Jackson plc, at the end of the year covered by the profit and loss account that we have just considered, is as follows:

Jackson plc
Balance Sheet as at 31 December 2006

	Cost £000	Depreciation £000	£000
Non-current assets			
Freehold land	550	–	550
Plant and machinery	253	(226)	27
Motor vehicles	102	(56)	46
	905	(282)	623
Current assets			
Stock	43		
Trade debtors (receivables)	96		
Prepaid expenses	12		
Cash	25	176	
Current liabilities			
Trade creditors (payables)	(45)		
Accrued expenses	(18)		
Taxation	(27)	(90)	
Net current assets			86
Total assets less current liabilities			709
Non-current liabilities			
10% secured loan stock			(300)
			409
Equity			
Ordinary share capital – 200 000 shares of £1 each			200
Profit and loss account			209
			409

This balance sheet tells us that the wealth of the business is £799 000. This is made up of non-current assets of £623 000 and current assets of £176 000. The business has obligations to transfer part of this wealth to outside groups: £90 000 is in respect of obligations that relate to day-to-day trading and are likely to be short term; £300 000 is in respect of longer-term obligations not directly related to trading.

The distinction between non-current and current assets is broadly concerned with the intended use of those assets. Non-current assets are those that business intends to use internally to help to generate wealth, not to be sold at a profit. Current assets are those that are acquired with the intention of turning them over in the normal course of trading. A particular non-current asset might be sold at a profit but this would not mean that it should have been treated as a current asset, provided that the primary reason for buying it was for using rather than selling it. Non-current assets can be seen as the tools of the business. Non-current assets were formerly known as *fixed assets*.

Depreciation recognises that certain non-current assets are not worth as much at the end of their life with the business as they cost at the beginning, and therefore that some part of the business's wealth will be lost. This is why depreciation appears in the profit and loss account as an expense, and why the balance sheet value of depreciating non-current assets is reduced below cost. The total amount of depreciation of a particular asset is calculated by taking its cost and deducting its estimated disposal value at the end of its life with the business. This total must then be apportioned among accounting periods in some reasonable manner. In practice in the UK this is typically accomplished by sharing the total equally across the number of accounting periods of the life of the non-current asset concerned.

It is considered useful to readers of balance sheets to deduct current (in essence short-term) liabilities from current assets and to show the net figure of net current assets or working capital. This is because, in normal circumstances, it is out of the assets included under current assets that the current liabilities will be met. Relating current liabilities to current assets in this way highlights the extent to which the business will find it easy to meet its short-term obligations. This is a particularly important matter since a failure to meet its short-term obligations can easily lead to the financial collapse of the business.

The bottom section of the balance sheet shows how the shareholders have contributed to the business's current wealth. This was by a combination of shareholders specifically putting assets, normally cash, into the business to acquire shares, and by allowing wealth generated within the business to remain there, rather than being paid to them as dividends. These ploughed-back profits, shown under the heading 'profit and loss account' are known as 'reserves'. Reserves represent part of the wealth of the shareholders just as much as dividends do.

The cash flow statement

→ The cash flow statement is simply an analysis of the cash (including short-term, highly liquid investments) received and paid out by the business during a period. It is arranged in such a way that it will enable readers to derive helpful insights to the sources and uses of cash over the period. It may seem strange that one particular asset – cash – is highlighted in this way when others, for example stock, are not. What is so special about cash? The answer to this question is that cash tends to be at the heart of most aspects of business. A business's ability to prosper and survive is likely to depend on its ability to generate cash. This is not usually true for other types of asset.

The cash flow statement of Jackson plc is as follows:

Jackson plc
Cash flow statement for the year ended 31 December 2006

	£000	£000
Cash flows from operating activities		
Cash generated from operations	212	
Interest paid	(30)	
Corporation tax paid	(18)	
Dividend paid	(20)	144
Cash flows from investing activities		
Payments to acquire non-current assets		(33)
Cash flows from financing activities		–
Net increase in cash and cash equivalents		111
Cash and cash equivalents at 1 January 2006 (overdraft)		(86)
Cash and cash equivalents at 31 December 2006		25

This statement shows that the business generated a net cash inflow of £212 000 from its trading activities. That is to say that during the year the receipts of cash from sales exceeded payments of cash to pay wages and salaries, suppliers of goods and services, and so on, by £212 000. You should be clear that this is not the same as profit. Profit is the net increase in wealth generally as a result of trading – not just cash.

The remainder of the statement shows where any other cash has come from (none in the case of Jackson plc in 2006) and gone to. In this case, cash has been spent on paying the interest, tax and dividend. In addition, some cash was spent acquiring non-current assets.

Had any cash been raised through an issue of shares or loan stocks, or had any cash been paid to redeem shares or loan stocks, the effect of these would have appeared under the 'cash flows from financing activities' heading in the statement.

The net cash generated during the year was £111 000 which had the effect of bringing the cash balance up from a negative (overdraft) of £86 000 to a positive balance of £25 000 between 1 January and 31 December 2006.

3.3 Definitions and conventions of accounting

Accounting is a language that is used to store and communicate economic information about organisations. It has a set of rules. It is particularly important that anyone trying to read accounting statements and draw conclusions from them is clear on the rules of accounting. Severe misunderstandings could arise for someone not familiar with the rules.

Accounting definition of an asset

An asset has a particular meaning in accounting, which is rather more restrictive than the general one that we use in everyday speech. To be included in a balance sheet as an asset of a particular business, the item would need to have the following attributes:

- It is likely to produce future economic benefits to that business.
- It has arisen from some past transaction or event involving that business.
- The right of access to it by others can be restricted by that business.
- It must be capable of measurement in monetary terms.

The benefit of having a loyal workforce has the characteristics of an asset, to the extent of it being capable of producing probable future economic benefits, for example through savings in recruitment costs as a result of low labour turnover. It would not, however, be included on the business's balance sheet because it has almost certainly not arisen as a result of any particular transaction or event. It would also be extremely difficult to put a monetary value on the benefit of the loyal workforce. It is also the case that the business would probably find it impossible to deny rival businesses access to members of the staff to try to employ them. It can be persuasively argued that failure to take account of such assets gives accounting a limited view of reality.

Money measurement convention

Accounting defines things in terms of money, and can do nothing else. Thus information that cannot be expressed in monetary terms cannot be included in accounting statements. This can also be seen as a deficiency of accounting.

Historic cost convention

Assets are shown in the balance sheet at a value that is based on their cost to the business when they were first acquired, not their current market value or any other value. This means that attempts to use the balance sheet to place a value on a business are likely to lead to misleading results. Some businesses break the historic cost convention and show certain assets, particularly those relating to land and buildings, at an estimate of their current market value. A particular asset may have a low market value but be worth much to the business itself. This could arise where the asset is highly specialised or specific to a business, and has little or no use to any other business.

Adherence to the historic cost convention means that the reader of accounting statements is unable to assess the opportunity cost of using a particular asset for some purpose. For example, when the historic cost of some stock sold is included in a profit and loss account, as an expense, the reader is not able to judge how much more the wealth of the business would have been increased had the stock been deployed in some other way.

Stable monetary unit convention

Accounting tends to assume that the value of the currency remains constant in terms of its ability to buy goods and services. In other words, financial statements are prepared as if there were no price inflation or deflation, either generally or in relation to particular goods and services. The fact that inflation is a constant feature of almost every economy in the world means that this is likely to lead to financial statements giving impressions that could be misleading. Attempts have been made to agree an approach that allows for the distortions of price changes in financial statements. So far, no major economy in the world has developed an approach that is consistently and widely used by its businesses.

Realisation convention

The realisation convention is concerned with the point in time at which a revenue, that is, an increase in wealth arising from trading, is recognised. For example, if a customer orders goods in one month, receives them in the next, and pays for them in the third month, when should the business supplying the goods treat the revenue (sale) as having taken place? This is not an academic question where the business is preparing financial statements for each month and comparing one month's performance with that of another, or where the three months do not all fall within the same accounting year.

The realisation convention says that the revenue should be recognised at the point where:

- the amount (value) of the revenue is capable of being measured with substantial accuracy;
- the necessary work to earn the revenue has substantially been completed; and
- it is reasonably certain that the cash will be received.

This is usually taken to be the point in time at which the customer takes delivery of, and accepts, the goods or service. Thus recognition of the revenue and receipt of the cash do not occur at the same point, except in the case of cash sales. Outside the retail trade, cash sales are rare. Thus, for most businesses, cash receipts from sales revenues tend to lag behind recognition of sales revenues.

Matching convention

Expenses (trading events leading to reductions in wealth) are matched to the particular revenues that they helped to generate in the same accounting period. For example, where the sale of some goods is recognised as a revenue in a particular accounting period, the cost of acquiring those goods should be treated as an expense of the same period.

The objective that the matching convention pursues is to assess the net effect on wealth that the revenues of a particular period generate.

Accruals convention

Profit or loss is concerned with net increases or decreases in wealth, not with increases or decreases in cash. Thus when deriving the amount of the expenses that are to be matched to particular revenues, the fact that cash may not yet have been paid is not relevant. For example, the cost of stock sold for inclusion in the profit and loss account will be the same, irrespective of whether payment for the stock concerned has yet been made.

Prudence convention

Accounting should err on the side of caution. For example, if an item of stock in trade has a sales value that is below cost, this should be reflected by reducing its value in the balance sheet to the lower figure, with the same reflection of the loss of wealth being shown in the profit and loss account. Following the same philosophy, a gain in the value of an asset is not taken into account until it is realised as a result of a disposal of the asset concerned to some person or organisation outside the business. In this way the prudence convention tends to underpin both the historic cost and the realisation conventions.

It has been argued that adherence to the prudence convention tends to lead to a fairly consistent bias in accounting information, which could mislead a reader of financial statements.

Going concern convention

In the absence of evidence to the contrary, it is assumed that the business will continue indefinitely. This means, for example, that it will be assumed that a non-current asset will be capable of being used by the business for the whole of its useful life, rather than it being assumed that the business will be forced to dispose of the asset as a result of the business suffering financial collapse. Thus a business can base its depreciation policy on the cost, expected life and disposal proceeds of the particular asset, rather than on the current value of the asset at intermediate points of its life. As a result, the fact that many non-current assets have a current market value below their balance sheet value does not cause the prudence convention to be invoked.

3.4 Problems with using accounting information for decision making

There are significant problems with using accounting information to help to make decisions. In this section we shall be considering financial statements drawn up in good faith. The problems here fall under two headings: income measurement and balance sheet values.

Income measurement

A major problem here is concerned with the costs that are matched against revenues. The costs are normally not expressed in the same terms as the revenues where there are changing prices (historic cost and stable monetary unit conventions). Since the costs tend to be incurred before the revenues are recognised, during a period of price inflation, there is a tendency for costs to be understated, causing profit to be overstated. Depreciation is often a particular problem here. Depreciation expenses are based on costs that may have been incurred many years earlier; also, depreciation is often a significant expense. The fact that historic costs are used rather than opportunity costs means that only a partial impression of the effect of a particular transaction on wealth is given. Again the distortion is consistently likely to overstate profit, that is, to imply that more wealth has been created than is justified by the facts.

Balance sheet values

Adherence to the historic cost, prudence, going concern and stable monetary unit conventions, coupled with the use of a fairly restricted accounting definition of an asset, tends to cause financial statements to understate the amount of wealth that is invested in the business. This tends to be the case both asset by asset and taking the business overall. Many assets have a greater value than is represented by the balance sheet. Some things that are of economic value to the business may not even be included in the balance sheet at all. Many businesses have goodwill, that is, an ability to earn abnormally high profits due to some factor, like a loyal workforce or loyal clientele. This asset is rarely included in the balance sheet since its inclusion would contravene one or other of the accounting conventions. Yet a distorted impression of the wealth committed to the business is given if most assets are either understated or are excluded.

It is perhaps worth noting that accounting's deficiencies for decision-making purposes stem from the fact that financial accounting did not evolve to meet the needs that decision makers currently try to satisfy. Rather, it developed to provide an historic financial record of the business's transactions. On the one hand, this was a record of where funds had come from – shareholders, creditors and so forth – and how much each had contributed. On the other hand, there was a record of how these funds had been deployed. Therefore, when shareholders subscribed for shares of £1m and the business used the cash to buy a building, this appeared on the balance sheet as share capital £1m and freehold land £1m. The fact that five years later the land might have a market value of £10m is not relevant, because the balance sheet simply records the transaction. For one reason or another, accountants have never really sat down with a clean sheet of paper and tried to design a system that would be more useful to decision makers. From time to time they have grafted on additional features, such as the profit and loss account, but these features were always underpinned by the same approach that had been taken with the balance sheet.

Despite the deficiencies of financial statements, they remain a major, if not the only, source of information for many decision makers. Provided that accounting information is used with care, it should be helpful, despite its limitations.

There is no reason of principle why a particular business should not prepare financial statements for its internal purposes in such a way as to correct for the distorting factors. Undoubtedly some businesses do this, but probably most do not.

3.5 Creative accounting

In the previous section we considered the problems that the accounting conventions raise for those trying to interpret financial statements. In addition, there can be other concerns about financial statements. There is evidence that the directors of some companies have used particular accounting policies or structured particular transactions in a way that portrays a picture of financial health that is in line with what they would like users to see rather than what is a true and fair view of financial position and performance. This practice is referred to as creative accounting and it poses a major problem for accounting rule makers and for society generally.

There seem to be various reasons for the existence of creative accounting, including:

- getting around restrictions (for example, to report sufficient profit to be able to pay a dividend);
- avoiding government action (for example, the taxation of excessive profits);
- hiding poor management decisions;
- achieving sales revenue or profit targets, thereby ensuring that performance bonuses are paid to the directors;
- attracting new share capital or loan capital by showing a healthy financial position; and
- satisfying the demands of major investors concerning levels of return.

Creative accounting methods

There are several approaches that unscrupulous directors have adopted with the aim of manipulating the financial statements. Some of these methods concern the overstatement of revenue. This often involves the early recognition of sales revenue or the reporting of sales transactions that have no real substance.

One case of overstating revenue is said to have been carried out by the **Xerox Corporation**, a large US business and a leading player in the photocopying industry. It is alleged that Xerox brought forward revenues in order to improve reported profits as its fortunes declined in the late 1990s. These revenues related to copier equipment sales, particularly in Latin America. Following the uncovering of the overstatement of revenues, Xerox had to restate its equipment sales revenue figures for a five-year period. The result was a reversal in reported revenues of a staggering $6.4 billion, although $5.1 billion was reallocated to other revenues as a result. This restatement was one of the largest in US corporate history.

Some creative accounting methods focus on the manipulation of expenses, and certain types of expenses are particularly vulnerable. These are expenses that rely heavily on the judgement of directors concerning estimates of the future or concerning the most suitable accounting policy to adopt.

The incorrect 'capitalisation' of expenses may also be used as a means of manipulation. Capitalisation is treating expenses as if they are part of the cost of a non-current asset. Businesses that build their own assets are often best placed to undertake this form of malpractice. The effect of capitalisation of expenses is falsely to boost both profit and the balance sheet value of non-current assets.

One particularly notorious case of capitalising expenses is alleged to have occurred in the financial statements of **WorldCom** (now renamed **MCI**), a large US telecommunications business. WorldCom is alleged to have overstated profits by treating certain operating expenses, such as basic network maintenance, as if they were the acquisition of a non-current asset. This happened over a fifteen-month period during 2001 and 2002. When this overstatement was revealed, net profits had to be reduced by a massive $3.8bn.

Some creative accounting methods focus on the concealment of losses or liabilities. The financial statements can look much healthier if these can somehow be eliminated. One way of doing this is to create a 'separate' entity that will take over the losses or liabilities.

Perhaps the most well-known case of concealment of losses and liabilities concerned the **Enron Corporation**. This was a large US energy business that used 'special purpose entities' (SPEs) as a means of concealment. SPEs were used by Enron to rid itself of problem assets that were falling in value, such as its broadband operations. In addition, liabilities were transferred to these entities to help Enron's balance sheet look healthier. The business had to keep its gearing ratios (the relationship between borrowing and equity) within particular limits in order to satisfy credit-rating agencies, and SPEs were used to achieve this. The SPEs used for concealment purposes were not independent of the business and should have been included in the balance sheet of Enron, along with their losses and liabilities.

When these, and other accounting irregularities, were discovered in 2001, there was a restatement of Enron's financial performance and position to reflect the consolidation of the SPEs, which had previously been omitted. As a result of this restatement, the business recognised $591m in losses over the preceding four years and an additional $628m of liabilities at the end of 2000. The business collapsed at the end of 2001.

Finally, creative accounting may involve the overstatement of asset values. This may involve revaluing the assets, using figures that do not correspond to their fair market values. It may also, as we have seen, involve the capitalising of costs that should have been written off as expenses, as described earlier.

Checking for creative accounting

When examining the financial statements of a business, a number of checks may be carried out on them to help gain a feel for their reliability. These can include checks to see whether:

- the reported profits are significantly higher than the operating cash flows for the period, which may suggest that profits have been overstated;
- the corporation tax charge is low in relation to reported profits, which may suggest, again, that profits are overstated, although there may be other, more innocent explanations;
- the valuation methods used for assets held are based on historic cost or current values, and, if the latter approach has been used, why and how the current values were determined;
- there have been any changes in accounting policies over the period, particularly in key areas such as revenue recognition, stock valuation and depreciation;
- the accounting policies adopted are in line with those adopted by the rest of the industry;
- the auditors' report gives a 'clean bill of health' to the financial statements; and
- the 'small print', that is, the notes to the financial statements, is not being used to hide significant events or changes.

Although such checks are useful, they are not guaranteed to identify creative accounting practices, some of which may be very deeply seated and subtle.

Is creative accounting a permanent problem?

A few years ago, there was a wave of creative accounting scandals in both the USA and Europe, but this now appears to have subsided. It seems that accounting scandals are becoming less frequent and that the quality of financial statements is improving. It is to be hoped that trust among users in the integrity of financial statements will soon be restored. As a result of the actions taken by various regulatory bodies and by accounting rule makers, creative accounting has become a more risky and difficult process for those who attempt it. However, it will never disappear completely and a further wave of creative accounting scandals may occur in the future. The recent wave coincided with a period of strong economic growth, and during good economic times, investors and auditors may become less vigilant. Thus, the opportunity to manipulate the figures becomes easier. We must not, therefore, become too complacent. Things may change again when we next experience a period of strong growth.

3.6 Ratio analysis

As well as gaining information about, and insights into, a business's trading and position by reading the published financial statements, it is also useful to calculate ratios relating particular figures to one another. It can even be useful to relate certain accounting figures to non-accounting measures, such as the number of employees. One reason for calculating ratios is to attempt to summarise quite complex accounting information into a relatively small number of key indicators. An associated reason for calculating ratios is to make figures more easily comparable. For example, if Business A made a profit last year of £1m and Business B made a profit of £2m, what does this tell us? Clearly it tells us that B made the larger profit, but does it tell us that B was better managed or more efficient? The answer is that it does not give us any impression of relative efficiency. B may be much larger than A. If we were to relate each one's profit to its size, a more valid comparison of efficiency could be made. The amount that the shareholders have invested (share capital plus reserves, which equals total assets less total liabilities) is a commonly used indicator of size, so we could use that.

Comparison between businesses is not the only one that we may wish to make. We may want to compare a business's current performance with its past performance to try to identify trends. We may wish to assess the business's performance against what it had planned.

Calculating ratios from a set of financial statements is a relatively easy task. A suitably primed computer will do it almost instantaneously. The hard part of interpretation lies in using skill and experience to draw valid and useful conclusions from the ratios.

Traditionally, ratios are classified into five groups, and we shall look at a selection of ratios under those same five headings. As we proceed to consider each ratio we shall calculate each one for Jackson plc for 2006. When this is completed, to give us some basis of comparison, we shall also look at the same ratios for 2005.

Profitability ratios

Profitability ratios are concerned with the effectiveness of the business in generating profit. A very popular means of assessing a business is to assess the amount of wealth generated for the amount of wealth invested.

 ### Return on net assets (return on capital employed)

$$\frac{\text{Net profit before long-term interest and tax}}{\text{Total assets less current liabilities}} \times 100\%$$

The ratio for Jackson plc for 2006 is:

$$\frac{135}{709} \times 100 = 19.0\%$$

This ratio looks at the return on the non-current and current assets less current liabilities. The logical profit figure to use in calculating this ratio is the operating profit. This is because we are considering the effectiveness of the assets financed both by the shareholders and by the long-term creditors (non-current liabilities), and therefore we should logically use the profit that is shared between these two groups.

Provided that short-term profit is not being generated at the expense of the long term, this ratio should probably be as high as possible. In Chapter 2 we saw that it might be open to most businesses to increase current accounting earnings and, with it, the return on assets ratio, through taking actions that could adversely affect long-term profitability, or at the expense of taking on higher levels of risk.

Since this ratio goes to the heart of what most private sector businesses are trying to achieve it is sometimes known as the *primary ratio*.

Return on equity (return on shareholders' funds)

$$\frac{\text{Net profit after long-term interest and tax}}{\text{Share capital and reserves}} \times 100\%$$

The ratio for Jackson plc for 2006 is:

$$\frac{78}{409} \times 100 = 19.1\%$$

This ratio is quite similar to the previous one, but considers matters more specifically from the shareholders' viewpoint. For this reason, the profit figure is that which is earned by the shareholders after all charges have been met.

Gross profit margin

$$\frac{\text{Gross profit}}{\text{Sales revenue}} \times 100\%$$

The ratio for Jackson plc for 2006 is:

$$\frac{359}{837} \times 100 = 42.9\%$$

This shows what percentage of the sales revenue remains after the expense of making the stock available to the customers is taken into account. There is a range of pricing and output strategies that a business can employ. At one end of the range is the strategy of charging very low prices for the output, so that customers are attracted, leading to a high sales revenue (turnover). At the other end is the strategy of charging a fairly high price, leading to a relatively low sales turnover. In principle neither strategy is preferable to the other. Where in the range the business seeks to operate is a matter of managerial judgement. In making this judgement, managers will need to take account of the nature of the market and of the business's own cost structure.

Net profit margin

$$\frac{\text{Net profit before long-term interest and tax}}{\text{Sales revenue}} \times 100\%$$

The ratio for Jackson plc for 2006 is:

$$\frac{135}{837} \times 100 = 16.1\%$$

This ratio shows what is left of sales revenue after all of the expenses of running the business for the period have been met. Once again it should be as large as possible, provided that high profit margins are not being earned at the expense of some other aspect. Again a 'short-termist' attitude to profit could lead to an apparently impressive net profit margin, but one that may not be sustainable into the future.

Activity ratios

Activity ratios are used to try to assess the effectiveness of a business in using its assets.

Net asset turnover

$$\frac{\text{Sales revenue}}{\text{Total assets less current liabilities}}$$

The ratio for Jackson plc for 2006 is:

$$\frac{837}{709} = 1.18 \text{ times}$$

This ratio enables a judgement to be made on the extent to which the business has generated revenue. As in the return on capital employed ratio, the net assets figure is used as a measure of the size of the business. This ratio is a measure of the effectiveness with which assets are being used to generate sales. The size of this ratio will be a reflection of the business's strategy on margins and turnover, discussed above in the context of the gross profit margin ratio. A high ratio is not necessarily beneficial if margins are so small that the net profit generated is unsatisfactory.

It is worth noting the direct relationship between return on net assets, net profit margin and net asset turnover. If you look back at the definition of each of these ratios you will see that:

$$\text{Return on net assets} = \text{Net profit margin} \times \text{Net asset turnover}$$

Looking at these ratios for Jackson plc for 2006 (see above), we have:

$$\text{RONA}(19.0\%) = \text{NPM}(16.1\%) \times \text{NAT}(1.18)$$

It can be quite helpful to look at sales revenue relative to various elements of the net assets. For example, if there is a relatively small net asset turnover ratio, further analysis can be undertaken to assess non-current asset turnover, current asset turnover, and so forth. This may enable an analyst to make a judgement about the reason for the low net asset turnover figure. This in turn may reveal that the business has an abnormal balance between the various elements of net assets, for example relatively high non-current assets.

Stockholding period

$$\frac{\text{Stock held}}{\text{Stock used}} \times 365 \text{ days}$$

Jackson plc is a manufacturer that makes things to order and therefore has no stock of finished goods. Let us assume that all the stock at the year end is of raw materials (rather than work in progress).

The ratio for Jackson plc for 2006 is:

$$\frac{43}{253} \times 365 = 62.0 \text{ days}$$

This ratio indicates the average number of days for which stock remains in the business before it is taken into production. Good stock management would cause this figure to be as low as possible, consistent with there being sufficient stock available to meet production needs.

The stock turnover ratio is the reciprocal of this, that is:

$$\frac{\text{Stock used}}{\text{Stock held}}$$

The management of stock and the other working capital elements is discussed in some detail in Chapter 13.

Debtor collection period (days debtors)

$$\frac{\text{Trade debtors}}{\text{Credit sales}} \times 365 \text{ days}$$

Assuming that all of the business's sales are on credit, the ratio for Jackson plc for 2006 is:

$$\frac{96}{837} \times 365 = 41.9 \text{ days}$$

This ratio tells us how long, on average, following the sale on credit, trade debtors take to meet their obligation to pay. A well-managed debtor policy will lead to debtors taking as short a time as possible to pay, without damaging good customer relations.

Creditor payment period (days creditors)

$$\frac{\text{Trade creditors}}{\text{Credit purchases}} \times 365 \text{ days}$$

Assuming that all of the purchases are on credit and that the trade creditors relate only to purchases of raw materials stock, the ratio for Jackson plc for 2006 is:

$$\frac{45}{255} \times 365 = 64.4 \text{ days}$$

This ratio tells us how long, on average, following a purchase on credit, the business takes to meet its obligation to pay for the goods or service bought. A well-managed creditor policy will lead to as much 'free' credit being taken as possible without damaging the goodwill of suppliers.

Liquidity ratios

Liquidity ratios are used to try to assess how well the business manages its working capital.

Current ratio

$$\frac{\text{Current assets}}{\text{Current liabilities}}$$

The ratio for Jackson plc for 2006 is:

$$\frac{176}{90} = 1.96 : 1$$

Note that this ratio is usually expressed by stating the amount of current assets per £1 of current liabilities.

The current ratio provides some measure of how the balance has been struck between the two aspects of working capital. Usually, businesses seek to have current ratios higher than 1 : 1, that is, they try to avoid having current assets financed entirely from current liabilities. In this way they hope to give the short-term creditors confidence that there are sufficient liquid assets comfortably to cover their claims.

Rule-of-thumb figures for this ratio tend to be bandied about in the literature and in financial management folklore, a popular figure being 2 : 1. In fact, actual figures tend to vary widely but there seem to be characteristic figures for different industries. The high street supermarket chains typically seem to have ratios below 1 : 1, whereas manufacturers have very much higher levels. The difference is almost certainly explained by the make-up of the current assets. In supermarkets, current assets consist of cash and fast-moving stock in trade; supermarkets do not sell on credit (therefore they have no trade debtors), and, typically, stock does not stay long on the shelves. Thus all their current assets are in a fairly liquid state, being either cash or, in the normal course of events, items naturally turning into cash within a week or two. Manufacturers, by contrast, typically sell on credit and, since they need to hold stocks of raw materials, finished goods and some amount of work in progress (WIP), many of their current assets are perhaps several months away from turning into cash.

See Table 13.1 on page 352 for some impression of current ratios in practice.

Quick assets (liquid or acid test) ratio

$$\frac{\text{Liquid assets}}{\text{Current liabilities}}$$

The ratio for Jackson plc for 2006 is:

$$\frac{133}{90} = 1.48 : 1$$

The quick assets ratio addresses itself fairly directly to the question: if short-term creditors were to demand payment of their claims more or less immediately, would there be sufficient liquid assets to meet them? We might ask ourselves whether it is likely that all the short-term creditors would demand their money at once. The answer is probably no, provided that they remained confident that payment would be forthcoming at the normal time. Those advancing credit without cast-iron security, which would be the position of the typical provider of short-term credit, do so for their own commercial advantage (for example, in order to sell their products) and they do so because they have reasonable confidence that they will be paid. Signs, including a weak quick assets ratio, that the business may not be able to pay are likely to erode that confidence, triggering demands for immediate payment.

What is included in *liquid assets* in the calculation of the quick assets ratio is a matter of judgement. For a supermarket, these would probably include all current assets, since none of them is likely to be too far away from turning into cash. For a manufacturer, they would probably exclude stocks and possibly some debtors.

We can probably say that, in theory, irrespective of the nature of business involved, this ratio should be about 1 : 1. The difference between the types of business is in effect adjusted in the definition of liquid assets. As can be seen in Table 13.1 on page 352, in practice they tend not to be as high as this for well-established businesses.

No credit period

$$\frac{\text{Cash (and near cash)}}{\text{Average daily cash running costs}}$$

The ratio for Jackson plc for 2006 is:

$$\frac{25}{(478 + 111 + 113 + 30 - 63)/365} = 13.6 \text{ days}$$

The numerator (top of the fraction) is cash. The denominator (bottom of the fraction) is the average expenses, excluding depreciation (£63 000 for the year). Depreciation is excluded because it is not an expense that gives rise to a cash flow.

This is a more dynamic measure of liquidity than is the quick assets ratio. It asks for how many days the business could continue to operate without any further injection of cash. In this way it relates the level of the business's liquid assets to that required to enable normal operations to be maintained.

This ratio should be as large as possible, consistent with not having too much unproductive cash at the bank. There is some discussion of the advantages and disadvantages of holding cash in Chapter 13.

Capital gearing ratios

Capital gearing is concerned with the relative sizes of the funds provided by shareholders, on the one hand, and by loan creditors on the other. This is an important issue in business finance, about which there are various theories and a body of empirical evidence. This is discussed in some detail in Chapter 11.

For reasons that are raised in Chapter 11, loan financing tends to be cheaper than equity financing. On the other hand, loan financing exposes the shareholders to greater risk than does equity financing. Ratios in this area tend to be concerned with assessing the level of capital gearing.

Debt to equity ratio

$$\frac{\text{Borrowings (long- and short-term)}}{\text{Total equity (shares plus reserves)}}$$

The ratio for Jackson plc for 2006 is:

$$\frac{300}{409} = 0.73 : 1$$

It is not easy to say whether a particular figure represents a high figure. 'High' is probably defined as significantly larger than is typically found in the industry in which the business operates.

Times interest covered

$$\frac{\text{Profit before interest and tax}}{\text{Interest charges}}$$

The ratio for Jackson plc for 2006 is:

$$\frac{135}{30} = 4.5 \text{ times}$$

This ratio looks at how many times the interest could be met from the profits. It is therefore some measure of how easily the business is able to cover its interest payment obligations out of its profits.

Investors' ratios

Investors' ratios are concerned with looking at the business from the point of view of a shareholder, perhaps owning shares in a stock exchange listed business. These ratios are of the type that appear in the financial pages of newspapers. Two of those that we shall be considering are partly based on the current market price of the shares. We shall work on the basis that Jackson plc's ordinary shares had a market value of £5.10 on 31 December 2006.

Earnings per share

$$\frac{\text{Profit after interest and tax}}{\text{Number of ordinary shares}}$$

The ratio for Jackson plc for 2006 is:

$$\frac{78}{200} = £0.39 \text{ (or 39p) per share}$$

The earnings per share figure is the profit attributable to each share. It is not the dividend paid per share, unless all of the profit is paid as a dividend, which would be unusual. We should bear in mind that the profit, or at least the wealth represented by that profit, belongs to the shareholders whether it is paid to them or not. In Chapter 12 we shall consider whether shareholders prefer to receive dividends or to 'plough back' their profits.

Price/earnings ratio

$$\frac{\text{Current market price per share}}{\text{Earnings per share}}$$

The ratio for Jackson plc at 31 December 2006 is:

$$\frac{5.10}{0.39} = 13.1$$

The price/earnings (P/E) ratio can be seen as the number of years that it would take, at the current share price and rate of earnings, for the earnings from the share to cover the price of the share. This has been a very popular means of assessing shares.

A share with a high P/E ratio is one that has a high price compared with its recent earnings. This implies that investors are confident of growth in future earnings. It will, of course, be on the basis of expectations of future profits that investors will assess the value of shares.

Dividend yield

$$\frac{\text{Dividend per share (grossed up for tax)}}{\text{Current market price per share}} \times 100\%$$

The ratio for Jackson plc at 31 December 2006 is:

$$\frac{(20/200) \times (100/90)}{5.10} \times 100 = 2.2\%$$

This ratio seeks to assess the cash return on investment earned by the shareholders. To this extent it enables a comparison to be made with other investment opportunities available. It is necessary to 'gross up' the dividend received because it is received as if income tax at 10 per cent had been deducted before payment. Since rates of return on investment are usually quoted in gross (pre-tax) terms, it makes for a more valid comparison.

Whether a high or a low figure is to be preferred for dividend yield depends greatly on the needs and investment objectives of the shareholders.

Dividend cover

$$\frac{\text{Profit after interest and tax}}{\text{Total dividend}}$$

The ratio for Jackson plc for 2006 is:

$$\frac{78}{20} = 3.9 \text{ times}$$

The dividend cover ratio indicates how comfortably the business can meet the dividend out of current profits. The higher the ratio, the more confident shareholders can be that the dividend will be maintained, at least at the current level, even if there were to be a downturn in profits.

We can now go on to assess Jackson plc through its accounting ratios. To give us a basis for comparison we shall assess the 2006 results against those for 2005. The profit and loss account and balance sheet for the earlier year are given in the appendix to this chapter. The following is a table of the 2006 ratios with their 2005 counterparts:

Jackson plc
Accounting ratios for the years ended 31 December

	2005	2006
Profitability ratios		
Return on net assets (%)	14.9	19.0
Return on equity (%)	13.1	19.1
Gross profit margin (%)	43.8	42.9
Net profit margin (%)	13.8	16.1
Activity ratios		
Net asset turnover (times)	1.08	1.18
Stockholding period (days)	78.8	62.0
Debtor collection period (days)	56.2	41.9
Creditor payment period (days)	83.9	64.4
Liquidity ratios		
Current	0.99 : 1	1.96 : 1
Quick assets	0.73 : 1	1.48 : 1
No credit period (days)	(54.0)	13.6
Capital gearing ratios		
Debt to equity	1.10 : 1	0.73 : 1
Times interest covered (times)	2.9	4.5
Investors' ratios		
Earnings per share (£)	0.23	0.39
Price/earnings	15.2	13.1
Dividend yield (%)	2.4	2.2
Dividend cover (times)	3.1	3.9

Comment on Jackson plc's ratios

In 2006 there was a significantly higher ratio for return on net assets than was the case in 2005, which would normally be seen as desirable. This has been achieved mainly through an increased net asset turnover, which more than overcame the small decrease in the gross profit margin. Thus the business was more effective at making sales in 2006 than it was in 2005. Net profit margin rose because of the strong increase in turnover, despite an increase in the amounts spent on overheads.

Liquidity improved dramatically from a level that was probably an unhealthy one, to one that would probably be considered fairly strong. This was achieved through the reduction in both the amount of time for which stock was held and the time taken to collect trade debts. Creditors were more promptly paid in 2006 than they were in 2005. This represents a reduction over the year in the extent to which the business took advantage of the availability of this theoretically cost-free form of finance. This may have been done deliberately with a view to improving relations with suppliers.

Partly through the elimination of the overdraft, and partly as a result of relatively high ploughed-back profit expanding reserves, the gearing ratio dropped significantly.

The increased profit with no increase in the number of shares issued led directly to an increase in earnings per share. The price/earnings ratio diminished despite a much better profit performance by the business in 2006. This can be explained by the fact that the share price is driven by investors' expectations of the future of the business. Thus the price in 2005 reflected the future, rather than the 2005 profits, which were used in the calculation of that year's ratio. The increased profit led to an increase in the dividend cover despite the raised dividend in 2006.

Generally we have a picture of a business that has significantly improved in most aspects of its performance and position over the year. It was more profitable, which led to strong cash flows (see the cash flow statement) and, therefore, to much better liquidity and lower capital gearing.

Apart from the problems of ratio analysis, which we shall consider shortly, it must be recognised that this analysis is very limited in its scope. We have considered only two years' figures. It would probably be much more instructive to have looked at ratios stretching over a number of years. We have only used another period for the same business as our basis of comparison. It would be at least as useful to compare Jackson plc's performance with that of other businesses in the industry; perhaps the industry averages for the various ratios. Possibly best of all would be to compare actual performance with the planned one. We know that the debtor collection period was shorter for Jackson plc in 2006 than it had been in 2005, but this is not to say that this represented a satisfactory performance compared with the industry average, or compared with the business's budgeted debtor collection period.

Other ratios

There is an almost limitless number of ratios that can be calculated from one set of financial statements. Those that we have considered represent only a sample, though they are what seem to be the more popular ratios used in practice. Certain ratios may be particularly appropriate in certain types of business. Obviously a stockholding period ratio is appropriate to a business that deals in stock in some way. To a business offering a service, it would be inappropriate.

Ratios need not be derived exclusively from financial statements. The sales revenue per employee ratio is widely used. Cost per tonne/mile (that is, the cost of transporting a tonne of cargo for one mile) is widely used in the transport industry. Sales revenue per square metre of selling area is widely used in the retail trade.

Caution in interpretation of ratios

It must be obvious from what we have seen so far that ratio analysis is not a very exact science. The choice of the ratios that are calculated, the precise definition of these ratios and the conclusions that are drawn are very much matters of judgement and conjecture. Ratios tend to raise questions rather than answer them. Ratios can highlight areas where this year's performance was different from last year's, or where one business's performance was different from that of other businesses in the industry. They will not tell you whether this year's performance was better than planned, better than that of other years, or whether Business A is better than the rest.

It follows that it is not appropriate to be dogmatic in interpreting ratios. For example, the debtor collection period for Jackson plc was shorter for 2006 than it was for 2005. This cannot automatically be interpreted as an improvement, however. It might be that a lot of pressure has been put on debtors to pay promptly and that this has led to some loss of customer goodwill, which will, in due course, have an adverse effect on the business's profitability.

Problems with accounting figures

Earlier in the chapter, we considered the nature of accounting information and problems with using it. In the context of accounting ratios, there are probably two particularly significant weaknesses. First there is a tendency for the profit and loss account to overstate profit, relative to a more true assessment of the amount of wealth created. Second there is a tendency for balance sheet figures to understate the amount of wealth that is tied up in the business. This is a particular problem when we are dealing with ratios that are calculated using one figure from the profit and loss account and one from the balance sheet. A good example of this is the return on net assets ratio. For example, would it be wise to conclude that Jackson plc's return on net assets of 19.0 per cent for 2006 represents a better return than bank deposit account interest of, say 5 per cent, even ignoring the disparity in the level of risk?

Another problem with using balance sheet figures is that they represent the position at a single, defined, point in time. This point in time, the particular business's accounting year end, may not be typical of the business throughout the rest of the year. This may be true by design: for example, management may choose a particular year-end date because stocks tend to be low at that time. It is quite common for businesses to have to carry out a physical count of the stock at the accounting year end, and this task will be made easier if stock levels are low. Using year-end balance sheet figures may therefore result in ratios which are unrepresentative of the business's performance during the year and may, in turn, lead to inappropriate decisions being made about the future course of the business.

Cadbury Schweppes plc, the confectionary and drinks business, mentions in its 2003 annual report that the balance sheet date represents a low point in the business's seasonal borrowing cycle. This is presumably to warn readers that the business's borrowings, shown in the year-end balance sheet, are unusually low compared with the position at other times in the year.

Where a particular ratio relates a balance sheet figure to one from the profit and loss account, there is a further problem. The balance sheet represents the position at a particular point in time, but the profit and loss account summarises a series of transactions over the period. If the balance sheet figure is not typical of the period, this can lead to distorted ratios. For example, we calculated the return on net assets for Jackson plc by relating the profit before interest and tax to net assets at the *end* of the year. Yet it is clear that at other times in the year the net assets were not the same as the year-end figure (see the 2005 balance sheet, in the appendix to this chapter). In other words, the net assets that were invested to generate the £135 000 were probably less than £709 000 for almost all the year.

An obvious solution to this problem is to average the opening and closing net assets figures and use this in the calculation of the ratio. This would give a ratio for 2006 of 19.9 per cent (that is, $\{135/[(651 + 709)/2] \times 100\%\}$), compared with the original calculated figure of 19.0 per cent. As we have already seen, it is not necessarily the case that the balance sheet figures are representative of the rest of the year. Here simply averaging the start-of-year and end-of-year figures may not do much to remove the distortion. This will not pose a problem to those who have access to the underlying figures, because they can deduce a more representative average figure. Outsiders can do no more than average the figures that are available.

Although International Accounting Standards seek to promote the extent to which financial statements are prepared on a consistent basis from one business to another, there are still areas where one business may legitimately deal with the same transaction, or event, differently from another. This creates yet another problem for the analyst when trying to use accounting information to make inter-business comparisons.

Other limitations of accounting ratios

Accounting ratios are derived by dividing one figure by another. As with all such indicators, information is lost. A significant reason for using ratios is to enable comparison to be made between factors that are not of the same scale. Sometimes, however, it is important to be aware of scale. For example, the size of a business could double from one year to the next, yet ratios alone would not reveal this fact.

It can be instructive just to look at the financial statements, trying to take a critical and enquiring approach. For example, if we look back at Jackson plc's balance sheet for 2006, several points are worthy of note, none of which would be picked up from using the standard accounting ratios.

The first of these relates to non-current assets, specifically to plant and machinery. The depreciation provision, that is, that part of the cost that has already been treated as an expense, is almost as large as the cost figure (£226 000 compared with £253 000). This implies that the plant is coming close to the end of the life that was predicted for it by the business. This, in turn, has several implications:

- The business is operating with old plant. This may mean it is not using the most sophisticated methods available to it. This may or may not be an important factor. Nevertheless it is something that someone trying to make an assessment of the business might find useful to know in building up the picture.

- Perhaps, more significantly, it seems likely that there will be a need to replace various items of plant in the fairly near future. This will probably lead to a major outflow of cash. This raises the question of where the cash will come from. Has the business got the levels of cash required or will it need to borrow or to raise new share capital?

- In a period of inflation, old non-current assets imply a low annual depreciation expense charged in the profit and loss account. Thus profits may be overstated relative to that which would result if newer plant were to be used.

The next point relates to the reserves. It would be perfectly legal for the shareholders to be paid a dividend of £209 000 at 31 December 2006, perhaps selling some of the non-cash assets to raise the necessary funds. This massive outflow of assets could have disastrous effects on the business in terms of its ability to continue to trade. Although this large dividend is not a likely outcome, the possibility is there and it should be recognised.

A third point is that, according to the balance sheet, there is a reasonable amount of scope for further secured borrowing. The loan stock is probably secured on the freehold land. The freehold land is probably understated on the balance sheet in terms of its market value. This could mean that the business would be able to double the amount of its secured borrowings. Since it is very much easier to borrow when the security of an asset, such as land, can be offered, this might be a significant point. Perhaps the business does not want to raise further loan capital. Perhaps there are separate reasons why it would find it difficult to borrow. On the other hand, the point about unused security might be an important one.

Similar points could be identified by further careful scrutiny of the financial statements, without even bothering to calculate any ratios.

3.7 Using accounting ratios to predict financial failure

One objective of ratio analysis is to try to make a judgement about a particular business's ability to survive and to prosper. Analysts have shown much interest in ratios that may be able to indicate businesses that are in danger of getting into financial difficulties. The reason for this is that several groups who have relationships with the business stand to suffer significantly should it collapse. Creditors may find that they will not receive the money they are owed, employees will probably lose their jobs, suppliers will probably lose a customer, and shareholders will probably lose some or all of their investment. If these parties were able to identify 'at risk' businesses, they could take steps to try to put things back on a sounder footing, or they could take damage limitation actions such as getting their money repaid quickly, changing their jobs, finding new customers or selling their shares.

Originally, interest focused on identifying individual ratios that might represent good indicators of likely financial collapse. Researchers, therefore, sought to be able to make statements such as: if the value for a particular ratio (such as the quick assets ratio) fell below a particular threshold figure, the business was then significantly at risk. They attempted to do this by identifying particular ratios that might be good discriminators between potential failures and survivors.

The researchers then found a group of businesses that had actually collapsed. They matched this with a second group of non-failed businesses, one of which was as like one of the collapsed group as possible in size, industry and so forth. This provided them with two groups, as far as possible identical, except that all the members of one group had collapsed and none of the second group had. Using past data on all the businesses, attempts were made to examine whether the particular ratios selected were significantly different between the two groups during the period (say, five years) leading up to the date of the collapse of the failed businesses. Where there were significant differences for a specific ratio, it was possible to say that a figure of above a particular level implied that the business was safe, whereas a figure below this benchmark implied that it was at risk.

Although researchers achieved some success at identifying ratios that were reasonably good discriminators, thoughts turned to the possibility that combining several quite good discriminator ratios might produce a **Z-score** (so called) that would be a very good discriminator. The most notable UK researcher in this field, Taffler, derived the following model:

$$Z = C_0 + C_1 \frac{\text{Profit before tax}}{\text{Current liabilities}} + C_2 \frac{\text{Current assets}}{\text{Total liabilities}}$$
$$+ C_3 \frac{\text{Current liabilities}}{\text{Total assets}} + C_4 \frac{\text{Liquid current assets}}{\text{Daily cash operating expenses}}$$

where C_0 to C_4 are constants.

According to Taffler (1995) a positive Z-score means that the business is sound, at least in the medium term. A negative Z-score implies a relatively high risk of failure. As might be expected, the higher or lower the Z-score, the more powerful is the indication of the potential survival or failure of the business concerned.

The recommended reading at the end of this chapter provides some discussion on the benefits and problems of using Z-scores.

Summary

Financial statements of three kinds are produced by the typical UK business

- Profit and loss account – summarises operating performance for a period.
- Balance sheet – summarises the position at a point in time.
- Cash flow statement – summarises cash movements during a period.

The rules of accounting lead to financial statements showing

- A restrictive definition of an asset, tending to mean that assets are understated.
- Only aspects measurable in monetary terms.
- A prudent or cautious view of profits and shareholders' wealth.
- A view that assumes the business is a going concern.
- A view that ignores inflation.
- Revenues as occurring on the date the work was done, and that their value is established and there is confidence that the cash will be received.
- A match between revenues and linked expenses in the same accounting period.
- A view that wealth consists of more than just cash.

Creative accounting

- There have been recent cases of managers (directors) taking actions to make the business appear more buoyant and profitable than it really is.
- This represents a problem to analysts since it is difficult to know whether a business's financial statements are reliable or not.
- Steps have been taken by the relevant regulatory authorities to tighten up the rules and avoid creative accounting.

Ratio analysis

- Compares two related figures, usually both from the same set of financial statements.
- An aid to understanding what the financial statements are saying.
- An inexact science, so results must be interpreted cautiously.
- Suffers from the weaknesses of financial statements.
- Can be used to predict financial failure – Z-scores.

Ratios are divided into five groups

- Profitability ratios – concerned with effectiveness at generating profit.
- Activity ratios – concerned with efficiency of using assets.
- Liquidity ratios – concerned with the ability to meet short-term debts.
- Capital gearing ratios – concerned with the relationship between equity and debt financing.
- Investors' ratios – concerned with returns to shareholders.

Further reading

Most books on accounting provide an introduction to accounting and to accounting ratios. Many business finance books include a chapter on accounting ratios. McLaney and Atrill (2005) provide an introduction to accounting and accounting ratios. Taffler (1995) describes research into the use of Z-scores in the identification of businesses that are potential financial failures.

Relevant websites

The Financial Times/WILink site enables you to order the annual reports and accounts of many listed businesses, including some overseas ones.
http://ft.ar.wilink.com

The Companies House site gives access to the addresses of all UK companies. You can write to them to ask for a copy of their annual report and accounts.
www.companieshouse.gov.uk/info/

Most major businesses put a copy of their annual report and financial statements on their website. If you go to any of the websites listed at the end of various chapters you can use the menu to bring up the financial statements. These can be read online or downloaded.

The websites of the businesses featured in this chapter are:

Cadbury Schweppes plc	www.cadburyschweppes.com
Enron Corporation	www.enron.com
MCI	www.mci.com
Xerox Corporation	www.xerox.com

REVIEW QUESTIONS

Suggested answers to review questions appear in Appendix 3.

3.1 What is a balance sheet? Does the balance sheet tell us how much the business is worth?

3.2 The first entry in the standard-layout cash flow statement is 'cash flow from operating activities'. How is this figure different from the net profit before interest and tax for the same period?

3.3 People often refer to a business as having a 'strong balance sheet'. What do they mean by this?

(Note that the answer to this question is not really provided in the chapter. However, a combination of background knowledge and common sense should enable you to come up with some relevant points.)

3.4 What does the matching convention of accounting say?

3.5 The quick assets ratio is not included in Taffler's Z-score model for identifying potentially failing businesses. Why is this?

(Note that the answer to this question is not really provided in the chapter. However, a combination of background knowledge and common sense should enable you to come up with some relevant points.)

3.6 Why is ratio analysis of financial statements considered to be so useful? Why is a careful reading of the statements not enough?

PROBLEMS

Sample answers to problems marked with an asterisk appear in Appendix 4.

(Problems 3.1 and 3.2 are basic-level problems, whereas problems 3.3 to 3.6 are more advanced and may contain some practical complications.)

3.1* Counterpoint plc, a wholesaler, has the following accounting ratios for last year and this year:

	Last year	This year
Return on net assets (RONA) (%)	28.25	13.51
Return on equity (ROE) (%)	51.95	18.35
Gross profit margin (%)	50.00	40.00
Net profit margin (%)	20.00	10.00
Debtors collection period (days)	73	91
Creditors payment period (days)	37	46
Current ratio	1.63 : 1	1.37 : 1
Quick assets	0.72	0.60
Debt to equity (%)	128.87	141.28

On the basis of these ratios, comment on the performance of the business this year as compared with last year.

3.2 The following are the highly simplified financial statements of Duration Ltd for last year:

**Profit and loss account for
the year ended 31 December**

	£000
Turnover	80
Cost of sales	(60)
Gross profit	20
Operating expenses	(10)
Operating profit	10

Balance sheet as at 31 December

	£000	£000
Non-current assets		70
Current assets	20	
Current liabilities	(12)	
Net current assets		8
		78
Equity (Capital and reserves)		78

Calculate as many accounting ratios as the information provided will allow.

3.3* The following are the financial statements of Persona Ltd for last year and this year:

Profit and loss account for the year ended 31 December

	Last year £000	This year £000
Turnover	499	602
Cost of sales	(335)	(423)
Gross profit	164	179
Operating expenses	(127)	(148)
Operating profit (before interest and taxation)	37	31
Interest payable	(13)	(22)
Profit before taxation	24	9
Taxation	(8)	(3)
Profit after taxation	16	6
Dividend paid	(6)	(6)
Retained profit for the year	10	–
Retained profit brought forward from the previous year	74	84
Retained profit carried forward	84	84

Balance sheet as at 31 December

	Last year £000	Last year £000	This year £000	This year £000
Non-current assets		110		125
Current assets				
Stocks	68		83	
Debtors	80		96	
Cash	6		2	
	154		181	
Current liabilities				
Creditors	(71)		(116)	
Taxation	(8)		–	
	(79)		(116)	
Net current assets		75		65
		185		190
Non-current liabilities				
Loan stocks		(55)		(60)
		130		130
Equity				
Ordinary shares of £0.50 each		13		13
Capital reserves		33		33
Retained profit		84		84
		130		130

Calculate the following ratios for both years:

- *Return on net assets*
- *Return on equity*
- *Gross profit margin*
- *Net profit margin*

- *Current ratio*
- *Quick assets ratio*
- *Stockholding period*.

3.4 The following is the balance sheet (in abbreviated form) of Projections Ltd for last year:

Balance sheet as at 31 December

	£000	£000
Non-current assets		
Cost		290
Less: Accumulated depreciation		(110)
		180
Current assets		
Stock	26	
Debtors	35	
Cash	5	
	66	
Current liabilities		
Trade creditors	(21)	
Taxation	(27)	
	(48)	
Net current assets		18
		198
Equity		
Share capital		150
Retained profit		48
		198

The following plans have been made for next year:

1 Sales revenue is expected to total £350 000, all on credit. Sales will be made at a steady rate over the year and two months' credit will be allowed to customers.

2 £200 000 worth of stock will be bought during the year, all on credit. Purchases will be made at a steady rate over the year and creditors will allow one month's credit.

3 New non-current assets will be bought, and paid for, during the year at a cost of £30 000. No disposals of non-current assets are planned. The depreciation expense for the year will be 10 per cent of the cost of the non-current assets owned at the end of the year.

4 Stock at the end of the year is expected to be double what it was at the beginning of the year.

5 Operating expenses, other than depreciation, are expected to total £52 000, of which £5000 will remain unpaid at the end of the year.

6 During the year, the tax noted in the start-of-the-year balance sheet will be paid.

7 The tax rate can be assumed to be 25 per cent. The tax will not be paid during the year.

8 A dividend of £10 000 will be paid during the year.

Prepare a projected profit and loss account for next year and a balance sheet as at the end of next year, to the nearest £1000.

3.5* The following are the financial statements of Prospect plc for last year and this year:

Profit and loss account for the year ended 31 December

	Last year £000	This year £000
Turnover	14 006	22 410
Cost of sales	(7 496)	(11 618)
Gross profit	6 510	10 792
Operating expenses	(4 410)	(6 174)
Operating profit (before interest and taxation)	2 100	4 618
Interest payable	(432)	(912)
Profit before taxation	1 668	3 706
Taxation	(420)	(780)
Profit after taxation	1 248	2 926
Dividend paid	(600)	(800)
Retained profit for the year	648	2 126
Retained profit brought forward from the previous year	722	1 370
Retained profit carried forward	1 370	3 496

Balance sheet as at 31 December

	Last year £000	Last year £000	This year £000	This year £000
Non-current assets		8 600		16 470
Current assets				
Stocks	2 418		4 820	
Trade debtors	1 614		2 744	
Other debtors	268		402	
Cash	56		8	
	4 356		7 974	
Current liabilities				
Trade creditors	(1 214)		(2 612)	
Other creditors	(848)		(1 202)	
Taxation	(420)		(780)	
Bank overdraft	–		(3 250)	
	(2 482)		(7 844)	
Net current assets		1 874		130
		10 474		16 600
Non-current liabilities				
Loan stocks		(3 600)		(7 600)
		6 874		9 000
Equity				
Ordinary shares of £0.50 each		3 600		3 600
Capital reserves		1 904		1 904
Retained profit		1 370		3 496
		6 874		9 000

Calculate the following financial ratios for Prospect plc for last year and this year. (Use year-end figures where balance sheet items are involved.)

- *Return on net assets*
- *Return on equity*
- *Gross profit margin*
- *Net profit margin*
- *Stockholding period*
- *Debtors collection period (days)*
- *Current ratio*
- *Quick assets ratio*
- *Gearing (debt to equity) ratio.*

Use these ratios to comment on the performance and position of Prospect plc from the point of view of:

(a) a 10% owner of the equity; and

(b) the business's bank.

3.6 The following are the financial statements of High Street Enterprises plc for last year and this year:

Profit and loss account for the year ended 31 December

	Last year £000	This year £000
Turnover	15 600	24 160
Cost of sales	(8 740)	(12 564)
Gross profit	6 860	11 596
Operating expenses	(5 296)	(8 572)
Operating profit (before interest and taxation)	1 564	3 024
Interest payable	–	(132)
Profit before taxation	1 564	2 892
Taxation	(316)	(518)
Profit after taxation	1 248	2 374
Dividend paid	(500)	(600)
Retained profit for the year	748	1 774
Retained profit brought forward from the previous year	996	1 744
Retained profit carried forward	1 744	3 518

Balance sheet as at 31 December

	Last year		This year	
	£000	£000	£000	£000
Non-current assets		8 072		10 456
Current assets				
Stocks	1 850		3 166	
Trade debtors	976		1 992	
Cash	624		52	
	3 450		5 210	
Current liabilities				
Trade creditors	(1 320)		(2 236)	
Other creditors	(1 142)		(1 434)	
Taxation	(316)		(518)	
Bank overdraft	–		(360)	
	(2 778)		(4 548)	
Net current assets		672		662
		8 744		11 118
Non-current liabilities				
Loan stocks		–		(600)
		8 744		10 518
Equity				
Ordinary shares of £0.50 each		6 500		6 500
Capital reserves		500		500
Retained profit		1 744		3 518
		8 744		10 518

Calculate the suitable financial ratios for High Street Enterprises plc for last year and this year (use year-end figures where balance sheet items are involved) and use the ratios to comment on the performance and position of the business.

There are both a set of **multiple-choice questions** and **missing-word questions** available on the website. These specifically cover the material contained in this chapter. These can be attempted and graded (with feedback) online.

There are also **two additional problems**, with solutions, that relate to the material covered in this chapter.

Go to **www.pearsoned.co.uk/atrillmclaney** and follow the links.

APPENDIX **Jackson plc's profit and loss account and balance sheet**

Jackson plc
Profit and loss account for the year ended 31 December 2005

	£000	£000	£000
Revenue			701
Cost of sales (including depreciation £22 000			
and raw materials stock usage £190 000			
Raw material purchases totalled £187 000)			(394)
Gross profit			307
Distribution costs			
Salaries and wages	(35)		
Motor expenses	(41)		
Depreciation of motor vehicles	(16)		
Sundry distribution expenses	(14)	(106)	
Administrative expenses			
Salaries and wages	(53)		
Motor expenses	(21)		
Depreciation of motor vehicles	(18)		
Sundry administrative expenses	(12)	(104)	210
Operating profit for the year			97
Interest payable			(33)
Profit on ordinary activities before taxation			64
Tax on ordinary activities			(18)
Profit on ordinary activities after taxation			46
Retained profit brought forward from last year			120
			166
Dividend paid on ordinary shares			(15)
Retained profit carried forward to next year			151

Jackson plc
Balance sheet as at 31 December 2005

	Cost £000	Depreciation £000	£000
Non-current assets			
Freehold land	550	–	550
Plant and machinery	232	(198)	34
Motor vehicles	90	(21)	69
	872	(219)	653
Current assets			
Stock	41		
Trade debtors (receivables)	108		
Prepaid expenses	10	159	
Current liabilities			
Bank overdraft	(86)		
Trade creditors (payables)	(43)		
Accrued expenses	(14)		
Taxation	(18)	(161)	
Net current liabilities			(2)
Total assets less current liabilities			651
Non-current liabilities			
10% secured loan stock			(300)
			351
Equity			
Ordinary share capital – 200 000 shares of £1 each			200
Profit and loss account			151
			351

The market price of the ordinary £1 shares was £3.49 at 31 December 2005.

PART 2

Investment decisions

Investment decisions are at the heart of the management of all businesses, except the very smallest. Errors in these decisions can, and do, prove fatal for many businesses.

Chapter 4 starts with an explanation of the nature and importance of investment decisions. It continues with some fairly detailed explanations of the major investment appraisal methods used in practice. It concludes with some discussion of the extent of the use of these methods in practice.

Chapter 5 is concerned with some of the practical aspects of making investment decisions. These include taxation, inflation, the problem of dealing with shortages of investment finance and real options. Chapter 5 also looks at how investment decisions fit in with the business's overall strategy.

Chapters 6 and 7 are concerned with various approaches to trying to make investment decisions where, as is always the case in reality, the outcome of an investment is not known with certainty. Chapter 7 is particularly concerned with attempting to assess the likely effect of the risk of a particular investment on the business's owners.

Chapter 4

Investment appraisal methods

Objectives In this chapter we shall deal with the following:

→ the importance of the investment decision

→ the derivation of the concept of net present value

→ an explanation of the meaning of net present value

→ a consideration of the other approaches used to assess investment projects

→ a consideration of some recent research bearing on the investment appraisal techniques used by businesses in the UK and elsewhere in the world

4.1 Introduction

Businesses operate by raising finance from various sources, which is then invested in assets, usually 'real' assets such as plant and machinery. Some businesses also invest in 'financial' assets, like the shares of another business or loans to businesses and individuals. Investment involves outflows (payments) of cash causing inflows (receipts) of cash. It is in the nature of things that cash flows (out and in) do not all occur at the same time: there is some time lag, perhaps a considerable one, between them. The typical investment project opportunity involves a relatively large outflow of cash initially, giving rise to a subsequent stream of cash inflows.

The business's balance sheet gives, at any particular point in time and subject to the limitations of such financial statements, the types of investment that it still has running. Balance sheets group assets by type (non-current assets, current assets and so on) rather than by investment project. Thus it is not possible from the standard balance sheet to discern which part of the non-current and current assets relate to any particular project. Nonetheless, a glance at a business's balance sheet would give us some idea of the scale of investment and to some extent an idea of its nature.

Selecting which investment opportunities to pursue and which to avoid is a vital matter to businesses because:

- individual projects frequently involve relatively large and irreversible commitments of finance; and

- they involve this commitment for long, often very long, periods of time.

Clearly, the investment decision is a central one. Costly and far-reaching mistakes can, and probably will, be made unless businesses take great care in making their investment decisions. Bad decisions usually cause major financial loss, and any particular business can make only a limited number of misjudgements before collapse occurs.

In this chapter we consider how such decisions should best be made, after which we shall go on to consider how they appear to be made in practice.

Note that, for the time being, we shall continue to assume that all cash flows can be predicted with certainty and that the borrowing and lending rates of interest are equal to one another and equal between all individuals and businesses.

4.2 Net present value

A basis for decision making

Given the crucial importance of businesses' investment decisions, managers need a logical and practical assessment procedure by which to appraise the investment opportunities that come to their notice. This procedure must promote the shareholders' wealth maximisation objective, though in the final decision other objectives may well be taken into account.

We discovered in Chapter 2 that if we assume that interest rates are equal, both as between borrowing and lending and as between businesses and individuals, an investment project undertaken by the business that will increase the spending power of any one particular shareholder in the business, at one particular point in time, will also increase the spending power of all other shareholders at any other point in time. (We may remember that in Example 2.2 in Chapter 2 all three of our shareholders were advantaged by acceptance of Project X, despite having different attitudes to the timing of their spending.)

It seems, therefore, that it does not matter whether our assessment procedure focuses on the effect on present wealth or on wealth in a year's time, or indeed at any other time. If undertaking a particular project will increase present wealth, it will also increase future wealth; that project that will most increase present wealth will most increase future wealth. Thus, both for accept/reject decisions and for ranking projects in order of desirability, it does not matter in respect of which point in time the effect on wealth is assessed, provided that consistency is maintained.

Since we are always at 'the present' when making the decision, to consider a project's effect on present wealth is probably most logical. This tends to be the approach taken in practice.

The time value of money

Suppose that a business is offered an opportunity that involves investing £10m which will give rise to a cash receipt of £12m. Should it make the investment? Obviously if the cash expenditure and the cash receipt are to occur at the same time (most unlikely in real life) this represents a good investment since it will work towards the assumed objective of maximising shareholders' wealth. It will increase the value of the business by £2m.

Now suppose that the opportunity means investing £10m now, which will give rise to a £12m cash inflow after one year. Here the decision is not so straightforward because we cannot directly compare £1 now with £1 after a year (or any other period of time). Each £1 of present expenditure is not equal in value to each £1 receipt in the future. This is for three reasons:

- *Interest forgone.* If the £1 is tied up in the investment for a year, the business cannot invest it elsewhere, so there is an interest *opportunity cost.*

- *Inflation.* Owing to the loss of purchasing power of money if there is inflation in the economy (which has been the case in each of the past fifty years in the UK and in most other countries), £1 will not buy as many goods and services next year as it will this year.

- *Risk.* The £1 paid out today is certain but the £1 anticipated receipt next year is not. However confident we may be of the receipt, we can never be sure of it. In many business contexts the degree of uncertainty about future receipts is profound.

At present we shall concentrate on only the first of these three, namely interest forgone, leaving issues involving inflation and risk to be dealt with in later chapters. At this point it must be emphasised that even if there were no inflation and the investment were regarded as risk free, it would still be true that £1 today is not equivalent to £1 tomorrow simply because of the opportunity cost of interest forgone.

Given that money has a 'time value' (£1 today is not equivalent to £1 after some period of time), how are we to make a comparison between the £10m now and the £12m in a year's time, and so reach a decision?

Net present value

One possible approach would be to add the interest forgone to the £10m, that is, to assess the amount to which the £10m would have grown after one year, with interest, and then to compare it with the £12m. Suppose that the current rate of interest is 10 per cent, then the value of the £10m after one year would be £11m (£1m interest). In other words, if the business were to pursue the alternative opportunity of putting the money into an interest-yielding bank deposit account, it would have £11m by the end of the year, whereas it will get £12m if it makes the investment under consideration. This is a totally logical and correct approach to take, and the conclusion that the investment should be made because it will lead to a *net future value* of £1m (£12m – £11m) is a correct one (that is, the business will be £1m better off at the end of the year than had it pursued the alternative of putting the money in a bank deposit account for the year).

Another approach is to ask: if it is possible to borrow money at 10 per cent, how much could be borrowed immediately against the £12m such that the £12m would exactly repay the borrowing plus interest thereon? Put another way, if the business could compare the £10m outflow with the present equivalent of £12m, an alternative basis for the decision could be achieved. The present value of the £12m is not necessarily a theoretical notion since it would be possible for the business to borrow and have the present value of £12m immediately if it wanted to do so. Indeed, it could even do this to raise the finance with which to make the £10m investment (assuming that the present value of the £12m is greater than £10m).

The next question is: what is the present value of £12m receivable after one year with an interest rate of 10 per cent p.a.?

If we let the amount that could be borrowed (the present value of £12m in a year's time) be B, then:

$$£12m = B + \left(B \times \frac{10}{100} \right)$$

which represents the borrowing plus the interest for one year. This can be rewritten as:

$$£12m = B \left(1 + \frac{10}{100} \right) = B \times 1.10$$

$$B = \frac{£12m}{1.10}$$

$$= £10.9m$$

If we now compare the present value of the future receipt with the initial investment, the result is an investment with a **net present value** (NPV) of £0.9m (that is, £10.9m – £10m). Since this is positive, the investment should be undertaken assuming that there is not a mutually exclusive alternative with a higher positive NPV.

The £0.9m NPV tells us that the business can invest £10m immediately to gain a benefit whose present value is £10.9m, that is, a £0.9m increase in the value of the business. In principle, the business could borrow £10.9m, use £10m to make the investment and immediately pay out the £0.9m to the shareholders as a dividend. When the £12m is received, it will exactly pay off the £10.9m plus the interest on it.

More generally, we can say that the NPV of an investment opportunity lasting for one year is:

$$NPV = C_0 + \frac{C_1}{1 + r}$$

where C_0 is the cash flow immediately (time 0) (usually negative, that is, an outflow of cash), C_1 is the cash flow after one year and r is the interest rate.

In practice we tend to use the NPV approach (that is, *discounting* future cash flows) for investment decision making rather than the net future value approach (*compounding* present cash flows), though in essence neither is superior to the other.

The reasons for favouring NPV are twofold:

● When comparing investment opportunities (choosing between one and the other), if net future value is to be used, a decision must be made on when in the future the value should be assessed (that is, how many years compounding). If the opportunities are of unequal length (say, one lasts three years, the other five years), this can cause difficulties.

● If the opportunity is to be assessed by looking at its effect on the value of the business, it seems more logical to look at the present effect rather than the future effect.

Investment opportunities lasting for more than one year

In reality, few investment opportunities last for only one year. Suppose that an investment opportunity involves an immediate cash outflow C_0, which will give rise to inflows C_1 and C_2 after one and two years, respectively. We already know that the present value of C_1 (effect on the present value of the business) is:

$$\frac{C_1}{(1 + r)}$$

By the same logic that we used to derive this, we could borrow an amount, say A, which would exactly be repaid with interest compounded annually out of C_2. Then:

$$C_2 = A + Ar + (A + Ar)r$$

which is the original borrowing A plus interest on that amount for the first year plus interest on these two during the second year.

This expression expands to:

$$C_2 = A + Ar + Ar + Ar^2$$

Taking A outside brackets,

$$C_2 = A(1 + 2r + r^2)$$

$$C_2 = A(1 + r)^2$$

$$A = \frac{C_2}{(1 + r)^2}$$

Following this logic, it can be shown that the present value (PV) of any amount of cash receivable after n years (C_n) would be:

$$PV = \frac{C_n}{(1 + r)^n}$$

Thus the NPV of any investment opportunity is given by:

$$NPV = \sum_{n=0}^{t} \frac{C_n}{(1 + r)^n}$$

where t is the life of the opportunity in years. In other words, the NPV of an opportunity is the sum, taking account of plus and minus signs, of all of the annual cash flows, each one discounted according to how far into the future it will occur. The value n in this equation need not be a whole number. The present value of a cash receipt expected in 18 months' time would be:

$$\frac{C_{18/12}}{(1 + r)^{18/12}}$$

There is no reason why the interest rate should be the same from one year to the next; in practice, financing costs alter over time. If the financing cost were r_1 for year 1 and r_2 for year 2, the present value of the year 2 cash flow would be:

$$\frac{C_2}{(1 + r_1)(1 + r_2)}$$

Note that it is as logical to discount future *payments* as it is to discount future receipts, where the investment opportunity involves a future payment.

Example 4.1

Seagull plc has identified that it could make operating cost savings in production by buying an automatic press. There are two suitable such presses on the market, the Zenith and the Super. The relevant data relating to each of these are as follows:

	Zenith £	Super £
Cost (payable immediately)	20 000	25 000
Annual savings:		
Year 1	4 000	8 000
2	6 000	6 000
3	6 000	5 000
4	7 000	6 000
5	6 000	8 000

The annual savings are, in effect, opportunity cash inflows in that they represent savings from the cash outflows that would occur if the investment were not undertaken.

Which, if either, of these machines should be bought if the financing cost is a constant 12 per cent p.a.?

Solution

The NPV of each machine is as follows:

	Zenith £	Super £
Present value of cash flows:		
Year 0	(20 000)	(25 000)
1	$\dfrac{4000}{(1 + 0.12)} = 3\ 571$	$\dfrac{8000}{(1 + 0.12)} = 7\ 143$
2	$\dfrac{6000}{(1 + 0.12)^2} = 4\ 783$	$\dfrac{6000}{(1 + 0.12)^2} = 4\ 783$
3	$\dfrac{6000}{(1 + 0.12)^3} = 4\ 271$	$\dfrac{5000}{(1 + 0.12)^3} = 3\ 559$
4	$\dfrac{7000}{(1 + 0.12)^4} = 4\ 449$	$\dfrac{6000}{(1 + 0.12)^4} = 3\ 813$
5	$\dfrac{6000}{(1 + 0.12)^5} = \underline{3\ 405}$	$\dfrac{8000}{(1 + 0.12)^5} = \underline{4\ 539}$
	$\underline{478}$	$\underline{(1\ 163)}$

The process, shown in Example 4.1, of converting future cash flows to their present value is known as *discounting*.

The business should buy the Zenith, as this would have a positive effect on its wealth, whereas the Super would have a negative effect. It would not be prepared to buy the Super even if it were the only such machine on the market, as to do so would be to the detriment of the business's wealth. The value of the business would, in theory, fall as a result of buying the Super. Only if it were possible to negotiate a price lower than £23 837 (the sum of the discounted savings) would the value of the annual savings justify the cost of that machine, given the financing cost. Similarly, up to £20 479 could be paid for a Zenith and it would continue to be a profitable investment.

It is important to recognise that the size of the initial investment is not of any direct relevance to the decision (except to the extent that it is used in the calculation of the NPV); only the NPV is important. Thus if the Super had a positive NPV of £480 it would be selected in preference to the Zenith. The only occasion where we would need to consider the size of the NPV in relation to the amount of investment is when there is a shortage of investment finance and projects need to compete for it. This is an aspect that we shall consider in Chapter 5.

The use of tables and annuity factors

Tables are readily available that will give the discount factor $1/(1 + r)^n$ for a range of values of r and n. Such a table appears in Appendix 1 to this book. Note that it is not necessary to use the table for discounting; the calculation can easily be done from first principles.

Sometimes an investment involves a series of identical annual cash flows (known as an **annuity**) and a constant discount rate. In these circumstances there is a short cut to the present value of those cash flows.

Example 4.2

A business is faced with an investment opportunity that involves an initial investment of £35 000, which is expected to generate annual inflows of £10 000 at the end of each of the next five years. The business's cost of finance is 10 per cent p.a. What is the NPV of this opportunity?

Solution

If we discounted the cash inflows using the table of discount factors in Appendix 1, the calculation would be as follows:

$$(10\ 000 \times 0.909) + (10\ 000 \times 0.826) + (10\ 000 \times 0.751) + (10\ 000 \times 0.683) + (10\ 000 \times 0.621)$$

This could be rewritten as:

$$10\ 000(0.909 + 0.826 + 0.751 + 0.683 + 0.621)$$

where the figures in brackets are the discount factors at 10 per cent for a series of annual cash flows of £1 for five years. In cases like this, the calculation is made easier for us in that tables giving the sum of discount factors, for specified periods of years and discount rates, are readily available. There is one shown in Appendix 2 to this book. Such tables are usually known as *annuity tables*. Even if such a table is not available, you can easily deduce the appropriate annuity factor. It is:

$$\frac{1}{r}\left[1 - \frac{1}{(1 + r)^n}\right]$$

where r is the annual interest rate and n the number of years into the future that the annuity will persist.

According to the table, the annuity factor for five years and 10 per cent, is 3.791. (This only differs from the sum of the five discount factors through rounding.)

Thus the NPV of the investment opportunity is:

$$-£35\ 000 + (£10\ 000 \times 3.791) = +£2910$$

It is probably fair to say that investments that give rise to a steady stream of cash flows are, in real life, relatively rare.

How a positive NPV leads to an increase in shareholder wealth

It has been said, quite reasonably, that the essence of good investment is to buy assets for less than they are worth. Clearly, doing this will enhance the value of the business. When assessing an investment opportunity like the Zenith, it comes down to the question of how much the estimated future benefits of owning the Zenith are worth to Seagull plc. The future benefits obviously are the potential operating cost savings (£4000 in year 1, £6000 in year 2 and so on).

To be able to assess whether the value of these future benefits exceeds the cost of the asset (£20 000), it is necessary to place some value on them. As we have just seen, the most logical way to value them is to discount each one according to how far into the future the benefit will occur, and to sum the discounted values. Thus NPV is an entirely logical approach to investment decision making, assuming that enhancing the value of the shareholders' wealth is the objective being pursued.

Discounting – a slightly different view

Staying with Example 4.1, a superficial assessment of the Zenith might be that it should be bought because it cost £20 000 but would yield total savings of £29 000 (the sum of the annual savings), that is, a benefit of £9000. A second look reveals, however, that this cannot be a correct assessment as no rational investor regards all of the £s in the question as equivalent to one another. We should all prefer £1 today to £1 next year and we should prefer it still more to £1 in five years' time, even if we assume no erosion of value through inflation. This is because if we have the £1 today we could, if we wished, lend it so that after a year we should have not only the £1 but the interest on it as well.

Simply adding the annual savings and comparing the total with the initial outlay would be illogical. It would be like saying that a certain item is more expensive to buy in France than in the UK because it costs 8 in France and only 5 in the UK, without mentioning that the 8 is euros whereas the 5 is pounds sterling. To make a sensible price comparison we should need to convert the euros to pounds sterling or vice versa.

Similarly, it is necessary to undertake a conversion exercise to make the various cash flows associated with the Zenith comparable. As we have seen, we usually convert the future cash flows to their present value and then make the comparison. The conversion exercise is, of course, achieved by discounting, by multiplying each of the cash flows by

$$\frac{1}{(1 + r)^n}$$

NPV can thus be viewed as a *time adjusted* measure of financial benefit.

Conclusions on NPV

We have seen that NPV is a totally logical way of assessing investment opportunities. It is logical, and, therefore, useful, because it possesses the following attributes:

- It is directly related to the objective of maximisation of shareholders' wealth (value of the business).

- It takes full account of the timing of the investment outlay and of the benefits; in other words, the time value of money is properly reflected. Put yet another way, NPV properly takes account of the cost of financing the investment.

- All relevant, measurable financial information concerning the decision is taken into account.

- It is practical and easy to use (once the anticipated cash flows have been identified), and it gives clear and unambiguous signals to the decision maker. It should be emphasised that accurately identifying future cash flows is usually difficult to do in practice.

Despite NPV's clear logic in appraising investments, research shows that there are three other approaches that are widely used in the UK and elsewhere. These are:

- internal rate of return;
- payback period; and
- accounting rate of return.

We shall now consider these three in turn.

4.3 Internal rate of return

The internal rate of return approach seeks to identify the rate of return that an investment project yields on the basis of the amount of the original investment remaining outstanding during any period, compounding interest annually. The **internal rate of return** (IRR) is the discount rate that gives the project a zero NPV. Identifying the IRR, at least by hand, can be laborious.

Example 4.3

What is the IRR of a project where an initial investment of £120 is followed a year later by a cash inflow of £138 with no further inflows?

Solution

Obviously it is:

$$\frac{138 - 120}{120} \times 100 = 15\%$$

What, though, if the project were £120 initial outlay, followed by inflows of £69 at the end of each of the following two years?

Despite the total inflows still being £138, the IRR is not 15 per cent because this project runs over two years, not one. Nor is it 7.5 per cent (that is, 15 ÷ 2) because much of the £120 is repaid in year 1 and so is not outstanding for both years. In fact, the first £69 represents a payment of the *interest* on the investment during the first year plus a repayment of part of the *capital* (the £120). By the same token, the second £69 represents interest on the remaining capital outstanding after the end of year 1, plus a second instalment of capital such that this second instalment will exactly repay the £120 initial outlay.

A moment's reflection should lead us to conclude that the IRR is closely related to the NPV discount rate. In fact, the IRR of a project is the discount rate that if applied to the project yields a zero NPV. For Example 4.3 it is the solution for r to the following expression:

$$-120 + \frac{69}{(1 + r)} + \frac{69}{(1 + r)^2} = 0$$

This equation could be solved using the standard solution to a quadratic equation: not a difficult matter. (The answer, incidentally, is $r = 0.099$, or 9.9 per cent.)

When we look at, say, the Zenith (from Example 4.1), the IRR of an investment in that machine is r in the following equation:

$$-20\,000 + \frac{4000}{(1 + r)} + \frac{6000}{(1 + r)^2} + \frac{6000}{(1 + r)^3} + \frac{7000}{(1 + r)^4} + \frac{6000}{(1 + r)^5} = 0$$

Solving for r here is not so easy, and in fact some iterative (trial and error) approach becomes the only practical one. Thus we solve for r by trying various values of r until we find one that satisfies, or almost satisfies, the equation. On page 82, we calculated that the Zenith has an NPV of +£479 when discounted at 12 per cent. This tells us that it must have an IRR of above 12 per cent, because the higher the discount rate, the lower the present value of each future cash inflow. How much above 12 per cent we do not know, so we just pick a rate, say 14 per cent.

Year	Cash flow £	Present value £
0	(20 000)	(20 000)
1	$\dfrac{4000}{(1 + 0.14)}$	3 508
2	$\dfrac{6000}{(1 + 0.14)^2}$	4 614
3	$\dfrac{6000}{(1 + 0.14)^3}$	4 050
4	$\dfrac{7000}{(1 + 0.14)^4}$	4 144
5	$\dfrac{6000}{(1 + 0.14)^5}$	3 114
		NPV (570)

As the NPV when the cash flows are discounted at 14 per cent is negative, the discount rate that gives this project a zero NPV lies below 14 per cent and apparently close to the mid-point between 14 and 12 per cent. We can prove this by discounting at 13 per cent:

Year	Cash flow £	Present value £
0	(20 000)	(20 000)
1	$\dfrac{4000}{(1 + 0.13)}$	3 540
2	$\dfrac{6000}{(1 + 0.13)^2}$	4 698
3	$\dfrac{6000}{(1 + 0.13)^3}$	4 158
4	$\dfrac{7000}{(1 + 0.13)^4}$	4 291
5	$\dfrac{6000}{(1 + 0.13)^5}$	3 258
		NPV (55)

Given the scale of the investment, an NPV of –£55 is not significantly different from zero, so we can conclude that, for practical purposes, the IRR is 13 per cent.

If we wanted to have a more accurate figure, however, we could make an approximation based on the following logic. Increasing the discount rate by 1 per cent (from 12 to 13 per cent) reduced the NPV by £534 (from +£479 to –£55). Thus, increasing the NPV from –£55 to zero would require a reduction in the discount rate of 55/534 of 1 per cent, that is, about 0.1 per cent. So the IRR is 12.9 per cent. This approach is not strictly correct because it assumes that the graph of NPV against the discount rate is a straight line. This assumption is not correct, as can be seen in Figure 4.1 below. The graph is close enough to being a straight line for this not to be important, however.

Where IRR is used to assess projects, the decision rule is that only those with an IRR above a predetermined hurdle rate are accepted. Where projects are competing, the project with the higher IRR is selected.

The IRR approach so closely resembles the NPV method that at first glance it appears that they are completely interchangeable. This might lead us to assume that they will always come to similar conclusions on any particular decision. This is not true, as can be seen by the following comparison of methods.

Comparison of IRR and NPV methods

● IRR is *not* directly related to the wealth maximisation criterion. If the hurdle rate used in conjunction with IRR is the cost of borrowing then in most cases the two methods will give identical results. Certainly this will tend to be the case on straightforward accept/reject decisions (that is, those where the decision is either to invest or not to invest). With competing projects the two methods sometimes give conflicting signals. This can happen where two mutually exclusive projects involve a different scale of investment.

Example 4.4

Two mutually exclusive projects have the following features:

| | | Cash flows | |
	Year	Project A £	Project B £
	0	(10 000)	(6 000)
	1	6 000	3 650
	2	6 000	3 650
	NPV @ 10%	413	334
	IRR (approximately)	13%	14%

If the cost of finance to support the project is 10 per cent p.a., which of these two projects should the business pursue (assuming no shortage of finance)?

Solution

There is obviously a conflict here. Both NPV and IRR are based on discounting cash flows. Both Projects A and B have IRRs in excess of 10 per cent, and yet there are different signals coming from the NPVs and the IRRs. Figure 4.1 shows a graph of NPV against discount rate for these two projects. Not surprisingly, as the discount rate is increased the NPV falls. The points where the curves cross the horizontal axis are the respective IRRs for each of the projects.

It is possible to read off, for each project, the NPV for any particular discount rate. For example, at an 8 per cent discount rate the NPV for Project A is about £700 and for Project B about £500. At discount rates up to about 11.3 per cent Project A has the higher NPV. Beyond 11.3 per cent, Project B has the higher NPV.

Going back to the question as to which project should be selected, the correct answer (from a wealth maximisation viewpoint) is Project A. Although Project B would be more attractive if the cost of finance were over 11.3 per cent, the fact of the matter is that in Example 4.4 it is 10 per cent, and since the business is pursuing wealth maximisation, Project A is the one that should be selected. The conflict arises because of an incorrect implicit assumption made by those who use the IRR method. The discount rate used with NPV should be the *opportunity* cost of finance. That is, it is the cost of funds raised to support the project or, if funds are available already, it is the rate that they could alternatively earn. According to the basic principles of NPV, referred to earlier in this chapter, this is the borrowing/lending rate. Using IRR, on the other hand, requires the assumption that the opportunity cost of finance is equal to the IRR, so that funds generated by the project could either be used to repay finance raised at the IRR or be reinvested at that rate. Clearly this is illogical: why should it be the case in Example 4.4 that if Project A is undertaken the opportunity cost of finance is 13 per cent, whereas if Project B is pursued it suddenly becomes 14 per cent? The choice by a particular business of specific projects would not alter the economic environment so that either the cost of finance or the investment alternatives change with the business's decision.

What IRR fails to recognise in Example 4.4 is that if finance is available at 10 per cent the business's wealth would be more greatly increased by earning 13 per cent on a £10 000 investment than 14 per cent on a £6000 one. IRR fails to recognise this because it does not consider value; it is concerned only with percentage returns.

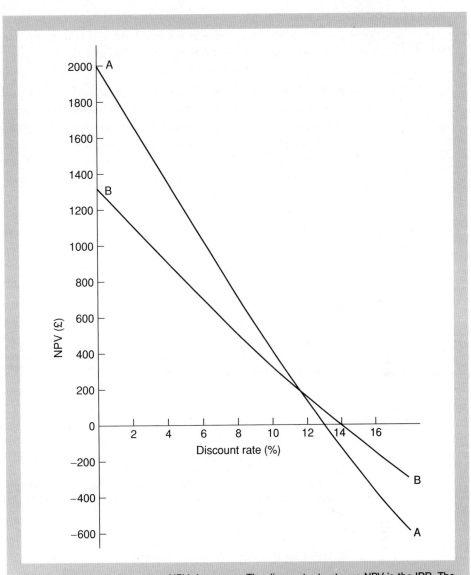

As the discount rate increases, NPV decreases. The discount rate at zero NPV is the IRR. The rate at which NPV decreases differs from one project to another. Whereas Project A has the higher NPV where the discount rate is below about 11.3 per cent, Project B has the higher NPV where the discount rate is higher than 11.3 per cent. This leads to a conflict between the signals given by NPV and IRR, where the discount rate is less than 11.3 per cent. At about 11.3 per cent the NPVs of the two projects are equal (at about £200).

Figure 4.1
Graph of the NPV against the discount rate for two projects (A and B)

- Like NPV, IRR takes full account both of the cash flows and of the time value of money.

- All relevant information about the decision is taken into account by IRR, but it also takes into account the irrelevant, or perhaps more strictly the incorrect, assumption (which we discussed in the first point above) made by IRR.

- IRR can be an unwieldy method to use, if done by hand. This is not a practical problem, however, since computer software that will derive IRRs is widely available: most spreadsheet packages are able to perform this function. The trial and error process, which is the only way to arrive at IRRs, can be very time consuming, especially where long projects are involved, if it is done by hand. Computers also try and err, but they can do it much more quickly than humans, so deriving IRRs is not usually a great difficulty in practice.

- IRR cannot cope with differing required rates of return (hurdle rates). IRR provides an average rate of return for a particular investment project. This rate is normally compared with a required rate of return to make a judgement on the investment. If financing costs are expected to alter over the life of the project, this comparison might cause difficulties. The reasons why the required rate may differ from one year to the next include the possibility that market interest rates might alter over time. If the IRR for a particular project is consistently above or below all of the different annual required rates of return, there is no difficulty in making the decision. Where, however, the IRR lies above the required rate in some years but below it in others, the decision maker has a virtually insoluble problem. This situation poses no problem for NPV because, as we saw in section 4.2 of this chapter, it is perfectly logical to use different discount rates for each year's cash flows.

- The IRR model does not always produce clear and unambiguous results. As we have seen, the IRR for a particular project is the solution to an equation containing only one unknown factor. This unknown factor is, however, raised to as many powers as there are time periods in the project. Any project, therefore, that goes beyond one time period (in practice one year) will usually have as many IRRs as there are time periods. In practice, this is not often a problem because all but one of the roots (IRRs) will either be unreal (for example, the square root of a negative number) or negative themselves, and therefore of no economic significance. Sometimes, though, all of the roots can be unreal so that there is no IRR for some projects. Sometimes a project can have more than one real root (IRR).

These problems of multiple and no IRRs can arise with projects that have *unconventional* cash flows. Projects A and B in Example 4.4 have conventional cash flows in that, chronologically, a negative cash flow is followed by positive ones, that is, there is only one change of sign in the cumulative cash flow total (from negative to positive between years 1 and 2 in both projects.)

However, now consider the following two projects:

	Cash flows	
Year	Project C	Project D
	£	£
0	(10 000)	10 000
1	33 000	(16 000)
2	(24 000)	12 000

Both of these projects are unconventional in that they each have two changes of sign in the cumulative cash flows. Project C changes from negative to positive between years 0 and 1 and from positive to negative between years 1 and 2. Project D does precisely the opposite.

The graphs of NPV against discount rate for each of these unconventional projects are shown in Figures 4.2 and 4.3. Project C has two IRRs (8 per cent and 122 per cent), both of which are equally correct. Which of these should be taken as being the appropriate one for investment decisions? There is no answer to this question and so here

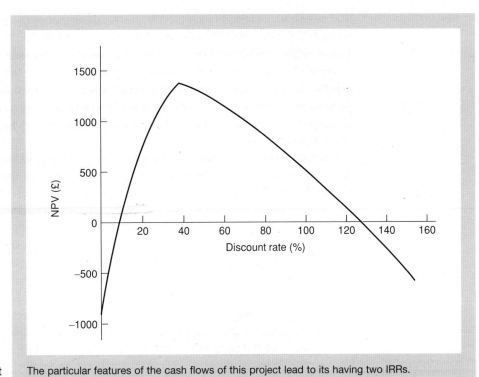

Figure 4.2
Graph of the NPV
against the discount
rate for Project C

The particular features of the cash flows of this project lead to its having two IRRs.

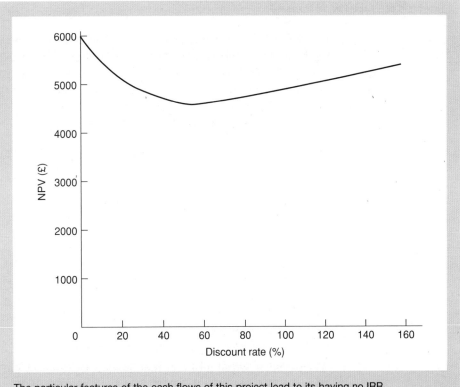

Figure 4.3
Graph of the NPV
against the discount
rate for Project D

The particular features of the cash flows of this project lead to its having no IRR.

IRR gives an ambiguous result. NPV can be used though: with any cost of finance between 8 per cent and 122 per cent the project is favourable; if the business's cost of finance is below 8 per cent or above 122 per cent the project should be rejected.

Trying to find the IRR of Project D by trial and error would be a frustrating experience because there simply is not one, at least not a real one. The graph shows there to be no intercept between the horizontal axis and the curve. Once again, IRR is incapable of assessing the project despite the fact that it has a large NPV at all discount rates.

It would be wrong to imagine that projects with unconventional cash flow profiles do not occur in practice. Probably they form a minority of the total of all projects, but nonetheless they do exist. For example, many projects involving mineral extraction would show something like the cash flow characteristics of Project C. Such projects frequently involve large commitments of cash in order to restore the land to its original contours after the mine or quarry has been fully exploited.

As a general conclusion on IRR, we can say that if the opportunity cost of finance is used as the hurdle rate, it will usually give the same signals as the NPV model. Sometimes, though, IRR will give false, ambiguous or incoherent signals, which if heeded could lead to sub-optimal decisions being made. It seems that IRR is a mathematical result rather than a reliable decision-making technique. Usually, by coincidence, it will give the right signal, but not always. There are means of modifying IRR to overcome some of these problems, but is there any point in our doing so? NPV always gives logical and clear signals and so we might as well use it as the primary assessment method all the time.

4.4 Payback period

The payback period technique asks the simple question: how long will it take for the investment to pay for itself out of the cash inflows that it is expected to generate?

Continuing to assess the investment opportunity in Example 4.1, page 82, the cash flows for which were:

Year	Zenith £	Super £
0	(20 000)	(25 000)
1	4 000	8 000
2	6 000	6 000
3	6 000	5 000
4	7 000	6 000
5	6 000	8 000

we should find that the anticipated payback periods would be:

Zenith
 4 years (assuming that the cash flows occur at year ends)
 or $3\frac{4}{7}$ years (assuming that the cash flows occur evenly over the year)

Super
4 years

→ The **payback period** (PBP) for the Zenith is represented in Figure 4.4.

The decision rule for the PBP method is that projects will be selected only if they pay for themselves within a predetermined period. Competing projects would

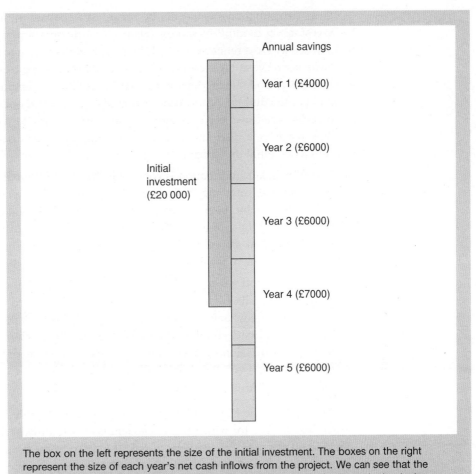

Annual savings

Year 1 (£4000)

Year 2 (£6000)

Initial investment (£20 000)

Year 3 (£6000)

Year 4 (£7000)

Year 5 (£6000)

The box on the left represents the size of the initial investment. The boxes on the right represent the size of each year's net cash inflows from the project. We can see that the total of the inflows will equal the initial investment at some point between the beginning and end of the fourth year.

Figure 4.4
Payback period for the Zenith machine

be assessed by selecting the one with the shorter PBP (provided it was within the predetermined maximum). Thus PBP favours the Zenith over the Super (if cash flows are assumed to occur evenly).

Comparison of PBP and NPV methods

- The PBP method is badly flawed to the extent that it does *not* relate to the wealth maximisation criterion: it is not concerned with increases in wealth. It promotes the acceptance of shorter-term projects and thus promotes liquidity rather than increased value.

- The PBP method takes account of the timing of the cash flows only in the most perfunctory way. The method divides the life of the project into two portions: the payback period and the period beyond it. PBP does not therefore treat cash flows differently depending on when they arise. It merely puts any particular cash flow into one of two categories: the relevant category and the irrelevant one. We can see this incompleteness of consideration of the timing of cash flows by reference to Example 4.1. With the Super, the PBP would be identical (four years) if there were no savings in each of the first three years but a £25 000 saving in year 4. Clearly, these two situations would not be regarded as equally desirable by any rational investor, yet the PBP method is incapable of distinguishing between them. Some businesses use a refinement of the PBP method that to some extent overcomes this weakness. These businesses look at the discounted figures when assessing the payback period. Taking the discounted figures for the Zenith from page 82 we can see that the discounted payback period is $4\frac{2925}{3404}$ years (about 4.86 years), assuming that the cash flows occur evenly over the year; otherwise it is 5 years. The Super does not have a discounted payback period, that is, its discounted inflows never sum to its initial investment.

- Not all relevant information is considered by the PBP method. The method completely ignores anything that occurs beyond the payback period. For example, the PBP method is incapable of discriminating between the anticipated cash flows for the Super and those of some other project with identical outflows and inflows until year 4 and then annual savings of £20 000 each year for the next ten years. This point is also true of the discounted payback approach, outlined above.

- The PBP method is very easy to use, and it will almost always give clear results. How those results are interpreted is not so straightforward though. How does the business decide what is the maximum acceptable payback period? Inevitably this is a pretty arbitrary decision, which means that the PBP method itself will tend to lead to arbitrary decision making, unless it is used for comparing competing projects and the project with the shortest PBP is always selected. Even then it would promote quick returns rather than wealth maximisation.

Advocates of the PBP method argue that it will tend to identify the less risky projects, that is, those for which the investment is at risk for least time. Even so, the PBP method takes a very limited view of risk. It only concerns itself with the risk that the project will end prematurely. It ignores such risks as sales being less than anticipated or costs being greater than planned.

We may generally conclude that PBP is not a very good method for selecting investment projects, and its use is likely to lead to sub-optimal decisions. It can, however, give insights into projects that the NPV method fails to provide, particularly on the question of liquidity. Thus the PBP method is seen by some as a useful complement to NPV.

4.5 Accounting (unadjusted) rate of return

→ The **accounting rate of return** (ARR) compares the average annual profit increase, after taking the cost of making the initial investment into account, with the amount of the initial investment. The outcome is usually expressed as a percentage.

Some users of ARR define it as average profit divided by *average* investment. Provided that the definition adopted is consistently applied, neither is superior to the other.

For the two opportunities in Example 4.1, and using the first definition of the ARR, it would be:

Zenith:

$$\frac{(4000 + 6000 + 6000 + 7000 + 6000) - 20\ 000}{5} \div 20\ 000 = 9.0\%$$

(The £20 000 is deducted from the total annual savings to take account of the cost of the depreciation of the machine over the five years.)

Super:

$$\frac{(8000 + 6000 + 5000 + 6000 + 8000) - 25\,000}{5} \div 25\,000 = 6.4\%$$

The decision rule would be that projects would only be accepted where they are expected to yield an ARR higher than some predetermined rate. With competing projects, the one with the higher ARR (Zenith in this case) would be selected. It should be noted particularly that ARR deals with accounting flows, *not* with cash flows. This is to say that ARR looks at the effect on future reported profits that a particular project will cause.

Although in Example 4.1 it has been assumed that, apart from depreciation, cash flows and accounting flows arising from the purchase of either of the presses (Zenith or Super) are the same for the years concerned, this will not always be the case for all projects to be assessed, as is explained shortly.

→   ARR is also known as the **unadjusted rate of return** and as **return on investment** (ROI).

Comparison of ARR and NPV methods

- ARR does not relate directly to wealth maximisation but pursues maximisation of a rate of return measured by accounting profits.

- ARR almost completely ignores the timing of the cash flows and hence the financing cost. The above ARRs for the Zenith and the Super would be identical irrespective of when within the five years they fell, provided that they had the same totals. With the Zenith, for example, the alternative cash flows shown below would give the same ARR as the original ones.

Year	Original £	Alternative £
0	(20 000)	(20 000)
1	4 000	25 000
2	6 000	1 000
3	6 000	1 000
4	7 000	1 000
5	6 000	1 000

Any rational investor would prefer the alternative, yet ARR cannot distinguish between them. The method makes no attempt to adjust the cash flows to reflect their timing.

- Typically, all relevant information on the cash flows (except their timing) is used in arriving at the ARR of an investment prospect. However, ARR often picks up some irrelevant data as well. This is because accounting profit is calculated on a basis that, for example, apportions a share of overheads to a particular project, even where the overheads do not vary according to whether or not the project is undertaken. In practice, it can be misleading to use accounting information to make decisions about the future in the way that the ARR approach does. This is not to say that measuring accounting profit is not a useful activity, simply that it is not a useful approach to assessing future real investment opportunities.

● ARR is easy to use, but the fact that it can be defined in two different ways can lead to confusion.

Like the PBP method, ARR seems likely to lead to poor decisions. Also, like PBP, there is the question of how the business arrives at a minimum ARR that it is prepared to accept. One of its features is the fact that it does not reflect repayments of the original investment. Take, for example, the 'alternative' cash flows for the Zenith given above. Here all of the original investment would be repaid in the first year, and it is thus a very attractive investment with a very high rate of return. Yet despite this, if the devotee of ARR decided to use the cost of borrowing (say 12 per cent) as the hurdle rate, the project would be rejected because its ARR is only 9 per cent. Perhaps, more logically, the net profit to net assets ratio taken from recent profit and loss accounts and balance sheets would be used, as this is the approach that ARR uses (hence its name). This would still be an arbitrary approach though, for why should past accounting returns on assets be felt to be a useful basis for decisions relating to the future? In any case, maximisation of accounting rates of return will not, except by coincidence, promote value maximisation.

It is possible to overcome a major problem of ARR, that is the timing problem, by using accounting profits that take full account of the finance cost involved with investment. In practice, however, this can be very unwieldy.

Table 4.1 summarises the relative merits of the four investment appraisal techniques.

Table 4.1 Summary of the relative merits of the four investment appraisal techniques

	NPV	IRR	PBP	ARR
Directly related to the wealth maximisation objective	Yes	No	No	No
Fully accounts for timing of cash flows and the time value of money	Yes	Yes	No	No
Takes account of all relevant information (other than timing)	Yes	Yes	No	Yes
Practical, easy to use and provides clear signals	Yes	Usually	Yes	Yes

4.6 Investment appraisal methods used in practice

Having considered the attributes and the theoretical strengths and weaknesses of the methods used in practice, it seems appropriate to consider the extent to which these methods are actually used by businesses.

The past 30 years have seen a large volume of research into the methods of investment appraisal used in practice. The more relevant of these for UK businesses were conducted by Pike (1982, 1996), by Pike and Wolfe (1988) (P&W), by Arnold and Hatzopoulos (2000) (A&H), by McIntyre and Coulthurst (1985) (M&C) and by Drury, Braund, Osborne and Tayles (1993) (DBOT).

Pike and P&W concentrated on very large businesses, in fact 100 of the largest 300 UK businesses. A&H surveyed 100 of the largest 1000 UK businesses, so their survey results are broadly comparable with the other surveys of large businesses. M&C looked at a sample of 141 businesses that fell within the Companies Act 1985 definition of a medium-sized company. These are businesses that satisfy two of the following three criteria: annual turnover between £1.4m and £5.75m, gross assets between £0.7m and £2.8m, and total number of employees between 50 and 250 people. Compared with the largest UK businesses, those in the M&C study would be rather small whatever the formal legal designation of their size. A&H also surveyed 100 smaller businesses, but these would have tended to be larger than those in the M&C study. The DBOT survey was of 260 UK manufacturing businesses of various sizes.

The results of these studies may be summarised as shown in Table 4.2.

Table 4.2 Investment appraisal methods used in practice in the UK

| Date of survey: | Large businesses | | | | | Smaller businesses | Manufacturing businesses (various sizes) |
	1975[1] %	1981[1] %	1986[2] %	1992[3] %	1997[4] %	1985[5] %	1993[6] %
Net present value	32	39	68	74	80	36	71
Internal rate of return	44	57	75	81	81	28	80
Payback period	73	81	92	94	70	82	86
Accounting rate of return	51	49	56	50	56	37	77
Total	200	226	291	299	287	183	314

Sources: 1 Pike (1982); 2 P&W (1988); 3 Pike (1996); 4 A&H (2000); 5 M&C (1985); 6 DBOT (1993).

These results suggest a number of factors that we shall consider next.

Appraisal methods and corporate objectives

An important point that we should bear in mind as we consider these research findings is that the choice of investment appraisal methods can quite logically be seen as evidence of the financial objective that businesses are following. This is because, when making investment decisions, businesses are frequently making judgements that will have the most profound effect on their future welfare and success.

We have already seen in section 4.2 of this chapter that NPV's major theoretical justification stems from an assumption that businesses pursue the objective of shareholder wealth maximisation. If this is the objective that they pursue in fact, we should expect to find strong adherence to NPV as the primary appraisal technique in practice. A&H found that 80 per cent of the large businesses surveyed used NPV, in almost all cases in conjunction with at least one other method. They also found that all of the large businesses surveyed used either NPV or IRR or both. In most circumstances, IRR is a good proxy for NPV.

It would probably be wrong, however, to conclude that, since NPV is not used by all businesses, shareholder wealth maximisation is not the primary objective. Indeed, Pike and Ooi (1988) found that there was no significant association between the importance to a particular business of shareholder wealth maximisation and the use of NPV. It may be that there is a lack of sophistication among some financial decision makers that causes them not to relate a particular objective to the appraisal method that will, in theory, promote it. The fact that NPV is much less popular with the smaller businesses, where less sophistication would be expected, may provide evidence for this point. On the other hand, the disparity in the use of NPV between the larger and the smaller businesses may be explained by them following different objectives.

Some businesses refer to their use of NPV and how this relates to wealth maximisation, in their annual reports. In its 2003 annual report, **Rolls-Royce plc**, the engine and power systems manufacturer, said: 'The group continues to subject all investments to rigorous examination of risks and future cash flows to ensure that they create shareholder value.' The report goes on to say that it uses discounted cash flow analysis to assess investment decisions.

Multiple appraisal methods

The fact that the totals in Table 4.2 are all greater than 100 per cent reveals that many of the businesses surveyed use more than one method. This does not necessarily mean that more than one method is consistently being used by a particular business in respect of each decision. It seems that businesses vary their approach according to the nature of the capital investment decision concerned. For example, A&H found that 80 per cent of their large business respondents used NPV. Within that 80 per cent, however, nearly three-quarters of those businesses used NPV for all decisions. At the other extreme, about 4 per cent of that 80 per cent rarely used it. It seems likely, however, that many businesses use more than one method concurrently to assess a particular investment project.

The extent of the use of multiple methods seems to be greater among large businesses than among smaller ones. A&H found that 34 per cent of larger businesses surveyed used all four methods, 42 per cent used three of the four, and 17 per cent used two of the four. M&C found that almost half of their sample of smaller businesses used only one method, and that only 13 per cent of that group used a discounting technique (NPV or IRR); 74 per cent of the single-method businesses relied entirely on the payback method.

The incidence of multiple use seems to have increased over time. According to Pike's 1975 survey of larger businesses, the average number of methods used was two. By the time of the three latest surveys of large businesses (1986 to 1997), this had grown to nearly three.

The fact that the use of multiple appraisal methods is so widespread may provide evidence that businesses pursue multiple financial objectives. On the other hand, as was suggested above, a lack of managerial sophistication may be the reason for this phenomenon.

Discounting techniques

Both NPV and IRR have shown strong growth in popularity over time with large businesses. Although the Pike and P&W studies show increasing popularity of all four methods, it is the discounting methods, particularly NPV, that have made the greatest progress. It seems likely that all, or all but a few, large businesses now use a discounting method in respect of most investment decisions. By contrast, only 44 per cent of the smaller businesses surveyed by M&C used a discounting method.

The increasing popularity of the discounting techniques is comforting to the theorists who have long argued the merits of NPV and, to a lesser extent, IRR. Why IRR remains the more popular of the discounting methods, despite its theoretical weaknesses, is not clear. It is felt by some observers that financial decision makers respond more readily to a percentage result than to an NPV expressed in £s.

It is also felt by some that decision makers prefer to leave the question of the 'hurdle rate' (minimum acceptable IRR) until after the analysis: something that NPV will not allow since the NPV cannot be deduced without selecting a discount rate. Since most discounted cash flow analysis will now be done using a computer spreadsheet or similar device, this point does not seem totally valid. This is because it is very easy to enter the predicted cash flows for a particular project and then try various discount rates to see their effect on the NPV figure.

The suggestion has also been made that some businesses may prefer to keep the minimum acceptable IRR as information confidential to senior management, and that by leaving it out of the quantitative analysis it need not become accessible to less senior staff who may be involved in deducing the IRR for particular projects.

From the popularity of NPV and the fact that, in most circumstances, IRR will give exactly the same decision as NPV, there is some evidence that businesses do, in fact, pursue shareholder wealth maximisation as a primary objective.

Boots Group plc, the chemist, seems to be an example of a user of several methods. In its 2004 annual report, Boots said: 'We also implemented a new investment appraisal process based upon a range of cash flow and accounting measures to assess value and risk. These include cash flow based criteria, such as net present value and payback, as well as return on capital employed and time to break even. The process is being rigorously applied to our store-opening programme in particular.' 'Return on capital employed' is presumably ARR. 'Time to break even' is not too clear since PBP is mentioned separately. Perhaps it is how long it will take before the takings from a new store start to make an accounting profit.

Payback period

The continued popularity of PBP has confounded finance academics for decades. As we have seen, it has serious theoretical flaws: perhaps most significantly it ignores the shareholder wealth maximisation objective. Despite these flaws it is very widely used by both large and smaller UK businesses. For 50 businesses (74 per cent) out of the 68 in the M&C study of smaller businesses that used only one method of investment appraisal, PBP was that method. It is also very popular with large businesses.

There has been much conjecture as to why PBP remains so popular. Some have suggested that it provides evidence that not all businesses pursue shareholder wealth maximisation, or at least that some couple it with 'short termism', a point that was discussed in Chapter 2. Thus shareholders may well be bearing an agency cost, in that decisions may be made that do not maximise their wealth, but could maximise the welfare of the business's managers. Pike (1985) found that businesses whose objectives emphasise shareholders' interests tend to place less reliance on PBP.

Others (for example, Boardman, Reinhart and Celec 1982) have suggested that PBP may fit into a strategic framework involving matching returns from investments with the need to repay a term loan of some description. If, in such 'capital constrained' businesses, cash inflows do not arise early in the life of the investment, the business may collapse before the anticipated cash flows arrive. The evidence seems not to support this suggestion, however. Graham and Harvey (2001) undertook a survey (in 1999) of practices in a large number of larger US businesses. They found no evidence that capital constrained businesses are more likely to use PBP.

Another possible reason for PBP's continued popularity may lie with its simplicity and therefore usefulness as a means of one manager arguing the case for a particular project when confronted by opposition to that project from other managers who do not have a financial background. Perhaps it is used in conjunction with a discounting method or is used only for relatively minor decisions. Another possibility is that PBP is used as an initial 'screening' device through which all project proposals must pass before the detailed analysis is conducted. This point is somewhat undermined, however, by the fact that both PBP and the discounting methods use the same basic inputs (predicted cash flows). Having identified these inputs it is little additional effort to apply discount factors to them.

Chen and Clark (1994) undertook a survey of US manufacturing businesses and found that the use of PBP is strongly linked to the extent to which managers believe that accounting profits are important to the way in which their performance is assessed, particularly where their remuneration is linked to accounting profit. PBP tends to favour projects that will generate fairly high operating cash flows and, therefore, profits, in the short term.

A further, and perhaps more likely, reason for PBP's continued popularity may lie in the fact that the discounting methods whose theoretical development mostly occurred during the 1960s have only recently fully established themselves. This may be particularly so with non-financial managers. The popularity of PBP may stem from a lack of managerial sophistication. This point is supported by the fact that PBP is overwhelmingly the most popular approach taken by the smaller businesses, according to M&C. It would be expected that there would be a narrower range of financial management skills in such businesses than in the larger ones. The more recent decline in the popularity of PBP coupled with the increasing use of the discounting methods may indicate increasing managerial sophistication.

Graham and Harvey (2001) found that businesses at the smaller end (in terms of sales turnover) of those surveyed were likely to use PBP almost as frequently as they used NPV or IRR. They also found that, among such businesses, PBP was most likely to be of importance where the most senior management was older and less well qualified. This seems to support the suggestion that PBP tends to be used by less sophisticated managers.

One well-known, and very successful, business that seems to use PBP is **Next plc**, the high street retailer. It says in its 2004 annual report: 'Every new store aims to pay back the net capital invested in less than 24 months.' It is interesting to note that Next states its financial objective as to 'maximise sustainable growth in earnings per share', rather than to maximise shareholder wealth.

Accounting rate of return

Despite its almost complete lack of theoretical justification ARR continues to be widely used. As with PBP, this fact could call into question whether businesses do actually seek a shareholder wealth maximisation objective. The widespread use of ARR may indicate that businesses are in fact pursuing some accounting return objective, possibly in conjunction with some wealth-enhancing one (also discussed in Chapter 2). However, as with PBP, use of ARR may imply a lack of managerial sophistication. Most managements are fairly used to financial statements: profit and loss accounts and the like. It may be that they prefer to think in accounting terms rather than in discounted cash flow terms, despite the fact that accounting measures are inappropriate for assessing individual investment opportunities, certainly where shareholder wealth maximisation is the goal. It may simply be that managers are concerned with the effect on the financial statements of undertaking a particular project. The research cited in Chapter 2 (page 22) suggests that some businesses pursue a percentage rate of return on investment objective. This is a measure based on the financial statements.

International experiences

Survey research undertaken in the USA shows that the same broad usage of the investment appraisal methods applies there as in the UK (Scapens, Sale and Tikkas 1982; Moore and Reichert 1983; Levy and Sarnat 1988; Chen 1995; Graham and Harvey 2001). There seems to be a greater incidence of the use of discounting methods than in the UK but, in contrast with the UK, NPV is more popular than IRR with US businesses. Interestingly, PBP seems to be as popular in the USA as it is in the UK.

According to evidence cited by Horngren, Bhimani, Foster and Datar (2001), methods used in investment appraisal differ markedly from country to country. In most countries cited, PBP is very popular; NPV and IRR are fairly widely used. ARR is not very popular anywhere, except in South Korea and the UK. Interestingly, the discounting methods hardly seem to be used at all in Japan.

Hodder (1986) also found little usage of discounting techniques of investment appraisal in Japan. He did, however, encounter widespread use of a net future value assessment. As we discussed earlier in this chapter, this approach is a logical alternative to NPV, and will give the same signals. Another widely used approach that Hodder found to be used in Japan was a version of ARR which included an allowance for interest on the investment finance in deducing the annual accounting profit. Hodder noted an emphasis on 'consensus' decision making, where managers at various levels discuss major investments at length, and where the results of formal financial appraisal are only part of the process of reaching a decision.

Non-financial appraisal of investment decisions

There is evidence that many businesses, perhaps most of them, base their investment decisions only partly on quantitative, financial assessments of each opportunity. Chen (1995) surveyed 115 stock market listed, large US manufacturing businesses. He found much the same popularity of the established financial appraisal methods as previous US researchers. He also found heavy reliance on non-financial methods. Overall, the discounting methods (NPV and IRR) were more popular than either PBP or ARR, but, for all types of investment, non-financial methods ranked almost as highly as the discounting methods, and well ahead of either PBP or ARR.

Non-financial methods here included such matters as whether the particular investment under consideration fitted in with the general strategy of the businesses, whether it seemed to have growth potential and whether the competitive position of the product and the business would be improved.

It can be argued that these so-called non-financial issues are simply financial ones that are particularly difficult to quantify. For example, a business would be keen to invest in a way that fitted in with its general strategy because it believes that this will tend to lead it into areas that are likely, in the long run, to be those with the greatest wealth enhancement potential.

The relationship between corporate strategy and investment appraisal is explored in Chapter 5.

Summary

Net present value (NPV)

- NPV = the sum of the discounted values of the cash flows from the investment.

- Money has a time value.

- Decision rule: All positive NPV investments enhance shareholders' wealth; the greater the NPV, the greater the enhancement and the more desirable the project.

- PV of a cash flow $(C_n) = C_n/(1 + r)^n$, assuming a constant interest rate.

- The act of discounting brings cash flows at different points in time to a common valuation basis (their present value), which enables them to be directly compared.

- Conclusions on NPV:

  - Relates directly to shareholders' wealth objective.

  - Takes account of the timing of cash flows.

  - Takes all relevant information into account.

  - Provides clear signals and practical to use.

Internal rate of return (IRR)

- IRR = the discount rate that causes a project to have a zero NPV.

- It represents the average percentage return on the investment, taking account of the fact that cash may be flowing in and out of the project at various points in its life.

- Decision rule: Projects that have an IRR greater than the cost of capital are acceptable; the greater the IRR, the more desirable the project.

- Usually cannot be calculated directly; a trial and error approach is usually necessary.

- Conclusions on IRR:

  - It does not relate directly to shareholders' wealth. Usually it will give the same signals as NPV, but it can mislead where there are competing projects of different scales.

  - Takes account of the timing of cash flows.

  - Takes all relevant information into account.

- Does not always provide clear signals and can be impractical to use:
  - Often cannot cope with varying costs of finance.
  - With unconventional cash flows, problems of multiple or no IRR.
- Inferior to NPV.

Payback period (PBP)

- PBP = the length of time that it takes the cash outflow for the initial investment to be repaid out of resulting cash inflows.
- Decision rule: Projects with a PBP up to defined maximum period are acceptable; the shorter the PBP, the more desirable the project.
- Can be refined a little by using discounted future inflows to derive a discounted PBP.
- Conclusions on PBP:
  - It does not relate to shareholders' wealth; ignores inflows after the payback date.
  - The undiscounted version takes little account of the timing of cash flows.
  - Ignores much relevant information.
  - Does not always provide clear signals and can be impractical to use.
  - Much inferior to NPV, but it is easy to understand and can offer a liquidity insight, which might be the reason for its widespread use.

Accounting rate of return (ARR)

- ARR = the average accounting profit from the project expressed as a percentage of the average (or initial) investment. The denominator needs to be defined and the definition consistently applied.
- Decision rule: Projects with an ARR above a defined minimum are acceptable; the greater the ARR, the more desirable the project.
- Conclusions on ARR:
  - It does not relate directly to shareholders' wealth. Its use can lead to illogical conclusions.
  - Takes almost no account of the timing of cash flows.
  - Ignores some relevant information and may take account of some irrelevant.
  - Relatively simple to use.
  - Much inferior to NPV.

Use of appraisal methods in practice

- All four methods widely used.
- The discounting methods (NPV and IRR) show a strong increase in usage over time.
- Many businesses use more than one method.
- Larger businesses seem to be more sophisticated than smaller ones.

Further reading

There are literally dozens of good texts covering topics discussed within this chapter, including those by Brealey and Myers (2002), Lumby and Jones (2003), Drury (2004) and Atrill (2006), all of which clearly and thoroughly deal with the basic principles of the investment appraisal techniques. The reports by Drury, Braund, Osborne and Tayles (1993) and Pike (1996), and the article by Arnold and Hatzopoulos (2000) provide very readable and interesting accounts of the research evidence on investment appraisal methods used in the UK that was cited in this chapter.

Horngren, Bhimani, Foster and Datar (2001) give an interesting summary of the results of a number of surveys of appraisal methods used in nine different countries. Graham and Harvey (2001) provide a very readable article reporting a major and far-reaching survey of business finance practices (including investment appraisal) in the USA.

Relevant websites

The websites of the businesses featured in this chapter are:

Boots Group plc **www.boots-plc.com**
Next plc **www.next.co.uk**
Rolls-Royce plc **www.rolls-royce.com**

REVIEW QUESTIONS

Suggested answers to review questions appear in Appendix 3.

4.1 Is the objective of discounting to take account of inflation? Explain.

4.2 When we say that future cash flows should be discounted at a rate that takes account of the *opportunity* cost of finance, what do we mean by *opportunity*?

4.3 What is the key point about the net present value approach to investment decision making that makes it the most correct method, in theory?

4.4 The payback period method of assessing potential investment projects is badly flawed, but it is widely used nonetheless. Why is it so widely used?

4.5 What is the fundamental flaw of using the internal rate of return method? Is it a problem in practice?

4.6 Evidence shows that many businesses use more than one of the four methods of investment appraisal found in practice. What could be the reason for this?

PROBLEMS

Sample answers to problems marked with an asterisk appear in Appendix 4.

(Problems 4.1 to 4.4 are basic-level problems, whereas problems 4.5 and 4.6 are more advanced and may contain some practical complications.)

4.1* Barclay plc is assessing an investment project. The estimated cash flows are as follows:

Year	£m	
0	10	Outflow
1	5	Inflow
2	4	Inflow
3	3	Inflow
4	2	Inflow

The business's cost of finance is 15 per cent p.a. and it seeks projects with a three-year maximum discounted payback period.

Should the project be undertaken on the basis of NPV and discounted PBP?

4.2 Branton & Co. Ltd is choosing between two mutually exclusive investment opportunities, Project A and Project B. The estimated cash flows for the two projects are as follows:

	Project A £000	Project B £000
Investment (immediate cash outflow)	50	36
Net annual cash inflows:		
Year 1	39	28
2	9	8
3	12	14
Cash inflow from residual value year 3	7	6

The business's cost of finance is estimated at 10 per cent.

Calculate:
(a) the net present value for both projects.
(b) the approximate internal rate of return for Project A.
(c) the payback period for both projects.

4.3* Turners Ltd is considering the purchase of a new machine that is expected to save labour on an existing project. The estimated data for the two machines available on the market are as follows:

	Machine A £000	Machine B £000
Initial cost (year 0)	120	120
Residual value of machines (year 5)	20	30
Annual labour cost savings:		
Year 1	40	20
2	40	30
3	40	50
4	20	70
5	20	20

Which machine will be selected under the following criteria?

(a) NPV, assuming a cost of finance of 10 per cent p.a.
(b) IRR
(c) ARR
(d) PBP.

Ignore taxation throughout, and treat the savings as if they will occur at the end of the relevant year.

4.4 RTB plc has recently assessed a potential project to make and sell a newly developed product. Two possible alternative systems have been identified, either one of which could be used to make the product. The results of the assessment can be summarised as follows:

	NPV £m	IRR %	Initial investment £m
Using System A	4.0	16	4.0
Using System B	6.0	13	6.0

The business's cost of finance is 10 per cent p.a.

Which system should the business select?

Explain what assumptions you have made about the business and your reasons for the selection made.

4.5* Cantelevellers plc's primary financial objective is to maximise the wealth of its share-holders. The business specialises in the development and assembly of high quality television sets. It normally subcontracts manufacture of the components of each set, carrying out the final assembly itself.

Recently the business has developed a new TV set that has been named Flatview, and a decision now needs to be taken as to whether to take it into production. The following data are available:

1   If the decision is taken to go into production with the Flatview, production and sales will start on 1 January 20X4 and end in 20X8. It is estimated that each set will be

sold for £2000. It is also estimated that the annual production and sales of Flatview televisions will be a steady 1500 units for each of the five years.

2 Development and market research in relation to the Flatview were undertaken during 20X3. The cost of these totalled £3m. It is the business's policy to write off all such costs against profits as they are incurred. Of the £3m, £1.8m was an apportionment of development department overheads. The remaining £1.2m was spent on materials and services, including a market survey, which were purchased specifically in respect of the Flatview project.

3 Assembly of the Flatview would take place in premises leased specifically for the assembly work, separate from the business's main premises. The directors believe that suitable premises could be leased at an annual rent of £450 000, payable annually in advance.

4 Labour for the Flatview project is available from the business's existing staff. If the project is not undertaken the staff involved will be declared redundant on 31 December 20X3 and paid a total of £250 000 in compensation at that time. If the project goes ahead the total incremental cost of employing the staff concerned is estimated at £200 000 per annum throughout the duration of the project. At the end of the project the staff concerned will all be made redundant, with estimated total compensation cost of £300 000 payable at that point.

5 Assembly of each Flatview set requires the use of a number of different bought-in components. Tenders have been obtained from the business's normal suppliers, and the lowest total purchase cost of all of the components necessary to make one Flatview is £380. This figure includes £120 for component F451. This component is the only one of which the business already has a stock since 500 units of F451 are held in stock as the result of a surplus from a previous project. These originally cost £80 each. If the Flatview project does not proceed, the only possible use for these stock items has been identified as selling them back to the original manufacturer at a price of £100 each, with the buyer bearing transport costs. Since the manufacturer cannot use these items until the end of 20X5, delivery and payment will not take place before that time. There are no incremental storage costs involved with retaining this stock until 20X5.

Each Flatview set requires the use of one component F451.

6 Incremental overheads associated with the Flatview project are expected to cost £200 000 for each year of production.

7 Plant and machinery will have to be bought and paid for on 1 January 20X4. The total cost will be £5m, which includes all installation costs. It is estimated that at the end of the Flatview manufacturing project (20X8) the plant will have a disposal value of £1m.

8 The directors judge that the Flatview project will cost 15 per cent per annum to finance.

Prepare a schedule that derives the annual net relevant cash flows arising from the Flatview project, and use this to assess the project on the basis of its net present value.

Ignore any factors (such as taxation) that are not referred to in the question.

4.6 Cool Ltd's main financial objective is to maximise the wealth of its shareholders. Cool specialises in providing a service for its clients. All of the work that it undertakes is of a similar type for similar clients.

Cool's management is contemplating offering a new service. This will require the acquisition of an item of plant on 1 June 20X4.

Cool intends to buy the plant for £300 000, payable on the date of acquisition. It is estimated that the asset will have a negligible market value by 31 May 20X8 and will be scrapped on that date.

A study of likely sales demand for the new service suggests that it will be as follows:

Year ending 31 May	£000
20X5	220
20X6	250
20X7	300
20X8	260

Variable operating costs associated with the new service are estimated at 30 per cent of the sales figure.

The introduction of the new service is planned to coincide with the discontinuance of an existing activity. This discontinuance will release labour. If the new service is introduced, the staff currently employed on the existing activity can all be fully employed throughout the four years at a total salary bill of £45 000 p.a.

If the new service is not introduced, it is estimated that the existing activity could be kept going until 31 May 20X7, generating revenues as follows:

Year ending 31 May	£000
20X5	100
20X6	80
20X7	80

Variable operating costs associated with the existing service are also estimated at 30 per cent of the sales figure.

If the new service is not introduced, it is envisaged that the staff will be made redundant and paid total redundancy pay of £20 000 on 31 May 20X7. This item was taken into account in the analysis, on which the original decision to start the existing service was based, several years ago. If the new service *is* introduced, staff will be made redundant upon its conclusion on 31 May 20X8, and paid total redundancy pay of £22 000 at that time.

Labour is a fixed cost (that is, it does not vary with the level of output). Exactly the same staff will be employed in the provision of either service.

Apart from those that have already been mentioned, there are estimated to be no incremental operating costs involved with offering these services.

The cost of finance to support the project is expected to be 10 per cent p.a.

(a) *Prepare a schedule that derives the annual net relevant cash flows associated with the decision as to whether Cool should acquire the plant and offer the new service, based on the information provided above, and use it to draw a conclusion about this decision on the basis of the project's net present value.*

(b) *Estimate the internal rate of return for the project.*

(c) *Discuss the factors that Cool needs to take into account in respect of the decision, other than the NPV and IRR.*

There are both a set of **multiple-choice questions** and **missing-word questions** available on the website. These specifically cover the material contained in this chapter. These can be attempted and graded (with feedback) online.

There are also **six additional problems**, with solutions, that relate to the material covered in this chapter.

Go to **www.pearsoned.co.uk/atrillmclaney** and follow the links.

Chapter 5

Practical aspects of investment appraisal

Objectives In this chapter we shall deal with the following:

→ the importance of cash flows rather than accounting flows for investment decision making

→ the relationship between cash flows and accounting flows

→ the importance of assessing the timing as well as the magnitude of cash flows

→ the need to identify only those cash flows that differ according to the decision and to identify all of them even where they are not obvious

→ the treatment of inflation in the investment decision

→ how the basic NPV rule must be adapted to deal with situations where there are shortages of investment finance

→ replacement decisions

→ the importance of establishing routines to try to identify possible projects

→ the link between strategic planning and investment decision making

→ value-based management

5.1 Introduction

In the previous chapter we established that the most theoretically correct approach to assessing investment opportunities is on the basis of their net present values. This involves identifying the cash flows and their timing and then discounting by an appropriate factor.

In this chapter we shall examine how the business should go about identifying the cash flows and assessing them, particularly in the NPV context. We shall also consider some other practical problems, including how a business should deal with a situation of having insufficient finance to support all of the projects that appear desirable.

While the focus will be on the more practical aspects of using NPV, many of the points relate equally well to the other techniques for assessing investment projects, and particularly to IRR.

5.2 Cash flows or accounting flows?

When assessing a particular business investment opportunity, should the business identify and discount cash payments and receipts or should it discount profits arising from the project? This is an important question, as it seems that many businesses use projections of accounting figures as the starting point for an investment appraisal. As we saw in Chapter 4, cash flows from a particular project, in a particular time period, will rarely equal the accounting profit for the project during the same period.

If we go back to the principles on which the concept of NPV is based, we see that discounting takes account of the opportunity cost of making the investment. It is not until cash needs to be expended in the project that the opportunity for it to produce income from some other source will be lost. Only when cash flows back from the project can the business use it to pay dividends, repay borrowings, lend it or reinvest it in another project.

Over the life of a project the accounting profits will equal the net cash flows (undiscounted) in total; it is the timing that will be different. Why should this be the case?

The roles of financial accounting and investment appraisal

Financial accounting, as we saw in Chapter 3, sets out to assess the profit (increase in wealth) for a period, perhaps a year. In doing so it needs to treat each period as a self-contained unit. This is despite the fact that most of the business's investment projects will not be self-contained within that same period. Non-current assets (for example, an item of machinery), perhaps acquired in a previous period, may be used in the period and continue to be owned and used in future periods. Stock in trade acquired in a previous period may be sold in the current one. Sales made (on credit) in the current period may be paid for by customers in the following period. Financial accounting tends to ignore the timing of payments and receipts of cash and concentrates on wealth generated and extinguished during the period. Costs, less anticipated disposal proceeds, of non-current assets are spread in some equitable way (depreciated) over their lives so that each period gets a share of the cost, irrespective of whether or not any cash is actually paid out to suppliers of non-current assets in the particular accounting period under consideration. Sales revenues are usually recognised and credit taken for them by the selling business when the goods change hands or the service is rendered even though the cash receipt may lag some weeks behind. The reduction in wealth suffered by using up stock in trade in making sales is recognised when the sale is made – and not when the stock is purchased or when it is paid for.

These points are not weaknesses of financial accounting. Its role is to seek to measure income (profit) over time periods so that interested parties can obtain a periodic assessment of the business's progress. As projects will not usually be self-contained within time periods as short as a year, it is necessary for financial accounting to take some consistent approach as to how to deal with the problem; the approach taken seems a very logical one.

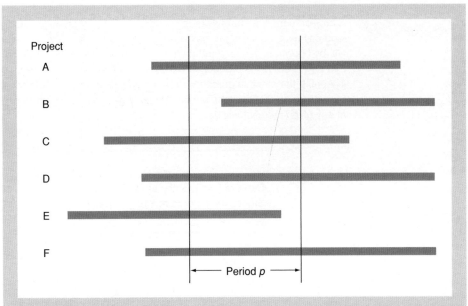

Figure 5.1
Six investment projects of a business. All of these projects operate during at least two accounting periods

The problem of financial accounting is to try to make an assessment of the amount of wealth generated by all of the business's projects during a particular period when not all of each project's cash flows are self-contained within that period.

Investment appraisal has a somewhat different objective from that of financial accounting, however. This is to assess a project over its entire life, not to assess it for a particular portion of that life. This difference of purpose is represented graphically in Figure 5.1. This shows a business with six investment projects (A to F), each of which starts and ends at a different time. Financial accounting seeks to assess the profit for a period such as *p*. During this period one project ends (Project E), one starts (Project B), while the other four run throughout period *p*. Investment appraisal seeks to assess whether any particular project is a viable one, before it starts. Profit measurement tends to be cross-sectional, investment appraisal longitudinal.

Converting accounting flows to cash flows

When using the NPV approach it is projected cash flows, not accounting profits, that should be discounted; yet frequently when projects are being assessed in advance of possible implementation they are expressed in terms of anticipated profit, so we need to convert such information to cash flows.

There are two areas where accounting profit needs to be adjusted:

 ● working capital; and

● depreciation.

As regards the operating items, that is, those items concerned with sales revenue and material, labour and overhead costs, the adjustment to convert accounting flows to cash flows can be done by taking account of the working capital requirement of the project.

Example 5.1	A project to manufacture widgets, if undertaken, will start on 1 January with the purchase of (and payment for) a widget-making machine. Materials for use in the manufacture of widgets will be bought in January and paid for in February, and these will be used in production in February. February's production will be sold in that month, on credit, and customers will pay in April. If the monthly purchase of raw materials is £10 000 and the monthly sales revenue from widgets £20 000, then once the project gets under way the working capital investment at any given moment will be

	£
Debtors (two months at £20 000 p.m.)	40 000
Stocks (one month at £10 000 p.m.)	10 000
	50 000
Less: Creditors (one month at £10 000 p.m.)	10 000
	40 000

(This assumes that the level of activity, the stockholding and the credit periods remain constant.) So to take account of the difference between operating accounting flows and cash flows we could treat the £40 000, which is the magnitude of the difference between accounting and cash flows, as an initial investment of the project.

We should also need to treat it as a receipt at the end of this project. This is logical because, during the last few months of the project, more cash would be received from sales revenue than sales revenue made; debtors will continue to pay after the end of the project for two months. Stocks will not be bought during the last month of production, though creditors for stocks bought the previous month will need to be paid during that last month.

Provided that this recognition of the timing difference (the £40 000), is correctly adjusted for, operating accounting flows can be used as a surrogate for the (more strictly correct) cash flows.

Failure to make this adjustment to accounting flows will tend to cause a bias in the appraisal, usually giving a more favourable impression than justified by the facts. It will tend to give this more favourable impression because accounting flows do not reflect the fact that, as in Example 5.1 (above), sales are usually made on credit so that the cash inflows may lag some time behind the sale. While it is true that an opposite effect is caused by the fact that the business is likely to buy its raw materials on credit, this opposite effect is itself likely to be offset by the fact that the business probably holds stocks of raw materials and perhaps finished goods as well.

In any case, for projects that are likely to be favourably considered by the business, the sales revenues will tend to be larger than the operating costs. Also, sales are usually made on credit whereas some significant operating costs (for example, wages) are payable more or less immediately.

With capital expenditure, and any possible disposal proceeds, it is necessary to identify specifically when these cash flows occur. Depreciation charged in arriving at operating profits needs to be eliminated.

Example 5.2

A project that involves an initial outlay of £200 000 on a machine is expected to generate annual profits of £60 000 (after deducting depreciation) each year for four years. Depreciation is calculated on an even (straight line) basis, assuming that the disposal proceeds of the original investment will be £40 000 receivable at the end of year 4. This means that the annual depreciation expense will be £40 000 [(£200 000 − £40 000)/4]. The initial cost is an outflow in year 0 (immediately) and the disposal proceeds are an additional inflow in year 4. The working capital requirement is estimated to be a constant £30 000. The estimated cash flows will be

Year	£	
0	(230 000)	(i.e. machine £200 000 + working capital £30 000)
1	100 000	(i.e. pre-depreciation profit £60 000 + depreciation £40 000)
2	100 000	
3	100 000	
4	170 000	(i.e. £100 000 + disposal proceeds £40 000 + working capital released £30 000)

and it is these figures that should be discounted, using an appropriate rate, to arrive at the NPV.

Discounting cash flows rather than profits does not really mean that depreciation is ignored. It is in effect taken into account by treating the initial investment as an outflow of cash and the disposal proceeds as an inflow, thus in effect charging the difference between these amounts to the project.

5.3 Do cash flows really occur at year ends?

In the examples that we have considered so far, all of the cash flows have occurred exact numbers of years after the start of the project. This obviously is not very representative of real life.

Most investments undertaken by businesses are in land, buildings, plant, machinery, trading stocks and so forth. The returns from these are in the form of sales revenues against which have to be set costs of labour, materials and overheads. Clearly, these cash flows are not likely to occur at year ends. They tend to be spread throughout the year, perhaps fairly evenly or perhaps more concentrated at some parts of the year than at others, reflecting the seasonal aspect of certain trades.

Strictly, the precise timing of the cash flows should be identified and they should be discounted accordingly. The discount factor $1/(1 + r)^n$ would be the same; however, the n would not necessarily be a whole number.

Although it would be perfectly feasible to recognise the precise timing of cash flows, it seems not usual to do so. The simplifying assumption that cash flows occurring within a year occur at the year end is thought to be popular in practice. Making this assumption tends to introduce an element of bias in that it usually treats cash flows as occurring a few months later than they actually do. This tends to have the effect of systematically understating NPVs. Strictly, it is probably better in practice to identify the forecast cash flows month by month and to discount them according to when they actually are expected to occur. The extent of bias of the year-end assumptions and the working capital adjustment is assessed and discussed by Atrill, McLaney and Pointon (1997).

5.4 Which cash flows?

As we saw in Chapter 2, only those cash flows relevant to the decision should be brought into the appraisal. Cash flows will be relevant only where they will be different, depending upon the decision under review. Items that will occur whatever the decision should be ignored. For example, where a decision involving a choice as to whether or not to make a new product would not have an effect on the fixed overheads, the fixed overheads should be disregarded when making the decision; they will be unaffected by it.

Similarly, past costs are irrelevant as they will inevitably be the same whatever happens in the future. For example, where a machine costing £50 000 one year ago is under review as to whether or not it should be replaced, the decision should not take the £50 000 into account. All that should be considered are the future benefits that could be derived from the machine, in terms of either proceeds of disposal or cash flow benefits of its retention. The present decision is not whether or not to buy the machine a year ago; that decision was made over twelve months ago and was either a good or a bad one. In either case it is not something that can now be altered.

Opportunity cash flows

It is not only cash flows that are expected actually to occur that should be taken into account. Opportunity cash flows are as important as actual cash flows. In the above example, if the machine has a current market value of £10 000 then one of the cash flows associated with retaining the machine will be a £10 000 outflow at whatever time it would be disposed of if the alternative action (disposal) were followed. Obviously, if the machine is retained this cash flow will not actually occur; nonetheless it should be taken into account because retention of the machine deprives the business of the opportunity to dispose of it. The £10 000 represents a difference arising from the decision. Some opportunity cash flows may be fairly remote from the project under review and so can quite easily be overlooked unless care is taken. An example of such opportunity cash flows is losses of sales revenue (and variable costs) of one of the business's existing activities as a result of introducing a new one. For example, a chain store contemplating opening a new branch should not just assess the cash flows of that branch. It should also consider cash flow changes that might occur in other branches in the locality as a result. Sales revenue might be lost at existing branches if a new one is opened.

Next plc, the high street retailer, makes the point in its 2004 annual report that, 'When appraising new stores we account for downturn in neighbouring stores . . .'

We shall meet other practical examples of relevant and irrelevant costs in Example 5.5 on page 120.

Forecasting cash flows

Investment appraisal deals with forecasts of future cash flows. Forecasting the cash flows associated with particular courses of action is likely to be difficult, and subject to error. Details of the techniques and problems of forecasting go beyond the scope of this book. These techniques include the use of statistical data on past events (generated inside and outside the business), market research projects and soliciting the opinions of experts.

Financing costs – the cost of capital

One type of cash flow that should not be included in the appraisal is the cost of finance to support the project. Discounting deals with the financing cost in a complete and logical manner in that future cash flows are reduced (discounted) to take account of the time for which finance will be tied up and the relevant interest rate.

So far we have referred to the cost of financing as 'interest', as though all finance is provided through borrowing. In practice, most businesses are financed by a mixture of funds provided by the owners (shareholders in the case of limited companies) and borrowing. Thus the financing cost is partly the cost of equity and partly interest

→ cost. We tend to use the expression cost of capital for the overall cost of financing and for the basis of the discount rate. This expression will generally be used from now on.

We shall review in some detail how an appropriate cost of capital figure is derived later in the book, particularly in Chapter 10.

5.5 Taxation

Cash flows associated with taxation must be brought into the assessment of the project. Most projects will cause differences in corporation tax. This may be because of capital expenditure attracting relief (capital allowances), profits from the project attracting additional tax or losses attracting tax relief. These differences must be taken into account in investment appraisal.

The taxable profit

Businesses are taxed on the basis of the profit shown by a profit and loss account (income statement) drawn up following the generally accepted accounting rules and conventions. This profit figure is, however, subject to some adjustment. There are certain items of expense and revenue that, though legitimately appearing in the profit and loss account, have been singled out by the law as being illegitimate for tax purposes.

Most of these items are fairly unusual in occurrence or relatively insignificant in effect, though there is one that is typically neither rare nor trivial. This is depreciation, the accounting device for spreading capital costs of non-current assets over their useful lives. For tax purposes, depreciation must be added back to the profit revealed by the profit and loss account, to be replaced by capital allowances.

Capital allowances

→ Capital allowances are set against the taxable profit to give tax relief for expenditure on non-current assets. There are several categories of asset into which the law has placed the various types of business non-current asset. Each of these has its own rules for granting the allowance. In practice, two of these, dealing with plant and machinery and with industrial buildings, are by far the most important to the typical business.

Plant and machinery

This includes a wide range of assets, from industrial machinery to the reference books of a lawyer, and includes motor vehicles. For expenditure on plant and machinery, businesses are allowed to deduct 25 per cent of the cost of the asset from the (otherwise taxable) profit of the period during which the asset was acquired. In each subsequent year of ownership of the asset, 25 per cent of the balance brought forward may be deducted.

Example 5.3

In 2006, Carriers Ltd buys a delivery van for £12 000. The capital allowances would be claimable as follows:

Year	Opening balance £	Capital allowance £
2006	12 000	3000 [25% of £12 000]
2007	9 000	2250 [25% of (£12 000 – £3000)]
2008	6 750	1688 and so on
2009	5 062	1266
	and so on	

This pattern will continue until the van is sold or scrapped.

When the asset is disposed of, in broad effect, any unrelieved expenditure is relieved, and any excess of relief is 'clawed back' by the Inland Revenue.

For example, if Carriers Ltd (in Example 5.3) disposed of the van for £6000 in the year 2009, tax would be charged on £938 (that is, £6000 – £5062). On the other hand, were the disposal proceeds to be £4000, additional relief of £1062 (that is, £5062 – £4000) would be given to the business.

The broad effect of capital allowances is to give tax relief on the difference between the acquisition cost of the asset and its disposal proceeds (if this is a lower figure), spread over the life of the asset.

Industrial buildings

These are buildings used directly or indirectly in manufacturing, the transport industry and other restricted purposes. Not included in the definition are shops and offices.

Relief is granted by allowing businesses to deduct 4 per cent of the cost of the building from the taxable profit in each year of its ownership and use. On disposal the proceeds will cause a claw-back of excess allowances or an additional allowance, if the difference between cost and the disposal proceeds has not already been fully relieved.

Having considered the basis on which business profits are taxed in the UK, it will be useful to proceed to an example.

Example 5.4

The profit and loss account of Amalgamated Retailers plc, for the year ended 31 March 2006, showed a net profit of £2 640 000. In arriving at this figure, depreciation was charged as follows:

	£
Shop premises	120 000
Shop equipment	85 000

During the year the business purchased new computerised cash registers for all its branches at a total cost of £500 000 and spent £850 000 on acquiring the freeholds of several new shops, all of which started trading during the year. The tax written down value of the shop equipment at 1 April 2005 was £210 000.

The business always claims all possible allowances and reliefs at the earliest opportunity. The taxable profit would be as follows:

		£
Net profit (from the profit and loss account)		2 640 000
Add: Depreciation:		
Premises	120 000	
Equipment	85 000	205 000
		2 845 000
Less: Capital allowances (see below)		177 500
Taxable profit		2 667 500

Capital allowances – shop equipment

	£
Written down value at 1.4.05	210 000
Add: Additions	500 000
	710 000
Less: Allowance @ 25%	177 500
Written-down value at 31.3.06	532 500

No capital allowances would be given on the acquisition of the freeholds, as they do not fall within the definition of any of the classes of asset for which capital allowances are given.

Rates of tax and dates of payment

The taxable profit is taxed at 30 per cent for businesses (trading as companies) earning large profits, and 19 per cent where their profits are lower.

Thus the liability of Amalgamated Retailers in the above example will be:

$$30\% \times \pounds2\ 667\ 500 = \pounds800\ 250$$

This tax will be payable in four equal instalments.

As is evident from the above, the tax cash flows can, in the case of investment in certain non-current assets, lag well behind the cash flow events giving rise to them. It is important to recognise this time lag, particularly as the cash flows concerned are likely to be large.

5.6 Inflation

Throughout almost the whole of the twentieth century, and continuing into the twenty-first, the UK has experienced erosion of the purchasing power of the pound. Much has been written on the causes of and possible cures for it, neither of which falls within the scope of this book. The effects of inflation, the problem that it causes to capital investment decision makers, and how they might cope with the problem are our concern here, however.

Even with relatively low levels of inflation (say, less than 3 per cent), over long periods prices will be greatly affected. An item costing £100 today would cost £115.93 after five years if its price increased by 3 per cent each year.

The principal problem facing the decision maker is whether to forecast future cash flows associated with an investment project in real terms or in money (or nominal) terms. Real terms here means in terms of today's (the date of the decision) price levels; money (or nominal) terms refers to price levels that are forecast to exist at the date of the future cash flow.

Seeking to forecast in real terms is probably going to be easier because it does not require any estimation of rates of inflation. Forecasting in money terms is not simply taking the real-terms forecasts and adjusting for 'the' rate of inflation because different types of cash flows will be differently affected by inflation. We tend to view inflation as operating at one rate across all commodities; this is incorrect. Inflation acts differentially. An index such as the Retail Price Index (RPI), by which inflation is quite often assessed, is simply a weighted average of the inflation rates of commodities bought by a 'typical' household. Within that, some commodities may have static or even declining prices though the average may still be increasing.

Assessing projects in money terms requires forecasts of future price levels for each element of the decision. In many instances, however, it probably will not materially affect the issue if prices of all elements are assumed to grow equally. In other cases, this simplifying assumption may cause unreasonable distortions.

The other element of the decision that inflation will affect is the discount rate. The cost of capital generally reflects expectations of the general level of inflation rates. Suppliers of finance require compensation for being prepared to delay consumption. They tend to require additional compensation where they not only delay consumption by lending, but also reduce the amount, which they can ultimately consume as a result of price rises of goods and services during the period of the loan.

The relationship between the real and money rates of interest and the inflation rate is:

$$1 + r_n = (1 + r_r)(1 + i)$$

where r_n is the money (or nominal) rate of interest (the actual rate of interest payable by borrowers), r_r is the real rate of interest (the rate that would be payable if the inflation rate were zero), and i is the expected rate of inflation in the economy generally. Where no inflation is expected, r_n will equal r_r.

Consistency of approach

In principle it does not matter whether money cash flows or real ones are used in the NPV analysis, provided each is used in conjunction with the appropriate discount rate.

Where the cash flows are estimated in money terms (that is, incorporating the forecast effects of inflation), then the discount rate must also reflect inflation expectations. Therefore the discount rate should be based on the money cost of capital.

If the cash flows are to be assessed in real terms, then the discount rate must be based on the real cost of capital.

It is important that there is consistency of approach. To use real cash flows in conjunction with a money discount rate, for example, would be to understate the NPV of the project, which could quite easily lead to desirable projects being rejected. A survey conducted in the UK during the 1970s by Carsberg and Hope (1976) suggested that this rejection of desirable projects, resulting from wrongly dealing with inflation, was indeed a problem.

Drury, Braund, Osborne and Tayles (1993), in their survey of 260 UK manufacturing businesses, found that only 27 per cent of those businesses dealt correctly with inflation, and 13 per cent of the businesses surveyed made an error that was probably not very significant. This left 60 per cent of businesses dealing with inflation in such a manner as to give a significantly misleading result. However Al-Ali and Arkwright (2000) found that only 3 per cent of the 73 respondents to their survey of large UK businesses, conducted in late 1997, mishandled inflation. This could imply an increasing level of sophistication among financial managers. Al-Ali and Arkwright also found that about half of their respondents took a 'real' approach, and the other half a 'money' one.

Dealing with cash flows and the discount rate in real terms does not completely avoid forecasting the rate of inflation. Real costs of capital are not directly identifiable in the way that money rates are. Money rates on government stocks, for example, are quoted daily in several national newspapers. Money rates can be converted into real rates by adjusting for expectation of future inflation rates that are incorporated in them. To identify inflation rate expectations, it is probably best to take some average or consensus view from the various economic forecasts that are published regularly by a number of commercial and academic institutions, also by the Bank of England for the UK.

The central point regarding inflation in investment decisions is that it cannot be ignored, not as long as inflation runs at significant rates. Not only must it be confronted but also consistency of approach must apply. Money cash flows must be discounted at money discount rates and real cash flows at real discount rates.

For some purely practical reasons, that we need not pursue here, using real cash flows and a real discount rate tends to make the calculations problematical. It is normally more straightforward to use their money counterparts.

5.7 An example of an investment appraisal

Having considered the practical aspects of applying the NPV rule in principle, we shall now go on to see how it would be applied to a practical example.

Example 5.5

Kitchen Appliances plc is assessing an investment project that involves the production and marketing of a sophisticated household food mixer, the Rapido. The annual sales volume is expected to run at 10 000 Rapidos for five years.

The development department has produced the following estimate of annual profit from the project:

	£000
Sales revenue	2000
Raw materials	600
Labour	600
Depreciation	240
Rent	60
Overheads	200
Interest	100
	1800
Annual net profit	200

The following additional information is relevant:

1 The production will require the purchase of a new machine at a cost of £1 200 000, payable on delivery. The machine will be depreciated on a straight-line basis over the five years. It is not expected to have any second-hand value at the end of that time.

2 Production of Rapidos will take place in a building currently used for storage. Apportioning the rent of the entire site occupied by the business on the basis of area, the building has a rental cost of £60 000. If production goes ahead, the business can rent a small warehouse, which will be adequate for storage purposes, for £10 000 p.a. payable annually in arrears.

If Rapido production is not undertaken there are plans to sublet the building to another business at a rent of £40 000 p.a. payable annually in arrears and to rent the small warehouse for £10 000 p.a.

3 £36 000 has been spent on developing the Rapido and £10 000 on a market survey to assess demand.

4 The overheads of £200 000 p.a. represent an apportionment of the overheads of the entire business on the basis of labour hours. The operating overheads will be increased by £90 000 p.a. as a result of Rapido manufacture. This includes £30 000 p.a. salary to a manager who is due to retire immediately on a pension of £10 000 p.a. If Rapido manufacture goes ahead, the manager will not retire for another five years. Staying on for the additional period will not affect the pension that the manager will ultimately receive. Pensions are paid by the business and the amounts are charged to non-operating overheads.

The remaining £60 000 represents salaries payable to two managers who will be taken on for the duration of the project, should it go ahead.

5 If Rapidos come on to the market there is expected to be a reduction in anticipated demand for the existing food mixer, the Whizzo, which the business also manufactures. The reduction in the volume of Whizzo sales would be expected to be:

Year	Units
1	10 000
2	10 000
3	5 000
4	5 000
5	5 000

Whizzos sell at £80 each with variable costs of £40 each. Lower Whizzo sales volumes would not be expected to affect overhead costs, which are fixed.

6 The business's corporation tax rate is 30 per cent and payment may be assumed to fall due at the end of the year concerned.

7 The expenditure on the new machine would attract capital allowances at the rate of 25 per cent p.a. with any unrelieved expenditure being allowed on disposal.

8 All of the data given are expressed in current terms. Inflation is expected to run at about 5 per cent p.a. over the next decade. All of the relevant cash flows are expected to increase at this annual rate.

9 The business's after-tax cost of capital is (and is expected to remain at) 12 per cent p.a. in money terms.

10 Working capital of £100 000 will be required from the start of the project and will be returned at the end of year 5.

(All of the above cash flows have been expressed in real terms, that is, in terms of prices at the date of the start of the project.)

On the basis of NPV should the project be undertaken or not?

Solution

Kitchen Appliances plc

Assessment of Rapido project

Despite the fact that using either a 'real' or a 'money' approach will give identical results if they are correctly applied, in practice the money approach tends to be a lot easier to use. We shall, therefore, use the money approach.

In the assessment of the project our guiding principles must be:

● to identify the cash flows relevant to the decision (that is, differences between the cash flows that will occur if the project is undertaken and those that will arise without the project) and convert them into money terms;

● to identify the timing of those relevant cash flows; and

● to discover the NPV of the project by applying the adjustment for the time value of money (in other words, discounting) to the relevant cash flows according to when it is anticipated that they will occur.

Annual operating cash flows

	£000
Sales revenue	2000
Raw materials	600
Labour	600
Rent	40
Overheads	80
Contributions lost from Whizzo sales	400 (200 for years 3, 4 and 5)
	1720
Annual net operating cash flow (in real terms)	280 (480 for years 3, 4 and 5)

Notes

1 *Depreciation*. This is irrelevant, as it does not represent a cash flow.

2 *Rent*. The appropriate figure here is the rent from the subtenant should the project not go ahead. Irrespective of the decision, both the rent of the entire site (of which £60 000 is

part) and the £10 000 rent of the outside warehouse will be paid: thus they are irrelevant to the decision.

3 *Overheads*. The retiring manager's salary makes a difference of £20 000 p.a. depending on the decision. Irrespective of the decision the manager will be paid £10 000 p.a., so it is the £20 000 that is relevant. The other £60 000 is also relevant. The apportionment of overheads is not relevant as this is not the amount of the difference in overheads associated with rejection or acceptance of the project.

4 *Interest*. This will be taken into account by discounting.

5 *Contributions from lost Whizzo sales*. These amount to £400 000 [that is, 10 000 × £(80 − 40)] for years 1 and 2, and £200 000 [that is, 5000 × £(80 − 40)] for years 3, 4 and 5.

Since lost Whizzo sales do not affect overheads, only sales revenue lost (£80 per unit) and variable costs saved (£40 per unit) are relevant to the decision.

This aspect must be accounted for, as accepting the project will affect Whizzo sales.

Corporation tax cash flows

The relevant operating cash flows will also be the basis of the differential tax charges. Capital allowances on the initial investment will be as follows:

Year	Balance £000	Allowance claimed £000	Tax savings (at 30%) £000
1 Acquisition	1200		
Capital allowance (CA) (25%)	(300)	300	90
	900		
2 CA (25%)	(225)	225	68
	675		
3 CA (25%)	(169)	169	51
	506		
4 CA (25%)	(127)	127	38
	379		
5 CA (balancing allowance)			
(nil proceeds)	379	379	114

The tax payable will be as follows:

Year	Operating cash flow surplus (adjusted for inflation) £000	Tax payable (at 30%) £000
1	294 (280 × 1.05)	88
2	309 (280 × 1.05^2)	93
3	556 (480 × 1.05^3)	167
4	583 (480 × 1.05^4)	175
5	613 (480 × 1.05^5)	184

Notes

1 Each of these payments will be treated as occurring at the end of the year concerned.

2 The tax-payable amounts represent the difference between the tax that would be payable if the project were accepted and that which would be payable if it were rejected. It is not necessary for us to know what the tax payable would be in total; we need only know the difference.

Discounting

Year	Initial investment £000	Working capital £000	Operating profit £000	Tax on operating profit £000	Capital allowance tax relief £000	Net cash flows £000	Discount factor @ 12%	Discounted cash flows £000
0	(1200)	(100)				(1300)	1.000	(1300)
1		(5)	294	(88)	90	291	0.893	260
2		(5)	309	(93)	68	279	0.797	222
3		(6)	556	(167)	51	434	0.712	309
4		(6)	583	(175)	38	440	0.636	280
5		122	613	(184)	114	665	0.567	377
							Net present value	148
See Note	2	3	4	5		6	7	

As the NPV is positive and significant, from a financial viewpoint, the production of the Rapido should be undertaken.

Notes

1 The costs of developing the product and of the market survey will not vary with the present decision and must therefore be ignored. They exist irrespective of the decision.

2 Treating the working capital commitment in the way shown takes account, in a broadly correct way, of the timing difference between operating cash flows and accounting flows. In 'money' terms, the investment in working capital will increase as inflation increases the stock and sales prices. Each of the outflows of years 1 to 4 (inclusive) comprises the additional amount necessary to invest to bring the working capital up to the higher level. In each case the figure is 5 per cent of the previous year's working capital figure.

3 The operating profits are simply the 'real' figures, adjusted for inflation at 5 per cent, for as many years into the future as is relevant.

4 The tax figures are simply the operating profits multiplied by 30 per cent (the CT rate).

5 The CA tax reliefs are taken directly from the table showing capital allowances on the initial investment. (See page 122.)

6 The discount factor reflects the 'money' cost of capital. Quite how the discount rate is established (that is, where the 12 per cent came from) is a question that we shall consider in some detail later in the book, particularly in Chapter 10.

7 Note that the NPV using 'real' cash flows would be identical to the NPV using 'money' cash flows. Note also that the present value of each year's net cash flow would have been identical, no matter whether 'real' or 'money' cash flows were used.

8 All the calculations in this example have been rounded to the nearest £1000. While this is not strictly correct, the accuracy to which cash flows, timings and discount rates can be predicted is such that this rounding is not out of place. It could be argued that doing other than this in such calculations would give the result an air of precision not justified by the levels of probable inaccuracy of the input data.

9 This example (except to the extent of the rounding mentioned in point 8 above) has completely ignored the question of risk.

How reliable are the predictions of labour costs? What if the bottom fell out of the domestic food mixer market? Would the increased level of activity that this project engenders prove too much for the competence of management?

These and many other matters are present with this project, and similar ones with any other project. These risks should be formally assessed and their effect built into the decision-making process. How this can be done will be addressed in the next two chapters.

10 The net cash flow figures in the example could be used as the basis of an IRR or a PBP assessment of the project without modification. IRR and PBP would simply use them differently.

5.8 Capital rationing

In Chapter 4 we saw that businesses will maximise the wealth of their shareholders by undertaking all investment opportunities that have a positive NPV when discounted at the appropriate cost of capital.

In some circumstances the business may be unable or unwilling to undertake all such opportunities because it cannot or does not wish to raise finance to the level required. This is known as capital rationing. Where it cannot raise the finance because sources of supply are limited, the situation is known as hard capital rationing. Where the constraint is self-imposed because, for example, the business feels that it does not have sufficient management talent to expand beyond a certain point, it is referred to as soft capital rationing.

Soft capital rationing may also arise where, though finance is available, the business might find it expensive or inconvenient to raise it at the time that the investment opportunity is first recognised. The business may, for example, find it more economic to raise the finance in large blocks rather than piecemeal. Research evidence suggests that, in real life, hard capital rationing is rare, finance seeming to be available for viable projects (Pike and Ooi 1988). Most instances of capital rationing seem to be of the soft variety, and Arnold and Hatzopoulos (2000) found that with nearly half of the businesses that they surveyed, soft capital rationing sometimes leads to rejection of viable projects.

It can be argued that there is no such thing as hard capital rationing since it is always possible to raise finance from somewhere to finance a project. If the project is viewed as risky, the finance may be expensive in terms of the cost of capital, but finance is always available at some price. If the project's anticipated cash flows, when discounted at this high cost of capital, cannot produce a positive NPV, the project should be rejected. This, however, is always the position with any type of project at any time: if it cannot produce a positive NPV it should be rejected.

One way or another, capital rationing means that there are more calls on finance than there is finance available.

Irrespective of whether there are hard or soft constraints, capital rationing requires that the basic NPV rule cannot be applied without modification. The modification depends on whether the constraint is to operate for one year only or is to persist over several years.

Single-period capital rationing

Where there is single-period capital rationing, projects should be ranked according to the NPV per £ of scarce initial investment capital.

Example 5.6

A business is unable or unprepared to invest more than £500 000 in the current year, but has the following projects available to it:

Project	Initial investment £	NPV £
A	100 000	15 000
B	150 000	29 000
C	140 000	31 000
D	210 000	22 000
E	180 000	36 000

Solution

The NPV per £ of investment and thus the ranking of the projects is as follows:

Project	NPV/£ of investment	Ranking
A	0.15	4
B	0.19	3
C	0.22	1
D	0.10	5
E	0.20	2

The business should therefore take on the projects in the order shown until the capital is exhausted. This would mean taking on projects as follows:

Project	£
C	140 000
E	180 000
B	150 000
A (30/100 thereof)	30 000
	500 000

This solution assumes that it is possible to take on 30/100 of Project A and that the cash flows of that project will simply be reduced to 30 per cent of their original figures, giving an NPV of 30 per cent of the original NPV. In reality this assumption may well be without foundation. If this is the case, the decision maker would have to look at the various combinations of the projects that have total initial investment outlays of £500 000 and then choose the combination with the highest total NPV. Some trial and error is likely to be involved with finding this combination. Obviously, use of the NPV per £ of investment approach (usually known as the profitability index) will cause NPV to be maximised for the level of investment finance involved.

Multi-period capital rationing

Where the constraint operates for more than one time period, a more sophisticated approach needs to be adopted. Linear programming (LP) is such an approach.

Example 5.7

Listed below are the cash flow characteristics of four investment projects. Investment finance is rationed at years 0 and 1 to £100 000 at each time. Projects cannot be delayed nor can they be brought forward. The cost of finance is 10 per cent.

Project	Year 0 £000	Year 1 £000	Year 2 £000	Year 3 £000	NPV (at 10%) £000
W	(70)	(20)	60	60	6.44
X	–	(90)	60	50	5.30
Y	(80)	10	60	30	1.18
Z	–	(50)	30	30	1.86

(Note that the NPVs are as at year 0 (now) even for Projects X and Z, which, even if selected, will not commence until year 1. Also note that Project W requires cash outflows in both year 0 and year 1.)

Solution

We should seek to undertake such a combination of the four projects as would give the highest possible total NPV, subject to the capital constraints at years 0 and 1. Letting w, x, y and z be the proportions of each of the four projects that it is desirable to undertake, we are seeking to maximise the function:

$$NPV = 6.44w + 5.30x + 1.18y + 1.86z$$

subject to:

$$70w + 80y \leq 100$$

that is, the total outlays at year 0 on W and Y being £100 000 or less, and:

$$20w + 90x - 10y + 50z \leq 100$$

that is, the total outlays on projects W, X and Z, less the inflow from Project Y at year 1, must not exceed £100 000.

In fact, further constraints will have to be applied since each of the proportions must be positive or zero and cannot (presumably) exceed 1. Thus:

$$1 \geq w \geq 0$$

$$1 \geq x \geq 0$$

$$1 \geq y \geq 0$$

$$1 \geq z \geq 0$$

There is no mathematical reason why the optimal solution should not completely exclude one of the projects. Note that the above formulation assumes that any uninvested funds cannot be carried forward from one year to be invested in the next, but it does assume that inflows from existing projects can be reinvested. It need not make these assumptions, however.

The optimal solution can be derived manually or by computer through the LP technique, finding the maximum value of the objective function subject to the various constraints. In addition to providing the proportion of each project that should be undertaken to achieve the maximum NPV, the LP output will also show, directly or indirectly, the following:

● the value of the maximum NPV;

● how much it is worth paying for additional investment funds in order to undertake more investment and so increase the NPV; and

● how much capital would be needed in each year before that year's shortage of investment funds ceased to be a constraint.

LP will give results that assume that the projects can be partially undertaken. As with the profitability index approach to single-period constraints, this will not be practical to apply in many real-life situations because many business investments cannot be made in part. Real-life instances of businesses going into partnership on large projects can be found. Some of these are clearly the pooling of expertise, but some provide examples of businesses undertaking only part of a project, because capital is rationed.

→ An alternative technique, integer programming, can be applied, which derives the optimal combination of complete projects.

Most texts on operations research and quantitative methods in business explain how to arrive at a solution to the above example through linear programming.

5.9 Replacement decisions

A particular type of investment decision is determining when to replace an existing asset with an identical one.

Example 5.8

A business owns a fleet of identical motor vehicles. It wishes to replace these vehicles after either three or four years. Each one costs £10 000 to replace with a new vehicle. If the business replaces the vehicles after three years it can trade in the old vehicles for £5000 each £5000. If it retains the vehicles for a further year the trade-in price falls to £4000. Assuming that the business regards a 15 per cent discount rate as appropriate, which trade-in policy will be cheaper?

Assume that the running costs of the vehicles, ignoring depreciation, are identical each year.

Unhelpful 'solution'

The relevant cost of owning one vehicle, expressed in present value terms, as at the date of buying a new vehicle, is:

	Replace after 3 years £	Replace after 4 years £
Cost of the vehicle	(10 000)	(10 000)
Present value of the disposal proceeds:		
£5000 × [1/(1.00 + 0.15)^3]	3 288	
£4000 × [1/(1.00 + 0.15)^4]		2 287
Net present cost of owning the vehicle	6 712	7 713

For a wealth-maximising business, it would appear at first glance that the three-year replacement cycle offers the better option. These two figures cannot, however, be directly compared because one of them is the net present capital cost of owning a vehicle for three years, whereas the other is the net present capital cost of owning the vehicle for four years.

One solution to this problem is to look at the position over 12 years. This is because whichever of the two replacement periods (after three years or after four years) is selected, after 12 years the business would be on the point of replacing the vehicle and would have had continual use of a vehicle throughout this period. In other words we should be comparing two costs that have both led to a similar provision.

Helpful but laborious solution

Year		Replace after 3 years £	Replace after 4 years £
0	Cost of a new vehicle	(10 000)	(10 000)
1		–	–
2		–	–
3	PV of the disposal proceeds:		
	£5000 × [1/(1.00 + 0.15)^3]	3 288	
	PV of the cost of a new vehicle:		
	£10 000 × [1/(1.00 + 0.15)^3]	(6 575)	
4	PV of the disposal proceeds:		
	£4000 × [1/(1.00 + 0.15)^4]		2 287
	PV of the cost of a new vehicle:		
	£10 000 × [1/(1.00 + 0.15)^4]		(5 718)
5		–	–
6	PV of the disposal proceeds:		
	£5000 × [1/(1.00 + 0.15)^6]	2 162	
	PV of the cost of a new vehicle:		
	£10 000 × [1/(1.00 + 0.15)^6]	(4 323)	
7		–	–
8	PV of the disposal proceeds:		
	£4000 × [1/(1.00 + 0.15)^8]		1 308
	PV of the cost of a new vehicle:		
	£10 000 × [1/(1.00 + 0.15)^8]		(3 269)
9	PV of the disposal proceeds:		
	£5000 × [1/(1.00 + 0.15)^9]	1 421	
	PV of the cost of a new vehicle:		
	£10 000 × [1/(1.00 + 0.15)^9]	(2 843)	
10		–	–
11		–	–
12	PV of the disposal proceeds:		
	£5000 × [1/(1.00 + 0.15)^{12}]	935	
	£4000 × [1/(1.00 + 0.15)^{12}]		748
	Net present cost of owning the vehicles	15 935	14 644

Now that we are able to make a valid comparison we can see that it is less costly to replace the vehicles after four years.

In this case using this approach was not too laborious because the lowest common multiple (LCM) is only 12 years. Suppose, however, that we were considering replacement after either eight or nine years? Here the LCM is 72 years. If we were also considering a seven-year possibility, the LCM would be 504 years. Clearly, we need a more practical approach.

An alternative approach is to imagine that we were able to rent a vehicle, to be replaced with a new one either after three years or after four years. In either case also imagine that the rent is of a fixed annual amount and that payment is made at the end of each year. If we could deduce the annual rent that would represent the equivalent cost, in NPV terms, to £6712 (three-year replacement) and £7713 (four-year replacement) (see 'Unhelpful solution' above), we could make a valid comparison between the two replacement policies.

One way to do this is by trial and error. We could try to find an amount such that the NPV of three payments of that amount, one at the end of each of the next three years, equals £6712. Fortunately there is a quicker way, using the annuity table (Appendix 2 of this book).

Helpful and practical solution

You may care to look back to page 83 for an explanation of the annuity table.

Looking at the annuity table for 15 per cent and 3 years we find an annuity factor of 2.283. This means that the present value of £1 payable (or receivable) at the end of this year and of the next two years totals £2.283. Thus the amount payable at the end of this year and of the next two years, which has an NPV of £6712, is £6712/2.283 = £2940.

The four-year annuity factor (from the table) is 2.855. Thus the equivalent annual cost of replacing the vehicle after four years is £7713/2.855 = £2702.

Again we find that the four-year replacement cycle is the less costly option. Note that the equivalent annual cost approach gives the same result as the LCM approach because they follow exactly the same principles, even though they seem quite different. (£15 935 is 8.8 per cent higher than £14 644 (LCM), and £2940 is 8.8 per cent higher than £2702 (equivalent annual cost).

The example we have used is a very basic one. In reality there would probably be a tax aspect, different running costs of the vehicle in each of the four years and the effects of inflation. All these can be incorporated without any great difficulty. There may well also be non-quantifiable factors such as the effect on the image of the business of having its staff driving relatively new vehicles.

5.10 Routines for identifying, assessing, implementing and reviewing investment projects

In Chapter 2 we saw how the decision-making process involves six steps. These are:

1 Identifying the business's objectives

2 Identifying possible courses of action

3 Assembling data relevant to the decision

4 Assessing the data and reaching a decision

5 Implementing the decision

6 Monitoring the effects of decisions.

Accepting that wealth maximisation is the principal financial objective for all decisions, we can now look at the other five of these in the context of investment decisions.

Identifying possible investment opportunities

The assessment of possible investment projects is only one step in a process of the search for opportunities. This process should not be regarded as one that should be undertaken at, say, five-yearly intervals, but as one that should be part of the routine of the business. Good investment opportunities do not tend to beat a path to the business's door; they must be sought out. Business tends to be highly competitive, so opportunities overlooked by one business will probably be taken up by another. Any business that regularly overlooks opportunities must sooner or later fall by the wayside.

Members of staff need to be encouraged to identify new products, new markets, new ways of supplying those markets and new approaches to production. Technical help should be available to help staff to develop ideas into formal investment proposals.

Assembling the relevant data for an investment proposal

Estimates of the relevant costs associated with the proposal must be made. This probably needs to be carried out by a financial manager. Care must be taken to gather all relevant costs and benefits. There is a danger that bias can influence some of the cost estimates, particularly where a manager is strongly in favour of or against the proposal. If an independent financial manager can carry out this task, it may help to promote freedom from bias.

Assessing the data and reaching a decision

The data must be fed into the decision-making model that the business is using. Assuming that the business is a wealth maximiser, this model should be NPV. Once again this process demands certain technical skill and freedom from bias, so it is best carried out by someone who has those attributes, such as a member of the business's finance staff.

Implementing the decision

Action needs to be taken to get the project under way. A project team may well be established to take the necessary steps.

Monitoring the effects of the decision

Reviews, sometimes known as **post audits**, need to be carried out to try to assess the effectiveness of the project. One of the reasons for this is to assess the quality of the decision-making process, so that improvements in this process can be sought and instigated in respect of future decisions.

The progress of the project must also be monitored to assess whether or not it is economic to continue with it. Periodically, over the life of the project, the question as to whether the project should be abandoned needs to be raised. The project will not be able to continue indefinitely – plant wears out, markets decline – so identifying the economically optimum moment for its abandonment is important. For the wealth-maximising business, this process logically involves an NPV analysis of the relevant costs and benefits of continuation relative to those associated with abandonment.

Investment decisions in practice

Pike (1996) found that 72 per cent of the 100 large UK businesses surveyed by him in 1992 carried out a post audit on 'most major projects'. The 1992 study was a continuation of a longitudinal study of investment practices of large UK businesses. The extent of the use of post audits had increased from 33 per cent in 1975 to 46 per cent in 1980, to 64 per cent in 1986, and to 72 per cent by 1992. This had risen to 95 per cent by 1997 according to Arnold and Hatzopoulos (2000) who surveyed a similar group of businesses to Pike. Clearly, the use of post audit has expanded strongly over the years.

Given these research findings it would be expected that major businesses would have fairly sophisticated routines surrounding all aspects of investment decisions. Many businesses comment on what they do.

Rolls-Royce plc, the engine and power systems manufacturer, seems to be a business that follows a policy of reassessing existing investment projects. It said in its 2003 annual report: 'The group has a portfolio of projects at different stages of their life cycles. Discounted cash flow analysis of the remaining life of projects is performed on a regular basis.' Presumably, any projects that have a negative NPV are abandoned.

Reckitt Benckiser plc, the household goods manufacturer (for example, Dettol and Harpic), in its 2003 annual report says: 'there is a structured process for the appraisal and authorisation of all material capital projects'.

Greene King plc, the regional brewer and pub owner, said in its 2004 annual report: 'there are clearly defined evaluation and approval processes for acquisitions and disposals, capital expenditure and project control. These include escalating levels of authority, detailed appraisal and review procedures and post completion reviews of all major projects to compare the actual with the original plan.'

GKN plc, the engineering business, said in its 2003 annual report: 'there are clearly defined management authorities for the approval of capital expenditure, major contracts, acquisitions, investments and divestments, together with an established framework for their appraisal, which includes a risk analysis and post-implementation plan, and where appropriate, a post-acquisition review'.

Some criticism has been made of researchers in capital investment appraisal implying that they have tended to concentrate on the minutiae of the quantitative assessment of projects, leaving largely untouched questions surrounding the search for possible projects.

The quantitative appraisal is a purely technical process, even though a complicated one at times. The real test of managers' talent is whether they can identify good projects that will promote the achievement of the business's objectives. Reliable appraisal is vital, but it is a low-level task by comparison.

5.11 Investment appraisal and strategic planning

So far, we have tended to view investment opportunities as if they are, more or less, unconnected independent entities, which follow no particular pattern. It seems that in practice, however, successful businesses are those that establish some framework for the selection of projects. Without such a framework it may be difficult to identify projects for which the business is sufficiently well placed for them to be beneficial, that is, to have a positive NPV. Such beneficial projects can only exist where a combination of the business's internal strengths (for example, skills, experience, access to finance) match the opportunities available and, probably, match them better than those of its competitors. In areas where this match does not exist, other businesses, for whom the match does exist, are likely to have a distinct competitive advantage. This advantage means that they are likely to be able to provide the product or service more cheaply and/or of a better quality and/or market it more successfully.

Establishing what is the best area or areas of activity and style of approach for the business is popularly known as strategic planning. In essence, strategic planning tries to identify the direction in which the business needs to go, in terms of products, markets, financing and so on, to best place it to generate profitable investment opportunities. In practice, strategic plans seem to have a time span of around five years and generally tend to ask the question: where do we want our business to be in five years' time and how can we get there?

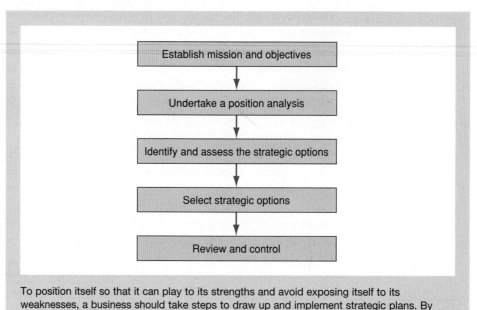

To position itself so that it can play to its strengths and avoid exposing itself to its weaknesses, a business should take steps to draw up and implement strategic plans. By doing so it stands the best chance of being able to identify investment opportunities that can yield positive NPVs.

Figure 5.2
The strategic
planning framework

Strategic planning is typically seen to follow a series of steps, which are set out diagrammatically in Figure 5.2.

Establish mission and objectives

The mission is a broad statement of the business's general direction and aspirations. It tends to identify what the business is trying to do, in the broadest terms, usually identifying the commercial activities that the business wants to be involved in.

Objectives are much more precise and operational. We reviewed possible objectives in Chapter 2 and concluded that, for most businesses, maximisation of wealth seems to be a major objective, if perhaps not the only one. The essential feature of objectives is that courses of action must be capable of being assessed against them. In other words, identifying objectives is not helpful unless the business can distinguish between meeting them and failing to meet them.

Undertake a position analysis

This step seeks to identify how the business is currently placed relative to its environment (competitors, markets, technology, the economy, political climate and so on), in the context of the business's mission and objectives. This is often formally approached through an analysis of strengths, weaknesses, opportunities and threats (a SWOT analysis). The first two of these are factors that are internal to the business. Strengths might include such matters as technical expertise, strong finances and access to markets. Weaknesses are such things as lack of experience, lack of access to new finance and lack of access to raw materials. Opportunities and threats are external factors. Opportunities might include a new market opening, some new technology developing or a competitor leaving the market. Threats could be factors such as a new competitor entering the market, the decline of a market or a change in the law that will make it harder for the business to operate.

→ It is not essential that the position analysis be carried out in the SWOT framework, though this seems to be a popular approach.

Identify and assess the strategic options

This step is concerned with pursuing the business's mission and objectives by trying to identify courses of action that use the business's strengths to exploit opportunities, and at the same time avoid, as far as possible, the business's weaknesses being exposed to the environmental threats.

Note that however good the strategic 'fit' of making a particular investment, if that investment does not have a positive NPV, it should not be undertaken. **Associated British Foods plc**, the UK food business, clearly recognises this point. It said in its 2004 annual report: 'The future will see us continue to build on those parts of our business that put forward clear growth strategies. We will invest heavily in support of these strategies and, where appropriate, acquire businesses that fit in well with these growth plans. Acquisitions grab the headlines, but we are less interested in the headlines than in ensuring that, when we spend our money, it is our shareholders who benefit in the short, medium and long term.'

Select strategic options

Here the best strategic option or options are selected and formed into a strategic plan.

Review and control

The performance of the business should be measured against the strategic plan. This is rather like the post audit for an individual investment project, but for the entire strategy rather than for just one of its building blocks.

5.12 Value-based management

Traditional accounting-based measures of management effectiveness, like the return on capital employed (ROCE) ratio and the earnings per share (EPS) value, have been criticised for not focusing sufficiently on what businesses ultimately seek to do: to generate wealth or value for their shareholders. The problem with the accounting measures is that they tend to focus on sales revenue and profit increases, not on value generation. For example, it is always open to a business to increase its ROCE and EPS, at least in the short term, by taking on more risky activities. Such activities may well have the effect of reducing value.

→ The increasing emphasis on the wealth of the shareholders as a corporate goal,
→ which we discussed in Chapter 2, has led to the emergence of ideas like shareholder value analysis (SVA) and economic value added (EVA®).

Shareholder value analysis

SVA is based on the, totally logical, principle that the value of the business overall is equal to the sum of the NPVs of all of its activities. This is to say, that at any particular point in time, the business has a value equal to the projected future cash flows from all of its existing projects, each discounted at a suitable rate. The shareholders' financial stake in the business is the entire value of the business less the value of its outstanding debt. Thus if the value of the NPVs of the business's various activities can be increased, this should mean greater value for shareholders, either to be paid out as dividends or to be reinvested in other projects that will, in turn, result in still more shareholder value.

The claimed advantages of SVA, as a philosophy of business decision making, are that the actions of managers can be directly linked to value generation, and the outcomes of decisions can be assessed in that context. SVA was first suggested by Rappaport (1986).

The principles of SVA

A business has a value at a particular time because of the projected cash flows from its activities. The particular value will be based on their timings and discount rate. According to the philosophy of SVA, the value of the business is affected by or driven by just seven factors known as value drivers. To increase the value of the business, that is, to generate additional value, one or more of these value drivers will need to alter in a favourable direction. These value drivers, and their effect on shareholder value, are shown in Figure 5.3.

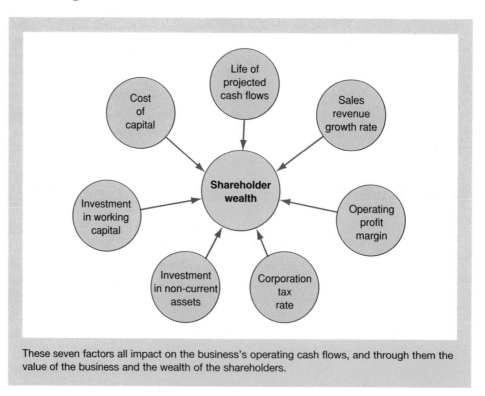

Figure 5.3
The seven drivers of cash flows and shareholder value

These seven factors all impact on the business's operating cash flows, and through them the value of the business and the wealth of the shareholders.

We shall now look at these value drivers and relate them to individual parts of the business.

Sales revenue growth rate

If a greater level of sales revenue can be generated in the future than was expected, then this should create more cash flows and, therefore, more value. The greater level of sales revenue could come from a new product and, provided that this did not have an adverse effect on one of the other value drivers, greater value would necessarily be created. Similarly, arresting an expected decline in sales revenue levels for some existing product has the potential to generate value.

Operating profit margin

The operating profit margin is the ratio of net profit, before financing charges and tax, to sales revenue. The higher this ratio, the greater the net positive cash flows from each sale. Thus, if costs can be controlled more effectively, more cash will tend to flow from each sale and value will be enhanced.

Corporation tax rate

The corporation tax rate clearly affects cash flows and value because, broadly, tax is levied directly on operating cash flows. Management's ability to influence the tax rate and the amount of tax paid by the business tends, at best, to be marginal.

Investment in non-current assets

Normally, cash has to be spent on additional non-current assets in order to enhance shareholder value. Wherever managers can find ways of reducing the outlay on plant, machinery and so on, without limiting the effectiveness of the business, this will tend to enhance shareholder value.

Investment in working capital

Nearly all business activities give rise to a need for working capital (stocks, debtors, creditors and cash). As we shall see in Chapter 13, the amounts tied up in working capital can be considerable. Steps that can be taken to reduce the investment in working capital, for example, by encouraging trade debtors to pay more quickly than expected, will bring cash flows forward and tend to generate value. We shall consider many of these steps in Chapter 13.

The cost of capital

The cost of funds used to finance the business's activities will typically be a major determinant of shareholder value. So, if the business could find cheaper sources of long-term finance, value would tend to be enhanced. How this would be achieved is discussed later in the book, particularly in Chapters 8 and 11.

The life of the projected cash flows

Clearly, the longer that any cash-generating activity can continue, the greater its potential to generate value.

How can SVA be used?

Probably, SVA's most helpful contribution to managing the business is that it highlights the key drivers of value. This enables managers to set targets for achieving value-enhancing strategies in each area. It can help to create an environment where value enhancement is at the top of the agenda for managers in all areas of the business. In this way the primary financial objective of the business is linked directly to managers' day-to-day decisions and actions.

SVA can be used as a basis for valuing shares and, thereby, assessing the increase in shareholder value as a result of adopting particular strategies. Doing this, however, tends to rely on making some simplifying assumptions that rather call the results into question.

An assessment of using the SVA approach to management

SVA's positive points include:

- SVA encourages managers to take actions that will lead to enhancement of shareholder value, so that their actions link directly to the principal corporate objective of most businesses.
- Managerial targets can be set in the area of each value driver.

SVA's problems include:

- Possible conflicts between value drivers, such that actions to enhance value in one area lead to a net destruction of value. For example, reducing the debtor collection period (working capital reduction) might lead to a loss of sales revenue if customers react adversely to shorter credit periods.
- The management information systems of many businesses are not geared to producing what is necessary in an SVA environment.

Economic profit and economic value added

The use of economic profit as a performance indicator reflects the notion that, for a business to be profitable in an economic sense, it must generate returns that exceed the required returns by investors. It is not enough simply to make an accounting profit because this measure does not take full account of the returns required by investors. The economic profit approach has a long history and is widely used.

Economic value added (EVA®) is a refinement of the economic profit approach that has been developed and trademarked by a New York management consultancy firm, Stern, Stewart and Company (SS).

The principles of EVA®

EVA® is a measure of the extent to which the after-tax operating profit of the business for a period, exceeds the required minimum profit, which in turn is based on the shareholders' minimum required rate of return on their investment multiplied by the amount of that investment. Thus if there is an excess of actual profit over the required minimum, economic value will have been added, and the shareholders will be more wealthy. If there is a shortfall, the shareholders will be less wealthy because they will not have earned an adequate return given the amount of investment and the required minimum rate of return.

The formula for EVA® is as follows:

$$EVA® = NOPAT - (R \times C)$$

where NOPAT is the net operating profit after tax, R is the required rate of return for investors and C is the capital invested (that is, the net assets of the business).

Only when EVA® is positive can we say that the business is increasing shareholder wealth. To maximise shareholder wealth, managers must increase EVA® by as much as possible.

How can EVA® be used?

As we can see from the formula, in order to increase EVA® managers need to achieve one or more of the following:

- Increase NOPAT. This may be done either by reducing expenses or by increasing sales revenue.

- Use capital invested more efficiently. This includes selling off any assets that are not generating returns that reflect their value and investing in assets that will do so.

- Reduce the required rate of return for investors. This might be achieved by borrowing to supply part of the total funding of the business. However, this strategy can create problems, as we shall see in Chapter 11.

Targets can be set for EVA® for a business as a whole or for individual parts of it. These target EVA®s can then be assessed against the actual value added, once the relevant planning period has ended.

EVA® relies on conventional financial statements to measure the wealth created for shareholders. However, the NOPAT and capital figures shown on these statements are used only as a starting point. They have to be adjusted because of the problems and limitations of conventional accounting measures. According to SS, the major problem is that profit and capital are understated because of the conservative bias in accounting measurement. As we saw in Chapter 3, the prudence convention tends to encourage this bias.

Capital is understated because assets are reported at a value based on their original cost (historic cost convention), which can produce figures considerably below current market values. In addition, certain assets, such as internally generated goodwill and brand names, are omitted from the financial statements because no external transactions have occurred.

SS has identified more than 100 adjustments that could be made to the conventional financial statements in an attempt to correct for the conservative bias. However, SS believes that, in practice, only a handful of adjustments will usually have to be made to the accounting figures of any particular business. Unless an adjustment is going to have a significant effect on the calculation of EVA®, it is considered not worth making. The adjustments made should reflect the nature of the particular business. Each business is unique and so must customise the calculation of EVA® to its particular circumstances.

The most common adjustments that have to be made are as follows:

- *Research and development costs.* R&D costs should be written off (treated as an expense) over the period that they benefit. In practice, however, these costs are often written off in the period in which they are incurred. This means that any amounts written off immediately should be added back to the assets on the balance sheet, thereby increasing invested capital, and then written off over time.

- *Goodwill.* In theory, goodwill should receive the same treatment as R&D. However, SS suggests leaving goodwill on the balance sheet. One argument in favour of this treatment is that goodwill is really a 'catch all' that includes intangible items such as brand names and reputation that have infinite lives. Thus, any amounts written off should be added back to assets.

- *Restructuring costs (that is, costs of reorganising the business's operations or finances).* This item can be viewed as an investment in the future rather than as an expense to be written off. Supporters of EVA® argue that, by restructuring, the business is better placed to meet future challenges, and so restructuring represents an asset. Any amounts written off should be added back to assets.

- *Marketable investments.* Investments in shares and loan capital of other businesses are not included as part of the capital invested in the business. This is because the income from marketable investments is not included in the calculation of operating profit. (Income from this source will be added in the profit and loss account *after* operating profit has been calculated.)

It is perhaps worth noting that SS believes that bonuses, calculated as a percentage of EVA®, should form a very large part of the total remuneration package for managers. Thus, the higher the EVA® figure, the higher the rewards to managers – with no upper limits.

An assessment of the EVA® approach to management

EVA®'s positive points include:

- Managers are subjected to a charge for the capital that has been invested. Before any increase in shareholder wealth can be recognised, an appropriate deduction is made for the use of business resources. Thus, EVA® encourages managers to use these resources efficiently. Where managers are focused simply on increasing profits, there is a danger that the resources used to achieve any increase in profits will not be taken properly into account.

- EVA® is based on conventional financial statements, adjusted to try to remove biases. There is no requirement for a separate management information system.

EVA®'s problems include:

- The adjustments to the financial statements are matters of judgement, which can call into question the calculation of the economic value added for a period.

Value-based management in practice

Value-based management, the main examples of which are SVA and EVA®, seems to be fairly widely used by larger businesses in practice. Ernst and Young (2003) undertook a major survey of management accounting practices in US businesses. The survey tended to be of larger businesses. It showed that 52 per cent of the businesses were, in 2003, using some value-based approach to management, with a further 40 per cent considering adopting such an approach in the future. There appears not to be similar information on the position in the UK and elsewhere. However, there is no reason to believe that the UK position differs greatly from the US one.

One UK business that uses a value-based approach to management is **Cadbury Schweppes plc**, the confectionary and drinks manufacturer. In its 2003 annual report it said:

In 1997, Managing for Value (MFV) was introduced into the business. MFV is an holistic management process, designed to focus the organisation more effectively on the delivery of superior shareholder returns. This remains the key management process within the business and includes the adoption of value based management principles in both strategic and operational management, raising capabilities at all levels of the organisation, setting stretching targets and aligning management rewards with the interests of shareholders.

5.13 Real options

Before we complete this consideration of the practical aspects of investment decision making, we are going to take a quick look at an approach to investment decisions that is gaining influence in the real world. Many business decisions can be seen to involve options and should, therefore, be assessed in that light.

An option is normally defined as the right, but not the obligation, to do something. In Chapter 1 we took a brief look at currency options. This is an example of a *financial* option. What we are talking about here is known as a **real option**. Probably the easiest way to explain real options is through a simple example.

Example 5.9	Wessex Mining owns a site in Dorset on which there is an oil well. The business does not pump oil any longer because the price of oil is such that it is not economic to do so. Furthermore, projections for oil prices are such that it may never be worthwhile to exploit the well. Recently, a property developer has offered £500 000 for the site, which it has plans to develop for domestic housing.
	What should Wessex Mining do?

Solution	On the face of it, the well has no economic value, so accepting the offer would make the shareholders more wealthy by £500 000. On the other hand, Wessex Mining owns an option. It has the right (because it owns the well) to pump oil whenever it wants, but it has no obligation to do so. Although projections for the future price of oil may suggest that it is unlikely that the business would ever choose to produce oil, oil prices can be volatile and could rise to a price at which production would become economic. This option, therefore, has a value, and this must be set against the £500 000. Retaining the site does not oblige the business to produce oil, but it enables it to keep the right to do so. Unfortunately, putting a value on this option is very difficult, but such a difficulty is not unique to this decision. All decisions involve trying to value future outcomes.
	In this case, as in many in real life, it may be reasonable to turn down the offer from the property developer and to wait and see what happens to the price of oil. It seems likely, given the demand for housing in the UK, that the site could be sold for development at virtually any time in the future. Obviously there is an opportunity cost here. Having the £500 000 would enable the business to gain income from it, so delaying would have a cost. It would all be a matter of commercial judgement.

This was a very simple example, and you need not even have heard the word 'option' to recognise that the well has a value because the price of oil might rise. There are, however, situations where the existence of a real option is less obvious but no less important to the decision.

Graham and Harvey (2001) found that 27 per cent of the US businesses surveyed by them incorporate a consideration of real options in their investment decisions 'always or almost always'. See the further reading at the end of this chapter for references to examples of real options.

Summary

Cash/accounting flows

- Net present value (NPV), internal rate of return (IRR) and payback period (PBP) all require the use of cash flows.
- Need to adjust accounting flows for:
  - depreciation, add it back to accounting profit;
  - capital expenditure and disposal proceeds cash flows need to be identified as to amount and timing; and
  - working capital (WC) needs to be treated as a cash outflow early in the project and an inflow at the end.

Relevant cash flows

- Only those that will differ according to the decision should be taken into account. This means that:
  - all past costs should be ignored;
  - all future costs that will be the same irrespective of the decision should be ignored; and
  - differential opportunity costs should be included.

Taxation

- Taxation must be taken into account where the decisions will lead to different tax cash flows.
- Depreciation is not a tax-deductible expense. Capital allowances replace depreciation for tax purposes.

Inflation

- Inflation must be taken into account when using NPV. Either:
  - real cash flows must be discounted using a real discount rate; or
  - money (nominal) cash flows must be discounted using a money (nominal) discount rate.

  The two cannot be mixed.
- In practice, it is usually easier to use money cash flows and discount rate.
- (1 + Money discount rate) = (1 + Real discount rate) × (1 + Inflation rate)

Carrying out an NPV appraisal involves five steps

1 Identify all the relevant cash flows and their timing.
2 Total the cash flows for each point in time.
3 Discount each total, according to the appropriate time into the future that the cash flow will occur.
4 Total the present values of the various discounted values to derive the NPV for the project.
5 If the NPV is positive, the project is acceptable, presuming a shareholder wealth maximisation objective.

Capital rationing

- May be self-imposed (soft) or imposed by the financial market (hard).
- May be single-period or multi-period.
- For single-period, decision rule is: maximise the NPV per £ of capital investment.
- For multi-period, needs to be approached through linear programming.

Replacement decisions involve four steps

1 Derive the present value (cost) of owning the asset for each of the time periods concerned.

2 Find (from the annuity table) the annuity factors for the relevant discount rate and time periods.

3 Divide each of the PVs by the relevant annuity factor to derive the equivalent annual cost (EAC).

4 The replacement period with the lowest EAC will be the most economical, though other factors may influence the final decision.

Investment and strategy

- Investment decisions should be taken in the context of the business's strategic plans.

Value-based management

- Shareholder value analysis (SVA) is an approach to management that focuses attention on the business objective of shareholder wealth maximisation and the seven key drivers of value.
- Can also be used to value businesses.
- Value (wealth) will be enhanced by improvement in any one of seven value drivers:
    1 Sales revenue growth rate
    2 Operating profit margin
    3 Corporation tax rate
    4 Investment in non-current assets
    5 Investment in working capital
    6 Cost of capital
    7 Life of the projected cash flows.
- Problems of SVA:
    - Possible conflicts between value drivers so enhancing value in one area can lead to losses of value in others.
    - Many businesses do not have management reporting systems that provide the information necessary in an SVA environment.
- EVA® is an approach to management that seeks to promote businesses earning more than the shareholders' required return and so increase value.

→

- Uses standard accounting profit and capital invested, but adjusts both of these for the innate conservatism of accounting measures.
- Benefits of EVA® include:
  - Managers are subjected to a charge that is based on capital invested by them and the shareholders' required minimum return.
  - There is no requirement for a separate management information system.
- A problem is that adjusting the accounting figures to remove the biases is subjective.

Real options

- Nearly all business situations offer strategic options, for example delaying a decision until information becomes more available.
- Traditional decision-making approaches tend to ignore or underplay these options.
- The value of the real options involved in a decision should be included in the analysis.

Further reading

Most texts on business finance and capital investment appraisal deal to a greater or lesser extent with the practical aspects. The following tend to deal with those aspects to a greater extent: Samuels, Wilkes and Brayshaw (1998), Arnold (2002), Brealey and Myers (2002). Bancroft and O'Sullivan (2000) give clear coverage of linear programming. Bowman and Asch (1995) provide a very readable introduction to strategic planning. Atrill and McLaney (2005) give more detail of value-based management. For a very readable introduction to real options, see Dixit and Pindyck (1995), and for some real-life examples of real options, see Leslie and Michaels (1998).

Relevant websites

The websites of the businesses featured in this chapter are:

Associated British Foods plc	www.abf.co.uk
Cadbury Schweppes plc	www.cadburyschweppes.com
GKN plc	www.gknplc.com
Greene King plc	www.greeneking.co.uk
Next plc	www.next.co.uk
Reckitt Benckiser plc	www.reckittbenckiser.com
Rolls-Royce plc	www.rolls-royce.com

The website of Stern, Stewart and Company, the organisation that developed EVA®, contains information about this approach.
www.sternstewart.com

REVIEW QUESTIONS

Suggested answers to review questions appear in Appendix 3.

5.1 'Depreciation is taken into account when deducing profit (in the profit and loss account), but ignored in NPV assessments. If both accounting profit and NPV are meant to be decision-making tools, this difference is illogical.' Is it illogical?

5.2 Is it logical to include interest payments on cash borrowed to finance a project as cash outflows of the project in an NPV assessment? Explain your answer.

5.3 Is it true that the 'money' rate of interest is equal to the 'real' rate, plus the rate of inflation? Explain your answer.

5.4 When inflation is predicted over the life of a project under assessment, there are two approaches to dealing with inflation. What are these? Which is the better one to use?

5.5 How can it be argued that hard capital rationing does not exist in real life?

5.6 What is meant by a 'profitability index'? Is it a helpful approach to dealing with multi-period capital rationing problems?

PROBLEMS

Sample answers to problems marked with an asterisk appear in Appendix 4.

(Problems 5.1 to 5.4 are basic-level problems, whereas problems 5.5 to 5.8 are more advanced and may contain some practical complications.)

5.1* Dodd Ltd is assessing a business investment opportunity, Project X, the estimated cash flows for which are as follows:

	£000
Investment (cash outflow on 1 January 20X2)	250
Net annual cash inflow (arising on the last day of the year):	
20X2	160
20X3	160
20X4	100
Cash inflow from residual value 31 December 20X4	50

All of the above figures are expressed at 1 January 20X2 prices. Inflation is expected to operate at 5 per cent p.a. throughout the project's life.

The business's 'real' (that is, not taking account of inflation) cost of finance is estimated at 10 per cent p.a.

Corporation tax is charged on profits at the rate of 30 per cent, payable during the year in which the profit is earned (assume that the taxable profit equals the net operating cash flow). The asset, which will be bought in 20X2 and disposed of in 20X4, is of a type that does not give rise to any tax relief on its cost nor a tax charge on its disposal.

Calculate (using 'money' cash flows), the net present value of Project X.

5.2 Lateral plc has a limit of £10 million of investment finance available to it this year, and it has the following investment opportunities available to it:

Project	Investment required this year (£m)	Net present value (£m)
U	8.0	3.3
V	3.2	0.9
W	5.3	1.2
X	2.0	0.5
Y	4.5	2.0
Z	0.5	0.4

Assuming that the capital shortage relates only to the current year and that each project can be undertaken in part, with the NPV scaled down in direct proportion to the proportion undertaken, which projects should Lateral plc undertake?

5.3 The management of Roach plc is currently assessing the possibility of manufacturing and selling a new product. Two possible approaches have been proposed.

Approach A

This involves making an immediate payment of £60 000 to buy a new machine. It is estimated that the machine can be used effectively for three years, at the end of which time it will be scrapped for zero proceeds.

Approach B

This involves using an existing machine, which cost £150 000 two years ago, since when it has been depreciated at the rate of 25 per cent p.a., on cost. The business has no use for the machine, other than in the manufacture of the new product, so if it is not used for that purpose it will be sold. It could be sold immediately for £48 000. Alternatively there is a potential buyer who will pay £60 000 and take delivery of the machine in one year's time. There are no additional costs of retaining the machine for another year.

If the machine is retained for manufacturing the new product, it will be scrapped (zero proceeds) in two years' time.

The staff required under Approach B will be transferred from within the business. The total labour cost involved is £25 000 for each of the next two years. The employees concerned will need to be replaced for two years at a total cost of £20 000 for each of those years. The operating profit estimates, given below, are based on the labour cost of the staff that will actually be working on the new product.

The estimated operating profits, before depreciation, from the new product are as follows:

	Year 1 £000	Year 2 £000	Year 3 £000
Approach A	30	50	60
Approach B	60	40	–

The new production will require additional working capital. This is estimated at 10 per cent of the relevant year's operating profit, before depreciation. It is required by the beginning of the relevant year.

The business's cost of finance to support this investment is 20 per cent p.a.

On the basis of NPV which, if either, of the two approaches should the business adopt? (Hint: You will need to make the decision about what to do with the old machine if Approach B is adopted, before you can go on to compare the two approaches.)

5.4* Livelong Ltd has the continuing need for a cutting machine to perform a particular function vital to the business's activities. There are two machines on the market, the Alpha
and the Beta. Investigations show that the data relating to costs and life expectancy of
each machine are as follows:

	Alpha	Beta
Acquisition cost	£50 000	£90 000
Residual value at the end of the machine's useful life	£5 000	£7 000
Annual running cost	£10 000	£8 000
Useful life	4 years	7 years

The two machines are identical in terms of capacity and quality of work.
The relevant cost of finance is 10 per cent p.a. Ignore taxation and inflation.

Produce workings that show which machine is the most economical.

*By how much, and in which direction, would the acquisition cost of an Alpha need to
alter in order for the two machines to be equally economical?*

5.5* Mega Builders plc (Mega), a civil engineering contractor, has been invited to tender
for a major contract. Work on the contract must start in January 20X6 and be completed by 31 December 20X7. The contract price will be receivable in three equal
annual instalments, on 31 December 20X6, 20X7 and 20X8. Mega's management has
reason to believe that the client will probably not accept a tender price in excess of
£13.5m.

It is estimated that the contract will require 500 000 hours of non-management
labour, in each of the two years 20X6 and 20X7, paid at an hourly rate of £5 and hired
for the duration of the contract.

Staff that would be hired only for the duration of the contract would undertake management of the contract. Employment costs of the management staff (including travel
and subsistence) would be £250 000, in each of 20X6 and 20X7.

Materials for the contract will be bought at an estimated cost of £1.3 million, in each
of the two years 20X6 and 20X7.

The contract would follow on from an existing contract, which will be completed
at the end of 20X5. The new contract requires the use of an item of plant that is
being used on the existing contract and could be moved for the new contract. This
item of plant was bought in May 20X4 for £6m. Were it not to be used on the new
contract it would be sold on 31 December 20X5 for an estimated £2.5m (in 'money'
terms), payable on that date. Transporting the plant to the new site would cost an
estimated £100 000, payable on 31 December 20X5. This cost would be expected to
be treated as part of the capital cost of the plant for tax purposes. It is estimated that
at the end of the new contract this plant would be disposed of for a zero net realisable
value.

Full capital allowances (at the rate of 25 per cent reducing balance) have in the
past been claimed at the earliest opportunity. This is expected to be continued in the
future.

For taxation purposes, it is the business's normal practice to recognise revenues
in the accounting periods in which it receives the cash. Mega matches the costs of
contracts with the revenues on a pro-rata basis. This is done by taking the total known
and expected future costs of the contract (excluding financing costs and capital

→

allowances) and allocating this to accounting years, as the contract price is received. The Inland Revenue accepts this approach. Capital allowances are given in the normal way. Mega's accounting year ends on 31 December.

Mega's corporation tax rate is expected to be 30 per cent. Assume that tax will be payable during the accounting year to which it relates.

Mega's management regards the 'real' cost of capital for the new contract to be 10 per cent p.a. (after tax).

There are not thought to be any other incremental costs associated with the new contract.

Forecasts of the general rate of inflation are 3 per cent for 20X6, 4 per cent for 20X7 and 5 per cent for both 20X8 and 20X9. It is estimated that the labour (both management and non-management) and material costs will increase in line with the general rate of inflation.

(a) Would the new contract be financially advantageous to Mega at a tender price of £13.5m? (Use a 'money', rather than a 'real' approach to your analysis.)

(b) What is the minimum price at which Mega should tender for the contract?

(c) What other factors should be taken into account in deriving the tender price?

Assume that all cash flows occur on 31 December of the relevant year, unless another date is specified in the question.

5.6 Marine Products Ltd has identified three possible investment projects. Two of these would have to be started very shortly (year 0), the third in a year's time (year 1). None of these projects can be brought forward, delayed or repeated.

The estimated cash flows for the possible projects, none of which will generate cash flows beyond year 5, are as follows:

Year	Project A £m	Project B £m	Project C £m
0	(1.6)	(2.3)	–
1	(0.8)	0.6	(2.5)
2	0.7	0.9	0.8
3	1.5	0.9	1.5
4	1.5	0.5	1.4
5	0.4	–	0.5

All of these projects are typical of projects that the business has undertaken in the past. The business's cost of capital is 15 per cent p.a.

The entire cash flows of Project A for years 0 and 1, of Project B for year 0, and of Project C for year 1 are capital expenditure. The subsequent net cash inflows are net operating cash surpluses.

The business is not able to raise more than £2m of investment finance in each of years 0 and 1. However, to the extent that the business does not invest its full £2m in year 0, it will be allowed to use it in year 1. The business can also use any operating cash surpluses from previously undertaken investments as new investment finance.

In past years the business has used all of its investment finance. It is expected that past investments will produce operating cash surpluses as follows:

Year	£m
1	0.5
2	0.5
3	0.3
4	0.2
5	0.1
6 and thereafter	0.0

*Set out the various statements (equations and/or inequalities) that can be subjected to linear programming to provide the management of the business with guidance on the best investment strategy for years 0 and 1. (The solution to the linear programming problem is **not** required.)*

Work to the nearest £100 000. Assume that all cash flows occur on 31 December of the relevant year. Ignore inflation and taxation.

5.7 Prentice Products Ltd's products development department has just developed a new product, a cordless hair dryer for use in hairdressing salons. Were production to go ahead it would start on 1 January 20X1.

Manufacturing the hair dryer would require the purchase of some new plant costing £500 000, payable on 31 December 20X0. At the end of 20X4, this plant would be scrapped (zero disposal proceeds). The business's policy is to depreciate plant in equal instalments over its estimated lifetime. For tax purposes, the equipment would attract annual capital allowances of 25 per cent, reducing balance. The funds for purchasing this plant would come from a bank loan, which would be raised on 31 December 20X0 and repaid on 31 December 20X4. Interest on the loan would be at a fixed rate of 10 per cent p.a. (gross), payable at the end of each year. The business's after-tax weighted average cost of capital is expected to be 15 per cent for the foreseeable future.

Prentice Products Ltd would not undertake manufacturing and selling the hair dryers unless the project could generate an increase in the present wealth of the shareholders of at least £200 000.

Based on an estimated constant annual demand of 10 000 hair dryers, the unit cost of a hair dryer has been determined by one of the business's employees as follows:

	£
Labour: 5 hours at £5/hour	25.00
Plastic: 2.5 kg at £10/kg	25.00
Supervision	3.00
Various bought-in parts	12.70
Loan interest	5.00
Depreciation	12.50
Electrical power	2.20
Apportionment of company-wide fixed overheads	23.80
	109.20

The supervision cost refers to the salary of an existing employee, who would be moved from her present work to manage production and sales of the hair dryer. This person's existing work will be undertaken by someone employed on a four-year contract at an annual salary of £25 000.

It is considered that manufacturing and selling the hair dryers would not have any net effect on the amount of working capital required by the business. Assume that all operating cash flows occur at the end of the relevant year.

The business's accounting year is to 31 December and its corporation tax rate is 30 per cent. Assume that tax cash flows occur on 31 December of the year in which the events giving rise to them occur.

Identify the minimum price per hair dryer that the business will need to charge in order for manufacturing and selling the hair dryers to meet the target of increasing the shareholders' wealth by £200 000.

Ignore inflation.

5.8 Penney Products plc has a manufacturing plant devoted exclusively to production of one of the business's products, a toy known as Zapper. The product is produced only at this factory. Recently demand has declined owing, managers believe, to the product's rather old-fashioned image.

The lease on the factory is due to expire on 31 December 20X8, and the company's management has identified two possible courses of action:

- Cease production of the Zapper and close the factory on 31 December 20X6.
- Keep up production of the Zapper until 31 December 20X8 and close the factory on that date.

You have been asked to make an assessment of the relative merits of the two possible closure dates. Your investigations have revealed the following:

1 Annual sales revenue of Zappers is estimated at £5m for 20X7 and £4m for 20X8. Both of these amounts are stated at 1 January 20X7 prices, but are expected to increase at the general rate of inflation. Variable manufacturing and distribution costs average 40 per cent of sales revenue value. Zapper production will be charged an allocation of head office costs at an estimated £1m for each of the two years.

2 The annual rent of the factory premises is £0.9m, payable annually in advance. If the factory were to be closed in 20X6, it appears that the landowner would be prepared to accept just one payment of £0.9m on 31 December 20X6 to terminate the lease.

3 Plant at the factory had a tax written down value of £1.2m at 1 January 20X6. For tax purposes, the plant will attract capital allowances on a reducing balance basis at 25 per cent p.a., starting in the year of acquisition irrespective of the exact date of acquisition during the year. In the year of disposal, no annual writing-down allowance will arise, but the difference between the written-down value and the disposal proceeds is either given as an additional tax allowance or charged to tax according to whether the written down value exceeds the disposal proceeds or vice versa.

The plant is old and specialised, and would not be transferred to the business's other factories. It is expected that it could be sold for £0.6m on 31 December 20X6, but by 20X8 it would have no market value.

4 If sales of Zappers were to cease in 20X6, it is estimated that sales revenues from other products of the business would benefit to the extent of 50 per cent of the lost sales revenues from Zappers. These other products have variable costs that average 30 per cent of sales revenue.

5 Working capital equal to 10 per cent of each year's sales revenues is required for all of the business's products. This needs to be in place by the start of each year.

6 Redundancy and other closure payments will be £0.8m if production ceases in 20X6, and £1.0m if it ceases in 20X8. In either case, the payment will be made on 31 December of the year concerned.

7 The business's rate of corporation tax is 30 per cent, and it is expected to remain at this rate for the foreseeable future. The cash flow effects of tax are expected to occur at the end of the year of the event giving rise to them.

8 The directors have a target return of 8 per cent p.a. in 'real' terms for all activities.

9 The business's accounting year end is 31 December.

   General inflation is expected to run at the rate of 3 per cent for 20X7 and 4 per cent for 20X8 and subsequent years.

Assume that all sales occur on the last day of the year concerned.

Prepare a schedule that derives the annual net incremental cash flows of ceasing Zapper production and closing of the factory in 20X6, relative to continuing production until 20X8, and use this to assess the decision on the basis of net present value.

Work to the nearest £10 000.

There are both a set of **multiple-choice questions** and **missing-word questions** available on the website. These specifically cover the material contained in this chapter. These can be attempted and graded (with feedback) online.

There is also an **additional problem**, with solution, that relates to the material covered in this chapter.

Go to **www.pearsoned.co.uk/atrillmclaney** and folow the links.

Chapter 6

Risk in investment appraisal

In this chapter we shall deal with the following:

→ the importance of risk and of its formal consideration in the decision-making process

→ the use of sensitivity analysis to try to assess the riskiness of a particular project

→ the use of statistical probabilities to try to assess risk

→ expected value and its deficiencies in the treatment of risk

→ systematic and specific risk

→ utility theory

→ risk aversion

→ the logic of the expected value/variance criterion for selecting risky investments in some circumstances

→ evidence on dealing with risk in practice

6.1 Introduction

Until this point in the book we have all but ignored questions of risk. We are now going to start to confront the issue, and though this is the only chapter with the word 'risk' in its title, much of the remainder of the book is concerned with problems of making decisions about a future in which we just do not know what is going to happen. Some events we can predict fairly confidently (for example, the population of the UK in five years' time, give or take a million). Other matters (such as how many of that population will buy our business's product) are rather more difficult to predict. None of the input data for decisions is known with absolute certainty, so risk is a constant problem for decision makers.

Despite this awkward environment, decisions must still be made. Delaying decisions until the mist of doubt lifts will not be a very fruitful approach, since it never will lift. In the context of a particular decision, it might be that delay may remove some major uncertainties but it will never remove them all. For example, a business manufacturing armaments might await an expected major policy statement by the government on the future of UK defence policy before making a decision on a significant investment in its own manufacturing capacity.

Risk and uncertainty

Some observers have sought to distinguish between risk and uncertainty. Risk is seen as the phenomenon that arises from circumstances where we are able to identify the possible outcomes and even their likelihood of occurrence without being sure which will actually occur. The outcome of throwing a true die is an example of risk. We know that the outcome must be a number from 1 to 6 (inclusive) and we know that each number has an equal (1 in 6) chance of occurrence, but we are not sure which one will actually occur on any particular throw.

Uncertainty describes the position where we simply are not able to identify all, or perhaps not even any, of the possible outcomes, and we are still less able to assess their likelihood of occurrence. Probably most business decisions are characterised by uncertainty to some extent.

Uncertainty represents a particularly difficult area. Perhaps the best that decision makers can do is to try to identify as many as possible of the feasible outcomes of their decision and attempt to assess each outcome's likelihood of occurrence.

The importance of taking account of risk

It is vital that we take account of risk. This should be done in the most formal possible way, not as an afterthought. The level of risk fundamentally affects a decision. We should view very differently the opportunity to wager on a throw of a die and to wager on the spin of a coin. If on payment of £1, we could either guess which face of the die would land upward or which side of a coin would land upward, in either case the prize for a correct guess being £5, which would we choose? Most people would probably be happy to enter the coin-spinning wager, but few would be eager to go in for the die throwing. This is because the level of risk attaching to each wager would cause us to view them differently, even though they both have only two possible outcomes (lose £1 or gain £4). It is the likelihood of each possible occurrence that would cause us to distinguish between them.

We shall now go on to consider some ways in which risk in investment decisions can be dealt with.

6.2 Sensitivity analysis

All business investment decisions have to be made on the basis of predictions of the various inputs. One approach is to assess the decision on the basis of the 'best estimate' (that is, what the decision maker believes to be the most accurate prediction) of each of the input factors. Assuming that the NPV is positive, the risk of the project can be assessed by taking each input factor and asking by how much the estimate of that factor could prove to be incorrect before it would have the effect of making the decision a bad one. This approach is known as sensitivity analysis.

Example 6.1

Greene plc has the opportunity to invest in plant for the manufacture of a new product, the demand for which is estimated to be 5000 units a year for five years. The following data relate to the decision:

- The machine is estimated to cost £50 000 (payable immediately) and to have no residual value.
- The selling price per unit is planned to be £10.
- Labour and material costs are estimated to be £4 and £3 per unit respectively.
- Overhead costs are not expected to be affected by the decision.
- The cost of capital for such a project is estimated to be 10 per cent p.a.
- The project is not expected to require any additional working capital.
- In the interests of simplicity, taxation will be ignored.
- Assume, also in the interests of simplicity, that all cash flows occur at year ends.

Required:

(a) Assess the project (via NPV) on the basis of the above estimates.

(b) Carry out a sensitivity analysis of the above estimates.

Solution

The annual cash flows will be 5000 × £[10 − (4 + 3)] = £15 000 each year. Thus the project's cash flows are estimated to be:

Year	£
0	(50 000)
1	15 000
2	15 000
3	15 000
4	15 000
5	15 000

The annuity factor for five years at 10 per cent is 3.791 (see Appendix 2). The NPV is therefore:

$$-50\ 000 + (15\ 000 \times 3.791) = +£6865$$

Thus on the basis of the estimates the project is favourable (it has a positive NPV) and should be undertaken.

The estimates are not certain, however, so we shall now go on to look at each of the input factors, one by one, to see how sensitive the decision is to each of them, that is, to see by how much each factor could vary from the original estimate before the project would become unfavourable (negative NPV). While we consider each factor we shall assume that the others will all be as originally estimated.

The project's NPV is given by:

$$-50\ 000 + \{5000 \times [10 - (4 + 3)] \times 3.791\} = +6865$$

To carry out the sensitivity analysis, just one of the factors on the left-hand side of this equation needs to be altered to a value that will make the NPV equal to zero. After this has been done with the first factor, the process goes on to the next one, restoring the first one to its original value and so on.

(1) *Original investment*

Starting with the initial investment, putting the symbol *I* into the equation, instead of £50 000, and setting the right-hand side of the equation to zero gives:

$$-I + \{5000 \times [10 - (4 + 3)] \times 3.791\} = 0$$

$$I = £56\ 865$$

Thus the initial investment could increase by £6865 before the project would become marginal.

Now the other factors will be assessed inserting an appropriate symbol and setting the right-hand side equal to zero.

(2) *Annual sales volume*

$$-50\ 000 + \{V \times [10 - (4 + 3)] \times 3.791\} = 0$$

where *V* is the annual sales volume.

$$V = \frac{50\ 000}{(10 - 7) \times 3.791} = 4396 \text{ units}$$

(3) *Sales revenue/unit*

$$-50\ 000 + \{5000 \times [S - (4 + 3)] \times 3.791\} = 0$$

where *S* is the sales revenue per unit.

$$S = 7 + \frac{50\ 000}{5000 \times 3.791} = £9.64$$

(4) *Labour cost/unit*

$$-50\ 000 + \{5000 \times [10 - (L + 3)] \times 3.791\} = 0$$

where *L* is the labour cost per unit.

$$L = 7 - \frac{50\ 000}{5000 \times 3.791} = £4.36$$

(5) *Material cost/unit*

$$-50\ 000 + \{5000 \times [10 - (4 + M)] \times 3.791\} = 0$$

where *M* is the material cost/unit.

$$M = 6 - \frac{50\ 000}{5000 \times 3.791} = £3.36$$

(6) *Cost of capital*

$$-50\ 000 + \{5000 \times [10 - (4 + 3)] \times A\} = 0$$

where *A* is the annuity factor.

$$A = \frac{50\ 000}{5000 \times 3} = 3.333$$

The annuity table (Appendix 2) for five years shows that 3.333 falls between the 15 per cent figure (3.352) and the 16 per cent one (3.274). Thus a 1 per cent increase in the discount rate (from 15 per cent to 16 per cent) causes a reduction in the annuity factor of 0.078 (from 3.352 to 3.274). The value of 3.333 lies 0.019 below the 15 per cent value, so the discount rate applying to 3.333 is about $15\frac{19}{78}$ per cent, that is, about 15.24 per cent.

(7) *Life of the project*

Of course, the same 3.333 annuity value must be used to deduce the life of the project, this time assuming that the discount rate remains at 10 per cent (the original estimate).

The 10 per cent column in the annuity table shows that 3.333 falls between the four-year figure (3.170) and the five-year one (3.791). This means that an extra year causes the annuity factor to increase by 0.621 (from 3.170 to 3.791). The value of 3.333 lies 0.163 above the four-year figure, so the period applying to 3.333 is about $4\frac{163}{621}$, that is, about 4.26 years.

(Note that this approach to finding the cost of finance and the life of the project is not strictly correct as the relationship between these factors (cost of capital and time) and the annuity factor is not linear. It is, however, fairly close to linear over small ranges so the above figures are a reasonable approximation. An alternative to using this approach in this particular case (because it is an annuity) is to use the equation for an annuity, introduced in Chapter 4, page 83.)

The results can now be tabulated, as follows:

Factor	Original estimate	Value to give zero NPV	Difference as percentage of original estimate for the particular factor (%)
Initial investment	£50 000	£56 865	13.7
Annual sales volume	5000 units	4396 units	12.1
Sales revenue/unit	£10	£9.64	3.6
Labour cost/unit	£4	£4.36	9.0
Material cost/unit	£3	£3.36	12.0
Cost of capital	10%	15.24%	52.4
Life of the project	5 years	4.26 years	14.8

From this it can be seen at a glance how sensitive the NPV, calculated on the basis of the original estimates, is to changes in the variables in the decision. This provides some basis on which to assess the riskiness of the project. If the decision makers concerned can look at the table confident that all of the actual figures will fall within a reasonable safety margin, then they would regard the project as much less risky than if this were not the case. If, on the other hand, they felt that all other factors seemed safe but that they were doubtful about, say, labour costs, the fact that only a 9 per cent rise would cause the project to become unfavourable might reduce their confidence in the investment.

Note that in this example, since there were constant annual cash flows (that is, an annuity), apart from the life of the project and the discount rate, all of the sensitivities could be calculated directly. Where cash flows differ from one year to the next, deriving the sensitivities is a little more laborious.

The most practical approach, where the cash flows are not an annuity, is trial and error, much the same approach as was used to derive IRR in Chapter 4. (Of course, the 15.24 per cent cost of capital figure is the IRR.)

As an example of this trial and error approach, let us look at material cost per unit. The original value was £3, and this, in combination with the other best estimates, leads to a positive NPV. The value for this factor that leads to a zero NPV is obviously higher than £3, so a higher value, say £4, could be tried. Depending on the result of this trial, either other values could be tried (if the NPV using £4 is a long way from zero) or the approach that was used with the cost of capital (and life of the project) could be applied to calculate an approximate value. In practice, a computer spreadsheet would normally be used in a sensitivity analysis.

Practical use of sensitivity analysis

Sensitivity analysis is a type of break-even analysis in which, in respect of each factor, we can assess the *break-even point* and the *margin of safety*.

Since it is most unlikely that all but one of the variables will turn out as estimated, the rather static approach taken in our example gives a very limited perspective on the project.

If the essentials of the project being assessed are put on to a computer spreadsheet, the decision maker can, fairly effortlessly, take the analysis a lot further than we have just done. A series of assumptions can be made about the variables, and the effect on the project's NPV of each combination of assumptions can be assessed. This approach is known as scenario building.

Irrespective of the depth to which sensitivity analysis/scenario building is taken, it enables the decision maker to 'get inside' a project, see which are the crucial estimates and get a feel for its riskiness. It is clear that sensitivity analysis can be a very useful approach to gaining an impression of a project.

Knowledge of the more sensitive factors might enable us to reassess those factors or even take steps to reduce or eliminate their riskiness. In Example 6.1 we discovered that the project's success, in NPV terms, is very sensitive to the estimates both of sales volume and of sales revenue per unit. We may feel that undertaking additional market research would be a way either of reinforcing our confidence in the original estimates or of changing our view of the project.

The results from a sensitivity analysis might cause us to take more positive steps to deal with particularly sensitive factors. The analysis in the example shows the project's success to be fairly sensitive to material costs. It would be quite possible to place orders at fixed prices for the raw material or to take out insurance cover against the possibility of a material price increase. Alternatively, it might be possible to purchase an option (that is, a right, but not an obligation) to buy the material at a set price on a future date. This is an example of a *derivative*. In its 2004 annual report, the airline business **British Airways plc** explains how it uses derivatives to set a maximum price on its future fuel requirements.

Clearly, these approaches to risk reduction are not without cost. Market research costs money. A supplier who is required to be committed to a fixed price contract, or option, would need that fixed price, or the price of the option, to take account of the risk that its own costs might increase. Insurance businesses do not cover risks for nothing. We may feel, however, that these are prices worth paying to reduce the risk to a point where the project would become acceptable.

Problems of using sensitivity analysis

Despite its benefits to the decision maker, sensitivity analysis has its weaknesses.

- Sensitivity analysis does not provide us with any rule as to how to interpret the results. We could carry out more research and possibly reinforce our confidence in the original estimates, but often the doubt can never be completely removed.

- The sensitivities are not directly comparable from one factor to the next. In our example, it might seem that the life of the project (14.8 per cent sensitive) is less of a problem than the amount of the original investment (13.7 per cent sensitive).

However, this is not true. The original investment is to be made immediately and, for that reason alone, is likely to be known with more certainty than the life reaching well into the future. Also, if it is found that the cost of making the original investment creeps to above £56 865, the project could be cancelled. Only when the project has been undertaken and finance committed would we discover whether or not the estimate of the project's life was over optimistic.

6.3 Use of probabilities

Perhaps more useful than looking at the amount by which a particular factor may vary from its estimate, before it renders a project unprofitable, is to look at how likely it is to do so. If the whole range of possible outcomes for each factor could be estimated together with each one's statistical probability of occurrence, a much fuller picture would be obtained. These could be combined to discover the range of possibilities and probabilities for the NPV of the project as a whole. Before we go on to look at how this could be done, it should be pointed out that reliably identifying possible outcomes and their probabilities is very difficult to achieve in practice.

In ascribing probabilities to various aspects, decision makers might use either or both of the following:

→ ● **Objective probabilities.** These are based on past experience of the outcomes and their likelihood of occurrence. For example, if we know what the annual demand for a particular product has been over the years, we could assume that this would define the possible outcomes and their probabilities for next year. Suppose that during each of six of the past ten years the demand for the product had been 2m units and it had been 3m for each of the other four years, we could conclude that next year's demand will either be 2m or 3m with a 0.6 and 0.4 probability, respectively. If we have reason to believe that the past is not a good guide to the future because, for example, the product has just been superseded by a more technologically advanced version, this approach could not be justified.

→ ● **Subjective probabilities.** These are based on opinions, preferably of experts, on the possibilities and on their probability of occurrence.

However ascribed, the use of probabilities enables a fuller picture of the range of outcomes to be considered.

Example 6.2

Using the data from Example 6.1, let us assume that all the factors are known with certainty (impossible in real life) except sales volume.

Extensive market research suggests that annual demand will be:

● 4000 units (0.2 probable), or

● 4500 units (0.5 probable), or

● 5000 units (0.3 probable).

What are the possible outcomes (in terms of NPV) and how probable is each one?

Solution

$$\text{NPV at 4000 units p.a.} = -50\,000 + [4000 \times (10 - 7) \times 3.791]$$
$$= -£4508 \text{ (probability 0.2)}$$

$$\text{NPV at 4500 units p.a.} = -50\,000 + [4500 \times (10 - 7) \times 3.791]$$
$$= +£1179 \text{ (probability 0.5)}$$

$$\text{NPV at 5000 units p.a.} = -50\,000 + [5000 \times (10 - 7) \times 3.791]$$
$$= +£6865 \text{ (probability 0.3)}$$

Thus we have a description of the range and probabilities of the outcomes. (Remember that it has been assumed that sales volume is the only factor whose value is not known with certainty.)

Example 6.2 vastly oversimplifies the situation, both by assuming that there are only three possible outcomes for sales volume and by assuming that there is only one possible outcome for each of the other factors. Let us, however, take one more small step towards reality.

Example 6.3

Still staying with the data in Example 6.1, let us assume not only that the sales volume has the same three possible outcomes, but that, independent of the sales volume, the cost of labour will be:

● £3/unit (0.1 probable), or
● £4/unit (0.7 probable), or
● £5/unit (0.2 probable).

What are the possible outcomes and how likely is each one?
(Note that the word 'independent' in the above context means that the actual outcome as regards sales volume implies nothing about the labour cost that is most likely.)

Solution

This situation is rather more complicated in that there are now nine possible outcomes. Each of the three possible sales volume outcomes could occur in conjunction with each of the three possible labour costs.

The outcomes might usefully be represented in a diagram (see Figure 6.1). For ease of reference the nine possible outcomes are labelled A to I inclusive. Outcome F, say, will occur if 4500 units p.a. are sold and the labour cost is £5/unit. As the probability of the first is 0.5 and of the second 0.2 then the joint probability is the product of these, which is 0.10 (that is, 0.5×0.2).

Note that the sum of the probabilities of all the nine possibilities is 1.00, that is, one of them is certain to occur, though we do not know which one.

The NPVs of each possibility are:

$$A: \text{NPV} = -50\,000 + \{4000 \times [10 - (3 + 3)] \times 3.791\} = +£10\,656$$
$$B: \text{NPV} = -50\,000 + \{4000 \times [10 - (4 + 3)] \times 3.791\} = -£4508$$
$$C: \text{NPV} = -50\,000 + \{4000 \times [10 - (5 + 3)] \times 3.791\} = -£19\,672$$
$$D: \text{NPV} = -50\,000 + \{4500 \times [10 - (3 + 3)] \times 3.791\} = +£18\,238$$
$$E: \text{NPV} = -50\,000 + \{4500 \times [10 - (4 + 3)] \times 3.791\} = +£1179$$
$$F: \text{NPV} = -50\,000 + \{4500 \times [10 - (5 + 3)] \times 3.791\} = -£15\,881$$

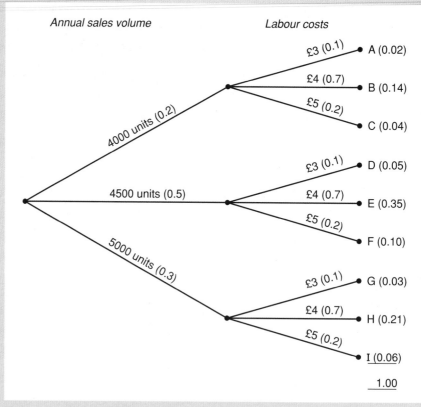

**Figure 6.1
Possible
outcomes of
Greene plc's
investment
opportunity**

This shows the nine possible outcomes (A to I) that could result from this project. Each one's likelihood of occurrence is found by multiplying the probability of the relevant outcome for sales volume with its counterpart for labour cost.

G: NPV = −50 000 + {5000 × [10 − (3 + 3)] × 3.791} = +£25 820

H: NPV = −50 000 + {5000 × [10 − (4 + 3)] × 3.791} = +£6865

I: NPV = −50 000 + {5000 × [10 − (5 + 3)] × 3.791} = −£12 090

Listing these in order of size, we get:

Possible outcome	NPV £	Probability
C	−19 672	0.04
F	−15 881	0.10
I	−12 090	0.06
B	−4 508	0.14
E	+1 179	0.35
H	+6 865	0.21
A	+10 656	0.02
D	+18 238	0.05
G	+25 820	0.03
		1.00

Note that, given the data, one of the above nine outcomes must occur, and only one can occur.

As we have seen, a very modest attempt at reality causes complications. We can well imagine the number of possible outcomes were we to explore a more realistic set of possibilities for each of the input factors, even with our simple example.

How useful to us is the array of nine outcomes and probabilities shown above? The NPV rule is to accept projects with positive NPVs and reject those with negative ones. Here we know that four of the nine possible outcomes will yield a negative NPV, yet the other five give positive ones. One of these nine possibilities will occur, but which one? One way forward on the problem of the vast array of possible outcomes and the subsequent problem of making the decision once we have them, is through the notion of expected value.

6.4 Expected value

As ever, when we are confronted by a mass of data, it can be useful if we can find some way of summarising it so that we can more readily absorb and use it.

One way of summarising is to calculate a weighted average or *expected* value. This involves multiplying each possible outcome by its probability of occurrence. Taking the array of outcomes from Example 6.3 gives us the following result:

Possible outcome	NPV £	Probability (p)	NPV × p £
C	−19 672	0.04	−787
F	−15 881	0.10	−1588
I	−12 090	0.06	−725
B	−4 508	0.14	−631
E	+1 179	0.35	+413
H	+6 865	0.21	+1442
A	+10 656	0.02	+213
D	+18 238	0.05	+912
G	+25 820	0.03	+775
		Expected value	+24

Incidentally, if the decision maker were not interested in the individual outcomes (A to I), there is a much more direct approach to arriving at the expected value. This is to calculate the expected value of the risky factors and then to calculate the NPV, incorporating these expected values.

$$\text{Expected sales volume} = (4000 \times 0.2) + (4500 \times 0.5) + (5000 \times 0.3)$$
$$= 4550 \text{ units}$$

$$\text{Expected labour cost} = (£3 \times 0.1) + (£4 \times 0.7) + (£5 \times 0.2)$$
$$= £4.10$$

$$\text{NPV} = -50\,000 + \{4550 \times [10 - (4.1 + 3)] \times 3.791\} = +£22$$

The difference between this figure and the original expected NPV (+£24) is entirely due to rounding errors in the original calculation.

We now have one single factor to which we could apply the NPV rule. (In this case the expected NPV (ENPV) is very close to zero and thus the project would be on the margin between acceptance and rejection if ENPV were the decision criterion.)

There are some obvious weaknesses in the ENPV approach.

- As with all averaging, information is lost. The figure of +£24 for the ENPV of the project in the example does not tell us that there is a 4 per cent chance of the project yielding a negative NPV of £19 672. It also fails to tell us that the single most likely outcome, outcome E, gives a positive NPV of £1179.

  How could we distinguish between this project and one with a certain NPV of +£24? We need some measure of dispersion, such as range or standard deviation.

- The ENPV is likely to represent a value that could not possibly exist. In our example an NPV of +£24 is certain not to occur: the possible outcomes are A to I, one of which must occur, and +£24 is not among these. In this sense, expected value is a misnomer as it could not possibly occur, let alone be expected in the normal meaning of the word. Does this invalidate ENPV as a decision-making criterion?

  We know that the probability of a fair coin landing heads up is 0.5. If we were offered a wager such that we should gain £1 if a coin landed heads up and nothing if it landed tails up, one such throw would have an expected value of £0.50 (despite the fact that the outcome could only be £1 or nothing). If the wager were repeated 100 times we should be very surprised if the expected value (£50) and the actual outcome differed by much. In other words, where there is a large number of projects, the expected value and the actual outcome are likely to be close, provided that the projects are independent, that is, they are not affected by common factors.

The portfolio effect

→ Businesses typically hold portfolios of investment projects: they have a number, perhaps a large number, of projects in operation at any given time. They do this, among other reasons, to diversify risk, that is, to seek to achieve the expected value of the sum of the projects. Managers know that the expected value of each project probably will not (probably cannot) actually occur but that 'swings and roundabouts' will cause the sum of the expected values to be the outcome. Greene plc (in Example 6.3) may well have many other projects, and it expects that the unlikely event of outcome C occurring will be matched by an unexpectedly favourable outcome in another project. The business would expect this in the same way as a coin landing heads up five times in a row is possible (a 1 in 32 chance) but, over a reasonably large number of throws, chance will even out so that heads will face upwards in only about 50 per cent of the total number of throws.

Diversification

Holding a portfolio of investment projects, with the aim of risk reduction is known as
→ diversification.

There are three important points to note about the effect of diversification in Example 6.4. These are:

- Diversification does not change the expected value (+£0.1m).

- Diversification does not alter the highest or lowest outcome (still +£0.4m or −£0.2m).

- Diversification does, however, introduce two new possibilities, both of which would combine a favourable outcome from one project with an unfavourable one from the other. These two possibilities, between them, are 0.5 probable.

Example 6.4

A business has two investment opportunities in each of which it can invest any amount up to £2m. It has £2m to invest. The characteristics of the two opportunities are as follows:

Project	Outcome (NPV as % of investment)	Probability
A	(i) +20%	0.5
	(ii) −10%	0.5
B	(i) +20%	0.5
	(ii) −10%	0.5

The outcomes from these two projects are independent of one another. This is to say that outcome (i) occurring in Project A tells us nothing about the outcome of Project B.

Solution

If all of the £2m is invested in either project the outcome will be either +£0.4m (that is, £2m × 20%) or −£0.2m (that is, £2m × −10%). However, if part, say half, is invested in each project then there are four possible outcomes:

A(i) and B(i): Total NPV = (£1m × 20%) + (£1m × 20%)
$$= £0.4m$$

Probability = 0.5 × 0.5 = 0.25

A(i) and B(ii): Total NPV = (£1m × 20%) + (£1m × −10%)
$$= +£0.1m$$

Probability = 0.5 × 0.5 = 0.25

A(ii) and B(i): Total NPV = (£1m × −10%) + (£1m × 20%)
$$= +£0.1m$$

Probability = 0.5 × 0.5 = 0.25

A(ii) and B(ii): Total NPV = (£1m × −10%) + (£1m × −10%)
$$= −£0.2m$$

Probability = 0.5 × 0.5 = 0.25

The expected NPV if either of the projects is undertaken in full with a total investment of £2.0m is:

$$(£2.0m × 20% × 0.5) + (£2.0m × −10% × 0.5) = +£0.1m$$

We can see that, as far as this example is concerned, diversification means that the expected value starts to become a likely outcome. Diversification has also reduced the chance of the best outcome occurring, and the worst outcome is also less likely (in both cases down from 0.5 to 0.25 probability).

We shall see a little further on that most investors will readily accept a reduction of expectations of high returns in order to reduce the likelihood of low ones.

Systematic and specific risk

How likely in real life is it that investment projects are independent of one another in the way that spins of a fair coin are? Is it not quite likely that the very factors that will cause one project to turn out unfavourably will similarly affect each of the others? In

Example 6.4, is it not true that outcome (ii) occurring in Project A, in real life, implies outcome (ii) occurring in Project B as well, meaning that there would be no advantage from diversification?

The answer to these questions seems to be that while there are factors specific to each individual investment such that they will affect only its outcome, there are also underlying factors that will affect just about all projects.

→ **Specific risk** is the expression used to describe the part of the risk that relates to the particular project. This portion of the risk can be eliminated by diversification, in the way that the example suggests, because specific risk factors for separate projects are independent of each other.

Consider the perhaps unlikely example of a business whose investments are diversified between making light bulbs and making chocolate. Project X might fail if a new means of making light bulbs is discovered by a competitor; Project Y might fail if there is a world shortage of cocoa. These are specific risk factors for separate projects that are independent of each other. There is no reason to believe that the world market for cocoa could possibly affect light-bulb making.

That part of the risk that cannot be diversified away because it is caused by factors
→ common to all activities is known as **systematic risk**. Such factors would include the general level of demand in the economy, interest rates, inflation rates and labour costs. Few, if any, activities are unaffected by these factors so diversification will not remove the risk. These factors seem likely to affect both light bulb and chocolate manufacture.

Clearly, businesses eager to eliminate specific risk by diversifying between industries must have more than half an eye on the fact that this is likely to have the effect of taking them into areas in which they have no expertise or experience.

The existence of systematic risk means that expected value is not the whole answer to dealing with risk. Not all of the risk is susceptible to elimination through diversification. Systematic factors mean that expected value may well not occur for the business as a whole, even though forecast assessments of financial effect and probability of occurrence of the various possible outcomes may be impeccable.

Before going on to consider another reason why expected value may not be a complete way of dealing with risk, let us take a brief look at a useful way of expressing attitudes towards risk.

6.5 Utility theory

Trading off preferences

The notion of utility provides a means of expressing individual tastes and preferences. This is an important aspect of business finance and something to which we shall return on several occasions in this book. Utility is the level of satisfaction that an individual derives from some desirable factor, for example going away on holiday, having drinking water available, eating caviar or having wealth. Utility and differing levels of it are frequently represented graphically by *indifference curves*, each one showing a constant level of utility or satisfaction for differing combinations of related factors.

The curve UU in Figure 6.2 represents the utility curve of the attitude of some individual towards holidays and how much money the person is prepared to devote to them. 0S represents the total of the person's cash resources, all of which could be spent

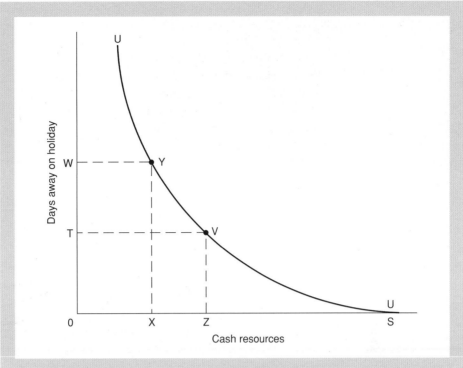

Figure 6.2
Utility of going
away on holiday for
some individual

All points along the curve UU represent combinations of days of holiday and money used up that could generate equal amounts of utility. For example, spending ZS to get 0T days of holiday, represented by point V, would yield exactly as much satisfaction, to this individual, as would spending XS to get 0W days of holiday, represented by point Y.

on going away on holiday this year. Alternatively, all or part of this money could be retained for other purposes. The curve suggests that this particular individual is prepared to spend some money to go on holiday. In fact the person is prepared to spend a lot of savings in order to go for a short time (the curve is fairly close to being horizontal at the bottom right). As we move up the curve (bottom right to top left), less and less utility is derived from each extra day of holiday so that the individual is prepared to give up less and less money for it. In fact, this individual reaches a point towards the top of the curve where there is a reluctance to spend any more money to get extra days of holiday (the curve becomes vertical). This suggests that once this person has had a certain amount of holiday there is an unwillingness to spend more money on extra days. It is important to recognise that the curve depicted applies only to this individual and reflects his or her personal tastes; any other individual may see things very differently – perhaps even not liking being away from home very much and so being unwilling to devote any money to it.

For the individual whose preferences are depicted in Figure 6.2, all points along the curve UU represent combinations of days away on holiday and money retained that will give equal satisfaction. Thus points V and Y on curve UU represent just two of the many combinations of days of holiday and money retained that would be of equal satisfaction or utility to our individual. This person would view having 0T days of holidays and retaining 0Z of money as equally satisfying to going on holiday for 0W days, leaving only 0X of money. The person would be indifferent as to which of these

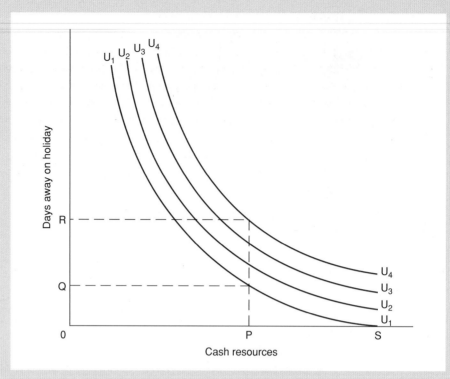

Figure 6.3
Various levels of utility of going away on holiday for some individual

All points along any particular curve U_1U_1, U_2U_2, etc., would generate equal amounts of utility. Being able to indulge in the combinations represented by a higher curve would yield greater satisfaction. For example, spending PS to get 0Q days of holiday would be less desirable than spending the same amount to get 0R days.

two combinations, or indeed of any other combinations lying along curve UU, were to be taken.

Higher levels of satisfaction

Figure 6.3 shows the same combinations of days of holiday and money retained but at varying levels. Each of the curves U_1U_1, U_2U_2, U_3U_3 and U_4U_4 of themselves show combinations that yield equal satisfaction or utility, but the higher the curve, the higher the level of utility. For example, any point along U_2U_2 is more satisfactory than any point along U_1U_1 for our individual. This is because, at any level of spending, more days of holiday could be taken; or, at any number of days of holiday, the inroads into the person's cash resources would be smaller. For example, if PS of money were devoted to paying for a holiday (leaving 0P to save or spend other than on holidays), 0Q days of holiday would be obtained if the state of the world implied curve U_1U_1, but the much longer period 0R days if it implied curve U_4U_4. Different levels of utility imply different states of the world: for example, U_4U_4 implies that holidays are cheaper, as compared with the U_1U_1 position. Thus the individual would prefer the range of possibilities portrayed by U_2U_2 to those shown on U_1U_1. To be on U_3U_3 would be even better, and on U_4U_4 even better still. Thus while the individual is indifferent to where he or she is on any particular curve, there is a clear preference to be on the highest possible curve (that is, the one furthest to the top right) as this gives the maximum possible level of satisfaction or utility.

Figure 6.3 represents just four of an infinite number of similarly shaped curves, parallel to the curves shown. Note that the shape of these curves is determined by our individual's preferences; which curve actually applies is decreed by the state of the world (for example, price of holidays). This example concerning the trade-off between money spent and days away on holiday illustrates a phenomenon that seems to apply generally to human behaviour. The more that individuals have of a particular factor they find desirable, such as going away on holiday, the less they are willing to pay for additional amounts of it. Thus the worth (in financial terms) of an additional day of holiday not only varies from individual to individual, it probably also depends on how much holiday the individual already has.

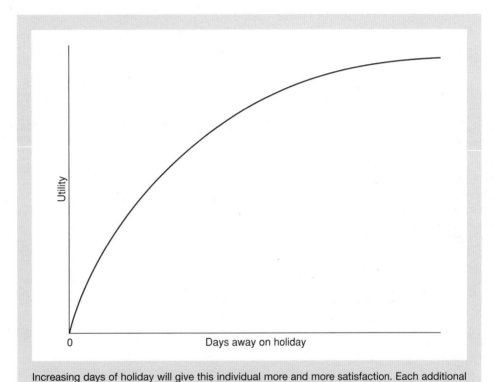

Figure 6.4
Utility function of some individual for going away on holiday

Increasing days of holiday will give this individual more and more satisfaction. Each additional day gives a decreasing amount of additional satisfaction, however.

An alternative way in which we could represent this individual's attitude to holidays is shown in Figure 6.4. Here utility itself is plotted against days of holiday. We can see from Figure 6.4 that our individual derives great utility from increases in days of holiday at the lower end but, as more days are obtained, the additional utility given by each extra day diminishes. Figure 6.4 raises the question of how utility is measured, and how we actually draw such a graph in practice. In fact, utility is not a readily measurable factor and therefore graphs of it are difficult to construct. Utility is in the mind of the individual.

Utility theory has been criticised for the fact that utility is difficult to measure. Most observers agree, however, that the notions represented in the theory have an inexorable logic. For our present purposes it is sufficient that we accept these notions; we shall not need to concern ourselves further than that.

6.6 Attitudes to risk and expected value

Let us now go back to expected value and the other reason why it is apparently not as useful as it might be to decision makers in businesses.

Like the attitude of our individual to holidays, depicted in Figure 6.4, most people's attitude to wealth varies with the amount of it that they have. On the face of it, the expected value of a risky venture is what a rational person would pay for it. For example, the expected value of a wager on the spin of a fair coin that pays out £200 for a head and nothing for a tail is £100 [that is, (£200 × 0.5) + (0 × 0.5)]. We might expect that a rational person would be prepared to pay £100 to take part in this wager. In fact it would appear that only a minority of people would be prepared to risk losing £100 in order to stand a one in two chance of winning £200. This is because most of us are

→ risk averse.

Risk aversion

Figure 6.5 shows the utility of wealth curve for a risk-averse individual. Utility, as we saw in the previous section, is a level of satisfaction. W on the horizontal axis

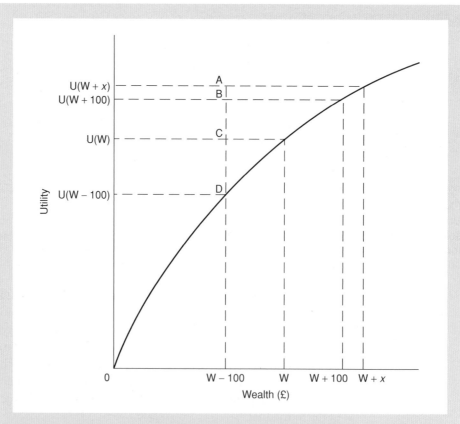

Figure 6.5
Graph of the utility of wealth against wealth for some risk-averse individual

This person prefers more wealth to less wealth, because the curve shows increasing utility for increasing wealth. It also shows the individual to be risk averse, because each successive increase of £1 of wealth yields a smaller increase in satisfaction. This person would lose more satisfaction from losing £1 than they would gain from gaining £1.

represents the present level of wealth of an individual. To this individual, increasing wealth by £100 would increase personal satisfaction (utility) by CB, but losing £100 would reduce that satisfaction by CD, a rather larger amount. This individual would only become indifferent to the wager if the potential gain were x, so that the increase in utility from the gain (should it arise) would equal the potential loss of utility from the loss of the money (that is, CA = CD). The risk-averse person would need the prize for the coin landing heads to be in excess of £200 to make the wager attractive.

The precise shape of a utility curve (and thus how much the prize in the above wager needs to be) depends on the personal preferences of the individual concerned. The curve in Figure 6.5 represents the preferences of just one hypothetical individual, though all risk-averse individuals will have a curve of roughly the same shape. Note that how much the prize in the wager would need to be, to tempt any particular individual, depends both on that person's utility curve and on the level of wealth of that individual at the time when the wager is on offer.

Figure 6.6 shows the general shapes of the utility curves of (a) a risk-averse investor, (b) a **risk-loving** investor and (c) a **risk-neutral** investor. A risk-neutral investor views equally entering a wager whose expected value is zero, and doing nothing.

There may be some individuals in the world who are risk lovers. Such an individual might, for example, be prepared to enter a coin-spinning wager standing to lose £100 with only a 50 per cent chance of gaining £190. Such might be the desire to be exposed to risk that he or she would be willing to take on wagers with negative expected value. Most of us are not.

Looking back at Example 6.4 on page 160, most people, because they are risk averse, would prefer a combination of Projects A and B rather than an investment in just one or the other. This is despite the fact that both strategies give the same expected value. It is also despite the fact that the single project strategy offers a 50 per cent probability of an NPV of £0.4m, whereas the diversification strategy (A and B) offers only a 25 per cent probability of that desirable outcome. This preference for the diversification strategy is connected with the relatively low probability of the negative outcome.

Evidence of risk aversion

There is quite a lot of evidence around us to support the assertion that most people are risk averse. People's general desire to cover potential disasters by insurance is an example. Most house owners, with no legal compulsion, choose to insure their property against destruction by fire. Clearly, taking account of the potential financial loss and the risk of fire, the premium must be more than the expected value of the loss, otherwise the fire insurance companies would consistently lose money. For example, if the potential damage from a fire for a particular house is £30 000 and the probability of a serious fire during a year is 1 in 1000 (that is, a 0.001 probability), the expected value of the loss is £30 (that is, £30 000 × 0.001). Unless the house owner is prepared to pay a premium higher than £30 p.a. the insurance company would not accept the risk, yet most house owners seem to insure their houses at a cost, presumably more than the expected value of the potential loss. They are prepared to do this because the loss of utility caused by paying the premium is less than the anticipated loss of utility caused by the cost of a fire (if the house is uninsured) multiplied by its probability of occurrence. This arises from the fact that, for risk-averse individuals, utility of wealth curves are not straight lines: in other words, there is not a linear relationship between wealth and utility of wealth.

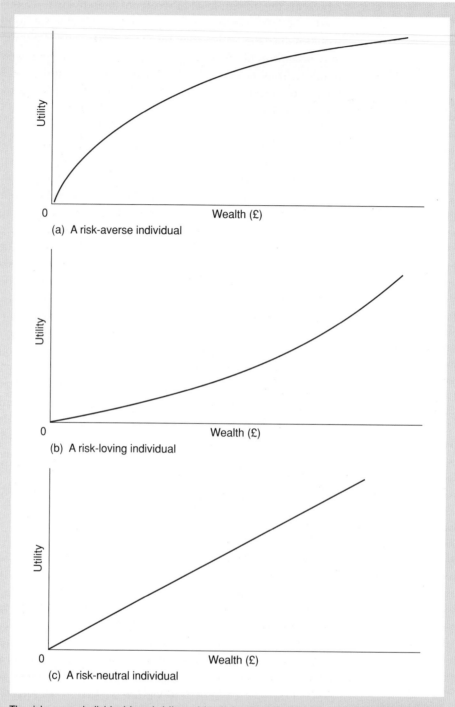

Figure 6.6
Graphs of the
utility of wealth
against wealth for
individuals with
different attitudes
towards risk

The risk-averse individual (graph (a)) would gain less satisfaction from having an additional
£1 than the satisfaction that would be lost from having £1 less. The risk-loving individual
(graph (b)) would gain more satisfaction from having an additional £1 than would be lost from
having £1 less. To the risk-neutral individual (graph (c)), the gain in satisfaction from having
an additional £1 is equal to the loss in satisfaction of having £1 less.

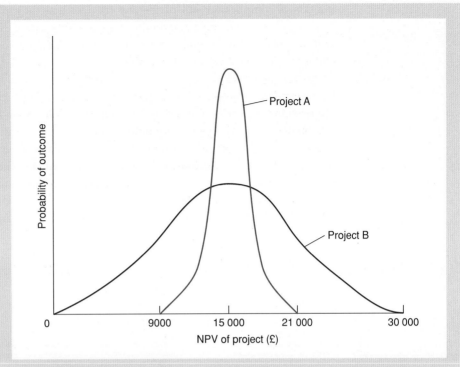

Figure 6.7
Graph of the probabilities of the NPV for two projects each having equal expected NPVs

Although both projects have identical expected NPVs, the ranges of possibilities differ between them. A risk-averse investor would prefer Project A. This is because the worst possible outcome is an NPV of £9000, which is quite a lot higher than the minimum outcome from Project B.

Figure 6.7 shows the range of possible outcomes for two investment projects, A and B. Both have expected values of £15 000 (the outcomes of each are symmetrically arrayed around this value); in fact, £15 000 is the single most likely outcome (the mode) in each case.

Both of these projects would be acceptable to the investor as they both have a positive NPV, irrespective of where in the range the actual outcome falls. Since most of the human race seems to be risk averse, Project A would be most people's first choice if they had to choose between the projects. This is despite the fact that Project B holds the possibility of an NPV as high as £30 000 whereas Project A's maximum is only £21 000. The risk-averse investor's eyes would be drawn to the lower end of the scale where that person would note that Project A gives a guaranteed minimum NPV of £9000 whereas Project B's outcome could be as low as zero. To the risk averse, the so-called *downside risk* looms larger than the *upside potential*. By contrast, a risk lover would be more attracted to Project B. A risk-neutral investor would be unable to distinguish between these two projects.

Expected value and the business's investment decisions

From what we have seen above, in deciding on risky investment projects we cannot directly translate the wealth maximisation rule into one of expected wealth maximisation: in other words, we cannot simply take on all available projects with a positive expected NPV. The reason for this is that shareholders are probably all risk averse. The situation is complicated still further by the fact that they probably show different degrees of risk aversion (differently shaped utility curves and different levels of wealth). An investment whose risk/return profile might be acceptable to one shareholder may not be acceptable to another.

This potential lack of unanimity may seem familiar. It is, of course, analogous to the investment decision without the borrowing/lending facility (a matter that we discussed in Chapter 2), and it poses the same problem. How do managers make their investment decisions when shareholders take different attitudes to risk? As before, it is really the utility, or satisfaction of wealth, that shareholders want maximised, but shareholders will not necessarily all agree on what satisfies them most. Maximisation of the utility of wealth involves some consideration of the range of possible outcomes (as is evident from Figure 6.5).

In the next section we shall look at a partial solution to management's problem.

6.7 The expected value/variance (or mean/variance) criterion

→ A popular statistical measure of dispersion is the **variance** (or its square root, the
→ **standard deviation**). The variance (σ^2) is defined as follows:

$$\sigma^2 = \sum_{i=1}^{n} p_i [x_i - E(x)]^2$$

where p_i is the probability of outcome x_i, $E(x)$ its expected value or mean, and there are n possible outcomes.

Example 6.5

A project will yield one of three NPVs whose amount and probabilities of occurrence are as follows:

NPV £	Probability
−1000	0.2
+1000	0.5
+2000	0.3

What is the expected NPV of the project and its variance?

Solution

ENPV = (0.2 × −1000) + (0.5 × 1000) + (0.3 × 2000)
$\qquad$ = £900

$\sigma^2 = 0.2(-1000 - 900)^2 + 0.5(1000 - 900)^2 + 0.3(2000 - 900)^2$
$\qquad$ = (0.2 × 3 610 000) + (0.5 × 10 000) + (0.3 × 1 210 000)
σ^2 = 1 090 000 (in £²)

The variance is a particularly useful device for our present purposes. It can be shown (Levy and Sarnat 1988) that if we assume that the range of possible outcomes from a decision is distributed symmetrically (as with the distributions in Figure 6.7) around the expected value, then knowledge of the expected value and the variance (or standard deviation) is all that risk-averse investors need to enable them to select between two risky investments. In other words, provided that the investor is risk averse and that the dispersion of possible outcomes is symmetrical, then selecting investments on the basis of their expected (or mean) value and variance will maximise the investor's utility of wealth.

Example 6.6

A risk-averse investor is faced with two competing investment projects, dispersions of both of whose possible outcomes are *symmetrical* about their expected values. Which should the investor select?

Project	A	B
Expected value (£)	20 000	20 000
Variance (£²)	10 000	12 000

Solution

Project A would be selected since this offers an equal expected value to Project B but with less risk. By selecting Project A, maximisation of the utility of wealth of any risk-averse investor will be promoted.

The expected value/variance criterion (EVC) may be summarised as follows:

● where the expected value of Project A is equal to or greater than that of Project B, A should be preferred to B if A has a lower variance; and

● where the variance of Project A is equal to or smaller than that of Project B, A should be preferred to B if A has a higher expected value.

What EVC does not tell us is how to choose between two investments where both the expected value and the variance of Project A are greater than those of Project B. We shall look at how this dilemma can be addressed in the next chapter.

6.8 Particular risks associated with making investments overseas

In principle, investing in a project based overseas is the same as investing in a similar one in the UK. There are several respects in which the overseas project is likely to be more risky. These issues will be discussed at length in Chapter 15, which deals with various aspects of international investment and financing.

6.9 Some evidence on risk analysis in practice

To gain some insight into the extent to which, and how, risk is taken into account in practical investment decision making we shall rely on the researches of Arnold and Hatzopoulos (2000) (A&H), whose findings are consistent with similar studies conducted recently. This evidence relates to a survey of the largest businesses in the UK, conducted in 1997.

The evidence seems to suggest that:

● Formal consideration of risk is not a universal practice. Of the businesses surveyed by A&H, 94 per cent formally considered risk in relation to their major capital investment decisions. Earlier research by Pike and Wolfe (1988) suggests that it is unlikely that many of the businesses surveyed, formally assessed risk in respect of every investment decision. It seems reasonable to suppose that among the businesses that do not formally assess risk all the time, there is a greater tendency to assess it in respect of larger investment decisions.

A reason suggested for the popularity of the use of the payback method of investment appraisal (see Chapter 4) is that it provides an assessment of the riskiness of the project. Though the validity of using this method of investment appraisal as a means of dealing with risk is theoretically somewhat dubious, its widespread use by businesses of all sizes may imply that consideration of risk is also widespread. It is difficult to believe that many businesses completely ignore the question of risk in investment decision making, even though decisions may be taken on an informal basis in many cases.

● There is an increasing tendency formally to take account of risk. As we have seen, 94 per cent of the businesses surveyed in 1997 formally accounted for risk. However, Pike (1982) found (with a similar survey sample) that in 1975 only 26 per cent of businesses formally accounted for risk: a figure that had grown to 38 per cent by 1981 (Pike 1983) and to 87 per cent by 1986 (Pike and Wolfe 1988).

● Some of the businesses that formally take account of risk use more than one approach to dealing with it.

● There are two main approaches to assessing the riskiness of projects:
  – sensitivity analysis, used by 85 per cent of A&H's respondents; and
  – use of probabilities, used by 31 per cent.

● There are also two main approaches to distinguishing between projects on the basis of their riskiness:
  – shortening the payback period for riskier projects (used by 20 per cent); and
  – requiring higher rates of return (presumably discount rate or IRR hurdle rate) for riskier projects (used by 52 per cent).

Both of these methods seem fairly popular among those who tackle the problem of risk in a formal way.

Conclusions on practice in risk analysis

It is perhaps surprising that not all businesses formally account for risk. If we bear in mind that the evidence relates to large businesses, it seems possible that little consideration of it will occur in the smaller ones.

It is not clear why the risk-adjusted rate of return has become so popular (speaking relatively, of course). Perhaps it is intuition based partly on observation that high risk seems to engender high returns.

In the next chapter we shall go on to see that the practice of requiring higher rates (discount rates) for riskier projects can be seen as a rational way of taking account of risk and of selecting investments. We shall also see that there is a theoretically correct way for management to make decisions on risky investment projects with which all the business's shareholders will agree.

Summary

Risk

Risk is of vital concern to decision makers.

Sensitivity analysis (SA)

- In the context of an NPV appraisal, SA involves six steps:

    1 Identify and estimate the various input factors to the decision.

    2 Assess the project on the basis of the best estimates.

    3 Take each input factor in turn and determine the value for it that will give a zero NPV for the project when the other factors are left at their original estimated values.

    4 Compare each of the values determined in step 3 with the original best estimate to gain an impression of the riskiness of the factor under consideration.

    5 Carry out any necessary research (for example, market research) to reassess the risk in sensitive areas.

    6 Make the decision and take any appropriate actions to reduce the risk in sensitive areas (for example, entering fixed-price contracts for raw material purchases).

- Benefits of SA:

    - Enables the decision maker to 'get inside' the project and see what are the key issues.

    - Conceptually easy to carry out and understand.

- Problems with SA:

    - No decision rule provided.

    - Sensitivities are not directly comparable from one input factor to the next.

    - Rather static approach, 'scenario building' might be better.

Expected value (EV)

- EV = the weighted (by probabilities) average of the possible outcomes.

- In the context of NPV appraisal, EV can be deduced either by:

    1 finding the EV of each input factor and then using the single EV of each factor in the NPV assessment; or

    2 identifying the NPV and probability of occurrence for each of the possible outcomes for the project (probably an enormously large number, in practice) and then finding the weighted average of these.

- Route 1 (above) is much easier, but only the EV is known; information on the spread of possible results is not revealed.

- Route 2 gives all of the results but in practice it can be impossible to cope with the volume of data.

- EV can be helpful because it summarises a large amount of data into one value.

- Problems of EV:
  - The averaging process hides information, e.g. on the NPV and probability of occurrence in the worst-case scenario.
  - The calculated EV could easily be a value that is not capable of occurring.

Diversification

- Diversification = the combining of investments with others whose returns are independent of one another.
- Tends to increase the probability that the EV for the portfolio is close to the sum of the EVs of the individual investments, thereby reducing risk.
- In practice, most investments are not independent; they are affected by common factors, to some extent.
  - Specific (unsystematic) risk = the risk of an investment arising from factors that are independent of other investment returns.
  - Systematic risk = the risk that is common to most investments.

Utility theory

- A way of representing an individual's preferences between two competing desires.
- Individuals seek to reach their highest level of satisfaction or utility.
- Individuals are generally risk averse, that is, they require increasingly large increments of wealth to compensate them for increasing their risk.
- Risk aversion = an unwillingness to pay as much as the expected value of a risky project to invest (or wager) in it.

Mean/variance criterion

- Making certain assumptions, all that needs to be known about an investment is its expected value of returns and how those returns array around that expected value.

Risk analysis in practice

- Increasingly, businesses formally consider risk when making investment decisions.
- Larger businesses seem to pay more formal attention to risk than smaller ones.

Further reading

Risk generally is dealt with very thoroughly in a number of texts, including those by Emery and Finnerty (2004) and Atrill (2006). The subject of probabilities is well explained by Bancroft and O'Sullivan (2000), which also deals with expected values. The research studies of Pike and Wolfe (1988), which were cited in the chapter, and of Pike (1996) are well worth reading.

Relevant websites

The website of the business featured in this chapter is:

British Airways plc   www.bashares.co.uk

REVIEW QUESTIONS

Suggested answers to
review questions appear
in Appendix 3.

6.1 What are the limitations of the results of a sensitivity analysis such as the one carried out in Example 6.1 (Greene plc)?

6.2 When deducing the expected NPV of a project, you can:

(a) identify all possible outcomes (and their individual NPVs) and deduce the expected NPV from them; or

(b) deduce the expected value of each of the inputs and use these to deduce the expected NPV directly.

What are the advantages and disadvantages of each of these two approaches?

6.3 What is the difference between the 'specific' and 'systematic' risk of a project? Why might it be helpful to distinguish between these two?

6.4 What does the word 'utility' mean in the context of utility theory?

6.5 What is a risk-averse person? Are most of us risk averse?

6.6 Which two assumptions need to be made if the expected value/variance criterion of investment decision making is to be applied?

PROBLEMS

Sample answers to
problems marked with
an asterisk appear in
Appendix 4.

(Problems 6.1 to 6.3 are basic-level problems, whereas problems 6.4 to 6.7 are more advanced and may contain some practical complications.)

6.1* Easton Ltd needs to purchase a machine to manufacture a new product. The choice lies between two machines (A and B). Each machine has an estimated life of three years with no expected scrap value.

Machine A will cost £15 000 and Machine B will cost £20 000, payable immediately in each case. The total variable costs of manufacture of each unit are £1 if made on Machine A, but only £0.50 if made on Machine B. This is because Machine B is more sophisticated and requires less labour to operate it.

The product will sell for £4 each.

The demand for the product is uncertain but is estimated at 2000 units for each year, 3000 units for each year or 5000 units for each year. (Note that whatever sales volume level actually occurs, that level will apply to each year.)

The sales manager has placed probabilities on the level of demand as follows:

Annual demand	Probability of occurrence
2000	0.2
3000	0.6
5000	0.2

Presume that both taxation and fixed costs will be unaffected by any decision made.

Easton Ltd's cost of capital is 6 per cent p.a.

(a) Calculate the NPV for each of the three activity levels for each machine, A and B, and state your conclusion.

(b) Calculate the expected NPV for each machine and state your conclusion.

6.2* In problem 6.1, assume that the 2000 level is the 'best estimate' of annual demand for Easton Ltd, and that only Machine A is available.

(a) Should the business acquire Machine A on the basis of its NPV?

(b) Carry out a sensitivity analysis on the decision recommended in (a).

6.3 Plaything plc has just developed a new mechanical toy, the Nipper. The development costs totalled £300 000. To assess the commercial viability of the Nipper a market survey has been undertaken at a cost of £35 000. The survey suggests that the Nipper will have a market life of four years and can be sold by Plaything plc for £20 per Nipper. Demand for the Nipper for each of the four years has been estimated as follows:

Number of Nippers	Probability of occurrence
11 000	0.3
14 000	0.6
16 000	0.1

If the decision is made to go ahead with the Nipper, production and sales will begin immediately. Production will require the use of machinery that the business already owns, having bought it for £200 000 three years ago. If Nipper production does not go ahead the machinery will be sold for £85 000, there being no other use for it. If it is used in Nipper production, the machinery will be sold for an estimated £35 000 at the end of the fourth year.

Each Nipper will take one hour's labour of employees who will be taken on specifically for the work at a rate of £8.00 per hour. The business will incur an estimated £10 000 in redundancy costs relating to these employees at the end of the four years.

Materials will cost an estimated £6.00 per Nipper. Nipper production will give rise to an additional fixed cost of £15 000 p.a.

It is believed that if Plaything plc decides not to go ahead with producing the Nipper, the rights to the product could be sold to another business for £125 000, receivable immediately.

Plaything plc has a cost of capital of 12 per cent p.a.

(a) On the basis of the expected net present value, should the business go ahead with production and sales of the Nipper? (Ignore taxation and inflation.)

(b) Assess the expected net present value approach to investment decision making.

6.4 Block plc has £6m of cash available for investment. Four possible projects have been identified. Each involves an immediate outflow of cash and is seen as having two possible outcomes as regards the NPV. The required initial investment, possible NPVs and probabilities of each project are as follows:

Project	Initial outlay £m	NPV £m	Probability
A	6.0	3.0 (positive)	0.5
		1.5 (negative)	0.5
B	2.0	1.0 (positive)	0.5
		0.5 (negative)	0.5
C	2.0	1.0 (positive)	0.5
		0.5 (negative)	0.5
D	2.0	1.0 (positive)	0.5
		0.5 (negative)	0.5

The outcomes of the projects are completely independent of one another.
The business has decided to adopt one of two strategies.

- Strategy 1: Invest all of the cash in Project A.
- Strategy 2: Invest one-third of the cash in each of Projects B, C and D.

Deduce as much information as you can about the effective outcome of following each strategy.

Which of the two investment strategies would you recommend to the directors? Why?

What assumptions have you made about the directors and the shareholders in making your recommendation?

Would your recommendation have been different had more or less finance been involved in the decision?

6.5* Hi Fido plc manufactures high fidelity sound reproduction equipment for the household market. It has recently incurred £500 000 developing a new loudspeaker, called the Tracker.

A decision now needs to be taken as to whether to go ahead with producing and marketing Trackers. This is to be based on the expected net present value of the relevant cash flows, discounted at the business's estimate of the 20X0 weighted average cost of capital of 8 per cent (after tax). Management believes that a three-year planning horizon is appropriate for this decision, so it will be assumed that sales will not continue beyond 20X3.

Manufacture of Trackers would require acquisition of some plant costing £1m, payable on installation, on 31 December 20X0. This cost would attract the normal capital allowances for plant and machinery. If the company makes the investment, for tax purposes, the plant will be depreciated on a reducing balance basis at 25 per cent p.a., starting in the year of acquisition irrespective of the exact date of acquisition during the year. In the year of disposal, no tax depreciation is charged, but the difference between the written down value and the disposal proceeds is either given as an additional tax allowance or charged to tax depending whether the written down value exceeds the disposal proceeds or vice versa.

For the purposes of assessing the viability of the Tracker, it will be assumed that the plant would not have any disposal value on 31 December 20X3.

The first sales of Trackers would be expected to be made during the year ending 31 December 20X1. There is uncertainty as to the level of sales that could be expected, so a market survey has been undertaken at a cost of £100 000.

The survey suggests that, at the target price of £200 per pair of Trackers, there would be a 60 per cent chance of selling 10 000 pairs and a 40 per cent chance of selling 12 000 pairs during 20X1.

If the 20X1 volume of sales were to be at the lower level, 20X2 sales would be either 8000 pairs of Trackers (30 per cent chance) or 10 000 pairs (70 per cent chance). If 20X1 volume of sales were to be at the higher level, 20X2 sales would be estimated at 12 000 pairs of Trackers (50 per cent chance) or 15 000 pairs (50 per cent chance).

In 20X3 the volume of sales would be expected to be 50 per cent of whatever level of sales actually occur in 20X2.

Sales of Trackers would be expected to have an adverse effect on sales of Repros, a less sophisticated loudspeaker, also produced by the business, to the extent that for each two pairs of Trackers sold, one less pair of Repros would be sold. This effect would be expected to continue throughout the three years.

Materials and components would be bought in at a cost of £70 per pair of Trackers.

Manufacture of each pair of Trackers would require three hours of labour. This labour would come from staff released by the lost Repro production. To the extent that this would provide insufficient hours, staff would work overtime, paid at a premium of 50 per cent over the basic pay of £6 an hour.

The Repro has the following cost structure:

	Per pair £
Selling price	100
Materials	20
Labour (4 hours)	24
Fixed overheads (on a labour-hour basis)	33

The management team currently employed would be able to manage the Tracker project, except that, should the project go ahead, four managers, who had accepted voluntary redundancy from the company, would be asked to stay on until the end of 20X3. These managers were due to leave the business on 31 December 20X0 and to receive lump sums of £30 000 each at that time. They were also due to receive an annual fee of £8000 each for consultancy work which the business would require of them from time to time. If they were to agree to stay on, they would receive an annual salary of £20 000 each, to include the consultancy fee. They would also receive lump sums of £35 000 each on 31 December 20X3. It is envisaged that the managers would be able to fit any consultancy requirements around their work managing the Tracker project. These payments would all be borne by the business and would qualify for full tax relief.

Tracker production and sales would not be expected to give rise to any additional operating costs beyond those mentioned above.

Working capital to support both Tracker and Repro production and sales would be expected to run at a rate of 15 per cent of the sales value. The working capital would need to be in place by the beginning of each year concerned. There would be no tax effects of changes in the level of working capital.

Sales should be assumed to occur on the last day of the relevant calendar year. The corporation tax rate is expected to be 33 per cent throughout the planning period.

On the basis of expected NPV, should Hi Fido plc go ahead with the Tracker project?

6.6 Focus plc has several wholly owned subsidiaries engaged in activities that are outside the business's core business. A decision has recently been taken to concentrate exclusively on the core business and to divest itself of its other activities.

One of the non-core subsidiaries is Kane Ltd, which operates in an activity that the board of Focus believes to be fast declining. It seems likely that it will be difficult to find a buyer for Kane as a going concern, and its break-up value is considered to be small. In view of these points it has been decided to retain Kane, allowing it to run down gradually over the next three years as its product demand wanes.

Estimates of the various factors relating to Kane, assuming that it continues to be a subsidiary of Focus, have been made, and these are shown in notes 1 to 8 below. All of the cash flows are expressed in terms of current (that is, beginning of year 1) prices. The years referred to are the accounting years of Focus (and Kane).

1 Sales revenue for year 1 is estimated at either £6m (60 per cent probable) or £5m (40 per cent probable). If sales revenue in year 1 is at the higher level, year 2 sales revenue is estimated at either £4m (80 per cent probable) or £3m (20 per cent probable). If year 1 sales revenue is at the lower level, year 2 sales revenue is estimated at either £3m (20 per cent probable) or £2m (80 per cent probable). If year 2 sales revenue is at the £4m level, year 3 sales revenue is estimated at either £3m (50 per cent probable) or £2m (50 per cent probable). At any other level of year 2 sales revenue, year 3 sales revenue is estimated at £2m (100 per cent probable).

2 Variable costs are expected to be 25 per cent of the sales revenue.

3 Avoidable fixed costs are estimated at £1m p.a. This does not include depreciation.

4 It is expected that Kane will operate throughout the relevant period with zero working capital.

5 When the closedown occurs at the end of year 3, there will be closedown costs (including redundancy payments to certain staff) estimated at £0.5m, payable immediately on closure. The premises will be put on the market immediately. The premises can be sold during year 4 for an estimated £2m, and the cash would be received at the end of year 4. This is not expected to give rise to any tax effect. The plant is old and would not be expected to yield any significant amount. The tax effects of the plant disposal are expected to be negligible.

6 The corporation tax rate for Focus is expected to be 30 per cent over the relevant period. It may be assumed that tax will be payable at the end of the accounting year to which it relates.

7 Focus's cost of capital is estimated for the next few years at 14 per cent p.a., in 'money' terms.

8 The rate of inflation is expected to average about 5 per cent p.a. during the relevant period. All of Kane's cash flows are expected to increase in line with this average rate.

Senior managers at Kane disagreed with the Focus directors' pessimistic view of Kane's potential. Shortly after the announcement of Focus's intentions for Kane, the Focus board was approached by some of Kane's managers with a view to looking at the possibility of an immediate management buyout, to be achieved by the managers' buying the entire share capital of Kane from Focus. The managers had taken steps to find possible financial backers and believed that they could find the necessary support and produce cash at relatively short notice. The board of Focus was asked to suggest a price for Kane as a going concern.

The Focus board was sympathetic to the Kane managers' proposal and decided to set the offer price for the buyout at the economic value of Kane to Focus, as if Kane remained a group member until its proposed closedown in three years' time. The economic value would be based on the expected present value of Kane's projected cash flows, Focus's tax position and Focus's cost of capital. Put another way, Focus was prepared to sell the Kane shares at a price that would leave the Focus shareholders as well off as a result of the management buyout as they would be were Kane to wind down over the next three years as outlined above.

(a) How much will the Kane managers be asked to pay for the shares? (Work in 'money' terms.)

(b) Assuming that the estimates are correct, does this seem a logical price from Focus's point of view? Why?

(c) What factors may cause the managers of Kane to place a different value on the business? Why? What direction (higher or lower) is the difference likely to be? (Assume that all cash flows occur at year ends.)

6.7 Tufty plc produces a small range of industrial pumps using automated methods. The business is now considering production of a new model of pump, starting on 1 January 20X3. The business wishes to assess the new pump over a four-year timescale.

Production of the new pump will require the use of automated production equipment. This production equipment could be bought new, on 31 December 20X2, for a cost of £1 000 000. As an alternative to buying new production equipment, some equipment already owned by the business could be used. This is proving surplus to requirements, owing to a recent downturn in demand for another one of the business's products, and this is expected to continue for the foreseeable future.

The surplus production equipment could be sold for an estimated £400 000 on 1 January 20X3. This was bought new in 20X0 for £1 000 000. If it were used on production of the new pumps, it would be expected to have a zero market value by 31 December 20X6.

If the equipment for the new pumps were to be bought new in 20X2, it would be disposed of on 1 January 20X7. It is expected to have a total realisable value of £400 000 on that date.

The production equipment has been, and/or will be, eligible for capital allowances, calculated on a reducing balance basis, at 25 per cent p.a., starting in the year of acquisition irrespective of the exact date of acquisition during the year. In the year of disposal, no tax depreciation is charged, but the difference between the written-down value and the disposal proceeds is either given as an additional tax allowance or charged to tax according to whether the written-down value exceeds the disposal proceeds or vice versa.

Fixed annual incremental costs, excluding depreciation, of producing the new pump would total £80 000. Variable annual costs would be £200 000, if the new production equipment is to be used, but £300 000 were the existing production equipment to be used, since the existing production equipment is less automated and would require a higher labour input.

Sales of the new pumps would be expected to generate revenues of £600 000 for each of the four years.

Production of the new pump is expected to give rise to an additional working capital requirement of 10 per cent of annual revenues. These amounts will need to be in place by 1 January of the relevant year, and will be released on 31 December 20X6.

It is not expected that any other incremental costs would be involved with the decision to produce the new pump.

The directors have a target after-tax return of 10 per cent p.a. for all activities.

All revenues and expenses should be treated as if they occurred on the last day of the relevant calendar year, except where the date is specifically stated. The corporation tax rate is estimated at 30 per cent for the relevant period. Tax cash flows occur on 31 December in the year in which the events giving rise to them occur.

(a) *Prepare a schedule that derives the annual net relevant cash flows arising from producing the new pump and use this to assess the decision on the basis of net present value. You should make clear whether the surplus production equipment should be sold or used on production of the new pump on 1 January 20X3.*

(b) *Assess, and comment on, the sensitivity of the estimate of the fixed annual incremental costs of producing the new pump to the decision reached in (a).*

(Ignore inflation.)

There are both a set of **multiple-choice questions** and **missing-word questions** available on the website. These specifically cover the material contained in this chapter. These can be attempted and graded (with feedback) online.

There are also **three additional problems**, with solutions, that relate to the material covered in this chapter.

Go to **www.pearsoned.co.uk/atrillmclaney** and follow the links.

Chapter 7

Portfolio theory and its relevance to real investment decisions

Objectives

In this chapter we shall deal with the following:

→ the effect on risk and return of holding risky assets in portfolios

→ efficient portfolios and the efficient frontier

→ the risk-free rate and two-fund separation

→ the relationship between the risk and expected return on individual assets

→ the implications of this relationship, particularly on the discount rate that must be applied to expected cash flows to assess real investment projects through NPV

→ the arbitrage pricing model

7.1 Introduction

The relevance of security prices

Most of the developed countries of the world have a market in which shares in local and international businesses may be bought and sold. These capital markets, known typically (in English) as stock markets or stock exchanges, also provide a forum for the purchase and sale of loan stock, of both private sector businesses and governments. Research evidence shows that in many of these markets (including the UK one), the market forces that set the prices of individual securities (shares and loan stocks) cause pricing efficiency to occur. 'Efficiency' in this context means that all available information concerning a particular security's future prospects is at all times fully and rationally reflected in the security's price. In Chapter 9 we shall take a more detailed look at the workings of the UK capital market and at the evidence for the efficiency of its pricing. At present it is sufficient that we appreciate that such a market exists and that its pricing mechanism tends to be efficient.

In this chapter we are going to consider how securities traded in capital markets seem to be priced. We might feel that this is at most only of passing interest to us in the study of business finance since our main concern is that of businesses' investment and financing decisions. That would, however, be an incorrect view of the topic, for the following reasons:

- Financial managers are concerned with the way that their businesses' securities are priced in the free market as this might well have some impact on their financing decisions, for example at what price to issue new shares.

- Financial managers are also concerned with the relationship between how securities are priced in the capital market, on one hand, and their businesses' investment decisions, on the other. Businesses make decisions concerning investment in real assets on the basis of anticipated returns and of the risk attaching to those returns. The capital market is a free market, which deals in precisely those two commodities: return and risk. Thus we have a free and apparently efficient market that sets prices for return and risk. A vast amount of historical data is available on security prices and dividends, so we can readily observe what has happened in the past and draw conclusions on how return and risk seem to be related. In other words, we can see how risk is dealt with in the pricing mechanism of a free market. This should be useful to financial managers since there seems no logical reason why they should take a different view of return and risk from that taken by investors in the capital market.

The market's pricing mechanism for securities becomes even more relevant to us when we remind ourselves that managers are seeking, through their investment and financing decisions, to increase the wealth of the shareholders, partly through the business's value on the capital market. It seems even more logical, therefore, that managers should take a similar attitude to risk and return to that of security investors in the market.

If we can come to some sensible conclusion on the way in which risk and return are priced in the capital market, this should provide us with a useful basis for the business to assess real investment opportunities.

What we are now going to discuss is generally referred to as portfolio theory.

A reminder

In the previous chapter we saw that diversification can reduce investment risk. We also saw that, given the assumption that possible returns are symmetrically distributed around the expected value and that investors are risk averse, the mean (or expected value) and the variance (or its square root, the standard deviation) are valid and practical, though sometimes incomplete, bases on which to assess and rank investment opportunities.

7.2 Security investment and risk

If we were to select a number of marketable securities at random, form them into portfolios of varying sizes, measure the expected returns and standard deviation of returns from each of our various-sized portfolios, and then plot standard deviation against size of portfolio, we should obtain a graph similar to that in Figure 7.1.

Before we go on to consider the implications of Figure 7.1, just a word of explanation on its derivation. The expected returns, r, referred to are the monthly returns of a security or a portfolio of securities. These are calculated as:

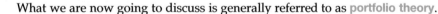

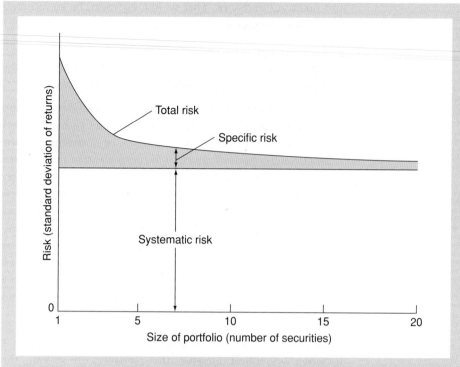

As the size of the portfolio is increased, the level of total risk diminishes, but at a decreasing rate such that, for a portfolio consisting of more than about 15 to 20 securities, adding more securities does little or nothing to reduce the total risk further. The element of the total risk that cannot be reduced through diversification is known as *systematic risk*. The element that can be removed by diversification is known as *specific risk*.

Figure 7.1
The risk of various-sized, randomly selected portfolios

$$r_t = \frac{P_t - P_{t-1} + d_t}{P_{t-1}}$$

where P_t is the market value of the security or portfolio at the end of month t, P_{t-1} the value at the start of the month, and d_t the dividend (if any) arising from the security or portfolio during the month. The expected value of returns for a security or portfolio is based on past experience, say of returns over the past 60 months. Thus the expected value could be the average (mean) of the monthly returns for the past five years.

The various-sized portfolios are constructed randomly. Several portfolios of each size are constructed, and the returns and standard deviations depicted in Figure 7.1 are the average of the returns and standard deviations of all of the portfolios for each size (see Evans and Archer 1968).

As standard deviation of returns around the mean is a reasonable measure of risk, Figure 7.1 suggests that a large reduction in risk can be achieved merely by randomly combining securities in portfolios. This provides empirical support for the maxim 'Do not put all your eggs in one basket', which is often applied to investment in securities.

Two features might surprise adherents to the eggs and baskets maxim, however. These are:

● Very limited diversification yields large reductions in the level of risk. Even spreading the investment funds available into a couple of different securities successfully eliminates a large amount of risk. Each additional different security added to the portfolio yields successively less by way of risk reduction.

- Once the portfolio contains about 15 to 20 securities there is little to be gained by way of risk reduction from further increases in its size. There seems to be some risk that is impervious to attempts to reduce it through diversification.

That part of the risk that is susceptible to removal by diversification is specific risk; the stubborn part is systematic risk. Total risk is the sum of these two.

As we saw in the previous chapter, specific (or unsystematic) risk arises from factors that are random as between one business's securities and those of another business. As these factors are random, a reasonably small amount of diversification will cause them to cancel one another.

The systematic (or portfolio) risk is concerned with economy-wide (macroeconomic) factors that affect all businesses.

The implications of the phenomenon represented in Figure 7.1 are as follows:

- Investors should hold securities in portfolios as, by doing so, risk can be reduced at little cost.
- There is limited point in diversifying into many more than 15 to 20 different securities as nearly all the benefits of diversification have been exhausted at that size of portfolio. Further diversification means that the investor will have to pay higher dealing charges to establish the portfolio and then will have more cost and/or work in managing it.

If systematic risk must be borne by investors because it is caused by economy-wide factors, it seems likely that some securities are more susceptible to these factors than are others. For example, a high street food supermarket would seem likely to suffer less as a result of economic recession than would a manufacturer of capital goods (business non-current assets).

Is the level of risk attaching to the returns from all securities the same, even though no one is forced to bear any specific risk? This question and several others relating to it will now be examined.

7.3 Portfolio theory

If we assume both that security returns are symmetrically distributed about their expected value and that investors are risk averse, then we can completely describe securities by their means and standard deviations and so represent them graphically, as in Figure 7.2.

In Figure 7.2, all risk-averse investors would prefer investment B to investment C as it has higher expected value for the same level of risk. All risk-averse investors would prefer investment A to investment C as it has lower risk for the same level of expected return. Thus both A and B are said to 'dominate' C. The choice between A and B, however, depends upon the attitude to risk of the investor making the decision (that is, on the shape of the particular investor's utility curve).

The positions of A and B in Figure 7.2 are dictated by their expected values and standard deviations. B is expected to yield higher returns than A (14 per cent as against 10 per cent), but it is also expected to be more risky (standard deviation of 12 per cent as against 10 per cent). Assuming that all investors have similar expectations

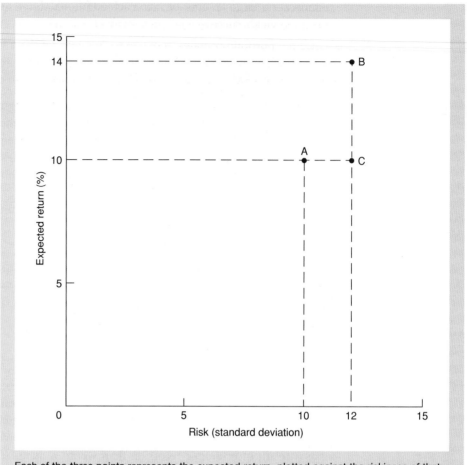

Figure 7.2
The risk/return profiles of three securities, A, B and C

Each of the three points represents the expected return, plotted against the riskiness of that return, for three independent securities.

of these and other securities, then they would all see these securities as occupying the same position on the graph.

Expected return and risk of a portfolio

Suppose that we were to form a portfolio containing a proportion (α) of each of A and B. The expected return from that portfolio would be:

$$r_P = \alpha_A r_A + \alpha_B r_B$$

where r_P, r_A and r_B are the expected returns from the portfolio, security A and security B, respectively: in other words, the returns of the portfolio are simply the weighted average of the returns of the constituent securities. The standard deviation of the portfolio would be:

$$\sigma_P = \sqrt{\alpha_A^2 \sigma_A^2 + \alpha_B^2 \sigma_B^2 + 2\alpha_A \alpha_B R \sigma_A \sigma_B}$$

where σ_P, σ_A and σ_B are, respectively, the standard deviation of the expected returns of the portfolio, security A and security B. R is the **coefficient of correlation** between the expected returns of the two securities.* If R were +1 it would mean that the expected returns would be perfectly correlated one with the other: an increase of x per cent in the returns of A would always imply a y per cent increase in the returns of B, and vice versa. If R were −1 it would imply as close a relationship but a negative one: an x per cent increase in the returns of A would always mean a y per cent decrease in the returns from B. An R of between −1 and +1 means less direct relationships, with a value of zero meaning that there is no relationship at all between the returns of the two securities. (Note that there would be a separate R for any two variables. The particular value of R for A and B would be peculiar to A and B and not the same, except by coincidence, for any other two securities, not even between A or B and a third security.)

Table 7.1 shows the expected returns and standard deviations for a selection of possible portfolios of A and B for a range of hypothetical correlation coefficients (R).

Table 7.1 Risk and expected returns for various portfolios of securities A and B with differing assumptions as to the correlation coefficient

Proportion of security A in portfolio %	Expected returns of portfolio (r_P) %	Standard deviation for various correlation coefficients (R)				
		−1.0 %	−0.5 %	0.0 %	+0.5 %	+1.0 %
0	14	12.0	12.0	12.0	12.0	12.0
25	13	6.5	8.0	9.3	10.5	11.5
50	12	1.0	5.6	7.8	9.5	11.0
75	11	4.5	6.5	8.1	9.4	10.5
100	10	10.0	10.0	10.0	10.0	10.0

To illustrate where the figures in Table 7.1 come from, let us take the case where the proportions of the securities in the portfolio are 25 per cent security A and 75 per cent security B, and the correlation coefficient between the returns of the two securities is +0.5 (i.e. the figures in row 2, columns 2 and 6 of the table).

Remember that security A has an expected return of 10 per cent with a standard deviation of 10 per cent, and that security B has an expected return of 14 per cent with a standard deviation of 12 per cent.

The expected return on the portfolio is given by:

$$r_P = \alpha_A + \alpha_B$$
$$= (0.25 \times 10\%) + (0.75 \times 14\%)$$
$$= 13\%$$

The standard deviation of the portfolio is given by:

$$\sigma_P = \sqrt{\alpha_A^2 \sigma_A^2 + \alpha_B^2 \sigma_B^2 + 2\alpha_A \sigma_A R \alpha_B \sigma_B}$$
$$= \sqrt{(0.25^2 \times 10\%^2) + (0.75^2 \times 12\%^2) + (2 \times 0.25 \times 10\% \times +0.5 \times 0.75 \times 12\%)}$$
$$= 10.476\%, \text{ say } 10.5\%$$

$* R = \dfrac{\text{Covariance (A, B)}}{\sigma_A \sigma_B}$

Readers who are not too confident with these statistical measures should refer to Bancroft and O'Sullivan (2000) or one of the other texts that cover the ground.

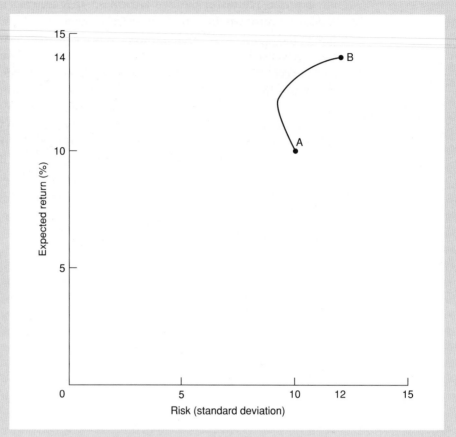

Figure 7.3
The risk/return profiles of portfolios of securities A and B, assuming a 0.5 positive correlation coefficient

By combining securities A and B into a portfolio, risk is reduced because the two securities have a correlation coefficient of less than +1.0.

Other portfolios of A and B

The expected return/risk profile of portfolios of various proportions of A and B, assuming a correlation coefficient of +0.5, is shown in Figure 7.3. This is a plot of column 2 values against those from column 6 (Table 7.1). Each of the points along this line represents the combination of return and risk for a portfolio containing particular proportions of A and B. We can see that the risk is at a minimum where the portfolio contains between 50 and 75 per cent of A.

Figure 7.4 shows the profiles of expected return and risk following the five assumed correlation coefficients (–1.0, –0.5, 0.0, +0.5 and +1.0), rather than just the one (+0.5) shown in Figure 7.3. Here we can see that the greatest risk reduction possibilities occur with negatively correlated securities. In fact there is a combination* of A and B

---

* This is discoverable by finding the minimum value for σ_P by means of differential calculus. Writing α_B as $1 - \alpha_A$, we get:

$$\sigma_P^2 = \alpha_A^2 \sigma_A^2 + (1 - \alpha_A)^2 \sigma_B^2 + 2\alpha_A(1 - \alpha_A)R\sigma_A\sigma_B$$

Differentiating with respect to α_A gives:

$$\frac{d\sigma_P^2}{d\alpha_A} = 2\alpha_A\sigma_A^2 + 2\alpha_A\sigma_B^2 - 2\sigma_B^2 + 2R\sigma_A\sigma_B - 4\alpha_A R\sigma_A\sigma_B$$

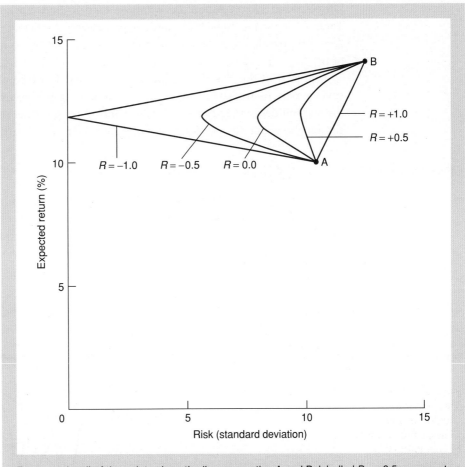

Figure 7.4
The risk/return profiles of various portfolios of securities A and B, with differing assumptions regarding the correlation coefficient

For example, all of the points along the line connecting A and B, labelled $R = -0.5$, represent the risk and return of a portfolio containing some combination of securities A and B, assuming a correlation coefficient of -0.5 between the two securities.

that has no risk when the correlation coefficient is assumed to be -1. In reality such perfectly *negatively* correlated securities would be impossible to find. Their existence would imply that it would be possible to form portfolios possessing no risk at all, which is not likely to be the case. It is probably equally unlikely that securities whose expected returns are perfectly *positively* correlated exist in the real world. If they did, forming portfolios of them would do nothing to reduce risk, since the risk of the portfolio is simply a linear combination of the risks of the constituent securities. This is evidenced by the straight line connecting A and B, representing the profile of expected return/risk for $R = +1$ in Figure 7.4. In reality, securities with positive, but less than

---

Setting this equal to zero and putting in the actual values for σ_A and σ_B and assuming $R = -1$, we get:

$$(2\alpha_A \times 100) + (2\alpha_A \times 144) - (2 \times 144) - (2 \times 10 \times 12) + (4\alpha_A \times 120) = 0$$

$$200\alpha_A + 288\alpha_A + 480\alpha_A = 288 + 240$$

$$\alpha_A = \frac{528}{968}$$

that is, about 55 per cent security A and 45 per cent security B.

perfect positive, correlation are what we tend to find. To that extent, column 6 of Table 7.1 is the most realistic. Here the correlation coefficient is +0.5, and combining A and B provides some reduction in the total risk but by no means total elimination of it.

That part of the risk that reduces when A and B are combined in a portfolio is specific risk. As we saw from Figure 7.1, combining two securities far from exhausts the possibilities of specific risk reduction. Introducing further securities in appropriate combinations into the portfolio would reduce the risk still further.

Extending the range of investments

Figure 7.5 shows three more securities, C, D and E, brought into the reckoning. The various curved lines show the expected return/risk profiles of various combinations of any two of the five securities. The line XB furthest to the top left of the graph shows the expected risk/return profile of a portfolio containing various proportions of each

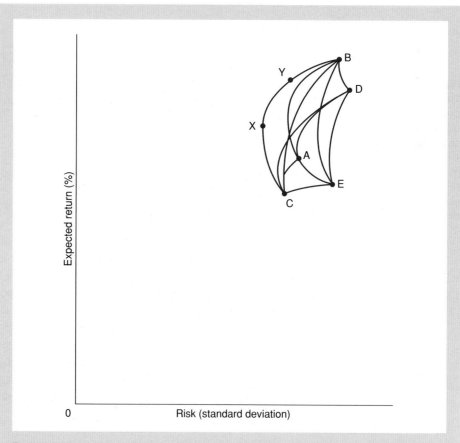

Figure 7.5
The risk/return profiles of various portfolios of securities A, B, C, D and E

Each point along any of the solid curved lines represents the risk and return of a portfolio containing some proportion of *some* of the securities. The curve that passes through points X and Y represents the risk and return of a portfolio containing some proportion of *all* of the securities. The portfolios that lie along this line between B and X are said to *dominate* all other possible combinations of these five securities. This means that they have either a higher expected return for the same (or a lower) level of risk, or lower risk for the same (or a higher) expected return.

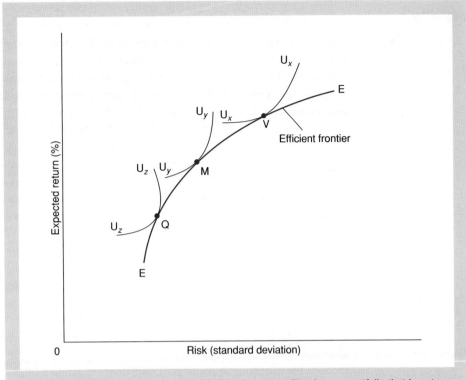

Each point along the line EE represents the risk/return profile of some portfolio that is not subject to any specific risk. The curves U_xU_x, U_yU_y and U_zU_z are the utility curves of three different individuals. The graph indicates that each individual will seek to hold a different portfolio of securities.

Figure 7.6
The efficient frontier

of these five securities. Note that every combination of expected return and risk along this line 'dominates' any other position in which the investor could be with these five securities. Take point X along this line, for example. No other combination available will either yield higher expected return for X's level of risk, or has less risk for X's expected return. Consider the portfolio represented by point Y: although this has a higher expected return than X, it also has higher risk. Thus X does not dominate Y, nor does Y dominate X.

Efficiency

Of course, the five securities in Figure 7.5 neither represent the total of financial investment opportunities nor, therefore, the maximum specific risk reduction opportunities available. There is an efficient frontier for securities as a whole. This is represented in Figure 7.6. Each point on the line EE represents some portfolio constructed from some or all of the securities available in the economy as a whole. Efficient in this context means that there is no specific (unsystematic) risk present; it has all been diversified away.

None of the many portfolios represented by the efficient frontier has any specific risk; if they did, it would be possible to diversify further and get rid of it, thus pushing the frontier further to the top left.

Utility

Let us remind ourselves of what we discussed in Chapter 6 on the subject of utility. It is possible (in theory at least), in respect of any particular individual and of any two related factors, to represent that individual's preferences as regards the trade-off between the factors by a set of utility curves. If we assume both that investors are risk averse and that they are expected utility-of-wealth maximisers, then they would have utility curves similar to those depicted in Figure 7.6 (U_xU_x, U_yU_y and U_zU_z).

Note that each of these three utility curves relates to different individuals (X, Y and Z), all of whom are prepared to take on some risk, but who require compensation in the form of increased expected returns for doing so. In each case, the investors whose attitudes are depicted require increasingly large increments in expected return for each successive increment of risk that they are prepared to accept. This is why each of these curves slopes upwards to the right.

According to his or her utility curve, individual Z is rather more risk averse than individual X. The latter is prepared to accept much more risk to achieve any given level of expected return than is the former. Individual X is still risk averse and therefore needs increasing amounts of expected return for each additional increment of risk, but less so than individual Z.

Irrespective of their personal preferences, all of the investors (X, Y and Z) whose attitudes are represented in Figure 7.6 would reach the highest level of utility (satisfaction) by investing in some portfolio that lies along the efficient frontier (EE). No one would want to invest in individual securities or portfolios lying below or to the right of the efficient frontier because these all have some specific risk. It would be possible either to obtain a higher return or have lower risk by investing in a portfolio lying on EE.

A risk-free asset

We now make another assumption, which is that there is a financial market that will lend to and borrow from all investors. It will do this in unlimited amounts of money, at an equal, **risk-free rate** (r_f). This would transform the position from that shown in Figure 7.6 to that of Figure 7.7. Now all investors would locate on the straight line r_fS.

Investors whose preferences are similar to those of individual Z would choose to put some wealth into risky securities and lend the remainder at the risk-free rate (see Figure 7.7). Individual Y would invest entirely in risky securities despite the existence of the **risk-free asset**. This is because this person's utility curve just happens to be tangential to r_fS where r_fS itself is tangential to EE. Investors whose preferences are similar to those of individual X (who is the least risk averse of the three) would choose to borrow at rate r_f, so that an amount even greater than their wealth can be invested in risky securities.

Note that two of our investors will achieve a higher level of utility (a higher level of expected return for a given level of risk, or lower level of risk for a given level of expected return) through the existence of the risk-free borrowing/lending opportunity. Compare point P with point Q (where individual Z would invest without the opportunity to lend – see Figure 7.6), or point T with point V (where individual X would invest without the opportunity to borrow) in Figure 7.7. For the third investor the position is unchanged. Only investors who happen to have preferences that cause their highest level of utility to be tangential with r_fS at M will be unaffected by the

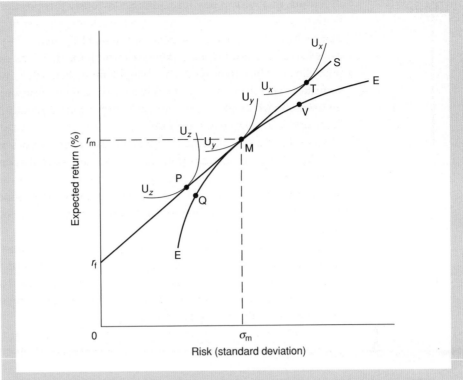

Figure 7.7
The efficient frontier with borrowing and lending

The graph indicates how most investors will be able to reach a higher level of utility as a result of the existence of the availability of borrowing and lending.

existence of the risk-free borrowing/lending opportunity, and this seems likely to be a very small minority. Every other investor will be better off.

Two-fund separation

→ The result of this is what is known as **two-fund separation**. Irrespective of the personal preferences of individuals they will all choose to invest their wealth in some combination of the portfolio M and the risk-free asset. This state of affairs is somewhat analogous to Fisher separation, which we met in Chapter 2. Fisher separation implies that irrespective of personal preferences as regards investment and consumption, all investors will concur about the optimum level of real investment provided that a borrowing/lending opportunity exists. Two-fund separation means that all investors will concur on the same portfolio of risky securities (portfolio M) if a risk-free borrowing/lending opportunity exists.

What is portfolio M?

The foregoing raises the questions: what is this portfolio in which we all want to invest, and what securities does it contain?

Let us attack these questions from the other direction. What happens to a security that does not form part of portfolio M? If we all want portfolio M, the prices of securities excluded from it will be zero. Any commodity that no one wants has a zero price (in a free market, at least). This means that there would be securities, with expectations of returns, that we can buy for nothing. Obviously this position would be too good to be true. Capital market efficiency, which we know at least broadly to exist, demands that such anomalies just could not occur in real life; such zero-priced or merely under-priced securities would offer superior returns for their risk and would enhance the portfolio M. Thus they would be bought until their price, relative to the prices of securities generally, was a reasonable one. The only logical conclusion from this is that the portfolio M strictly must contain a proportion of all securities on the market, in other words, it is the **market portfolio**.

More strictly still, since the capital market for securities is not a self-contained, sealed entity, the market portfolio should contain a proportion of all capital assets in existence. It is possible, and often practical, to sell securities and use the proceeds to buy (for instance) gold, land, a painting, or some vintage wine, and thus such assets must be regarded as possible substitutes for securities, and logically they must form part of the market portfolio.

Clearly, no one can hold the strict market portfolio. Most of what we know of capital market efficiency (and which we shall review in Chapter 9) suggests, however, that securities are priced logically one against another. To that extent they are sub-stitutes for one another and so failure strictly to hold the market portfolio may not invalidate the principles so far established.

The capital market line

The line r_fS in Figure 7.7 is known as the **capital market line** (CML). The CML defines the relationship between risk and return for efficient portfolios of risky securities. Note that this line will shift up and down, closer to or further from the horizontal, as interest rates change over time.

We can see from Figure 7.7 that the expected return available to an investor is:

$$r_f + \text{Risk premium}$$

The amount of the risk premium is dependent on how much of the investment is in the portfolio of risky securities.

7.4 Capital asset pricing model

The CML defines the risk/return trade-off for efficient portfolios. What is probably of more interest and value to us is the relationship between expected return and risk for individual securities. In fact, this is:

$$E(r_i) = r_f + [E(r_m) - r_f]\frac{\text{Cov}(i, M)}{\sigma_m^2}$$

where $E(r_i)$ is the expected return from i, a particular individual security, r_f is the risk-free borrowing/lending rate, $E(r_m)$ the expected return on the market portfolio, $\text{Cov}(i, M)$ the covariance of returns of security i with those of the market portfolio, and σ_m^2 the variance (square of the standard deviation) of the market returns.

This statement, known as the **capital asset pricing model** (CAPM), can be derived directly from what is known about the CML. (The appendix to this chapter gives the detailed derivation of CAPM.)

Note that, in using CAPM to discover the expected return for any particular security i, we use only one factor that refers specifically to i. This is $\text{Cov}(i, M)$. All of the other factors $[E(r_m), r_f$ and $\sigma_m^2]$ are general to all securities. The only factor that distinguishes the expected returns of one security from those of another is the extent to which the expected returns from the particular security co-vary with the expected returns from the market portfolio.

This ties in pretty well with what we have discovered so far about specific and systematic risk. We know that specific risk can easily be avoided; it is not therefore surprising to find that the returns that we expect to get from a particular security bear no relation to specific risk. Even though higher risk usually engenders higher expectations of returns, it is entirely logical that someone who is needlessly exposed to specific risk should not expect higher return.

Suppose that an office block window cleaner went to his employer to demand higher wages on the grounds that by choosing not to wear the safety harness provided by the employer, the window cleaner was exposed to greater risk than the other employees who wore the harness. No doubt the employer would answer emphatically that the window cleaner was not being asked to bear this risk and that it was unnecessary to bear it since, by the simple expedient of wearing the safety harness, it could be completely avoided. In effect, the capital market says the same to the misguided bearer of specific risk; consequently it will not compensate that investor for bearing that risk.*

CAPM tells us that expectations of returns will be enhanced by the extent of the covariance of expected returns from the particular security with those of the market portfolio. Again this ties in with what we already know in that systematic risk, which the investor is forced to bear, relates to factors that tend to affect all securities. The greater their effect on a particular security, the greater the systematic risk, and logically, the greater the returns expected from that security. It is not surprising that covariance with the generality of securities is a measure of systematic risk.

Beta: a measure of risk

CAPM tells us that the capital market prices securities so that no higher returns are expected for bearing specific risk. Bearing systematic risk is expected to be rewarded by a risk premium (over the risk-free rate) of:

$$[E(r_m) - r_f] \times \text{Cov}(i, M) / \sigma_m^2$$

→ The last term is usually known as **beta** (β), so CAPM is typically written as:

$$E(r_i) = r_f + [E(r_m) - r_f]\beta_i$$

The greater the beta that characterises a particular security, the higher are that security's expected returns.

---

* Some readers might be mystified as to how the capital market sets the returns from a particular security.

Remember that return in this context is dividend (if any) plus appreciation in value of the security over a period divided by the value of the security at the start of the period. The capital market, through the actions of buyers and sellers, sets the current market price of each security. If investors feel that 15 per cent p.a. is the appropriate level of return for the level of risk involved, the capital market will set the price of the security accordingly.

After the event, the actual return may prove to be other than 15 per cent. This difference is in the nature of risk; what is anticipated may not occur.

Securities with a high beta are by no means guaranteed high returns. It is in the nature of risk that nothing is guaranteed. However, before the event, high-beta securities are expected to have higher returns than low-beta ones. If the generality of investment in securities (the market portfolio) does well, then portfolios containing high-beta securities will prosper: the higher the beta, the more they will prosper. On the other hand, should securities generally fare badly, high-beta securities will fare particularly badly. In other words, beta is a measure of volatility of returns relative to those of the market portfolio. Betas above 1.0 are regarded as high and those below 1.0 as low. High-beta securities are sometimes referred to as *aggressive*, and low-beta ones as *defensive*. In real life, equity shares can be found having betas of up to about 2.0; they can also be found with betas as low as around 0.4.

Negative betas

There is no reason of principle why some securities should not have a negative beta. Systematic risk is caused by a number of macroeconomic factors, such as the level of interest rates, or the price of fuel. Some securities are greatly affected by most of these in an adverse way (high-beta securities). Other securities are little affected by these factors (low-beta securities). There could be some securities that are favourably affected by these factors, at a time when the factors are adversely affecting most securities; such securities would have a negative beta.

Probably, most businesses are adversely affected by high interest rates and high fuel prices. However, banks and fuel-producing businesses, respectively, might tend to be favoured by high levels of those two factors. This does not necessarily mean that the securities of banks and fuel producers have a negative beta. A security's beta is related to all of the macroeconomic factors affecting it. In the case of a particular security, while there may be one or two of these factors that have the opposite effect to the one they have on the majority of securities, most factors will have a similar effect on that security to their effect on the majority. The bank may be favoured by high interest rates, but it is still adversely affected by high fuel costs, high labour costs, trade recession and so on. In practice, negative-beta securities seem not to exist.

It should be particularly noted that betas only indicate the effect of a particular security on a well-diversified portfolio. A security with a low beta may be very risky, but much of its risk may be specific risk.

Security market line

Figure 7.8 shows CAPM represented diagrammatically. Here risk is measured by beta. The risk/return profile of all assets should lie somewhere along the line r_iT, which is known as the **security market line** (SML).

It is important to recognise the difference between the capital market line and the security market line. The CML shows expected returns plotted against risk, where risk is measured in terms of standard deviation of returns. This is appropriate because the CML represents the risk/return trade-off for efficient portfolios, that is, the risk is all systematic risk. The SML, on the other hand, shows the risk/return trade-off where risk is measured by beta, that is, only by the systematic risk element of the individual security. No individual security's risk/return profile is shown by the CML because all individual securities have an element of specific risk, that is, they are all inefficient.

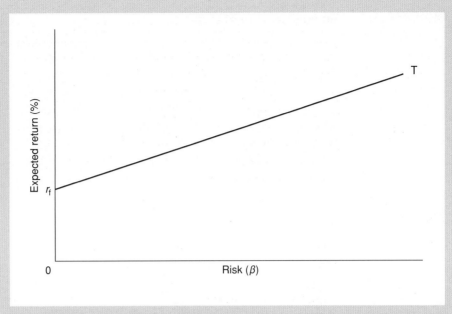

Figure 7.8
Graphical
representation
of CAPM – the
security market line

Where there is no risk, the expected return is the risk-free rate. As systematic risk (measured by β) increases, an increasingly large risk premium, over the risk-free rate, is expected.

Thus all individual securities (and indeed all inefficient portfolios) lie to the bottom-right of the efficient frontier (Figure 7.6).

CAPM was developed by Sharpe (1963), though others independently reached similar conclusions.

7.5 CAPM: an example of beta estimation

We shall now take a look at how the beta for the ordinary shares of a particular business may be derived.

Example 7.1

The year-end level of a representative stock exchange index and of the price of an ordinary share of Ace plc were as follows:

Year	Index	Ace plc (£)
1995	218	1.09
1996	230	1.20
1997	248	1.33
1998	250	1.40
1999	282	1.80
2000	297	1.99
2001	288	1.81
2002	290	1.98
2003	320	2.25
2004	356	2.55
2005	371	2.80

You are required on the basis of the above to calculate beta. (Ignore dividends throughout.)

Solution

Estimation of market factors

Year (1)	Index (2) p_{mt}	Return (3) $r_{mt} = \dfrac{p_{mt} - p_{mt-1}}{p_{mt-1}}$	Return deviation (4) $r_{mt} - S_m$	Return variance (5) $(r_{mt} - S_m)^2$
1995	218			
1996	230	0.055	(0.001)	0.0000
1997	248	0.078	0.022	0.0005
1998	250	0.008	(0.048)	0.0023
1999	282	0.128	0.072	0.0052
2000	297	0.053	(0.003)	0.0000
2001	288	(0.030)	(0.086)	0.0074
2002	290	0.007	(0.049)	0.0024
2003	320	0.103	0.047	0.0022
2004	356	0.113	0.057	0.0032
2005	371	0.042	(0.014)	0.0002
		0.557		0.0234

$$S_m = \frac{0.557}{10} = 0.056, \quad \text{Var } r_m = \frac{0.0234}{10} = 0.0023$$

Estimation of beta of Ace plc

Year (1)	Share price (2) $£p_{it}$	Return (3) $\dfrac{p_{it} - p_{it-1}}{p_{it-1}}$	Return deviation (4) $r_{it} - S_i$	Covariance with market (5) $(r_{it} - S_i)(r_{mt} - S_m)$
1995	1.09			
1996	1.20	0.101	(0.002)	0.0000
1997	1.33	0.108	0.005	0.0001
1998	1.40	0.053	(0.050)	0.0024
1999	1.80	0.286	0.183	0.0132
2000	1.99	0.106	0.003	(0.0000)
2001	1.81	(0.090)	(0.193)	0.0166
2002	1.98	0.094	(0.009)	0.0004
2003	2.25	0.136	0.033	0.0016
2004	2.55	0.133	0.030	0.0017
2005	2.80	0.098	(0.005)	0.0001
		1.025		0.0361

$$S_i = \frac{1.025}{10} = 0.103, \quad \text{Cov}(i, M) = \frac{0.0361}{10} = 0.0036$$

Since:

$$\beta_i = \frac{\text{Cov}(i, M)}{\text{Var } r_m}$$

then:

$$\beta_{Ace} = \frac{0.0036}{0.0023} = 1.56$$

Thus Ace plc equity has a fairly high beta.

The explanation of the calculation of the market factors shown in the first table above is as follows:

- p_{mt} is the value for the index used as a surrogate for the market, and is shown in column 2.
- r_{mt} is the return for the year on the market. It is calculated as the gain during the year, that is, the end-of-year value (p_{mt}) less the start-of-year value (p_{mt-1}) divided by the start-of-year value (p_{mt-1}). For example, the return during 1996 was the increase in the index from 1995 to 1996 (12) divided by the value at the start of 1996 (218).
- S_m is the mean of the annual returns, that is, the sum of them divided by the number of returns (10).
- Column 4 is deduced by deducting the mean annual return (0.056) from each year's return (column 3).
- Column 5 is column 4 squared.

The figures in the table relating to Ace plc are similarly derived.

7.6 Assumptions of CAPM

In developing CAPM several assumptions need to be made. These are as follows:

1 Investors are risk-averse, and maximise expected utility of wealth.

2 The capital market is not dominated by any individual investors.

3 Investors are interested in only two features of a security, its expected returns and its variance (or standard deviation).

4 There exists a risk-free rate at which all investors may borrow or lend without limit at the same rate.

5 There is an absence of dealing charges, taxes, and other imperfections.

6 All investors have identical perceptions of each security.

Let us briefly consider these in terms of their validity. Assumption 1 seems to be true; certainly most people seem to prefer more wealth to less (all things being equal) and most of us are risk averse. Assumption 2 also is broadly true, with investors, even the large ones, not usually dominating the market in any one security. There has been much discussion in the literature (for example, Levy and Sarnat 1988) of the validity of the *mean variance* criterion and it seems that in the context of security returns, assumption 3 is probably reasonable. Levy and Sarnat (1995) discuss evidence that suggests that while security returns are not strictly 'normal' in their distribution, they are roughly so.

Clearly, assumptions 4, 5 and 6 are invalid. Whether or not their invalidity seriously weakens the model is probably discernible only by looking at how well CAPM works in practice.

7.7 Tests of CAPM

For most of us, certainly for most financial managers, the only important feature of a theoretical derivation like CAPM is how well it explains, and more particularly how well it predicts, real events.

Beta as an explainer of past events

CAPM has been subjected to a large number of empirical tests. Most of these have sought to estimate the beta for a security by regressing the monthly returns (capital gain plus dividend expressed as a fraction of the security price at the beginning of the month) against returns from the *market portfolio* (as we did for Ace plc in Example 7.1). Since the market portfolio is strictly unobservable (it contains some of every possible capital investment), a surrogate is used. Typically this is some representative capital market index (in the UK the Financial Times Actuaries Index is sometimes used for this purpose). Betas tend to be calculated on the basis of monthly returns over fairly protracted periods such as five years (60 months). The tests have then gone on to assess whether or not CAPM explains the returns for securities over the period following the one that was used to estimate the beta.

Until recently, it was possible to say that the various tests had broadly supported CAPM. Doubts had been expressed about the validity of using short-term bills of stable governments, like those of the UK and USA, as a risk-free rate, since it did not really fit with the evidence. However, researchers found beta to be a valid and fairly complete measure of risk. Despite the fact that CAPM deals with expected returns (which are impossible to test) and tests had, of necessity, dealt with actual past events, it was concluded that CAPM was broadly valid as a useful explainer of what happened.

Recently, however, evidence has emerged that calls the validity of CAPM into question. Fama and French (1992, 1996) carried out a major study of US stocks covering the period 1962 to 1989. They found that beta could not always completely explain the level of investment returns. They found the returns from the shares of some businesses were greater than CAPM predicted. Such businesses were small ones and/or ones that had a high ratio of balance sheet (book) value of equity to the market value of equity. Fama and French concluded that investors viewed such businesses as being more risky (hence a higher return) than larger ones and/or those with a lower book-to-equity ratio. They further concluded that this was because investors saw it as more likely that small businesses and those with high book-to-equity ratios would get into financial difficulties, for example in an economic downturn, than other businesses. Such financial difficulties tend to be costly to shareholders. It seems that small businesses are less resilient to hard times than are larger ones. The market value of the equity of most businesses (that is, current share price multiplied by the number of shares issued) is greater than the figure found in their balance sheets for share capital plus reserves. This is because balance sheets tend not to include as assets such items as goodwill and the value of brand names, whereas market share prices tend to reflect these items. Broadly, where the market value of equity is very high compared with its book value, investors have faith in the business's future, particularly its ability to survive and expand. Conversely, where a business's book-to-market ratio is relatively high, investors' confidence in its future tends to be relatively low.

Fama and French proposed a revision to CAPM, broadly as follows:

Expected return from an investment = Risk-free rate + Normal CAPM risk premium
+ A second risk premium related to size
+ A third risk premium related to book to market ratio

Broadly, for a large business with a low book-to-market ratio, the standard CAPM will be a good predictor of expected returns. For businesses that are small and/or have relatively low share prices compared with the balance sheet value of equity, one or both of the other two risk premiums will need to be included. Davies, Fama and French (2000) tested their three-factor model using US data over the period 1929 to 1997 and found that it was significantly more reliable than the basic CAPM. Davies, Unni, Draper and Paudyal (1999) tested the Fama and French model using UK data. They took the period 1976 to 1995, using data from the first part of the period to establish beta and the factors for the other two risk premiums (size and book-to-market), and assessed how well the model predicted actual returns during the second part of the period. They found that the model worked significantly better than the basic CAPM. Chi-Hsiou Hung, Shackleton and Xu (2004), also using UK data, concluded that beta remains highly significant in explaining returns on shares even where the Fama and French factors (size and book-to-value) are taken into account.

Beta as a predictor of future events

An important issue, as regards the usefulness of CAPM to financial managers, concerns how well the beta of a particular security calculated from past data predicts that security's beta for a future period: in other words, how stable are betas over time?

The evidence suggests that the betas of individual securities calculated over one time period are not very good predictors of the betas for those individual securities over the following and subsequent periods. On the other hand, where securities are combined into portfolios, the beta of the portfolio for one period seems a reasonable predictor of that portfolio's beta during the next period. (Incidentally, the beta of a portfolio is the weighted average of the betas of the constituent securities, that is:

$$\beta_{P} = \sum_{i=1}^{n} \alpha_{i}\beta_{i}$$

where security i represents proportion α_i, by market value, of the portfolio.)

The stability of portfolio betas is particularly of interest to financial managers when it is considered that the portfolios concerned could be made up entirely of ordinary shares of businesses in some particular industry. That is to say, there is a characteristic beta for each industry, which remains fairly stable over time.

Why should it be the case that betas of individual securities are not very stable, whereas those for a portfolio tend to be? There are perhaps two reasons for this:

● Measurement errors. The beta calculated for a security may well not be the 'true' beta for that security owing to errors in estimating the beta including, for example, using a capital market index as a surrogate for the market portfolio.

● Actual changes in the security's risk profile over time. There is absolutely no reason why the capital market's perceptions of a security should remain constant when the business concerned may, for example, be changing its real investment patterns. As we shall see in Chapter 11, the extent to which the particular business is reliant on long-term borrowings also affects its securities' beta, so changes in the extent of this reliance over time will tend to make the beta look unstable.

Each of these factors will probably tend to be fairly random in nature (from one security to another), so that combining securities in portfolios would have a 'portfolio' effect leading to a more stable picture emerging.

7.8 Implications of CAPM

For security investors

The implications of CAPM for investors in securities seem to be the following:

- Investors should diversify sufficiently to eliminate most of the specific risk from their portfolios. There seem to be no rewards for bearing specific risk.

- They should decide whether they wish to invest in high-risk ($\beta > 1$), medium-risk ($\beta = 1$) or low-risk ($\beta < 1$) securities. There are lists of betas of the leading Stock Exchange listed equities published regularly by a number of commercial organisations, including the London Business School, which subscribers may use to help them to construct portfolios reflecting their personal risk/return preferences. The published betas are updated quarterly and are believed to be derived from comparing monthly returns of the immediately preceding five years with those of a representative Stock Exchange index, acting as a surrogate for the market portfolio. (Several commercial organisations in the USA offer a similar service in relation to US securities.)

While the evidence on capital market efficiency indicates that it is impossible to spot winners systematically, this does not mean that one business's securities are much the same as those of another. The evidence on CAPM suggests that it is possible to distinguish between those securities that will perform better than average if the market does well – and worse if the market does badly – on the one hand, and less volatile, less risky securities on the other. Thus investors are able to select the level of risk that suits their situation and personality and to expect returns commensurate with that risk level.

The instability of betas for individual securities is probably not too significant here since investors are well advised to hold portfolios in any case.

For financial managers in deriving the discount rate for real investment projects

At this point the question arises as to how businesses should select the rate at which to discount the expected cash flows of prospective real investment projects, in order to discover their NPVs.

In our discussion of shareholder wealth maximisation in Chapter 2, we introduced the idea that the appropriate discount rate is the borrowing/lending interest rate. In the real world such an approach is not tenable because the comparable alternative to real investment is not risk-free lending. The opportunity with which the project under consideration must logically be compared is one of equal risk to that project.

Let us remind ourselves of three factors that bear on the discount rate decision:

- The value of a business is the sum of the NPVs of all of the projects that it currently has in operation, so that undertaking a new project with a positive NPV should increase the value of the business by the amount of the positive NPV (see Chapter 4).

- Capital market efficiency research suggests that events of economic significance occurring within the business reflect in the share price, so that taking on projects with positive NPVs should actually increase the market value of the business's securities (see Chapter 9).

● CAPM tells us that expected return is directly proportional to the level of risk for each individual investment. Furthermore, the only part of risk that matters (assuming investors hold efficient portfolios) is systematic risk (measured by beta).

Between them, these three lead to the assertion that the logical discount rate for an individual real (and inevitably risky) investment project should be derived from CAPM. The beta value to be used would reflect the covariance of expected returns from the project with those from the generality of risky investments (the 'market' portfolio).

After all, the capital market is one where the commodities traded are risk and expected return, and to use a market-derived price of risk (which is what CAPM does) seems a reasonable way of pricing individual real investments. This is particularly logical where shareholder wealth maximisation is the business's goal.

Whether it is very practical actually to seek to assess betas of individual real investment projects is less certain. It is difficult enough trying to estimate the cash flows, without trying to assess the degree of covariance these might have with the market portfolio.

A more practical approach probably is to try to use characteristic (average) betas for the industry in which the real investment is to be made, to derive the discount rate for the project. This might, at first sight, appear to be too much of a broad-brush approach in that there are risks attaching to any particular project that may not apply to the area of activity more generally. A brief reflection, however, will reveal that the non-general factors relate to specific risk that the individual investor can diversify away.

For example, a business, most of whose real investments are in newspaper publishing, intends to make a real investment in the manufacture of kitchen furniture. To derive the appropriate discount rate for the project it should use the average beta of businesses that are completely engaged in the same activity. By doing so, the discount rate would reflect the capital market's perceptions of the systematic risk attaching to kitchen furniture manufacture.

Since the business is seeking to enhance its shareholders' wealth, presumably, mainly through the market value of the shares, the perceptions of the market are very important.

We should note that by advocating a capital-market-derived discount rate, we are saying that we should use an opportunity cost discount rate, just as the cash flows to be discounted are the opportunity cash flows. This is true since an investment alternative of equal systematic risk to the real investment under consideration is buying shares of another business of equal beta to that of the project. Thus we should only be prepared to make the real investment where we expect a positive NPV, when expected cash flows are discounted at the expected rate of return from the security investment alternative.

7.9 Lack of shareholder unanimity on risky investment

In the previous chapter we identified a problem facing managers in respect of selecting risky investment projects. The problem is that individual shareholders may not all see a particular risky project in the same light. While the project may increase the utility of one shareholder, it may reduce that of another. This simply reflects different levels of risk aversion among shareholders.

In theory, discounting the expected cash flows [Σ(possible cash flows × each one's probability of occurrence)] using a discount rate derived from CAPM will overcome this problem. All shareholders, irrespective of their individual attitude to risk (provided that they are risk averse), will be unanimous that projects having a positive NPV when expected cash flows are discounted at a CAPM-derived rate will increase their utility of wealth, and therefore should be undertaken. Note that this theoretical unanimity depends on the assumption that all shareholders hold the shares as part of a well-diversified portfolio.

7.10 Using CAPM to derive discount rates for real investments – the practical problems

There are three factors that need to be estimated for the future in order that the logic of using the basic CAPM to derive the discount rate can be carried into practice. We shall now take a look at each in turn to try to assess the difficulty of arriving at reasonable estimates for them. Really what we shall need to ask ourselves is whether the past is likely to be a useful guide to the future in respect of each of them, and if it seems that it is not, what, if anything, can we use as an alternative?

The risk measure (β)

The risk measure is perhaps the least problematical of the three factors, in that the average betas for ordinary shares of businesses in particular industries do seem to be reasonably stable over time. It certainly seems that the beta of a portfolio, calculated over a five-year period, is a fairly good predictor of the beta of that same portfolio over the subsequent five years (Chi-Cheng, Fuller and Chen 2000; Groenewald and Fraser 2000).

In practical terms, a reasonable approach seems to be to estimate or, more easily, to use some commercial service's estimate of, the betas for several businesses whose principal activity is similar to that in which the particular real investment under consideration lies These individual betas should then be averaged.

The risk-free rate (r_f)

For the risk-free rate we should need to identify a risk-free asset and to make some estimation of its likely future value. While there is strictly no such thing as a risk-free asset, short-dated UK government bills probably are as safe an asset as we can find in the real world. The historical interest rates on these are readily accessible to us. Our problem remains one of estimating likely future rates. Fortunately, government bill rates are fairly stable from year to year, and seem to be predicted with a fair degree of accuracy by the leading economic forecasters. Al-Ali and Arkwright (2000) found that nearly all businesses that use CAPM base the risk-free rate on historic returns on government securities. The current (2005) real (ignoring inflation) return on UK government bills is about 2 per cent p.a.

The expected return on the market portfolio ($E(r_m)$)

The expected return on the market portfolio is something of a problem area. This factor tends to be pretty volatile from year to year and difficult to forecast accurately. We could use an average of returns for the immediate past periods as a surrogate for future expectations but, as was shown by Ibbotson and Sinquefield (1979) on the basis of US data, vastly different results could be obtained depending on which starting point is selected, for example annual rates of 6.5 per cent in the period 1960 to 1978, 4.5 per cent for 1970 to 1978 and 0.9 per cent for 1973 to 1978.

Dimson, Marsh and Staunton (2002) show that the average excess of equity returns over that from treasury bills (the risk premium) was 4.5 per cent p.a. (in real terms) in the UK during the period 1900 to 2001, though it varied from year to year. Dimson *et al.* also show that the equity premium varied significantly on an international basis over this period, as they also do for shorter recent periods.

Probably the best approach to the problem of estimating the risk premium for the market is to base it on this long-term average of about 4.5 per cent p.a. (for UK investments).

CAPM and tax

The point emerged clearly in Chapter 5 that, in practice, we should predict after-corporation-tax cash flows and discount them at an after-corporation-tax cost of capital. This raises the crucial question, in the context of using CAPM to derive the discount rate: is the CAPM derived rate before corporation tax or after corporation tax? The answer is that, as it is normally derived, it is after tax. This is because the expected return on the market portfolio, $E(r_m)$, which is directly used in CAPM, is an after-corporation-tax return. Returns on individual securities, and on portfolios of securities, are calculated using dividends (which are paid out of after-corporation-tax income) and capital gains (which are based on future expectations of dividends). Thus the $E(r_m)$ is an after-corporation-tax rate. It is essential that the risk-free rate (r_f) is also expressed in after-corporation-tax terms.

CAPM and real life

Nothing that we have discussed so far in this chapter should lead us to the conclusion that CAPM (even if we extend it as advocated by Fama and French (see page 200)) is a perfect description of the real relationship between risk and return in the context of marketable securities. Tests of CAPM have found some inconsistency between fact and theory that seems unlikely to be accounted for completely, if at all, by inadequacies in the testing methods.

At the same time the logic of the derivation of CAPM and the reasonableness of the major assumptions on which that derivation is based, plus the general tendency of the evidence to support it, strongly suggest that its basic tenets are justified. It does seem reasonable for us to believe that risk is divided into that which is specific and susceptible to elimination, and that which is systematic and unavoidable. Furthermore, there does seem to be a clear relationship between risk, as measured by beta, and return.

Even if CAPM is less than perfect, its broad approach seems well worth taking into account.

It certainly seems as if those making real investment decisions in practice use CAPM to help them to derive the appropriate discount rate for NPV appraisals. Pike (1996) found that while none of his survey respondents used CAPM in 1975 and 1980, by 1986, 16 per cent reported using it, and by 1992, 20 per cent. Three surveys were conducted in 1997 involving large UK businesses. McLaney, Pointon, Thomas and Tucker (2004) undertook a postal survey of a sample of 193 of the 1292 businesses fully listed on the London Stock Exchange and found that 47 per cent of them used CAPM. Gregory, Rutterford and Zaman (1999) interviewed financial managers of 18 of the largest 100 UK businesses and found that 13 of these (78 per cent) used CAPM. Al-Ali and Arkwright (2000) postal surveyed 73 of the largest 450 UK businesses and found that 85 per cent of the respondents used CAPM. The discrepancy between these findings may well be explained by the sizes of businesses involved. The last two of these three studies involved the very largest UK businesses, whereas the first involved a wider range of sizes of businesses. In general, other research suggests that larger businesses tend to be more sophisticated in their approach to most aspects of business finance.

In the USA, Graham and Harvey (2001) found that 73 per cent of the larger US businesses surveyed in 1999 used CAPM 'always or almost always'. They found larger businesses more likely to use CAPM than smaller ones.

It seems that in both the UK and USA, CAPM is used by nearly all large businesses. It seems likely that this is true in much of the rest of the world as well. The existence of numerous commercial services providing betas adds further weight to the evidence that CAPM is an important approach in practice.

When we come to consider how useful CAPM can be to us in the real investment appraisal context, it is then that our problems arise. As we have just seen, reliably estimating the three factors (five factors in the case of the Fama and French model) to plug into the model to obtain the expected return from an asset is rather difficult. This seems particularly problematical with the expected return on the market portfolio, or at least its proxy, a representative market index.

This probably means that CAPM is severely limited in its operational usefulness to financial managers when they are making real investment decisions. It is not easy to use it in practice to derive the discount rate. However, what is the alternative? If we are not to use CAPM, despite its problems, what are we to do? The answer must be to make some guess at a discount rate, a guess based on no particular logic. In the face of this situation, an approach that is logical, even if problematical, must be preferable.

7.11 Arbitrage pricing model

The fact that tests of CAPM have shown beta not to be a perfect explanation of the relationship between the level of risk and the expected risk premium caused researchers to look at other approaches. One such approach led to the development of the arbitrage pricing model (APM). The logic of this model is that there is not a single explainer of the risk/risk premium relationship, as is suggested by CAPM (three explainers in the Fama and French version), but a number of them. The APM, which was developed by Ross (1976), holds that there are four factors that explain the risk/risk premium relationship of a particular security.

Basically, CAPM says that:

$$E(r_i) = r_f + \lambda \beta_i$$

where λ is the average risk premium $[E(r_m) - r_f]$.

However, APM holds that:

$$E(r_i) = r_f + \lambda_1 \beta_{i1} + \lambda_2 \beta_{i2} + \lambda_3 \beta_{i3} + \lambda_4 \beta_{i4}$$

where λ_1, λ_2, λ_3 and λ_4 are the average risk premiums for each of the four factors in the model, and β_{i1}, β_{i2}, β_{i3} and β_{i4} are measures of the sensitivity of the particular security i to each of the four factors.

The four factors in the APM relate to future macroeconomic factors, including industrial output and levels of inflation. Other versions of the APM have also been developed that have more factors than the four in the Ross version.

Tests conducted on APM appear to show it to be superior to CAPM as an explainer of historical security returns. However, it contains four (or more) factors rather than one (three in the Fama and French version). This limits its practical usefulness (in deriving a discount rate to be applied in NPV analyses) even more than that of CAPM. APM seems not to be used in practice, to any significant extent.

7.12 Diversification within the business

CAPM and the principles from which it is derived tell us that investors, holding securities in efficient portfolios, can eliminate specific risk. The same is true of APM. Evidence suggests that investors typically hold fairly well diversified portfolios.

As the typical individual or institutional investor in securities is diversified (not too exposed to specific risk), there seems no advantage to the shareholder in businesses diversifying their own real investments across industries. Indeed, it has been argued that businesses should take on real investments that they know best how to manage (in other words, within their own area of expertise) and leave the diversification to their shareholders.

This theoretical argument is strongly supported by the available evidence. Walker (2000) looked at takeovers (where one business buys another) in the USA between 1980 and 1996. He found that takeovers that took businesses into areas outside of their expertise caused a loss of shareholder value. Conversely, takeovers that expanded market share or geographical reach in the existing activity led to a gain in shareholder value. This was supported by Lamont and Polk (2002) who found, using data from various US businesses that had diversified, that those businesses that had diversified across different industries tended to have destroyed shareholder value as a result.

Despite the strength of the evidence, the fact remains that many businesses are diversified across industries. This contradiction may arise for one or both of two reasons:

- Managers are unfamiliar with the principles of modern portfolio theory (MPT), and believe that the interests of shareholders are best served by inter-industry diversification. This seems increasingly unlikely to be the case as managers become more familiar with MPT over time.

- Managers are, not unnaturally, concerned with how risk affects themselves. Whereas shareholders tend to hold securities in portfolios, this is not very practical for managers as regards their employments. They usually have only one employment at a time and are thus exposed to both the specific and the systematic risks of their businesses. To individual shareholders, the demise of the business will be unfortunate but not crucial, to the extent that they each hold only perhaps 5 per cent of their wealth in that business. To managers, the failure of their employer will probably be something of a disaster, to the extent of loss of employment.

This second point identifies a possible area of conflict between the best interests of the shareholders and those of the managers, and provides another example of the agency problem.

Summary

Diversification

- Diversification can eliminate specific risk but not systematic risk. In practice:
  - very little diversification (just two or three different investments with equal values of each investment) can lead to large risk reduction;
  - once the portfolio consists of 15 to 20 different investments there is little scope for further risk reduction.
- With sufficient diversification, an 'efficient' portfolio is formed, that is, one with no specific risk.
- Without a borrowing/lending opportunity individuals will have different efficient frontier preferences, depending on their utility for wealth.

Capital asset pricing model (CAPM)

- If there is a borrowing/lending opportunity at a 'risk-free' rate, all individuals will have the same preference as to location on the efficient frontier.
- Individuals will achieve their maximum utility through borrowing or lending.
- CAPM says that the expected return from a risky investment is equal to the risk-free rate (r_f) plus a risk premium.
- The CAPM risk premium equals the average risk premium for all risky assets (the expected level of return for all risky assets (r_m), less the risk-free rate (r_f)) multiplied by the riskiness of the particular asset concerned relative to the average level of risk (β).
- CAPM concerns itself only with systematic risk, that is, it says that there are no rewards (in terms of enhanced returns) for bearing specific risk. This is logical because the latter can be avoided by diversification.
- It is reasonable to look to the risk/return profiles of stock market equities and to use this to determine discount rates for risky projects because:
  - the stock market is a free and efficient market where the prices of assets with known risk/return profiles can be observed;
  - for shareholder-wealth-enhancing businesses, it is through the market price that this goal will substantially be achieved.
- CAPM can be (and in practice is) used by businesses to derive discount rates, particularly for an investment of a type that the business does not usually do, by looking at the betas of businesses that specialise in that type of investment.

- Managers diversifying within the business may represent an agency cost to the shareholders.
- Fama and French found that the basic CAPM is deficient and that it needs to include further risk premiums: one for smaller businesses and another one for businesses with high book to market equity values.

Further reading

Levy and Sarnat (1988) give a clear explanation of the derivation of CAPM and its implications for real investment appraisal. This is also clearly covered by Sharpe (1998). Arnold (2002) is also worth reading on the derivation of CAPM and empirical tests of the model. Copeland, Weston and Shastri (2004) give a rigorous coverage of CAPM and APM and discuss empirical tests of them. Davies, Unni, Draper and Paudyal (1999) provide a practical and readable guide to using CAPM and the Fama and French three-factor model to derive the cost of capital, in a UK context.

Relevant websites

For the very readable Dimson, Marsh and Staunton article on business returns over time, cited in the chapter, see:

http://faculty.london.edu/edimson/Jacf1.pdf

Hemscott's site will allow you to extract lots of information about Stock Exchange listed businesses, including individual business's share prices over time.

www.hemscott.co.uk/hemscott/

REVIEW QUESTIONS

Suggested answers to review questions appear in Appendix 3.

7.1 Modern portfolio theory tends to define risky investments in terms of just two factors: expected returns and variance (or standard deviation) of those expected returns.

What assumptions need to be made about investors and the expected investment returns (one assumption in each case) to justify this 'two factor' approach? Are these assumptions justified in real life?

7.2 'The expected return from a portfolio of securities is the average of the expected returns of the individual securities that make up the portfolio, weighted by the value of the securities in the portfolio.'

'The expected standard deviation of returns from a portfolio of securities is the average of the standard deviations of returns of the individual securities that make up the portfolio, weighted by the value of the securities in the portfolio.'

Are these statements correct?

7.3 What can be said about the portfolio that is represented by any point along the efficient frontier of risky investment portfolios?

7.4 What is meant by 'two-fund separation'?

7.5 'The capital asset pricing model tells us that a security with a beta of 2 will be expected to yield a return twice that of a security whose beta is 1.' Is this statement true?

7.6 What justification can there be for using the rate of return derived from capital (stock) market returns as the discount rate to be applied in the appraisal of a real investment project within a business?

PROBLEMS

Sample answers to problems marked with an asterisk appear in Appendix 4.

(Problems 7.1 to 7.4 are basic-level problems, whereas problem 7.5 is more advanced and may contain some practical complications.)

7.1* What sort of factors relating to a business specialising in operating ferries crossing the English Channel would tend to give rise to (a) specific risk and (b) systematic risk?

7.2 You have overheard the following statement: 'If an investor holds shares in about 20 different businesses all of the risk is eliminated and the portfolio will give a return equal to the risk-free rate.'

Is this statement correct? Explain.

7.3 You have overheard the following statement: 'According to modern portfolio theory, shares are priced on the basis of their systematic riskiness. This means, therefore, that a piece of bad news relating only to a particular business will not affect the market price of that business's shares.'

Is this statement correct? Explain.

7.4 'Recently, equity returns have been lower than the returns available from short-term government securities. Clearly, in such a period, the capital asset pricing model doesn't work because equity returns are supposed to be more than the risk-free rate.'

Is this statement correct? Explain.

7.5* The following are the annual returns for the ordinary shares of Court plc and for a representative equity price index:

Year	Court plc %	Index %
1	19	13
2	(8)	(7)
3	(12)	(13)
4	3	4
5	8	8
6	17	10
7	14	15
8	14	16
9	14	16
10	1	(2)

(a) What is the beta for Court plc's ordinary shares?

(b) If the risk-free rate is 6 per cent p.a. and the expected return for equities generally was 12 per cent p.a., what would be the expected return on Court plc's ordinary shares?

There are both a set of **multiple-choice questions** and **missing-word questions** available on the website. These specifically cover the material contained in this chapter. These can be attempted and graded (with feedback) online.

There are also **three additional problems**, with solutions, that relate to the material covered in this chapter.

Go to **www.pearsoned.co.uk/atrillmclaney** and follow the links.

APPENDIX Derivation of CAPM

In Figure 7.9:

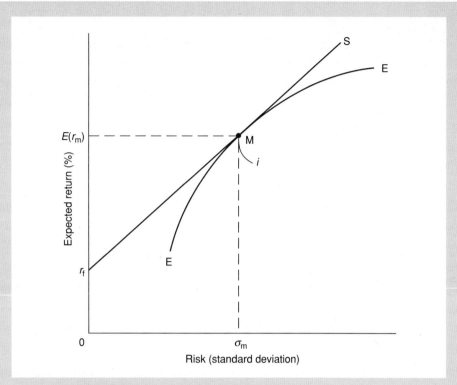

Figure 7.9
The relationship of an individual security *i* with the market portfolio M and the capital market line

The line *i*M is a series of various combinations of individual security *i* and the market portfolio M.

- EE is the *efficient frontier* of risky assets;
- r_f is the risk-free rate;
- r_fS is the efficient frontier of possibilities once the risk-free asset is introduced; and
- *i*M is the risk return profile of various portfolios containing proportions of an individual *inefficient* asset *i* and the *market* portfolio M.

Let α be the proportion of *i* in the portfolio (P) of *i* and M. Then:

$$E(r_P) = \alpha E(r_i) + (1 - \alpha)E(r_m) \tag{A7.1}$$

and

$$\sigma_P = \sqrt{[\alpha^2\sigma_i^2 + (1 - \alpha)^2\sigma_m^2 + 2\alpha(1 - \alpha)\text{Cov}(i, M)]} \tag{A7.2}$$

The slope of *i*M at any point is given by:

$$\frac{dE(r_P)}{d\sigma_P}$$

which equals:

$$\frac{dE(r_P)}{d\alpha} \times \frac{d\alpha}{d\sigma_P}$$

Hence:

$$\frac{dE(r_P)}{d\alpha} = E(r_i) - E(r_m)$$

If we set x to be the expression within the square root sign in equation (A7.2), then:

$$\frac{d\sigma_P}{d\alpha} = \frac{dx}{d\alpha} \times \frac{d\sigma_P}{dx}$$

and

$$\sigma_P = x^{1/2}$$
$$\frac{d\sigma_P}{dx} = \frac{1}{2}x^{-1/2}$$

or

$$\frac{1}{2} \times \frac{1}{\sqrt{[\alpha^2\sigma_i^2 + (1-\alpha)^2\sigma_m^2 + 2\alpha(1-\alpha)\text{Cov}(i, M)]}}$$

$$\frac{dx}{d\alpha} = 2\alpha\sigma_i^2 + 2\alpha\sigma_m^2 - 2\sigma_m + 2\text{Cov}(i, M) - 4\alpha\text{Cov}(i, M)$$

so

$$\frac{dE(r_P)}{d\sigma_P} = [E(r_i) - E(r_m)] \times \frac{2\sqrt{[\alpha^2\sigma_i^2 + (1-\alpha)^2\sigma_m^2 + 2\alpha(1-\alpha)\text{Cov}(i, M)]}}{2\alpha\sigma_i^2 - 2\alpha\sigma_m^2 - 2\sigma_m + 2\text{Cov}(i, M) - 4\alpha\text{Cov}(i, M)}$$

If the market is in equilibrium, then M will already contain the appropriate proportion of i and so the portfolio of i and M will contain no excess i. Thus the only point on iM that would be expected to occur will be M, that is, the point where $\alpha = 0$.

When $\alpha = 0$, $dE(r_P)/d\sigma_P$ (above) reduces to:

$$[E(r_i) - E(r_m)] \times \frac{\sigma_m}{\text{Cov}(i, M) - \sigma_m^2} \qquad (A7.3)$$

At M, the chord iM is tangential to (has the same slope as) the capital market line r_fS. The slope of r_fS is $[E(r_m) - r_f]/\sigma_m$. Equating this with (A7.3) above and simplifying gives:

$$E(r_i) = r_f + [E(r_m) - r_f]\frac{\text{Cov}(i, M)}{\sigma_m^2}$$

or

$$E(r_i) = r_f + [E(r_m) - r_f]\beta$$

where $\beta = \text{Cov}(i, M)/\sigma_m^2$. This is the CAPM, which says, in effect, that the expected return from a risky asset depends on the risk-free rate of interest, the expected returns from the market portfolio, and the degree of correlation between the risky asset's returns and those of the market portfolio.

PART 3

Financing decisions

Investment requires finance, and there are many sources available. This part of the book considers how decisions are made on the most appropriate sources to finance particular investments.

Chapter 8 reviews the principal sources of finance and their particular features. The role and effectiveness of the market for finance is discussed in Chapter 9. Here, the theory that share prices always reflect the economic reality is examined in some detail. In Chapter 10, assessing the cost of finance is examined. The relationship between the investment and the financing decision is also considered. Chapter 11 is concerned with the extent to which it is likely to be beneficial for businesses to borrow funds as an alternative to raising them from shareholders. Raising funds from shareholders can be done in broadly two possible ways. These are ploughing back past profits, instead of paying them to shareholders as dividends, and raising fresh money from shareholders by asking them to buy new shares. Chapter 12 considers which of these two approaches, if either, is likely to be the more appropriate.

Chapter 8

Sources of long-term finance

Objectives   In this chapter we shall deal with the following:

→ the major issues to consider in respect of each type of financing

→ equity financing

→ methods of raising equity finance

→ preference shares

→ loan stocks and debentures

→ convertible loan stocks

→ warrants

→ term loans

→ the use of finance leasing

→ financial grants from public funds and their importance

→ the attitude that businesses should take to deciding on their financing method

8.1 Introduction

In previous chapters we have seen that businesses raise their long-term finance either from equity shareholders or from borrowings. Within each type of financing (equity or borrowing) are several subtypes. In fact, one fairly important financing method → (convertible loan stock) has elements of both equity and borrowing.

In this chapter we shall consider the various subtypes. Given the financial objective of maximisation of shareholders' wealth we shall consider each of them in the context of how they will affect the interests of existing equity shareholders. We shall also try to assess their attractions to potential investors.

The primary capital market

We shall in fact be considering the capital market in its primary function, as a market for *new* capital. The primary capital market does not reside in a single location. It is a somewhat nebulous market; in fact, any point of contact between a supplier and a user of capital is part of the primary capital market. In the UK this includes the London Stock Exchange (LSE) which, as well as its more familiar role as probably the most important part of the secondary market (that is, the market for 'second-hand' shares and loan stocks), is also a very important sector of the primary market. However, the primary market also includes a large number of other institutions and organisations. We shall be looking at the secondary capital market in Chapter 9.

An important financial source in the modern UK is grants given by the government and the European Union. We shall therefore be considering these in broad terms.

The factors

From the point of view of the business and its existing shareholders there are several important factors relating to any particular source of new finance. These include:

- the administrative and legal costs of raising the finance;
- the cost of servicing the finance, for example interest payments;
- the level of obligation to make interest or similar payments;
- the level of obligation to repay the finance;
- the tax deductibility of costs related to the finance; and
- the effect of the new finance on the level of control of the business by its existing shareholders and on their freedom of action.

To the supplier of new finance to the business, the following are likely to be important factors:

- the level of return that is expected by investors;
- the level of risk attaching to the expected returns;
- the potential for liquidating the investment either through direct repayment by the business or by using the secondary market;
- the personal tax position of investors in relation to returns from their investment; and
- the degree of control or influence over the business's affairs that the investor is likely to acquire as a consequence of investing.

In this chapter we shall assess each of the financial sources reviewed, in the context of these factors. We should note that those relating to suppliers of finance are of more than passing interest to the business's financial managers and existing shareholders. Those factors have a considerable bearing on the attractiveness of any particular type of finance (as an investment) and therefore on the likely success of an attempt to raise new finance in that particular way.

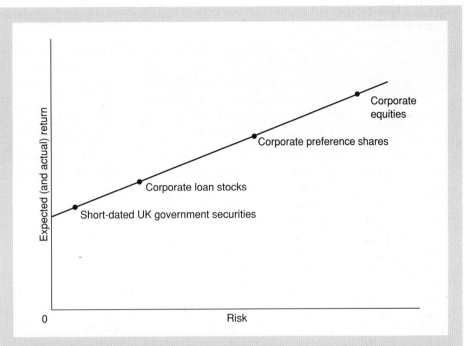

Figure 8.1
The risk/return relationship for various types of security

The more risky the security the higher will be the expected return. Thus, for example, short-dated UK government securities, which tend to engender very low risk, command only a very small expected risk premium over the risk-free rate. The shares of commercial businesses (corporate equities) tend to command quite a high expected risk premium.

Risk and return

Both intuition and the results of several research studies suggest that investors expect, and actually get, on average, higher returns where higher risk is involved. The relationship appears to be something like that depicted in Figure 8.1.

For the business, the position is the opposite of that of the investors: sources of finance that are relatively risky tend to be cheap in terms of servicing cost; safe sources tend to be expensive. The level of returns required by secured lenders is relatively low but the existence of such loans represents, as we shall see, a potential threat to the welfare of the shareholders. Equity investors expect high returns, but issuing additional ordinary shares does not tend greatly to increase the risk borne by the original shareholders.

8.2 Ordinary (equity) capital

Equity financing is overwhelmingly the most important in the UK corporate private sector. Both as regards the cumulative financing arrangements and the raising of new capital, equity finance has tended to be by far the largest source. Equities seem to attract a wide range of investors, both private and institutional. In recent years, new issues by LSE listed businesses have tended towards loan finance (see Table 8.1). Nevertheless, equity finance dominates most businesses' financing. It should be remembered that most equity finance comes from businesses retaining profit (rather

Table 8.1 New security issues, net of redemptions, by LSE listed UK non-financial businesses (by type of security)

Year	Total issues	Ordinary shares	Preference shares	Percentage of issues that were:				
				Loans				
				Total	Convertible	Other	Issued in sterling	Issued in other currencies
	(£m)							
1991	14 570	67	3	30	6	24	28	2
1992	8 239	62	3	35	1	34	30	5
1993	16 283	78	3	19	6	13	15	4
1994	13 467	74	3	23	8	15	21	2
1995	15 903	48	8	44	6	38	24	20
1996	13 201	58	(1)	43	(4)	47	29	14
1997	16 941	32	(2)	70	2	68	34	36
1998	14 563	29	(4)	75	1	74	35	40
1999	26 224	26	0	74	6	68	44	30
2000	39 229	41	0	59	0	59	15	44
2001	33 782	44	0	56	4	52	35	21
2002	20 427	60	0	40	n/a	n/a	n/a	n/a

Note that the detailed information on loan stocks is not available after 2001.

Source: Adapted from Bank of England (2005), *Capital Issues and Redemptions*, table 23.13.

than paying it all out as dividends), not from issues of new shares. This is a point that Table 8.1 does not capture.

There are three striking features of Table 8.1:

- New issues of loan finance have represented the majority of new issues in most years since 1997. This probably reflects a lowering of interest rates from the late 1990s.

- Preference shares as a source of new finance, though never very significant in recent years, have most recently become a negligible source. Reasons for this are discussed later in the chapter in section 8.4.

- The massive increase in the proportion of borrowings made in non-sterling currencies since 1995. This probably reflects a tendency for interest rates to be lower in many overseas countries, for example the USA and EU member states. It may also reflect an increasing tendency of businesses to take a more international perspective on both investing and fund-raising. We shall look in detail at reasons for this increasing internationalisation in Chapter 15.

The nature of equity

The ordinary shareholders are the owners of the business, who, through the voting rights attaching to their shares, exercise ultimate control over it.

As owners of the business, the ordinary shareholders bear the greatest risk. If the business trades unsuccessfully, the ordinary shareholders are the first to suffer in terms of lack of dividends and, probably, declines in the market value of their shares. If the business collapses (it is put into liquidation) it is the ordinary shareholders who will be at the bottom of the list with a claim for repayment of their investment.

On the other hand, the fruits of the business's success principally benefit ordinary shareholders; other participants – labour, lenders, suppliers and so forth – tend to earn returns not related to the business's success. Thus, once the claims of these other participants are met, the balance accrues to the ordinary shareholders.

Nominal values

When the business is first established, a decision is made about how much equity finance (the law requires that there is some) it wishes to raise and into how many shares this is to be divided. If, for example, the decision is that £1m needs to be raised, this could be in the form of two shares of nominal value (or par value) £500 000 each, 1m shares of £1 each, 200 000 shares of £5 each, or (more likely) 2m shares of £0.50 each. Which of these, or of any one of the almost infinite number of other possibilities, is decided upon, is a matter of the judgement of the promoters of the business.

In making this decision, probably the major factor is marketability. Most investors would not find shares of very large nominal value very attractive, as this would make it difficult to set aside an amount of money to be exactly invested in the business. If the shares were of nominal value £50, an investor who wishes to invest £275 could not do so. The choice would be between five or six shares. Even if the shares were £10 nominal value the investor could get fairly close to the target of £275 (27 or 28 shares). It seems to be believed that large nominal value shares are not as readily marketable as those of smaller denomination. Certainly large-denomination shares are very rare in practice. Few ordinary shares have nominal values larger than £1 each.

Once the business has invested its capital and has started to trade, the market value of its ordinary shares will probably move away from the nominal value, as a result of market forces. Further issues of ordinary shares will normally be priced by reference to current market prices: that is, businesses will seek to issue further ordinary shares at the highest price that the market will bear. In fact, nominal values cease to have much significance once the business has started trading. This is evidenced by the fact that, in the USA, which has similar corporate financing arrangements to those encountered in the UK, shares of no par (or nominal) value are not unusual.

The decision on nominal value is not irrevocable; businesses may subsequently *split* or *consolidate* nominal values. For example, a business whose ordinary shares have a nominal value of £1 each may split them into shares of £0.50 each. In practice this is easily accomplished, and culminates in each ordinary shareholder being sent a replacement share certificate showing twice as many £0.50 shares as the investor previously had £1 ones. As we have seen, the objective of such a move seems to be to reduce the unit price to make the shares more marketable.*

Enterprise Inns plc, the UK public house operator, had a two-for-one share split in January 2004. The objective was to increase the marketability of the shares.

Investment ratios

Several ratios are used by, or at least made available to, investors that give measures of some aspects of the ordinary shares' performance. For leading businesses, these

---

* If the shares are, in fact, rendered more attractive by splitting, logically the split would increase the market value of a particular investor's holding. The evidence seems to indicate that this does not happen in practice. See Copeland, Weston and Shastri (2004) for a discussion of some tests relating to this point.

are published daily, together with the daily share price, by most of the more serious national newspapers. The three principal ratios (which were introduced in Chapter 3) are described below.

Price/earnings ratio (P/E)

Here the current price per share is expressed as a multiple of the earnings per share (net, after-tax profit available for ordinary shares divided by the number of ordinary shares that the business has issued). The profit figure used in the calculation of the ratio is that for the most recently reported year.

Shares with large P/Es are those that are highly priced for their historical earnings level, indicating the market's faith in the future of the business and its ability to grow.

Dividend yield (DY)

The dividend yield expresses the gross equivalent of dividends per share paid in the most recent year as a percentage of the current market price. It gives some idea of the rate of return that the dividend represents. This may be compared with returns from other investments to try to assess the particular share. To the extent that, over a period, capital gains and losses may be as important in amount per share as dividends, DY is (to say the least) an incomplete measure of the benefits of ownership of the share.

Dividend cover (DC)

Dividend cover expresses the earnings per share, after prior claims have been satisfied, as a multiple of the actual dividend per share paid from those earnings. It gives some indication of the extent to which the business's profits are paid out as dividends and to what extent they are ploughed back into the business.

Much of what we have already discussed in this book on such matters as the importance of risk calls into question the value of relying on the above ratios. It must be said, however, that such ratios are widely available to investors and, therefore, are probably used by them. We shall discuss the issues relating to the choice of dividend levels in Chapter 12.

Factors for the business to consider on equity financing

Issue costs

Issue costs vary considerably according to the method used to raise the new equity and the amount raised, ranging from virtually nothing up to about 15 per cent of the new finance raised (Jenkinson 1990). We shall consider this in more detail when dealing with the various methods in the following section.

Servicing costs

Equity holders expect relatively high returns in terms of capital appreciation and dividends. Dividends represent an explicit cost. The capital appreciation results from the fact that sooner or later profits not paid out as dividends are expected to end up in the hands of the shareholders, even if they have to wait until the business is liquidated before this happens. Thus, one way or another, the entire profits will eventually be paid out to shareholders.

Obligation to pay dividends

Dividend payment levels are a question of the discretion of directors and financial managers. As we saw under 'Servicing costs' above, ultimately the dividend must be paid, but shareholders cannot directly force payment of a particular level of dividend in a particular year.

Obligation to redeem the investment

There is no such obligation unless (or until) the business is liquidated. Because of this, and to some extent because of the flexibility on dividend levels, finance provided by ordinary shareholders does not normally impose a legally enforceable cash flow obligation on the business.

Tax deductibility of dividends

In contrast to the servicing of virtually all other types of finance, dividends are not tax deductible in arriving at the business's corporation tax liability. This tends to make dividends more expensive than a similar gross equivalent loan interest rate.

Effect on control and freedom of action

Where new equity finance is raised from other than the existing shareholders in the same proportions as their original investment, voting power will shift to some extent, perhaps to a large extent, and possibly with it control of the business. This is not necessarily a feature of all increases in equity financing. In fact, the two most important means of raising equity finance for most businesses, retained profits and rights issues (each discussed below), generally avoid this problem.

It is doubtful whether this shift in power is really of much concern to typical ordinary shareholders, since they seem not to use their votes in any case. The annual general meetings of most businesses are characterised by a distinct absence of most of those entitled to be present and to vote. Control is a factor that is more likely to be of concern to ordinary shareholders in small businesses, a point that we shall discuss in Chapter 16.

Factors for the potential investor to consider on equity financing

Level of return

The level of return on equity financing would be expected to be higher than the level of return associated with 'safe' investments such as UK government securities. This has historically been the case, with real returns from UK equities averaging around 7 per cent p.a. from 1900 to 2001 (Dimson, Marsh and Staunton 2002), contrasting with an average real return from government securities of about 3 per cent p.a. over the same period. Compared with other types of security, ordinary shares have on average provided the best, though often an incomplete, hedge against inflation.

Equities provide an opportunity to make investments where returns are related fairly directly to commercial success. Direct ownership of the assets of a business normally requires investors to spend time managing those assets. It normally also exposes investors to unlimited liability. However, equities enable delegation of day-to-day management to the directors and protect the investors' other assets.

Riskiness of returns

Returns, in terms both of capital gains and of dividends, are not certain by any means. Negative returns are very common over short periods, though, historically, above-average positive returns in other periods compensate for these. A period of adverse trading could, in theory, cause the value of a particular business's ordinary shares to fall to zero, losing the shareholder the entire amount invested in those shares. Extensive losses of value of the shares of particular businesses are by no means rare.

Ease of liquidating the investment

Typically, when investors take up part of an issue of new equity of a business, they have no particular thoughts of the business ever repaying that investment. However, the average investor would be reluctant to take up equities unless it were clear that there would be the opportunity to liquidate the investment in some other way. This is where the secondary capital market comes in. It is clearly in the interest of the business to have its ordinary shares regularly traded on a recognised stock exchange so that the facility to liquidate the investment exists.

Equities and personal tax

In the UK, dividends are taxed as *income* in the hands of the shareholder, at marginal rates up to 40 per cent. Capital appreciation is subject to capital gains tax at rates similar to those applied to income.

Degree of control

Ordinary shares typically carry voting rights. This tends not to be too important to the typical shareholder but it does put him or her in a position, perhaps acting together with other shareholders, to apply pressure to the business's senior management on any matter of concern.

8.3 Methods of raising additional equity finance

There are broadly three ways of raising new equity finance. These are: retaining profits rather than paying them out as dividends; making issues of new shares to existing shareholders; and making new share issues to the public. Evidence shows, despite some fluctuation from year to year, the clear dominance of retained profits over other methods. Over recent years, new shares issued to existing shareholders as rights issues have tended to be more important, in terms of value, than issues to the general public (Bank of England).

Retained profit

It may seem surprising to mention retained profits as a source of new equity finance. However, profits certainly lead to a net increase in funds, and retaining these, or part of them, rather than paying them out as dividends, is in effect a way of raising finance. After all, if the full profit were paid out as dividends and then shareholders bought new shares with their dividend money, this would have much the same effect as retaining the funds in the first place.

In fact, retained profits are a very important source of finance, probably accounting for about half of all the long-term finance raised by UK businesses over recent years.

A free source of finance?

At first sight, retained profits seem to be a source that costs nothing to service. A moment's reflection, however, shows this not to be true. From the ordinary shareholder's point of view, there is a clear opportunity cost in that, if cash dividends were paid, that cash could be invested in some income-yielding way. As the obvious comparison is an investment in equities of similar risk to those of the business under consideration, retained profits logically have a cost similar to that of the original ordinary shares.

Bonus shares

In much the same way as businesses can and do split nominal values, they can convert retained profits into ordinary shares, which are then distributed to existing shareholders free of charge.

Example 8.1

The following is a highly abbreviated balance sheet of a business that has been trading for some period of time and which has retained at least some of its profits.

Balance sheet as at 30 June 2006

Sources of finance (claims)	£m	Uses of finance (investments)	£m
Ordinary shares of £1 each	4	Non-current assets	5
Retained profits	3		
Equity	7	Working capital	4
Long-term loan	2		
	9		9

It is open to the business, with only the minimum of administrative difficulty, to convert all or part of the £3m retained profits to shares, which may be issued pro rata to the ordinary shareholders. Let us assume for our example that £2m of the £3m retained profits is so converted. The revised balance sheet would be:

Balance sheet as at 30 June 2006

Sources of finance (claims)	£m	Uses of finance (investments)	£m
Ordinary shares of £1 each	6	Non-current assets	5
Retained profits	1		
Equity	7	Working capital	4
Long-term loan	2		
	9		9

Note that the conversion of retained profits into shares leaves the uses of funds totally unaffected. It also leaves completely untouched the equity figure: in other words, the contribution of the ordinary shareholders is not altered by the bonus issue. All that will occur is that for every two shares held before the bonus issue, the shareholder will hold three after it. As with splitting, the economic effect of a **bonus issue** should logically be zero. If in this example the price of an ordinary share were £1.80 before the issue, it should be £1.20 (that is, £1.80 × $\frac{2}{3}$) afterwards.

If they have no economic consequences, why do businesses make bonus issues? Do directors believe that shareholders will be fooled into thinking that they have got something for nothing? If so, the evidence (discussed in Chapter 9) suggests that those directors are wrong. Possibly, bonus issues are intended to transmit information. Bonus issues are sometimes thought to indicate a confidence on the part of management in the investments that it has made. A third possible reason is, as with splits, simply to reduce the unit price of the shares to (what management may regard as) a more marketable size.

Clinton Cards plc, the UK greetings card business, made a two-for-one bonus share issue in 2003 in an attempt to increase the liquidity of its shares.

Factors to consider in respect of raising finance by retention of profits

Does dividend policy affect the net wealth of the shareholder?

If it does, then retaining one proportion of the profit, rather than another proportion, will have some effect on the sum of the dividend paid and the ex-dividend price of the share, that is, on the net wealth of the shareholders. We shall review the debate and evidence on this topic in some detail in Chapter 12.

No issue costs

Other means of raising additional equity have explicit issue costs not applicable to retained profits.

Profits are uncertain

Once the need for raising further finance has been identified, there is no guarantee that sufficiently large profits will subsequently be made to meet the requirements. On the other hand, once the funds have been generated from profits, their existence is certain and their retention just a matter of a management decision. This latter point contrasts with other methods of raising equity finance.

No dilution of control

Retaining profits does not alter the voting strength of any individual shareholder.

Rights issues

Rights issues are offers to existing ordinary shareholders to take up additional shares, for cash, at a price usually significantly below the current market price of already existing shares. In November 2004, **Prudential plc**, the UK insurance business, made a 1-for-6 rights issue that raised £1 billion.

Rights issues have generally represented by far the most important method of raising new equity finance in the UK, after retained profits, over recent years. In fact, the law requires, in normal circumstances, that any new equity issue must be offered first to existing shareholders in proportion to their individual shareholdings. Shareholders can agree to waive these 'pre-emption rights', and some businesses ask their shareholders to agree to do so. **J. D. Wetherspoon plc**, a business that manages a number of public houses in the UK, announced in its 2004 annual report its intention to ask its shareholders to agree to waive their pre-emption rights. The existence of pre-emption rights is sometimes seen as a restriction on the ability of directors to take advantage of some other source of equity finance.

Once the business has decided on the amount of finance it needs and has set a price, it simply offers shares to existing shareholders. The number of new shares that any individual shareholder has the *right* to take up depends on the number of shares already owned.

If the shareholder wishes not to take up this entitlement, the rights may be sold to someone who does wish to take them up (irrespective of whether or not the buyer is an existing shareholder). Usually rights may be sold in the capital market. Their buyer acquires the same right to take up the shares as did the shareholder to whom they were originally granted.

Example 8.2	A business has in existence 4m ordinary £1 shares whose current market price is £1.80 each. It wishes to raise £1.2m by a rights issue at £1.50 per share. The number of shares to be issued will be £1.2m/£1.5, that is, 800 000 shares. These will, therefore, be offered on a 1-for-5 basis to existing ordinary shareholders. For example, a shareholder owning 200 shares will be given the right to buy an additional 40 shares.

In Example 8.2, the value of the entire equity of the business immediately before the rights issue was £7.2m (4m × £1.80). Immediately following the issue, this should rise by £1.2m (the amount of *new* money raised). The total value of the equity should then be £8.4m (4m + 800 000 = 4.8m shares) or £1.75 per share (£8.4m/4.8m).

This is the price at which the shares should trade immediately following the rights issue, assuming that everything else remains equal. Thus the value of the right to buy one share is likely to be £0.25, that is, the difference between the rights issue price and the ex-rights price. Market forces would tend to ensure that this is broadly true, since if it were not, it would imply that it is possible to make abnormal gains by buying rights, on the one hand, or that no one would be prepared to buy them, on the other.

Let us consider a shareholder who starts with 100 ordinary shares and as a result is offered 20 new shares in the rights issue. This person has three choices:

- Pay £30 (20 × £1.50) to the business and take up the entitlement. If this is done, the value of the shareholding will go up from £180 (100 × £1.80) to £210 (120 × £1.75). This increase of £30 is exactly the amount that has just been paid to take up the rights, so the rights issue leaves the shareholder neither richer nor poorer than before.

- Sell the rights, presumably for £5 (20 × £0.25). This would leave a shareholding worth £175 (100 × £1.75) and £5 in cash, a total value of £180, once again leaving the shareholder neither better nor worse off.

- Allow the rights to lapse, in which case the value of the shareholding will fall from £180 to £175. Thus the shareholder will lose wealth by failing to act either to take up the rights or to sell them within the time allowed by the business to do so. In practice, however, the business will typically sell the rights, on the shareholder's behalf, and pass on the proceeds, if the rights look likely to lapse.

The importance of the rights issue price

How important is it that the business gets the price right? In the above example, would existing ordinary shareholders be worse off, better off or unaffected if the rights issue price had been, say, £1 per share instead of £1.50?

Obviously, to raise £1.2m would require issuing 1.2m shares if the issue price were to be £1 each. The value of the equity immediately following the issue would still be

£8.4m, but the market price per share would be £1.615 (£8.4m/5.2m). This would put the value of the rights at £0.615 per share. Let us again consider the position of a holder of 100 of the original ordinary shares who chooses to take up the entitlement of 30 new shares (remember that 1.2m new shares will now have to be offered to the holders of the original 4m shares, that is, 3-for-10).

The value of our shareholder's increased holding will be £210. Again the increase from the original value of the holding (£180) is entirely accounted for by the cash that our shareholder has had to pay. Thus the wealth of the shareholder is not affected by the price at which the rights issue is made. It can equally well be shown that the shareholder who chooses to sell the rights will similarly be unaffected.

Businesses typically price rights issues at about 21 per cent below the current pre-rights share price (Armitage 2000). As we have seen, doing this should not really advantage the shareholder. However, since allowing the rights to lapse disadvantages shareholders, a rights issue priced at a discount puts pressure on them either to take up the issue or to sell the rights. In either case this is likely to lead to the issue being successful in terms of all of the shares being taken up and the desired amount of money being raised.

Another reason for pricing rights issues at a discount is to try to ensure that any possible fall in the market price of the shares already issued, between the date of the announcement of the rights issue (and of the rights issue price) and the date of the issue, still leaves the rights issue price below the market price. If, on the issue date, shares were cheaper to buy in the capital market than by taking up the rights, the issue would almost certainly fail.

Factors to consider in respect of rights issues

Rights issues are a relatively cheap way of raising equity finance

It is estimated that the issue costs average 5.8 per cent of the funds raised (Armitage 2000). This estimation was based on an examination of a large number of UK rights issues during the period 1985 to 1996. Note that many of these issue costs are fixed, that is, they are the same irrespective of the amount of funds raised by the issue. As a result, the cost (as a proportion of the value of the funds raised) will be more for smaller issues and less for larger ones.

Pricing of issues is not a critical factor

As we have seen, shareholders who either sell or take up their rights are left in more or less the same position as regards wealth irrespective of the issue price.

Rights issues are fairly certain

It is rare in practice for a rights issue to fail. This is an important factor since many of the issue costs are committed in advance and are lost if the issue fails.

Existing shareholders are forced either to increase or to liquidate part of their shareholding

To shareholders given rights to take up additional shares, doing nothing is not a sensible option. To preserve their wealth they must either take up the shares, and so increase their investment in the business, or sell the rights, thus in effect liquidating part of their investment. Neither of these may be attractive to some shareholders. This could cause the shares of businesses that make frequent rights issues to become unpopular, thus adversely affecting their market value.

It is, of course, always open to an individual shareholder to sell some of the rights to obtain sufficient cash to take up the rest. This still requires action on the shareholder's part. In practice the vast majority of rights are taken up by existing shareholders (90 per cent on average, according to the Wilson Committee (1980)). Ninety-two per cent of the rights issue shares of **Prudential plc** (referred to above) were taken up by the shareholders.

Dilution of control

Dilution of control need not occur with rights issues as existing shareholders are given the opportunity, usually accepted, to retain the same voting power after the issue as they had before.

Some shareholders may not have the funds available to take up the rights issue

This can be a particular problem with businesses whose shares are not listed on a recognised stock exchange, since it may be difficult to sell the rights to a third party.

Equity issues to the public

Equity issues to the public are rare in practice and do not account for a very large proportion of total equity fund-raising – probably less than 10 per cent of all new equity finance in the UK over recent years. While there are not many such issues, those that do occur tend to be large in size. They seem to occur most with businesses that have newly been listed by a stock market for a quotation and dealing, that is, those making their first significant public issue of ordinary shares, known as their initial public offering (IPO). Seasoned equity offerings (that is, issues of shares of businesses that have been stock market listed for some time) are less common.

Technically there are two ways of making public issues:

- The issuing business can sell the shares to an *issuing house*, usually a merchant bank that specialises in such work. The issuing house then sells the shares to the public. This is known as an *offer for sale*.

- The issuing business sells the shares direct to the public. Often such businesses are advised by a merchant bank on such matters as the pricing of the issue. Here the offer is known as an *offer by prospectus*.

Irrespective of which of these methods is used, the general procedure is the same. Basically, the shares are advertised in newspapers and/or elsewhere. The advertisement is required by law and by the regulations of the LSE, to give a large volume of detailed information. This is very expensive to prepare, including, as it does, reports from independent accountants and such like. The objective of including such voluminous and detailed information is to protect the public from the type of sloppy and sometimes fraudulent claims that were made by businesses' managements in the earlier days of the LSE.

There is a variation on the issuing house selling the shares to the general public by advertising. This is known as a 'placing'. Here the issuing house 'places' (that is, sells) the shares with several of its own clients, such as insurance businesses and pension funds. This is still a public issue, but here 'public' does not have its usual meaning. The advantage to the business raising the equity finance is that certain costs, such as adverts and underwriting (see above) are saved. There is still the need to provide the extensive and costly information of a more traditional public issue, however. In October 2001, **Somerfield plc**, the supermarket business, raised £51m through a placing.

Smaller businesses may not wish to be subjected to the rigours, and the accompanying cost, of obtaining a full LSE listing for their shares. For such businesses the LSE provides a separate market in which shares may be traded. This is the *Alternative Investment Market (AIM)*, which tends to cater for businesses whose shares have a total market value of around £20m, though many are either much larger or much smaller than this.

The fact that a particular business's securities are traded in the AIM should warn potential investors that the requirements to obtain, and retain, a full listing for its shares have not been met, though less rigorous ones will have been complied with. This implies that such securities represent a more hazardous investment than would those of a similar business that had obtained a full listing.

AIM has been seen as a step towards a business obtaining a full listing. Recently, however, several fully listed businesses have transferred their listing to AIM. The objective has clearly been to save the larger annual fee for being fully listed and, perhaps, to avoid the cost and inconvenience of meeting the more stringent requirements of a full listing.

AIM is discussed in greater detail, in the context of smaller businesses, in Chapter 16.

Pricing of issues to the public

In contrast with the position of rights issues, the pricing of issues of ordinary shares to the public is of vital importance to existing shareholders.

If the new shares are priced at a discount on the value of the existing shares, unless existing holders were to take up such a number of new shares as would retain for them the same proportion of the total as they had before, it would be the equivalent of a shareholder allowing all or some of the allotment in a rights issue to lapse (see the example on page 225 for the effect of this).

Since issues to the public tend to occur where the business is significantly extending its equity base, it is most unlikely that an existing shareholder will be able to take up sufficient new shares to avoid being penalised by an issue at a discount.

It is a matter of judgement as to how well the issue price strikes the balance between attracting the maximum amount of cash per share on the one hand, and avoiding a very costly failure to raise the required funds, after spending large amounts on promoting the issue, on the other. There are two ways in which the pricing problem can be mitigated. One is to have the shares underwritten. For a fee, underwriters will guarantee to take up shares for which the public do not subscribe. This ensures the success of the issue. The underwriters' fee or commission is fixed by them according to how many shares they are underwriting, the offer price and, naturally, how high the underwriter believes the probability to be that some shares will not be taken up by the public. Underwriters are, in effect, insurers. Most issues to the public are underwritten. Underwriting costs tend to be in the order of 2 per cent of the capital raised.

The second way of dealing with the pricing problem is for the shares to be open to tender. This is much like an auction where the shares are sold to the highest bidders, usually subject to a pre-stated reserve price (that is, a price below which offers will not be accepted). When all of the offers have been received (the closing date for offers has been reached), the business or the issuing house assesses what is the highest price at which all of the shares could be issued. This can probably best be explained with a simple example.

Example 8.3

A business wishes to issue 10m shares by tender. After publishing the advertisement in the required form it receives offers as follows:

1m	shares at £5.00 each (that is, offers for 1 million shares at £5 per share)
1m	shares at £4.50 each
2m	shares at £4.00 each
2m	shares at £3.50 each
3m	shares at £3.00 each
5m	shares at £2.50 each
10m	shares at £2.00 each

The highest price at which all of the 10m shares could be issued yet each offerer be required to pay the same price per share is £2.50. This is known as the striking price, and is the price at which all 10m shares will be issued: 9m to those who offered above £2.50 and the other 1m to some of those who offered £2.50 exactly. Note that all of the 10m shares are issued at £2.50 each.

Issues by tender seem to be increasingly popular. There have been several of them in recent years.

Share issues in depressed markets

It is argued by some observers that it would be unfair to sell new shares to the public when either capital market prices generally, or the shares in a particular business, are depressed. This is because it would allow outsiders to buy shares 'on the cheap' at the expense of the existing shareholders. If a rights issue were made under such circumstances, it is claimed, this advantage would go only to existing shareholders.

This seems an illogical view in the light of the evidence on capital market efficiency, which will be reviewed in the next chapter. Such evidence strongly supports the hypothesis that the current market price of a share is the consensus view of its value at the time. There is no reason to believe that because it has recently fallen in value it is about to increase, any more than it should cause us to feel that it is about to suffer a further decrease in value or to remain static.

Factors to consider in respect of equity issues to the public

Issue costs

Issue costs are very large, estimated at 12.5 per cent of the proceeds for a £5m issue in the UK (Jenkinson 1990). This compares with 4 per cent for a rights issue and zero cost for retained profits. Lee, Lockhead, Ritter and Zhao (1996) estimate that the issue costs for an IPO in the USA average 11 per cent of the funds raised, and that those for a public issue of seasoned shares average 7 per cent.

Most issue costs are fixed, irrespective of the size of the issue, so they can be proportionately more costly, as a percentage of the funds raised, for a small issue.

At these levels of issue cost, the effect on the cost of equity is profound. We saw in Chapter 7 that the average cost of equity over the twentieth century averaged about

7 per cent p.a. This means £7 for each £100 of equity. If issue costs are, say, £10, the net proceeds are only £90. Thus the effective cost of equity would be £7/£90, or 7.78 per cent. This probably explains the small number of public issues and why they tend mainly to occur in cases where neither the rights issue nor retained profits option exists.

Uncertainty of public issues

The relative certainty of success associated with rights issues does not exist with issues to the public. As we have discussed already, the use of underwriters and/or issuing by tender can overcome the problem to some extent, but at a cost.

Pricing of issues is critical

If the interests of existing ordinary shareholders are to be protected, the pricing question is one of vital importance. Issuing by tender does, to some extent, overcome the problem. Capital market efficiency suggests that offers will rationally and fairly price the issue.

Dilution of control

Clearly, dilution of control for existing shareholders is going to occur with issues to the public. It is probably the price that the original shareholders have to pay to obtain access to additional equity finance when rights issues and retained profits are not possibilities.

8.4 Preference shares

Preference shares form part of the risk-bearing ownership of the business, but preference shareholders usually have the right to the first slice (of predetermined size) of any dividend paid. As a result, they are less risky, from an investor's perspective, than are ordinary shares. Investors' expectations of returns from preference shares are therefore lower than expectations from ordinary shares in the same business. Historically, preference shares have been a significant source of corporate finance.

More recently they seem to have fallen from favour and have tended to be of very little importance as a source of new finance (see Table 8.1, page 218). Many businesses are still partly financed by preference shares issued some years ago, however.

Preference shares are usually *cumulative*. This means that if the preference dividend is not met in full in any particular year, ordinary shareholders are not entitled to dividends in any future year until preference share dividends have been brought up to date.

Nominal value

Preference shares have a nominal value but, as with ordinary shares, its size is not usually of much importance. However, the preference dividend is usually expressed as a percentage of the nominal value (though it need not be).

Investment ratios

Dividend yield and dividend cover are important ratios to the preference shareholder. Dividends would normally be by far the most significant part of the preference shares' returns, so the effective rate and its security are important matters.

Factors for the business to consider on preference share financing

Issue costs
Issue costs are similar to those associated with raising new equity finance and similarly variable with the method used.

Servicing costs
Servicing costs tend to be lower than those relating to ordinary shares, since preference shares expose their holder to rather less risk.

Obligation to pay dividends
Preference shares do not impose on the business the legal obligation to pay a dividend. They do, however, impose the obligation to meet the preference dividend before any dividend may be paid to ordinary shareholders. Where preference shares are cumulative, arrears of unpaid preference dividends must also be made good before ordinary shareholders may participate in dividends. In practice, despite the lack of legal obligation, businesses seem reluctant to miss paying a preference dividend.

Obligation to redeem preference shares
Some preference shares are expressly issued as redeemable, and where this is the case the business must be mindful of the necessity to finance this redemption. By no means are all preference shares redeemable, and where they are not, the position is similar to that of ordinary shares. Where preference shareholders cannot demand redemption, this type of financing is a relatively safe one from the ordinary shareholders' viewpoint.

Tax deductibility of preference share dividends
The UK tax system does not distinguish between ordinary and preference dividends, so preference dividends, like ordinary share dividends, are not deductible from profit for corporation tax purposes.

Effect on control and on freedom of action
Normally, preference shares do not impose much by way of restriction on the ordinary shareholders. Many preference shares give the holders the right to vote only where their dividends are in arrears. Generally, preference shareholders have no voting rights.

Factors for the potential investor to consider on preference shareholding

Level of return
The level of return to preference shareholders tends to be low, significantly below that of equities of the same business. The return tends also to be entirely in the form of dividends since preference shares do not normally experience significant changes in values.

Riskiness of returns
Typically, this risk lies between that attaching to ordinary shares and to loan stocks. This is mainly because preference dividends have priority over ordinary ones.

Ease of liquidating the investment

Where preference shares are redeemable and/or traded in the capital market, liquidation is possible. Failure for at least one of these to be the case will usually make investors reluctant to take up preference share issues.

Preference shares and personal tax

Dividends are taxed as income.

Degree of control

Unless dividends are in arrears, preference shareholders typically have no voting rights and hence no real power.

Methods of raising preference share capital

The methods used to raise preference share capital are more or less identical to those available with ordinary shares, including bonus issues to ordinary shareholders created from retained profits. In practice, rights issues seem to be the most popular method of issuing preference shares.

8.5 Loan stocks and debentures

Many businesses borrow by issuing securities with a fixed interest rate payable on the nominal or face value of the securities (known as the **coupon rate**) and a pre-stated redemption date. Such securities are known as **loan stocks**, **debentures** or **bonds**. They are typically issued for periods ranging from 10 to 25 years, though some are issued for periods outside that range. Indeed, perpetual loan stocks (no redemption date) do exist.

The popularity of loan stocks, as a means of raising long-term finance, seems to fluctuate rather wildly from year to year. In 1998, 75 per cent of the value of all securities issued by LSE listed businesses (net of redemptions) was loan stocks of some description or another, yet just five years earlier, in 1993, net of redemptions, the figure was only 19 per cent (see Table 8.1, page 218).

Many businesses obtain a capital market listing for their loan stocks, so that potential lenders can *buy* part of a business's borrowings from a previous lender. The new owner of the loan stock will, from the date of acquiring it, receive interest payments as well as the capital repayment if the stock is held until the redemption date.

Loan stocks attract all types of investors who seek relatively low-risk returns. Institutional investors are particularly attracted by them, especially those institutions that need regular cash receipts to meet recurring payment obligations, for example pension funds.

Most loan stocks are secured, either on specified assets of the borrowing business or on the assets generally. For example, **easyJet plc**, the UK 'no-frills' airline business, has, according to its 2003 annual report, pledged £74m of the value of its aircraft as security for loans. This can be compared with the balance sheet value of easyJet's fleet of £137m. These loans were used to finance acquisition of the aircraft concerned. Alternatively, the loan stockholder may simply have the security that the law of contract gives any unsecured creditor to enforce payment of interest or capital if the business defaults. Whether a loan stock is secured or not determines where in the queue for payment the loan stockholder will stand in the event of the liquidation of the borrowing business.

Since it is not usually practical for individual loan stockholders to monitor their security at all times, trustees are often appointed by the business to do this for them. Businesses will be prepared to do this so that the issue will attract lenders.

Loan stock (bond) ratings

Where loan stocks are listed on the LSE, they tend to be rated by two independent assessors, Moody's and Standard and Poor's. These two are commercial financial services providers. The rating indicates the assessors' opinion of the quality of the loan stocks in terms of the commercial and financial prospects of the business that issued the loan stock concerned. The rating views things from the potential investors' perspective. It is, therefore, the ability of the business concerned to pay interest and redeem the loan stock, in full, on the contracted dates, that is the key factor. The assessors keep their loan stocks ratings constantly under review and alter them as circumstances change. Businesses with high ratings will find it comparatively easy to borrow and/or can borrow more cheaply.

Both of these assessors rate loan stock into one of ten classes. Table 8.2 shows the Standard and Poor's classification.

Standard and Poor's sees the demarcation line between BBB and BB loan stocks as a key one. BBB and higher are seen as 'investment grade' loan stocks and broadly represent a safe investment. BB and below are considered risky and speculative. BB and lower are often known as **junk bonds**.

Table 8.2 Standard and Poor's loan stock credit ratings

Rating	Explanation
AAA	The capacity of the issuing business to meet its obligations is extremely high
AA	Slightly lower rated than 'triple-A' (AAA), but still very high
A	More susceptible to changes in the business/environment than 'double-A' loan stocks, but still a high rating
BBB	Such loan stocks are fairly safe but still more susceptible to adverse changes than 'single-A' loan stocks
BB	Major uncertainties as to its safety in the event of adverse changes to the business/economic environment
B	More risky than 'double-B' loan stocks, but currently able to meet its commitments
CCC	Currently vulnerable to non-payment of its obligations. Is reliant on business/economic conditions being favourable
CC	Highly vulnerable to non-payment
C	Currently highly likely not to be able to meet its obligations
D	Currently not meeting its obligations

Source: Information taken from the Standard and Poor's website (www.standardandpoors.com).

LRS: Somerset College

The *Financial Times* on 21 October 2004 made the following comments: 'Standard and Poor's credit ratings are proving as fluid as J Sainsbury's [**J Sainsbury plc**] forecasts. The food retailer has issued two profit warnings in 10 days. Twice S&P has downgraded in response, most recently, to one notch above "junk".'

In its 2004 annual report, **British Energy plc**, the troubled electricity generator, reported that its loss of investment grade status had caused it problems. It had to provide collateral to those with whom it dealt on credit and this caused liquidity problems for the business.

Investment ratios

Since profitability per se is of no direct interest to loan stockholders, ratios dealing with the effective rate of interest (yield) are likely to be of more concern to them.

Two ratios that tend to be widely reported in the media are:

- *Flat yield.* This is simply the gross interest receivable expressed as a percentage of the current market value of the relevant amount of loan.

- *Redemption yield.* Where, as is usually the case, the loan stock is redeemable, the effective return from owning it may include some capital gain or even loss. (A capital loss would arise where the current market price is above the redemption value. This would tend to occur where prevailing rates of interest are below the coupon rate for the loan stock.)

The gross redemption yield (r) would be given by the following expression:

$$\text{Current market value} = \sum_{t=1}^{n} I/(1 + r)^t + RV/(1 + r)^n$$

where I is the annual gross interest payment, RV is the redemption value and n is the remaining life (in years) of loan stock. Using the annual net (of tax) interest payment as I in the expression would give the net redemption yield. This is, in effect, the IRR of the loan stock, taking account of the current market price, the interest payment during the rest of the life of the loan stock and the amount that will be received on redemption. This can be expressed before tax (gross redemption yield) or after tax (net redemption yield). Examples of calculations involving this equation are given in Chapter 10.

Methods of issuing loan stocks

Loan stocks can be issued in several ways, including direct issues to the public by newspaper advertisement and so on. Quite often, businesses wishing to issue loan stocks will approach an issuing house and ask it to try to place the issue with its clients, often institutional ones.

Factors for the business to consider on loan stock financing

Issue costs

Issue costs tend to be relatively low; they have been estimated at about 2.5 per cent of the value of the cash raised on a £2m issue (Wilson Committee 1980). Lee, Lockhead,

Ritter and Zhao (1996) found that, in the USA, issue costs of loan stocks average 2 per cent of funds raised.

Servicing costs

Since loan stock represents a relatively low-risk investment to investors, expected returns tend to be low compared with those typically sought by equity holders. Historically, this has been reflected in actual returns.

Obligation to pay interest

Loan stockholders have the basic right under the law of contract to take action to enforce payment of interest and repayment of capital on the due dates, should they not be forthcoming. In many cases, loan stockholders have the contractual right to take some more direct action (such as effective seizure of an asset on which their loan is secured), should the borrowing business default on payments.

This clear obligation to pay interest, with potentially dire results for defaulting, can make servicing the loan stock finance a considerable millstone around the neck of the borrowing business.

Obligation to redeem loan stocks

Irrespective of whether loan stocks are issued as redeemable or not, it is always open to the business to buy its own loan stock, in the open market, and to cancel what it buys. Thus loan stocks offer a level of flexibility not so readily available with ordinary and preference shares. On the other hand, if loan stocks are issued as redeemable with a stated redemption date, which will usually be the case, the business is under a contractual obligation to redeem. This could put the business into a difficult cash flow position as the due date for redemption approaches.

Tax deductibility of loan stock interest

Interest is fully deductible from profit for corporation tax purposes. This has tended in the past to make loan interest payments cheaper, pound for pound, than ordinary and preference share dividends. This is a point that we shall return to in Chapter 11.

Effect on control and on freedom of action

The severity of the consequences of failing to meet interest payments and capital repayments can considerably limit the freedom of action of the business. While control, in the sense of voting rights, is not usually involved with loan stock financing, the issuing of loan stocks may well seriously erode control in the sense of being able to manage affairs without impediment.

It is common for those who lend money to impose conditions or **covenants** on the business. Failure to meet these covenants could, depending on the precise contract between the lenders and the business, give the lenders the right to immediate repayment of the loan.

Typical covenants include:

- a restriction on dividend levels;
- maintenance of a minimum current asset/current liability ratio;
- a restriction on the right of the business to dispose of its non-current assets; and
- a restriction on the level of financial (capital) gearing.

In its 2003 annual report **Arriva plc**, the transport business (mainly buses and trains) referred to its covenants. It said: 'Arriva remains comfortably within the principal covenants set out by its lenders, which require net tangible assets to exceed £140 million and gearing to remain below 200 per cent.'

We shall go more fully Chapter 11 into the effect on the position of the ordinary shareholders as borrowings increase in.

Factors for the potential investor to consider on loan stocks

Level of returns

The returns from loan stocks tend to be low compared with those expected from equities and preference shares.

Riskiness of returns

Although the level of risk associated with default by the borrowing business tends to be low, the loan stockholder is usually exposed to another risk, namely interest rate risk. This is the risk of capital losses caused by changes in the general level of interest rates.

Example 8.4	An investor has £100 nominal value of perpetual (irredeemable) loan stock, which has a coupon rate (the rate that the borrowing business is contracted to pay on the nominal value of the stock) of 6 per cent. The prevailing interest rates and the level of risk attaching to the particular loan stock cause the capital market to seek a 6 per cent return from it. Since the loan stock's return on its nominal value is 6 per cent, the capital market would value the holding at £100 (the nominal value).
	If the general level of interest rates were to increase so that the capital market now sought a 7.5 per cent return from this loan stock, its value would fall to £80 (that is, the amount on which the 6 per cent interest on £100 represents a 7.5 per cent return). Thus our loan stockholder would be poorer by £20.
	If the loan stock were not perpetual but redeemable at £100 at some date in the future, the price would probably not drop as low as £80 on the interest rate change. The closer the redemption date, the smaller the fall; but irrespective of the redemption position some loss of value would occur. Clearly, the investor would gain similarly from a general fall in prevailing interest rates, but a risk-averse investor (and most investors seem to be risk averse) would be more concerned with the potential loss than with the potential gain.

The relatively low interest rate risk associated with *short-dated* loan stocks tends to mean that lower returns are available from them as compared with those from stocks not due for redemption for some time.

Ease of liquidating the investment

Businesses that wish to make public issues of loan stocks must seek a capital market listing for them if they are to have any serious hopes of success. Thus, publicly issued loan stocks can be liquidated by sale in the market.

Loan stocks and personal tax

Interest is subject to income tax in the hands of individual loan stockholders. Capital gains are also taxed. Since all, or almost all, of the returns from loan stocks are usually in the form of interest, capital gains tend not to be significant.

Degree of control

Loan stocks do not give their holders any control over the business, except that which is necessary to enforce payment of their dues in the event of the business defaulting and to enforce any loan covenants.

Eurobonds

→ **Eurobonds** are unsecured loan stocks denominated in a currency other than the home currency of the business that made the issue. They are foreign currency loans. Businesses are prompted to make eurobond issues to exploit the availability of loan finance in an overseas country. Also, eurobonds can offer innovative features making them more attractive, both to the lenders and to the issuing business. This latter point arises from the fact that the bonds are traded in an unregulated market. **Boots Group plc**, the chemist, is an example of a UK business with a large eurobond loan (£300 million), according to the business's 2004 annual report.

Interest rate swaps

→ A business may have borrowed money where the contract specified a **floating interest rate**, that is, an interest rate that varies with the general level of interest rates in the
→ economy. It may have preferred a loan with a **fixed interest rate** but has been unable to negotiate such an arrangement.

Under these circumstances, it may be possible for the business to find another business with exactly the opposite problem, that is, with a fixed rate loan but a preference for a floating rate loan. Having identified one another, each of the businesses might agree to service the loan of the other. In practice they would probably make contact first and then issue the loan stock or undertake the borrowing in some other form.

→ **Interest rate swaps** have practical relevance because different businesses have different credit ratings. One may be able to negotiate a floating rate loan at a reasonable rate, but not a fixed rate one. The other business may find itself in the opposite position. Swaps are another example of a derivative.

Tesco plc, the supermarket business, uses interest rate swaps to limit its exposure to interest rate risk. In its 2004 annual report, the business says that its policy is to have about 40 per cent of its long-term borrowings on fixed rates.

8.6 Convertible loan stocks

Convertible loan stocks are securities that bear all of the features of loan stocks, which we have just discussed, except that at a pre-stated date they may be converted by the holders, at their discretion, into ordinary shares of the same business. The conversion rate is usually expressed as so many ordinary shares in exchange for £100 nominal value of loan stock. If there are any splits or bonus issues of ordinary shares during the life of the loan stock, the conversion rights are usually adjusted to take account of them.

A convertible loan stock is an example of a financial derivative.

Cable and Wireless plc, the telecommunications business, made an unsecured convertible bond issue in July 2003. The issue raised funds of £258m. The bonds have a coupon rate of 4 per cent p.a. and are convertible at the rate of 457.93 shares for every £1,000 (par value) of the bonds at any time before 9 July 2010.

Convertible issues have not been popular over recent years (see Table 8.1, page 218), though a number of businesses are partially financed by them.

Since convertibles are a hybrid of loan stocks and equities, the factors important both to the issuing business and to potential investors will basically be those that we have already considered. However, a couple of features of convertibles are worth mentioning.

Issue costs

The fact that loan stocks are cheaper to issue than are equities means that convertibles may be a cheap way to issue ordinary shares, particularly where the business is keen to have some loan finance in any case.

Loans are self-liquidating

There is no need for the business to find cash to redeem the loan stock since it is redeemed with ordinary shares. This does not, of course, make it free. Issuing shares to redeem loan stock represents an opportunity cost to the business and its existing shareholders. Convertible loan stocks tend to be used to raise finance where investors prefer to have the security of a loan stock, with the option to convert to equity should the business perform well.

8.7 Warrants

→ Warrants are, in effect, options granted by the business that entitle the holder to subscribe for a specified quantity of ordinary shares, for a specified price at, or after, a specified time – usually several years following their issue.

The business would usually issue the warrants in one of two ways:

- sell them, in which case it would derive a cash inflow; or
- attach them to a loan stock issue as a 'sweetener' or incentive to investors to take up the loan stock.

Where a business attaches the warrants to loan stocks, which is probably the most common means of issuing them, the arrangement very much resembles a convertible, except that the loan stock continues after the warrant has been used to subscribe for shares. Thus the loan stock is not 'self-liquidating' as it is with a convertible loan stock.

Like convertible loan stocks, warrants are financial derivatives. In most ways, warrants so resemble convertibles that the important factors are much the same.

8.8 Term loans

→ Term loans are negotiated between the borrowing business and a financial institution such as a clearing bank, an insurance business or a merchant bank. This sort of finance is extremely important, perhaps accounting for as much as 25 per cent of new finance raised by businesses other than through retained profits.

In many ways, term loans are like loan stocks in that security is usually given to the lender and loans are made for up to 20 years. They differ from loan stocks in that they are not usually transferred from lender to lender in the way that loan stocks typic-ally are. They are not traded in the capital market. Some term loans are repayable in instalments so that each monthly or annual payment consists of part interest, part capital repayment, in a similar manner to mortgage loan payments made by private house purchasers under repayment mortgages.

Term loans tend to be very cheap to negotiate, that is, *issue costs* are very low since the borrowing business deals with only one lender (at least in respect of each loan) and there is room for much more flexibility in the conditions of the loan than is usually possible with an issue of loan stock.

Clearly, term loans so closely resemble loan stocks that, with the exception of the points concerning transferability and the possible spreading of capital repayment, the factors concerning both borrower and lender are much the same as those that we reviewed in respect of loan stocks.

8.9 Leasing

It may seem strange to see leasing referred to as a source of long-term finance, but in fact it is very similar to secured lending.

Leases may be divided into two types:

- *Operating leases*. It is often possible to hire an asset, say an item of plant, that is perhaps required only occasionally, rather than purchasing it. Usually, the owner carries out any maintenance necessary. The decision whether to buy the asset or to lease it will perhaps be affected by financing considerations. Basically, though, it is an operating decision, which would be made according to which approach would be cheaper.

- *Finance leases*. Here the potential user identifies an asset in which it wishes to invest, negotiates price, delivery and so on, and then seeks a supplier of finance to buy it. Having arranged for the asset to be purchased, the user leases it from the purchaser. Naturally, the lease payments will need to be sufficient to justify the owner's expenditure, in terms both of capital repayment and of interest.

The nature of finance leasing

→ It is *finance leases* that concern us here since they are effectively term loans with capital repayable by instalments. This is an important source of finance, which has been estimated to provide as much as 20 per cent of the total finance for new capital expenditure by businesses over recent years (Drury and Braund 1990).

In the past, finance leasing has been believed to be popular with users partly because, while it is tantamount to borrowing, neither the asset nor the obligation to the owner appeared on the balance sheet of the user business. Those trying to assess the business's financial position could overlook such a source of off balance sheet finance. However, accounting regulations have now put leasing *on the balance sheet*. Businesses are now required to show both the leased assets and the capital value of the obligation to the owner on the face of the balance sheet.

Another feature of finance leasing, which was apparently a major reason for the growth in its popularity during the late 1970s and early 1980s in the UK, was its considerable *tax efficiency* in some circumstances. Lease payments are fully deductible for corporation tax purposes by the borrowing business. This includes the capital portion of the payment.

Until 1984, the capital cost of items of plant attracted 100 per cent first-year capital allowance in their year of acquisition. As far as the borrowing business was concerned, leasing rather than buying a non-current asset would deny it the opportunity to claim the first-year allowance. On the other hand, leasing would still enable the business to claim 100 per cent of the cost of the asset, but over its life, rather than in the first year. In many cases, however, even where businesses were to buy the asset by raising finance from, say, a term loan, profits were insufficient for the full benefit to be gained from the large first-year allowance. This was particularly true where recession restricted profitability.

With leasing, the right to claim capital allowance passed to the 'lender'. If the profits from leasing and other activities were such as to put the 'lender' in a position to take full advantage of them, some of this advantage could be passed on to the 'borrower' in lower lease payments. Thus the 'borrower' could give up some of the advantage of the first-year allowance in exchange for a lower lease charge.

Evidence on leasing

The advent in the mid-1980s of lower corporation tax rates and the abolition of the 100 per cent first-year tax capital allowance greatly reduced the benefit of finance leasing. This, taken together with the requirement for the 'borrower' business to disclose in its annual accounts the extent of its indulgence in this source of finance, seemed likely to reduce the level of use of finance leasing.

In fact, far from decreasing in popularity since the accounting and tax changes of the mid-1980s, finance leasing has expanded massively in popularity since the late 1980s. The reasons for this fact are not obvious. Drury and Braund (1990) conducted a survey of UK businesses of various sizes on the reasons why they frequently prefer to acquire assets on finance leases rather than buying them. There were two principal reasons given for the popularity of leasing. The first was that the interest rate implied in leasing contracts was lower than the rate that the businesses would have to pay to raise finance to buy the assets themselves. The other main reason given was that they believed it still to be more tax efficient to lease rather than to buy, despite the changes in the tax treatment of non-current assets. **British Airways plc**, according to its 2004 annual report, leases a significant part (32 per cent) of its fleet of aircraft.

Although in some cases, one or both of the principal reasons given in the Drury and Braund survey could be valid, for the majority of businesses this seems unlikely to be so. Drury and Braund discovered one factor that could cast some light on the subject. This was an alarmingly high incidence of mishandling of the analysis of the decision whether to lease, on the one hand, or to borrow and purchase, on the other. Even among larger, and presumably more financially sophisticated, businesses, about 30 per cent were taking an incorrect approach to the analysis such as to bias the results in favour of a decision to lease.

Although it would be unreasonable to conclude that the continued popularity of finance leasing is based on wholesale mishandling of the decision data, it remains far from clear as to why leasing is so popular.

To lease or not to lease – a financing decision

When a business is considering the acquisition of an asset, it should estimate the cash flows that are expected to arise from its ownership. These should then be discounted at a rate that reflects the level of risk associated with those cash flows. If the NPV is positive the asset should be acquired; if negative it should not, at least from a financial viewpoint.

Whether the asset should be financed by a finance lease or by some other means is a completely separate decision. The first is an investment decision, the second a financing one.

Only by coincidence will the appropriate discount rate be equal to the rate inherent in the finance lease. This latter rate will tend to reflect the relatively risk-free nature of lease financing from the lender's point of view. To the user of the asset, the level of risk is likely to be rather greater than that borne by the lender. It would therefore be illogical to discount the cash flows from the asset at the rate implicit in the finance lease.

We shall consider more fully in Chapter 11 the importance of separating the investment and the financing decision.

Finance leasing is so similar in practical effect to secured borrowing that the factors that both 'borrower' and 'lender' need to consider are much the same in respect of each of them.

Sale and leaseback

→ **Sale and leaseback** is a variation on a finance lease. Where a business needs finance, and has a suitable asset, it can sell the asset to a financier, with a leaseback deal as part of the sale contract. Thus the business retains the use of the asset yet gains additional funds. Again this is very similar to a secured loan.

Land and buildings are often the subject of sale and leaseback deals. Recently, several major UK businesses have sold off freehold properties in this way. **Travelodge**, the budget hotel chain owned by the venture capital business **Permira Advisors Ltd**, sold 136 of its freehold properties to raise £400m. This represented the whole of its freehold properties. Numerous UK supermarkets, public house and hotel chains have sold and leased back some of their freehold properties over recent years. This is now a significant source of finance for many businesses.

Surprising subjects of sale and leaseback deals are professional footballers. The playing contracts of several English Premier League footballers are owned by the leasing arm of **Barclays Bank plc**, rather than by the club concerned. Perhaps the best-known player to whom this applied was Rio Ferdinand, the England defender, who was leased from Barclays Bank by Leeds United when he played for that club (Fletcher 2002).

8.10 Grants from public funds

In the UK there are many different grants or sources of finance that are given at little or no direct cost to businesses. The bulk of such finance emanates either from UK government sources or from the European Union.

Each of the grants is formulated to encourage businesses to act in a particular way. Examples of such action include:

- investment in new plant;
- development of the microelectronics industry;
- training and retraining staff;

- energy conservation; and

- research and development.

Many of the grants available apply only, or particularly, to businesses located in specified parts of the UK.

Since there are so many different schemes, and since they tend to alter quite frequently, it is probably not worth our looking at any individual ones here. It must be emphasised, however, that the amounts that individual businesses may claim can be highly significant, and that every effort should be made by financial managers to familiarise themselves with the grants available and how to claim them. The Department of Trade and Industry will provide information on most sources of grant finance. (See Relevant websites at the end of this chapter.) Local authorities, particularly county councils, tend to produce guides to grants available in their own areas.

8.11 Conclusions on long-term finance

The apparent existence of an efficient capital market, coupled with the evidence on the relationship between risk and expected return, suggest that businesses are unlikely to be advantaged significantly by selecting one type of finance rather than another.

An increase in equity financing, which does not expose existing ordinary shareholders to increased risk, tends to be expensive. Secured loan finance, which does expose them to increased risk, tends to be cheap. This suggests that there is no advantage or disadvantage to existing ordinary shareholders in raising further finance in one way rather than another. One method may increase expected returns of existing ordinary shareholders but it is also likely to increase their risk commensurately.

However, the situation in real life is probably not quite as suggested by Figure 8.1 (page 217). There are anomalies in the primary capital market that can mean that using one form of financing rather than another can be to the advantage of equity holders. For example, loan finance attracts tax relief in a way that equity finance does not. Convertibles are probably a cheaper way of issuing ordinary shares than is a direct offer of equities to the public.

These points and those that will be discussed in the context of the gearing and dividend debates later in the book perhaps explain why we find that businesses seem to devote much effort to deciding on the most appropriate means of raising long-term finance.

Perhaps we could generally conclude that businesses should assess all possible methods of raising long-term finance. They should look for anomalies like the ones mentioned above and then seek to exploit them as far as is practical, given the particular circumstances of the business.

Summary

Risk and return are key issues in financing

- To the business (that is, the shareholders) sources that are cheap, in terms of servicing costs (for example, loans) tend to be risky; those that are less risky (for example, equities) tend to be expensive.

- To the provider of finance, risk and reward are positively linked, that is, high returns mean high risk, and vice versa.

Ordinary shares

- The owners' (shareholders') stake in the business.
- The largest element of business financing, much of it from retained profits.
- Risky for the shareholders, low risk for the business; high levels of return expected by investors, expensive for the business.
- Typically no legal or contractual obligation on the business either to pay dividends or to redeem the shares.
- Dividends are not tax deductible to the business, but are taxable in the hands of shareholders.
- Retained profits can be slow and uncertain, but no issue costs.
- Rights issue = issue to existing shareholders at a discount on the current market value. Shares offered pro rata the existing holdings.
  - Issue costs about 6 per cent of funds raised, but there are economies of scale.
  - Issue price is not a big problem.
  - Tend to be successful.
  - Control stays in the same hands if existing shareholders take up their entitlement.
  - Rights can be sold by a shareholder who does not want to take them up.
- Issues to the public:
  - Relatively rare in the life of the typical business.
  - Significant issue costs, perhaps 13 per cent of funds raised, though there are economies of scale.
  - Pricing is an important issue.
  - Not always successful, though underwriter (in effect, insurer) may be used.
  - Control may shift from the original to the new shareholders.
- Shares easy to liquidate if listed on a stock exchange; otherwise could be very difficult.

Preference shares

- Shares that have a right to the first part of any dividend paid, up to a maximum level.
- Relatively little used in recent years.
- Relatively low risk for the shareholders, some risk to the ordinary shareholders since preference shareholders are usually entitled to any backlog of dividends as well as that for the current year before an ordinary share dividend can be paid.
- Relatively low cost to the business and low returns to the preference shareholder.
- Ratios used by preference investors are dividend yield and dividend cover.
- Typically no legal or contractual obligation on the business to pay dividends, but sometimes there is an enforceable one to redeem the shares.

- Dividends are not tax deductible to the business, but are taxable in the hands of shareholders.
- Issue methods and costs similar to those of equities.
- Shares easy to liquidate if listed on a stock exchange; otherwise could be very difficult.

Loan stocks and debentures

- Long-term borrowings, with contractual interest payments and typically redemption payments as well, though some loans are perpetual.
- Typically an important source of finance.
- Usually very low risk for the lenders, high risk for the business; low levels of return expected by investors, cheap for the business.
- Interest is tax deductible to the business (makes them seem even cheaper), and taxable in the hands of lenders.
- Issued to the public through advertising or investment intermediaries, like stockbrokers, costing up to about 2.5 per cent of the funds raised.
- The existence of loan finance can severely restrict a business's freedom of action.
- Loan stock easy to liquidate if listed on a stock exchange; otherwise could be difficult.
- Loan covenants (or restrictions) likely to be involved.

Convertible loan stocks

- Loan stocks that entitle the holders to convert to ordinary shares on or after a particular date at a particular rate of conversion.
- Not a very important source of finance in recent years.
- Tend to be used where investors prefer the certainty of a loan, with the option to convert should the equities perform well – it is an option to convert, not an obligation.
- Loans are self-liquidating; they do not require a cash outflow from the business.
- The relatively low issue costs of loan stock means that, ultimately, convertibles are a cheap way of issuing equities.
- Other factors similar to those of loans before conversion and equities afterwards.

Warrants

- Options sold by, or attached to loan stocks issued by, the business. They entitle the holder to subscribe for new shares issued by the business at a specified price at, or after, a certain date.

Term loans

- Loans negotiated between the business and financial institutions, for example a clearing bank.

- Very important source of finance for businesses of all sizes.
- Cheap to negotiate – very low issue costs.
- Usually able to be negotiated to suit the borrower business's precise needs.
- Most aspects of term loans are the same as loan stocks.

Finance leases

- An arrangement where a financial institution buys an asset which it leases to the user for a substantial proportion of the asset's life.
- Quite an important source of finance.
- In effect this is a loan secured on the asset concerned, and the factors relating to loan finance apply to finance leases.

Sale and leaseback

- An arrangement with a financial institution that it will buy an asset already owned by the business and lease it back.
- Quite an important source of finance.
- This too is quite like a loan secured on the asset concerned and the factors relating to loan finance also apply to finance leases.

Grants from public funds

Further reading

Samuels, Wilkes and Brayshaw (1998) and Brealey and Myers (2002) give full treatment, from both a theoretical and practical perspective, of corporate financing. Rutterford and Montgomerie (1993) is a comprehensive collection of articles on various types of corporate finance sources. Drury and Braund (1990) give an account of their survey of finance leasing and a general discussion of the subject.

Relevant websites

The site for the London Stock Exchange contains a lot of information and statistics about the exchange.
www.londonstockexchange.com

The sites of Moody's and Standard and Poor's are, respectively:
www.moodys.com
www.standardandpoors.com

The site for the Department of Trade and Industry gives information about grants.
www.dti.gov.uk

The websites of the businesses featured in this chapter are:

Arriva plc	www.arriva.co.uk
Barclays Bank plc	www.barclays.co.uk
Boots Group plc	www.boots-plc.com
British Airways plc	www.bashares.com
British Energy plc	www.british-energy.com
Cable and Wireless plc	www.cw.com
Clinton Cards plc	www.clintoncards.co.uk
easyJet plc	www.easyjet.com

Enterprise Inns plc	www.enterpriseinns.com
Permira Advisors Ltd	www.permira.com
Prudential plc	www.prudential.co.uk
J Sainsbury plc	www.sainsbury.co.uk
Somerfield plc	www.somerfield.co.uk
Tesco plc	www.tesco.com
J. D. Wetherspoon plc	www.jdwetherspoon.co.uk

REVIEW QUESTIONS

Suggested answers to review questions appear in Appendix 3.

8.1 From the point of view of the borrowing business, loan capital tends to be cheap but risky. In what sense is it risky?

8.2 Why are retained profits not a free source of finance?

8.3 If retained profits are not a free source of finance, why are they nonetheless such a popular source of finance?

8.4 A loan stock, listed on the stock market, has a 'coupon' rate (interest rate specified in the contract between the business and the lenders) of 10 per cent. Does this necessarily mean that the current pre-tax cost of the loan stock is 10 per cent?

8.5 What factors tend to affect the market value of a particular convertible loan stock?

(Note that the answer to this question is not really provided in the chapter. A combination of background knowledge and common sense should enable you to come up with some relevant points, however.)

8.6 In what way can it be said that finance leasing is a source of long-term finance?

PROBLEMS

Sample answers to problems marked with an asterisk appear in Appendix 4.

(Problems 8.1 to 8.3 are basic-level problems, whereas problems 8.4 and 8.5 are more advanced and may contain some practical complications.)

8.1* Many businesses issue loan stocks, which carry the right for holders to convert them into ordinary shares in the same business at a later date.

Why might a business choose to issue convertible loan stocks rather than make an issue of equity in the first place?

8.2* Most businesses, particularly larger ones, have outstanding claims (financial obligations) of a wide variety of types from a wide variety of claimants at any given moment.

Why is there this diversity?

8.3 Polecat plc has 18m £0.50 ordinary shares in issue. The current stock market value of these is £1.70 per share. The directors have decided to make a one for three rights issue at £1.25 each.

Julie owns 3000 Polecat ordinary shares.

Assuming that the rights issue will be the only influence on the share price:

(a) *What, in theory, will be the ex-rights price of the shares (that is, the price of the shares once the rights issue has taken place)?*

(b) *For how much, in theory, could Julie sell the 'right' to buy one share?*

(c) *Will it matter to Julie if she allows the rights to lapse (that is, she does nothing)?*

8.4* Memphis plc has 20m £0.10 ordinary shares in issue. On 7 June the stock market closing price of the shares was £1.20. Early on the morning of 8 June, the business publicly announced that it had just secured a new contract to build some hospitals in the Middle East. To the business, the contract had a net present value of £4m. On 9 June the business announced its intention to raise the necessary money to finance the work, totalling £10m, through a rights issue priced at £0.80 per share.

Assuming that the events described above were the only influence on the share price, for how much, in theory, could a shareholder sell the right to buy one of the new shares?

8.5 The management of Memphis plc (Problem 8.4) is reconsidering its decision on the rights issue price. It is now contemplating an issue price of £1 per new share. One of its concerns is the effect that the issue price will have on the wealth of its existing shareholders. You have been asked to advise.

Calculate the effect on the wealth of a person who owns 200 shares in Memphis plc before the rights issue, assuming in turn a rights issue price of £0.80 and £1.00. In each case make your calculations on the basis both that the shareholder takes up the rights, and that the shareholder sells the rights.

Taking account of all of the factors, what would you advise Memphis plc to do about the rights issue price?

There are both a set of **multiple-choice questions** and **missing-word questions** available on the website. These specifically cover the material contained in this chapter. These can be attempted and graded (with feedback) online.

There is also an **additional problem**, with solution, that relates to the material covered in this chapter.

Go to **www.pearsoned.co.uk/atrillmclaney** and follow the links.

Chapter 9

The secondary capital market (the stock exchange) and its efficiency

In this chapter we shall deal with the following:

→ the role of the capital markets in their secondary function

→ the mechanisms of the London Stock Exchange

→ the efficiency of the secondary capital market

→ tests of efficiency

→ the implications of capital market efficiency

9.1 Introduction

The capital market is a title given to the market where long-term finance is raised by businesses and by local and national governments. Businesses raise this type of finance through the issue of equity (shares) and debt (loan stocks, debentures or bonds) to members of the public and to investing institutions (unit trusts, insurance businesses and so forth), usually in exchange for cash. It is also a market where holdings of equity or debt (securities) may be transferred from one investor to another. The new finance market is known as the primary capital market, whereas the market in which second-hand securities are traded is referred to as the secondary capital market. We have already considered this primary role in Chapter 8. In this chapter we shall confine ourselves to consideration of the secondary aspect.

Secondary capital markets

The most important secondary capital markets throughout the world tend to be the official stock exchanges or stock markets. They are not the whole of the secondary capital market, however – certainly not in the UK, as we shall see later in the chapter. Nonetheless, the world's official stock exchanges are the major forums for trading local, and increasingly international, securities. Most of these official stock exchanges fulfil a primary function as well as a secondary one.

The existence of a secondary capital market is vital to businesses wishing to raise long-term finance. Potential long-term investors will not generally be prepared to take up issues of shares or loan stocks, unless the opportunity exists to liquidate their investment at any time. Since it is not practical for businesses themselves constantly to hold cash in readiness to redeem the securities, it is necessary for there to be a secondary capital market where security holders may sell their investments. The absence of secondary market facilities tends to make the raising of long-term finance impossible or, at best, very expensive in terms of returns demanded by investors. It is thought by some observers that underdeveloped countries are often restrained in their industrial and commercial development by the lack of an established secondary capital market and therefore by the lack of long-term investment finance.

Price efficiency

Potential investors will not only require the existence of the opportunity to liquidate their securities as and when they wish; they will also be interested in whether their investment is *efficiently* priced. Efficiency in the context of pricing implies that, at all times, all available information about a business's prospects is fully and rationally reflected in that business's security prices. That is to say, the market price of a particular security is the present (discounted) value of the future economic benefits that ownership of the security will bestow on its owner. This will interest investors as they would generally prefer that the price at any particular moment be set rationally and not be a matter of sheer chance. Perhaps more important is the fact that, as the capital market is the interface between managers and investors, efficiency means that financial decisions made by managers will reflect in the business's security prices and so have a direct effect on shareholders' wealth. As maximisation of shareholders' wealth is generally accepted as the principal criterion for management decisions, this reflection of management action is a significant matter, with several implications.

In this chapter we shall look briefly at the mechanisms of the London Stock Exchange (LSE) in its secondary role before going on to see that it seems to be efficient to a large extent. Lastly we shall consider the implications for investors and for financial managers of the efficiency (or otherwise) of the LSE.

9.2 The London Stock Exchange

As with all capital markets in their secondary role, the LSE is basically a marketplace where securities of private businesses and public bodies may be bought and sold.

LSE members

Whereas in many types of markets members of the public may directly buy and sell on their own behalf, in the LSE they are barred from entry. Only members of the LSE have direct access to buy and sell securities. When members of the public wish to buy or sell securities through the LSE, they can do so only by using a member as an agent.

The rules governing the conduct of the members are laid down and enforced by a Council elected by the membership. One of the functions of the Council is to authorise specific securities as suitable to be dealt on the LSE. Authorised (*listed*) securities are those that satisfy a number of criteria established by the Council. The object of screening securities before authorising them is to try to avoid members of the investing public from losing money by buying very hazardous securities.

There are currently about 2000 businesses whose shares are listed by the LSE, with about 100 of these accounting for about 80 per cent of the total value of the shares of all 2000 businesses (Coggan 2003).

LSE members have two roles:

- As market makers or dealers, equivalent in principle to a trader in a street market. Each dealing business specialises in a particular group of securities, in much the same way as traders in street markets tend to specialise in fruit, or meat, or fish.

- As agents of the public who wish to buy or sell through the LSE (stockbrokers).

Dealing on the LSE

Dealers

Dealers will usually be prepared to buy or sell irrespective of whether they are immediately able to *close the deal*. Thus dealers will normally be ready to sell securities that they do not at the time possess or to buy those for which they have no immediate customer. It is only with very rarely traded securities and with exceptionally large orders that dealers may not be prepared to deal either as a buyer or seller. Any unwillingness on a dealing business's part to make a market in a particular security on a particular occasion may damage the dealer's reputation. This could have an adverse effect on the future trade of that dealer. There is therefore a sanction against dealers who fail properly to fulfil their function as market makers.

At any given time, a particular dealing business will typically hold a *trading* stock, either a positive or a negative one, of some of the securities in which it deals. Where the stock is a positive one it is said to hold a *bull position* in that security, and where securities have been sold that the dealer has yet to buy in, it is said to hold a *bear position*.

Dealers are risk-taking market makers. When dealers buy some securities they judge that they can subsequently sell them at a higher price. Similarly, when they sell securities that they do not possess (where they take a bear position), their judgement is that they can buy the securities that they have an obligation to deliver, at a lower price. If they are wrong in this judgement it could be an expensive mistake, as they may have to offer a very high price to encourage a seller into the market. Members who act only as dealers make their living through profits from trading.

The dealing process

Until the mid-1980s virtually all LSE transactions were conducted on the floor of the Exchange. Here, each dealer business would have its own 'stall' to which stockbrokers could go to deal on their clients' behalf. To deal at the most advantageous prices it would have been necessary for the stockbroker to call at the stalls of all, or at least a good sample of, dealers who dealt in the particular security concerned, to compare prices. Now the 'floor' of the LSE is, in effect, a computerised dealing system, though in essence the dealing process remains the same. The Stock Exchange Automated Quotations system (SEAQ) allows dealers to display their prices to interested parties, both members and non-members, and constantly to update those prices. It also enables LSE members to deal directly using a terminal linked to SEAQ, without leaving their offices.

When members of the investing public wish to buy or to sell a particular security, they typically e-mail or telephone their stockbroker. The stockbroker can immediately display the prices at which various dealers are prepared to trade. These prices will normally differ from one dealer to another. This is because estimates of the value of the security concerned will vary from dealer to dealer. The 'stockholding' position of the particular dealer at that particular moment will also influence the prices on offer. A dealer with a bear position may well be prepared to pay a higher price to buy the particular securities than one with a bull position. In respect of a particular security and a particular dealer, the SEAQ screen will display two prices. At the lower of these the dealer is prepared to buy and at the higher one to sell. The same information is available to all members and to others who wish to subscribe. The stockbroker can tell the client what is the best price in the security according to whether the client is a potential buyer or a potential seller. The client can then immediately instruct the stockbroker to execute the trade at this best price or to do nothing. If the client wishes to go ahead with the deal, the stockbroker executes the transaction immediately and without any direct contact with the relevant dealer business (using the SEAQ terminal). The effective contact between the stockbroker and the dealer is through SEAQ. The system automatically informs the dealer concerned that the trade has taken place and provides a record of the details of the transaction. Although anyone can be provided with the SEAQ information, only LSE members can use that information directly to trade through SEAQ.

Stockbroking businesses charge their clients a commission, which is their source of income. These dealing costs tend to be significant, particularly on small transactions, though they typically become proportionately lower on larger ones.

Stockbrokers offer their clients a range of professional services related to investment, rarely viewing their role in the narrow sense of buying and selling agents. They are, of course, competing with each other for investors' business. Those giving the best service, in terms of advice and guidance, are likely to attract most dealing commissions.

Derivatives

Not only can investors buy and sell securities, they may also buy and sell derivatives linked to security prices. Investors may, for example, buy and sell security options. They can buy the right (but not the obligation) to buy or sell specified securities at predetermined prices before a stated date. Where, for example, an investor believes that **Boots Group plc** (the Chemist) shares are due to rise in price, an option to buy a certain quantity at a specified price before a stated date can be bought. This would be known as a 'call' option, and the price of such an option would depend on the quantity, the call price and the exercise date. If, by the exercise date, the market price of Boots Group were above the call price, the investor would take up the option to buy the shares. An option giving the right to sell is known as a 'put' option. In certain securities the option itself may even be bought and sold (traded options). Share options are another example of derivatives (see Chapter 1), and just one of many derivatives linked to security prices.

The place of the LSE in the UK secondary market

There is no legal requirement in the UK that all secondary market activities must be carried out through the LSE. While it has long been and still remains the case that the

LSE dominates the UK secondary market in terms of business transacted, there are other markets, albeit limited ones.

There are, for example, commercial organisations that operate *over the counter (OTC)* markets, where the organisations act as a market maker in a range of securities. Securities are bought from and sold to the investing public, in much the same way as dealers in second-hand furniture do with their wares, without an agent being involved.

There is some evidence – for example, the emergence of the OTC market – that suggests that members of the investing public will readily look elsewhere if they feel that the LSE is not providing the service they need, at a price they are prepared to pay.

9.3 Capital market efficiency

When security prices at all times rationally reflect all available, relevant information, the market in which they are traded is said to be **efficient**. This implies that any new information coming to light that bears on a particular business will be incorporated into the market price of the security

● quickly, and

● rationally, in terms of size and direction of security price movement.

To say that a secondary capital market is efficient is not necessarily to imply that the market is 'perfect' in the economists' sense, although to be efficient the market has to display most of the features of the perfect market to some degree. It is also important to note that efficiency does not mean perfect powers of prediction on the part of investors. All it means is that the current price of a security is the best estimate of its economic value on the basis of the available evidence. Note that 'efficient' in the current sense is not related to 'efficient' in the sense of having no specific risk (see Chapter 7). It is unfortunate that the same word has become the standard term to describe two different concepts.

Why should capital markets be efficient?

Prices are set in capital markets by the forces of supply and demand. If the consensus view of those active in the market is that the shares of a particular business are underpriced, demand will force the price up.

In a secondary capital market such as the LSE, security prices are observed by large numbers of people, many of them skilled and experienced, and nearly all of them moved to do so by that great motivator – financial gain. Information on the business comes to these observers in a variety of ways. From the business itself come financial statements, press releases and leaks (deliberate or otherwise). Information on the industry and economy in which the business operates will also be germane to assessment of the value of a particular security, and this will emerge from a variety of sources.

Where observers spot what they consider to be an irrational price, in the light of their assessment of, say, future projected dividends, they tend to seek to take advantage of it or to advise others to do so. For example, an investment analyst employed by a unit trust assesses the worth of a share in **Tesco plc** at £3.50 but notes that the current share price is £3.00. The analyst might then contact the investment manager to advise the purchase of some of these shares on the basis that they are currently underpriced and there are gains to be made. The increase in demand that some large-scale buying would engender would tend to put up the price of the shares. Our analyst is just one of a large number of pundits constantly comparing the market price of Tesco shares with their own assessment of their worth. Most of these pundits will take action themselves or cause it to be taken by those whom they advise if they spot some disparity. The market price of the shares at all times represents the consensus view. If people feel strongly that this price is irrational, they will take steps to gain from their beliefs: the greater they perceive the irrationality to be, the more dramatic the steps that they will take.

Efficiency and the consensus: predicting American football results – ask the audience or phone a friend

Efficiency has been interpreted by some people as requiring that there is at least one person active in the market who has great knowledge, skill and judgement. This need not be the case. Beaver (1998) points out that all that is needed for efficiency is many observers with most having some rational perceptions even if their other perceptions about the security are misguided. He argues that the misguided perceptions will be random and probably not held by others. The rational perceptions, on the other hand, will be common, perhaps not to all, but nonetheless to a large number of observers. As the security price reflects a *weighted average* of the perceptions of all of those active in the market for that particular security, the misconceptions, because they are random, will tend to cancel each other out and so have no overall effect on the price. The correct perceptions will not be random and so will not cancel each other and will therefore be reflected in the share price.

Beaver illustrates and supports this point with what is at first sight an irrelevant account of some predictions of results (win, lose or draw) of American football games. The *Chicago Daily News*, on each Friday over the period 1966 to 1968, reported the predictions of each of its 14 or 15 sports staff of the outcome of the games to be played over the forthcoming weekend. The newspaper also published the consensus view of the sports staff, that is, the single most popular view on each game. When the success of the predictions was summarised for the three years, the results were as shown in Table 9.1.

It is interesting to note that the consensus view outperforms all *individuals* over the three years and indeed outperforms all but one or two in any particular year (it tied with two individuals in 1966 and was beaten by one individual in 1967 and 1968). It is

Table 9.1 Performance of forecasters of American football games

	1966	1967	1968
Number of forecasters (including the consensus)	15	15	16
Number of forecasts per forecaster	180	220	219
Rank of leading forecasters:			
J. Carmichael	1 (tie)	8	16
D. Nightingale	1 (tie)	11	5
A. Biondo	7	1	6
H. Duck	8	10	1
Rank of the consensus	1 (tie)	2	2

Source: *Chicago Daily News*.

clear from the table that the performance of the successful individuals is inconsistent, suggesting some element of luck in their successful year. Luck may not be the only reason for the success, since Biondo performed better than average in all three years. Yet despite the possible presence of skill in one individual, over the three years the consensus easily beat them all.

It would appear that some forecasters are more skilled than others. It also seems that the consensus performs even better than the best individual. This is despite the fact that the consensus combines the forecasts of all the individuals, skilled and not so skilled. Far from having the effect of dragging down the quality of the forecasts of the best individuals, combining the forecasts, to find the consensus, actually improves the quality of forecasting. Beaver suggests that this is because idiosyncratic factors (such as personal loyalties to a particular football team), which might influence the forecasts of even the best forecaster, tend to cancel out when a reasonably large number of different individuals is involved in forming the consensus. Thus the consensus represents a rather more clear-sighted and objective forecast than any individual can provide, on a consistent basis. This is rather like the portfolio effect of equity investing that we met in Chapter 7. Random factors (specific risk, in the case of investing) cancel out, leaving only the common factor (systematic risk).

Beaver (1998) also refers to a similar effect with predictions of UK gross domestic product by 30 economists. Here the consensus beat 29 and tied with one of the economists.

Another example of this seems to arise in the context of the TV quiz show *Who Wants To Be A Millionaire?* According to Surowiecki (2004), the 'friends' (who are selected by the contestant for their expertise) answer correctly 65 per cent of the time, whereas the audiences (each one a random selection of quite a large number of people) supply the correct answers to 91 per cent of the questions asked of them. This is again explained by the portfolio effect. It may be that contestants choose to ask the audience the easier, more obvious questions, but this difference in success rate is still striking.

Efficiency and speed of reaction

Efficiency requires not only that prices react rationally to new information, but also that they react speedily. Certainly, the rate at which data can be transmitted, received, analysed, the analysis transmitted, received and acted upon by buying or selling is very rapid, particularly in this era of cheap electronic data communication and processing.

Since there are large numbers of informed, highly motivated observers who are capable of quick action, we have good reason to believe that a sophisticated secondary capital market like the LSE would be efficient in its pricing of securities. The question now becomes: is it efficient in practice?

9.4 Tests of capital market efficiency

Forms of efficiency

Attempts to assess efficiency have addressed themselves not so much to whether the capital markets are efficient or are not efficient but rather to what extent they are efficient. Roberts (1967) suggested that efficiency and tests of it should be dealt with under three headings:

- **Weak form**. If the market is efficient to this level, any information that might be contained in past price movements is already reflected in the securities' prices.

- **Semi-strong form**. This form of efficiency implies that all relevant publicly available information is impounded in security prices.

- **Strong form**. If present this would mean that all relevant information, including that which is available only to those in privileged positions (for example, managers), is fully reflected in security prices.

These are ascending levels of efficiency such that, if a market is strong-form efficient it must, therefore, also be semi-strong and weak-form efficient.

Approach taken by the tests

Propositions such as that relating to capital market efficiency are *not directly testable*. How can we test whether all available information is reflected in security prices? The researcher may not personally have all of the available information or even know that some of it exists. We can, however, test whether or not security price behaviour seems consistent with efficiency. Generally, the tests that have been carried out have tried to do this.

The tests have sought to assess whether or not it seems possible to make *abnormal* returns by exploiting any possible inefficiency. Abnormal returns in this context means returns in excess of those that could be made, over the same period in which the test was conducted, from securities of similar risk. Returns typically means capital gain plus dividend received over a period, expressed as a percentage of a security's price at the start of that period.

Tests of this type pose several methodological problems. Such is the number of factors acting simultaneously on the price of a particular security that it is difficult to know to what extent prices are affected by the specific factor in which the researcher is interested and to what extent other factors are involved. For our present purposes, let us accept what most qualified observers believe, that the major researchers in this area, some of whose work we shall consider, have sufficiently well overcome the practical problems for their results to be regarded as providing significant insights. Where this seems not to be the case, we shall discuss it. Readers who are interested in looking at the methodological problems in detail should take up some of the references given during and at the end of this chapter.

Tests of weak-form efficiency

Technical analysis

It has long been popularly believed that security prices move in cycles or patterns that are predictable by those who study the matter closely enough. Many feel that past patterns of security price behaviour repeat themselves, so that spotting a repeat starting to occur can put the investor in a position to make abnormally large investment returns. Not surprisingly, adherents to this philosophy use graphs and charts of past security prices to facilitate recognition of the pattern early enough to benefit from it. These people are often referred to as *chartists*.

Others seek to develop trading rules that are perhaps easier to apply than those of the chartists. For example, it is believed by some that the price of a particular security tends to hover around a particular value, rarely deviating from it by more than a small percentage. If the price starts to *break out* from the ±*x* per cent band, they believe that this implies a large movement about to occur. This they feel can be taken advantage of by buying or selling according to the direction of the breakout. Such dealing rules are usually called *filter rules*. More generally, the use of techniques such as filter rules and charts is known as technical analysis.

If the market is efficient this should mean that no gains could be made from technical analysis because there are so many observers at work that if any information were contained in past price movements it would be impounded in the current price as a result of buying and selling. Only new information would affect share prices. As new information is random, security prices would be expected to follow a random path or random walk. New information must be random or it would not be new information. That the sales of a Christmas card manufacturer were greater towards the end of the year than at other times during that year is not new information because this pattern tends to occur every year and is predictable.

Spotting repeating patterns

Let us suppose that the price of a particular security has followed the cyclical pattern shown in Figure 9.1 over a number of years. There is obviously a regular pattern here. What should we do if we spotted this pattern at time *t*? Surely we should buy some of the securities and hold them until the next peak, sell them and buy some more at the following trough and so on until we became bored with making money! It seems too good to be true and, of course, it is. In real life we should not be the only ones to spot this repetition of peaks and troughs; in fact there would be a very large number

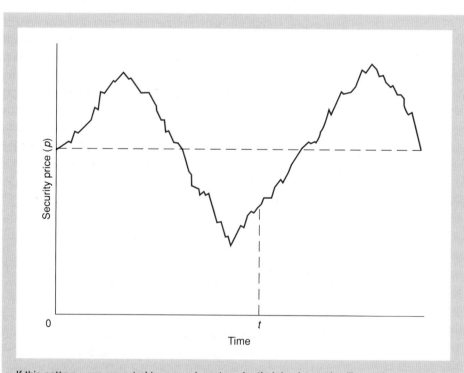

Figure 9.1
Graph of the daily share price against time for a hypothetical security

If this pattern were expected to occur, investors, by their buying and selling actions, would cause the pattern not to occur.

of us who would notice it. As we try to sell at the peak, so would the others. Since few potential buyers would be interested at the peak price, the price would drop. Realising this, we should all try to sell earlier to try to beat the drop in price, which would simply cause it to occur still earlier. The logical conclusion of this is that the price would not in fact ever rise to the peak. Expecting the trough to be reached and eager not to miss it, we should be buying earlier and earlier, thus keeping the price up and ensuring that the trough is never reached either.

The net result of all this is that if there are sufficient investors following past price patterns and seeking to exploit repetitions of them, those repetitions simply will not occur. In practice, the more likely price profile of that security would approximate to the horizontal broken line shown in Figure 9.1.

Weak-form efficiency test results

The first recorded discovery of randomness in a competitive market was by Bachelier when he observed it as a characteristic of commodity prices on the Paris Bourse as long ago as 1900. His discovery went somewhat unnoticed until interest in the topic was rekindled some years later.

Kendall (1953), accepting the popular view of the day that LSE security prices move in regular cycles, tried to identify the pattern, only to discover that there was none; prices seemed to move randomly.

Efficiency and randomness imply that there should be no systematic correlation between the price movement on one day and that on another. For example, it seems to be believed by some observers that if the price of a security rises today then it is more likely than not to rise again tomorrow: in other words, there are price trends. Similarly, there are those who feel that the opposite is true and that a price rise today implies a fall tomorrow. These attitudes do not, of course, reflect any belief in efficiency.

Figures 9.2, 9.3 and 9.4 depict the scatter of the price movement of one day (t) plotted against that of the following day ($t + 1$) for a particular security over a period. Each of the dots on the graphs is one day's price movement for a particular security, plotted against that of the following day for the same security. Figure 9.2 reflects a positive correlation, that is, it suggests that an increase in the security price on one day will be followed by another increase on the following day. Figure 9.3 implies a negative correlation so that an increase in price on one day would mean a fall on the following day, and vice versa. Figure 9.4 shows what we should expect if the security were traded in a weak-form efficient market: there appears to be randomness between one day's price movement and that of the next. Sometimes an increase is followed by an increase, sometimes by a decrease, but with no patterns.

Many tests have sought to identify relationships between price movements on consecutive days, two or more days or weeks, and found no such relationships, either positive or negative, of significant size. This research shows that security price movements closely resemble the sort of pattern that would emerge from a random number generator. Probably the most highly regarded of these serial correlation tests was conducted by Fama (1965). Brealey (1970) and Cunningham (1973) conducted similar tests on security prices in the LSE and found evidence of weak-form efficiency.

Most of the rules used by technical analysts have been tested. For example, Alexander (1961) used a filter rule and found that abnormal returns could be made, but as soon as dealing charges are considered the gains disappear. Dryden (1970), using filter tests on UK security prices, came to similar conclusions.

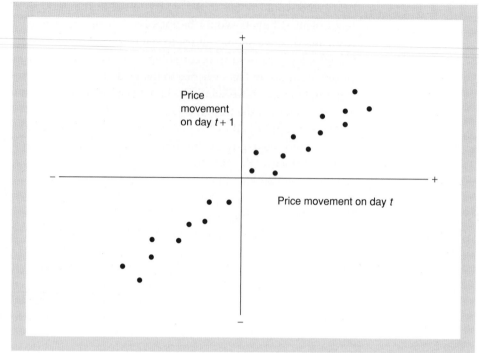

Figure 9.2
Graph of a
security's price
on one day (day *t*)
against that of the
following day (day
t + 1) where the two
movements are
positively correlated

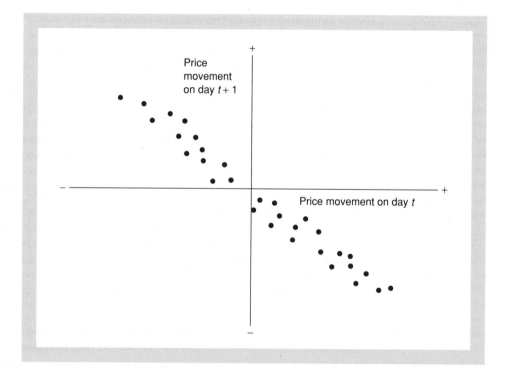

Figure 9.3
Graph of a
security's price
on one day (day *t*)
against that of the
following day (day
t + 1) where the
two movements
are *negatively*
correlated

Counter-evidence on weak-form efficiency

There is an increasingly large body of evidence of an apparent tendency for investors
to overreact to new information. There seems, for example, to be evidence that the
release of an item of news that reduces the price of a particular share tends to cause

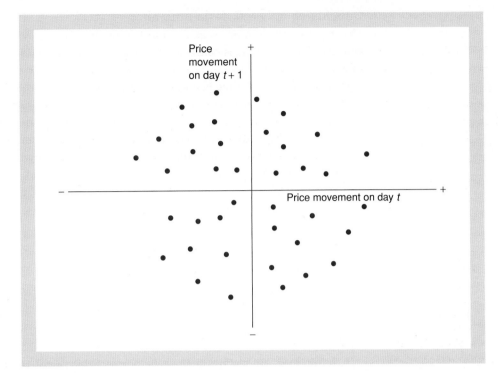

Figure 9.4
Graph of a security's price on one day (day *t*) against that of the following day (day *t* + 1) where the two movements are uncorrelated

the price to reduce more than is justified. This overreaction is subsequently corrected by the price increasing by a small but significant amount. It seems that investors who exploit the tendency to overreact, by, for example, buying shares immediately following some 'bad' news, can make abnormally large returns as the overreaction is corrected (see, for example, Dissanaike 1997, 1999).

There is also evidence of a 'weekend' or 'Monday' effect, where there are significantly higher returns from either buying shares on a Monday morning and selling them on a Monday evening, or selling them in the morning and buying them back in the evening, than the normal expected returns from the shares over one day (see, for example, Mehdian and Perry (2001), Sun and Tong (2002) and Brusa, Liu and Schulman (2003)). The problem with generating abnormal returns from exploiting this apparent weakness is that the effect seems inconsistent. Over some periods (and for the shares of some sizes of business), returns are positive, but over other periods (and for different sizes of business) they are negative. Although the Monday effect seems to be an anomaly, it falls short of providing evidence of a lack of market efficiency.

Fama (1998) makes the point that some of these apparent anomalies may result from using a 'bad model'. Where researchers are saying that abnormal returns result from a particular investment technique, they are comparing returns from using that technique with those that would be *expected* for the particular securities concerned. Typically, the capital asset pricing model (CAPM) would be used to determine these expected returns. As we discussed in Chapter 7, Fama and French (1992, 1996) showed that, for the securities of many businesses, the basic CAPM tells only part of the story. Fama (1998) argues that, were the Fama and French version of CAPM to be used to determine the expected returns, the anomalies would disappear.

Conclusion on weak-form efficiency

The broad conclusion on weak-form tests must be that the evidence on capital markets, including the LSE, is consistent with weak-form efficiency. While there might be minor inefficiencies, they are generally not of any economic significance since they cease to exist when dealing charges are considered.

It is particularly important to note that randomness does *not* mean that prices are set irrationally. On the contrary, since new information becomes available randomly, its reflection in security prices should also be random if the market is efficient. After a particular price movement it may well be possible to explain, by reference to real events, why the movement took place. Randomness should not be confused with arbitrariness here. Prices moving in trends and repeating past patterns would point to available information not being fully reflected in those prices, that is, to inefficiency and arbitrary pricing.

Tests of semi-strong-form efficiency

Tests of semi-strong-form efficiency have centred on questions of whether new information, which could reasonably be expected to affect a security's price, actually does so, in the expected direction, by the expected amount, and with the expected rapidity.

A fertile area for testing to see whether security prices react rationally to new information, is where some action of management might superficially seem to indicate something that, on closer examination, is not the case. If security prices seem to reflect the superficial view of the action, and not the rational one, it would imply that the market was not efficient (in the semi-strong form) owing to the naïvety of investors. In other words, it would imply that the managers would be able to fool the investors by window-dressing activities.

Bonus share issues

Capitalisation or *bonus share issues* involve little more than a bookkeeping entry that gives existing equity shareholders an increase in their holding of shares without increasing each individual's slice of the ownership of the business. For example, an investor owning 100 ordinary shares in a business whose total shares issued is 1 000 000 owns one ten-thousandth of the equity value of that business. If the business makes a bonus issue of one for two, our shareholder now has 150 shares but, as the total number of shares at issue will now be 1 500 000, this still represents one ten-thousandth of the equity. As the total value of the equity has not changed as a result of the bonus issue, logically share prices should adjust so that three shares after the issue are worth as much as two were before. Naïve investors might feel that this was a real gain and see the post-issue price of two-thirds of the pre-issue one as a genuine bargain. This would cause them to come into the market as buyers, forcing the price up. Research conducted on the LSE and on Wall Street by Firth (1977a) and by Fama, Fisher, Jensen and Roll (1969) respectively found no such naïvety, and that security prices reacted in the logical way.

Change in accounting procedures

Another example where the superficial interpretation of events could be the wrong one is where profits appear to improve as a result of a change in accounting procedures.

Sunder (1973) looked at a number of US businesses that had changed their method of stock-in-trade valuation so that they appeared to show higher profits than if the old method had been adhered to. This would appear to be the perfect trap in which to catch the naïve investor, in that the economic consequences of the change would be adverse since the businesses' tax charges (which are based on accounting profits) would increase. Rationally, the change in accounting policy should cause a drop in equity share prices for those businesses because the change would adversely affect their cash flows (increased tax payments). Sunder found that reason appeared to have prevailed in that, for these businesses, the change had an adverse effect on share prices. Sunder also took a group of businesses that had altered their stock-in-trade valuation method in exactly the opposite way and found this had, as reason would demand, caused the opposite effect on share prices.

Using UK data, Morris (1975) found that share prices had adjusted to take account of a reduction of earnings figures to adjust for inflation, even before the adjustment had been published.

Speed of reaction

Testing speed of reaction of security prices to new information presents great practical difficulties. It is hard to identify precisely when the new information becomes known, and in some markets, including the LSE, it is difficult to know after the event precisely when the price movement occurred. On Wall Street, records are available of all transactions and their timing, to the minute. Thus if a particular transaction is itself regarded as having possible informational content, researchers could know the timing of that transaction and the timing and price of subsequent transactions. Dann, Mayers and Raab (1977) conducted some research on the effect of trades of large blocks of shares of a particular business, much larger than the number of shares traded in the typical stock market transaction. Among other things they noted that the *turbulence* caused by such trades, the period during which the market assessed the effect of the trade, lasted about fifteen minutes at most. This is to say that an unexpected event, albeit an event occurring in the heart of the capital market (Wall Street in this particular case), had been assessed and was reflected in the new price within a quarter of an hour. Large block trades are felt to have possible informational content in that a purchase or a sale of a large quantity of the security might imply that the investor initiating the trade has some new information that has precipitated the action.

More recently, Busse and Green (2002) found that good news is typically impounded in the relevant share price within one minute. Bad news can take up to fifteen minutes before it is fully reflected. The 'news' in these cases was the opinions of analysts broadcast on television during Wall Street's normal trading hours.

Conclusion on semi-strong-form efficiency

From the studies that we have reviewed here, the results of which are typical of the conclusions drawn from the research conducted on the world's secondary capital markets, the evidence seems consistent with the view that security prices adjust rationally and speedily to new information. Just as importantly, they seem to ignore bogus new information, that is, data that appear to be relevant but which in fact are not. Thus the general conclusion is that the capital markets, including the LSE, are efficient in the semi-strong form.

Tests of strong-form efficiency

Strong-form efficiency would imply that there is no such thing as private information in the context of information relevant to the setting of security prices. As soon as information is available to any one person or group it is reflected in the price of the particular security or securities to which it relates.

Those who might have access to information that is not generally available include:

- *insiders* who have privileged positions with regard to such information (this might include managers, staff, auditors and other professional advisers); and
- *expert and professional investors.*

Intuition suggests that managers who have information not yet publicly available could turn this knowledge into investment returns that are abnormally high compared with those of investors not possessing the information. Similarly, we might expect that investment fund managers would be more successful, given their experience and research resources, than if they were to select investments with a pin.

Insiders

In the UK, insider dealing is much frowned upon by public opinion, by law, and by ethical standards of professional bodies. Thus, if insider dealing goes on, it is done furtively and is, therefore, not readily observable by researchers. In the USA a different attitude used to be taken (until the 1960s) to insider dealing, although insiders were required to register their status when dealing. Tests on the success of insiders dealing on Wall Street have been conducted. Both Jaffe (1974) and Finnerty (1976) found that insiders could consistently earn abnormal returns as a result of their greater access to information.

Professionals

As regards professional investors, much research has been conducted into the performance of unit and investment trusts. These are organisations that attract funds from the investing public, which are then invested predominantly in marketable securities. These studies, including one conducted by Firth (1977b) on UK unit trust performance during the period 1965 to 1975, have found no superior performance. Some researchers have found that the results of investment by these experts are in fact less good than would be the outcome of an investment strategy based on selecting securities at random. For example, Blake and Timmermann (1998) looked at the performance of 2300 UK professionally-managed investment funds over a 23-year period. They found that the average fund performed less well, in terms of investment returns, than would have been expected for the risk levels involved.

The advice of professional investment advisers has also been assessed and found not generally to lead to consistently abnormal returns.

Conclusion on strong-form efficiency

The conclusion on strong-form efficiency would seem to be that insiders who have genuine new information can use it to advantage, revealing an inefficiency of the capital markets. However, those not having access to such information are not, on a continuing basis, able to achieve better than average returns irrespective of whether they are 'experts' or not.

We have reviewed by no means all of the research that has been conducted; however, other studies have reached similar conclusions to those that we have considered.

9.5 The efficient market paradox

A notable paradox of capital market efficiency is that if large numbers of investors were not trying to earn abnormal returns by technical analysis and by the analysis of new information (fundamental analysis), efficiency would not exist. It is only because so many non-believers are actively seeking out inefficiencies to exploit to their own advantage that none exists that is, in practical terms, exploitable.

9.6 Conclusions on, and implications of, capital market efficiency

The conclusions of tests on the efficiency of the LSE and of capital markets generally is that the evidence is consistent with efficiency in all forms, except that only publicly available information seems to be reflected in security prices. Information not yet publicly available is not necessarily reflected. Results of research, emerging from the USA particularly, may be indicating some minor capital market inefficiencies. Some observers believe that if evidence of inefficiency is emerging, it may reflect a change in the nature of LSE investors. Efficiency requires a large number of independent investors. Increasingly, LSE investment has tended to concentrate in the hands of a relatively few large institutional investors, most of whom are based in and around the City of London. This, it is believed by some, leads to prices being determined not so much by independent market forces as by 'herd instinct'. Welch (2000) found evidence that recommendations from analysts about particular securities tend to have an effect on the subsequent recommendations from other analysts.

Despite some contrary evidence, it remains true that, for most practical purposes, we can say that the LSE efficiently prices securities that are traded there.

It might be worth remembering that, given the way that stock markets operate, which we discussed earlier in the chapter, this conclusion on the evidence is not surprising. Logically, we should expect it to be efficient.

Implications for investors

Capital market efficiency implies that investors should not waste time seeking to obtain abnormally high returns from investment, either by observing historic information on security price movements or by analysis of new economic information. Only where an investor has access to as-yet unreleased information can above-average returns be made – except by sheer chance. Even putting trust in investment analysts or investing through one of the investing institutions will not, on a regular basis, be advantageous, and it may well be costly.

Why, if the above statement is true, do so many investors indulge in precisely the activities that appear to be futile? There are several possible explanations for this apparently irrational behaviour.

● *Ignorance of the evidence on efficiency.* Many investors seem to be unfamiliar with the evidence on capital market efficiency so, quite reasonably, they do not take account of it. Few people or organisations have a vested interest in publicising the evidence, and many have the opposite interest. Newspapers and journals that deal partly or mainly in giving advice on which securities to buy or sell do not have an interest in pointing out that this advice is only going to prove valuable by sheer chance so that, on average, it will be of no value. Other investment advisers, stockbrokers and such like, are similarly placed.

● *Close examination of charts of past security price movements shows patterns repeating themselves.* This is undoubtedly true in some cases, but it is equally true that plotting random numbers will also sometimes do exactly the same. In other words, chance alone will sometimes cause a pattern to repeat itself; this does not imply that gains can be made by trying to spot repeats.

● *Proponents of certain technical rules have been shown to be successful.* Efficiency does not imply that investment cannot be successful, simply that being more than averagely successful is a matter of good luck. During some particular periods, and generally throughout the twentieth century, investment in securities dealt on the LSE will have given positive returns. The value of securities generally has increased, not to mention the dividends or interest receipts from which the investor will also have benefited. It should not therefore surprise us that, despite efficiency, following most investment advice over a substantial period yields positive returns. Indeed, efficiency implies that it would be impossible to find investment advice to follow that would yield lower-than-average returns in the long run, for the level of risk involved, except by sheer chance.

● *We all know of cases of people who have been extremely successful in capital market investment.* Those who are particularly successful tend to be noticed; those who are disastrously unsuccessful tend to keep quiet about it. In both cases it seems to be sheer luck – good and bad, respectively. Those who are unsuccessful tend to acknowledge this fact; the successful ones – being human – may prefer to believe that skill in selection and timing of investment was the cause of their success.

Even in matters of sheer chance, someone can still be successful, even staggeringly successful. Suppose that a coin-tossing championship of the UK were to be held and that all 60 million inhabitants entered. The rules are that we are all grouped into 30 million pairs, each of which tosses a coin. The member of each pair who calls correctly goes into the next round, and the process is repeated until the winner emerges. We know that a winner must emerge, but would we really believe that skill was involved? We should more likely judge the winner to have had remarkably good fortune in the face of a very small probability of success.

A strategy for an investor in marketable securities

The evidence that we reviewed in this chapter, and what we found about diversification and risk reduction in Chapter 7, leads to the following strategy as being preferable:

● Divide the total to be invested by between 15 and 20, and invest the resultant amounts in different securities. Try to invest over a range of different industries. By doing this the investor will eliminate almost all of the specific risk attaching to the individual securities.

- Invest in securities whose betas suit the investor's risk/return preferences.

- Do not trade in securities. Only alter the securities in the portfolio to 'rebalance' should the values of the holdings of individual securities become significantly different from one another as the result of relative security price movements within the portfolio. This is to maintain the broad equality of value of the 15 to 20 different holdings. Do not be tempted to take profits on securities that are performing well or to get rid of badly performing ones. Efficient market evidence is clear that the current price is the best available estimate of the value of a security, given the projected future. The evidence is also clear that, unless the investor is an insider, the current market value is a better estimate of the security's worth than the investor's estimate. The evidence is clear that active trading is costly in terms of dealing costs and does not yield security price value (see, for example, Barber and Odean (2000)). A buy-and-hold policy has been shown to be the best.

Small investors may find it uneconomic, in terms of dealing costs (stockbrokers fees), which tend to have economies of scale, to follow the first of the above recommendations. Here, the use of an investment fund may be the best approach. Investment fund managers charge an annual fee, usually based on the size of each investor's holding, but they can achieve dealing economies of scale. If this approach is taken, the investor should select a fund that has a buy-and-hold strategy.

Implications for financial managers

These are vitally important and the main reason why we are discussing capital market efficiency in this book. Broadly the implications are:

- *It is difficult to fool the investors.* Investors rationally interpret what the business's management does, and 'window dressing' matters will not cause security prices to rise.

- *The market rationally values the business.* If the management wants to issue new equity shares, then the existing equity price is the appropriate issue price. If the general level of prices were low on a historical basis, it would be illogical to wait for a recovery before issuing new equity. If security prices follow a random walk, there is no reason to believe that just because prices have been higher in the past they will return to previous levels.

- *Management should act in a way that maximises shareholder wealth.* As this is the generally accepted criterion for making investment decisions within the business, if managers make decisions that logically should promote it, then provided that they release information on what they have done, security prices will reflect the managers' actions. In other words, if managers act in a way that promotes the interests of shareholders, this will in fact promote their interests through the share price.

- *Managers may have an interest in withholding unfavourable information.* The strong-form inefficiency revealed by research shows that not all information that exists is impounded in security prices. Thus management might have a vested interest in withholding unfavourable information. Whether this would in fact be valid in the long run is doubtful since most information emerges sooner or later. Probably, a widespread feeling among investors that managers are prepared to suppress unfavourable information would ultimately be detrimental to those managers.

● *The secondary capital markets provide a reliable guide to required returns from risky investments.* In the same way that if we wish to value a second-hand car we might look at the price for similar cars in the second-hand car market, it is logical to try to assess the value of assets with particular risk and return expectations by looking at prices of similar assets in the secondary capital markets. This provides a major justification for the use of CAPM, in deriving an appropriate discount rate to apply to cash flows, in the assessment of real investment decisions made by businesses.

The general conclusion on efficiency is that management and security holders are directly linked through security prices. Significant actions of management immediately reflect in security prices. The evidence is clear that security prices react rapidly and rationally to new information. The implications of secondary capital market efficiency for managers will be referred to at various points throughout the remainder of this book.

Summary

Capital market efficiency (CME)

● CME means that the market rationally prices securities so that the current price of each security at any given moment represents the best estimate of its 'true' value.

● CME would imply that all available information bearing on the value of a particular security is taken into account in its price:

  ● rapidly; and

  ● rationally.

● It is reasonable to believe that CME could exist in practice because many skilled individuals with the financial weight to affect security prices constantly assess the value of those securities and monitor their market prices.

● The current price of any security represents a consensus view of the security's current worth – its price is the result of the actions of buyers and sellers, each with different perceptions of the value of the security.

The evidence on CME

● Research studies have been conducted that look at efficiency at three different levels:

  ● weak form (WF);

  ● semi-strong form (SSF); and

  ● strong form (SF).

● WF efficiency would exist if it were not possible to make abnormal profits from security investing relying on past security price movements (for example, with the use of charts) or technical rules to indicate when to buy and sell.

● Evidence shows that the world's leading markets are WF efficient.

● SSF efficiency would exist if it were not possible to make abnormal profits from security investing relying on the analysis of publicly available information to indicate when to buy and sell.

- Evidence shows that the world's leading stock markets are SSF efficient.
- SF efficiency would exist if it were not possible to make abnormal profits from security investing relying on the analysis of information available only to insiders to indicate when to buy and sell.
- Evidence shows that the world's leading markets are *not* SF efficient.

Implications of CME

- Implication for investors: only if they have access to information not available to the public can they expect, except by chance, to make better-than-average returns, given the risk class of the securities concerned.
- Implications for financial managers:
  - It is difficult to fool investors.
  - The market rationally values the business.
  - Efforts to enhance share value should have that effect.
  - Managers may have a short-term interest in withholding information.
  - The LSE rationally values assets with risky returns.

Further reading

The role and operation of the LSE are covered by a number of texts including Samuels, Wilkes and Brayshaw (1998). Facts and figures on the LSE are published annually in *The Stock Exchange Fact Book*.

Capital market efficiency is well reviewed in the literature, for example in Emery and Finnerty (2004).

For an impressive review of empirical studies of market efficiency, see Dimson and Mussavian (1998).

Relevant websites

The site for the London Stock Exchange is:
www.londonstockexchange.com

The Dimson and Mussavian (1998) article cited in the Further reading, can be accessed and downloaded. This is Professor Dimson's website, which also gives access to a number of his other articles.
http://faculty.london.edu/edimson/market.pdf

The websites of the businesses featured in this chapter are:

Boots Group plc   **www.boots-plc.com**
Tesco plc   **www.tesco.com**

REVIEW QUESTIONS

Suggested answers to review questions appear in Appendix 3.

9.1 What are the two roles of members of the LSE in respect of their secondary market activities?

9.2 When UK shareholders have shares that they wish to sell, must the sale be made through the LSE?

9.3 What is 'price efficiency' in the context of stock markets?

9.4 Is a market that is 'strong-form efficient' necessarily 'semi-strong-form efficient'?

9.5 Without any knowledge of the evidence surrounding the efficiency of the LSE, would you expect it to be efficient? Explain your response.

9.6 Must all of the world's stock markets be price efficient? Explain your response.

PROBLEMS

Sample answers to problems marked with an asterisk appear in Appendix 4.

(Problems 9.1 to 9.6 are all basic-level problems.)

9.1* 'The shares of XYZ plc are underpriced at the moment.'

How logical is this statement about some shares quoted on the LSE?

9.2* 'Capital market efficiency in the semi-strong form implies that all investors have all of the knowledge that is publicly available and which bears on the value of all securities traded in the market.'

Comment on this statement.

9.3* 'In view of the fact that the market is efficient in the semi-strong form, there is no value to investors in businesses publishing financial reports, because the information contained in those reports is already impounded in share prices before that information is published.'

Comment on this statement.

9.4 'A graph of the daily price of a share looks similar to that which would be obtained by plotting a series of cumulative random numbers. This shows clearly that share prices move randomly at the whim of investors, indicating that the market is not price efficient.'

Comment on this statement.

9.5 'A particular professionally managed UK equity investment fund produced better returns last year than any of its rivals. This means that it is likely to outperform its rivals again this year.'

Comment on this statement.

9.6 'An efficient capital market is one in which the market portfolio contains no systematic risk.'

Is this statement correct? Explain.

There are both a set of **multiple-choice questions** and **missing-word questions** available on the website. These specifically cover the material contained in this chapter. These can be attempted and graded (with feedback) online.

There are also **four additional problems**, with solutions, that relate to the material covered in this chapter.

Go to **www.pearsoned.co.uk/atrillmclaney** and follow the links.

Chapter 10

Cost of capital estimations and the discount rate

In this chapter we shall deal with the following:

→ estimating the cost of individual sources of capital

→ the difficulties of estimating the cost of equity finance

→ target gearing ratios

→ the weighted average cost of capital and its relevance as a discount rate

→ WACC and CAPM derivation of cost of capital compared both in theory and in practice

10.1 Introduction

In Chapter 8 we took a brief look at typical sources of long-term finance of UK businesses. Now we shall see how it is possible to make estimates of the cost to the business of each of these individual sources.

Since, logically, the discount rate to be applied to the expected cash flows of real investment opportunities within the business should be the opportunity cost of finance to support the investment, this discount rate must be related to the costs of individual sources in some way. In fact, using an average cost of the various sources of finance, weighted according to the importance of each source to the particular business, seems to be regarded as a standard means of determining discount rates. Evidence (Petty and Scott 1981; Corr 1983; Al-Ali and Arkwright 2000; Arnold and Hatzopoulos 2000) suggests that this weighted average cost of capital (WACC) approach is widely used in practice. McLaney, Pointon, Thomas and Tucker (2004) found that WACC is used in investment appraisal by 53 per cent of UK listed businesses. They also found that nearly 80 per cent of businesses reassess their cost of capital annually or more frequently.

The standard approach to estimating the cost of specific sources of capital is based on the logic that the discount rate is implied by the current value of the financial asset concerned, and by future expectations of cash flows from that specific asset. This is a popular approach in practice, although for estimating the cost of equity its popularity is decreasing.

In Chapter 7 we saw that the capital asset pricing model (CAPM) is a logical device for deriving the cost of individual financing elements. CAPM deduces the cost of capital from capital market information, dealing explicitly with risk through a risk premium. This risk premium is based on the covariance of specific security returns with those from the generality of risky investments. CAPM is increasingly the standard way for most businesses, particularly larger ones, to derive their cost of equity (see the evidence cited in section 7.10 of Chapter 7 on the extent of CAPM usage).

The traditional WACC approach is also capital market based (we use current security values in the calculation), but it deals much less formally with risk than CAPM.

After having considered the traditional approach we shall try to reconcile it with the CAPM philosophy, and attempt to reach some conclusion on the theoretical appropriateness of each and of their relative practicality.

10.2 Cost of individual capital elements

An economic asset (which loan stocks, equities, and so on, are to their owners) has a current value equal to the value of the future cash benefits from ownership of the asset discounted at a rate commensurate with the timing and risk of each of those cash benefits, that is:

$$v_0 = \Sigma C_n / (1 + r)^n \qquad (10.1)$$

where C is the cash flow associated with the asset, r the rate of return and n the time of each cash flow. To a loan creditor or shareholder, the future cash flows, at any given moment, will be the future interest or dividend receipts (payable annually, biannually, or perhaps quarterly) and, perhaps, a repayment of the principal at some future specified date.

Logically, a rate of return to the investors represents a cost to the business concerned. Therefore we can make the general statement that:

$$p_0 = \Sigma C_n / (1 + k)^n \qquad (10.2)$$

where k is the cost of capital to the business and p_0 is the security's current market price.

Loan stocks

With Stock Exchange listed loan stocks we should know the current market value of the loan stock, the contracted interest payments and dates, and the contracted amount and date of the repayment of the principal. Thus, in the valuation expression above, we should know all of the factors except k. Solving for k will give us the cost of capital figure that we require.

Example 10.1

A loan stock that was originally issued at par is currently quoted in the capital market at £93 per £100 nominal value, repayment of the nominal value in full is due in exactly five years' time, and interest at 10 per cent on the nominal value is due for payment at the end of each of the next five years. What is the cost of the loan stock?

Assume a 30 per cent rate of corporation tax.

Solution

Since we are seeking to deduce a rate that can be used to discount after-tax cash flows, we need an after-tax cost of capital. The loan stock interest would attract tax relief, but the capital repayment would not because it is not an expense.

The following statement holds true:

$$93 = \frac{10(1 - 0.30)}{(1 + k_L)} + \frac{10(1 - 0.30)}{(1 + k_L)^2} + \frac{10(1 - 0.30)}{(1 + k_L)^3} + \frac{10(1 - 0.30)}{(1 + k_L)^4} + \frac{10(1 - 0.30)}{(1 + k_L)^5} + \frac{100}{(1 + k_L)^5}$$

where k_L is the after-tax cost of the loan stock.

Solving for k_L will give us the required cost of capital figure. We have met this situation before when deducing the internal rate of return of an investment opportunity. k_L is of course the IRR of the loan stock, and hence the solution is only discoverable by trial and error. As annual returns of a net £7 are worth £93, a rate of less than 10 per cent is implied. Let us try 8 per cent.

Year	Cash flow £	Discount factor	Present value £
0	(93.0)	1.000	(93.0)
1	7.0	0.926	6.5
2	7.0	0.857	6.0
3	7.0	0.794	5.6
4	7.0	0.735	5.1
5	107.0	0.681	72.9
			3.1

It seems that the cost of capital is above 8 per cent; let us try 9 per cent.

Year	Cash flow £	Discount factor	Present value £
0	(93.0)	1.000	(93.0)
1	7.0	0.917	6.4
2	7.0	0.842	5.9
3	7.0	0.772	5.4
4	7.0	0.708	5.0
5	107.0	0.650	69.6
			(0.7)

Thus the cost lies very close to 8.8 per cent.

Some readers may be puzzled as to why, when the original amount borrowed was £100, the amount to be repaid is equally £100 and the coupon interest rate is 10 per cent, the cost of the loan stock is not 10 per cent before tax or 7.0 per cent after tax.

We should remember that our purpose in calculating the cost of capital is to derive a discount rate to apply to investment projects. In previous chapters we have seen that the appropriate discount rate is the opportunity cost of capital. This means either the saving that would follow from repaying the capital source, or the cost of further finance raised from that source. At the present time this amount would be 8.8 per cent after tax. If the business wishes to cancel the loan stock, it can do so by buying the stock in the capital market at £93 (per £100 nominal). This would save the annual interest payments of 7.0 per cent on the nominal value, and avoid the necessity to repay the capital after five years. If further finance is to be raised, presumably the same business could raise £93 for a loan stock that pays £10 at the end of each of the next five years plus £100 at the end of the fifth year. So in either case, 8.8 per cent is the appropriate rate.

We might also ask why investors were at one time prepared to pay £100 (for £100 nominal value) for a loan stock that yields £10 p.a. in interest (a 10 per cent return). The difference must arise either from interest rates having increased generally and/or from the capital market having changed its perceptions of the risk of default (by the business) in payment of interest or principal. Thus a particular business's cost of capital is not necessarily static over time. Given capital market efficiency, the cost of any element of capital is the market's best estimate of that cost for the future.

Perpetual loan stocks are occasionally issued by businesses. These are loan stocks that have no repayment date and which will, in theory, continue paying interest for ever. Their cost of capital calculation is similar to, though simpler than, the calculation for redeemable loan stocks.

Where each of the C_n values is identical and n goes on to infinity,

$$p_{L0} = \sum_{n=1}^{\infty} \frac{C_n(1-T)}{(1+k_L)^n}$$

where T is the rate of corporation tax. This can be written as:

$$k_L = \frac{C_n(1-T)}{p_{L0}}$$

Thus in the above example, if there were to be no repayment of principal but the annual £10 interest payments were to continue indefinitely, then

$$k_L = \frac{10(1-0.30)}{93}$$

$$= 7.5\%$$

Term loans

With term loans and unlisted loan stocks, there is no readily accessible figure for p_0 that can be put into the valuation model (equation (10.2) above) to deduce k. Logically p_0 should be the amount that the borrowing business would need to pay immediately to induce the lender to cancel the loan contract. Alternatively, it is the amount that could currently be borrowed, given the future payments of interest and capital it is obliged to make under the terms of the loan in question. In theory these two should be alternative routes to the same value for p_0; in practice they may not be.

The real problem is that, equal or not, in practice p_0 is not readily observable, so some estimate of it needs to be made. In practical terms, unless the value of the loan is particularly large and/or there have been major changes in interest rates since the loan was negotiated, the contracted rate of interest would probably serve adequately as the present opportunity cost of the source. Alternatively, an estimate, based on observation of current interest rates, could be made.

Finance leases

As we saw in Chapter 8, a finance lease is in effect a secured term loan with capital repayments at intervals during the period of the loan, rather than all at the end. Where it is not explicit in the lease contract, we can discover the interest rate fairly easily.

The value of the lease at the date of its being taken out is the cost of the asset that is the subject of the lease. Since this figure and the amount and timing of the future lease payments can be discovered, k can be discovered. To identify the present cost of a lease later in its life we should need to take a similar attitude to that which is necessary in respect of term loans and unlisted loan stocks. We could try to put some current value on the lease and solve for k in the valuation expression (equation (10.2) above). We could, however, assume that the current opportunity cost of the lease finance is more or less the same as it was when the lease was first taken out.

Trying to value the lease at some date after it has been in operation for a while is likely to be a fairly difficult task, so we are probably left with making the assumption that the interest rate implied by the original contract is still appropriate. Alternatively, some estimate of rates applying to current new leases could be used.

Preference shares

The calculation of the cost of preference shares is almost identical to that for loan stocks. The major differences between the two financing methods are as follows:

- Loans stock interest attracts corporation tax relief; preference dividends do not.
- Loan interest is paid under a contractual obligation; preference dividends are paid at the discretion of the business's directors.

The first point simply means that tax should be ignored in the calculation of the cost of preference shares. The second implies that rather more uncertainty is involved with predicting preference dividends than with predicting loan interest payments, although this creates no difference in principle.

Ordinary shares

Ordinary shares too are similar to loan stocks in the basic calculation of the cost of capital. Ordinary shares have a value because they are expected to yield dividends. How, if at all, the pattern of dividends affects the value of equities, we shall discuss in Chapter 12.

Ex dividend and cum dividend

Before we start detailed discussion of dividends and how they are linked to share prices, a few words need to be said about the basis on which shares are traded in the secondary capital market. Normally, shares are traded cum dividend, which means that anyone who buys the shares will receive the next dividend paid by the business concerned. When a dividend is imminent, the business concerned will 'close' its list of shareholders and pay the dividend to those shareholders appearing on the list, in other words the shares go ex dividend. This means that anyone buying the shares after that date will not receive that particular dividend; it will, however, be paid to the previous shareholders who have sold their shares since the close date. This is despite the fact that those investors will no longer own the shares on the dividend payment day. Not surprisingly, the price of the share falls, by the value of the forthcoming dividend, as the share moves from being traded cum dividend to being traded ex dividend.

Whenever the current market price of a share, p_{E0}, is used in any equation relating to dividends and the cost of equity, we must use the ex-dividend price. If a dividend is soon to be paid and the shares are being traded cum dividend, we need to deduct the amount of the forthcoming dividend per share to arrive at the equivalent ex-dividend price.

Deriving the cost of equity

To say that equities should be valued on the basis of future dividends is not to assume that any particular investor intends to hold a particular share for ever, because the proceeds of any future disposal of the share will itself depend on expectations, at the date of disposal, of future dividends.

If a business is expected to pay a constant dividend d per share, at the end of each year indefinitely, the value of each ordinary share will be:

$$p_{E0} = \sum_{n=1}^{\infty} \frac{d_n}{(1 + k_E)^n}$$

to the investor who intends to hold the shares for ever.

Suppose, however, that the investor intends to sell the share at time t; its value at that time will be:

$$\sum_{n=t+1}^{\infty} \frac{d_n}{(1 + k_E)^n}$$

This would mean that the value to our shareholder would be:

$$p_{E0} = \sum_{n=1}^{t} \frac{d_n}{(1 + k_E)^n} + \left(\sum_{n=t+1}^{\infty} \frac{d_n}{(1 + k_E)^n} \times \frac{1}{(1 + k_E)^t} \right)$$

that is, the value depends on the dividends to be received until time t (suitably discounted) plus the market value at time t [discounted at $1/(1 + k_E)^t$] to bring this market value to the present value.

This expression reduces to:

$$p_{E0} = \sum_{n=1}^{\infty} \frac{d_n}{(1 + k_E)^n}$$

Hence, irrespective of whether disposal at some future date is envisaged or not, provided that valuation always depends on dividends, the current value will be unaffected.

Unlike loan interest, which is usually fixed by the contract between borrower and lender, and preference dividends, which businesses usually endeavour to pay (and for which there is a defined ceiling), ordinary share dividends are highly uncertain as to amount. This poses a major problem in the estimation of the cost of equity. The prediction of future dividends is a daunting task. One of two simplifying approaches may be taken, however:

- assume that dividends will remain as at present; or
- assume some constant rate of growth in them.

If the first of these is adopted, a similar approach is taken to that for a perpetual loan stock, that is:

$$p_{E0} = \sum_{n=1}^{\infty} \frac{d_n}{(1 + k_E)^n} \qquad (10.3)$$

which, when all dividends are equal, means:

$$k_E = \frac{d_n}{p_{E0}} \qquad (10.4)$$

If we assume a constant rate of growth (g), then:

$$p_{E0} = \frac{d_1}{1 + k_E} + \frac{d_1(1 + g)}{(1 + k_E)^2} + \frac{d_1(1 + g)^2}{(1 + k_E)^3} + \ldots \text{(to infinity)} \qquad (10.5)$$

which reduces to:

$$p_{E0} = \frac{d_1}{k_E - g} \qquad (10.6)$$

so:

$$k_E = \frac{d_1}{p_{E0}} + g \qquad (10.7)$$

where d_1 is the expected dividend per share, payable next year. This is known as the Gordon growth model, after the person who derived it (Gordon 1959).

McLaney, Pointon, Thomas and Tucker (2004) found that 28 per cent of listed UK businesses use a dividend approach to estimating the cost of equity. Of these, 75 per cent include a growth factor, almost always a rate of growth based on a past trend. Al-Ali and Arkwright (2000) found that 21 per cent of larger UK businesses use the dividend approach. Graham and Harvey (2001) found that 16 per cent of the US businesses surveyed use this approach, with smaller businesses more likely to adopt it than larger ones. Note that increasingly CAPM is the standard way to derive the cost of equity, in practice.

Example 10.2

A business's ordinary shares are currently trading at £2.00 (ex dividend) each in the capital market. Next year's dividend is expected to be £0.14 per share, and subsequent dividends are expected to grow at an annual rate of 5 per cent of the previous year's dividend. What is the cost of equity?

Solution

$$k_E = \frac{d_1}{p_{E0}} + g$$

$$= \frac{0.14}{2.00} + 0.05$$

$$= 12\%$$

If a fixed proportion (b) of funds generated by trading each year is retained (as opposed to being paid as a dividend), and the funds are reinvested at a constant rate (r), then:

$$\text{Rate of growth } (g) = b \times r$$

Assuming either that dividends will be constant, on the one hand, or that the rate of growth will be constant, on the other hand, is clearly unrealistic. In practice, dividends tend to increase from time to time, and to remain steady at the new level for a period before the next increase. These particular assumptions need not be made, although they provide a practical, if inaccurate, way of estimating the cost of equity.

Retained profit

As was made clear in Chapter 8, retained profit is not a free source of finance. It has an opportunity cost to shareholders because, if such profits were to be distributed, shareholders could use them to make revenue-generating investments. It would be incorrect, however, to deal with retained profit separately in deducing its cost. When we derive the cost of equity, we are deriving the cost of the share capital *and* of the retained profit. The current market price of a share (p_{E0}) used in the dividend valuation model (above) would reflect any retained profits attaching to the particular share. Thus, provided that the cost of equity is properly derived, the fact that the equity is part share capital and part retained profit will automatically be taken into account.

Convertible loan stocks

Convertible loan stocks may be viewed as redeemable loan stocks on which interest will be paid until a date in the future when they will be *redeemed* by their conversion into equities. Estimating the cost of convertibles is, therefore, a similar operation to valuing loan stocks, except that the redemption amount is unknown, to the extent that we do not know what the equity share price will be at the conversion date. As with estimating the cost of equities, we can make some assumptions – for example, that the equity dividends will remain constant or that they will grow at a steady rate.

Example 10.3

A convertible loan stock of Tower plc currently trades in the capital market at £140 per £100 nominal. The stock pays annual interest of £11 per £100 nominal and may be converted in exactly five years' time at a rate of 50 ordinary shares in the business per £100 nominal of loan stock. The present price of the ordinary shares is £2.20, which is expected to grow by 5 per cent p.a. over the next five years. What is the cost of the convertible loan stock?

Note that corporation tax is charged at 30 per cent.

Solution

The price of the convertible p_{C0} is given by:

$$p_{C0} = \sum_{n=1}^{t} \frac{i}{(1 + k_C)^n} + \frac{p_{E0}(1 + g)^t R_C}{(1 + k_C)^t}$$

→

where i is the interest payment in each year until conversion in year t, p_{E0} is the current market price of an equity share, g is the growth rate of the equity price, R_C the conversion rate and k_C the cost of the convertible. In this example we have:

$$£140 = \frac{£11(1 - 0.30)}{1 + k_C} + \frac{£11(1 - 0.30)}{(1 + k_C)^2} + \frac{£11(1 - 0.30)}{(1 + k_C)^3} + \frac{£11(1 - 0.30)}{(1 + k_C)^4}$$

$$+ \frac{£11(1 - 0.30)}{(1 + k_C)^5} + \frac{(1 + 0.05)^5 \times £2.20 \times 50}{(1 + k_C)^5}$$

Solving for k_C (by trial and error) gives about 5.5 per cent as the cost of the convertible finance. Note that 5.5 per cent is an opportunity cost since:

- Tower plc should be able to issue some more convertibles with similar terms and expect to issue them at £140 per £100 nominal; or

- if the business were to buy back its own convertibles, for an investment of £140 it could gain £11 (less tax) each year for five years and issue the shares for cash in five years instead of using them to 'redeem' the loan stock. This would represent an annual return of 5.5 per cent to Tower plc.

Warrants are valued similarly except that the returns from the warrant continue after the equity is taken up.

10.3 The overall cost of capital to the business

We have seen how the cost of individual elements can be estimated from current capital market prices and predictions of future cash flows associated with the element concerned. Most businesses use at least two of the financing methods that we have considered, and each is likely to have a different cost. For example, to the capital market investor, loan stock tends to be much less risky than equities in the same business. Expectations of returns from equities are therefore higher. Given this disparity in the cost of the various elements, which discount rate should be applied to the estimated cash flows of prospective investment projects?

Target gearing ratios

Evidence shows that, generally, businesses have a target ratio, based on capital market values, of the various financing elements. In other words, a particular business seeks to keep equity finance as a relatively fixed proportion (by market value) of the total finance. Similarly, it seeks to keep loan-type finance as more or less a fixed proportion. Minor variations may occur from time to time, but businesses are believed to take steps to get back to target as soon as it is practical to do so.

Marsh (1982) found that, in practice, most businesses maintain a stable capital structure and appear to have a target gearing ratio. Ozkan (2001), studying 390 UK businesses over the period 1984 to 1996, concluded that, generally, businesses have a long-term target gearing ratio. Businesses seem rapidly to readjust their gearing to meet this target whenever they find themselves diverging from it. Graham and Harvey (2001) found that 81 per cent of the US businesses surveyed by them in 1999 had a target gearing ratio. Just under half of these had a 'flexible' target. Larger businesses and those with investment grade loan stocks tended to have more rigid target ratios.

It is believed that such target ratios exist because businesses, taking account of such factors as levels of interest rates, tax advantages of loan interest relative to dividends, and the stability of their operating cash flows, decide on an optimal mix of financing methods, which they then try to establish and maintain. Such targets are not, presumably, established for all time; changes in interest rates, tax rules and so on, may cause a change to a new target, which may then rule for several years.

Targets will also vary from one business to another, partly because of differences of opinion from one set of management to another. Such differences may also partly, perhaps mainly, arise from differences in the nature of the trade in which the particular business is engaged.

The objective of trying to establish and maintain an optimal balance between various sources of finance; indeed, raising finance from other than equities at all, is presumably to try to minimise the cost of capital, which will maximise shareholder wealth. Whether such attempts actually work is a matter to which we shall return in Chapter 11. Meanwhile let us go back to the question of the choice of the discount rate.

Weighted average cost of capital

If we make three assumptions:

- there is a known target ratio for the financing elements, which will continue for the duration of the investment project under consideration;
- the costs of the various elements will not alter in the future from the costs calculated; and
- the investment under consideration is of similar risk to the average of the other projects undertaken by the business

then using the weighted average cost of capital (WACC) as the discount rate is logical.

Using opportunity cost implies looking at the savings in financing cost that would arise if finance were to be repaid instead of undertaking the investment project. Alternatively, it could be seen as the additional cost of raising the necessary finance to support the project. If there were a target, repayment of finance or additional financing would be carried out in accordance with the target. For example, suppose that a particular business has a target debt/equity ratio of 50/50 (by market value). If that business is to take on extra finance to support an investment project, it will in principle do so in the same 50/50 proportion, otherwise it will disturb the existing position (presumably 50/50). Similarly, if the finance for the project is available but it could alternatively be repaid to suppliers, presumably 50 per cent would be used to cancel loan stocks and 50 per cent paid to ordinary shareholders, perhaps as a dividend.

The three assumptions stated at the start of this section are all concerned with the fact that in investment project appraisal, and in any other case where we may wish to assess the cost of capital, it is the future cost that we are interested in. The third assumption, relating to risk, perhaps needs a comment. We know from a combination of intuition, casual observation of real life and from a robust theoretical proposition (CAPM, examined in Chapter 7), that the required rate of return/cost of capital depends partly on the level of risk surrounding the cash flows of the investment project concerned. It is not appropriate, therefore, to use a WACC, based on a past involving investment projects of one risk class, as the discount rate for investments of an entirely different class.

Example 10.4	**Calculation of WACC**

Hazelwood plc is financed by:

(a) 1 million ordinary shares (nominal value £1 each), which are expected to yield a dividend of £0.10 per share in one year's time; dividends are expected to grow by 10 per cent of the previous year's dividend each year; the current market price of the share is £1.80 each; and

(b) £800 000 (nominal) loan stock, which pays interest at the end of each year of 11 per cent (of nominal) for three years, after which the loan stock will be redeemed at nominal value. Currently the loan stock is quoted in the capital market at £95 (per £100 nominal).

The corporation tax rate is 30 per cent.
What is the business's WACC?

Solution	

First we must find the cost of each of the individual elements.

(a) *Ordinary shares*. Here we can apply the Gordon growth model (see equation (10.7), page 276)

$$\text{Cost of equity, } k_E = \frac{£0.10}{£1.80} + 10\%$$

$$= 15.6\%, \text{ say } 16\%$$

(b) *Loan stock*. We must use our IRR-type trial and error here. We have the equivalent of an investment project where an investment of £95 now will bring in interest of £11 (less tax) that is, £7.70 net, at the end of each of the next three years plus £100 at the end of the third year.

The discount rate that will give a zero NPV looks as if it is below 10 per cent. Try 8 per cent:

Year	Cash flow £	Discount factor	Present value £
0	(95.00)	1.000	(95.0)
1	7.70	0.926	7.1
2	7.70	0.857	6.6
3	107.70	0.794	85.5
			4.2

The appropriate discount rate lies above 8 per cent. Try 9 per cent:

Year	Cash flow £	Discount factor	Present value £
0	(95.00)	1.000	(95.0)
1	7.70	0.917	7.1
2	7.70	0.842	6.5
3	107.70	0.772	83.1
			1.7

Clearly the appropriate rate lies close to 9 per cent; a closer approximation may be obtained, but it is doubtful whether there is any point in seeking more accuracy than the nearest whole percentage (9 per cent). This is because:

● the cost of the other element in the financing (ordinary shares) has been calculated making some fairly sweeping assumptions about future dividends; *and*

● the cash flows that will be discounted by the resulting WACC cannot be predicted with any great accuracy.

We may say, then, that the cost of the loan stock, $k_L = 9\%$.
Next we need to value the two elements:

(a) *Ordinary shares*. The total value of the ordinary shares:

$$V_E = 1 \text{ million} \times £1.80 = £1.80\text{m}$$

(b) *Loan stock*. The total value of the loan stock:

$$V_L = 800\,000 \times \frac{95}{100} = £0.76\text{m}$$

$$\text{WACC} = \left(k_E \times \frac{V_E}{V_E + V_L}\right) + \left(k_L \times \frac{V_L}{V_E + V_L}\right)$$

$$= \left(16 \times \frac{1.80}{1.80 + 0.76}\right) + \left(9 \times \frac{0.76}{1.80 + 0.76}\right)$$

$$= 11.25 + 2.67$$

$$= 13.92\%, \text{ say } 14\%$$

Note that we used market values rather than the nominal values of the two elements as the weights. This correctly reflects the fact that we are seeking the opportunity cost of capital. Market values reflect or indicate current opportunities; nominal values do not. Despite this, Al-Ali and Arkwright (2000) found that 21 per cent of large UK businesses use nominal values as the weights.

Realities of raising (and repaying) finance and the discount rate

Although businesses seem to establish and maintain a target gearing ratio, the practical realities of raising and repaying finance are that it is not always economic to raise (or repay) each £1 of additional (or reduction in) finance strictly in the target proportions. This is because, as we have already seen in Chapter 8, there are fairly large fixed costs associated with share and loan stock issues. In practice, businesses seem to raise fairly substantial sums from each issue in order to take advantage of the economies of scale regarding the issue costs. This would tend to have the effect that the target is a factor around which the actual ratio hovers.

In the last example, the current ratio of loan stock to total finance for Hazelwood plc is 29.7 per cent [that is, 0.76/(1.80 + 0.76)]. Equity currently accounts for 70.3 per cent of the total. This suggests a target ratio of about 70/30. If the business wished to raise £100 000, say, to finance a new investment project, it is most unlikely that it would raise £70 000 in ordinary shares and £30 000 in loan stock. It is much more likely that

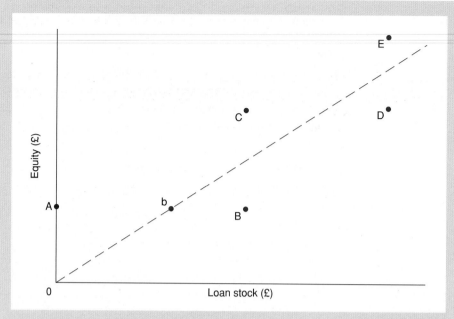

Figure 10.1
Graph of the capital structure of a geared business over time

Since there are economies of scale in share and loan stock issue costs, businesses tend not to raise each tranche of new finance in the same proportion as the target gearing ratio, but either totally from equities or totally from debt. This means that the actual gearing ratio will tend to follow a path that wanders from one side of the target to the other. Rarely will the actual and the target gearing ratios coincide. Points A, B, C, D and E represent actual gearing at various times, whereas the dotted line represents the target.

it would raise the whole £100 000 from one source or the other. This would move its gearing ratio away from the 70/30 (approximately) that currently exists. The business would get back nearer its target by raising the following increment of finance from the other source. The pattern would probably be something like that depicted in Figure 10.1. Here the broken line represents the target ratio, with the points A to E representing consecutive actual financing configurations. The business starts by raising some initial equity capital (0A) followed by an issue of loan stock of amount AB. It presumably chooses not to raise amount Ab because sufficient economies of scale as regards loan stock issue cost would not be available on such a small issue.

The next issue is of equities (amount BC) and so on until the present position (E) is reached.

Specific cost or weighted average

The fact that a particular increment of finance is to be used in some particular project should not lead the business to use the specific cost of that finance as the discount rate. Say, in the case of Hazelwood plc, that the funds to finance the project were to be raised from an issue of loan stock at a cost of 9 per cent. It would clearly be wrong to use 9 per cent as the discount rate in assessing the project, in the same way as 16 per cent would be inappropriate were the finance to be raised by an ordinary share issue. To use 9 per cent would mean that a project that might be acceptable if the business were moving from point C to point D in Figure 10.1 might be rejected if it were moving from point D to point E, when a 16 per cent (cost of equity) rate would be used.

This would clearly be illogical and could lead to some bizarre investment decisions. It would be much more logical to use WACC, provided that the business intends to maintain a broadly constant gearing ratio.

10.4 The discount rate: CAPM versus the traditional approach

We have seen two means of deducing the cost of the individual elements of long-term finance:

- the increasingly popular CAPM approach, explained in Chapter 7, which can be applied equally well to any element of financing, though we tended to concentrate on equity financing in that chapter; and

- the increasingly less popular 'traditional' approach adopted in this chapter, which bases the costs of the elements on the market price of the element, that is, we created equations that contained the market price of the particular element (such as loan stock, equity), the cash returns that investors would expect to receive from the element, and the cost of the element. Only the last of these was unknown and not estimated, so its value could be easily deduced.

Whichever of these two approaches is adopted, if the business is not totally equity financed, as we have seen in this chapter, the WACC must be used. Some people seem to believe that CAPM and WACC are alternative approaches. In fact, WACC is the correct approach whether or not CAPM is the means of estimating the cost of the individual elements.

The principles of the WACC calculation would be identical, whether the 'traditional' or the CAPM approach is used. So, in the Hazelwood plc example above, we could derive k_E and k_L using CAPM and then calculate WACC exactly as shown on page 281.

Although both approaches must consider risk, CAPM probably has the advantage that it tends to focus more clearly on the risk of the specific project under consideration. With the traditional approach, there might be a tendency to make the implicit assumption that the risk of the project under consideration is similar to that of existing activities.

In Figure 10.2 the horizontal line represents the WACC for a particular business. Logically, the weighted average risk of the business's existing projects must be β' as that is the risk level that, CAPM tells us, is consistent with the particular WACC. Only if projects under consideration were of exactly β' risk would WACC be the appropriate discount rate. If Project A (Figure 10.2) were under consideration, it should be accepted since it would have a positive NPV when discounted at r_A (the appropriate discount rate for its level of risk) even though if discounted at WACC its NPV would be negative. Similarly, Project B, whose required rate of return is r_B, would have a positive NPV if discounted at WACC, yet a negative one if discounted at the more appropriate rate, r_B. Thus, using WACC, based on projects currently in progress, irrespective of the risk attaching to the particular project under review, will cause some favourable projects (for example, Project A in Figure 10.2) to be rejected, whereas others that would diminish the wealth of the shareholders (Project B) could be accepted.

In practice, businesses tend to specialise in similar projects with, presumably, similar risk, so that the current WACC might well be appropriate in most cases. Where a project under consideration is not of similar risk level to that of the existing projects,

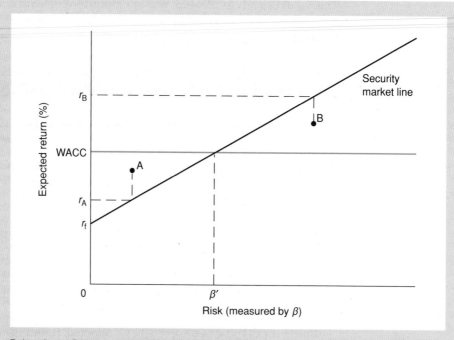

Points A and B represent the risk/return profiles of two investment projects. The discount rate should correctly be determined from the security market line (CAPM). Since Project A has relatively low risk, a relatively low return is required, and therefore a relatively low discount rate should be applied. Project B, on the other hand, is relatively risky, which implies a relatively high discount rate. Using a blanket, WACC-derived, discount rate could lead to wrong decisions on both projects. Project A would be assessed using too high a discount rate and Project B's cash flows would be discounted at too low a rate.

Figure 10.2
Graph of the expected return against risk for a particular business

it might be possible to obtain the appropriate discount rate by looking at the WACCs of businesses whose activities (and therefore presumably risk) are all similar to the project under review. This is a similar approach to using the beta of another business whose activities are all of the same type as the project under review, where the project is not typical of the existing projects of the investing business, when deriving the discount rate through CAPM.

Practicality of using the traditional approach compared with using CAPM

Traditionalists seem to regard CAPM as a rather fanciful approach to deducing discount rates, even though they may not disagree with CAPM in theory. The objection seems to lie in their recognition of the difficulty of estimating the parameters of CAPM (the risk-free rate, the expected market return and the beta). The traditionalists are right to be sceptical of our ability to estimate these reliably (see Chapter 7). Where perhaps they are misguided is to believe that the estimates necessary to arrive at the cost of capital by the 'traditional' route are any less susceptible to error than are those for CAPM.

Typically it would seem that the traditional approach uses estimates, either from expectations of future cash flows from the various elements of long-term finance, or from recent history of what the costs of each element have been. If based on future expectations, these estimates are not more reliable than those required when using

CAPM. If WACC, to be used as a rate to discount future cash flows of a project, is derived from evidence of the recent past, this too seems pretty dubious. Merely to extrapolate unquestioningly from the past to the future is not always a good idea, and seems a particularly poor one in this context.

Research evidence shows an increasing use of CAPM to derive the discount rate, particularly among larger businesses (see Chapter 7, page 206).

CAPM can be particularly helpful to small businesses in deriving their cost of capital. These businesses typically do not have a known market value. Published betas of large businesses in the same industry can act as useful benchmarks for small businesses.

WACC values used in practice

To put things into perspective, Dimson, Marsh and Staunton (2002) estimate that real (that is, inflation-free) returns on equity, for UK businesses over the whole of the twentieth century, averaged about 7 per cent p.a. This is, in effect, the average cost of equity. Since most businesses have an element of debt financing, and debt tends to lower WACC, we might expect that the rates actually used by UK businesses would not be higher than about 6 per cent.

Recent survey evidence (Gregory, Rutterford and Zaman 1999; Al-Ali and Arkwright 2000; McLaney, Pointon, Thomas and Tucker 2004) indicates the mean real WACCs found in practice in the UK to be in the range 7 to 9 per cent, though many individual businesses estimate their WACCs at values outside this range. These values seem on the high side given the findings of Dimson *et al.* Presuming that WACC is used by the businesses surveyed as their discount rates for assessing investments, it would appear that valuable investment opportunities may be being rejected as a result of businesses having too high an expectation of acceptable returns.

Kingfisher plc, the home improvement business (B&Q DIY stores among others) records in its 2004 annual report an estimated cost of capital for the business at 8.4 per cent p.a. This puts Kingfisher in the mainstream of UK businesses regarding cost of capital, but well above that which Dimson *et al.* would suggest. Kingfisher is unusual in making its cost of capital public.

Some further points on WACC

There are some other points that need to be made about using WACC as the discount rate, but since these require some understanding of the contents of Chapter 11, we shall leave them until the end of that chapter.

Summary

Cost of capital estimations

- Cost of capital (k) is the IRR for a set of cash flows, such that current market price of the investment equals the sum of the discounted values of all future cash flows relating to the investment, from the business's point of view.
- Market price used – opportunity k required.
- With a perpetuity, k = annual interest (or dividend) payment/current market price.

Loan stocks

- Interest payments are tax deductible; effective interest payment is 70 per cent of the coupon rate.
- May be redeemable; redemption payment not tax deductible.

Preference shares

- Treated like loan stocks, except:
  - dividends are not tax deductible;
  - dividends need not always be paid.

Ordinary shares

- Need to make an assumption about future dividends, usually either:
  - constant (perpetual) – treat like a preference share; or
  - assume a constant rate of dividend growth, g [g = proportion of profits retained (b) times the rate of return on those retained profits (r)].
- Assuming constant growth,

$$\text{Cost of equity, } k_E = \frac{d_0(1 + g)}{p_0} + g$$

where d_0 is the current dividend per share (top part of fraction is next year's dividend, that is, this year's dividend plus the growth over the next year) and p_0 is the current ex-dividend price per share, that is, the price that does not include the current year's dividend.

- Retained profit automatically included as part of k_E.

Weighted average cost of capital (WACC)

- WACC (of a business with two types of finance, A and B) is:

$$\text{WACC} = \frac{(k_A \times \text{Value of A}) + (k_B \times \text{Value of B})}{\text{Value of A} + \text{B}}$$

- Use of WACC as discount rate requires three assumptions:
  - business has a target gearing ratio that will be maintained;
  - cost of individual elements will remain constant; and
  - investments to be appraised are of similar risk to the general risk of the business's investments.

Other issues

- Specific cost of capital should not be used as the discount rate, even where investment funded from that specific element – use WACC.
- CAPM can be used to derive cost of different elements, but WACC needs still to be applied.
- CAPM is particularly useful for small businesses since they do not have a market price – an essential element in the 'traditional' approach to deriving the cost of equity.

Further reading

Most finance texts include fairly comprehensive treatment of the material discussed in this chapter. Samuels, Wilkes and Brayshaw (1998) give an interesting coverage of it; Brealey and Myers (2002) deal with it clearly and go into quite a lot of detail, particularly with regard to the costs of various types of finance. Gregory, Rutterford and Zaman (1999) provide a very readable account of their research into the cost of capital and of the background to this topic, including many insights to how real businesses approach various aspects of investment decision making.

Relevant websites

The Dimson, Marsh and Staunton (2002) article cited in the chapter, can be accessed and downloaded.
http://faculty.london.edu/edimson/Jacf1.pdf

The website of the business featured in this chapter is:

Kingfisher plc   www.kingfisher.com

REVIEW QUESTIONS

Suggested answers to review questions appear in Appendix 3.

10.1 What determines the value of an economic asset (as opposed to an asset that has value for reason of sentiment)?

10.2 If we know the projected cash flows from a loan stock and its current market value, what approach would we take to deducing the cost of the loan stock?

10.3 Why does it seem likely that businesses have a 'target' gearing ratio?

10.4 What is wrong with using the cost of the specific capital used to finance a project as the discount rate in relation to that project?

10.5 When calculating the weighted average cost of capital (WACC), should we use market values or balance sheet values as the weights of debt and equity? Explain your response.

10.6 When deducing the cost of equity through a dividend model, must we assume either a constant level of future dividends or a constant level of growth of dividends? Explain your response.

PROBLEMS

Sample answers to problems marked with an asterisk appear in Appendix 4.

(Problems 10.1 to 10.4 are basic-level problems, whereas problems 10.5 and 10.6 are more advanced and may contain some practical complications.)

10.1* Gregoris plc has some loan stock, currently quoted at £104 per £100 nominal value. This stock will pay interest at the rate of 8 per cent p.a. of the nominal value at the end of each of the next four years and repay £100 at the end of four years.

What is the cost of the loan stock? (Ignore taxation.)

10.2 Shah plc has a cost of equity of 17 per cent p.a. The business is expected to pay a dividend in one year's time of £0.27 per share. Dividends are expected to grow at a steady 5 per cent each year for the foreseeable future.

What is the current price of one share in Shah plc?

10.3* Fortunate plc's capital structure (taken from the balance sheet) is as follows:

	£m
Ordinary shares of £0.50 each	8
10% preference shares of £1.00	5
Reserves	6
12% debentures	10

The business pays corporation tax at the rate of 50 per cent and is expected to earn a consistent annual profit, before interest and tax, of £9m.

The current market prices of the business's shares are:

Preference shares	£0.65
Ordinary shares	£0.80

The debentures are irredeemable and have a market value of £100 per £100 nominal value.

What is the weighted average cost of capital, assuming that shareholders regard retained profit and dividends as equally valuable?

10.4 Doverdale plc has some convertible loan stock, with a current market value of £109 per £100 nominal value, on which it will pay interest at the rate of 12 per cent on their nominal value in one year's time and then annually until conversion. In four years' time the loan stock can be converted into ordinary shares at the rate of 25 shares per £100 nominal value of loan stock.

The cost of the loan stock is 15 per cent p.a.

What value does the market believe that the shares will have in four years' time, if it is assumed that conversion will take place at that time? (Ignore taxation throughout.)

10.5* Da Silva plc's shares are not traded in any recognised market. Its sole activity is saloon car hire. It is financed by a combination of 2 million £0.50 ordinary shares and a £1.5m bank loan. Very recently, Mavis plc, a national car hire group, offered a total of £5.5m to acquire the entire equity of Da Silva plc. The bid failed because the majority of shareholders rejected it since they wished to retain control of the business, despite believing the offer to represent a fair price for the shares. The bank loan is at a floating rate of interest of 10 per cent p.a. and is secured on various fixed assets. The value of the bank loan is considered to be very close to its nominal value.

Da Silva plc's current capital structure (by market value) represents what has been, and is intended to continue to be, its target capital structure.

Da Silva plc's management is in the process of assessing a major investment, to be financed from retained earnings, in some new depots, similar to the business's existing ones. An appropriate cost of capital figure is required for this purpose. The dividend growth model (DGM) has been proposed as a suitable basis for the estimation of the cost of equity.

Recent annual dividends per share have been:

Year	£
1	0.0800
2	0.0900
3	0.1050
4	0.1125
5	0.1250
6	0.1350
7	0.1450
8	0.1550

The business's rate of corporation tax is expected to be 33 per cent p.a., for the foreseeable future.

(a) Estimate Da Silva plc's weighted average cost of capital (WACC). (Ignore inflation.)

(b) What assumptions are being made in using the WACC figure that you have estimated as the basis for the discount rate?

10.6 Vocalise plc has recently assessed a new capital investment project that will expand its activities. This project has an estimated expected net present value of £4m. This will require finance of £15m. At the same time, the business would like to buy and cancel £10m of 15 per cent debentures, which are due to be redeemed at par in four years' time. It is estimated that the business will incur dealing costs of £0.3m in buying the debentures.

There are plans to raise most of the necessary finance for the investment project and for buying the debentures through a one-for-one rights issue of equity at an issue price of £0.50 per share. The remaining finance will come from the business's existing cash resources. The issue will give rise to administrative costs of £0.4m.

None of these plans has been announced to the 'market', which is believed to be semi-strong efficient.

Vocalise plc's capital structure is as follows:

	£m
Ordinary shares of £0.25 each	10
Reserves	14
	24
15% debentures	10
10% term loan	15
	49

The current and likely future rate of interest for loans to businesses like Vocalise plc is 10 per cent p.a. The business's ordinary shares are currently quoted at £0.85 each.

(a) Estimate the theoretical share price following the announcement of the plans and the issue of the new shares, assuming that the only influences on the price are these plans. (Ignore taxation.)

(b) Why might the theoretical price differ from the actual one?

There are both a set of **multiple-choice questions** and **missing-word questions** available on the website. These specifically cover the material contained in this chapter. These can be attempted and graded (with feedback) online.

There are also **five additional problems**, with solutions, that relate to the material covered in this chapter.

Go to **www.pearsoned.co.uk/atrillmclaney** and follow the links.

Chapter 11

Gearing, the cost of capital and shareholders' wealth

Objectives In this chapter we shall deal with the following:

→ the use of loan finance as part of businesses' long-term financial needs

→ the effect of capital gearing on WACC, the value of the business and the shareholders' wealth

→ the traditional view of this effect

→ the Modigliani and Miller view

→ the empirical evidence of the effects of gearing

→ gearing and CAPM

→ financial gearing and operating gearing

→ a conjectural conclusion on gearing – trade-off theory

→ pecking order theory

11.1 Introduction

At several points in this book so far we have encountered the fact that most businesses raise part of their long-term financing requirements through borrowing, often by the issue of loan stocks or debentures. These give lenders contractual rights to receive interest, typically at a predetermined rate and on specified dates. Usually such loan stocks are redeemable: thus the contractual rights extend to the amount to be repaid and to the date of redemption. Loan finance could also be provided by a bank or similar institution, which would acquire similar contractual rights. The central point about loan finance, in the present context, lies in the fact that neither interest nor redemption payments are matters of the borrowing business's discretion. Interest on loans is an annual charge on profit. This must be satisfied before the equity shareholders, who in the typical business provide the larger part of the finance, may participate.

In Chapter 2 we found, subject to several assumptions, that financing through borrowing rather than equity does not seem to make any difference to the wealth of the shareholders. In this chapter we shall review the traditional view, that capital gearing does have an effect on shareholders' wealth, before we go on to develop the point raised in Chapter 2. After this we shall review the evidence and try to reach some conclusion on the matter.

11.2 Is loan finance as cheap as it seems?

It is widely believed that the capital market prices securities so that expected returns from equities are higher than those from loan stocks. Historically, this belief has been valid over all but fairly brief periods (see, for example Dimson, Marsh and Staunton, 2002). Does the apparent cheapness of loan finance really mean that equity holders will benefit from the use of it in the business's capital structure?

Example 11.1

La Mer plc has one asset, a luxury yacht, which is chartered to parties of rich holiday-makers. Profits of the business over the next few years are expected to be £140 000 p.a. La Mer is financed entirely by equity, namely 1m ordinary shares whose current market value is £1 each. The business pays all of each year's profit to shareholders as a dividend. La Mer plc intends to buy an additional, similar vessel, also expected to generate annual profits of £140 000 p.a., at a cost of £1m. The finance for this is to be provided by the issue of £1m of 10 per cent loan stock. The loan is to be secured on the two vessels.

Without the new yacht, the return per share is expected to be:

$$\frac{£140\ 000}{1\ 000\ 000} = £0.14 \text{ per share}$$

If the second yacht is acquired, the annual return per share will be:

Profit from chartering (2 × £140 000)	£280 000
Less: Interest (£1m @ 10%)	100 000
	£180 000

that is:

$$\frac{£180\ 000}{1\ 000\ 000} = £0.18 \text{ per share}$$

Thus the expected return is increased by the use of loan stock. (Note that if the finance for the new yacht had been raised by issuing 1m ordinary shares of £1 each, the annual return per share, with the second yacht, would have remained at £0.14.)

Since the ordinary shares of La Mer plc are priced at £1 each, when returns are expected to be 14p per share, we may infer that investors regard 14 per cent as the appropriate return for such an investment. If the expected returns increase to 18p per share, as acquisition of the second vessel engenders, this seems likely to push up the price of an ordinary share to £1 × 18p/14p = £1.286 (18p represents a 14 per cent return on £1.286). This implies that, were the second vessel to be financed by an issue of equity, the value of each ordinary share would be £1, whereas if the second vessel were to be financed by loan stock, the ordinary shares would be worth £1.286 each. In short, the shareholders' wealth would be increased as a result of borrowing instead of issuing equity.

Too good to be true? Probably yes, yet there is nothing in the example that seems too unreasonable. Expected returns on equities tend to be greater than those on loan stocks, so the 10 per cent interest rate is not necessarily unrealistic. Surely though, such alchemy cannot really work. It cannot be possible in a fairly rational world, suddenly to turn a 14 per cent return into an 18 per cent one, to increase a share's price from £1 to £1.286, quite so simply. Or can it?

To try to get to the bottom of this enigma, let us look at the situation from the point of view of the suppliers of the loan finance. If there are 14 per cent returns to be made from investing in yacht chartering, why are they prepared to invest for a 10 per cent return? Why do they not buy ordinary shares in La Mer? Are they so naïve that they do not notice the 14 per cent possibility? Perhaps they are, but this seems rather unlikely.

The difference between investing directly in yacht chartering, through the purchase of shares in La Mer, and lending money on a fixed rate of interest is the different level of risk. In the example, of the £140 000 p.a. expected profits from the second yacht, only £100 000 would be paid to the providers of the new finance. The other £40 000 goes to the equity holders, but with it goes all of the risk (or nearly all of it).

As with all real investment, returns are not certain. Suppose that there were to be a recession in the yacht charter business, so that the profits of La Mer plc fell to £70 000 p.a. from each vessel. This would mean:

Profit from chartering (2 × £70 000)	£140 000
Less: Interest (£1m @ 10%)	100 000
	£40 000

that is:

$$\frac{£40\ 000}{1\ 000\ 000} = £0.04 \text{ per share}$$

(Note that, had the second yacht been financed by equity, the return per share would in the circumstances be £140 000/2 000 000 = £0.07, not quite such a disastrous outcome for equity holders.)

From this it seems clear that loan stocks provide an apparently cheap source of finance, but they have a hidden cost to equity shareholders.

11.3 Business risk and financial risk

Table 11.1 shows the annual dividend per share for La Mer (assuming the second vessel is acquired and that all available profit is paid as dividend) for each of the two financing schemes referred to above (all equity and 50 per cent loan financed) for various levels of chartering profits.

The inclusion of loan finance enhances returns on equity over those that could be earned in the all-equity structure, where annual profits are above £100 000 per vessel. Where annual profit per vessel falls below £100 000, however, the existence of loan finance weakens the ordinary shareholder's position. In fact, below a profit of £50 000 per vessel there would be insufficient profit to cover loan interest payments. Presuming that no other assets exist, the business might have to dispose of one of the vessels to provide the finance to meet the interest payments.

Table 11.1 Returns per share in La Mer plc for various levels of profit under each of two different financial structures

(a) Annual profit per vessel	0	£50 000	£100 000	£150 000	£200 000
All equity					
(b) Profit [(a) × 2]	0	£100 000	£200 000	£300 000	£400 000
(c) Return per share [(b) ÷ 2 000 000]	0	£0.05	£0.10	£0.15	£0.20
50% loan finance					
(d) Profit [(a) × 2]	0	£100 000	£200 000	£300 000	£400 000
(e) *Less:* Interest (£1m @ 10%)	100 000	100 000	100 000	100 000	100 000
(f) Net profit	(£100 000)	0	£100 000	£200 000	£300 000
(g) Return per share [(f) ÷ 1 000 000]	(£0.10)	0	£0.10	£0.20	£0.30

At virtually all levels of profit, the loan stockholders could view the situation confidently. After all, not only do they have the legal right to enforce payment of their interest and repayment of their capital, they even have the vessels as security. Only if there were major losses to the market value of the yachts would the loan stockholders' position be seriously threatened.

Where gearing exists, the risk to which equity holders are exposed clearly is increased over that which they would bear in the equivalent all-equity business. To **business risk**, the normal risk attached to investing in the real world, is added **financial risk**, the risk caused by being burdened with the obligation to meet fixed finance charges illustrated in Table 11.1.

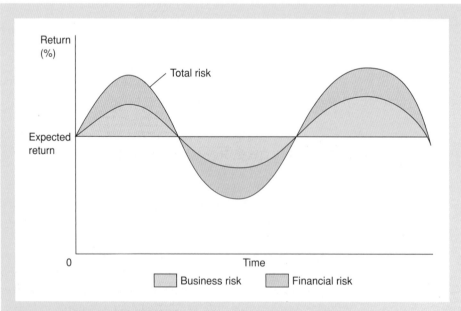

Figure 11.1
The return on equity over time for a financially geared business with fluctuating profits

Financial gearing has the effect of accentuating the fluctuations in the returns to equity holders. The basic fluctuations are related to *business risk*. Gearing adds the effect of *financial risk* to this.

Figure 11.1 depicts the relationship between business and financial risk where operating returns fluctuate. The amount of business risk depends on the commercial activities of the business; financial risk depends on how the business is financed.

Intuition and modern portfolio theory (MPT – see Chapter 7) both tell us that risk and return are related. Where investors perceive high risk, they require high returns. Hence, referring back to the above example, while gearing will lift expected dividend per share to ordinary shareholders from 14p to 18p, this will not necessarily increase the share price (and therefore the wealth of the shareholder). Accompanying the increased expected dividend is a wider range of possible outcomes (see Table 11.1).

Not all of the new possibilities that gearing brings to the returns to equity holders are bad news. For example, for La Mer, Table 11.1 shows that for any chartering profit per vessel above £100 000 p.a., ordinary share dividends would be enhanced. Most investors, however, are risk averse, which means that the possibility that profit per vessel could be below £100 000, by a particular amount, tends to be more significant to them than the possibility that profits could be greater, by the same amount.

La Mer's ordinary shareholders will only be better off through the introduction of gearing if the capital market, when it reassesses the situation, following the loan stock issue and the purchase of the second yacht, prices the ordinary shares so that their expected yield is less than 18 per cent.

Before La Mer's expansion these ordinary shares had an expected yield of 14 per cent. If, as a result of the higher risk level, after the expansion the market expected a return of, say, 16 per cent, the price per share would be:

$$\frac{£0.18}{0.16} = £1.125$$

that is, an increase in value per share.

If, on the other hand, capital market requirements for the level of risk rose to 20 per cent, the price per share would become:

$$\frac{£0.18}{0.20} = £0.90$$

The key question is, will the introduction of gearing lower the weighted average cost of capital (WACC) and therefore make the investments in which the business is involved more valuable, or not?

Given the business's overall objective of maximisation of shareholder wealth, how the capital market reacts, in terms of required returns, to the introduction of gearing is an important matter. Gearing is, presumably, undertaken only with the objective of increasing equity shareholders' wealth.

11.4 The traditional view

The traditional view seems to be that if the expected rate of return from equity investment in yacht chartering is 14 per cent, this will not be greatly affected by the introduction of capital gearing, at least not up to moderate levels. This view of the effect of gearing on capital market expectations of returns from equities, loan stocks and WACC is depicted in Figure 11.2.

Figure 11.2 shows that, as gearing is increased, both equity investors and lenders perceive additional risk and require higher returns. At lower levels of gearing,

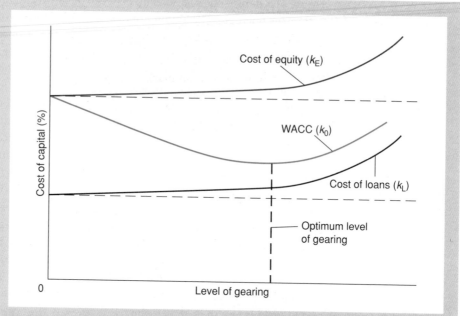

Figure 11.2
The cost of capital for varying levels of gearing – the traditional view

The logical conclusion of this view is that there is an optimum level of gearing, where there is a minimum weighted average cost of capital. This arises from the assumption that the cost of equity does not increase sufficiently to outweith the advantage of the low-cost loan finance until some significant level of gearing is achieved.

however, neither group requires greatly increased returns to compensate for this risk, and so WACC reduces. When gearing reaches higher levels, the risk issue becomes increasingly important to both groups, so required returns start to increase dramatically. Now WACC starts to rise steeply. Although the point at which each group's required return starts this steep rise is not necessarily the same, there is a point (or a range of points) where, according to traditionalists, WACC is at a minimum. This is the *optimal level of gearing* in Figure 11.2. At this point the shareholders' wealth is maximised, that is, the price per share would be at its peak. Note that a graph of share price against the level of gearing would resemble an inversion of the WACC (k_0) curve in Figure 11.2. This means that the share price, and with it, shareholders' wealth and the value of the business, would be maximised at the optimum level of gearing.

The rationale for the traditional view seems to be that lenders would recognise that, at high levels of gearing, their security is substantially lost and would begin to demand successively higher levels of interest to compensate them for the higher risk involved. It seems also to be believed that, up to a certain level of gearing, equity shareholders would not see the increased risk to their returns as too significant. After that point, however, they would start to demand major increases in returns for further increases in gearing.

Broadly, the traditional conclusion was that gearing is a good thing, in terms of shareholder wealth maximisation, at least up to a certain level, past which it would start to have an adverse effect on WACC and therefore on shareholder wealth.

During the 1950s some observers started to question the value of gearing, finding it difficult to reconcile the 'something for nothing' aspect of the traditional view with the rapidly growing belief that securities are efficiently and rationally priced.

11.5 The Modigliani and Miller view of gearing

In 1958, Modigliani and Miller (MM) published an article, now almost legendary, questioning the traditional approach to the issue of gearing. MM argued that, given rational pricing in the capital markets, it is not possible for a business to increase its total market value (lower its WACC) merely by doing what it is in theory open to any of us to do: borrow money. They asserted that if a particular business is expected to generate some level of income, this should be valued without regard to how the business is financed.

Example 11.2

To see how the MM assertion would work in the case of La Mer, let us assume that the business raised the £1m for the second vessel by issuing a 10 per cent debenture (that is, borrowing at 10 per cent p.a.). Let us also assume that there is another business, Sea plc, identical in every respect to La Mer, but completely financed by 2m ordinary shares of £1 each.

Franco, a holder of 1 per cent of the equity of La Mer (that is, 10 000 shares), would expect a return on them of £1800 p.a. since, as we have seen, each one is expected to yield 18p p.a. Franco could equally well obtain the same expected income by selling the shares for £10 000, borrowing an amount equivalent to 1 per cent of La Mer's borrowings (that is, £10 000) at the rate of 10 per cent p.a. and using this total of £20 000 to purchase 1 per cent of the ordinary shares in Sea (20 000 shares). The Sea shares would be expected to yield 14p each and so £2800 in total, which, after paying interest on the borrowing, would leave £1800 p.a. of expected income of equal risk (business and financial) as that of the expected income from La Mer. Franco's situation may be restated and summarised as follows:

	Investment £	Income £
Present position		
10 000 shares in La Mer		
(i.e. 1% of total shares)	<u>10 000</u>	<u>1800</u>
Alternative position		
Borrow £10 000	(10 000)	(1000)
Buy 20 000 shares in Sea		
(i.e. 1% of total shares)	<u>20 000</u>	<u>2800</u>
	<u>10 000</u>	<u>1800</u>

Since securities (indeed, all economic assets) are valued by reference only to their expected return and risk, each of the above positions must be equally valuable to Franco, or to any other investor. Both positions offer identical risk/return expectations.

If, in the above circumstances, Sea's share price fell below that of La Mer, Franco could make the switch from the original to the alternative position, have the same expected return and risk, but make a profit on the switch. Since the sale of the La Mer shares and purchase of the Sea shares could be achieved simultaneously (an action known as *arbitraging*), a risk-free gain would be available. The actions of Franco, and others spotting this opportunity, would increase both the demand for Sea's shares and the supply of those of La Mer. As a result, the price of the shares would equalise.

MM's central point is that, if Franco wants to be involved with gearing but wishes to hold shares in Sea, this can be achieved by personal gearing, that is, *homemade gearing*.

Similarly, another individual, Merton, who owns shares in Sea but wishes to invest in La Mer though not to be involved with gearing, can easily *ungear* an investment in La Mer. Merton can do this by selling the Sea shares, lending the same proportion of the money to be invested as La Mer borrows of its total financing (£10 000) and using the remaining £10 000 to buy La Mer shares.

	Investment £	Income £
Present position		
20 000 shares in Sea	20 000	2800
Alternative position		
Lend £10 000	10 000	1000
Buy 10 000 shares in La Mer	10 000	1800
	20 000	2800

Once again, a switch from the present to the alternative position would result in the same expected return with the same risk.

It would seem illogical for a business to be able to increase the wealth of its shareholders merely by *packaging* its income in a particular way.

This is made especially illogical by the fact that individual shareholders can adjust the packaging to their own convenience, merely by borrowing and/or lending. Income of similar risk and expected return should be similarly priced in a rational market, irrespective of the packaging.

It seems clear from these examples that:

$$\frac{\text{Total value of the equity of Sea}}{100} = \frac{\text{Total value of the equity of La Mer}}{100}$$

$$+ \frac{\text{Total value of the borrowings of La Mer}}{100}$$

Rearranging this gives:

Total value of the equity of Sea = Total value of the equity and borrowings of La Mer

and more generally,

$$V_U = V_G$$

where V_U and V_G are the total value of the ungeared and geared businesses respectively.

The implication of the MM proposition is that the value of the business is not affected by the financing method (that is, $V_U = V_G$): therefore the cost of capital is not reduced (or affected at all) by the introduction of gearing. The only matters on which the value of the business and its WACC depend are:

- the cash flows that the business's investments are expected to generate; and
- their risk (that is, their business risk).

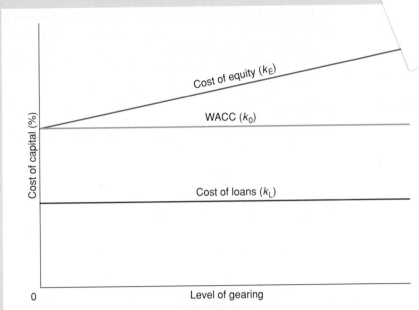

Figure 11.3
The cost of capital
for varying levels of
gearing – the MM
(pre-tax) view

The logical conclusion of this view is that there is no optimum level of gearing. WACC will be identical at all levels of gearing. This arises from the assumption that the cost of equity rises at a rate that precisely cancels the advantage of the low-cost loan finance at all levels of gearing.

This is another phenomenon following the same pattern as Fisher separation (see Chapter 2). MM were, in effect, saying that management should concentrate all its efforts on finding and managing investment opportunities, leaving the financing arrangements for individual shareholders to decide for themselves.

The effect suggested by MM is shown graphically in Figure 11.3. Here we can see that the potential that increasing amounts of *cheap* loan finance have for reducing WACC is exactly offset by the increasing cost of equity. Thus WACC is impervious to the level of gearing.

We see from Figure 11.3 that shareholders in geared businesses expect a return equal to the expected return from the identical ungeared business, plus a premium that is directly proportional to the level of gearing. Thus, while gearing increases earnings per share, it also increases capital market expectations of the share's returns because of higher risk. The net effect of these factors on the value of each share will be zero, that is, the effects will be equal and opposite (according to MM).

According to MM, the relationship between the return expected by the capital market and the level of gearing is:

$$k_{EG} = k_{EE} + (k_{EE} - k_L)\frac{L_G}{S_G}$$

where k_{EG} and k_{EE} are respectively the expected returns from shares in the geared and all-equity businesses; L_G and S_G are respectively the total market value of the loan stock and shares of the geared business; and k_L is the loan stock interest rate.

Thus the introduction of 50 per cent gearing into the capital structure of La Mer would push the capital market's expected return on the business's equities up to 18 per cent (k_{EG} = 14 + (14 − 10)(£1m/£1m) = 18%). The expected earnings per share of 18p (see page 292) would still only be worth £1.

MM's disagreement with the traditionalists was that MM saw the capital market's return expectations increasing as soon as gearing is introduced, and increasing in proportion to the amount of gearing. The traditionalists felt that this would not occur at lower levels of gearing.

The formal proof of the MM proposition is developed in Appendix I of this chapter.

The MM assumptions

The MM analysis is based on several assumptions, which we shall now consider.

Shares can be bought and sold without dealing costs

This is obviously unrealistic: brokers' commissions and other costs are involved with trading in shares. It is doubtful, however, whether the weakness of this assumption seriously undermines the proposition. It might mean that investors would be unable to make a profit by exploiting minor instances of mispricing of shares of geared businesses, relative to those of ungeared ones. The larger instances of mispricing could be exploited despite the existence of dealing charges.

Capital markets are efficient

The evidence seems to show that they are efficient, for practical purposes, in the weak- and semi-strong forms (see Chapter 9). This implies that investors would see through the financial packaging and realise that income of a particular risk class is equally valuable irrespective of how it is wrapped. It seems that this assumption is reasonable.

Interest rates are equal between borrowing and lending, businesses and individuals

Clearly, this is invalid. In particular, there is usually a difference between the rates at which individuals and businesses can borrow. Large businesses, in particular, can often offer good security, can borrow large amounts, and can exploit borrowing opportunities not open to most individuals (for example, borrowing overseas). The importance of this assumption lies in the question of homemade gearing, where the investor borrows on his or her own account and buys shares in the ungeared business.

There is no reason, however, why the investor who exploits any mispricing of shares need be an individual; it could be a large business such as a large unit trust or investment trust. After all, most investment in securities, in the UK at least, is undertaken by the institutions rather than by individuals. Nor is it necessary that every investor in the economy seeks to exploit any mispricing in order to correct it. The action of a couple of investors, well placed to exploit the situation, would be sufficient. Probably the weakness of this assumption is not sufficient to call the MM proposition too seriously into question.

MM also made the implicit assumption that the corporate cost of borrowing does not increase with the level of gearing. This seems less plausible, and is a point to which we shall return later in the chapter.

There are no bankruptcy costs

This assumption suggests that if a business were to be liquidated, the shareholders would receive, in exchange for their shares, the equivalent of their market value immediately before the liquidation. This assumption envisages a situation where, as a result of a business defaulting on interest and/or capital repayment, it is liquidated at the instigation of loan stockholders. This sort of action would obviously be more likely with very highly geared businesses.

The assumption is invalid since dealing costs would be involved in the disposal of the business's assets, legal costs would arise in formally bringing about the demise of the business and, perhaps most importantly, the market for real assets is not generally efficient in the same way that capital markets seem to be. This last point implies that a machine worth £1000 to Business A does not necessarily have that same value to Business B, because B, for some reason, may not be able to use it as effectively as A. Before the liquidation, A's equity value may have been based partially on a £1000 value for the machine, but when the machine comes to be sold it may realise only £500. Furthermore, there are costs of administering a potentially bankrupt business, even if it is saved.

This assumption's lack of validity undermines the MM proposition in its broad form. It is doubtful, however, whether the assumption is a very important one where gearing levels are moderate, which appears typically to be the case in practice. On the other hand, the existence of bankruptcy costs may well be the reason for the modest gearing levels that we tend to see in real life.

Two businesses identical in income (cash flow) and risk exist, one all-equity, the other geared

This assumption is most unlikely strictly to be true. It seems not, however, to be an important impediment to the validity of MM's proposition. CAPM, and modern portfolio theory in general, suggest that business risk can explicitly be dealt with so that it is possible to relate two businesses of different risk. That is, there is an established mechanism for pricing risk, which enables returns for one business's shares to be reconciled with those of another business. But even if CAPM etc. were questioned, Stiglitz (1974) showed that it is not necessary for two such businesses actually to exist in order for the proposition to be valid.

There is no taxation

This is clearly invalid. MM were much criticised for this fact and were forced to reconsider their proposition because of it.

The revised *after-tax* version asserts that market forces must cause:

$$V_G = V_U + TL_G$$

where L_G is the value of the business's borrowings and T is the relevant corporation tax rate, at which loan stock interest will be relieved. The derivation of the above is shown in Appendix II to this chapter. The term TL_G is often referred to as the tax shield of debt.

The after-tax proposition implies that the value of the geared business is greater than the value of the all-equity one; also that the greater the level of gearing, the greater the value of the business. The inevitable conclusion is that the value is highest and WACC lowest when gearing is at 100 per cent, that is, when the loan stockholders provide all of the finance.

Figure 11.4 shows the MM after-tax view of capital gearing. There is a contrast with the pre-tax position depicted in Figure 11.3. In the after-tax case, the cost of debt is low enough (owing to higher tax relief on loan interest) for increasing amounts of loan finance to reduce WACC at a greater rate than that at which the increasing demands of equity holders are raising it. Thus the WACC line slopes downwards.

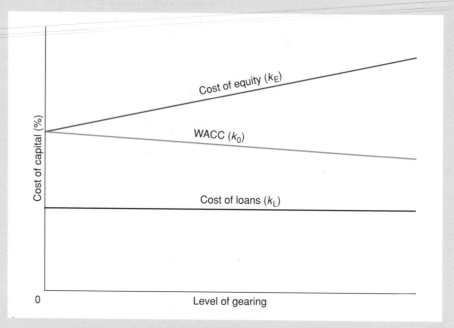

Figure 11.4
The cost of capital for varying levels of gearing – the MM (after-tax) view

The logical conclusion of this view is that there is an optimum level of gearing, and that this is located at 100% gearing. This arises from the assumption that the cost of equity rises at a rate that would precisely cancel the advantage of the low-cost loan finance at all levels of gearing, were it not for the fact that loan interest is tax deductible. The fact that interest is tax deductible means that the greater the amount of loan finance, the greater the tax benefit to the business.

It is doubtful whether this 100 per cent loan finance conclusion is tenable in practical terms, however. At very high levels of gearing the loan stockholders would recognise that their security had been substantially eroded and that, while they might be lenders in name, as risk takers they are equity holders in reality. They would therefore seek a level of return that would compensate them for this risk: a level of return similar to that which the equity holders seek. This would mean that at very high levels of gearing, both in the pre-tax and in the more important after-tax propositions, the cost of loans would rise significantly. For MM's conclusions to hold, this requires that the rate of increase in the cost of equity starts to fall. In Figure 11.4, if the cost of loans line is going to start turning upwards at some high level of gearing, the WACC line can only continue its downward path if the cost of equity line becomes less steep. (Remember that the WACC line is the average of the other two.)

The idea of the rate of increase in the cost of equity, as gearing is increased, suddenly starting to reduce at high gearing levels seems to defy logic. Why should investors start to behave contrary to all the theories and evidence of investor reaction to increasing risk? This suggests a weakness in the MM analysis.

11.6 Other thoughts on the tax advantage of loan financing

Miller (1977) showed that the tax benefits of gearing for a particular business will depend on the personal tax positions of both the loan stockholders and the shareholders. Thus businesses will tend to attract investors (both lenders and shareholders) who are suited to their capital structures. This is known as a clientele effect, where particular policies attract particular types of investor. If Miller is right about this, the implication is that businesses should probably try to avoid altering their capital structure because this would lead to investors selling their loan stocks or shares and investing their money in a business that matches their preferences. This is because the dealing costs involved with selling and buying securities would have an adverse effect on the wealth of the investors.

More recently, Dempsey (1991) showed, in the context of the UK tax and financial environment, that in theory gearing has a relatively small *adverse* effect on the wealth of shareholders.

For several decades of the late twentieth century, in the UK, provided that the business paid most of its profit as a dividend, and that it was in a normal tax-paying situation, the tax advantages of loan finance tended not to be too profound. To that extent, the original MM assumption of no corporate taxes was not an unreasonable one. There were taxes, but the advantage that they gave loan financing was not that great.

In 1997, the tax rules altered, such that now there are normally significant tax advantages for the business in having debt finance rather than equity.

It is probably fair to say that the question of the tax benefits of gearing remains unanswered.

11.7 Capital/financial gearing and operating gearing

We saw earlier in this chapter that the existence of debt finance in the capital structure accentuates the effect of variations in operating (that is, pre-interest) profits on returns to shareholders. This is because, at any significant level of gearing, the interest payment represents a large fixed commitment, which must be met irrespective of the level of operating profit.

There is also a gearing aspect to businesses' operating activities. That is to say, it is not just capital gearing that causes returns to shareholders to vary. Virtually all operations have costs that are fixed, irrespective of the level of sales revenue (fixed costs), and costs that vary with the level of sales revenue (variable costs). The relative proportions of each of these types of cost, in terms of the total costs, vary from one business to another, depending on the nature of the activities. This phenomenon is known as operating gearing. A business is said to be highly operationally geared when a large proportion of its total costs are fixed costs.

Example 11.3

Consider two businesses, High plc and Low plc. Their cost structures are as follows:

	Fixed costs per annum	Variable costs per £ of sales revenue
High plc	£100 000	£0.20
Low plc	£50 000	£0.50

For a range of sales revenue figures, operating results would be as shown in Table 11.2.

The table shows that the more highly operationally geared, High plc, shows much greater fluctuations with alterations in the level of sales revenue than does Low plc. You will remember that we saw a similar effect with capital gearing in Table 11.1 (page 294).

Table 11.2 Operating results for High plc and Low plc for various levels of sales revenue

	£	£	£	£
Sales revenue	0	200 000	300 000	400 000
High plc				
Fixed costs	100 000	100 000	100 000	100 000
Variable costs	0	40 000	60 000	80 000
Total costs	100 000	140 000	160 000	180 000
Operating profit	(100 000)	60 000	140 000	220 000
Low plc				
Fixed costs	50 000	50 000	50 000	50 000
Variable costs	0	100 000	150 000	200 000
Total costs	50 000	150 000	200 000	250 000
Operating profit	(50 000)	50 000	100 000	150 000

If a business is simultaneously highly geared in both operating and capital terms, relatively small fluctuations in the level of sales revenue can have a dramatic effect on returns to shareholders. This means that the risk of bankruptcy is greater with businesses that are highly geared in both senses, particularly where their sales revenue levels are susceptible to fluctuations from year to year. It is expected that businesses whose cost structure is such as to make them relatively highly geared on the operations side tend not to indulge in too much capital gearing.

11.8 Other practical issues relating to capital gearing

Agency costs

The fact that shareholders must, in practice, rely on the directors (the shareholders' agents) to manage the business can lead to its being managed in a way that may not always be in the best interests of the shareholders. Were the directors to act in a way that is less than optimal, from a shareholder wealth maximisation perspective, the shareholders would bear a cost.

In the context of capital gearing, such a cost can arise because gearing may be in the best interests of the shareholders yet be a less attractive proposition to the directors. If gearing lowers the cost of capital, shareholders would welcome this. The need to meet interest payments and to have the funds available to repay borrowings on the contracted date, however, imposes a discipline on the directors that they might prefer to avoid. On the other hand, Jensen (1986) pointed out that being forced to make interest payments, at a particular level, might dissuade the directors from making investments that would not be justified by the returns likely to be generated by those investments; in other words, the directors would tend to be more careful in taking on investments that might prove disadvantageous. Thus gearing might discourage the directors from making such investments as a means of expanding the business and with it their personal security and well-being.

Signalling

It has been suggested that raising loan finance can be interpreted, by the investing public, as signalling that the directors are confident enough of the future cash flows that are expected to be generated by the business's investments to be prepared to expose the business to the need to make regular interest payments to lenders.

Clientele effect

It seems likely that particular shareholders are attracted by or, at least, satisfied with a particular business's level of capital gearing. That is to say that those shareholders are content with the risk/return trade-off implied by the business's level of capital gearing. As we saw on page 303, investors' tax positions could also give rise to a clientele effect.

Were the business to alter the level of capital gearing by, for example, increasing or reducing the level of debt finance, the new level of capital gearing would not suit many, perhaps most, of the existing shareholders. This shift in gearing levels might cause some of the shareholders to sell their shares and to buy those of another business whose gearing levels were more satisfactory. By the same token, some investors might be inclined to buy the shares, whereas previously they would not have done, because they like the new gearing level. This buying and selling of shares would be likely to have a net adverse economic effect on the original shareholders.

Also, the uncertainty caused by the change in gearing level could make the shares less attractive, with an adverse affect on the share price.

11.9 Evidence on gearing

Some casual observations

Before going on to some of the sophisticated studies relating to gearing, it is well worth noting some important points that arise from casual observation.

- A very large proportion of businesses have some level of capital gearing. This seems to be particularly true among larger businesses. Few raise all of their financial requirements from equity shareholders. Assuming that managements are pursuing a shareholder wealth maximisation objective, they are presumably using gearing to promote that objective. Rightly or wrongly, therefore, managements seem to believe that gearing lowers WACC.

- Very high levels of gearing are rarely seen. Managements seem not to believe that the value of the business is maximised (WACC minimised) by very high gearing levels.

Some businesses make public comments about the benefits of financial gearing. **Cadbury Schweppes plc**, the drinks and confectionery business, said in its 2003 annual report: 'Net borrowing rose during the year, from £1846 million at the end of 2002, to £4211 million at the end of 2003, representing 50% of total market capitalisation. The group intends to manage its capital structure proactively to maximise shareholder value while maintaining flexibility to take advantage of opportunities, which arise to grow its business.'

Some formal evidence

The questions to which the answers are of real interest are:

- Does WACC change with gearing as MM (after-tax) suggested?
- Does it move to a minimum at some level of gearing of less than 100 per cent and then increase as gearing is further increased?

The publication of the MM articles on capital structure was followed by a number of studies bearing on the above questions.

Modigliani and Miller (1958) themselves took the lead with a study using data concerning a number of oil and of electrical utility businesses, and came to the conclusion that WACC is not dependent on the level of gearing (supporting their pre-tax proposition).

Weston (1963) criticised the MM results on the basis that they had made too many simplifying assumptions. Weston himself used data on electrical utility businesses to show that the MM after-tax proposition was valid in that WACC seemed to decrease with increased gearing. Miller and Modigliani (1966) returned to the scene and, again using the electrical utilities, they too found evidence to support the after-tax propositions.

Hamada (1972), using CAPM to deal with risk differences, found that the cost of equity increases with the level of gearing. Masulis (1980) found that announcements of a business's intention to increase the level of gearing tend to be associated with increases in the price of its equity, and that announcements of intentions to reduce gearing tend to have an adverse effect on the equity values. This clearly supports the MM after-tax proposition. It also implies that, if there *is* an optimal level of gearing, investors tend to believe that businesses are operating below it.

DeAngelo and Masulis (1980) found an increase in the value of the business as gearing increases up to a certain point, and a reduction as more debt is added. This was ascribed to the fact that the tax advantages can become decreasingly valuable with higher gearing since the business may not have sufficient taxable operating profits against which to set the interest expense: in other words, the tax deductibility of interest becomes irrelevant. Barclay, Smith and Watts (1995) found, based on US data, that the tax deductibility of interest is a factor in the levels of gearing, but not a very significant one.

Homaifar, Zeitz and Benkato (1994) found evidence based on US data that the level of gearing tends to be higher with businesses exposed to higher corporate tax rates: in other words, the greater the value of the tax shield, the higher the level of debt. They also found that larger businesses tend to be more highly geared than smaller ones, perhaps reflecting the greater ease with which larger businesses are able to raise external finance. These tax and size points were confirmed by Ozkan (2001), based on UK data. He also found evidence that businesses have a target gearing ratio that they try to return to quickly when they diverge from it. He inferred from the fact that they returned to the target quickly, that the costs of being away from their optimal gearing position were significant.

Graham and Harvey (2001) found that, among the US businesses that they surveyed, the tax benefit of debt finance is seen as an important factor in capital gearing decisions. This is particularly true among larger businesses where the tax rate is higher. They also found that businesses did not see the potential costs of bankruptcy as being an important issue, except for those businesses that were already relatively financially weak. On the other hand, many businesses were concerned about the credit rating of their debt (AAA, AA etc). This may indicate a concern about financial distress. Graham and Harvey also found that only 19 per cent of businesses had no target gearing ratio, although some of those that did had a fairly flexible one.

The formal evidence seems to answer the first question above: WACC decreases with increased gearing. It does not really deal with the second question, and so we do not know from the formal evidence whether or not WACC bottoms out at some point below 100 per cent gearing, after which it starts to increase.

Kester (1986) found dramatic differences between industrial sectors as regards levels of gearing. The highest average level of gearing was found in steel manufacturers (where debt was 1.665 times the market value of equity). The lowest occurred in pharmaceutical manufacturers (where the debt was only 0.097 times the market value of equity). It is not clear why there should be such differences, or why these two industries should occupy the positions indicated. One theory concerns the potential costs of bankruptcy. Some industries can liquidate their assets more easily than can others, with less difference between the value of the assets to the business on a 'going concern' basis and on a bankruptcy sale basis.

There also seem to be international differences in gearing levels. McClure, Clayton and Hofler (1999) looked at gearing levels in all of the G7 group of 'rich' industrial countries in 1991. They found that, by market value, debt to total value in the UK averaged 40.7 per cent. This contrasted with an average for all G7 countries of 45.1 per cent and quite wide variations between individual countries. These differences can probably be explained by international differences. For example, high corporate tax rates would tend to encourage loan finance; the UK has relatively low tax rates. Also, bank financing is more traditional in some countries than in others, for example, it is more so in Germany than in the UK.

11.10 Gearing and the cost of capital – conclusion

The central question on gearing is whether in reality it is the traditionalists or MM who best explain the effect of gearing.

The traditional view, that somehow equity shareholders do not pay much attention to the increased risk that rising amounts of gearing engender until it reaches high levels, seems naïve. It appears to conflict with most of the evidence on the efficiency of the capital market. Tests of capital market efficiency indicate that little of significance goes unnoticed. It is difficult to believe that increased levels of gearing are insignificant to equity shareholders, since gearing increases the range of possible returns. As most investors seem to be risk averse, increasing the range of possible outcomes will be unattractive to them.

The formal evidence on the effects of gearing cited above also cuts across the traditional view since it appears that gearing levels broadly affect equity returns and WACC in the manner suggested by MM (after-tax).

On the other hand, casual observation shows that businesses' managements do not seem to believe in very high levels of gearing, which rather supports the traditional view.

There is a conflict here, although perhaps it is possible to reconcile these two factors.

The MM (after-tax) analysis relies on a number of assumptions, most of which seem not to be so far-fetched as seriously to weaken their conclusions. Two of them, however, call their proposition into question. These are (1) that there are no bankruptcy costs, and (2) that the interest rate demanded by lenders remains the same at all levels of gearing. We shall now look more closely at these two assumptions.

There are no bankruptcy costs

The importance of this assumption lies in the fact that the existence of high levels of loan finance exposes the business to the risk that it will not be able to meet its payment obligations to lenders, not at least out of its operating cash flows, if the business should experience a particularly adverse period of trading. While it is equally true that the all-equity business might have difficulty paying dividends in similar economic circumstances, there is an important difference.

Lenders have a contractual right to receive interest and capital repayment on the due dates. If they do not receive these, they have the legal power to enforce payment. The exercise of such power can, in practice, lead to the liquidation of the assets and the winding up of the business. For the reasons we have already discussed (principally through an apparently inefficient market in real assets), this will usually disadvantage the ordinary shareholder to a significant extent.

This is supported by research evidence. Andrade and Kaplan (1998) estimate, from a study of 31 businesses that became financially distressed during the 1980s, that the costs of bankruptcy, or coming close to it, represent between 10 and 20 per cent of the businesses' value. If we take a hypothetical bankrupted business that is financed 50/50 by debt and equity, the cost to the shareholders (who would normally bear all of the cost) represents between 20 and 40 per cent of the value of their investment – a very significant amount.

By contrast, neither in a geared nor in an ungeared business do ordinary shareholders have any rights to enforce the declaration and payment of a dividend.

This bankruptcy risk is probably insignificant at low levels of gearing, if only because any shortage of cash for interest payments could be borrowed from some other source – a possibility probably not so readily available to highly geared businesses in distress.

The interest rate demanded by lenders remains the same at all levels of gearing

At very low levels of gearing the position of lenders is one of great security, with the value of their loan probably covered many times by the value of the business's assets. As gearing increases, this position erodes until at very high levels lenders, because they provide most of the finance, bear most of the risk.

Going back to Example 11.1 (La Mer), suppose that the unexpanded business (that is, just one yacht worth £1m) were financed 90 per cent by equity shares and 10 per cent by loan stock. Here the value of the yacht would have to fall by 90 per cent before the security of the lenders would be threatened. Even if the equity/loan ratio moved to 80/20, the lenders' security, while in theory slightly weakened, would not be less in practical terms than had they supplied only 10 per cent of the finance. If, however, the ratio moved to 10/90, only a small drop (10 per cent) in the value of the yacht would leave the lenders bearing all the risk. Naturally enough, lenders would demand high returns to induce them to buy loan stocks in such a highly geared business, presumably something like the returns expected by equity shareholders.

Logically, the loan stockholders would not see risk (and required return) increasing significantly with increases in gearing at the lower end. After all, unless the asset on which security rests is extremely volatile in its value, an asset value/loan ratio of 5/1 is probably as good as 10/1; the lenders need only to be paid once. If this ratio increased to nearer 1/1, lenders would no doubt start to see things differently.

The trade-off theory

It is notable that neither of the above two 'weak' assumptions of MM significantly affects the position at lower levels of gearing. At higher levels, however, they start to loom large. In the light of this, and taking account of the evidence that we briefly discussed, we may perhaps draw a tentative conclusion.

Up to moderate levels of gearing, the tax advantages of loan finance will cause the WACC to decrease as more gearing is introduced, as MM (after-tax) predicted. Beyond moderate levels, bankruptcy risk (to equity shareholders) and the introduction of real risk to lenders will push up the returns required by each group, making WACC a very high figure at high gearing levels.

Figure 11.5 depicts this conclusion with k_E, k_0 and k_L all following the same pattern as shown in Figure 11.4 (MM after-tax) up to a moderate level of gearing and then all starting to take off to very high levels as further gearing is introduced.

It is more likely that, in real life, *moderate* is not a fixed point for any particular business; it is, rather, a range below which MM's proposition holds, but above which it clearly does not. The key question, then, is what does 'moderate' mean? The problem

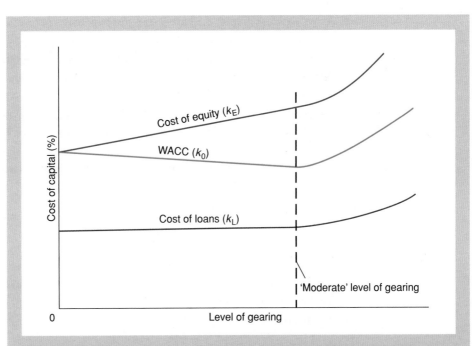

Figure 11.5
The cost of capital for varying levels of gearing – a possible reconciliation of the traditional view, the MM (after-tax) view and what appears to happen in practice

Here it is assumed that there is some logic in the MM case, and therefore WACC will fall as gearing increases. As the level of gearing increases above a 'moderate' level, however, both equity holders and lenders will become increasingly conscious of the risk. As a result they will seek higher returns in compensation. This will drive WACC steeply up. Thus there will be an optimum level of gearing.

is that 'moderate' is likely to be difficult to define and, as such, a matter of judgement for financial managers. It must be the point at which the balance is struck between the tax advantage, on the one hand, and bankruptcy cost and rising cost of borrowing, on the other. This will vary from industry to industry and will to some extent depend upon the business risk (perhaps measured by beta) of the investments in which the particular business is engaged.

More formally, the relationship between the value of the geared and ungeared businesses can be expressed as:

$$V_G = V_U + TL_G - \text{Present value of the expected cost of bankruptcy}$$

As gearing increases, the value of the tax shield (TL_G) increases but so does the expected cost of bankruptcy. At some point the latter will outweigh the former.

This conclusion, that choosing the level of gearing requires that a balance is struck between the tax shield and bankruptcy cost, has become known as the **trade-off theory** of capital gearing.

11.11 Pecking order theory

It has been suggested, first by Myers (1984), that businesses do not follow the trade-off theory or, at least, not to the letter.

The **pecking order theory** is really concerned with the idea that businesses are reluctant to make new share issues. There seem to be three reasons for this:

● As we saw in Chapter 8, share issues are expensive in terms of issue costs.

● It is believed that managers often feel that their business's share price understates its true value. Issuing new shares at this 'low' value would, in these circumstances, disadvantage existing shareholders to the advantage of those taking up the new shares issued.

● Arising from the preceding point, managers fear that the market may view making a share issue as a sign that the directors believe the shares to be overpriced in the stock market. It can also be viewed as an act of desperation, only to be undertaken when the business has no option. These points are likely to make it difficult to make an issue and may lead to a low issue price.

As a result, according to the pecking order theory, businesses will tend to finance their activities in the following sequence:

1 Retained profit.

2 Debt, which is relatively cheap to raise, particularly if it is in the form of a term loan from a bank or similar institution.

3 Equity share issue.

The pecking order theory is sometimes put forward as a strict alternative to the trade-off theory, but there is the possibility that they could work together. For example, businesses may broadly follow the principles of the trade-off theory but try to avoid new share issues and, perhaps, rely on debt finance rather more than strictly dictated by the trade-off theory.

Evidence on the pecking order theory

Graham and Harvey (2001) undertook a major survey of attitudes of senior managers in a large sample of larger US businesses in 1999. The range of the study was wide, but they paid quite a lot of attention to testing the pecking order theory. Graham and Harvey found that managers' behaviour seemed to be consistent with both theories. They found that businesses are reluctant to issue new shares where it is perceived that existing shares are undervalued, and that this is an important consideration in share issue decisions. They report that senior managers in more than two thirds of businesses believe that their shares are undervalued. This is consistent with the pecking order theory. Graham and Harvey also found that most businesses had a target gearing ratio, which is inconsistent with the pecking order theory.

Frank and Goyal (2003) tested the pecking order theory on the basis of what a broad cross-section of US businesses actually did (rather than what managers said that they felt) during the period 1980 to 1998. They found that the businesses behaved exactly in line with the trade-off theory and not as they would have been predicted to behave had the pecking order theory been valid.

Bunn and Young (2004) taking a similar approach to Frank and Goyal, but using UK data, found clear support for the trade-off theory.

11.12 Likely determinants of capital gearing

Having reviewed the theory and evidence on gearing, we can probably summarise the factors that will influence a business's decision on capital gearing. These are:

- *The rate of tax*. In the UK, there are clear tax advantages in paying £1 of loan interest rather than paying £1 of dividend. This will, in general, encourage debt finance.

- *Tax capacity*. A tax-deductible expense has no value unless there is taxable income against which to set it. Also, businesses with lower profits pay a lower rate of corporation tax. Businesses with low earnings tend to find high gearing less attractive.

- *Fluctuating sales revenue and/or high operating gearing*. Either of these factors, and particularly a combination of them, can lead to severe fluctuations in the returns paid to ordinary shareholders. This may confront the shareholders with an unacceptable level of risk in relation to their returns. It may also increase the risk of bankruptcy and its associated costs to the shareholders.

- *Nature of the business's assets*. Businesses with assets whose value is much greater on a 'going concern' than on a bankruptcy sale basis, i.e. those with potentially high bankruptcy costs, are likely to avoid high levels of gearing.

- *Reluctance to issue new shares*. Businesses typically feel that the market undervalues their shares and are not eager to issue new shares at 'undervalued' prices. There is also the fear that the market may perceive a share issue as a last resort, implying that the business is in difficulties.

- *Costs of raising the capital*. Most equity finance comes from retaining profits. Here 'issue' costs are zero, whereas issues of shares, even rights issues, are relatively expensive. Loan finance tends to be cheap to raise. Inevitably, these facts will affect most decisions on capital gearing.

- *Costs of servicing the capital*. The prevailing rates of interest will also be a relevant factor.

11.13 MM, MPT and CAPM

Before leaving the subject of capital gearing and its effect on WACC, perhaps we should consider how these matters relate to modern portfolio theory (MPT) in general, and the capital asset pricing model in particular.

Earlier in this chapter we saw that the introduction of capital gearing exposes the ordinary shareholder to two types of risk, namely business risk and financial risk. The question now arises as to how these two relate to specific risk and systematic risk.

We should recall from Chapter 7 that business risk has two components: the specific or diversifiable part and the systematic part that the investor must bear. Figure 11.1 (page 294) depicts the relationship between business risk and financial risk; it shows that financial risk simply augments or accentuates business risk. It seems logical therefore that, if business risk is part specific and part systematic, this must also be true for financial risk. This means that, as with business risk, part of financial risk can be diversified away. It also means that part of it cannot be eliminated by diversification.

The logical conclusion of this is that equity shares in geared businesses have higher betas than those in all-equity ones. Indeed, this is the case. We know that betas are additive, that is, the beta for a portfolio is the average (weighted by market value) of the betas of the constituents of the portfolio. Therefore (ignoring tax):

$$\beta_{EE} = \beta_{EG}\frac{S_G}{S_G + L_G} + \beta_{LG}\frac{L_G}{S_G + L_G}$$

where β_{EE} is the beta of the equities of the all-equity business, β_{EG} is the beta of the equities of the geared business and β_{LG} is the beta of the loan stock of the geared business. This assumes that the two businesses are identical in all respects except their financing method.

If we take account of the 'tax shield' of debt, the relationship between the betas is:

$$\beta_{EE} = \beta_{EG}\frac{S_G}{S_G + L_G(1 - T)} + \beta_{LG}\frac{L_G(1 - T)}{S_G + L_G(1 - T)}$$

where T is the corporation tax rate.

If we assume that the loan stock is without risk ($\beta_{LG} = 0$), then:

$$\beta_{EE} = \beta_{EG}\frac{S_G}{S_G + L_G} \text{ (ignoring tax)}$$

Rearranging gives:

$$\beta_{EG} = \beta_{EE}\left(1 + \frac{L_G}{S_G}\right)$$

$$\beta_{EG} = \beta_{EE} + \beta_{EE}\frac{L_G}{S_G}$$

or:

$$\beta_{EG} = \beta_{EE} + \beta_{EE}\frac{L_G(1 - T)}{S_G} \text{ (taking account of tax)}$$

In other words, the risk attaching to the equities in a geared business is equal to the risk to equities in the equivalent all-equity business plus a financial risk premium that depends on the basic all-equity risk and on the level of gearing. This is simply another way of saying:

Total systematic risk (of equities in a geared business)
= Systematic business risk + Systematic financial risk

Business risk can, as we know, be measured by beta, and financial risk is simply an accentuation of that same risk. This is entirely consistent with MM's assertions.

11.14 Weighted average cost of capital revisited

Towards the end of Chapter 10 it was said that there are two points about using WACC that it would be better to consider now.

The cost of capital of elements of financing at different levels of gearing

We have seen in this chapter that the cost of the various elements of long-term finance is partially dependent on the level of capital gearing. It is a basic tenet of both the MM and the traditional models that, as gearing increases, so does the cost of equity. Whether we deduce costs of capital using the traditional approach (based on market prices) or using CAPM, the figures that we calculate will be based on a particular level of gearing, and therefore that level of gearing will affect the deduced costs. If that level of gearing is not the level that will be relevant to the investment under consideration, the WACC to be used as the discount rate must reflect this difference in the gearing level.

For example, a business's equity may have been calculated to have a cost of 10 per cent p.a. This, however, assumes a particular level of gearing. Say that in this case we are talking about an all-equity business, that is, zero gearing. Suppose that the business is to take on some loan finance to fund a new project. This means that, all other things being equal, the cost of equity will increase. If we now want to calculate a WACC at which to discount the estimated cash flows of the new investment project, we must adjust the cost of equity from 10 per cent to reflect the level of gearing before we do the weighted averaging.

Adjusted net present value

Linked to the previous point is the fact that we have a problem in that undertaking a positive NPV project changes the level of gearing (unless the business is all-equity financed) and, therefore, the WACC. The value of a positive NPV project accrues entirely to the shareholders and increases the value of the equity. This alters the WACC. This means that the WACC that was used to deduce the NPV was the wrong one. The problem is that until we have deduced the NPV we do not know what the gearing ratio and, therefore, the correct WACC, are. Without knowing what the correct WACC is, we cannot calculate the correct NPV.

The most practical way to deal with this problem is to deduce the NPV in two stages. First we calculate the NPV assuming that the investment is all-equity financed and then, when we know the NPV on this basis, we adjust it for the tax effect of the debt finance. This is very similar (for good reason) to the relationship between the value of the geared and ungeared business that appears on page 301.

For the business as a whole:

$$V_G = V_U + TL_G$$

For the investment project:

$$NPV_G = NPV_U + TL_P$$

where: NPV_G = NPV if the project is undertaken by the geared business

NPV_U = NPV if the project is undertaken by the all-equity business

T = the corporation tax rate

L_P = the value of the loan finance used to finance the project.

Eleven per cent of the US businesses surveyed by Graham and Harvey (2001) use the adjusted NPV approach.

Summary

Capital (financial) gearing (CG)

- CG means financing partly through fixed-return finance (in practice, usually loans).

- Loan finance cheap because:

  - low risk to lenders; and

  - tax deductible.

- CG has the potential to increase returns to shareholders.

- CG has the effect of increasing the variability (risk) of returns to shareholders.

Traditional view

- The two reasons for loan finance being cheap lead to lowering WACC.

- Shareholders and lenders unconcerned about increased risk at lower levels of gearing.

- As gearing increases, both groups start to be concerned – higher returns demanded – WACC increases.

- WACC decreases (value of equity increases) as gearing is introduced – reaches a minimum – starts to increase again – optimum level of gearing.

Modigliani and Miller (MM) view

- Shareholders immediately concerned by the existence of gearing.

- Ignoring taxes, 'cheap' loan finance precisely offset by increasing cost of equity so WACC remains constant at all levels of gearing – no optimum level – managers should not concern themselves with gearing questions.

- With tax, interest cheap enough to cause WACC to fall despite increasing cost of equity – all-debt-financing conclusion – illogical since interest rates would increase at high levels of gearing.

Modern view: trade-off theory

- MM probably right that gearing is beneficial only because of tax relief.

- At high levels of gearing, the costs of the business going into enforced liquidation (bankruptcy) become significant.

- Generally well supported by the evidence.
- Conclusion: businesses should gear up to a point where the benefit[] relief are balanced by potential costs of bankruptcy – here WACC wil[] a minimum and value of the business at a maximum.

Pecking order theory

- Managers reluctant to make new share issues because:
  - high issue costs;
  - many managers believe that the market undervalues their business's shares; and
  - some managers believe that the market views a share issue as an act of desperation.
- The pecking order for raising funds is:
  - retained profit;
  - debt finance;
  - equity issues – as a last resort.
- Pecking order theory can be seen as a brake on the trade-off theory, rather than as a strict alternative to it.
- Evidence on the pecking order theory is not very strong.

Practical issues

- Most businesses seem to use gearing, but not to very high levels.
- High operating gearing businesses may be unsuitable for high capital gearing.
- Directors may not favour as high a level of gearing as is beneficial to share-holders (agency problem).
- Businesses may attract shareholders because of their gearing level (clientele effect).
- High tax rates will encourage high gearing.
- Tax capacity (having sufficient profit to be able to benefit from the tax relief on interest) may well affect gearing levels.
- Business may be reluctant to make share issues if they believe that they will disadvantage existing shareholders.
- The relative costs of raising funds (issue costs):
  - Equity from retained profit – virtually nothing.
  - Equity from rights or public issue – very expensive.
  - Debt finance – relatively cheap.

Further reading

The subject of capital gearing is well written up in the literature. There is good coverage of it by Levy and Sarnat (1995), Lumby and Jones (2003) and Atrill (2006). It is worth reading the original MM articles, which are reprinted in Archer and D'Ambrosio (1983).

Relevant
websites
The website of the business featured in this chapter is:

Cadbury Schweppes plc
www.cadburyschweppes.com

REVIEW QUESTIONS

Suggested answers to
review questions appear
in Appendix 3.

11.1 Why is loan finance usually cheaper than equity finance in the same business?

11.2 According to MM, what happens to the cost of equity as gearing increases (ignoring taxation)?

11.3 According to MM, and taking account of taxation, what happens to the cost of equity as gearing increases?

11.4 One of the MM assumptions is 'no bankruptcy costs'. What costs does this phrase represent?

11.5 How do we know that the managements of most businesses believe in the benefits of gearing?

11.6 What is the difference between the value of an ungeared and a geared business according to MM (taking account of taxation)?

PROBLEMS

Sample answers to
problems marked with
an asterisk appear in
Appendix 4.

(Problems 11.1 and 11.2 are basic-level problems, whereas problems 11.3 to 11.7 are more advanced and may contain some practical complications.)

11.1* Shiraz plc is financed by 10m shares, whose current market value is £2.40 a share, and 10 per cent debentures with a nominal and market value of £14m. The return on the ordinary shares is 20 per cent.

Making Modigliani and Miller's original assumptions (including that of no taxes), what would be the equity rate of return and the share price of an identical business that was all-equity financed?

11.2 Merlot plc is financed by 10m shares, whose current market value is £2.40 a share, and 10 per cent debentures with a nominal and market value of £14m. The business plans to issue additional shares to raise £14m and to use the cash generated to pay off the debentures. The corporation tax rate is 30 per cent.

(a) *Making Modigliani and Miller's assumptions (in a world with taxes), how would the restructuring described affect the value of the business?*

(b) *If the shareholders gain, who will lose, **or** if the shareholders lose, who will gain?*

11.3* Particulate plc is an all-equity financed business with a market value of £35m and a cost of capital (after tax) of 20 per cent p.a.

The business intends to purchase and cancel £8m of equity finance using the cash raised from issuing a 10 per cent irredeemable loan stock. The rate of corporation tax is 30 per cent.

Assuming that the assumptions of Modigliani and Miller (in a world with taxes) are correct, how will the capital restructuring affect:

(a) *the market value of Particulate plc;*
(b) *its cost of equity; and*
(c) *its weighted average cost of capital?*

11.4 Mile Long Merchants Limited (MLM) runs two small supermarkets. MLM's equity is owned entirely by members of the Long family.

The directors are keen to open an additional supermarket. The cost of doing this would be significant, perhaps equal to 30 per cent of the estimated current value of the business.

MLM generates profit at a level that leads to it paying corporation tax. This is likely to continue.

The business has limited cash available because most of the surpluses of the past few years have been distributed to the shareholders.

As finance director, you have been asked to prepare a paper to brief the other directors on the key issues before the next board meeting, where the question of finance to fund the additional supermarket will be discussed. The agenda for the meeting states that the decision is between asking the business's bankers to grant a term loan to cover the projected expenditure, on the one hand, and seeking the necessary funds from shareholders, through a rights issue, on the other.

Outline the main issues that you would include in your briefing paper.

11.5* Ali plc is a Stock Exchange listed business. It is all-equity financed by 40m 25p ordinary shares, which are currently quoted at £1.60 each. In the recent past, annual profit has been an average of £12.8m. The average rate of return on capital employed is expected to continue for the future. All of the profit is paid as a dividend each year. The business intends to raise some finance for expansion, either through a 1-for-4 rights issue at a price of £1.20 per share, or through the issue of 10 per cent unsecured loan stock to raise the same amount of cash.

Lee is an individual who owns 10 000 of the shares.

Making the same assumptions as were made by Modigliani and Miller in their original proposition on capital gearing (including a world without taxes), calculate and compare the effect on Lee's income of:

(a) *personally borrowing the cash necessary to take up the rights; and*
(b) *the business deciding to make the loan stock issue instead of the rights issue.*

What general conclusion do you draw from this comparison?

11.6 Cavendish plc is a Stock Exchange listed business whose main activity is producing a low-value material used in large quantities in the building/construction industries. Production is such that a large proportion of its costs are fixed relative to the level of output.

The business is financed by a combination of ordinary shares and loan stocks. At present the capital gearing ratio is a little below the average for businesses in the building materials industry.

Cavendish plc has identified a possible investment opportunity in taking over the operation of a smaller business, Darley Ltd, which is involved in producing another, more recently developed building material, which is increasingly being used as a substitute for a more traditional material. The decision has been taken to make the acquisition, and a price has been negotiated with the owners of Darley Ltd. The owners will only accept cash as the consideration for the acquisition. The acquisition will expand Cavendish plc's total funds invested by around 20 per cent.

Cavendish plc does not have sufficient cash to be able to finance the acquisition without making some form of capital issue. For various reasons, including potential loss of the economies of scale in respect of issue costs, the directors have decided either to make a rights issue of equities or a loan stock issue, rather than a combination of the two.

A board meeting has been scheduled to make a decision as to the means of financing the acquisition.

In advance of the meeting, individual directors of Cavendish plc have made the following comments:

● *Director A*: 'We don't want to make a rights issue of equities at present. With this depression in the construction industry dragging our share price down, we are going to have to issue a lot of shares to get the amount needed.'

● *Director B*: 'The trouble with a loan stock issue is that it will push our gearing level above the sector average and that won't help our share price.'

● *Director C*: 'My daughter is taking a business finance course as part of her degree, and she has told me that there's a theory that it doesn't make any difference to the existing shareholders whether new finance is raised from a share issue or by borrowing.'

Prepare some notes that will brief the directors, in advance of the meeting, on the likely key issues that they will need to consider, including the points that have already been made to you.

11.7 Arthur Graham plc (AG) is a Stock Exchange listed business that owns a chain of builders' merchants throughout the south of England. AG is currently financed principally by equity, as a result of organic growth.

An opportunity has arisen for AG to purchase all of the shares of an unlisted business, Sandboy Ltd, which owns a chain of builders' merchants with branches in many locations in the Midlands, an area into which AG's directors wish to expand. The price being asked by the shareholders equals about 25 per cent of AG's market capitalisation. Given the price and the prospects for Sandboy, the directors of AG are keen to acquire the shares.

The scale of the investment is such that AG could not raise the cash from internal sources and will have to make a rights issue of ordinary shares, an issue of preference shares or a loan stock issue. A decision now needs to be made on the method of funding.

Three of the directors have spoken to you about the funding decision and their comments have included the following:

● *Director A*: 'I'm not keen on loan finance because the interest will inevitably reduce our earnings per share and, therefore, our share price.'

● *Director B*: 'I don't favour a rights issue because inevitably many of our shareholders don't want to increase their investment and will lose out as a result. Irrespective of the direct effects of a rights issue on our share price, this will have an adverse effect on the total market value of our company. An issue of loan stock seems the best idea.'

● *Director C*: 'I favour a preference share issue, because it would be neutral as far as the capital gearing question is concerned; it will neither increase it nor reduce it.'

A board meeting has been arranged at which a final decision on the acquisition of Sandboy and, most importantly, the means of funding it will be discussed. As finance director, you have been asked to provide a briefing note for the directors to read in preparation for this meeting. Your briefing note should raise all relevant points about the funding arrangements and the points raised by the directors. The briefing note must be in simple, non-technical language. All of the relevant factors must be clearly explained and placed in the context of the particular circumstances of the question.

Prepare the briefing note requested by the directors.

There are both a set of **multiple-choice questions** and **missing-word questions** available on the website. These specifically cover the material contained in this chapter. These can be attempted and graded (with feedback) online.

There is also an **additional problem**, with solution, that relates to the material covered in this chapter.

Go to **www.pearsoned.co.uk/atrillmclaney** and follow the links.

APPENDIX I Proof of the MM cost of capital proposition (pre-tax)

The following symbols will be used:

$V_U = S_U$ = market value of the ungeared (all equity) business

S_G = market value of the equity of the geared business

L_G = market value of the loan capital of the geared business

$V_G = S_G + L_G$ = market value of the geared business

i = interest rate

X = net operating income of both businesses

α = the proportion of either business's securities owned by an individual.

Suppose that an individual owns proportion α of the shares of the ungeared business. This is an investment valued at αV_U (or αS_U), which will produce income of αX.

The same income could be obtained (with, according to our assumption, the same risk) by buying proportion α of both the equity and loan stock of the geared business:

	Investment required	Income produced
Buy proportion α of geared business's equity	$\alpha S_G = \alpha(V_G - L_G)$	$\alpha(X - iL_G)$
Buy proportion α of geared business's loan stock	$\underline{\alpha L_G}$	$\underline{\alpha i L_G}$
Total	$\underline{\underline{\alpha V_G}}$	$\underline{\underline{\alpha X}}$

If $V_U > V_G$, the investor would sell the equity shares in the ungeared business and buy equity shares and loan stock. Thus the investor would end up with the same income and make a profit on the difference between the price at which the equity shares of the ungeared business could be sold and what would have to be paid to buy the equity shares and loan stock of the geared business.

Such action by our investor (and by others similarly placed) will have the effect of reducing the value of the ungeared business's equity and increasing that of the geared one's securities. This would occur until the value of the two businesses was equal. Efficient capital market research suggests that such a process would not take long.

The commodity that is being traded here (as far as our individual is concerned) is annual income of amount αX. MM argued that it would be irrational for this to be priced differently merely because it is not packaged in the same way. They contended that the packaging of the income is irrelevant since the individual investor can repackage it personally without (according to MM's assumption on frictionless capital markets) any personal cost.

MM also tackled the proof from the other starting point.

Suppose that an individual owns proportion α of the equity shares of a geared business. This would have a market value of αS_G [or $\alpha(V_G - L_G)$, since $V_G = S_G + L_G$] and produce annual income $\alpha(X - iL_G)$.

In order to get the same income the individual could buy proportion α of the ungeared business's equity and finance it partly by personal borrowing:

	Investment required	Income produced
Buy proportion α of ungeared business's shares	$\alpha S_U = \alpha V_U$	αX
Borrow (personally) an amount equal to αL_G	$-\alpha L_G$	$-\alpha i L_G$
Total	$\underline{\alpha(V_U - L_G)}$	$\underline{\alpha(X - i L_G)}$

Thus by investing $\alpha(V_U - L_G)$ the investor can get the same income as had been obtained from an investment valued at $\alpha(V_G - L_G)$. If the market value of the geared business (V_G) is greater than that of the ungeared one (V_U), it will benefit our investor to sell the equity stake in the geared business and then go in for some 'personal' gearing.

Once again the action of investors in selling the geared business's equity and buying that of the ungeared business would, by the laws of supply and demand, quickly drive the two market values (V_U and V_G) back into equality.

The assumptions on which the above analysis is based are stated and discussed in the chapter.

APPENDIX II   Proof of the MM cost of capital proposition (after-tax)

It is proved below that:

$$V_G = V_U + T L_G*$$

Suppose that an individual owns proportion α of the shares of an ungeared business. This would be an investment valued at αV_U (or αS_U), which will produce income $\alpha X(1 - T)$, that is, proportion α of the after-tax income of the business.

The same income could be obtained by buying proportion α of the equity and proportion $\alpha(1 - T)$ of the loan stock of the geared business:

	Investment required	Income produced
Buy proportion α of geared business's equity	$\alpha S_G = \alpha(V_G - L_G)$	$\alpha(X - i L_G)(1 - T)$
Buy proportion $\alpha(1 - T)$ of the geared business's loan stock	$\underline{\alpha L_G(1 - T)}$	$\underline{\alpha i L_G(1 - T)}$
Total	$\underline{\alpha(V_G - T L_G)}$	$\underline{\alpha X(1 - T)}$

If $\alpha(V_G - T L_G) < \alpha V_U$, (that is, if $V_G < V_U + T L_G$), it means that the investor could retain the same income [$\alpha X(1 - T)$] by selling the ungeared equities and replacing them with the cheaper geared business's shares and loan stocks. The action of investors making this switch will tend to cause $V_G = V_U + T L_G$.

Tackling the proof from the other starting point, suppose that an investor holds proportion α in the equity of a geared business. This would give an income of $\alpha(X - i L_G)(1 - T)$. (This is because the loan interest ($i L_G$) is tax deductible.) The investor

---

* Note that
$$\sum_{n=0}^{\infty} \frac{i T L_G}{(1 + i)^n} = T L_G$$
that is, the present value of the tax saving on loan interest ($i T L_G$) is $T L_G$.

could obtain the same income from selling these shares and buying proportion α of the shares of the ungeared business and by borrowing amount $\alpha(1 - T)L_G$ to help finance the purchase of the shares.

	Investment required	Income produced
Buy proportion α of the ungeared business's shares	$\alpha S_U = \alpha V_U$	$\alpha X(1 - T)$
Borrow (personally) $\alpha(1 - T)L_G$	$-\alpha(1 - T)L_G$	$-\alpha(1 - T)iL_G$
Total	$\alpha[V_U - (1 - T)L_G]$	$\alpha(X - iL_G)(1 - T)$

If $\alpha[V_U - (1 - T)L_G] < \alpha S_G$, then $V_U < S_G + L_G(1 - T)$, which would encourage holders of the geared business's equity to switch to the ungeared business's equity (with personal borrowing) since they could continue with the same income but make capital gains on the switch. Such switching would cause:

$$V_U = S_G + L_G(1 - T)$$

Therefore this equality must hold.

Chapter 12

The dividend decision

Objectives   In this chapter we shall deal with the following:

→ the nature of dividends

→ the theoretical position of dividends as residuals

→ the Miller and Modigliani view that the pattern of dividends is irrelevant to the value of shares (and WACC)

→ the traditional view of dividends

→ the evidence on dividends

12.1 Introduction

Dividends are payments made by businesses to their shareholders. They seem to be viewed by both the directors and the shareholders as the equivalent of an interest payment that would be made to a loan creditor; a compensation for the shareholders' delaying consumption. Dividends are also seen as a distribution of the business's recent profits to its owners, the shareholders.

A share, like any other economic asset (that is, an asset whose value is not wholly or partly derived from sentiment or emotion), is valued on the basis of future cash flows expected to arise from it. Unless a takeover, liquidation or share repurchase is seen as a possibility, the only possible cash flows likely to arise from a share are dividends. So it would seem that anticipated dividends are usually the only determinant of share prices and hence of the cost of equity capital.

It would, therefore, appear that the directors would best promote the shareholders' welfare by paying as large a dividend as the law will allow in any particular circumstances.

This attitude begs several questions, however. Is it logical that directors can enhance the value of the business's shares simply by deciding to pay a larger dividend; can value be created quite so simply? What if the business has advantageous new investment opportunities; would it be beneficial to shareholders for the business to fail to pay a dividend in order to keep sufficient finance available with which to make the investment? Alternatively, should the business pay a dividend and raise the necessary finance for the investment opportunity by issuing additional shares to the investing public, perhaps including any of the existing shareholders who wish to be involved?

Even where the business cannot see any particularly advantageous investment opportunities, should it be cautious and pay less than the full amount of dividend that the law allows?

Just what should the business's dividend policy be, and does it really matter anyway? We shall consider these questions during this chapter.

12.2 Modigliani and Miller on dividends

In 1961, Modigliani and Miller (MM) published an important article dealing with dividends and their effect on shareholders' wealth (Miller and Modigliani 1961). Their theme further developed the principle, Fisher separation, which we discussed in Chapter 2. There we looked at a very simple example which suggested that directors need not concern themselves with the payment of dividends. Provided that the business takes on all available investment projects that have positive NPVs, when discounted at the cost of capital, shareholders' wealth will be maximised. Any funds left over should be paid to shareholders as dividends.

MM took this slightly further by asserting that the value of a share will be unaffected by the pattern of dividends expected from it. If shareholders want dividends they can create them by selling part of their shareholding. If dividends are paid to shareholders who would rather leave the funds in the business, they can cancel these dividends by using the cash received to buy additional shares in the business, in the capital market.

Let us use an example to illustrate the MM proposition.

Example 12.1

White plc has net assets whose net present value is £5m. This includes cash of £1m, which the directors have identified could be invested in a project whose anticipated inflows have a present value of £2m. Assuming that White plc is financed by 1m ordinary shares (no gearing) and that the investment is undertaken and no dividend paid, the value of each share should be £(5 + 2 − 1)m/1m = £6. If, instead of making the investment, the £1m cash were used to pay a dividend, each share would be worth £(5 − 1)m/1m = £4 and the holder of one share would have £1 (the dividend) in cash.

Clearly it would be to the shareholder's advantage for the business to make the investment and so it should be made. If White plc wanted both to pay the dividend (using up all available cash) and to make the investment, it would need to raise new finance. Assuming that it wished to retain its all-equity status it would need to issue new shares to the value of the dividend. Since the value of the business after paying the dividend and making the investment would be £5m, this would engender an issue price of the new shares of £5 each (200 000 of them to make up the £1m required).

It also means that the original shareholders would gain £1 per share by way of dividend and lose £1 per share, as each share would have a value of £5 instead of the

£6 that would apply if no dividend were paid. In other words, the dividend would make no difference to the wealth of the shareholders. On the other hand, making the investment makes a significant difference to their wealth.

Creating homemade dividends

Note that, provided the new investment is undertaken, the worth of the original shares would be £6 each. This value is in some combination of share price and dividend. Irrespective of the amount of dividend paid, the individual shareholder can choose how much dividend to take. Suppose that no dividend is paid on the White plc shares, but a particular shareholder owning 100 of the shares wants cash of, say, £60. The shareholder can create a 'homemade' dividend by selling 10 shares (at £6 each, their current value).

Cancelling dividends

Conversely, assuming that the business pays a dividend of £1 per share (and creates an additional 200 000 shares to finance it), shareholders who do not want a dividend but prefer to keep their investment intact could negate the effect of the dividend payment by using the whole of the dividend receipt in buying new shares. Let us again consider the holder of 100 shares who receives a £100 dividend. This cash could be used to buy 20 new shares (at £5 each), increasing the investment to 120 shares in total. These will be worth £600, the same as the 100 shares would have been worth had no dividend been paid. Using the whole of the dividend to buy new shares will ensure that our shareholder retains the same proportion of the ownership (120 of the 1.2m) as was held before the dividend and the new issue (100 of the 1.0m shares).

Dividends as a residual

Example 12.1 illustrates MM's central point, which is that the primary decision is the investment one. The business should make all investments that yield a positive NPV when discounted at the shareholders' opportunity cost of capital. Any funds remaining should be paid to the shareholders, enabling them to pursue other opportunities. Thus dividends are a *residual*. MM contended that it would be illogical for the capital market to value two, otherwise identical, businesses differently just because of their dividend policy. If the business wants to pay a dividend it can do so and raise any necessary finance by issuing new equity. Also, individual shareholders who do not like the business's dividend policy can alter it to suit their taste through 'homemade' creation or negation of dividends.

MM's assertion does, however, rely on several assumptions of dubious validity in the real world. We shall consider the limitations of these assumptions later in the chapter. A formal derivation of the MM proposition is contained in the appendix to this chapter.

What MM did not say

Before we go on to assess what MM said about dividends against the traditional view and against the evidence of what actually seems to happen in real life, it might be worth clarifying exactly what they said.

What they did *not* say is that it does not matter whether dividends are paid or not as far as the value of the business is concerned. If shareholders are never to receive a dividend or any other cash payment in respect of their shares, the value of those shares must be zero. What MM said is that the *pattern* of dividends is irrelevant to valuation. Provided that the business invests in all projects that have a positive NPV when discounted at the shareholders' opportunity cost of capital (and none with a negative NPV), and provided that eventually all of the fruits of the investment are paid in cash to shareholders, it does not matter when payment is made. 'Eventually' may be a very long time, but this in principle does not matter. Even if no cash is expected to be forthcoming until the business is liquidated, this should not, of itself, cause the shares to be less valuable than were there to be a regular dividend until that time. Thus MM do not cast doubt on the validity of the dividend model for valuing equities, which we discussed in Chapter 10 (page 275).

In principle, the timing of a particular dividend does not matter to the shareholder, provided that the later dividend is $(1 + r)^n$ times the earlier alternative, where r is the shareholder's expected return and n is the time lapse between the earlier and later dividends.

Suppose that a business could pay a dividend now of amount D. Alternatively, it could invest that amount now in a project that will produce one cash inflow after n years, which will be paid as a dividend at that time. The shareholders would be indifferent as to whether the dividend is paid now or in n years, provided that the later dividend is $D(1 + r)^n$. This is because $D(1 + r)^n$ has the present value D [that is, $D(1 + r)^n/(1 + r)^n$]. Thus dividend D now, or $D(1 + r)^n$ in n years, should have equal effect on the value of the shares and on the wealth of the shareholders.

If the business were able to invest in a project that yields an inflow of amount greater than $D(1 + r)^n$ (that is, a project with a positive NPV), then the value of the shares would be enhanced.

Of course, as MM pointed out, it is always open to individual shareholders to create dividends by selling part of their shareholding if the delay in the dividend does not suit their personal spending plans.

The key point here is that the business has funds that belong to the shareholders. If it is able to invest those funds more effectively, on the shareholders' behalf, than the shareholders can do for themselves, then it should do so. If it cannot do this, it should return the funds to the shareholders and let them do the investing. This is, of course, why businesses should use the shareholders' opportunity cost of capital as the discount rate in investment appraisal. If the business's potential investments cannot achieve that rate, the funds should be passed to the shareholders, who can achieve it.

12.3 The traditional view on dividends

Before MM made their assertion and presented a plausible proof of it, the view had been taken not only that dividends are the paramount determinant of share values but also that £1 in cash is worth more than £1 of investment.

The traditionalists would value the shares differently depending on whether or not a dividend was to be paid. Greater value would be placed on the share where a dividend was to be paid (and, for example, a share issue undertaken) than where this was not the case. This is a view based on 'a bird in the hand is worth two in the bush' approach, that is, the notion that a guaranteed receipt enhances the value of the asset from which it derives.

Going back to the White plc in Example 12.1, if the shares are priced at £6 before a £1 per share dividend, the price of the share will not fall to £5 ex dividend, according to traditionalists, but perhaps to, say, £5.50. Thus the wealth of a shareholder will be enhanced by £0.50 per share as a result of the dividend.

The traditional view implies that the payment of dividends reduces the capital market's perceptions of the level of risk attaching to future dividends. This means that the discount rate to be applied to expected future dividends will be lower and the market price will increase as a result.

12.4 Who is right about dividends?

The traditional view on dividends seems to suffer from a fundamental lack of logic. The only circumstances where shareholders should logically value £1 in cash more highly than £1 in investment is where they feel that the business is using retained cash to make disadvantageous investments (that is, those that have negative NPVs when discounted at a rate that takes account of the level of risk attaching to the particular project). Since, ultimately, the shareholders must receive all of the fruits of the investments, provided businesses invest only in projects with positive NPVs then investment is to be preferred to present dividends.

MM seem to have logic on their side, yet many businesses appear to behave as if the pattern of dividends does matter. Directors seem to devote quite a lot of thought to fixing the levels of dividends. Most businesses seem to maintain pretty stable levels of dividends, implying that they set aside a similar amount for dividends each year. Yet it would be a remarkable coincidence if each year there were a similar amount of cash for which profitable investment opportunities could not be found. We shall look at the dividend policies of some well-known businesses later, in section 12.6.

MM's assertion that the pattern of dividends does not matter is based, as we have seen, on several assumptions. The extent to which these weaken their analysis might explain why the logic of the MM proposition does not seem to be fully accepted in practice. We shall now review these assumptions.

- *There are frictionless capital markets, which implies that there are neither transactions costs nor any other impediments to investors behaving in practice as they might be expected to do in theory.* Obviously this is invalid and probably sufficiently so to call the MM view into question. MM rely on the ability of individual shareholders to sell their shares to create dividends or to buy shares to eliminate dividends. The fact that dealing in the capital market involves significant cost (agents' fees and so on) means, for example, that receiving a dividend, on the one hand, and liquidating part of an investment in the shares concerned, on the other, are not perfect substitutes for one another.

- *Securities are efficiently priced in the capital market.* The evidence (that we reviewed in Chapter 9) tends to support the validity of this assumption. The assumption is necessary, otherwise (in Example 12.1, above) White plc undertaking the investment will not necessarily increase the share price by £1, nor the payment of the dividend necessarily reduce the share price by £1.

- *Shares may be issued by businesses without any legal or administrative costs being incurred.* This assumption is not valid, and this is probably significant in the present context. MM see paying no dividend on the one hand, and paying a dividend and raising an equal amount by share issue on the other hand, as equivalent. This will not be true in practice. Issuing new shares tends to involve the business in fairly large legal and administrative costs (see Chapter 8). It seems likely that this is an important factor in making decisions on dividend payment levels.

- *Taxes, corporate and personal, do not exist.* Certainly this is untrue, and it is often a significant feature. From the business's point of view, its corporation tax liability is not dependent on the level of dividends.

    From the shareholders' perspective, the main question is whether it is more *tax efficient* to receive dividends or to make capital gains. The answer tends to depend on who the shareholders are and on their individual level of income and capital gains for the year concerned. For some shareholders (such as tax-exempt institutions), neither dividend nor capital gains will attract tax. For others, tax becomes significant. To the extent that it is possible to generalise, it is probably true to say that for individuals with high levels of dividends and capital gains, further dividends tend to be taxed at the same rate as capital gains.

    A feature of the UK investment scene is the increasing tendency for equities to be owned by the investing institutions. Many of these, for example pension funds and life assurance funds, are exempt from taxes both on income and on capital gains.

    The situation is complicated still further by the fact that the business's corporation tax liability will, to a large extent, depend on what it does with any funds that it retains. Some investments in real assets are more tax efficient than others; for example, an investment in a factory attracts tax relief whereas an investment in an office block does not.

    MM's 'no tax' assumption is perhaps not too significant provided that businesses show some consistency in their dividend policy: a point to which we shall shortly return.

The deficiencies of the individual assumptions do not seem sufficiently profound to destroy the MM case. Clearly, the existence of significant dealing and share issue costs must weaken it, but there seems no reason why MM's analysis should not reasonably represent the true position – not, at least, as far as their analysis goes.

12.5 Other factors

There are some other factors that might bear on the position and explain why directors seem to regard the dividend decision as an important one, despite the MM assertion that it is not.

Informational content of dividends

Some hold the view that the level of dividends, perhaps, more particularly, changes in the level of dividends, convey new public information about the business. For example, an increased level of dividend might be (and seems often to be interpreted as) a signal that the directors view the future of the business with confidence. (This contrasts strikingly with the conclusion that might be reached by following MM's analysis. Paying any dividend, let alone one that showed an increase over the previous year, might well indicate that the directors cannot find sufficient investment opportunities to use all the finance available to them, so they are returning some to shareholders. This would not suggest great confidence in the future on the part of the directors.)

Assuming this view to be correct, whether such a signal is meant as one or is inadvertent probably varies from case to case. Certainly, a typical tactic of an unwilling target business's management in a takeover battle is to increase its dividend level; perhaps this is a deliberate signal to inspire the shareholders' confidence in the business's future.

If dividend increases are meant to act as signals, it seems reasonable to ask why the directors do not simply issue a statement. Surely a statement would be much less ambiguous than an increased dividend. Perhaps the directors feel that actions speak louder than words.

Incidentally, if the signalling view of dividends were correct, it would be expected that an increased dividend would have a favourable effect on the share price in the capital market. Such a phenomenon would represent a further piece of evidence that the capital market is not efficient in the strong form (see Chapter 9), because it implies that information available to the directors may not be impounded in the share price.

Clientele effect

It is widely believed that investors have a *preferred habitat*, that is, a type of investment that they feel best suits them. In the context of dividends, their preference might well be dictated by their individual tax position. A person with a high marginal income tax rate might well be attracted to shares where dividend payouts are low. On the other hand, an investor such as a pension fund that is tax exempt, but which needs regular cash receipts in order to be able to meet payments to pensioners, might go for shares in businesses whose dividend payments are relatively high. Such an investor could, of course, generate cash by selling shares, but this would involve brokers' fees and such like, which obviously are best avoided.

If there really is a clientele effect it means that a proportion of any business's shareholders acquired their shares because they are suited by that business's dividend policy. If there is inconsistency in the policy on dividends, many investors would be put off the shares as they would not know whether the levels of dividends would suit their preferences or not. The lack of popularity of the shares would have an adverse effect on their price and, therefore, on the cost of capital. Even if a particular business were to be fairly consistent in its dividend policy, but then undertook a major change, those of its shareholders who particularly liked the previous dividend policy (this might be all of them) would probably seek to move to the shares of a business with a dividend policy more acceptable to them. While it might well be the case that a new clientele would find the dividend policy attractive, the friction caused by one set of investors selling to a new set of investors would have a net adverse effect on the shareholders. Not only this, but the uncertainty in the minds of investors that the change may precipitate, as to how consistent the dividend policy was likely to be in future, could also have a dampening effect on the share price.

Liquidity

It has been suggested that the level of dividends paid by a particular business, at a particular time, is largely dictated by the amount of cash available. Certainly this is what

MM suggest should be the case. On the other hand, if failure to pay a dividend is interpreted adversely by the capital market, the best interests of shareholders' wealth might be advanced by making sure that cash is available, perhaps by borrowing, or even by passing up otherwise beneficial investment opportunities.

Pecking order theory

In Chapter 11 we saw that a combination of factors might lead to businesses seeking to raise funds in the following order of preference:

1 Retained profit

2 Debt

3 Equity issue, only as a last resort.

This implies that, where the business has funds built up from profitable trading that it can dip into for investment purposes, it will tend to do so. If there are insufficient investment funds available from retained profit, debt financing will be favoured next, while equity financing through a new issue of shares will come last in the list of preferences. The preference for using retained profit for investment, combined with a firm resistance to making share issues, has implications for dividend policy. According to the pecking order theory, businesses may be less likely to pay dividends, where they have profitable (positive NPV) investment opportunities, as predicted by MM. If they have surplus cash, businesses would be likely to hold on to it rather than pay dividends, in contradiction to MM. Also, if they need more investment finance, they are more likely to borrow than to make a new share issue, again in contrast to what MM predict.

Agency

The theoretical principles of dividend decisions are clear, according to MM. If the business cannot identify profitable (positive NPV) investments, it should return any residual cash to the shareholders and let them use it more advantageously than it can on their behalf. In an effort to expand their empire, however, the directors may choose to make disadvantageous investments. Thus there is the danger that the agency problem of the separation of the ownership of the business from the directors can lead to agency costs to be borne by the owners – the shareholders.

In short, the agency problem could lead to dividends that are less than those that it would be in the shareholders' best interests to receive. As ever with the agency problem, the shareholders often do not have the necessary information that could lead them to make a reasoned challenge to the directors' dividend decision.

Share repurchase

One way for a business to transfer funds to shareholders is for it to buy back shares from individual shareholders, either through the Stock Exchange or by making direct contact with them. We should be clear that, in essence, this has the same overall effect on the business as would a dividend payment involving an equal amount of cash. The effect on shareholders is very different, and this is a major advantage. Shareholders who want to take part or all of their stake in the business (sell part or all of their shares to the business) can do so to the extent that they wish; those that do not wish to sell need not do so. Share repurchases allow the business to make significant cash distributions in a particular year without establishing any expectations of the future level of dividends.

It is common for businesses to make share repurchases involving a limited number of shareholders while paying 'normal' dividends.

12.6 Dividends: the evidence

The scale of dividends

Whatever the effect on overall shareholders' wealth of particular dividend policies, the evidence shows that, historically in the USA, dividends have contributed 52 per cent of returns to shareholders during the period 1872 to 2000, the remaining 48 per cent coming from increases in share values (Coggan 2001). More recently, the contribution of dividends has been rather less. In the period 1995 to 2000, they contributed only 20 per cent. There is no reason to believe that the relationship between capital gains and dividends is significantly different in the UK.

Benito and Young (2003) examined dividends paid by UK businesses between 1974 and 1999. They found that, since 1995, there has been an increasing tendency for businesses to pay no dividend. In 1995, 14.3 per cent of businesses paid no dividend, but this had increased to 25.2 per cent by 1999. Although the single most important factor in failing to pay dividends was a lack of profitability, the recent increase in the proportion of businesses failing to pay a dividend is associated with new, expanding businesses that have never paid a dividend. The latter point is entirely consistent with MM: finance that is needed for profitable investment is not used to pay dividends. Benito and Young also noted an increasing tendency to reduce dividends over recent years. On the other hand, the higher dividend payers in 1999 were paying out about twice as much by way of dividends, relative to sales revenue, as their high-paying counterparts in 1977. These findings suggest much more flexible dividend policies in recent years; more non-payers and larger big payments. This would be consistent with MM.

Fama and French (2001) found that, in the USA, the percentage of businesses paying dividends fell from 66.5 per cent in 1978 to 20.8 per cent in 1999. Like Benito and Young in the UK, they found that this decline partly related to the changing profile of stock market listed businesses towards younger, smaller businesses with low profitability and strong growth opportunities. They also found a general decline in the dividends among all businesses.

Deangelo, Deangelo and Skinner (2004), again with US data, supported the Fama and French finding that there is a decreasing number of businesses paying dividends. They also found, however, that total dividends paid by all businesses had increased. The larger dividends paid by the big payers has tended to outweigh the lower and no dividends at the other end of the range. These two US studies are consistent with Benito and Young's UK finding that there seems to be more flexibility in dividend policies than used to be the case.

The flexibility point is further supported by Julio and Ikenberry (2004). They found that the propensity of US businesses to pay dividends in the late twentieth century was reversed in the early 2000s. They attributed this reversal to several factors, including:

- a tendency for the younger, smaller businesses (mentioned by Benito and Young and by Fama and French (see above)) now to have become larger and more profitable with less requirement for investment capital, leaving them with spare cash;

- businesses using dividends as a means of reassuring investors that their profits are genuine, following the corporate governance scandals (such as Enron discussed in Chapter 3); and

- a more favourable tax treatment of dividends in the USA.

Stability of dividend policy

The evidence of casual observation is that directors treat the dividend decision as an important one. It also seems that they try to maintain dividends at previous levels; reductions in dividends seem relatively rare occurrences.

This is very much supported by more formal evidence. Baker, Powell and Veit (2002) undertook a survey (during 1999) of the opinions of 187 senior financial managers of larger US businesses that were regular dividend payers. They found that over 90 per cent of the managers felt:

- dividend increases should not occur unless there was confidence that the business could sustain the higher level in future (93 per cent);

- dividends should never be missed (95 per cent); and

- the market places a higher value on a business that maintains a stable level of dividends paid than on one that pays a constant proportion of its profit as a dividend (which, therefore varies with profit levels) (94 per cent).

Note that the managers surveyed were with businesses that paid regular dividends, so they were not a random sample. Whether these managers were correct in their judgements is, to some extent, not the issue. If they believe that investors are benefited by regular dividends that are never decreased or missed, then they are likely to strive to adopt such a dividend policy.

Effect of dividends on share price

Friend and Puckett (1964) tested the relationship between share prices and dividend policy. While they experienced some methodological problems they found no close correlation between dividends and share prices.

Black and Scholes (1974) undertook a similar study to that of Friend and Puckett but overcame some of the problems encountered. They too found no evidence that higher or lower dividend levels lead to higher or lower returns either before or after taxes.

Though numerous subsequent tests, conducted on both UK and US data, have failed to show a clear relationship between dividends and share prices, Fama and French (1998) did show one. These researchers inferred that increases in dividends are treated, by the market, as a signal of higher expectations of managers. This tends to lead to enhanced share prices as investors reassess the value of the business.

Informational content of dividends (signalling)

Pettit (1972) found clear support for the proposition that the capital market takes account of dividend announcements as information for assessing share prices.

This finding has fairly consistently been supported by subsequent studies, for example Aharoney and Swary (1980). Nissim and Ziv (2001) found that dividend changes provide information about the level of profitability in the years following the change. Increases in dividends tend to indicate increases in accounting profits in each of the two years following the increased dividend. This links in with the Fama and French (1998) finding (above). The evidence on the informational effect of dividends seems fairly conclusive.

Mougoue and Rao (2003) found that not all businesses seem to signal future profitability through dividend policy; only about one-quarter of the businesses that they examined did so. They noted that the 'signallers' tended to be smaller, have a lower asset-growth rate and have higher capital gearing than the average.

Dewenter and Warther (1998) compared signalling effects in the USA and in Japan. They concluded that dividends seem to have a greater informational content in the USA than in Japan. They inferred that this arose from a closer relation between investors and managers in Japan, which leads to better information flows from the latter to the former. This might indicate less of an agency problem in Japan. Lack of information by shareholders tends to be a major cause of agency costs.

Clientele effect

Elton and Gruber (1970) conducted a rather interesting study to test for the clientele effect. By looking at the fall in share price when a share goes from cum dividend to ex dividend (shortly before a dividend payment), they were able to infer an average marginal income tax rate for any particular business's shareholders. They found that lower income tax rates were associated with high dividend shares and higher income tax rates with low dividend shares: that is, they found a clientele effect.

Pettit (1977) gained access to information on the security portfolios of a large number of clients of a large US stockbroker. He found that low levels of dividends seemed to be preferred by investors with relatively high marginal income tax rates, by younger investors, and by those who were less than averagely risk averse (high-beta share owners).

However, Lewellen, Stanley, Lease and Schlarbaum (1978), using the same data but a different approach from that taken by Pettit, reached the dissimilar conclusion that there is only a very weak clientele effect. Litzenberger and Ramaswamy (1982) undertook a study that produced results that seemed to support the clientele effect. Crossland, Dempsey and Moizer (1991), using UK data, also found clear evidence of a significant clientele effect. Allen, Bernado and Welch (2000) identified an interesting link between the clientele effect and the agency issue. They argue that businesses that pay dividends tend to attract institutional investors, many of which are tax exempt (life insurance funds, pension funds and the like). Institutions, because they tend to be large investors and are professionally managed, tend to take steps to try to ensure that the businesses in which they invest are well managed. The various studies on the clientele effect broadly seem to support its existence.

Corporate taxes

A study by Siddiqi (1995) showed, as might be expected, that changes in tax rules that make dividends less costly to businesses tend to be related to increased dividends.

Cash flow and investment opportunities

Barclay, Smith and Watts (1995) found, based on a sample of US businesses, that dividends tend to be lower when there are more investment opportunities for the businesses, as the MM principles would suggest.

Examples of real businesses following the MM principles

Monsoon plc, the high street retailer, said in its 2004 annual report: 'it is unlikely that the Group will pay dividends in future years while it remains in a period of high capital expenditure'.

Michael O'Leary, the colourfully spoken chief executive of **Ryanair Holdings plc**, the 'no frills' airline, was rather more direct than Monsoon plc. He said: 'We are never paying a dividend as long as I live and breathe and as long as I'm the largest shareholder. If you are stupid enough to invest in an airline for its dividend flow you should be put back in the loony bin where you came from' (Osborne 2004). Presumably, Ryanair is expanding at a rate that eats up all available finances.

Examples of real businesses not apparently following the MM principles

Many businesses seem to base their dividends on the profit of the most recent accounting year, though with reference to future investment. For example, **Interbrew NV**, the international brewer (Bass, Beck's, Stella Artois), said in its 2003 annual report: 'Our policy is to retain the majority of our earnings to finance future growth. We intend to use between 25% and 33% of our net profit from ordinary activities, on average, to pay dividends.'

Some businesses seem keen to link their dividends to their level of profit. In its 2003 annual report, **Imperial Chemical Industries plc**, the chemicals and paints business, said: 'The group's dividend policy is that dividends should represent about one third of net profit before exceptional items and goodwill amortisation.'

Other businesses like to link their dividend to profit and, at the same time, to be in line with similar businesses. For example, **The Go-Ahead Group plc**, the transport business (Thameslink, Metrobus), in announcing an increase in dividend in its 2004 annual report, said: 'The total dividend for the year is increased by 52% compared to last year in accordance with the policy noted last year, dividend cover is proposed to be reduced to 2.9 times adjusted earnings from 3.2 times in 2003. Further reductions towards the peer group average currently estimated at 2.3 times, can be foreseen.'

Perhaps surprisingly, Ettridge and Kim (1994) found that where a change in accounting methods led to higher reported profits, and to a higher actual tax charge, dividend levels seemed to increase. This seems strange, since the investment opportunities and the level of operating cash flows were not affected by the accounting change. Higher tax payments were the only real effects of the change. This implies that businesses relate dividends more to the reported accounting profits than to the underlying economic reality.

Share repurchase and MM

Share repurchase is a very common activity in the UK and it seems to be increasing in popularity. Oswald and Young (2002) looked at UK buy-backs by UK listed businesses over the period 1995 to 2000. They found that buy-back activity in 2000 was seven times what it had been in 1995. It is estimated that in the USA, businesses spend out more on share repurchase than on dividends (Grullon and Michaely 2002). On the face of it, share repurchase is an example of businesses following the MM principles and returning funds which they are unable to invest profitably on the shareholders behalf, to those shareholders.

Some businesses seem to relate their share repurchase to the MM ideas. For example, **Marks and Spencer plc**, in its 2004 annual report said: 'The Company engages in share buybacks to create value for shareholders, when cash flow permits and there is not an immediate alternative investment use for the funds.' MM could almost have written this themselves! **Dixons Group plc**, the electrical appliance and IT retailer (Dixons, Currys, PC World), said in its 2004 annual report: 'Following the disposal of Wanadoo shares and Codic International, the Group has reviewed its capacity to return surplus cash to shareholders, whilst maintaining a robust balance sheet and protecting the Group's lenders and bondholders. The Board has concluded that this can be most effectively achieved by the repurchase of £200 million of shares. This decision has been taken after considering the Group's annual lease payment commitments, its credit rating and future opportunities available to the Group which require it to retain financial flexibility.' Again, the MM principles are being followed.

Some businesses seem to relate share repurchase more to capital gearing and enhancing earnings per share (EPS), than to following the MM ideas. Of course, buying back shares reduces the level of equity and, presuming no equivalent debt repayment, increases capital gearing. If a business can buy back some shares, without it affecting after-tax profit proportionately, EPS will inevitably increase. In its 2003 annual report, **Arriva plc**, the transport business (mainly buses and trains) said of a share repurchase that had already taken place: 'The purchase exercise was undertaken to further optimise the Group's capital structure'. **Boots Group plc**, the chemist, said in its 2004 annual report: 'We have reviewed our financial strategy during the year and intend to increase our debt levels over the next couple of years by returning surplus capital to shareholders through our on-going share buyback programme. This will improve the efficiency of our balance sheet and enhance Earnings per Share.' Boots's reference to 'surplus capital' implies that the business cannot find a profitable use for the cash.

Next plc, the high street retailer, said in its 2004 annual report: 'The long term growth in earnings per share continues to be one of our key objectives, and we will continue to buy back our shares when it is in the interests of our shareholders.'

Agency

Agency problems (and costs) tend to arise where shareholders and directors have different objectives. Schooley and Barney (1994) provide some evidence that where senior managers are also shareholders, the agency problem, in the context of dividends, tends to be reduced. See also the Allen, Bernado and Welch (2000) study mentioned under 'Clientele effect' (above).

Reinvestment of dividends

MM made the point that shareholders could negate the effect of dividends by reinvesting them in the business concerned. Some UK businesses make this relatively easy for their shareholders to do. For, example, both **Royal and Sun Alliance Group plc**, the insurance business, and **Kingfisher plc**, the retail business, give their shareholders the choice of a dividend in cash or in additional shares.

A number of businesses will use dividend cash to buy their own shares, in the Stock Exchange, on behalf of shareholders who wish to have this done for them, at low cost to the shareholder. These include, for example: **British Petroleum plc**, **Dixons Group plc**, **Rio Tinto plc**, **GKN plc**, **Manchester United plc** and **Scottish and Newcastle plc**.

Pecking order theory

The evidence on the pecking order theory was reviewed in Chapter 11. There we saw that there is not strong evidence that this theory applies in practice.

12.7 Conclusions on dividends

As with capital gearing, we do not know whether the traditionalists or MM are correct in their assertions. We do, however, have a certain amount of empirical evidence on the subject and so we might be able to reconcile the two views.

MM's assertion that patterns of dividends are irrelevant has some credibility. The assumptions are not entirely convincing but they do not seem sufficiently unreasonable to invalidate the irrelevancy assertion completely. Importantly, the evidence seems to support the MM view, in that valuation seems not to be closely related to levels of dividends.

From the evidence there does seem to be a clientele effect in that the dividend policy associated with particular shares appears to attract an identifiable group of investors. Recognition of the clientele effect by directors could well explain their reluctance to alter dividend payment levels.

Perhaps we can conclude that MM were broadly correct in saying that dividends do not affect values provided that investors know the dividend policy of the business. Probably the most effective way of informing investors of this policy is to establish a fairly constant pattern and to stick to it. Failure to show consistency is likely to lead to uncertainty for investors and to the necessity for shareholders to leave one habitat in favour of another, more preferred, one. In either case, the effect of changes in dividend policy seems likely to lead to lower share prices and higher costs of capital. This implies that liquidity may not be a particularly important factor in the dividend decision, and that businesses will make sure that sufficient cash is available for the dividend, one way or another.

Summary

Traditional view

- Dividend decision – a vital one for shareholder wealth effect.
- Shareholders value a dividend more highly than the equivalent amount retained in the business.

Modigliani and Miller (MM) view

- Dividends should be paid only where the business cannot use the available funds at least as effectively as shareholders can on their own account, that is, invest in all projects with a positive NPV when discounted at the shareholders' opportunity cost of capital.
- Only funds remaining after investing should be paid as dividend – dividend is residual.
- Share price is the PV of future dividends – shareholders will be indifferent as to how the PV is made up (size of each year's dividend). If paying less this year leads to more in later years such that PV (and share price) is increased, shareholders' wealth will be enhanced.
- Individual shareholders can adjust the business's dividend payments to meet their own needs.
  - If no (or low) dividend and they need funds, they can sell some shares to generate a cash inflow from the shares (homemade dividends).
  - If they prefer not to receive a dividend from the business, they can buy more shares with the cash and, thereby, leave the investment intact.

Practical issues

- Dividend levels might signal information – high dividends could imply confidence in the future of the business. Possibly an illogical argument – why not make a statement instead?
- Clientele effect – investors are attracted to particular shares because of dividend policy, perhaps because of their personal tax positions or need for regular cash inflows.
- The relative costs of raising funds (issue costs) – same as for gearing decision:
  - Equity from retained profit – virtually nothing.
  - Equity from rights or public issue – very expensive.
  - Debt finance – relatively cheap.
  - Tends to favour low dividends where business needs funds for investment.
- Agency problem – the best interests of shareholders may favour a large dividend (no positive NPV investment opportunities), but the directors may prefer to retain the funds and invest despite this.
- Share repurchase increasingly a popular alternative to dividend payments, but with much the same effect.

Further reading

Most business finance texts deal with the question of dividends and dividend policy. Both Arnold (2002) and Brealey and Myers (2002) contain interesting sections on it.

Emery and Finnerty (2004) discuss this topic in a practical and interesting way.

Relevant websites

The websites of businesses featured in this chapter are:

Arriva plc	www.arriva.co.uk
British Petroleum plc	www.bp.com
Dixons Group plc	www.dixons-group-plc.co.uk
GKN plc	www.gknplc.com
The Go-Ahead Group plc	www.go-ahead.com
Imperial Chemical Industries plc	www.ici.com
Interbrew NV	www.interbrew.com
Kingfisher plc	www.kingfisher.co.uk
Manchester United plc	www.manutd.com
Marks and Spencer plc	www.marksandspencer.com
Monsoon plc	www.monsoon.co.uk
Next plc	www.next.co.uk
Rio Tinto plc	www.riotinto.com
Royal and Sun Alliance Group plc	www.royalsunalliance.com
Ryanair Holdings plc	www.ryanair.com
Scottish and Newcastle plc	www.scottish-newcastle.com

REVIEW QUESTIONS

Suggested answers to review questions appear in Appendix 3.

12.1 According to MM, what is the difference between the value of a dividend received now and one received in the future, if the shareholders are indifferent as to whether they receive the dividend now or in the future?

12.2 According to MM, what rule should a business follow in paying dividends to its shareholders?

12.3 What are 'homemade dividends' in the context of MM? Why might a shareholder want such a dividend?

12.4 What, in outline, is the traditional view on the payment of dividends?

12.5 Why is the MM position on dividends partly dependent on their assumption of no taxes?

12.6 Why should we find that businesses attract a 'clientele' of shareholders as a result of their dividend policy?

PROBLEMS

Sample answers to problems marked with an asterisk appear in Appendix 4.

(Problems 12.1 to 12.5 are basic-level problems, whereas problems 12.6 to 12.9 are more advanced and may contain some practical complications.)

12.1* The shareholders of Distributors plc have an opportunity cost of capital of 20 per cent. The business makes a steady profit of £25m each year, which is all paid out as a dividend. The opportunity has arisen to invest the dividend that is about to be paid (£25m). This investment will give rise to a single payoff in three years' time. The normal £25m dividend will be paid next year and subsequently, in the normal way.

What dividend needs to be paid in three years' time so that the shareholders will be equally content to wait the three years, adopting the Modigliani and Miller assumptions on dividends?

12.2 'According to Modigliani and Miller, shareholders are indifferent between a dividend and a capital gain.'

Comment on this statement, which you have overheard.

12.3* HLM plc, an all-equity financed business, has just paid a dividend totalling £1.5m. This amount has been paid on a regular basis for many years, and the market expects this to continue. The business has 10m ordinary shares currently quoted at £1 each. The directors have identified the opportunity to invest £1m in one year's time, and a similar amount in two years' time, in a project that will generate an annual cash flow of £0.4m for ever, starting in three years' time.

The only possible way of financing this investment is by paying a reduced dividend for the next two years.

If the directors were to announce their intention to make this investment and to publish full details of it and the financing method, what would happen to the share price? Ignore taxation.

12.4 Durodorso plc is a Stock Exchange listed business that has built up a cash mountain equal in size to about 25 per cent of its market capitalisation as a result of the continuation of restricted dividend policy and a consistent failure to identify investment opportunities. Since the directors continue to see no investment opportunities, a decision has been made to use the cash to pay a 'special' dividend.

When the directors met to discuss the special dividend, the finance director told the other directors, 'We've always been modest dividend payers in the past so our shareholders would probably welcome a large dividend.'

What would you advise the directors to do regarding the special dividend?

12.5 'It is widely accepted that dividend valuation models are an acceptable way of valuing businesses. Modigliani and Miller said that dividends are irrelevant to valuation and so flew in the face of conventional wisdom.'

Is this statement correct? Explain.

12.6* Images plc is an all-equity financed, Stock Exchange listed business. It has been a steady profit and cash flow generator over recent years, and it has distributed all of its after-tax profit as dividends.

More recently, the business has been actively seeking new investment opportunities. In the financial year that has just ended, it reported profits of £5m, a figure similar to that of recent years.

Four potential investment projects have been identified, all of which could commence immediately. The estimated cash flows and timings of these projects are as follows:

Year	Project I £m	Project II £m	Project III £m	Project IV £m
0	(2.0)	(2.0)	(3.0)	(1.0)
1	0.75	0.65	0.80	0.50
2	0.75	0.65	0.80	0.50
3	0.75	0.65	0.80	0.50
4		0.65	0.80	
5		0.65	0.80	

Each of these projects falls within the same risk class as the business's existing projects.

It has been estimated that the cost of equity is 15 per cent p.a.

The directors would be very reluctant to raise outside funds to help finance any of the above projects.

What advice would you give the directors as to the level of dividend that should be paid this year?

12.7 The directors of Bellini plc, a Stock Exchange listed business, are contemplating purchasing some of its own shares in the market, and cancelling them, as an alternative to paying a dividend. Some of the directors believe that certain shareholders would prefer this.

What considerations should the directors particularly take into account when making this decision?

12.8 Breadwinner plc, a £500m market value, all-equity financed listed business, has been in the habit of making just one dividend payment each year. The business has just paid a dividend of 21p a share. This dividend represents an increase of 5 per cent on the dividend paid just over a year ago, and the share's current market price is thought to be based on the expectation that this growth rate will continue indefinitely. The business's cost of equity is 10 per cent p.a.

The directors have identified a major investment project which requires significant outlays of cash over the forthcoming two years. It is the business's policy to finance all investments from retained profits, which means that, to make the investment, there could be no dividend payment for the next two years. The next dividend would be in three years' time at an estimated 40p per share, but this would be expected to grow at an annual rate of 6 per cent indefinitely from that time. It is estimated that the riskier nature of the investment project would increase the overall cost of equity to 12 per cent.

The directors are about to announce their intention to go ahead with the investment.

Miss Jenkins owns some of the shares, the dividends from which she relies on to supplement her state retirement pension. This holding represents her only wealth apart from the freehold of the bungalow in which she lives.

(a) Show and explain calculations that indicate the theoretical expected alteration in the company's current share price when the announcement of the investment and dividend plans is made.

(b) Explain why the theoretical alteration in the business's share price may not occur in practice.

(c) Advise Miss Jenkins on what she should do in response to the announcement, presuming that she wishes to remain a shareholder in Breadwinner plc. This advice should include the theoretical and practical effects, on Miss Jenkins's wealth and income, of any actions that she might take.

(d) Advise Miss Jenkins more broadly on her investment strategy. This advice should clearly explain the issues involved and any costs that may result from taking your advice.

12.9 Butterworth plc is a UK listed business. For many years it has paid an annual dividend, on its ordinary shares, that was 8 per cent higher than that of the previous year. The market expects that this pattern will continue. The dividend paid just under a year ago was £0.43 per share. The current cum-dividend share price is £6.78.

An opportunity has arisen for the business to undertake a project that will require an immediate outflow of cash equal to the amount of the planned dividend. The cash that was to be used for the dividend is the only source of cash for the project. The project will have just one cash payoff, which will occur in three years' time. The directors intend that, if the project is undertaken, the cash payoff will all be paid to shareholders by increasing the dividend expected in three years' time.

If the project is undertaken, the amount of the payoff, and the directors' intention to use it all to augment the normal dividend due in three years' time, will be publicly announced.

(a) What amount will the dividend per share, in three years' time, need to be such that shareholders will be indifferent between receiving this year's dividend and the cash being used for the project? Assume that the Gordon dividend growth model and the assertion of Modigliani and Miller on dividends are both valid. (Ignore taxation in this calculation.)

(b) Explain the Gordon dividend growth model and the assertion of Modigliani and Miller on dividends.

(c) Explain why, in practice, the shareholders may not be indifferent to the company missing this year's dividend and undertaking the project, even if the increased dividend expected in three years' time equals the amount calculated in (a).

There are both a set of **multiple-choice questions** and **missing-word questions** available on the website. These specifically cover the material contained in this chapter. These can be attempted and graded (with feedback) online.

There is also an **additional problem**, with solution, that relates to the material covered in this chapter.

Go to **www.pearsoned.co.uk/atrillmclaney** and follow the links.

APPENDIX — Proof of the MM dividend irrelevancy proposition

In the proof of their assertion, MM considered business j during a period that starts at time t and ends at time $t + 1$. They used the following symbols:

D_{jt} = total dividend paid during the period starting at time t

d_{jt} = dividend per share paid during that period

P_{jt} = price per share at time t

r_t = return per share during the period starting at time t

n_t = number of shares of the business at time t

m_t = number of new shares issued during the period starting at time t

V_{jt} = value of the business at time t (that is, $V_{jt} = n_t \times P_{jt}$).

Now:

$$r_t = \frac{d_{jt} + P_{j(t+1)} - P_{jt}}{P_{jt}} \tag{A12.1}$$

that is, the return per share during the period is the dividend paid during it *plus* the increase in price per share ($P_{j(t+1)} - P_{jt}$) expressed as a fraction of the price at the start of the period. Rearranging (A12.1) gives:

$$P_{jt} = \frac{d_{jt} + P_{j(t+1)}}{1 + r_t} \tag{A12.2}$$

that is, the price per share is the discounted value of the dividend for the period plus the price per share at the end of the period.

Market forces will tend to ensure that equations (A12.1) and (A12.2) hold to the extent that the current price P_{jt} will be such as to cause r_t to be similar to that of other shares of similar risk to those of business j.

Further:

$$n_{(t+1)} - n_t = m_{(t+1)} \tag{A12.3}$$

that is, the difference between the number of shares at the start and end of the period is accounted for by those issued (or withdrawn) during the period:

$$V_{jt} = \frac{D_{jt} + n_t P_{j(t+1)}}{1 + r_t} \tag{A12.4}$$

From equation (A12.2), the value of the whole business is the discounted value of the total dividend payable during the period plus the value of the business at the end of the period.

Expressed another way:

$$V_{jt} = \frac{D_{jt} + V_{(t+1)} - m_t P_{(t+1)}}{1 + r_t} \tag{A12.5}$$

that is, the value of the business at the start of the period is the discounted value of the dividend for the period plus its value at the end less the value of any share capital raised during the period. This is because:

$$V_{(t+1)} = n_t P_{(t+1)} + m_t P_{(t+1)} \tag{A12.6}$$

From equation (A12.5) we can see that the value of the business at time t is dependent upon anticipated dividends, the value at the end and the value of any new shares issued. However, the quantity of new shares that it is necessary to issue is, in turn, dependent on the size of dividends paid:

$$m_t P_{(t+1)} = I_t - (X_t - D_t) \tag{A12.7}$$

where I_t is the real investment and X_t the operating cash flow surplus during the period. That is to say, the value of the finance that must be raised from new share issues is the excess of the funds invested over the operating cash flow surplus after dividends have been paid. In other words, the value of the new issues depends on the extent to which new investment exceeds retained profit.

Substituting equation (A12.7) into equation (A12.5) for $m_t P_{(t+1)}$ gives:

$$V_t = \frac{D_t + V_{(t+1)} - I_t + X_t - D_t}{1 + r_t}$$

The D_t terms cancel each other out to give:

$$V_t = \frac{V_{(t+1)} - I_t + X_t}{1 + r_t}$$

Thus V_t is independent of the amount of dividend paid during the forthcoming period, but depends on the anticipated value of the business at the end of the period, the anticipated level of investment and cash flow surplus.

Dividends can be at any level. Any cash deficiency caused by dividends being paid in excess of operating cash flows can be made up through capital issues of new equity.

The assumptions made and their validity are discussed in the chapter.

PART 4

Integrated decisions

There are some areas of business finance that do not fall distinctly into the categories of either investment or financing, but involve some combination of both. These are discussed in this part of the book.

Working capital, the subject of Chapter 13, consists of the business's short-term assets and liabilities. Since these are in a constant state of change, as the business carries out its normal activities, decisions on investment and finance are frequent and, for the most part, routine.

Progressive businesses in an open economy should be constantly seeking ways of reorganising themselves, so as best to be able to relate to their environment and to achieve their objectives. Such reorganisations are the subject of Chapter 14. These typically involve altering some fairly fundamental aspect of their investment or financing strategy.

Most businesses have some international aspect. Even those that do not themselves trade internationally can be significantly affected by aspects of international business finance. Chapter 15 considers the benefits and problems of international business from a financial point of view.

Small businesses are consistently seen as a major part of the future. Chapter 16 considers to what extent, if at all, small businesses should be treated differently from large ones, when making financial decisions.

Chapter 13

Management of working capital

Objectives
In this chapter we shall deal with the following:

→ the nature of working capital and the working capital cycle

→ its importance as a source and use of short-term finance

→ liquidity and working capital

→ the management of the individual elements of working capital: stocks, trade debtors, cash (and bank overdrafts), and trade creditors

→ the necessity for establishing policies on each element of working capital in order to provide a framework for its practical management

13.1 Introduction

The need for working capital

When businesses make investment decisions they must not only consider the financial outlay involved in acquiring the new machine or the new building, or whatever, but also take account of the additional current assets that any expansion of activity will usually entail. Increased production tends to engender a need to hold additional stocks of raw materials and work in progress. Increased sales revenue usually means that the level of debtors will increase. A general increase in the scale of operations tends to imply a need for greater levels of cash. As with any investment, working capital exposes the business to risk.

Financing working capital

The current assets (stock in trade, debtors and cash) tend not to be financed entirely from long-term sources of finance. Most businesses also have access to two major short-term sources. The first of these is trade credit, arising from the fact that purchases of goods and services are usually on credit; in other words, the buyer does not have to pay immediately on delivery but may be allowed to delay payment for a period, say 30 days. The second is a source with which many of us are all too familiar in our private lives, the bank overdraft.

Since the relationship between these short-term sources of finance (or current liabilities) and the current assets tends to be very close, it seems logical to deal with both of them in the same chapter, though there would also have been logic in dealing with short-term sources of finance, alongside long-term ones, in Chapter 8.

Particular features of the management of working capital

In the same way that it can be seen as illogical to discuss short-term finance separately from long-term finance, it can also be argued that it is wrong to separate discussion of current assets from discussion of the investment decision generally. The reason for taking the present approach is simply that there are features of the management of current assets and of current liabilities that particularly commend dealing with them together, yet separate from the longer-term investment and financing decisions. These features include the systematic nature of the management of the working capital elements and the frequency with which decisions have to be taken in respect of most of them.

Perhaps another reason for discussing current assets and current liabilities together is that care needs to be taken by financial managers to maintain a reasonable balance between them, so it is important not to lose sight of their interrelationship. In fact, so closely related are these two that they are frequently netted against one another and considered as a single factor, namely working capital (current assets *less* current liabilities).

The objective of working capital management is the same as that for non-current asset and long-term financing decisions. This is typically the maximisation, or at least the enhancement, of the shareholders' wealth. This will be achieved by optimising positive cash flows through striking an appropriate balance between costs and revenues, on the one hand, and risk, on the other.

13.2 The dynamics of working capital

The working capital cycle

The upper portion of Figure 13.1 depicts, in a highly simplified form, the chain of events in a manufacturing business as regards working capital. The chain starts with buying raw material stock on credit. In due course this stock will be used in production, work will be carried out on the stock, and it will become work in progress (WIP). Work will continue on the WIP until it eventually emerges as the finished product. As production progresses, labour costs and overheads will need to be met. Of course, at some stage trade creditors will need to be paid. When the finished goods are sold on credit, debtors are increased. They will eventually pay, so that cash will be injected into the business.

Each of the areas – stocks (raw materials, WIP and finished goods), trade debtors, cash (positive or negative) and trade creditors – can be viewed as tanks into and from which funds flow. Most of this chapter will be devoted to questions of why any of these 'tanks' need exist at all and, if they are necessary, what attitude managers should

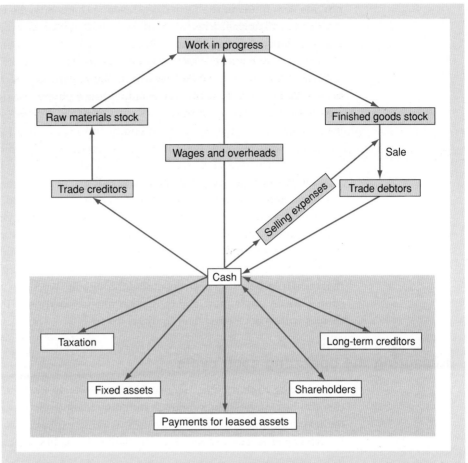

**Figure 13.1
The working
capital cycle for
a manufacturing
business**

Each of the boxes in the upper part of the diagram can be seen as a tank through which funds flow. These tanks, which are concerned with day-to-day activities, have funds constantly flowing into and out of them.

take on the amounts to be held in each tank at any given time. Here managers need to attempt to balance the costs involved with maintaining funds in the tanks, with the risks involved with having the tanks too full or too empty.

Note that the upper portion of Figure 13.1 would, with minor amendment, apply equally well to non-manufacturing businesses. For example, a retailer would not have raw materials stock or WIP. A service business would have neither raw materials nor finished goods stock, but may well have WIP. The figure takes a manufacturer as the example simply because manufacturers tend to have all elements of working capital.

The link between working capital and long-term investment and financing

Working capital is clearly not the only aspect of the business that impacts on cash. The business will have to make payments to government, both central and local, for taxation. Non-current (fixed) assets will be purchased and sold. Lessors of non-current assets will be paid their rent (lease payment). Shareholders (existing or new) may provide new funds in the form of cash, some shares may be redeemed for cash, and dividends will normally be paid. Similarly, long-term loan creditors (existing or new) may provide loan finance, loans will need to be repaid from time to time, and interest obligations will have to be met. Unlike movements in the working capital items, most of these 'non-working capital' cash transactions are not everyday events. Some of them may be annual events (for example, lease payments, dividends, interest and, possibly, non-current asset purchases and disposals). Others (such as new equity and loan finance and redemption of old equity and loan finance) would typically be less common events. A factor that most of these non-working capital transactions have in common is their size: they are likely individually to involve large amounts of cash. These non-working capital transactions are shown in the lower portion of Figure 13.1.

It is obvious that the management of working capital, and particularly of cash, is closely linked to financing decisions and to decisions involving investment in non-current assets. This linkage involves quantities of cash, the timing of cash flows and the level of risk involved. For example, if a particular long-term debt is to be redeemed under a contractual obligation, thought must be given to the question of the source of that cash. If cash has not been generated through the working capital cycle, some other source (for example, new equity or loan finance) will need to be considered. These themes will be developed later in this chapter.

Measuring the operating cash cycle

The working capital cycle, represented descriptively in the top part of Figure 13.1, can also be expressed in a more quantitative manner, as shown in Figure 13.2. Here the length of time that each element of working capital takes in the cycle is shown. Figure 13.2 also refers to a manufacturing business, but can easily be amended to fit non-manufacturers.

In Figure 13.2, raw materials (RM) stock is held for a period of time before it is taken into production: the stock now becomes part of the WIP, along with other costs (labour, overheads and so on) until such time as it is completed and forms part of finished goods (FG) stock. Finished stock is held until it is sold to become a trade debtor, which in due course is paid by the customer and the cycle is completed. The sum of the time taken from the payment for purchase of the raw material stock to the

Figure 13.2
The operating cash cycles for a manufacturing business

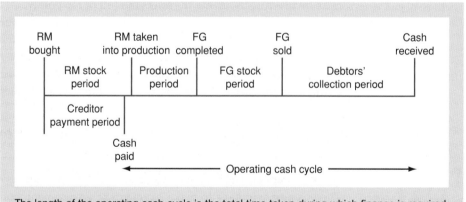

The length of the operating cash cycle is the total time taken during which finance is required from the business for normal trading operations.

receipt of cash from the customer is known as the operating cash cycle. This cycle must be financed by the business. Broadly, the shorter the operating cash cycle, the less finance is required. One of the objectives of working capital management is to keep this cycle to a minimum length. By doing so, the shareholders' wealth will tend to be enhanced, all other things being equal.

Example 13.1

The following information relates to Jittery plc for last year:

	£m
Purchases of raw materials	67
Usage of raw materials	65
Revenue from sales of finished goods (all on credit)	250
Cost of sales of finished goods	180
Average creditors	14
Average raw materials stock	12
Average work in progress	10
Average finished goods stock	21
Average debtors	47

What is the length of the operating cash cycle?

Solution

			Days
RM stock period	$\dfrac{\text{RM stock}}{\text{RM usage}} \times 365$	$= \dfrac{12}{65} \times 365 =$	67
Production period	$\dfrac{\text{WIP}}{\text{Cost of sales}} \times 365$	$= \dfrac{10}{180} \times 365 =$	20
FG stock period	$\dfrac{\text{FG stock}}{\text{Cost of sales}} \times 365$	$= \dfrac{21}{180} \times 365 =$	43
Debtors' collection period	$\dfrac{\text{Debtors}}{\text{Sales revenue}} \times 365$	$= \dfrac{47}{250} \times 365 =$	69
			199
Creditors' payment period	$\dfrac{\text{Creditors}}{\text{RM purchases}} \times 365$	$= \dfrac{14}{67} \times 365 =$	(76)
Operating cash cycle (days)			= 123

Notes to the solution

It should be noted that days in the above solution are not of equal importance in economic terms. For example, reducing the debtors' collection period by one day will save funding of £685 000 (£250m/365). Increasing the creditors' payment period by one day will save funding to the extent of only £184 000 (£67m/365). So, despite the fact that these two actions would leave the length of the operating cash cycle unchanged, they would have the effect of reducing the working capital investment by a net amount of £501 000 (£685 000 – £184 000).

13.3 The importance of the management of working capital

The scale of working capital

It is tempting to believe that with working capital we are dealing with relatively trivial amounts. Such a view is very wide of the mark for the typical UK business; the amounts involved tend to be vast.

Table 13.1 gives some idea of the scale of working capital. The investment in stocks, debtors and cash is typically a large figure looked at alongside the total investment, at book values, in non-current assets. This is, of course, offset to some extent by 'free' finance supplied by trade creditors and others.

Table 13.1 A summary of the balance sheets of five UK businesses

	Black Leisure Group plc	Scottish and Newcastle plc	Balfour Beatty plc	Tesco plc	Tate and Lyle plc
Balance sheet date	29.2.04	31.12.03	31.12.03	26.2.04	31.3.04
	%	%	%	%	%
Non-current assets	76	101	113	119	82
Current assets					
Stock	47	5	20	9	15
Trade debtors	10	14	76	0	12
Other debtors	6	7	69	7	7
Cash and near cash	11	2	36	8	9
	74	28	201	24	43
Current liabilities					
Trade creditors	(22)	(8)	(76)	(19)	(10)
Tax and dividends	(14)	(6)	(25)	(5)	(6)
Other short-term liabilities	(10)	(10)	(112)	(13)	(7)
Overdrafts and short-term loans	(4)	(5)	(1)	(6)	(2)
	(50)	(29)	(214)	(43)	(25)
Working capital	24	(1)	(13)	(19)	18
Total long-term investment	100	100	100	100	100

Notes: The non-current assets, current assets and current liabilities are expressed as a percentage of the total net investment (equity plus long-term loans) of the business concerned. The businesses were randomly selected, except that they were deliberately taken from different industries. Blacks acts principally as a retailer, through Blacks and Millets outlets. Scottish and Newcastle is a brewer, pub and hotel operator. Balfour Beatty is one of the UK's building and civil engineering businesses. Tesco is a food supermarket. Tate and Lyle makes sweeteners, starch products and animal foods.

The other striking feature of Table 13.1 is the variation from one type of business to the next. Consider stock in trade for example. **Blacks Leisure Group plc** is a retailer of goods that are, in the main, non-perishable. To be able to offer its customers choice, the business has to hold fairly high levels of stock in trade. **Balfour Beatty plc** tends to hold fairly large stocks because it has a lot of work in progress. Compared with its overall operations, **Scottish and Newcastle plc** stocks are small. **Tesco plc**'s and **Tate and Lyle**'s stocks tend to be perishable and therefore need to be relatively fast moving. This level of variation in the amounts and types of working capital elements is typical of the business world.

The relative vastness of the typical business's investment in working capital has led to the management of working capital increasingly being treated as fundamental to the welfare of the business and to its ability to survive and prosper.

The nature of decisions on working capital

We have just seen that the difference between working capital decisions and those involving non-current assets and long-term finance does not apparently lie in the amount of finance involved. To the extent that there is a difference, it lies in the tendency for working capital decisions to be short term, reversible at relatively short notice and more frequently made.

While they may be made more frequently, many working capital decisions are straightforward since they tend to be repetitive. There will (or should be) a policy that creates a set of rules to be followed. For example, each time a customer seeks to buy goods on credit, a decision will be needed as to whether to grant credit at all and, if so, how much. Most businesses will have decided on some formula that can be applied to help them to reach a decision. The existence of such formulae has the advantage that many decisions can be made by employees quite low in the management hierarchy, and therefore they can be made fairly quickly and cheaply.

In establishing these formulae or sets of rules for the day-to-day management of working capital, great care should be taken to assess which approach will most advance the business's objectives. Once a set of rules has been established it should be regarded as the framework within which all operating decisions must be made.

It is unlikely that rules established at one time will continue to represent the most beneficial approach over long periods of time. Circumstances, including the business's competitive position, interest rates and the economic environment generally, alter over time. Policies must therefore be reviewed periodically and, if necessary, revised.

The use of budgets

Control of working capital through the use of detailed plans in the form of budgets can be very beneficial. The ability to assess in advance the calls that will be made on the various elements of working capital enables managers to ensure that the 'tanks' are always adequately full.

Few businesses have steady and regular working capital requirements from week to week throughout the year. This is due, among other things, to seasonal factors. Prior knowledge of what the demands are likely to be at various times is of enormous value.

General attitude to working capital

Broadly, businesses should seek to minimise the level of each type of current asset that they hold and to maximise the benefits of cheap short-term finance. This is, of course, subject to the risks and costs involved with doing so to the extreme. For example, granting credit to customers is expensive (in lost interest on the funds, if nothing else), so, ideally, credit should not be given. However, failing to give credit is very likely to mean that the business will be unable to make sales (perhaps because competitors do offer credit). Clearly, the credit policy must seek to strike a balance between the costs and risks of taking one extreme view and those of taking the other extreme view.

Since working capital elements tend to be of high financial value, getting the balance between the extremes wrong tends to be an expensive matter. Indeed, as we shall shortly see, it can even be a fatal one.

13.4 Working capital and liquidity

The need for liquidity

Not only do businesses need to strike a reasonable balance between the extremes in respect of individual working capital elements, a balance should also be sought between exploiting 'cheap' sources of short-term finance (current liabilities) to the fullest possible extent, and the risks and possible costs involved with being heavily reliant on suppliers of finance who can demand repayment at short notice. That is to say, businesses need to maintain sufficient current assets to enable them to meet short-term claims as they become due. They need to be able to do this since failure to meet them would entitle the short-term claimants (the current liabilities) to take steps to put the business into liquidation. This would normally involve the forced sale of some or all of the business's assets, including its non-current assets.

If bankruptcy costs were not significant and if the market for real assets were efficient, from a shareholder wealth-maximisation perspective, the liquidation threat would be unimportant. This is because shareholders could expect, on the liquidation of the business, to receive an amount equal to the capital market price of the shares immediately before the liquidation. In other words, liquidation would not affect a shareholder's wealth. In reality, of course, since bankruptcy costs are likely to be significant and markets for real assets do not seem to be efficient, liquidation would usually be expected to have a severely adverse effect on shareholders' wealth.

Means of remaining liquid

One way to avoid the risk of liquidation is to maintain a large amount of cash on short-term interest-bearing deposit. In this way, should a need for cash to meet current liabilities suddenly arise, cash could be made available quickly to meet the demand. Obviously there would be no point in taking such an approach unless the funds used to establish the short-term deposit were provided from long-term sources. Otherwise the policy would have the effect of solving the original problem by creating another group of short-term claimants who could create the same difficulty.

The approach of using long-term finance to create a short-term fund would offer the perfect solution to the liquidity problem but for the nature of the capital market. This tends to mean, among other things, that businesses usually cannot lend at as high a rate of interest as they have to pay to borrow. Also, long-term interest rates are usually higher than short-term ones. So, for the average business, borrowing long term and lending short term, in an attempt to maintain good liquidity and avoid the risk of liquidation, is likely to be an expensive solution to the problem.

In practice, businesses seem to try to strike a balance between the levels of their current assets and current liabilities, that is, a balance between exploiting cheap sources of short-term finance and the risk inherent in doing so.

It is probably fair to say that, irrespective of the root problem (for example, lack of profitability), most business failures result immediately from a deficiency in working capital.

Financing working capital

The amount of funds tied up in working capital would not typically be a constant figure throughout the year. Only in the most unusual of businesses would there be a constant need for working capital funding. For most businesses there would be weekly fluctuations. Many operate in industries that are, to a significant extent, seasonal in demand pattern. This means that sales revenue, stocks, debtors, and so on, would be at higher levels at some predictable times of the year than at others.

In principle, the working capital need can be separated into two parts: a fixed part and a fluctuating part. The fixed part is probably defined in amount as the minimum working capital requirement for the year.

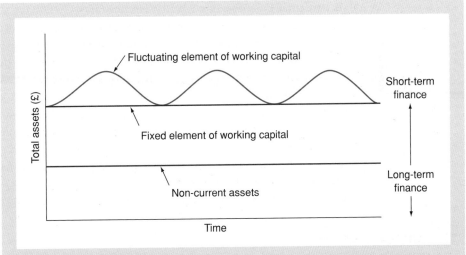

**Figure 13.3
Financing
the business**

The more permanent elements (non-current (fixed) assets and fixed working capital) should generally be financed by long-term sources. The fluctuating element of working capital should be financed from short-term funds.

It is widely advocated that the business should be funded in the way depicted in Figure 13.3. The more permanent needs (non-current assets and the fixed element of working capital) should be financed from fairly permanent sources (such as equity and loan stocks); the fluctuating element should be financed from a short-term source (such as a bank overdraft), which can be drawn on and repaid easily and at short notice.

Figure 13.3 assumes no basic alterations in the levels of any of the assets, except the fluctuating working capital. In practice, any expansion, contraction or structural alteration of its operations would also tend to alter the pattern of finance required by the business.

The use of accounting ratios in the management of working capital

Accounting ratios are widely used in the management of working capital. The following are some of the ratios used. You may care to look back at Chapter 3 for more details of these ratios:

- the current ratio (current assets/current liabilities);
- quick assets (acid test) ratio (liquid assets/current liabilities); and
- no credit period (liquid assets/average daily cash running costs).

Probably, managers can best use these ratios for monitoring the actual liquidity position and comparing it constantly with some standard or target figure, taking steps to correct any significant deviations. The standard might be one that emerges from within the business, or an industry average, or perhaps some combination of the two. One way or another, businesses should actively seek to maintain liquidity and the confidence of short-term creditors that they will be paid.

13.5 Overtrading

The problem

A particular business, in particular circumstances, will have particular working capital requirements, though precisely what these are is a matter of managerial judgement. For example, the management of a retailer, with a particular level of demand for its merchandise, will decide on a level of stock requirement. If demand were to alter, a different level of stockholding would normally be required. A doubling of the level of demand would not necessarily imply a need to double stock levels, but it would normally imply a need for a significant increase in the amount of stock available to customers. The same point is broadly true for all businesses in respect of all working capital aspects. It is obviously necessary not only that management decides on the level of working capital that will be required, but also that it ensures that it can finance that amount of working capital. Not to be able to provide the level of working capital required to sustain a particular level of trading is known as overtrading.

Expansion and overtrading

Problems arise in practice for businesses that experience an expansion of trading activity due to an upturn in demand, particularly when the increase in demand is rapid and unexpected. The temptation to exploit profitable new trading opportunities is frequently overwhelming. Yet increased activity without increased working capital to sustain it can lead to serious overtrading problems, possibly culminating in the business's complete financial failure. At first sight the problem seems capable of solving itself, since the increased profits from the additional activity will provide the finance necessary to expand the working capital. This view is usually misleading, however, since the working capital requirement (additional stocks, additional cash for labour and other costs) generally precedes any additional cash flows from the increased activity. This arises from the fact that the typical business, irrespective of its type of activity, has to pay cash to meet most of the costs of making a particular sale, before cash is forthcoming from the customer. The extent of this problem varies from one type of business to another. Clearly, it is a greater problem for a manufacturer, selling on credit (relatively large stock and debtor levels), than it is for a business providing services for immediate cash settlement, for example a hairdressing business. In fact, for a hairdressing business, rapid expansion of trading may pose no overtrading problems at all. Put another way, manufacturers tend to have long cash cycles whereas hairdressers do not.

13.6 Stock in trade (inventories)

As we saw in Figure 13.1, manufacturing businesses typically hold stocks at various stages of completion, from raw materials to finished goods. Trading businesses (wholesalers, retailers and so forth) hold stock in only one condition. Broadly speaking, the level of investment in stocks by manufacturers tends to be relatively large compared with that of traders.

Even with traders, there may be vast differences. A jeweller would normally hold much more stock (in value terms) than would a greengrocer with the same level of annual turnover. The perishable nature of the greengrocer's stock would partly account for this, as would the high value of the individual items in the stock of the jeweller. Another factor might be that when we buy jewellery we usually demand a choice, which is less likely to be the case when we buy potatoes.

With many businesses the requirement for stocks varies with the time of year. Firework manufacturers in the UK, who experience high sales volume in the period leading up to 5 November, may well find it necessary to hold very large stocks during each summer as they *stockpile* for the forthcoming period of high demand.

Irrespective of the nature of the trade, all businesses should seek to balance the costs and risks of holding stock with those of holding no or low levels of stock. While the costs of holding stocks tend to be fairly certain, if difficult to quantify, those of failing to hold stocks may or may not occur: in other words, there is a risk. Thus such costs are in the nature of *expected values*, where costs are combined with their probability of occurrence.

The costs and risks of holding stocks

Some of the costs and risks of holding stock are described below.

Lost interest
Interest could be earned on the finance tied up in the stocks. This cost is partly mitigated by a certain amount of free credit granted by suppliers of the stock, which would only be available if stock is bought. The existence of this aspect is very important to some types of business. Food supermarkets, because their stock turnover is rapid, typically have their entire stocks financed by suppliers of these stocks (see, for example, the position of **Tesco plc** in Table 13.1 on page 352). For other types of business, where stock is not financed by the suppliers, the opportunity cost of interest should be based on the returns from an investment of risk similar to that of investing in stocks.

Storage costs
Storage costs include rent of space occupied by the stock and the cost of employing people to guard and manage the stock. With some types of stock it might include the cost of keeping it in some particular environment necessary for its preservation. This is likely to be particularly true for perishables such as food.

Insurance costs

Holding valuable stocks exposes businesses to risk from fire, theft, and so forth, against which they will usually insure, at a cost.

Obsolescence

Stocks can become obsolete, for example because they go out of fashion or lose their value owing to changes in the design of the product in whose manufacture they were intended to be used. Thus apparently perfectly good stock can become little more than scrap. The business holding no stock is clearly not exposed to the risk of this cost.

The costs and risks of holding low (or no) stocks

The costs and risks of holding low (or no) stocks can also be substantial. The more common ones are described below.

Loss of customer goodwill

Failure to be able to supply a customer owing to having insufficient stock may mean the loss not only of that particular order, but of further orders as well. The extent to which this is a significant risk depends to a large degree on the nature of the trade and on the relative market power of supplier and customer.

Production dislocation

Running out of raw material when other production facilities (factory, machinery, labour) are available can be very costly. How costly depends on how flexible the business can be in response to a *stockout*, which in turn probably depends on the nature of the stock concerned. For example, a car manufacturer running out of a major body section probably has no choice but to stop production. If the business runs out of interior mirrors, it is probably quite feasible for these to be added at the end of the production cycle rather than at the scheduled stage, without too much costly dislocation.

Loss of flexibility

Businesses that hold little or no stock inevitably lead a 'hand to mouth' existence, where purchasing and manufacture must be very closely geared to sales. This may preclude maximising the efficiency of production runs or of buying materials in batches of economically optimum sizes. Such an existence also means that, unless things go precisely to plan, the business risks costly problems. There is also the risk that even a slight increase in sales demand cannot be met.

Stockholding creates a 'margin of safety' that can reduce risk, so that mishaps of various descriptions can occur without major and costly repercussions.

Reorder costs

Any business existing on little or no stock will be forced to place a relatively large number of small orders with short intervals of time between each one. Each order gives rise to costs, including the physical placing of the order (buyer's time, telephone, postage and so on) and the receipt of the goods (stores staff time, costs of processing the invoice and making payment).

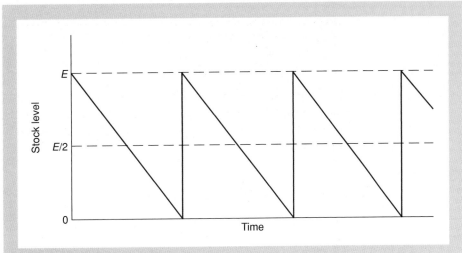

Figure 13.4
Graph of the stock
level against time
for some item
of stock

An amount (*E*) of stock is delivered at time 0. This is steadily used until the stock level drops
to 0, at which point a new consignment (amount *E*) arrives. The average level of stock is *E*/2.

Stock management models

Models have been developed to aid managers in their task of balancing costs. Each of
these models seems to have its strengths and its limitations.

One such model can be used to identify the optimum size of order to be placed for
the purchase of new raw materials, given a particular rate of usage of stock and other
relevant factors. The model is based on the assumption that the level of each stock item
will be as shown in Figure 13.4. This shows the stock level falling evenly over time
until just as the stock completely runs out it is replaced by quantity *E*. Since the stock
level falls evenly from *E* to zero, the average stockholding level is *E*/2. The model
seeks to balance stockholding costs with the cost of placing orders.

If *C* is the cost of placing each order, *A* the annual demand for (that is, usage of)
the stock item and *H* the cost of holding one unit of the stock item for one year, then
the annual cost of placing orders will be ($A/E \times C$) and the cost of holding the stock
will be ($E/2 \times H$). The total cost associated with placing orders and holding stock is
the sum of these two. (Note that we are not interested in the purchase price of the
stock itself as this is defined by the annual usage and the price per unit and is
independent, except for the question of possible discounts for bulk orders, of the size
of each order and the average stock level.)

Figure 13.5 shows the behaviour of the costs with various levels of stock. As stock
levels and, following our assumptions depicted in the graph in Figure 13.4, order size
increase, the annual costs of placing orders decrease but holding costs increase. Total
cost drops as stock level increases until, at point *M*, it reaches a minimum and starts
to increase. What we want to know is the size of order quantity *E* that will minimise
the total cost: in other words, we need to identify point *M*.

Since *M* is the same as *E*/2, that is, half of the optimum order quantity, the total cost
and, therefore, the expression plotted as such in Figure 13.5, is:

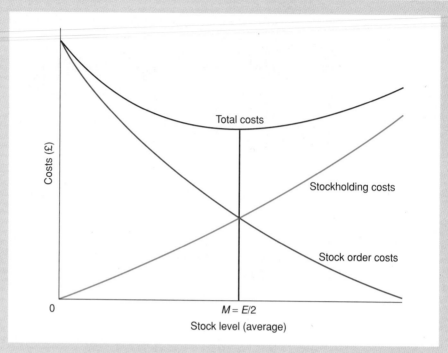

Figure 13.5
Graph of the stockholding costs and stock order costs against the average stock level for some item of stock

The larger the stock order, the larger the amount of the average stock level and the higher the stockholding costs. On the other hand, large stock orders mean relatively infrequent orders and, therefore, relatively low total order costs. There seems likely to be an optimum stock order size, which will balance the two types of cost.

$$\frac{AC}{E} + \frac{HE}{2}$$

that is, annual order placing cost plus annual stock storage cost.

We can discover where this total will be a minimum (point M) using differential calculus. It will be a minimum where the differential of the expression (with respect to E) is equal to zero, the point of zero slope.

Differentiating with respect to E gives:

$$\frac{-AC}{E^2} + \frac{H}{2} = 0$$

so:

$$E = \sqrt{\frac{2AC}{H}}$$

Example 13.2

Economic order quantity

A business uses 1000 units of a particular stock item each year. The costs of holding one unit of it for a year are £3 and the cost of placing each order is £30. What is the most economical size for each order?

Solution

$$E = \sqrt{\frac{2AC}{H}}$$

$$= \sqrt{\left(\frac{2 \times 1000 \times 30}{3}\right)}$$

$$= 141.4, \text{ say } 141 \text{ units}$$

Thus each order will be placed for 141 units (or perhaps a round figure like 140 or 150), necessitating about seven orders being placed each year.

We should note the weaknesses of this model, the most striking of which are as follows:

- Demand for stock items may fluctuate on a seasonal basis, so that the diagonals in Figure 13.4 may not all be parallel, or even straight.

- Annual demand may be (almost certainly is) impossible to predict with certainty, though it may be possible to ascribe statistical probabilities to possible levels of demand.

- The model ignores many of the costs associated with holding and failing to hold stocks. This particularly applies to some of the costs of holding low levels of stock, such as loss of customer goodwill, production dislocation and loss of flexibility.

Virtually all of these deficiencies are capable of being accommodated by increasing the sophistication of the model. For example, the loss of customer goodwill and production dislocation problems can to some extent be dealt with by revising the model to incorporate a safety margin reflecting a pattern of stock levels over time, following more closely that which is depicted in Figure 13.6 than the one shown in Figure 13.4. How large this margin of safety should be must be a matter of managerial judgement. Some estimate of the costs of holding the additional stock, the costs of a 'stockout' and the probability of its occurrence, must give some guidance in the exercise of the judgement.

Note that incorporating a safety stock means that the average stockholding level is no longer $E/2$ and so the basic model is not strictly valid; however, the model can quite easily be adjusted to cope with this.

Let us be clear that the model that we have derived is a highly simplified, even simplistic, attempt to balance the two types of cost. However, the model can be extended to deal with most factors that the simpler version ignores. Several of the references at the end of this chapter go into some of the sophistications that can be incorporated. The model may also be used with a little adaptation for WIP and finished stocks as well as for bought-in raw materials.

Some practical points on management of stocks

Optimum order quantities

These should be established for each item of stock, using either the model that we derived (above) or some more sophisticated version. These quantities should be periodically revised, but between revisions should be regarded as the size of order that should be placed, except in most unusual circumstances.

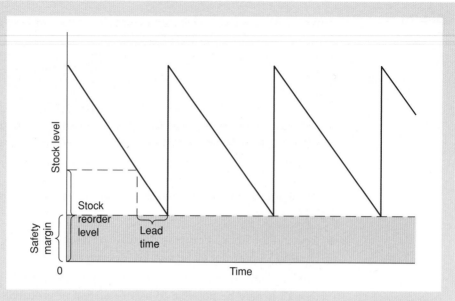

Figure 13.6
Graph of the stock level against time for some item of stock, assuming a safety margin

An amount of stock is delivered at time 0. This is steadily used until the stock level drops to the stock reorder level, at which point a new consignment will be ordered. The stock reorder level should be set at such an amount that there is enough stock to maintain operations until the new consignment arrives, and to provide a margin of safety. The size of the margin of safety will probably depend on the reliability of the supplier in delivering within the expected time period. It will also depend on the predictability of the rate at which stock will be used during the lead time. The lead time is the period that elapses between placing the order and receiving the stock.

Stock reorder levels

The level of stock at which the next order must be placed should also be established and adhered to. The actual level for a particular stock item largely depends upon the lead time (that is, how long it takes between placing the order and the stock actually arriving at the business's premises) and the rate of usage of stock. One way or another, the order should be placed early enough for the stock to arrive just as the safety level is expected to be reached. This is depicted in Figure 13.6.

To illustrate this, let us assume that, in the economic order quantity example (above), the lead time is three weeks. As the weekly usage is about 20 units (1000/52), if the order is placed when the stock level drops to about 60 units and all goes according to plan, the new stock will arrive just as existing stocks are running out. This, of course, leaves no safety margin, but as we have already seen, such devices can easily be incorporated. Such a safety margin is represented by a 'buffer' – a level below which stock should not normally fall.

Most computer packages dealing with stock records have a facility for incorporating reorder levels for each stock item so that the computer's output will draw attention to the need to place the next order.

Budgeting and planning

Much of successful stock management is concerned with knowing what to expect in terms of levels of demand for and costs associated with stocks. The importance, in cost and risk reduction, of forward planning and budgeting probably cannot be overestimated.

Reliable stock records

Unless businesses know what they have in stock, stock management becomes very difficult. It is rarely possible in practice to gain sufficient information on stocks from physical observation.

Ratios

Ratios can be useful in managing stocks, particularly the *stockholding period* ratio (average stock × 365/annual stock usage), which indicates the average period, in days, for which stock is held. The inputs for calculating the ratio may be stated either in terms of physical units of stock or in money terms. It is important that both inputs are stated in similar terms; usually cost is used.

The ratio may be calculated for a business's entire stock (in which case the inputs would need to be expressed in money terms), for a section of the stock (for example, stocks of tyres of a car manufacturer), or for specific items (such as stock of a particular size and quality of tyre). Such figures may be used as a check that policies laid down are in fact being followed.

Security and authorisation

Routine systems should be established in an attempt to ensure that stock may only be ordered (or manufactured) and used on the authority of some fairly senior employee. This involves specifying the employees who are empowered to authorise the placing of orders and ensuring that stock is kept in some enclosed area, only to be issued on the authority of other specified employees. Clearly, management needs to use some common sense here so as not to make the purchase and issuing of stock a major obstacle to the business's activities. However, a system where anyone can order stock and where it can be used without authority is likely to lead to chaos and loss.

To summarise, these practical points are really concerned with establishing routines to be applied systematically. Stock management should not be a haphazard operation.

13.7 Just in time stockholding

The just in time philosophy

There is a tendency, which seems to have originated in the USA, but to have been developed in Japan, for manufacturing businesses to operate a system where there is a fairly continuous flow of raw materials stock into the factory, of work in progress (WIP) through the factory and of finished stocks to the customer. In such a system, large amounts of stock (raw materials, WIP and finished stock) would never build up. Finished goods stocks would be produced just as they are needed to supply to customers, inputs of internally manufactured components and sub-assemblies would be produced and pass to the next stage of production just as they are needed to be used, and raw materials deliveries would arrive from suppliers just as they are needed in production. In essence, the just in time (JIT) approach means that production and purchasing are linked closely to sales demand on a day-to-day basis, avoiding the need to hold buffer stocks to see the business through unexpected demand peaks.

Although at first sight JIT is a technique of stock and production control, its effective implementation requires the acceptance of a particular philosophy and culture. An effective JIT system requires a flexible attitude on the part both of suppliers and of the internal workforce, to expand and contract output at short notice. It also requires close attention to quality of outputs at each stage, both by suppliers and by the internal workforce. If raw materials stocks are to arrive just in time to go straight into production, those stocks must be of guaranteed quality, which need not be tested or checked before being taken into production. The same general point about quality follows through each stage of production and into sales.

The practicalities of JIT

The JIT system can only be reliably established where there are very close relationships between users and suppliers. This requires that the user be prepared to guarantee only to buy from the one supplier in respect of a particular stock item and to give the supplier access to the user's production/sales plans. This enables the supplier to match its production to the needs of the user in much the same way as would a department of the user business supplying components or sub-assemblies to another internal department. To work well, the system probably requires that supplier and user be geographically fairly close to one another so that deliveries can be made frequently and, when necessary, at short notice.

Achievement of low stock levels of internally produced components and sub-assemblies, and of finished stocks, normally requires short production runs, that is, each production batch of a particular product or component is fairly small. To be economical, this normally means that the costs of setting up each production run are fairly low. High-technology production methods (robots and computer controlled manufacturing) typically have low set-up costs and considerable flexibility. This makes an effective JIT system more achievable than it was in the past.

An effective system of JIT also requires a workforce willing to increase and decrease its working hours from one period to another. This can pose serious problems for implementing a JIT system, particularly in some western countries where regular weekly working hours are an established feature of industrial employment. The existence of a pool of labour willing to come in at short notice to supplement the 'core' workforce during production peaks may provide a solution in some cases.

Clearly, a JIT policy will tend to lead to lower stock levels from the user's point of view and, therefore, to stockholding cost savings. The attention given to quality control and assurance is also likely to lead to net financial benefits. On the other hand, there may be additional opportunity costs arising from the fact that the user cannot, in the short term at least, buy from different suppliers according to price. Also, it may be fairly expensive to maintain a flexible workforce. However, the increasing popularity of the JIT approach implies that many businesses regard the policy as having net benefits for them.

JIT in practice

JIT seems to be used quite widely in practice.

Boots Group plc, the UK's largest healthcare retailer, recently improved the stock management at its stores. The business is working with a JIT system where a stock delivery from its one central warehouse in Nottingham will be made every day to each retail branch, with nearly all of the stock lines being placed directly on to the sales shelves, not into a branch stock room. The business says that this will bring significant savings of stores staff time and lead to significantly lower levels of stock being held, without any lessening of the service offered to customers. The new system is expected to lead to major economic benefits for the business.

Nissan Motors UK Limited, the UK manufacturing arm of the Japanese car business, has a plant in Sunderland in the north east of England. Here it operates a well-developed JIT system. **Tarkett Sommer Ltd** supplies carpets and soft interior trim from a factory close to the Nissan plant. It makes deliveries to Nissan once every 20 minutes on average, so as to arrive exactly as they are needed in production. This is fairly typical of all of the 200 suppliers of components and materials to the Nissan plant.

13.8 Trade debtors (accounts receivable)

With the exception of the retail trade, where immediate cash settlement predominates, most commercial sales are made on credit. When the goods or services pass to the customer business, that business becomes a trade debtor of the supplier until such time as it settles its debt by paying cash.

It appears that attitudes to the granting of credit vary from trade to trade, with time-honoured credit policies being perpetuated by virtue of the fact that individual businesses find it hard to break patterns with which their competitors intend to continue.

In determining credit policy the financial manager must try to strike the balance between the costs and risks of granting credit and those associated with denying or restricting credit.

The costs and risks of granting credit

The costs and risks of granting credit are outlined below.

Lost interest

Granting credit is equivalent to making interest-free loans. Since trade debtors are not usually secured, they tend to be fairly risky loans. Thus the interest lost is at a fairly high rate.

Loss of purchasing power

When price inflation is present, which in the UK (and most of the developed world) has been much of the twentieth century, including every single year since the Second World War, value transfers from lender to borrower. This is because the borrower (trade debtor in this context) pays the debt in £s of lower value than those that were borrowed. To some extent this point is covered in the previous one, but fairly recent experience of very high inflation rates showed that, at such times, interest rates do not necessarily increase fully to compensate lenders for the erosion of their money's purchasing power. Those granting trade credit should be aware that they are likely to be forgoing more than just interest in times of inflation.

Assessing the potential customer's creditworthiness

It is usual before granting credit to a new customer, or perhaps when increasing the credit limit of an existing customer, to assess creditworthiness. It would usually be done by seeking references from the customer's bank and from other traders who have already granted credit to that customer. The assessment might include examination of the customer's published financial statements, for clues as to liquidity and financial rectitude, and paying a credit rating agency for a report on the customer.

Carrying out these procedures reduces the risk of bad debts, but it costs money, though to a large extent the cost, once incurred, is unlikely to need to be repeated. Typically, businesses, once having granted credit to a customer, reassess that customer on the basis of their own experience of the customer's track record of payment.

Administration and record keeping costs

Most businesses that grant credit find it necessary to employ people to act in the role of credit controllers, that is, to devote themselves to the administration and collection of trade debts. Granting credit usually involves a greatly increased volume of accounting transactions.

Bad debts

Unless the business adopts an extremely cautious credit-granting policy it is almost inevitable that some trade debts will never be paid, owing, for example, to the defaulting customer's financial collapse. This risk can be insured against, though typically it is borne by the supplier; either way there is a cost.

Discounts

It is quite common for businesses to offer their credit customers a discount if they settle their debts quickly. For example, a 2.5 per cent discount may be offered if customers pay within 30 days of receipt of the goods or service. What the effective cost of such a policy would be depends upon how long the customers, who pay quickly and claim the discount, would take to pay were no discount available. If, say, in the above example they would on average take 40 days but the discount causes them to pay exactly on day 30, the effective cost of the discount is 2.5 per cent per 10 days, or about 100 per cent p.a. (compounded). Clearly, giving discounts for prompt payment can represent a significant cost, so its use should be treated with caution. We should bear in mind, however, that discount-induced prompt payment might well reduce some of the costs that we have already discussed, particularly those associated with the risk of bad debts and administration of debtors.

Exchange rate costs

Any business will expose itself to risk and cost by making credit sales in an overseas currency. The risk can be managed effectively, but this will involve further cost. This topic will be explored in Chapter 15.

The costs and risks of denying credit

There are various costs and risks associated with denying credit. These are considered below.

Loss of customer goodwill

If its competitors grant credit it will be difficult for a business to deny credit, unless it offers instead some special inducement (such as discounted prices), which itself may be as expensive as granting credit. Where the supplier is in a monopolistic, or near-monopolistic, position, it may be able to sell as much as it wishes without offering credit. In a competitive market, however, credit may be used as a basis of competition, so that it may be necessary to offer unusually extended credit to attract large and recurring orders.

Inconvenience and loss of security of collecting cash

Administratively, supplying goods or services on credit can be very convenient. Cash is not usually paid until the customer is satisfied that the goods are as ordered, which avoids the necessity for refunds in respect of defective goods. Cash is collected centrally, usually by cheques received by post, or by direct bank credit. It is unnecessary for delivery drivers to collect cash: thus the delay and potential administrative and security problems likely to arise from such decentralised cash collection may be avoided. The existence of trade credit tends to allow specialisation and segregation of duties; delivery drivers deliver the goods and credit controllers collect the cash.

Some practical points in management of trade debts

Establish a credit policy

The business should consider whether it judges it appropriate to offer trade credit at all, and if so, how much, to whom and under what circumstances. It might, for example, decide generally that trade credit is not a good idea, but nonetheless identify specific circumstances where it is prepared to offer it. For example, a retailer may be prepared to offer credit only for orders above £100.

One way or another, each business should establish a policy, not merely accept that credit is inevitable.

Assess customers' creditworthiness

Although in principle the business may have decided that it is in its best interests to offer credit, it should not offer unlimited credit to any potential customer who seeks it. Those seeking credit are, in effect, asking for an unsecured loan, and supplying businesses should assess matters in those terms.

The business should establish a policy for investigating creditworthiness, and should not be prepared to grant credit before satisfying itself that the risk of doing so in respect of each customer is an acceptable one. It is not just a question of either granting credit or not. Credit limits should be established, and these will almost certainly vary from customer to customer depending on the supplying business's confidence in each one's individual creditworthiness. Once established, each customer's credit limit should be rigorously applied until such time as there is some fundamental review by a senior employee.

The supplying business should try to establish some 'ear to the ground' routines so that signs that any particular established credit customer is experiencing liquidity problems can be picked up quickly and action taken. Such routines might include regularly monitoring the customers' financial statements (annual accounts). Another approach that could also be used is to look out for customers who are taking longer than they usually do to pay their debts; this may indicate a weakening liquidity position.

Establish effective administration of debtors

Systems should be established to ensure:

- that no goods are dispatched until it has been confirmed that the present order will not take the customer above the predetermined credit limit for that customer;

- that invoices for goods supplied on credit go off to the customer as soon as possible after the goods, thus encouraging the customer to initiate payment routines sooner rather than later; and

- that existing debtors are systematically reviewed and that slow payers are sent reminders.

Most computer packages for dealing with trade debtors can produce a list of debtors with each customer's debt analysed by length of time for which the debt has been outstanding. This (known as an ageing summary) and similar devices can usefully be used by credit controllers in the pursuit of trade debts.

Establish a policy on bad debts

At some stage it will often become more costly to pursue reluctant payers than their debt is worth. The business should decide on a policy for writing off bad debts. Once established, the policy should be followed except in unusual circumstances.

It is important that writing off a bad debt occurs only when all the steps identified in the policy have been followed. It is also important that writing off bad debts can only be authorised by a senior employee.

Consider offering discounts for prompt payment

A discount for prompt payment (or cash discount) is a reduction in the amount due for debtors who pay within a specified time, for example one month of the transaction concerned.

The costs and advantages of allowing discounts should be assessed. If the business establishes a particular policy of allowing discounts, care should be taken to ensure that customers are allowed to deduct discounts only when they have in fact paid within the specified period.

Consider factoring debts

It is possible to enter into an arrangement with a debt factor (many are subsidiaries of commercial banks). Here the factor collects the debts on behalf of the supplier business. The precise arrangements can vary considerably but, fairly typically, payment (at a discount) is made by the factor, immediately after the sale. The factor then goes on to collect the debt and to manage all accounting and administrative matters concerned with it. This relieves the supplier of the administrative and financial burden of granting trade credit, but at a cost. 'Invoice discounting' is a very similar arrangement.

Manage exchange rate risk

Where the business is involved with credit sales in a foreign currency there is the danger that an adverse shift in the exchange rate during the period from the credit sale to its settlement will reduce the value of the debt. This risk normally needs to be managed. This and other aspects of international transactions are dealt with in some detail in Chapter 15.

Ratios

These can be useful in debtor management. Probably the most widely used is *debtor collection period* (average debtors × 365/annual credit sales revenue) which indicates the average time taken between a sale being made and the cash being received. It gives an overall impression of what is actually happening with debtors, which can be compared with the business's policy on debtor collection to provide a control device. Where collection periods are in fact exceeding those specified in the policy, steps can be taken to try to correct matters.

In summary, trade debtor management should be thought through in advance and conducted in a systematic manner. Incidences, by accident or by design, of departure from the established credit policy should be highly exceptional.

Debtor payment periods in practice

UK businesses are required to indicate in their annual reports how long on average they take to pay their trade creditors. Since one business's trade creditors are another one's trade debtors, we can take the information provided by businesses on paying trade creditors as an indication of the typical trade debtor payment period.

Based on a sample of 30 randomly selected, UK Stock Exchange listed businesses' annual reports for 2003 and 2004, the following emerges:

Longest time taken	77 days
Mean time taken	37 days
Median time taken	34 days
Shortest time taken	10 days

This suggests a fairly wide variation. Businesses can expect to be paid after more than about 34 days by about half of their debtors and in less than about 34 days by the other half. Of course, individual policies on trade debtor management, like offering discounts for prompt payment, will normally have an effect.

13.9 Cash (including overdrafts and short-term deposits)

If we glance back at Figure 13.1 on page 349, we see that cash is sooner or later involved in everything that the typical business does. Some may not hold stock (perhaps because they sell services rather than goods), others may have no trade debtors or creditors (because they neither give nor receive credit), but all of them have cash. Admittedly, some businesses have negative cash balances (overdrafts), but a business with no cash balance at any given moment would be rare.

Cash tends to be held for three reasons:

- To meet planned needs to pay suppliers and labour.
- As a fund to meet unexpected obligations: for example, a short-term creditor demanding payment earlier than expected.
- To enable unexpected opportunities to be taken: for example, to place a larger than planned order for stock to exploit some temporary price advantage.

As we saw in our discussion of Figure 13.1, cash is much more than just one of the elements of working capital. As the medium of exchange and store of value it provides the linkage between all financial aspects of the business. More specifically, it links short- and long-term financing decisions with one another, and with decisions involving investment both in non-current assets and in working capital.

Clearly, cash management is one of the key roles in any organisation of any size or description. Treasury management, as this role is increasingly being called, requires a specialism of skills, knowledge and experience. This has led to a tendency for treasury managers in larger organisations to be specialists whose career path lies exclusively in that functional area. Not surprisingly, in smaller organisations the role of treasury manager is likely to be filled by the accountant.

We shall first have a look at the costs involved with holding cash/not holding cash, before we go on to the closely related topics of the use of bank overdrafts to overcome temporary cash shortages and of how temporary cash surpluses can be used.

The costs and risks of holding cash

The costs and risks associated with holding cash are described below.

Loss of interest

If cash is held in its most liquid form (notes and coins), it will yield no interest at all. Even if it is in a current account with a bank it will not yield income at a very high rate. It may be possible for a business to have some, perhaps most, of its cash on some very short-term deposit from which it can be withdrawn at short notice should the need arise. Even where this is done there is still a cost, since short-term interest rates tend to be lower than longer-term ones.

Loss of purchasing power

As with trade debts, during a period of inflation there is erosion in the value of money. This is not necessarily compensated for by interest rates.

Exchange rate cost

Businesses that hold cash in an overseas currency will incur a cost should that currency weaken against the home currency. This will be discussed at some length in Chapter 15.

The costs and risks of holding little or no cash

The costs and risks of holding little or no cash are described next.

Loss of supplier goodwill

'Supplier' here is used in its widest sense to include employees as suppliers of labour. Failure to meet financial obligations on time, owing to cash shortages, may mean the loss of further supplies from injured parties. This could be extremely damaging, especially where the particular commodity is one that is vital to continuing operations, such as labour. Failure to meet a financial obligation to a creditor puts that creditor into a position where it could take steps to instigate the defaulting business's liquidation. Given the bankruptcy costs and an inefficient market for real assets, such an outcome must be a matter of great concern to shareholders seeking to increase or at least to maintain their wealth. A shortage of cash could expose the business to this risk.

Loss of opportunities

Cash shortages tend to mean that it may be impossible to react quickly to an opportunity. For example, if a business is offered a contract that must be fulfilled at short notice by overtime working, it may have to be refused if cash is not available to meet the additional labour costs. Thus a shortage of cash exposes the business to the risk of incurring opportunity costs.

Inability to claim discounts

Discounts for prompt payment are very advantageous, in percentage terms, to the purchasing business. Cash shortages may preclude claiming such discounts.

Cost of borrowing

Shortages of cash will expose the business to the risk of having to borrow short term to be able to meet unexpected obligations. Interest costs for such borrowings can be expensive, particularly where the money has to be raised at very short notice and under pressure.

As ever, optimally balancing these two types of cost and risks is the aim of the financial (treasury) manager. There are some models that can be helpful in this task.

Cash management models

Several cash management models have been developed. The simplest one is substantially the same as the economic stock order quantity model that we derived on page 360. This cash model assumes that the business keeps all of its cash on an interest-yielding deposit from which it can make withdrawals as it needs. It also assumes that all receipts (from debtors and so forth) are put straight into the deposit and that cash usage is linear over time, following exactly the same pattern as Figure 13.4 (page 359) does for stocks. The model derives the amount of money to withdraw from the deposit so that the costs of withdrawal are optimally balanced with those of interest, etc., forgone by holding cash, rather than leaving the funds on deposit. The model can be stated as:

$$C = \sqrt{\frac{2WP}{H}}$$

where C is the optimum amount of cash to be withdrawn each time, W is the cost of making each withdrawal (a cost independent of the size of the withdrawal), P is the planned payments for the forthcoming time period and H is the interest forgone on the cash withdrawn (that is, the interest rate of the deposit).

Example 13.3

A business plans to use £20 000 of cash during the forthcoming year. It holds most of its cash in a deposit account from which it costs £30 to make each withdrawal and which pays interest at 10 per cent p.a. What is the optimal size for each withdrawal?

Solution

$$C = £\sqrt{\left(\frac{2 \times 30 \times 20\,000}{0.10}\right)}$$

$$= £3464$$

Therefore, about £3464 should be withdrawn from the deposit. When all that is spent, a further withdrawal of similar amount should be made, and so on.

As with its close relation, the economic order quantity, this model takes a very simple view of the world, though it is probably better than nothing.

Modifications to the basic model have been proposed by Miller and Orr (1966), and Beranek (1963) suggested another approach.

Bank overdrafts

Bank overdrafts are facilities allowed by commercial banks enabling customers to have negative balances on their current accounts. The bank overdraft is therefore a form of borrowing for which the bank will charge interest, typically at 1 or 2 per cent above the relevant base lending rate. Banks usually make a fixed charge for establishing the facility as well.

Once the facility is established, the customer may continue to conduct the bank account as normal, except that it can now incur a negative balance up to a specified limit. This tends to be a cheap form of finance, as the customer is required only to pay for the funds used for as long as they are being used. In fact, overdrafts are in essence short-term loans of fluctuating amounts, with fluctuating interest rates; the actual rate charged is likely to be low compared with those associated with longer-term loans.

As was discussed on page 355, businesses seem to use overdrafts particularly to overcome temporary cash shortages, caused perhaps by seasonal fluctuations. For example, a business whose main trading period is during the summer holiday season will tend to stock up during the late spring. This will put a temporary strain on its cash resources, which will gradually be relieved as the summer progresses. The alternative to overdraft finance may only be some long-term source. If the business made a debenture issue, it would then be saddled with interest payments throughout the year on funds that it only needs for a month or two. It could, of course, put the spare cash on deposit for the other 10 or 11 months, but the nature of the market for finance tends to mean that interest received will not match interest paid on those funds.

Bank overdrafts have a major disadvantage compared with long-term loans: they are usually repayable at call (that is, immediately) as a condition of the facility being granted. Where overdrafts are being used, as in our example, to overcome temporary shortages of cash, this is probably not a problem since 'immediately', in practice, probably means at a couple of months' notice. To the business seeking to use a bank overdraft as a more permanent source of finance, this can be a serious problem, however.

Despite this problem, many businesses are financed partially by overdraft, on a permanent basis. The overdraft remains at call, but is not repaid. To such businesses, the overdraft represents a relatively cheap, but risky, source of finance.

Short-term cash surpluses

Where the business is experiencing cash surpluses, normally evidenced by a build-up of cash in its current account, it will be necessary to determine whether this cash represents a permanent surplus or a temporary one. If it is a permanent one, consideration will need to be given to using it in some 'long-term' manner. This should involve further investment, if positive NPV projects can be found, or the repayment of some long-term finance, if they cannot.

Where the cash surplus seems to be a temporary one caused, for example, by the seasonality of the business's trade, steps need to be taken to use it in the most effective way. Possible options include the following:

- *Putting the cash on an interest-yielding deposit.* Generally, higher returns accrue from deposits requiring a period of notice of withdrawal, perhaps 30 days. Care must therefore be taken to assess for how long the spare funds are likely to be available and how likely it is that they will be needed unexpectedly.

- *Buying marketable investments.* These would need to be easily sold, so those listed on the Stock Exchange or a similarly liquid and efficient market would tend to be most appropriate. Equities may well be viewed as too risky a prospect in this context; the price could easily fall. It would be possible to use a financial derivative, for example a put option (see Chapter 7) to cover this risk, but at a cost. A loan stock, possibly a government one (gilt) might be appropriate. These tend to be less risky, though holders are exposed to interest rate risk (see Chapter 8). Again, a financial derivative could be used to hedge this risk.

  Dealing charges are likely to be involved with buying and selling marketable securities of both types, which will tend to mean that such investment will be inappropriate where small amounts and/or short investment periods are involved.

As with the treatment of any permanent cash surpluses, decisions here should be based on which action would lead to the greatest enhancement of shareholders' wealth.

Some practical points in the management of cash and overdrafts

Establish a policy

The business should, with the aid of models and other means, establish a policy for cash. This policy should be adhered to, except in the most unusual circumstances, until such time as it is formally reviewed.

Plan cash flows

Forward planning is vital in this area; failure to balance cash inflows with cash outflows can be fatal.

The formal statement of financial plans (the budget), can probably best be explained through an example.

Example 13.4

A business has the following plans for the next few months:

1 *Sales revenue:*

	£
September	60 000
October	60 000
November	70 000
December	90 000

All sales will be made on credit. Half of the debtors are expected to pay within the month of sale and to claim a 2 per cent cash discount. The remainder are expected to pay in the following month.

2 *Raw materials purchases:*

	£
September	20 000
October	40 000
November	40 000
December	30 000

The business plans to pay its creditors (in full) in the month following that of the purchase.

3 *Wages and salaries:*

	£
September	12 000
October	15 000
November	17 000
December	13 000

All employees are paid in full in the month in which the wage or salary is earned.

4 Rent of £10 000 each quarter is payable in March, June, September and December.

5 Other cash overheads of £2000 per month are payable.

6 Some new plant due for delivery in September will be paid for in November at a cost of £25 000.

7 On 1 October the business plans to have £10 000 in the bank.

A cash budget for the months of October to December (inclusive) is to be prepared.

Make judicious use of bank overdraft and deposit accounts

Bank overdrafts should be avoided if possible, by scheduling payments and receipts with a view to staying in credit. Use temporary cash excesses by putting the money on deposit or investing in marketable securities. Where the cash surplus looks more permanent, thought should be given to whether it should be used in real investment or repaid to suppliers of long-term funds, thus saving the cost of servicing those funds.

Solution

Cash budget for the three months ending 31 December:

	October £	November £	December £
Cash inflows:			
Debtors: Current month	29 400	34 300	44 100
Previous month	30 000	30 000	35 000
Total cash inflows (A)	59 400	64 300	79 100
Cash outflows:			
Creditors	20 000	40 000	40 000
Wages and salaries	15 000	17 000	13 000
Rent	–	–	10 000
Overheads	2 000	2 000	2 000
Plant acquired	–	25 000	–
Total cash outflows (B)	37 000	84 000	65 000
Cash surplus/(deficit) for the month (A – B)	22 400	(19 700)	14 100
Cumulative cash balance	32 400	12 700	26 800

Notes to the solution

1 The above statement reflects the timing and amount of cash payments and receipts and the resultant balance. It is not, and is not intended to be, a profit and loss account. The profit or loss for these months will almost certainly be different from the cash surplus or deficit.

2 Knowledge of the projected cumulative cash balance enables plans to be made to use the surplus to effect; even if the most effective prospect is putting it on short-term deposit, it is better than nothing.

Bank frequently

Promptly pay cheques received into the bank, thus saving overdraft interest or generating income. The business should encourage direct bank credit payment by its debtors, thus limiting the time before the bank reflects such receipts. Businesses with large receipts of notes and coin (for example, retailers) should consider banking several times each day, if only for security reasons.

Time transactions to the best cash flow effect

There are several areas, particularly relating to tax payments, where with a little forethought a payment can legitimately be delayed or a receipt hastened. For example, corporation tax is based on the individual business's accounting year, and the timing of capital allowances is dependent on the date of acquisition of non-current assets. If a new piece of plant is purchased at the end of an accounting year, the tax relief will first manifest itself in cash flow terms a year earlier than if the acquisition is delayed for the short period until the start of the new accounting year.

Manage exchange rate exposure

Where the business holds cash in an overseas currency, there is the danger that an adverse shift in the exchange rate will reduce the value of the funds. This will be discussed at some length in Chapter 15.

13.10 Trade creditors (accounts payable)

Trade creditors represents money owed for goods and services purchased on credit by the business. It is the other side of the coin from trade debtors; one business's trade debts are another's trade credit. As we saw in section 13.6, worldwide it will be true that:

Total of all trade debts = Total of all trade credits

As we also saw, a random sample of London Stock Exchange listed businesses indicates that average trade creditors represents about 5 weeks' purchases. The highest level of creditors in the survey represents 11 weeks' purchases, and the lowest 1.5 weeks. Table 13.1 (page 352) shows that trade credit is a significant source of finance for the five businesses highlighted. The table also shows how the use of trade credit seems to differ from one business to another. Thus, trade credit is an important source of 'free' finance, which should be taken seriously.

That trade credit is strictly free is doubtful, since businesses will build the cost of granting credit into the pricing policy. However, unless suppliers are willing to discriminate in their pricing between those who settle their bills immediately and those who do not, there is no obvious differential cost of taking credit. There may be less obvious costs involved so, as ever, the balance must be sought between that cost and the cost of not taking trade credit.

The costs and risks of taking credit

The costs and risks of taking credit are considered below.

Price

Some suppliers might offer cheaper prices for immediate settlement – in effect a discount for prompt payment. Cash-and-carry wholesalers in the grocery trade are examples of businesses that are prepared to offer lower prices because they do not offer credit (or delivery). The small retail grocer has the option of dealing with wholesalers who offer credit but who usually also charge higher prices.

Possible loss of supplier goodwill

If credit is overstepped, suppliers may discriminate against delinquent customers if supplies become short. As with the effect of any loss of goodwill, it depends very much on the relative market strengths of the parties involved.

Administration and accounting

Taking credit almost certainly engenders administrative and accounting costs that would not otherwise be incurred.

Restrictions

Many suppliers insist that, to be granted credit, orders must be of some minimum size and/or regularity.

Exchange rate costs

Businesses that buy on credit, where settlement is to be in an overseas currency, are exposed to risk and potential cost. Normally, buyers expect to be invoiced in their home currency, which means that the creditor does not face this problem, but there are exceptions to this. This will be discussed at some length in Chapter 15.

The costs and risks of not taking credit

The costs and risks of not taking credit are set out below.

Interest cost

Trade credit is, in effect, an interest-free loan, so failure to exploit it has an interest cost. It may be worth incurring some of the costs of taking credit, particularly when interest rates are high.

Inflation

In periods of inflation, borrowers are favoured over lenders with the levels of interest rates not seeming totally to redress the balance.

Inconvenience

It may be inconvenient, for the reasons discussed in the context of trade debtors, to pay at the time of delivery of the goods or performance of the service. It will probably also inconvenience the supplier. Indeed, insistence on paying on delivery may even be a cause of loss of supplier goodwill. If the supplier's systems are geared to deferred payment, a customer who insists on immediate settlement may not be welcome.

Some practical points in the management of trade credit

Establish a policy

After weighing the two types of cost, a policy should be established and followed. It may well be that suppliers are treated differently according to:

- the discounts offered for prompt payment;
- the attitude to credit taken by individual suppliers; and/or
- the weight of any possible repercussions arising from loss of supplier goodwill.

Exploit trade credit as far as is reasonable

For the typical business it is unlikely that the costs of claiming credit outweigh the considerable advantage of doing so.

Manage exchange rate risk

This is the other side of the coin from the similar problem related to trade debtors that we discussed in that context earlier in the chapter. This will be discussed at some length in Chapter 15.

Ratios

The most useful ratio in the monitoring of trade credit is the *creditor payment period* (average trade creditors $\times$ 365/annual credit purchases). This gives a view of how long, on average, the business is taking to pay its creditors, which can be compared with the planned period.

Summary

Working capital (WC)

- WC = stock + debtors + cash − creditors.
- An investment in WC cannot be avoided in practice – typically large amounts are involved.
- Management of WC is concerned with striking a balance between the risks and costs of having too much of each element, with those of having too little.
- Decisions on WC tend to be frequent and routine.
- WC must be managed as a whole, not just individual elements. Ratios (for example, current ratio) and operating cash cycle (see below) are useful here.
- Overtrading means operating at a level beyond the capacity of the working capital. Can be a particular problem for rapidly expanding businesses.

Operating cash cycles

- Operating cash cycle (for a manufacturer) = length of time from buying RM stock to receiving cash from debtors less creditors' payment period (in days).
- An objective of WC management is to limit the length of the operating cash cycles, subject to any risks that this may cause.

Stock in trade

- Costs of holding stock:
  - Lost interest.
  - Storage cost.
  - Insurance cost.
  - Obsolescence.
- Costs of not holding sufficient stock:
  - Loss of customer goodwill.
  - Production dislocation.
  - Loss of flexibility – cannot take advantage of opportunities.
  - Reorder costs – low stock implies more frequent ordering.
- Practical points on stock management:
  - Identify optimum order size – models can help with this.
  - Set stock reorder levels.
  - Use budgets.
  - Keep reliable stock records.
  - Use accounting ratios (for example, stockholding period ratio).
  - Establish systems for security of stock and authorisation.
  - Consider just in time (JIT) stock management.

Trade debtors

- Costs of allowing credit:
  - Lost interest.
  - Lost purchasing power.

- Costs of assessing customer creditworthiness.
- Administration cost.
- Bad debts.
- Cash discounts (for prompt payment).
- Foreign exchange losses.
- Costs of denying credit:
  - Loss of customer goodwill.
  - Inconvenience and loss of security.
- Practical points on debtor management:
  - Establish a policy.
  - Assess and monitor customer creditworthiness.
  - Establish effective administration of debtors.
  - Establish a policy on bad debts.
  - Consider cash discounts.
  - Manage exchange rate risk.
  - Use accounting ratios (for example, debtor collection period ratio).

Cash

- Costs of holding cash:
  - Lost interest.
  - Lost purchasing power.
  - Foreign exchange losses.
- Costs of holding insufficient cash:
  - Loss of supplier goodwill if unable to meet commitments on time.
  - Loss of opportunities.
  - Inability to claim cash discounts.
  - Costs of borrowing (should an obligation need to be met unexpectedly).
- Practical points on cash management:
  - Establish a policy.
  - Plan cash flows.
  - Make judicious use of bank overdraft finance – it can be cheap and flexible.
  - Use short-term cash surpluses profitably.
  - Bank frequently.
  - Time transactions to best cash flow effect.
  - Manage exchange rate risk.

Trade creditors

- Costs of taking credit:
  - Higher price than purchases for immediate cash settlement.
  - Administrative costs.

→

- Restrictions imposed by seller.
  - Foreign exchange losses.
- Costs of not taking credit:
  - Lost interest-free borrowing.
  - Lost purchasing power.
  - Inconvenience – paying at the time of purchase can be inconvenient.
- Practical points on creditor management:
  - Establish a policy.
  - Exploit free credit as far as possible.
  - Manage exchange rate risk.
  - Use accounting ratios (for example, creditor payment period ratio).

Further reading

Drury (2004) gives a full, yet clear, review of the various aspects of the management of working capital. Samuels, Wilkes and Brayshaw (1998) and Atrill (2006) both cover the topics of this chapter and deal with them in a UK context. An interesting article by Moyes (1988) discusses the features and problems of JIT. For a case study on aspects of JIT at Nissan, see Relevant Websites (below).

Relevant websites

A case study on Nissan and JIT can be found on the website of Partnership Sourcing Ltd (PSL). PSL was established by the Confederation of British Industries (CBI) and the UK government (Department of Trade and Industry) to promote partnership between businesses and other organisations.
www.pslcbi.com/studies/docnissan.htm

The websites of businesses featured in this chapter are:

Balfour Beatty plc	www.balfourbeatty.com
Blacks Leisure Group plc	www.blacksleisure.co.uk
Boots Group plc	www.boots-plc.com
Nissan Motors UK Ltd	www.nissan.co.uk
Scottish and Newcastle plc	www.scottish-newcastle.com
Tarkett Sommer plc	www.tarkett.com
Tate and Lyle plc	www.tateandlyle.com
Tesco plc	www.tesco.com

REVIEW QUESTIONS

Suggested answers to review questions appear in Appendix 3.

13.1 Why is working capital a particularly important area of concern for financial managers?

13.2 What is meant by 'overtrading', and how does it arise?

13.3 How is 'obsolescence' a cost of holding stock?

13.4 In what ways is the basic stock reorder model deficient in representing reality?

13.5 What credit checks would most prudent businesses take before dispatching goods in respect of a credit sale?

13.6 For a business, what (briefly) are the advantages and disadvantages of using a bank overdraft as a means of financing?

PROBLEMS

Sample answers to problems marked with an asterisk appear in Appendix 4.

(All the problems appearing in this chapter are basic-level problems.)

13.1* Dixon plc uses a component, which it buys in from a supplier, in its manufacturing process. The estimated annual usage is 23 000 units, and these are used fairly steadily throughout the year. It is estimated that the various stockholding costs amount to £1.50 per unit per year. Investigation indicates that it costs about £50 to process each order for the component. Experience shows that delivery always occurs within one week of placing an order.

(a) What is the economic order quantity for the component?

(b) At what stock level should the order be placed to be confident that delivery would occur before the existing stock of the components is all used?

13.2 Pithead Products Ltd plans to sell its single product for £35 a unit.

Credit plans for the next six months are as follows:

● 70 per cent of sales are made on credit and 30 per cent for cash.

Of the credit sales revenue:

● 40 per cent will be paid during the month of sale (with the customers claiming a cash discount of 2 per cent of their debt);

● 40 per cent will be paid during the month following the month of sale;

● 18 per cent will be paid during the second month after the sale; and

● the remaining 2 per cent will prove to be bad debts and are expected never to be paid.

Sales volumes for the next few months are budgeted as follows:

	Units
July	5100
August	5500
September	5200
October	5000
November	4800
December	4700

How much cash will be budgeted to be received from sales during October?

13.3* Arcadia Ltd has only one product, a garden gnome, for which it plans to increase production and sales during the first half of next year. The plans for the next eight months are as follows:

Month	Production (gnomes)	Sales volume (gnomes)
November	700	700
December	800	800
January	1000	800
February	1200	1000
March	1200	1200
April	1400	1300
May	1500	1400
June	1500	1600

The selling price for each gnome will be £10. The raw materials will cost £4 per gnome; wages and other variable costs are expected to be £3 per gnome.

Salaries and other fixed overheads are expected to amount to £1400 per month during November and December, to rise to £1600 per month from January to April (inclusive), and to increase to £2000 per month for May and June.

Sixty per cent of sales are made on a cash basis (paid on delivery). The remainder are sold on credit, debtors being expected to pay in full in the second month after the sale.

Payment is planned to be made for raw material purchases one month after delivery, and materials are expected to be held in stock for one month before they are used in production.

Wages and other variable costs are expected to be paid during the month of production. Salaries and other fixed overheads are planned to be paid 80 per cent in the month in which they are incurred and 20 per cent in the following month.

To promote the expanded sales volume, an advertising campaign is to be undertaken. This will involve payments to the advertising agency of £1000 in January and £1500 in April.

A new machine, to help cope with the increased production, has been ordered, and it should be delivered in February. The agreement is to pay the £6000 for the machine in three equal instalments of £2000 each in March, April and May.

Arcadia Ltd intends to pay a dividend of £600 to its shareholders in April.

It expects to have a bank current account balance (in funds) of £7500 on 1 January.

Produce a cash budget for the first six months of next year, showing the net cash position at the end of each month.

13.4 Antithesis Ltd sells its service on credit at the rate of £6m a year. Customers take varying lengths of time to pay, but the average is 65 days. The business does not experience any significant level of bad debts because it spends £50 000 a year on debt collection procedures.

Antithesis Ltd is considering a proposal to introduce a cash discount of 2 per cent of the amount due if customers pay within 30 days of the sale. It is estimated that 60 per cent of customers would pay on the thirtieth day and claim the discount. The remaining customers would be the slower payers, and they would be expected to take an average 75 days to pay. The cost of debt collection procedures would be expected to fall to £20 000 a year. The cost of funds to finance the debtors is 12 per cent p.a.

In terms of effect on net profit (after interest, before tax), should the proposed debtor policy be introduced?

13.5* North Anglia Engineering Ltd (NAE), a manufacturing business, has recently obtained the financial statements of some of its industry rivals and has discovered that it holds, on average, twice the level of stock for its output, compared with its rivals.

(a) *How should NAE set about trying to judge what levels of stock to hold?*
(b) *What approach would you take to investigating NAE's relatively high stock level?*

13.6 Supertraders Ltd is experiencing severe liquidity problems, which you, as a business consultant, have been asked to investigate. You have identified the problem as being caused principally by a very poor trade credit system, with no member of staff responsible for managing trade credit.

Your major recommendation is that the business appoints a credit manager.

(a) *Outline the job description of the person to be appointed as credit manager.*
(b) *Set out the main headings that you would advise the new credit manager to consider, in respect of each of the following:*
   (i) *assessing a particular customer's creditworthiness;*
   (ii) *major sources of information that can be used to assess a customer's creditworthiness; and*
   (iii) *addressing a proposal to alter the business's credit policy.*

There are both a set of **multiple-choice questions** and **missing-word questions** available on the website. These specifically cover the material contained in this chapter. These can be attempted and graded (with feedback) online.

There are also **two additional problems**, with solutions, that relate to the material covered in this chapter.

Go to **www.pearsoned.co.uk/atrillmclaney** and follow the links.

Chapter 14

Corporate restructuring (including takeovers and divestments)

Objectives In this chapter we shall deal with the following:

→ the nature of corporate restructuring

→ the background to mergers

→ the technicalities of mergers

→ the regulation of mergers in the UK

→ the economic success of mergers

→ divestments and the various means of achieving them

→ the means of financing divestments

14.1 Introduction

A striking feature of the post-war business scene, throughout the world but particularly in the UK, is the extent of the use of various corporate restructuring devices. This feature has become more evident over time, perhaps promoted by the emergence of increasingly sophisticated techniques for achieving corporate restructures.

Changes in the economic environment and in the objectives being pursued by a particular business may be seen by that business as necessitating significant changes in its structure. Such changes may be concerned with the assets employed or with the manner in which those assets are financed, or with some combination of both of these. Whatever the precise nature of a particular corporate restructuring, logically it should be pursued to work towards the achievement of the business's objectives. On the assumption that the business's major financial objective is the maximisation of the shareholders' wealth, it is against that objective that the effectiveness of any particular restructuring should be assessed. Corporate restructuring is clearly a necessary and desirable feature of any dynamic and flexible economic environment. Despite the bad publicity that has attached to some aspects of certain corporate restructures, corporate restructuring is in essence a means for businesses to pursue their legitimate objectives.

We shall start our consideration of the major restructuring devices that are found at present in the UK by concentrating on two of the more important areas, namely takeovers (mergers) and divestments. Following that we shall look briefly at some other corporate restructuring devices found in the UK today.

14.2 Takeovers and mergers

In recent years, buying existing businesses in their entirety has become a very popular way of investing and growing. For example, **Cadbury Schweppes plc** says in its 2003 annual report: 'Through a series of acquisitions it [the Group] has strengthened existing positions and extended its presence in higher margin, faster growing product categories or geographies within its core market.' Later in the annual report, Cadbury Schweppes says: 'One element of the Group's strategy is to make targeted, value-enhancing acquisitions.' Not all businesses seek to expand in this way, nor do those that have done so necessarily do it habitually. The city pages of the national newspapers frequently tell us of an attempt on the ownership of some business or another, often with quite large ones as targets.

In practice this type of investment is typically effected by one business (the *bidder*) buying sufficient ordinary voting shares in the other one (the *target*) to be able to exercise control or even to have complete ownership.

→ Whether a particular situation is described as a takeover or as a merger is a matter of semantics. Where the two businesses are of similar size and/or there is agreement between the two sets of managements as to the desirability of the outcome, then it tends to be referred to as a 'merger'; otherwise the expression 'takeover' tends to be used. In this chapter, for convenience, we shall use the word 'merger' irrespective of the circumstances.

Despite certain apparent differences, from the bidder's viewpoint, between a merger and the more traditional investment opportunity, the same basic principles should be applied to its appraisal. That is to say, a merger that would represent a net increase in the current worth of the bidder (a positive net present value) should be pursued, if its financial objective is to be achieved.

Reasons for mergers

In theory, a business will become a bidder when it sees an opportunity to make an investment with a positive incremental net present value. It is likely to perceive such an opportunity, either:

- where it considers that the incremental cash flows from the investment, when discounted at a rate consistent with the level of risk associated with those cash flows, are positive; and/or
- where the reduction in the level of risk associated with the bidder's existing cash flows causes the appropriate rate for discounting those cash flows to fall, thus increasing the NPV of the existing cash flows of the bidder.

Frequently, a particular merger is attractive to the bidding business for both of these reasons.

Example 14.1

Bidder plc is expected to generate net positive cash flows of £1m p.a. for ever. The level of risk associated with these cash flows is perceived by the capital market as justifying a rate of return of 15 per cent p.a. Thus the net present value of Bidder is £1m/0.15 = £6.67m.

Bidder sees an opportunity to acquire the entire equity of Target plc. Forecasts indicate that the annual net positive cash flows of the merged business would be £1.5m for ever, and that the required rate of return would be 12 per cent p.a. The net present value of Bidder after the merger, should it take place, would become £1.5m/0.12 = £12.5m.

This would imply that it would be worth Bidder paying any amount up to £5.83 (£12.5m – £6.67m) for Target. Note that part of this amount arises from the existing cash flows of Bidder being discounted at a lower rate than previously. This factor would arise only where the merger had the effect of reducing risk.

It is quite feasible that £5.83m exceeds the current market value of Target. The reasons why this could be the case include:

- Target's expected cash flows being less than £0.5m p.a., that is, the merged business might be able to generate more expected cash flows than the sum of the expected cash flows of the separate businesses; and
- the possibility of the risk attaching to the combined business being less than applies to the overall level of risk of the separate parts.

Over the years, many observers have sought to identify the factors that make mergers attractive, particularly to the bidder. Let us now consider some of these factors and discuss each of them in the context of the overall risk reduction and cash flow expansion mentioned above.

Elimination or reduction of competition

Where the bidder and target are in competition for the market for their output, a merger could lead to a monopoly or at least a larger market share for the merged unit. This strength in the marketplace might enable prices to be raised without loss of turnover – hence an increase in cash flows. (As we shall see later in this chapter, in the UK such a merger may well fall foul of the Competition Commission.)

Safeguarding sources of supply or sales outlets

A bidder may be attracted to a merger where the target is a supplier of some vital raw material, which is in short supply or which the target could stop supplying, beyond the control of the bidder. Similarly, where the target represents a major sales outlet for the bidder, the target could cause problems for the bidder if it started to promote sales of the product of one of the bidder's competitors. Here a merger may not increase annual cash flows but it may well lower the perceived risk because the cash flows of both parts of the combined business would become more certain.

Access to the economies of scale that a larger business could yield

Economies of scale may be envisaged in a wide variety of areas. Such economies might include:

- greater buying power may lead to lower prices being paid for raw materials;
- larger production runs may become possible, leading to savings in set-up costs and other overheads;

- combining administration and accounting activities may lead to savings in the associated costs; and

- raising (issue costs) and servicing finance would tend to be on a larger scale and, possibly, cheaper therefore.

These economies of scale would tend to give rise to decreased total cash outflows.

Access to some aspect of the target that the bidder considers underutilised

Assets considered to be underutilised might include:

- particular tangible assets, including land, plant and cash, that are not fully exploited; and

- particular intangible assets such as its standing in some market, perhaps an export market or a particular contract; or technological expertise, which could be better exploited.

Underutilisation of assets suggests poor management, and bidders will sometimes be attracted to such targets where they have an abundance of management skills themselves. Businesses must seek ways of promoting rising management talent, and expansion through merger with mismanaged businesses provides an excellent means of creating opportunities for promotion. Underutilisation of assets implies the possibility of acquiring assets at a discount on their potential economic value.

The overall effect of such mergers would be expected to be an increase in positive cash flows, through stronger management skills being brought to bear on the target's assets. They may also decrease uncertainty about the cash flows, in other words, reduce risk.

Risk spreading and reduction through diversification

Merging two businesses with different activities will reduce risk since the returns from the different activities are unlikely to be perfectly positively correlated with one another.

Although this factor is frequently put forward as the justification for such mergers, in the context of maximisation of shareholders' wealth it is invalid. This is because, as we saw in Chapter 7, such diversification could be, and probably is, undertaken by individual shareholders at little or no cost. Having this done for them will not increase their wealth, because security market prices seem to assume that such diversification will already have taken place. The evidence on the success of mergers in practice, which we shall review later in the chapter, seems to indicate that 'diversifying' mergers are not successful.

As we saw in Chapter 2, this provides us with an example of possible conflict of interests between shareholders and managers – an agency problem. Shareholders are unlikely to be benefited by the merger because they will typically have undertaken such risk-reducing diversification on a 'homemade' basis.

The managers, on the other hand, do not hold portfolios of employments, so the only way that they can achieve this risk reduction is through diversification within the business. A popular way to diversify is through merger, though this would by no means be the only way.

Legislation to protect the public interest from monopolies has meant that mergers within the same industry have sometimes been impossible to achieve. This could leave businesses that are ambitious to expand with diversification as their only possibility. It should be noted that, irrespective of the benefits of diversification, the other reasons for merger could still apply to a particular case involving businesses in different industries. Even economies of scale, particularly in the administration of the merged business, could apply.

Synergy

We can see then that, in theory, mergers can bring real benefits to shareholders owing to genuine increases in positive cash flows and/or risk reduction. These benefits are often referred to as arising from synergy, a 'two plus two equals five' syndrome with the whole being greater than the sum of the parts.

We should note that these synergy benefits accrue to the shareholders of the target as well as to those of the bidder. Merger can take place only where target shareholders are prepared to sell their shares. They will do this only where they are offered something in excess of what they perceive to be the current value (usually the Stock Exchange quotation) of those shares. Unless the capital market and the management of the bidder are basing their valuations on different information from one another, this excess can only exist due to the synergy benefits perceived by the bidder's management.

Going back to Example 14.1, the excess of £5.83m over the current market value of the equity of Target is a measure of the value of the synergy benefits. If the current market value of Target's equity is as high as £5.83m then there will be no synergy benefits of merger and, from a financial viewpoint, it should not take place. If the market value of Target's equity immediately before the merger is below £5.83m but Bidder has to pay as much as this to persuade the shareholders to sell, then all of the benefits from synergy would accrue to Target's shareholders, and none of it to those of Bidder. It is therefore unlikely that Bidder would offer as much as the £5.83m.

14.3 Mergers: the practicalities

Financing mergers

It is important to realise that mergers are basically open market transactions, with one party buying assets belonging to another. How much the bidder offers and how it proposes to pay are matters of judgement, which must be decided by the management. Often, in practice, such decisions are made only after taking advice from experts, usually merchant bankers. As regards financing, the bidder must seek a method that is both attractive to the target's shareholders and acceptable to itself.

The following are commonly encountered approaches to merger financing.

Cash

Cash has its attractions to the recipients as it gives something that they can use immediately, either for consumption or reinvestment, without having to incur any cost. Target shareholders receiving shares or loan stock that they do not wish to keep must incur cost and effort to turn them into cash. The receipt of cash will, however, in most cases be treated as a disposal for capital gains tax purposes, and many shareholders would not welcome the possibility of a charge arising from this.

From the bidder's point of view, cash may not be available and can only be obtained by making a public issue of shares or loan stock for cash, or borrowing in some other form – a course of action that, for various reasons including cost, the bidder may not wish to follow.

Ordinary shares in the bidder business

Ordinary shares may be attractive to the recipients, who would simply cease being shareholders in the target and become shareholders in the bidder. Before the merger they hold shares in one business (the target) so are obviously not hostile to equity investment per se. This is not to say that they wish to hold shares in the bidder, in which case the problems of disposal, mentioned above, will come into play. From the bidder's viewpoint, issuing shares to exchange for those of the target has its attractions. Cash will not need to be raised, and the business will not be taking on the contractual commitments to pay interest or to repay capital, as would be the case with loan stock issues.

It is important to be clear that share issues have a cost to the bidder's original share-holders. Issuing shares as the consideration in a merger represents an opportunity cost to the bidder. If the target shareholders are prepared to accept bidder's shares, they must see the shares as being worth owning. In view of this, the shares issued could equally well have been for cash, either as rights or a public issue.

Loan stocks of the bidder business

Loan stocks have their part to play but may have serious disadvantages from both viewpoints, depending on the circumstances. As we have seen, loan stocks create binding contractual obligations on the bidder as regards both interest and capital repayment. To the equity holder of the target they represent a distinct change of investment: a change to a risk/return profile that they may find unacceptable. Switching back to equities will involve them in inconvenience and cost, possibly including a capital gains tax liability. The advantages of loan stocks in the merger context would seem to be twofold:

- To the bidder they would not have the effect of diluting control as a result of extending its share ownership (loan stockholders do not usually have votes at the annual general meeting).

- To the recipient they may have the attraction that, as they will have fixed interest payments and usually have a fixed capital repayment date, their market value is supported. Target shareholders who are sceptical about the future success of the merged business may prefer an investment in it whose returns are more certain than those from the equity capital.

As well as the specific factors referred to in respect of each financing method, the bidder will need to have regard to its desired level of gearing. Perceptions as to what this should be may well change with the merger. The bidder's management may feel that, owing to perceived changes in risk caused by the merger, the merged business's gearing potential is different from that of the bidder alone.

Table 14.1 shows how recent UK mergers have been financed. Although the mix varies from merger to merger and over time, it is clear that cash and ordinary shares of the bidder business are very much more important than preference shares and loan stock.

Possible reasons for the reduction in the number of takeovers since the late 1980s will be discussed later in this chapter when we are assessing the evidence on the success of mergers.

Table 14.1 Recent takeovers and mergers by industrial and commercial businesses within the UK

Year	Total number	Mean value £m	Cash %	Ordinary shares %	Preference shares and loan stocks %
1987	1528	10.8	35	60	5
1988	1499	15.2	70	22	8
1989	1337	20.4	82	13	5
1990	779	10.7	77	18	5
1991	506	20.6	70	29	1
1992	432	13.8	63	36	1
1993	526	13.4	81	16	3
1994	674	12.3	64	34	2
1995	505	64.5	78	20	2
1996	584	52.6	64	35	1
1997	506	53.0	41	58	1
1998	635	46.5	53	45	2
1999	439	53.1	62	37	1
2000	587	182.1	38	61	1
2001	492	58.9	–*	–*	–*
2002	430	58.7	–*	–*	–*
2003	558	33.5	–*	–*	–*
2004	694	45.0	–*	–*	–*

* These values were not published after 2000.

Source: Adapted from Office for National Statistics (2004), *Financial Statistics*, Table 6.1B.

The mean value of mergers was distinctly greater in the late 1990s and beyond than it had been in earlier years. There were many mergers in recent years that involved some very large businesses (the major high street banks, for example).

Appraisal of the merger

By the bidder

A merger is simply an investment, and should be appraised as one. The expected cash flows from the merged business must be estimated and discounted according to a cost of capital factor that incorporates consideration of market perceptions of the risk of the merged business, that is, the systematic risk. The cash flows that must be assessed will include all of the normal operating cash flows of the new undertaking. In addition, any cash flows arising from disposing of any unwanted divisions of the target (or of the bidder) arising from the merger, including any cost of making employees redundant, must be taken into account. We must also include the amount paid to acquire the target's equity. Where payment is not all in cash, the amount should include the opportunity cost of the equity and/or loan stock issue, that is, it should include the amount of cash that would have been received for the share/loan stock issue had it been made for cash, assuming that all other factors would have been the same.

If the net present value calculated from the above is positive, then, logically, the investment should be made.

There will usually be non-financial factors to consider, such as the acceptability of declaring employees redundant in order to gain potential economies of scale. These factors will have to be balanced with the strictly financial aspects when reaching a decision.

By the target's shareholders

Appraisal of the offer by the target's shareholders is just as much a capital investment decision as it is for the bidder. Each shareholder must assess whether future cash benefits from accepting the offer, suitably discounted, will exceed the discounted cash flow benefits of retaining the shares of the target.

What level of expertise and sophistication will be applied to this appraisal and whether it will be done at all, on the basis suggested above, depends on the individual shareholder. The large investing institutions will, it is presumed, reach their decisions on the basis of reason and logic. This may be less the case with the individual private investor.

Hostile and friendly mergers

The directors of many target businesses resist any merger attempts: in other words the mergers are 'hostile'. This may be for a variety of reasons, including:

- a belief that there is a lack of commercial logic in the merger;
- a feeling that the price being offered to the target shareholders for their shares is too low; and
- an understandable desire by the target business's directors to protect their personal futures. The immediate outcome of many mergers is the departure of some or all of the target's directors.

Hostile mergers tend to capture the headlines, though ones involving major businesses seem increasingly rare. The unsuccessful attempted hostile takeover of **Marks and Spencer plc** by Philip Green, the retailing entrepreneur who owns **British Home Stores Ltd**, attracted a lot of media attention during 2004.

An increasing number of mergers are 'friendly' rather than hostile. Here the directors of both businesses negotiate the terms and conditions that will be offered to the target's shareholders. When the formal bid is made, it is recommended, by the target's directors, that it should be accepted. The weight of such a recommendation tends to be sufficient to sway the shareholders to accept. An example of a friendly merger occurred when **easyJet plc**, the 'no frills' airline business, took over its rival **Go Fly Ltd** in May 2002. Another involved **Scottish and Newcastle plc**, the brewing business, taking over **HP Bulmer Holdings plc**, the cider maker in July 2003.

Regulation of mergers in the UK

In the UK, mergers are regulated in two ways, each by a different agency. The way in which this is done provides an interesting example of statutory regulation and self-regulation working hand in hand.

The Competition (formerly the Monopolies and Mergers) Commission

The Competition Commission is a statutory body which derives its power from the Fair Trading Act 1973. It is concerned with the outcome of the merger, rather than with the conduct of the merger operation itself.

The Competition Commission is empowered by statute to delay and to investigate any merger referred to it by the Secretary of State for Industry. The Secretary of State will refer a merger to the Commission on the advice of the Director General of Fair Trading when it is considered that it may be against the public interest for it to proceed. The Secretary of State will not usually refer a particular merger to the Commission unless a monopoly is likely to result. The Commission publishes its findings in reports that are sometimes long and detailed (see Relevant Websites at the end of this chapter).

In fact, relatively few of the many mergers that have taken place since the Commission was established have been referred to it. Of those that have been investigated, few have resulted in the Commission exercising its statutory power of veto in respect of them.

It seems that the Commission does not have great effect in restricting merger activity, nor is it intended to. The general philosophy of the legislation and of the Commission is that it is up to businesses and shareholders to decide on the economic desirability of particular mergers, with the state stepping in only when it fears that the public interest is threatened by the outcome of a merger. The Commission perceived such a threat when **William Morrison plc**, the supermarket business, sought to take over its rival **Safeway plc** in 2003. The Commission blocked the deal initially, while it investigated any possible threat to competition. It concluded that the deal could go ahead provided that the new group sold 53 of its stores. These stores were in locations where the competition had previously been between Morrison and Safeway, so the takeover would eliminate this. The stores were sold to other rival supermarkets and the takeover went ahead.

The City Panel on Takeovers and Mergers

The Panel is a self-regulatory body which includes in its membership representatives of most of the leading financial institutions of the City of London. These include the London Stock Exchange and the Committee of London Clearing Banks. The Panel and the Code that it administers were established in 1968, following a number of merger battles in the 1960s, which many observers saw as involving tactics that did not reflect well on big business and the financial institutions. Many of the less savoury encounters involved businesses that are (or were) household names, thus attracting a high level of media attention.

The main fears were that actions of the bidders' and of the targets' managements, particularly in cases where the bid was opposed by the target's management, were having adverse effects on shareholders, more particularly small shareholders, of the target. Specifically, it seemed that there were differences in the treatment of different shareholders regarding the quality and quantity of information each received pertaining to the merger.

The Code, which is constantly under review, comprises a set of rules defining the steps to be followed by both bidder and target in the course of the merger negotiations. The Code does not address itself to wider questions of the desirability of the merger; it deals only with the conduct of the merger process. The Panel has no statutory powers to enforce the Code, but it is able to apply moral pressure on offenders. Ultimately it can request that one of its members – the London Stock Exchange – excludes the offending business from listing.

Whether the Panel and the Code have achieved their objectives is a question open to debate, though most observers appear to feel that much of the more extravagant behaviour evident in the 1960s is not obvious today.

Practical steps towards the merger

Most mergers are effected by the bidder buying, from the target's shareholders, sufficient ordinary shares to give control or even total ownership of the equity. This is usually done in two stages:

- by the bidder buying shares, for cash, through the Stock Exchange; and then
- by its making a formal offer to remaining shareholders by direct mailing and therefore outside the established capital market.

It is not common for bidders to acquire a large proportion of the required shares by buying them in the capital market. Once investors realise that there is a large buyer in the market, the share price will tend to rise in anticipation of a formal offer, making it uneconomical for the bidder to proceed further in this way. The formal offer to each shareholder becomes cheaper at the point where the capital market quotation reaches the proposed formal offer price. Of course, all capital market purchases have to be paid for in cash, which may be a disincentive to a bidder who wishes to finance the merger in some other way. The formal offer document, which is usually communicated to shareholders by post, contains the precise terms of the offer and a statement explaining why, in the view of the bidder's management, it should be accepted. The offer document must be submitted for the approval of the Director General of Fair Trading and of the City Panel.

Usually, offers are made on condition that they are accepted by the owners of a specified percentage of the shares concerned. In this way the bidder can ensure that, in the event of insufficient acceptances being forthcoming, it will not end up being forced to buy shares that it may not want. If, for example, the bidder wishes to obtain a minimum of 60 per cent of the shares of the target, it would probably prefer not to be forced to buy, say, 25 per cent if the owners of the other 75 per cent decide not to accept the offer. The proportion of 90 per cent is often stated on offer documents because UK company law gives any business that owns that percentage of the equity of another business the right to acquire the remaining 10 per cent, with or without the consent of their owners, on the same terms as those on which the others were acquired.

A question that the target shareholders must consider on receiving the offer is whether to accept this particular offer or to hope for an improved one. While the failure of an offer can cause the bidder to withdraw, frequently the bidder's reaction is to make an increased offer. This can be a difficult question for the shareholder because withdrawal by the bidder will probably result in the quoted share price of the target dropping back, from the high figure that it will probably have reached in the light of the offer, to the pre-offer price. On the other hand, rejection of the first offer is quite likely to result in a better one. Perhaps, though, this is no worse than the dilemma that all shareholders experience when they see their shares quoted at a high price: should they sell and take advantage of it or should they wait, in the hope that the price will go even higher?

The management of the target is most unlikely to react passively to advances made by a bidder to the target shareholders. Quite often the bidder will seek the support of the target management in advance of its formal offer. If the management supports the offer, perhaps because it feels that there is commercial logic in such a merger, it is likely that the offer document will include a statement by the target's management to that effect.

Frequently, however, the target's management will be hostile to the offer and will oppose it with some vigour. Typical tactics employed by hostile target management include:

- issuing statements countering the claims of the bidder and putting forward the arguments for remaining independent;
- revaluing the target's assets in an attempt to show that the bidder's offer under-values them; and
- releasing other information relevant to the target's future as an independent business.

The object of these tactics is probably to increase the share price of the target to a point where the bidder's offer looks low and will be rejected.

Quite often, these battles are long and bitter, with claims of one side being met with counter-claims from the other, and offers being increased, until eventually an offer is accepted or the bidder withdraws. The battles can be damaging; they are expensive and, if the merger finally takes place, much bitterness can be carried into the management of the merged business.

The results of the battle are not necessarily all bad. Much new information about both parties tends to be forthcoming in statements, and this enables the market to value the businesses better.

Are mergers successful?

Having looked at why and how mergers occur, it seems appropriate to ask whether or not they appear to be successful. Numerous studies have considered this question. These have fallen broadly into two types:

- those that have asked managers of merged businesses whether they consider the merger to have been successful or not; and
- those that have looked at the returns available to the shareholders of merged businesses to see whether these were better than they were likely to have been had the merger not taken place. Returns in this context are capital gains, plus dividends for the period as a percentage of the share's market value at the start of the period.

Opinions of managers

The general conclusion of managers seems to be that the mergers had not been beneficial. Coopers and Lybrand (1993) undertook a study during 1992, which comprised interviews with senior managers of 50 large UK businesses that had been involved in a merger. The conclusion was that 54 per cent of mergers were not financially successful. This was remarkably consistent with the results of an earlier Coopers and Lybrand study, conducted in 1973, and with those of Newbould (1970). The 1993 study identified several major causes of failure. These are set out in Table 14.2.

Stock market returns

The results from studies of stock market returns consistently show gains for the target business shareholders. The benefits to the bidders' shareholders are less clear.

Franks, Broyles and Hecht (1977) found significant gains to the target shareholders, particularly in the period leading up to the merger. They also found no detriment to

Table 14.2 Causes of failure of UK mergers

Cause of failure	% of interviewees who mentioned the factor as a cause of failure
Management attitudes	85
Lack of post-acquisition integration planning	80
Lack of knowledge by the bidder of the target and its industry	45
Poor management and management practices in the target	45
Little or no experience of the bidder management in acquiring other businesses	30

Source: Coopers and Lybrand (1993).

the bidder's shareholders, either before or after the merger; in fact this group made small gains.

Franks and Harris (1989), using a large sample of UK mergers, found gains for both sets of shareholders during the pre-merger and immediate post-merger periods. They also found, however, post-merger losses by the bidder's shareholders. Limmack (1991) came to a similar conclusion to that of Franks and Harris. Post-merger losses to bidder shareholders were also found by Gregory (1997) in his examination of a number of UK mergers. He found that, where cash was the consideration, there tended to be neither gains nor losses. Where, however, the bidder's equity was used, significant losses of bidder's shareholders' wealth were observed.

Draper and Paudyal (1999) found that shareholders in the target businesses benefit substantially from takeover activity, particularly where they are given the option to receive either cash or shares in the bidder as the consideration. It seems that the bidder's shareholders do not suffer from the merger. They also found that the benefits to target shareholders have declined in the recent past.

Walker (2000) found that US takeovers between 1980 and 1996 that were diversifications caused a loss of the bidder's shareholder value. On the other hand, takeovers that expanded the bidder's existing activity led to a gain in shareholder value.

Fuller, Netter and Stegemoller (2002) found that, in the USA, bidder shareholders gain when buying an unlisted business, but lose when buying a listed one. They also found that the gains were greater with larger targets and where the consideration is discharged in shares rather than cash.

Bruner (2004) argued that the approach taken by many of the studies based on US takeovers were flawed in that the research results were unduly influenced by a relatively small number of failures that involved particularly large businesses. He claimed that all takeovers benefit target shareholders and the overwhelming majority benefit bidder shareholders as well.

Conclusion on the success of mergers

The conclusion is unclear. It can be argued that, in the context of the objective of shareholder wealth enhancement, the opinions of managers (the subject of the first group of studies) are not important. It is economic returns that count. There seems to be evidence that takeovers can be economically beneficial to both sets of shareholders, but that this is not always the case for those of the bidder. As far as the evidence goes, it appears that mergers involving targets that operate in the same area of business as the bidder tend to be successful: in other words, diversifying mergers are not successful.

This lack of clarity on the benefits of mergers may well explain why the number of UK mergers seems to have reduced fairly dramatically since the late 1980s (see Table 14.1). Other possible reasons include:

- a greater professionalism among corporate management leading to fewer cheap targets; and

- a change in the perceptions of corporate managers of the desirability of large, diversified units. This point is raised again, in the context of divestment, later in this chapter.

International mergers

The increasing internationalisation of commerce has led to mergers between businesses in different countries. The EU's single market, which started in 1993, seems to have led to UK businesses being particularly active in mergers with those in other EU countries. For example, in 2001, **Lafarge Group** the French-based cement and building business, bought **Blue Circle Industries plc**, a similar UK business.

14.4 Divestments

In certain circumstances a business may wish to sell off some part of its operation, perhaps a division or subsidiary company. Possible reasons for this are considered below.

A desire to concentrate on its core activities

A business operating in a range of areas of business, either as a result of organic growth or following mergers, may decide that it would prefer to concentrate on its main area of expertise. Such rationalisations have become quite common recently and possibly reflect a view, which we shall discuss in Chapter 16, that the future lies with smaller, more focused businesses.

An example of a recent sell-off, where the reason given was a desire to concentrate on core activities, was provided by **Northern Foods plc**, the food products business that supplies prepared meals to several leading UK supermarkets. Northern Foods sold that part of its business that makes Fox's glacier mints, and some other well-known confectionery brands, to **Big Bear Ltd**, in September 2003.

Datta and Iskandar-Datta (1996), looking at UK data, found that divestments aimed at the sale of assets that do not strategically fit the business's core activities tend to be beneficial to shareholders' wealth.

A wish to get rid of some part of its business that is causing problems

One typical problem would be a lack of profitability. This reason, together with the desire to concentrate on core activities, perhaps provides an example of the opposite of synergy, that is, a 'five plus one equals four' syndrome, where the sum of the parts is greater than the whole.

A need to raise cash

The need to raise cash may arise from a desire to make investments in other parts of the business, perhaps including a merger. The reason given for many recent sell-offs has been the desire to raise cash to enable a reduction in the level of capital gearing.

Marks and Spencer plc, the UK retail business, sold off some of its financial services division (**M and S Money**) to **HSBC plc**, the banking business, in November 2004 for £762m. It was believed in this case that the funds were needed to help finance a major share repurchase that Marks and Spencer undertook in late 2004.

GKN plc, the engineering business, sold its 50 per cent of its helicopter division (**AgustaWestland**) to its co-owner, the Italian business **Finmeccanica SpA**. The deal, which took place in July 2004, raised £1bn in cash. GKN expected to use the cash to pay off some debt and to pursue possible acquisitions of new businesses.

Some sell-offs, particularly those involving smaller businesses might be caused by a need to raise cash to avoid being forced into liquidation (bankruptcy) as a result of an inability to meet financial obligations. The sale of leading players by some English Premier League football clubs (for example, **Leeds United**, who were subsequently relegated) over recent years provides examples of this.

→ In effect, divestments are the opposite of mergers. Indeed, many of the divestments that have occurred recently were of subsidiaries acquired by apparently rash mergers during the 1970s and 1980s.

When assessing the effectiveness of a divestment, the corporate objectives of both seller and buyer should be the touchstone. Assuming that shareholder wealth is the major financial criterion, both parties should undertake an NPV analysis of the financial benefits and costs.

There are various means that are used to effect divestments, the more important of which we shall briefly consider.

Management buyouts

→ In a management buyout (MBO), the managers of the part of the business that is to be disposed of buy it from the business. MBOs have grown enormously in number over recent years in the UK. In 1980, there were about 100 (KPMG Corporate Finance), but during 2000 there were over 600 (Centre for Management Buy-out Research 2004). The number has since dropped, to about 400 in 2004. The average value of the buyout has also increased dramatically, from a mean of £0.4m in 1980 to around £50m per buyout in 2000.

An interesting example of an MBO occurred in 2001 when **Go Fly Ltd** (Go), the low-cost airline operation, was bought from **British Airways plc** (BA), by a group of Go managers. Barbara Cassani, who had been the chief executive since BA created Go to compete with the independent low-cost operators, led the MBO. BA sold Go because it felt that Go did not fit in with its normal activity of providing full service to its passengers. The deal was worth about £100m. Go was subsequently the subject of a friendly merger with **easyJet plc** in 2002.

Some MBOs have proved to be very successful, and have led to stock market flotations of the bought-out undertakings. Some of these have made millionaires of the managers concerned. **office2office plc**, a business that provides office supplies, was floated on the London Stock Exchange in June 2004. Managers who had invested in the buyout of the business saw the value of their investment yield about six and a half times what they had paid for it in December 2000: a floated value of about £65m. These returns should be set against the risk that the managers took in making the investment.

Since the managers are unlikely to be able to raise all of the cash necessary to make the buyout, some fairly complicated financing arrangements have been developed. Loans have accounted for much of the finance: hence the label 'leveraged buyout' ('leverage' is another word for 'gearing'). The high level of gearing required has engendered relatively high-risk, high-coupon-rate lending, known as 'junk bonds'. 'Mezzanine' finance has also been a feature of a number of management buyouts. This is basically a high-coupon-rate loan with equity possibilities. Usually there is some right to convert the loan finance into equity, but only if the business, through which the MBO is effected, becomes listed on the Stock Exchange. The evidence on the success of MBOs is thin and inconclusive; however, it appears that managers taking over the business that they run is a phenomenon that is likely to continue to occur.

Buy-ins

→ In a buy-in a group of individuals puts together an offer for part, or possibly all, of a business with which they have previously had no particular connection. Like MBOs, buy-ins became increasingly popular in the 1980s and 1990s. According to the Centre for Management Buy-out Research, there was just one UK buy-in, worth £0.5m, during 1979. By 2000 this had increased to about 200 each year. Most of the features of MBOs are present with buy-ins, including the means of financing such deals. Many buy-ins involve very large sums of money.

The disposal of Fox's confectionery business by **Northern Foods plc**, mentioned above, was to a buy-in team. Another example was when **Caterham Cars Ltd** was sold to a buy-in team in January 2005. Caterham Cars makes specialist sports cars. It was founded (in 1973), managed and owned by the Nearn family, until the sale. Ansar Ali, who had worked for **Lotus Cars Ltd** as a senior manager, led the buy-in team. **Corven Ventures Ltd**, a venture-capital provider, financially backed the deal. (Venture capital is relatively low amounts of finance provided to growing small businesses. Chapter 16 discusses venture capital.)

Buy-ins seem to occur quite often where the majority shareholder of a small family-type business wishes to retire.

Sell-offs

→ Sell-offs involve one established business selling part of its operations (that is, a set of assets) to another established business, normally for cash. A sell-off can be an alternative to a merger. The assets of the selling business, perhaps all of its assets, are sold to another business, leaving the selling business with the debts to settle.

An example of a recent sell-off occurred in late 2004, when **Peninsular and Oriental Steam Navigation Company plc** (P and O), the UK shipping and transport business, sold off La Manga, the sports and leisure resort situated in Spain, to **MedGroup Leisure Investment MV**, a Spanish business, for £102m.

Spin-offs

→ In a spin-off, part of a business is floated (spun off) as a separate, new (probably listed) business, and the existing shareholders receive the appropriate number of shares in the new business. There is no change in ownership, except that the shareholders directly own the spun-off part, instead of owning it through the intermediary of the original business. The reasons for doing this might include:

- a desire to give the spun-off business its own distinct corporate identity; and
- to avoid a takeover attempt on the whole business. The value of the spun-off portion may have been underestimated as part of the value of the original business, except perhaps by a potential predator. By spinning off a particularly valuable part of the business, the market will have the opportunity to assess that part as a separate unit. This may make it unattractive to predators. This point implies a lack of belief in the efficiency of the capital market.

In 2000, **P and O plc**, spun off its cruise shipping activity. Here, P and O shareholders retained their original shares but were given one share in the spun-off business, **P and O Princess Cruises plc**, for each one that they held in P and O. Both businesses were listed from the date of the spin-off. In his letter to the P and O shareholders detailing the arrangements for the spin-off, the chairman said: 'It will enable both the future P and O and P and O Princess Cruises to pursue independently the strategies that best meet their long-term objectives. Furthermore, the demerger should ensure that the value of both businesses is more fully recognised by the market as investors are better able to assess each business's individual attributes.'

In 2001, **Kingfisher plc**, a UK group that owns a number of retail outlets, spun off **Woolworth Group plc**, the high street retailer. The purpose seems to be to enable Kingfisher to concentrate on what it sees as its core activity in the 'do-it-yourself' area of retailing.

Summary

Mergers (takeovers)

- Merger = buying sufficient shares in another business to control it.
- It is an alternative to organic growth (organic growth is where the business expands through new, internally generated, projects).
- Mergers assessed by bidder business and target shareholders on NPV principles, logically from a shareholder wealth perspective.
- Reasons for mergers:
  - Elimination or reduction of competition.
  - Safeguarding sources of supply or sales outlets.
  - Access to economies of scale.
  - Access to an underutilised asset.
  - Spreading risk through diversification.
  - Synergy ('2 + 2 = 5').
- Financing merger – needs to be acceptable to bidder and appealing to target shareholders.
  - Cash – gives the recipient options; may have tax ramifications for recipient.
  - Shares – can be popular with target shareholders, but control of bidder is diluted; also has gearing ramifications for bidder.

- Loan stock, may not be popular with investor who currently owns equities; also has gearing ramifications for bidder.
- The success of mergers is mixed, recent ones have tended to be less successful.

Divestment

- Divestment = a business parting with some aspect of itself to:
  - concentrate on 'core activities';
  - rid itself of a troublesome investment;
  - raise cash.
- Management buyouts (MBOs):
  - MBO = the sale of part of a business to a group of staff.
  - Often financed with quite a high level of debt – 'leveraged' buyouts.
- Buy-in = a group of people outside the business buys part of a business.
- Sell-off = one established business selling part of its operations to another established business.
- Spin-off:
  - Spin-off = taking a part of a business, placing it inside a new business and issuing shares to shareholders in the original business pro rata the number of shares owned by each.
  - Usually done for one of two reasons:
    - To give the spun-off business its own distinct corporate identity in an attempt to increase overall shareholder wealth.
    - To avoid a takeover of the whole of the business, by placing a particularly attractive part outside the rest of the business.

Further reading

Samuels, Wilkes and Brayshaw (1998) and Arnold (2002) both give good coverage of most aspects of corporate restructuring, in a UK context.

Relevant websites

The Centre for Management Buy-outs Research site gives access to up-to-date information on management buy-ins and buyouts.
www.nottingham.ac.uk/business/cmbor

The site of the Competition Commission contains access to information on the work of the Commission and to reports commissioned by it.
www.competition-commission.org.uk

The websites of businesses featured in this chapter are:

AgustaWestland	www.agustawestland.com
British Airways plc	www.britishairways.com
British Home Stores Ltd	www.bhs.co.uk
Cadbury Schweppes plc	www.cadburyschweppes.com
Caterham Cars Ltd	www.caterham.co.uk
Corven Ventures Ltd	www.corven.com

easyJet plc	www.easyjet.com
FinmeccanicaSpA	www.finmeccanica.it
GKN plc	www.gknplc.com
HP Bulmer Holdings plc	www.bulmer.com
HSBC plc	www.hsbc.co.uk
Kingfisher plc	www.kingfisher.co.uk
Lafarge Group	www.lafarge.com
Leeds United Football Club	www.leedsunited.com
Lotus Cars Ltd	www.lotuscars.com
Marks & Spencer plc	www.marksandspencer.com
Northern Foods plc	www.northern-foods.co.uk
office2office plc	www.office2office.biz
P and O Princess Cruises plc	www.pocruises.com
The Peninsular and Oriental Steam Navigation Company plc	www.p-and-o.com
Scottish and Newcastle plc	www.scottish-newcastle.com
William Morrison plc	www.morrisons.co.uk
Woolworth Group plc	www.woolworths.co.uk

REVIEW QUESTIONS

Suggested answers to review questions appear in Appendix 3.

14.1 Is corporate restructuring a good thing for businesses that are pursuing a shareholder wealth maximisation objective? Explain your response.

14.2 How should shareholders in a 'target' logically assess an offer for their shares (on a share-for-share exchange basis) from the bidder?

14.3 What is the general stance of UK monopolies regulation with regard to mergers and takeovers?

14.4 What is the difference between a management buy-in and a management buyout?

14.5 What is the difference between a sell-off and a spin-off?

14.6 Generally, have mergers in the UK been successful?

PROBLEMS

Sample answers to problems marked with an asterisk appear in Appendix 4.

(Problems 14.1 and 14.2 are basic-level problems, whereas problems 14.3 and 14.4 are more advanced and may contain some practical complications.)

14.1* ABB plc has a cost of capital of 20 per cent p.a., and it is expected to generate annual end of year cash inflows of £12m a year for ever.

The capital projects department has identified a smaller business, CDD Ltd, which it is believed would be a suitable takeover target for ABB plc. It is estimated that the combined operation would have a perpetual end-of-year cash inflow of £14m.

ABB plc's capital projects department analysts estimate that it would be worth the business paying up to £27.5m to acquire the entire equity of CDD Ltd.

What cost of capital must the analysts have estimated for the combined operation? (Ignore taxation.)

14.2 Taking the same circumstances as in Problem 14.1, without the takeover CDD Ltd had expected annual end-of-year cash inflows of £1.5m for ever, and an estimated cost of capital of 18 per cent p.a.

What is the minimum that the shareholders of CDD Ltd should logically accept for their shares in the takeover?

Logically, what should be the finally agreed total price for CDD Ltd's equity?

14.3* Thruster plc is a dynamic, expanding business. Relaxation plc is a solid but unambitious one operating in the same industry. Thruster plc has recently launched a takeover bid for Relaxation plc. The offer is that Thruster plc will give one of its shares to shareholders in Relaxation plc for every three of their shares.

After-tax cost savings are estimated to be £8m p.a. as a result of administrative efficiencies, compared with the total costs historically incurred by the two businesses.

Summarised financial statements for the two businesses for the year just ended are as follows:

Profit and loss account

	Thruster plc £m	Relaxation plc £m
Turnover	650	200
Profit before tax	72	17
Taxation	24	6
Profit after tax	48	11
Dividends	7	5
Retained profit for the year	41	6

Balance sheet as at the end of the year just ended

	Thruster plc £m	Relaxation plc £m
Non-current assets	350	200
Working capital	110	50
	460	250
Less: Long-term liabilities	180	60
	280	190
Equity		
Ordinary shares of £0.50 each	170	90
Reserves	110	100
	280	190
Pre-bid price/earnings ratio (P/E)	18	14

Observers believe that, following the takeover, the P/E ratio of Thruster plc will be 16.

Assuming that the market value of their shareholdings is the only factor of concern, would the shareholders of each business welcome a successful takeover?

14.4 Expansion plc has consistently expanded its activities over the past decade, partly through takeover and partly through retention of much of its operating profits. Consolidation plc operates in a mature, stable industry. Expansion plc is about to launch a takeover bid for the entire equity of Consolidation plc. The offer will be that Expansion plc will give one of its shares for every ten shares in Consolidation plc.

Analysts at Expansion plc believe that there are potential savings in total after-tax administrative costs of the merged operation, relative to the existing total administrative cost of the two businesses, totalling £10m.

Summarised financial statements for the year just ended are as follows:

Profit and loss account

	Expansion plc £m	Consolidation plc £m
Turnover	940	730
Profit before tax	156	75
Taxation	52	25
Profit after tax	104	50
Dividends	20	40
Retained profit for the year	84	10

Balance sheet as at the end of the year just ended

	Expansion plc £m	Consolidation plc £m
Net assets	1750	2400
Less: Long-term liabilities	870	1150
	880	1250
Equity		
Ordinary shares of £0.50 each	400	1000
Reserves	480	250
	880	1250
Pre-bid price/earnings ratio (P/E)	25	10

Observers believe that, following the takeover, the P/E ratio of Expansion plc will be 20. It seems likely that Expansion plc will continue to distribute the same proportion of its after-tax profits as in the most recent year.

Assuming that both sets of shareholders are concerned both with the level of dividends and with the market price of their shares, how would the shareholders of each business be likely to react to the takeover offer?

There are both a set of **multiple-choice questions** and **missing-word questions** available on the website. These specifically cover the material contained in this chapter. These can be attempted and graded (with feedback) online.

There is also an **additional problem**, with solution, that relates to the material covered in this chapter.

Go to **www.pearsoned.co.uk/atrillmclaney** and follow the links.

Chapter 15

International aspects of business finance

Objectives In this chapter we shall deal with the following:

→ the nature of international business

→ foreign exchange markets

→ theories and evidence on exchange rate relationships

→ exchange rate, economic and translation risk

→ foreign investment

→ modern portfolio theory and risks of internationalisation

15.1 Introduction

A striking feature of many modern businesses is the extent to which they are international in one or more aspects of their activities. Take, for example, **Cadbury Schweppes plc**, which specialises in making confectionery and soft drinks. This is ostensibly a UK business, to the extent that its head office is in London and its shares are listed, and principally traded, on the London Stock Exchange. According to the business's 2003 annual report, however:

- about 87 per cent of its employees are based outside the UK;

- about 84 per cent of its turnover is made outside the UK;

- about 90 per cent of its non-current (fixed) assets are located outside the UK;

- it has manufacturing plants in 36 different countries, in many parts of the world, as well as in the UK;

- some of its production, both UK and overseas, is exported to countries outside the country of manufacture;

- it obtains much of its raw materials from outside the countries of manufacture;

- a large part of its long- and short-term borrowing is from outside the UK; and

- its ordinary shares are listed on the New York Stock Exchange as well as the UK one, which implies that foreign institutions and individuals own a significant percentage of the shares.

Cadbury Schweppes is, perhaps, one of the more international of UK businesses, but it is by no means an unusual case. Most larger businesses, and a great number of smaller ones, resemble the internationalism of Cadbury Schweppes, to some extent.

A glance at Table 8.1 on page 218 indicates the extent to which UK listed businesses borrowed in non-sterling currencies recently.

Why do businesses internationalise?

Presumably, businesses become international in a bid to achieve their corporate objective of shareholder wealth maximisation.

Importing and exporting

Without certain raw materials only available, or more cheaply available, outside the home country, many businesses would not be able to produce their products or services. Cadbury Schweppes plc, for example, would not be able to manufacture chocolate in the UK, unless it imported cocoa.

Exporting enables the business to reach larger markets for its output. It may be that the home market is saturated with its product, and the only means of profitable expansion is into foreign markets. Possibly the business has the choice of expanding both in the home market and by exporting, but pursues the foreign market because it offers better returns.

Overseas investment

Direct investment in facilities in a foreign country may make it more economic to supply other local foreign markets with goods or services, or even the home one. Many UK businesses have call centres located outside the UK (India seeming to be a popular location) from which they supply services to UK customers.

Manufacturing in a location close to the market obviously reduces transport costs. Production costs may be lower at certain foreign locations, such that it might be cheaper to manufacture there for export to the home market. Local manufacture may be the only profitable means of entering certain markets. For example, the attraction of the UK as a manufacturing location for certain Japanese car producers is not just to avoid the transport costs that would be associated with manufacture in Japan. Were the cars not made in one of the EU member states, the businesses would face effective tariff barriers when trying to sell their cars anywhere in the EU. There might also be more willingness of EU citizens to buy a car that was locally made.

Overseas financing

The home capital market may not offer the cheapest or most suitable funding options. In theory, the relatively free movement of capital should mean that financing costs would be the same wherever the cash is raised, but imperfections in the market mean that this is not always the case.

It is probably true for many businesses, and for an increasing number of them, both large and small, that they see themselves as players on the world stage. For a UK business, a customer in Moscow is as important and desirable as one in Middlesborough, all things being equal. Similarly, a source of finance in Tokyo is more attractive than one in London, if the cost is less, again all other things being equal.

Internationalisation and risk reduction

Internationalisation can offer opportunities for diversification of risk, and, it seems, many businesses are attracted to it for that reason. The risk of an economic slump in the home market may be able to be countered by the possibility that the slump would not affect foreign markets. We shall pick up the arguments about risk and international diversification later in the chapter.

Internationalisation and shareholders' wealth

It seems then that refusing to be constrained by national boundaries can offer an increased number of investment opportunities. It can also provide the possibility of lowering the cost of capital. This is illustrated in Figure 15.1. The red curved line shows the investment opportunities available to a business, assuming that it buys its supplies in the home country and sells only in the home market. To the left are the most profitable opportunities, which the business will take first. As these are exploited, the business moves to the right, to the less advantageous ones. The red straight, horizontal line is the cost of finance, assuming that the business uses only home country sources of finance. It would choose to invest in all of the projects up to point A, where the return on the investment just equals the cost of financing it.

The two blue lines represent the investment opportunities and the financing cost where the business exploits overseas opportunities. There are higher-yielding investment projects, and the average cost of finance is less. This now means that the business would invest in all projects up to point B, and the return on the various investments is the vertical distance between the blue lines. Thus it will be more effective at generating wealth for its shareholders, both because it is confronted by a higher number of profitable opportunities and because the cost of finance is less.

Figure 15.1 is obviously very simplified and theoretical. In real life, at any particular point in time, the best investment opportunities may lie in the home country.

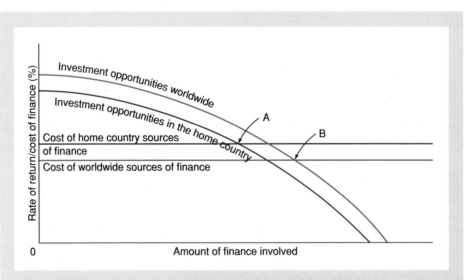

Figure 15.1
The investment opportunities and cost of finance for a business assuming (A) a strictly home country outlook and (B) an international one

When the business looks only to the home market, a home country productive base, and exclusively home country sources of finance, it will invest in all opportunities to the left of point A. It will earn returns equal to the vertical distance between the two red lines for each investment. If the business embraces internationalism, the number of profitable opportunities expands and the cost of finance reduces (the blue lines), leading to larger returns and greater wealth generation.

Similarly, at the particular time that the business is looking for new finance, the home country capital market may be the cheapest source. In the long run, however, businesses that widen their commercial horizons are likely to generate more wealth.

It would be wrong to see internationalisation of business as a new phenomenon. It is certainly true that internationalisation is, for various reasons, much easier than it used to be. Nevertheless, many businesses, in Europe and the USA in particular, have traded internationally on a large scale for over a century. Today's internationalisation is at a level that would have been unimaginable as recently as twenty years ago.

Having established that, in principle, internationalism is an economically beneficial approach, the remainder of this chapter will be concerned with identifying the problems associated with businesses being international, and with practical approaches to dealing with those problems.

15.2 Foreign exchange

One of the biggest and most obvious problems of internationalism is the fact that not all countries use the same currency and that the relative values of any two currencies may alter over time, sometimes with significant alterations occurring over very short periods. Between certain countries, in particular time periods, the individual national governments agree to 'peg' their currencies to those of the others in the agreement. For example, most EU countries (not including the UK) were in an agreement to keep their currencies pegged to one another, subject to minor fluctuations, for many years leading up to the introduction of the common currency (the euro) in 1999. Of course, the introduction of the euro was a move to a more permanent and concrete removal of the tendency for relative movements in currency values. Although such agreements and arrangements exist, were you to select at random any two of the world's trading nations, it is unlikely that they would both be members of the same currency group, and therefore you would expect exchange rate movements between the two currencies over time. This is a particular problem because the business does not know for certain the value of a particular transaction, in terms of the home currency.

Before we go on to look more closely at the problems of shifts in relative values of currencies, and at how businesses can manage this problem, it will probably be useful to take a brief look at the way in which foreign exchange markets operate, and why relative currency values can shift over time.

The need for foreign exchange markets

When a business sells goods or services to a foreign customer, the transaction will normally require some foreign currency be converted into the home currency, sooner or later. Although a sale may be made in the foreign currency, the seller will normally need to have its home currency to pay its employees and suppliers, to pay its taxes and to pay dividends. Those, in the home country, to whom the business has financial obligations, will not normally be prepared to accept anything other than the home currency in settlement. If the sale is made in the home currency, the foreign customer will normally need to convert its local (foreign) currency to that of the seller (home currency). The word 'normally' is used in the preceding sentences because, in particular circumstances, the conversion may not be necessary. For example, the foreign customer may have the required amount of the seller's home currency, perhaps from a sale that it has made to a home country customer. Possibly the seller has a financial obligation, unconnected with the present transaction, which will need to be met in the foreign currency. However, generally, and in the long run, a sale to a foreign customer will require that some foreign currency is 'sold' to 'buy' the required amount of the home currency.

What is the foreign exchange market?

The market in which one currency is converted into another is known as the *foreign exchange market*. This market is operated by commercial banks, national central banks (the Bank of England in the UK), brokers and others. The market does not have a particular location, but part of it exists anywhere that one currency is converted into another. When we are preparing to travel overseas and arrange to take some of the currency of the destination country with us, we might well do this through our normal bank. Here, we and the bank form part of the foreign exchange market. If you had a few dollar bills left following a visit to the USA and exchanged these for sterling with a friend who was shortly to go there, you and your friend would briefly form part of the foreign exchange market.

Dealing in foreign exchange

When dealing with foreign exchange professionals, it is normally possible to trade on either of two bases. The currencies can be exchanged immediately, at today's rate, known as the **spot rate**. Alternatively, the contract can be to exchange the currencies at some specified future date, at a rate determined today, known as the **forward rate**. For reasons that will be discussed shortly, the spot and forward rates are frequently different from one another.

When foreign exchange dealers are approached with a view to a spot foreign exchange transaction, they will quote two rates at which they will deal: one at which they will sell and one at which they are prepared to buy. For example, dealers may be prepared to accept $1.96 in exchange for £1, but only be prepared to give you $1.95 in exchange for £1. This is to say that they will sell you £1 for a price of $1.96, but will pay only $1.95 to buy £1 from you. In reality, for most commercial transactions, the difference between the two rates is usually rather closer than in this example. The 'spread' (difference between the two rates) represents the dealers' profit. The existence of this spread means that there is a cost involved in using the foreign exchange market. The size of the spread tends to reflect the efficiency of the market, the volatility of the exchange rate concerned, and the size of the transaction involved. Where the market is efficient, the volatility of the exchange rate low and the transaction a large one, the spread tends to be smallest.

How are foreign exchange rates determined?

If we had looked at the financial pages of our newspaper in early 2005, we should have seen that £1 sterling was worth about US$1.95. Why was that the rate at that time? The answer is that the free market, that is, a market subject to the laws of supply and demand, determines the rate. Relative supply and demand is caused, in turn, by the extent to which individuals, businesses and institutions want to convert dollars into sterling or sterling into dollars.

There are broadly five reasons why individuals, businesses or institutions may wish to convert the home currency into a foreign one or vice versa:

- To enable them to exchange cash, received from a sale of goods or services in a foreign currency, to the home currency.

- To enable them to pay for goods or services in the relevant foreign currency (including taking a holiday in the foreign country concerned).

- Because they may feel that they would rather hold part of their wealth in the foreign currency.

- To speculate, for example by buying a particular foreign currency in the expectation, or hope, that its value will appreciate in relation to the home one.

- In the case of a central bank, to enable it to manage, or to try to manage, the exchange rate between the two currencies.

The first and second of these are obvious enough. If these were the only reasons for the existence of foreign exchange markets, exchange rates would tend to reflect the relative exports and imports of goods and services between the two countries.

Individuals, businesses and institutions may prefer to hold part or all of their wealth in the foreign currency rather than in the home currency. This might be because they have a belief that the foreign currency will strengthen relative to the home one, so that they could convert back at a later date and have more of the home currency than they had originally.

They may alternatively prefer to convert to the foreign currency to enable them to lend money to a borrower in the foreign country, who pays a higher rate of interest than is obtainable in the home country. The relative strength of sterling in the late 1990s and early 2000s was ascribed to this factor. During that period, UK interest rates were relatively high compared with those of many other economies. Governments, through their central banks, ultimately determine interest rates. A government might choose to have high interest rates to strengthen its currency in an attempt to manage the exchange rate to achieve some objective, such as holding exchange rates relatively fixed ('pegged') against certain other currencies. This was not the case in the UK recently, however. The high UK rate of interest was the Bank of England's weapon in an attempt to curb inflationary tendencies in the UK economy. Most countries tend to use interest rates as the main tool of counter-inflationary policy.

The fourth reason, speculation, tends to be regarded as a parasitic and maligned activity. Speculators would argue that their activities tend to lead to more effective and rational markets, however.

The fifth reason why there might be a wish to convert the home currency into a foreign one is also concerned with managing the exchange rate. Governments, usually through their central banks, create supply and demand for their national currencies by selling them or buying them. Thus the UK government may convert some of its reserves of dollars into sterling (that is, sell dollars, buy sterling) in an attempt to strengthen sterling against the dollar. Alternatively, it may do exactly the opposite in an attempt to weaken sterling.

Both the adjustment of interest rates and intervention in the market are much-used practices of governments as they attempt to manage their exchange rates.

Some theoretical explanations of relative exchange rates

Various attempts have been made to explain and predict relationships between two national currencies. We shall now briefly review these and the research evidence of their existence in real life.

The law of one price

The theories explaining relative exchange rates are underpinned by the general notion that if there are lots of wealth-maximising buyers and sellers with access to information, then the prices of identical goods and services in two different countries (each with its own currency) must logically be the same, when expressed in the same currency, and the exchange rate will adjust to make sure that this is true. This is known as the law of one price.

For example, if the exchange rate were $1.95 = £1, then a product or service costing $19.50 in the USA should cost £10 in the UK. Were this temporarily not true, market forces would force it to be true. Suppose that a particular product costs £11 in the UK and $19.50 in the USA. Then traders would seek to make a profit by buying the product in the USA and selling it in the UK. This would have several effects simultaneously. It would create additional demand in the USA, which would force up the price of the product there. In the UK it would create additional supply, which would force down the price there. The action of selling a US-derived product in the UK market would also lead to the conversion of sterling into dollars, that is, increase the demand for dollars and increase the supply of sterling. This would have the effect of strengthening the dollar against sterling. These adjustments in the supply and demand, both of the product and of the two currencies, should drive the effective cost of the product to be the same on both sides of the Atlantic.

The law of one price should, in theory, extend to financial assets – loans, shares and so forth.

In practice, the law of one price does not always work as theory would suggest. This is for several reasons:

- There are currency conversion costs. This means that it would not be worth traders exploiting a very small pricing difference, where after meeting the costs of converting the currency, there would be no gain. This point is not a major one in economic terms.

- There may be some legal restriction on importing the particular product from the foreign country.

- Transport costs mean that buying a product in one country and selling in the other will not completely equalise the price in the two countries.

- The exchange rate, as we have seen, is not always entirely determined by independent traders in goods and services. Governments are often major interveners in the foreign exchange market.

From the law of one price come several subsidiary relationships.

Purchasing power parity

If an identical product has, in effect, the same price in two different countries, as the law of one price predicts, then differential inflation rates between the two countries must, in theory, affect the exchange rate.

Purchasing power parity (PPP) can be summarised as follows:

$$\frac{e_1}{e_0} = \frac{1 + i_h}{1 + i_f} \tag{15.1}$$

where e_0 is the value in terms of the home country currency of one unit of the foreign currency at the start of a period, e_1 is the value in terms of the home country currency of one unit of the foreign currency at the end of the period, i_h is the rate of inflation in the home country during the period and i_f is the rate of inflation in the foreign country during the period.

To illustrate how this works, continue to assume a current exchange rate of £1 = US$1.95. Let us also assume that the inflation rate during the next year will be 10 per cent in the UK and 5 per cent in the USA. At present, according to the law of one price, a product that costs £1 in the UK will cost $1.95 in the USA.

At the end of the year, the product will cost £1 (1 + 10%) = £1.10 in the UK and $1.95 (1 + 5%) = $2.05 in the USA. This should mean that, by the end of the year, £1 will be worth 2.05/1.10 = $1.86.

Going back to equation (15.1), and bearing in mind that at the start of the period $1 = £0.51 (that is, 1/1.95):

$$e_1 = \frac{(1 + i_h)e_0}{1 + i_f}$$

$$= \frac{(1 + 0.10) \times 0.51}{1 + 0.05} = 0.53$$

that is:

$$\$1 = £0.53 \quad \text{or} \quad £1 = \$1.86$$

Since the law of one price does not work strictly in practice, it is not surprising to find that PPP does not strictly operate in practice either. However, as Shapiro and Balbirer (2000) showed, those countries with the highest levels of inflation during the 1980s showed the highest rates of currency value depreciation, or decline, as PPP would predict.

Fisher effect

The law of one price would lead us to the conclusion that the real (ignoring inflation) interest rate should be the same in any country, assuming deposits with a similar level of risk. If this were not the case, funds would flow across borders seeking the best returns to such an extent that interest rates would alter and/or exchange rates would change making real interest rates equal. This phenomenon is known as the Fisher effect.

As we saw in Chapter 5, in the context of investment appraisal:

$$1 + r_n = (1 + r_r)(1 + i)$$

where r_n is the nominal (or money) interest rate (that is, the rate that we actually have to pay to borrow, which takes account of inflation), r_r is the real interest rate and i is the rate of inflation. Then:

$$1 + r_r = \frac{1 + r_n}{1 + i}$$

If real interest rates are equal in all countries, then:

$$\frac{1 + r_{nh}}{1 + r_{nf}} = \frac{1 + i_{nh}}{1 + i_{nf}}$$

where r_{nh} is the nominal (or money) interest rate in the home country, r_{nf} is the nominal (or money) interest rate in the foreign country, i_{nh} is the rate of inflation in the home country and i_{nf} is the rate of inflation in the foreign country.

Shapiro and Balbirer (2000) also show that, while this relationship seemed not to be precisely as the model suggests, countries with high nominal interest rates tended to have high levels of inflation.

International Fisher effect

→ The international Fisher effect combines the underlying principles of the general Fisher effect and PPP. Fisher implies that interest rates will move to take account of inflation rates:

$$\frac{1 + r_{nh}}{1 + r_{nf}} = \frac{1 + i_{nh}}{1 + i_{nf}}$$

PPP implies that exchange rates move in response to differences in inflation rates (see earlier in this section):

$$\frac{e_1}{e_0} = \frac{1 + i_h}{1 + i_f}$$

Since the interest rates referred to in the PPP model are nominal rates, putting Fisher and PPP together we have:

$$\frac{e_1}{e_0} = \frac{1 + r_{nh}}{1 + r_{nf}}$$

The international Fisher effect therefore implies that the exchange rate is, in theory, directly linked to nominal interest rates.

Again Shapiro and Balbirer (2000) show that this relationship is a broadly correct approximation to reality.

Interest rate parity

As we saw earlier in this section, there are two bases on which we can buy or sell foreign currencies. We can trade for immediate delivery of the currency, when we shall be trading at a 'spot' rate of exchange. Alternatively, we can buy or sell the currency under a forward contract. Here, delivery will take place on some specified date in the future, but the exchange rate at which the transaction is effected is set now. Naturally, the 'forward' rate will be linked closely to the spot rate. In theory, were the nominal interest rates the same, in the countries of both currencies, the spot and forward rates would be the same. Remember that nominal interest rates reflect both real interest rates and the rate of inflation.

→ Interest rate parity can be summarised, in this context, as saying that where nominal interest rates differ from one country to the other, the spot and future rates will not be the same. The relationship is as follows:

$$\frac{1 + r_{nh}}{1 + r_{nf}} = \frac{f_1}{e_0}$$

where f_1 is the future value, in the currency of the home country, of one unit of the foreign currency, and the other symbols are as previously specified.

The future rate will be higher than the spot rate where the interest rate in the home country is greater than that in the foreign country. For example, assuming that UK interest rates are higher than US ones, you would have to pay more in sterling for

US dollars if you were to take delivery of the dollars (and pay the pounds) at a date in the future, than if it were a spot transaction. This is because you would be able to benefit from the better UK interest rates for longer than if you were to exchange sterling for dollars immediately. The converse would also be true.

For example, assume that the spot rate is £1 = $1.95 or $1 = £0.51. Assume also that the rates of interest expected to prevail for the next year are 10 per cent in the USA and 5 per cent in the UK. If we convert £0.51 now, we should have $1, which we could invest in the USA and it would grow to $1.10 by the end of the year. The person who received our £0.51 could invest this in the UK such that it would grow to £0.54 by the end of the year. By that time, taking account of the interest that we could each earn, the effective rate of exchange is $1 = £0.49 (that is, 0.54/1.10). This would be the future rate for a transaction to be carried out in one year's time.

The above formula will give us the same result:

$$\frac{1 + 0.05}{1 + 0.10} = \frac{f_1}{0.51}$$

$$f_1 = \frac{1.05 \times 0.51}{1.10} = 0.49$$

Here we should say that the dollar is trading at a forward discount against sterling. Were the opposite state of affairs to apply (interest rates higher in the USA than in the UK), sterling would trade at a forward discount against the dollar. The size of the premium or discount depends partly on how far into the future the exchange will occur, as well as on the relative interest rates.

In practice, interest rate parity tends to follow the theoretical model very closely.

Foreign exchange markets and market efficiency

We saw in Chapter 9 that the secondary capital market, the stock exchanges of the world, tends to be price efficient to a significant degree. This means that new information is rapidly and rationally impounded in security prices. This leads to a situation where it is not possible consistently to make better than average returns without knowledge of things not available to investors generally.

Casual observation of the foreign exchange market might lead to the conclusion that this too would be efficient, such that it would not be possible consistently to make abnormal gains by trading in currencies. The same general factors seem to apply. There are lots of intelligent people studying the market closely and seeking profitable opportunities. They have access to the capital to exploit any anomalies and make a profit. In one significant respect, however, the foreign exchange and the secondary capital markets differ. This is that governments tend not to intervene in the secondary capital market, whereas governments sometimes, perhaps frequently, intervene to a significant extent in the foreign exchange market. This is done in an attempt to manage the exchange rate in some way.

Knowing that a government, or governments, have a particular exchange rate objective can enable speculators to predict what will happen in the foreign exchange market. The evidence seems to bear this out. Studies show that where there is a clear government policy never to intervene in the market, that is where the currency is allowed to 'float' freely, the markets seem to be efficient. Where governments have a known policy, such as raising interest rates, or buying their currency in the market, to support its value, the evidence shows that the market is not efficient.

15.3 Problems of internationalism

So far we have seen that businesses generally should benefit from taking an international perspective on all aspects of their activities. We have also looked at how the foreign exchange markets work, and at some theory and evidence of the factors that seem to affect the determination of exchange rates. We shall now go on to look at some of the problems involved with operating at an international level, and at how some of the risks can be eliminated or contained.

Problems with foreign exchange

Any business that trades in foreign markets is almost compelled to exchange currency as part of its day-to-day routine. The existence of problems surrounding foreign exchange is the spur to countries seeking to peg currencies against those of countries with whom they frequently deal, or adopting a common currency, as many of the EU countries have done with the euro.

The most obvious problem that confronts such businesses is the cost of foreign exchange dealing. When a business sells to a foreign buyer, usually payment will be in the currency of the buyer's country. Some part of the value of the sales proceeds will be lost to the foreign exchange market. In percentage terms this is not a very large figure, but it is a cost.

Exchange rate risk

→ Exchange rate risk is the risk that the rate of exchange between two currencies will move adversely to the particular business under consideration. Changing exchange rates can have the effect of reducing the business's wealth. Similarly, an exchange rate change can increase its wealth, where the change is favourable, given the type of exposure.

Exchange rate risk can be broken down into three areas: transaction risk, economic risk and translation risk.

Transaction risk

Suppose that a business buys something from a US supplier, which is priced in dollars, at $100 at a time when £1 = $1.95. At that point, the business has an obligation to pay the equivalent of £51.28 (that is, 100/1.95). Suppose also that, by the time that the business comes to settle the bill, the exchange rate has depreciated to £1 = $1.70. Now the amount that will actually have to be paid is £58.82. The problem here is that when the business made a decision to buy the item the price was £51.28, but it then
→ turns out to be £7.54 higher. This risk is known as transaction risk because it is the risk that the exchange rate will move in a direction adverse to the business partway through a transaction.

There are ways of dealing with transaction risk, which we shall now consider individually.

Doing nothing

The methods for dealing with transaction risk all seek to stop the worst happening, or to make sure that the business does not suffer if it does. To this extent they are like insurance policies, and they have costs associated with them. With most risks in our personal lives we tend not to insure them unless the adverse event is unlikely to occur and/or it will be very damaging if it does. The reason for this is that insurance premiums are likely to be unreasonably high compared with the potential loss where the loss is a likely one. Adverse exchange rate movements are very common. For example, an ice cream seller could insure against spells of bad summer weather, but in the UK there is such a likelihood of these occurring that the premiums would tend to be high. Ice cream sellers tend to 'self-insure', that is, they bear the risk themselves. It is only unlikely events or those that would lead to a very major disaster for the business that are generally considered to be worth insuring against.

Future directions of movement of exchange rates are difficult, if not impossible, to predict. If a business is owed money, denominated in a foreign currency, it is as likely that the exchange rate will move in a favourable direction for the particular business as it is that it will move in an unfavourable one – or it could stay the same. Thus a business with a lot of foreign transactions will gain from an exchange rate movement as often as it loses. It is only where the business is exposed to an unusually large, perhaps isolated, transaction risk that it might feel the need to take steps to manage that risk using one of the techniques explained below.

There is another issue, portfolio effect, which argues for not managing exchange rate risk. We shall deal with this in section 15.5.

Trading in the home currency

It is possible for the UK business to avoid the transaction risk by insisting that purchases and sales prices are denominated in sterling. This simply shifts the risk from the business to its suppliers and customers. To the extent that it is common for sellers to quote prices in the currency of the buyer, it will tend to be feasible to buy from abroad and be invoiced in the home currency. When the time for settlement arrives, sterling is paid. By the same token, however, foreign customers will usually expect to be invoiced in their own currency. Insisting on invoicing in the home currency, and shifting the transaction risk to the customer, may well lose sales (or be penalised by having to accept lower prices). Also, insisting that all suppliers invoice in the buyer's home currency may deny the business the opportunity to buy from certain foreign suppliers who are only prepared to invoice in their home currency.

The key point here is strength in the marketplace. If the business's goods or services are much sought after and in short supply, then foreign customers may well be prepared to accept being invoiced in the seller's home currency. Similarly, a foreign supplier, eager to make a sale, may be prepared to invoice in the customer's home currency, against that particular supplier's own normal practice. Even where the business can persuade both suppliers and customers to deal with it exclusively in the business's home currency, this may be a costly strategy in that the foreign businesses may expect the prices to compensate them for bearing the transaction risk.

Maintaining a foreign currency bank account

If the business maintains a separate bank account in each of the currencies in which it transacts foreign business, it may be possible to delay conversion until such time as it judges the rate to be particularly favourable. For example, if a UK business has US customers, it could open a bank account in US dollars and pay all dollar cash receipts into it. The account would then generate interest until such time as the business felt that the dollar was relatively strong, and convert the balance to sterling.

If a UK business tended to buy from US suppliers, it could convert some sterling to dollars periodically, when sterling was relatively strong. This could then be paid into an interest-bearing dollar bank account, to be used to make payments in dollars as and when they arose.

A problem with this strategy is a loss of liquidity by having cash tied up in the foreign currency bank account when it might be needed elsewhere in the business. Also, deciding on the best time to convert may be difficult. To the extent that the foreign exchange market for the two currencies is efficient, there will be no time when the business could be confident that the rate would, in the future, move in one direction rather than the other.

Netting the transactions

A business that trades both as a buyer and a seller in the same foreign currency may be able to set receipts from sales against payments for purchases, perhaps best effected by opening a bank account in the foreign currency. Even if precise netting were not possible because, for example, receipts in the foreign currency exceeded payments, only the balance would need to be converted.

In many ways this is almost the perfect solution to the problem, but it requires a particular set of circumstances that will only rarely occur, to any significant extent, for most businesses.

Forward exchange contracts

Earlier in this chapter, the point was made that it is possible to enter a foreign exchange contract today, at an exchange rate set today, where the currencies will not be exchanged until a specified date in the future. For example, where a UK business knows that it will receive $1m in three months' time, it can enter into a **forward exchange contract** immediately that will fix the rate of exchange and thus eliminate transaction risk. The rate will be closely linked to the spot rate. If interest rates are higher in the USA than in the UK, the rate will be at a discount to the spot price in sterling for $1. If interest rates are higher in the UK, the price will be higher than (at a premium to) the spot price.

One problem with using the forward market to solve the transaction risk problem is that the business cannot benefit should the exchange rate move favourably. The reason for a business, with an obligation to make a payment in a foreign currency, to use the forward market is to avoid the risk that the foreign currency will strengthen against the home currency during the period of the contract. This would leave the business with a larger home currency payment to make than if it converted the currency immediately or undertook the forward-market transaction. But what if the home currency strengthened against the foreign one? The business could have had a cheaper bill had it left the risk uncovered. Obviously, users of the forward market are prepared to accept the lack of ability to benefit from a favourable movement in exchange rates, if they can eliminate the risk of loss through an adverse one.

Another problem is that, because the contract is binding, both parties must complete it. If the UK business, expecting to receive the $1m, fails to receive it because the debtor defaults, the business is still left to fulfil its obligation under the forward contract.

The use of forward contracts seems to be very widespread, among larger businesses at least. Ricci and Di Nino (2000) in 1995 surveyed the largest 200 UK businesses listed on the London Stock Exchange. They found that 75 per cent of their respondents often used forward contracts and that a further 21 per cent used them, but less often.

Money market hedges

→ Businesses use **money market hedges** to avoid transaction risk by combining the spot foreign exchange market with borrowing or lending.

Suppose that a UK business is expecting to receive $1m in three months' time. It can borrow an amount in dollars that, with interest, will grow to $1m. The borrowed dollars can be converted to sterling immediately, thus eliminating the risk. If the interest rate for three months is 2 per cent, then the amount to be borrowed is $980 392 (that is, $1m × 100/102). This will be converted to sterling immediately. When the $1m is received, it will exactly pay off the loan, with interest.

Also, suppose that another UK business has to pay $1m to a US supplier in three months' time. It can immediately convert sterling into dollars such that the amount of dollars would be, with interest, $1m in three months' time. Again, assuming a 2 per cent interest rate, the amount necessary would be $980 392, so assuming an exchange rate of £1 = $1.95, £502 765 (that is, 980 392/1.95) would be necessary to convert into dollars on the spot market.

The disadvantages of this approach are much the same as those of using the forward markets. The first is losing the opportunity to gain from any favourable exchange rate movement. The second is that the business either has an obligation or an asset in a foreign currency and so is relying on a foreign currency receipt or payment to complete the hedge.

Currency options

As we have seen, the problem with some of the strategies for eliminating transaction risk is that both the downside and upside risks are eliminated. This means that there is no opportunity for the business to benefit from any favourable movement in exchange rates. They also leave the business exposed if the overseas debtor defaults.

→ **Currency options** offer a solution to both of these problems. Options were introduced in Chapter 1. A foreign exchange option gives the owner the right, but not the obligation, to exchange a specified amount of a particular currency for another one, at a rate and at a time specified in the option contract. For example, a business expecting to receive a sum in a foreign currency in three months' time could buy an option to exchange the specified amount of foreign currency for the home currency, in three months' time at a specified rate. This would be known as a 'put' option because it enables the holder to sell the foreign currency.

Note, particularly, that the owner of the option has the right to sell the currency to the grantor of the option, but does not have to do so. If the foreign currency has strengthened against the home one during the three months, the option holder would ignore the option and sell the currency in the spot market when it is received. Similarly, if the debtor defaults, the option is ignored. The option acts rather like an insurance policy. The business is prepared to pay to buy the option because, if the worst happens and the foreign currency weakens against the home one, it can exercise its option. If all goes well the option will simply lapse.

It is equally possible to buy a 'call' option, that is, the right to buy a specified amount of a foreign currency, at a specified rate to the home currency, at a specified time in the future. A business expecting to pay a bill denominated in a foreign currency might choose to avoid transaction risk by using a call option in the currency concerned.

The disadvantage of using foreign exchange options to avoid transaction risk is the cost. The grantor of the option does not have the right to insist that the business exercises the option. The option will be exercised only if the exchange rate movement is disadvantageous from the grantor's point of view. The grantor will therefore need a good incentive to be prepared to grant a particular option.

The Ricci and Di Nino (2000) survey showed options to be a popular means of dealing with exchange rate risk, with 75 per cent of respondents using them, at least some of the time.

Currency futures

→ Currency futures contracts are quite like forward contracts in that they bind the parties to the exchange of two amounts, at exchange rates and at a future date all specified in the contract. Where futures differ from forwards is that they exist only for exchanges between relatively few currencies, relatively few values and relatively few future points in time, in other words they are standardised contracts.

These restrictions tend to make futures unwieldy in that it may not be possible to hedge a particular exchange rate risk exactly because the standard values and maturity dates may not precisely match the needs of the business. On the other hand, the standardised nature of futures means they can be bought and sold, and there is a market for currency futures. This means that businesses can create a hedge without having to identify a counterparty: they can simply buy a futures contract in the market. Similarly, a futures contract that is no longer required can be sold.

The Ricci and Di Nino (2000) survey indicates that futures are not a very popular approach to dealing with exchange rate risk.

Futures, forward contracts and options are all examples of financial derivatives that can be used to reduce or eliminate risk.

Economic risk

The problem

→ When a business's fortunes are capable of being affected by movements in exchange rates, the business is said to be exposed to economic risk. Some people see transaction risk as a part of economic risk and, given the definition of economic risk that we have just met, this is correct. Generally, transaction risk is seen as being related to short-term debtors and creditors, whereas economic risk tends to be related to more long-term hazards of exchange rate movements.

Economic risk covers such areas as:

● long-term loans made in foreign currencies becoming costlier than expected to service (interest payments) and repay the principal of the loan, as a result of a shift in exchange rates;

● projects not having as high an NPV in practice as was planned, because the home currency has strengthened against the relevant foreign ones, so that the value of operating cash flows is less than planned; and

● the business finding it hard to compete in the foreign market, when it is supplying from the home country and the home currency strengthens against the relevant foreign one.

Most businesses affected by economic risk

We might think that it is only businesses that transact part of their activities in a foreign currency that are exposed to foreign exchange economic risk, but this is not necessarily the case. Take an imaginary business, Little England plc, that uses UK supplies and sells its product or service in the UK market. At first sight, such a business is immune from economic risk. What if it has a market competitor who supplies the product or service from Japan, and sterling strengthened against the yen? Now the Japanese product could become cheaper, in sterling terms, without the Japanese business receiving less for it in terms of yen. This could quite easily severely damage Little England's ability to sell, at least at prices that it was used to charging. To take another example, what if a major element of Little England's market is other UK businesses that are principally engaged in the export market, and sterling strengthens against most other currencies? Little England's main customers may well find that their markets are under pressure as a result of strong sterling. This might well lead to a fall in sales volumes and/or revenues for Little England, despite the fact that it does not sell overseas itself.

Managing economic risk

Managing economic risk is not as easy as managing transaction risk, which, to a great extent, is pretty straightforward. There are well-established techniques for managing transaction risk, such as options and forward contracts, which can solve the problem, though not without cost. While there are some similar techniques available for managing economic risk, much of economic risk management is concerned with strategic approaches that try to limit exposure. Such approaches include:

- avoiding being too exposed to one single foreign currency;
- trying to trade in foreign countries where there is known to be some intent on the home government's part to hold the home currency at a broadly constant exchange rate, relative to relevant foreign ones; and
- taking steps to try to balance payments and receipts in the same currency.

As with transaction risk, there are arguments for doing nothing about economic risk. One aspect of this (self-insurance) was discussed in the context of transaction risk earlier in this section. Another point is that taking the kinds of steps listed above might be commercially unsound. For example, it is not always easy to trade in the particular countries of the business's choice; businesses often have to make sales where they can. Another aspect will be picked up later in this chapter.

Currency swaps

A problem of borrowing funds in a foreign country is that exchange rate fluctuations can alter the sterling cost of servicing and repaying the debt. Currency swaps can overcome this problem. Here, two borrowers based in different countries, each having a similar-sized debt in the other one's currency, agree to swap the cash flow obligations of their debts. So a UK business may agree to take over paying interest and repaying the principal on a foreign one's debt in sterling. In exchange, the foreign business takes over the obligations regarding the UK business's debt in the foreign one's home currency.

The Ricci and Di Nino (2000) survey shows currency swaps to be a popular means of handling economic risk, being used by 81 per cent of respondents, at least to some extent.

Translation risk

The problem

→ The last element of exchange rate risk is translation risk. This is associated with the fact that a business that has assets in a foreign country whose currency weakens against the business's home currency suffers a reduction in its wealth, as measured in the home currency. This is not the same as either transaction or economic risk, where the risk is concerned with cash flows. There is not necessarily any reason why cash needs to flow from the foreign operation to the home country. The business may well be able use funds generated from trading to make local acquisitions (that is, in the foreign country) to expand the foreign operation.

Translation risk tends to give particular concern because, under the accounting rules that apply throughout much of the world, the performance and position of all of the business's operations, including foreign ones, have to be incorporated in its profit and loss account and balance sheet, respectively. In the case of foreign operations, this requires translating figures expressed in foreign currencies into the home one. If the foreign currency is weak relative to the home one, both profit figures and asset values will be below what would have been the case had the foreign currency been stronger.

It is a matter of some debate as to whether translation risk has any economic impact. If a business has assets in a foreign country whose exchange rate has weakened against its home currency, in terms of the home currency those assets are worth less and, all things being equal, so will be future profits that those assets might generate. The evidence seems to show that, in such circumstances, the business's stock market value will fall. Given that the objective of most businesses seems to be to enhance shareholders' wealth, it seems difficult to deny that translation risk is a real issue.

On the other hand, it can be argued that the assets in the foreign country are equally productive and valuable as measured by the local currency, irrespective of that currency's value relative to other currencies.

The question probably hinges on the location and local currency of the shareholders. If they are in the business's home country, the value of their assets in terms of the home currency will be less. If they are elsewhere this may not be a problem.

Managing translation risk

Translation risk is very difficult to manage and, as for economic risk, it tends to be more at the strategic level that managing it can best be attempted. The following might be possible:

● avoiding being too exposed to one single foreign currency by having operations in a range of countries each with different, unlinked, currencies;

● trying to trade in foreign countries where there is known to be some intent on the government's part to hold the home currency at a broadly constant exchange rate with the relevant foreign currencies; and

● taking steps to try to finance much of the foreign investment with funds borrowed in the local currency, so that translation losses of assets' values are matched by gains on liabilities.

Like transaction risk and, to a lesser extent, economic risk, there are arguments for ignoring translation risk. One reason is the commercial inconvenience and cost of taking the strategic steps listed above. For example, it may be very expensive to raise finance in a country where the business wishes to make an investment in a manufacturing plant. The other reason, which is concerned with portfolio effects, we shall consider later in the chapter, in section 15.5. Most UK businesses seem not to hedge translation risk.

15.4 International investment appraisal

In essence, all investments should be appraised in exactly the same manner. This is irrespective of whether cash flows from them will emanate, partly or fully, from a foreign country or from the home country. NPV is applicable to all investments, wherever they may be located, and in whichever currency the cash flows are generated. There are, however, aspects of international investments that need special attention. These are now considered.

Estimating exchange rates

Where some of the cash flows associated with the project will be in a foreign currency, appraisal requires that they be translated to a common currency, normally the business's home currency, so that an appraisal can be undertaken. This requires not just that future cash flows are estimated, but also that they are translated into the home currency using an estimate of the exchange rate prevailing at the point in the future when the cash flows will occur. In theory, the purchasing power parity (PPP) principle, discussed earlier in the chapter, should ensure that the exchange rate is not an issue. This is because any shift in exchange rates should be compensated for by movements in purchasing power of the two currencies concerned. We saw earlier in this chapter, however, that PPP does not strictly hold in the real world. Given the difficulties of estimating future exchange rates, it might be reasonable to assume PPP unless there is good reason to believe otherwise in the particular circumstances.

Taxation

Almost certainly there will be ramifications of foreign taxation where profits are generated outside the home country. There may well be taxes on other aspects as well as profit. There may, for example, be taxes on the occupation of property, as is the case in the UK.

In the case of taxes on profits, there may well be a double-taxation agreement with the home country, where, in effect, tax is paid at the higher of the home country's and the relevant foreign country's rate. For UK businesses, since UK corporation tax rates are low by international standards, this may mean higher tax than on a similar profit generated in the UK.

Obviously the appraisal of the investment must take account of the tax aspects.

Restriction of remittances

Some countries restrict the amount of profit that can be repatriated by foreign investors. This may be because converting funds to another currency weakens the first currency – something that the government of the foreign country concerned may be eager to avoid. Also, funds that cannot be remitted abroad can only be reinvested in the country where they were generated, an action likely to be beneficial to the country concerned. Whatever the reason for the restriction, it is a factor that needs to be taken into account.

Environmental factors

There may be particular factors that affect a particular foreign location and which need investigation. These would include such matters as environmental constraints (for example, anti-pollution laws) and ethical constraints (for example, resistance by the population to working in a particular way or to buying particular products). These need to be looked at carefully.

Risk assessment

There are likely to be risks inherent in a foreign environment that are not present at home. For example, there is political risk, that is, the risk concerned with dangers of war and civil unrest, unexpected increases in taxes, restriction of remitting funds to the UK and the seizing of the business's foreign assets. These risks may be no more, or even less, than those arising from investing in the home country. They are, however, additional to those faced at home. One way to avoid political risk is simply to avoid investing in those countries where the political risk is high. There are commercial services that provide information on political risk, country by country. Another way of avoiding political risk is to insure against it. It is quite common for businesses to insure their foreign investments.

15.5 Risks of internationalisation, management of those risks and portfolio theory

International investment and risk reduction

As we saw in Chapter 7, it is probably better for businesses to concentrate on the most profitable opportunities and to leave risk diversification to the shareholders at the portfolio level. This is because shareholders can eliminate nearly all specific risk from their portfolios by holding a reasonably large number (15 to 20) of holdings of shares in businesses across a range of industries. Logically, we can extend this principle to diversifying into international securities. This is because risks that are systematic within one country might be specific to that country and so can be eliminated by international diversification.

The evidence supports this assertion. Shapiro and Balbirer (2000) show that international portfolio diversification leads to a relationship between portfolio risk, on the one hand, and number of different holdings in the portfolio, on the other, as shown in Figure 15.2.

This shows the standard deviation (a measure of risk) for portfolios of increasing levels of diversification. We met this in Chapter 7. The risk of the portfolio decreases significantly as the number of securities making up the portfolio is increased. This decrease is significantly more pronounced when international securities are included in the portfolio.

Cooper and Kaplanis (1995) showed that there is a relatively low degree of correlation between the returns from equity investment in one country and those from others. For example, in the period January 1991 to December 1994, the correlation between the UK and Japanese equity markets was only 40 per cent (perfect positive correlation = 100 per cent). The correlation between the UK and the Netherlands was 80 per cent. So even diversification by a holder of UK equities into Dutch shares would

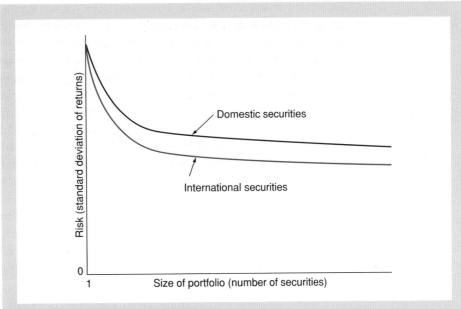

Figure 15.2
The risk of various sized, randomly selected portfolios, comparing a domestic share portfolio with an international one

As the size of the portfolio is increased the level of risk diminishes, but at a decreasing rate such that, for a portfolio consisting of 15 to 20 securities, adding more securities does little or nothing to reduce total risk further. This is true for both the domestic and the international portfolios, but the level of risk reduction is significantly greater with the international portfolio.

seem likely to yield some risk reduction, and diversification into Japanese ones would seem likely to lead to a fairly substantial amount of it.

Mathur, Singh and Gleason (2004) examined the accounting-based measures of performance of a set of chemical industry businesses that had diversified internationally over three years. They found there to be strong support for gains from international diversification.

International investment at the portfolio level

It can be argued that in view of the shareholders' ability to eliminate specific risk by internationalising their portfolios, businesses should not feel that it is worthwhile spending money to avoid specific risks associated with international activities. Exchange rate risk provides a very good example of a specific risk. By the nature of things, currencies weaken and strengthen relative to one another. If the US dollar is weakening against sterling, sterling is strengthening against the dollar. Exchange rate risk cannot be, on an international basis, a systematic risk since a decline in the strength of one currency cannot possibly go in step with a decline in all other currencies. This, from an internationally diversified shareholders' perspective, means that businesses should leave international specific risks uncovered and not waste money on managing them.

International investment and agency cost

The vast amount of trading in the international currency futures and options markets clearly implies that businesses do not follow the message of modern portfolio theory as applied to internationalised businesses. The reasons for this are not known with certainty. It may be that managements are not clear on the theory and evidence of risk reduction by portfolio diversification. Another possibility is that managers do not always act in the best interests of the shareholder, but have some regard to their own welfare. At the end of Chapter 7 we discussed the point that managers cannot normally diversify their employments. If their business suffers a major loss, perhaps as a result of being exposed to a significant exchange rate risk, and is forced out of business, the managers will lose their only employment. The well-diversified shareholder can be more relaxed about the situation, since this loss is likely to be matched by a larger than expected gain elsewhere. As we shall see in Chapter 16, this point may not be so relevant for smaller businesses, where diversification at the portfolio level may be impractical.

Irrespective of the theory, it seems that many businesses internationalise, at least partly, for risk diversification purposes. The, perhaps unnecessary, costs of managing exchange rate risks could provide another example of an agency cost.

Summary

Business internationalisation

- Many, if not most, businesses are international to some extent.
- Expanded investment opportunities and financing options can generate value.

Foreign exchange (forex)

- A market exists where prices are determined by supply and demand.
- The market is not necessarily price efficient because of predictable central bank actions.
- Currencies can be traded (exchanged) for immediate settlement (spot rate) or for settlement at a point in the future (for example, after a month or a year) at a different rate (forward rate).
- Currency dealers will quote two spot rates (for example, US$ per £1) – the first (lower figure) at which they will sell the foreign currency; the second (higher) at which they will buy.

Theoretical explanations of relative exchange rates

- Law of one price = a good or service will have the same price in all countries and foreign exchange rates will adjust to make this true.
- Purchasing power parity = different inflation rates in different countries will cause foreign exchange rates to alter so that the law of one price holds.
- Fisher effect = real interest rates are equal in different countries, so different inflation rates across countries should affect nominal (money) interest rates to make this true.
- Interest rate parity = where nominal interest rates are different between countries, the exchange rate will shift over time.

Exchange rate risk

- Transaction risk = problem that the exchange rate will alter during a credit period leading to a loss. Can be tackled in various ways:
  - Do nothing:
    - On average, a business will gain as often as it loses from foreign exchange movements.
    - Dangerous strategy where averaging may not work, for example with a particularly large or unusual transaction.
  - Trade in the business's home currency:
    - Often difficult to make sales in other than the customer's home currency, so there may be costs.
  - Maintain a foreign currency bank account:
    - Use it to make payments and bank receipts in the foreign currency concerned.
    - Make transfers to and from it (by converting from or to home currency) when the exchange rate is favourable.
    - Ties up cash (may cause an opportunity cost), also difficult to judge when rate is favourable.
  - Net transactions:
    - Set payments for purchases against sales receipts in the same currency, perhaps using a bank account in the currency.
    - Requires equal and opposite transactions in the same currency, which would be unusual – could work partially.
  - Use the forward market:
    - Deal done today at an agreed (forward) rate, but the currencies are not exchanged until a specified future date, when the foreign debt or obligation is due.
    - Advantage: business knows how much it will receive or pay in terms of home currency.
    - Disadvantage: business cannot gain from a favourable exchange rate movement because it is committed to the foreign exchange transaction.
  - Use currency futures:
    - Exactly the same as forward contracts, except they are for standard amounts and dates, which means that there can be a market for them.
    - Advantages: business knows how much it will receive or pay in terms of home currency and futures can be bought and sold as required.
    - Disadvantages: business cannot gain from a favourable exchange rate movement because it is committed to the transaction and futures are unwieldy (standardised amounts and dates).
  - Use the spot market and a money market (borrowing or lending) hedge. For example, business expecting a receipt in foreign currency at a known future date should:

1 borrow (in the foreign currency) amount that will grow with interest to the expected receipt amount;

2 exchange the borrowings for home currency immediately;

3 in due course, use the receipt exactly to pay off the loan.

- Advantages: conversion takes place at the time of the sale or purchase and rate is known.

- Disadvantage: cannot take advantage of any favourable movement in the rate because forex transaction undertaken at the beginning.

● Buy currency options – a right but not an obligation to exchange specified amounts of specified currencies on a specified date at a specified rate. For example, a business with a creditor to meet in a foreign currency in three months' time should:

1 buy a call option for the amount of currency and date concerned, at the best rate available;

2 on the due date, exercise the option, if the rate specified in the option is better than the spot rate at that time *or*, if the spot rate is better than the option rate, use the spot market and let the option lapse.

- Advantage: can benefit from a favourable shift in the rate – no obligation to exercise the option.

- Disadvantage: buying the option costs money.

● Economic risk

  ● Similar to transaction risk, but long term. Can be tackled in various ways:

    - Strategic approaches, such as avoiding being too exposed in a particular currency.

    - Currency swaps: two businesses with borrowings in different currencies agree to service each other's debt in, what is, each one's home currency.

● Translation risk

  ● Possibility that assets held abroad will lose value in the home currency with an exchange rate movement and so the shareholders' wealth reduced.

  ● Can be managed with strategic approaches.

International investment appraisal

● Raises problems additional to home country investment, for example assessment and estimating future exchange rates, foreign taxes, inability to repatriate investment returns.

International portfolio theory

● International security investment should increase the benefits of diversification because returns from securities in different countries tend to be relatively uncorrelated.

<table>
<tr><td>Further reading</td><td>Many business finance texts cover international aspects. Shapiro and Balbirer (2000) include a readable chapter. Two books specialising in international business finance that can be recommended for their readability are Buckley (2000) and Madura (2002). For a case study on how one major UK business deals with foreign exchange problems see Dhanani (2003).</td></tr>
</table>

Relevant websites

The Cadbury Schweppes website will give access to the company's annual report, which was mentioned at the beginning of the chapter.

www.cadburyschweppes.com

REVIEW QUESTIONS

Suggested answers to review questions appear in Appendix 3.

15.1 Why is it claimed that a UK business can achieve its objectives more effectively by internationalising its activities?

15.2 Broadly, there are four types of people or organisations that use the foreign exchange market. Who are they?

15.3 What are the four theoretical rules on foreign exchange rates that derive from the law of one price?

15.4 What causes foreign exchange markets not to be price efficient?

15.5 How are the three risks of being involved in international business usually described?

15.6 What is a 'money market hedge'?

PROBLEMS

Sample answers to problems marked with an asterisk appear in Appendix 4.

(All the problems appearing in this chapter are basic-level problems.)

15.1* Planters plc manufactures agricultural implements, components for which are acquired from a number of sources, including some overseas ones. The implements are marketed in the UK and, increasingly, overseas.

The directors are aware that the business is exposed to exchange rate risk, but in the past have been prepared to accept that this leads to losses and gains at a level that it has been prepared to accept. Recently, the scale of overseas trading has led the directors to consider the possibility of managing their foreign exchange risk exposure.

Draft a note for the directors explaining how buying and selling in foreign currencies exposes the business to risk. The note should then explain, in reasonable detail, how this risk might be managed in practice.

15.2* Pavlov plc has just made a sale to an Australian customer for A$500 000, the payment to be made in three months' time. The current exchange rate is £1 = A$2.6. Nominal interest rates for three months are 2 per cent in Australia and 3 per cent in the UK.

Pavlov plc is going to avoid transaction risk by using a money market hedge.

Describe, with exact figures, what action the business will take, and when it will take it, to achieve its objective. (Work to the nearest £ and/or A$.)

15.3 Lee plc has just made a sale to an Australian customer for A$500 000, the payment to be made in three months' time. The current exchange rate is £1 = A$2.6. Nominal interest rates for three months are 2 per cent in Australia and 3 per cent in the UK. Lee is going to avoid transaction risk by using a forward contract.

(a) What cash will change hands and when?

(b) Is the A$ at a forward discount or at a forward premium to sterling?

15.4 Precision Parts plc is a UK business that makes a small range of components for motor cars. These parts are sold to UK-based manufacturers. The components are made from steel, bought from a UK manufacturer, which obtains its raw materials from exclusively UK sources.

Explain how Precision Parts plc is exposed to exchange rate risk. What could the business do to protect itself from any exchange rate risk to which it is exposed?

There are both a set of **multiple-choice questions** and **missing-word questions** available on the website. These specifically cover the material contained in this chapter. These can be attempted and graded (with feedback) online.

There is also an **additional problem**, with solution, that relates to the material covered in this chapter.

Go to **www.pearsoned.co.uk/atrillmclaney** and follow the links.

Small businesses

In this chapter we shall deal with the following:

→ the importance of the small business sector of the economy, and a definition of 'small'

→ the objectives of small businesses

→ the likely legal form of the small business

→ taxation and the small business

→ risk and the discount rate to apply in appraising real investment opportunities for the small business

→ problems experienced by the small business with raising external long-term finance

→ valuing the shares of the small business

→ gearing in the small business

→ dividends and the small business

→ working capital and the small business

16.1 Introduction

Definition of a small business

What people mean by 'small' in the present context seems to vary widely: number of employees, total funds invested, and sales turnover are often used in the definition. For our present purposes, a strict definition probably does not matter. The sorts of business that we shall mainly be discussing are those displaying the following features:

- They are more substantial than the very small businesses that act as the medium for the self-employment of their owners:

- The business's securities are not quoted in any established capital market: i.e. they are not traded in an efficient market.

- The ownership of the business's equity and hence its control lie in the hands of a small close-knit group, that is, it is a *family-type* business.

The importance of small businesses

Small businesses, as we have defined them, are an important part of the UK private sector. According to the Bank of England (2003a, 2004), UK businesses with fewer than 50 employees accounted for:

	As a percentage of the UK private sector
People employed	44
Sales turnover	37
Gross value added	54
Net capital expenditure	40

This situation is similar in most EU countries individually, and for the EU as a whole.

There are good reasons to believe that small businesses will become increasingly important in the UK. The industrial restructuring that occurred in the 1980s and 1990s shifted the balance still further away from the traditional manufacturing, mineral extracting and power generation industries towards the service industries. Service industries, perhaps because they often do not depend so much on the economies of scale, tend to operate in smaller units. Even in manufacturing, the new computer-based technologies have tended to make smaller businesses more viable. This is because the flexibility of such technologies has meant that the economies of scale, in manufacturing, are much less profound than was the case with more traditional industrial methods. As we saw in Chapter 13 in the context of 'just in time' systems, flexibility is increasingly important in manufacturing industries. Small businesses have probably shown themselves to be more flexible.

There seems to be an increasing trend towards a future where businesses of all sizes will subcontract or buy in services and components, as they need them, from businesses specialising in such work, rather than seeking to do virtually everything 'in house' (this is known as outsourcing). Already there is an increasing number of examples of businesses outsourcing functions such as personnel and IT. For example, **Boots Group plc,** the chemist, has recently subcontracted both its IT systems management and the administration of its central warehouse to specialist businesses. This leaves Boots free to concentrate on its core activities. In fact, not surprisingly given the size of Boots, this outsourced work is being done by larger businesses. Nevertheless, outsourcing tends to promote a need for many small businesses, each one specialising in the provision of some product or service. Not only does outsourcing create a market for the output of small businesses, it also has the effect of providing labour to staff them. This is because larger businesses are tending to shed labour with skills other than in what they see as their core activity. The divestments, including management buyouts (which we discussed in Chapter 14), may be seen as part of a trend towards smaller units and a concentration on core activities.

Small businesses are also seen as being particularly important in that they provide an environment in which innovation tends to flourish. Claims are made that a very

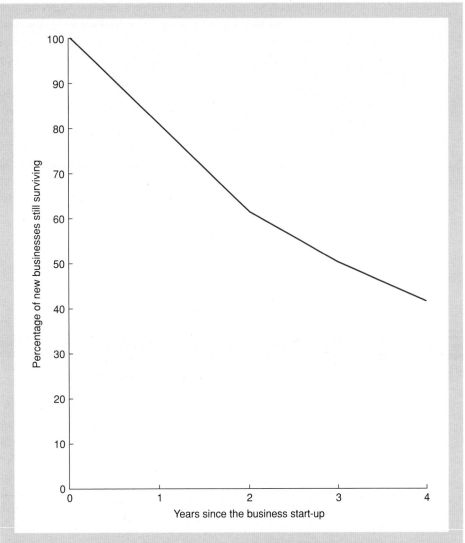

Figure 16.1
Survival of new businesses

Source: Adapted from Bank of England (2001).

The rate of failure of new businesses (presumably nearly all small ones) is such that after four years only 42 per cent still survive.

high proportion, perhaps a majority, of new ideas emerge and are first tried in the small business sector.

There are few areas of business finance where the broad principles that apply to large businesses do not equally well apply to small ones, but there are certainly some areas where the emphasis is different and where small businesses tend to have their own particular problems. In this chapter we shall consider these areas.

Failure of small businesses

A sad fact about small businesses is the failure rate. The Bank of England (2001) cites evidence on survival rates of new businesses. This is shown in Figure 16.1. By the end of four years, only 42 per cent of new businesses still survive. Though the rate of failure seems to reduce as the lifetimes increase, it seems pretty certain that further failures occur beyond the first four years. Other EU countries show a similar pattern of new business failures. Thus failure is very much the normal, though far from inevitable, fate of a new business. Not all new businesses are small, but it is very likely that most of them will be.

Storey (1994) cites evidence that seems to show consistently that size is a big issue in businesses failing. For example, a business employing less than 20 people is statistically nearly twice as likely to fail as one employing over 1000 people. As we saw in Chapter 7, Fama and French (1996) showed that investors require an additional risk premium, related inversely to the size of the business, to compensate them for investing in smaller businesses. In this case the businesses were at the smaller end of the range of stock market listed ones, but the point seems likely to be valid for unlisted businesses.

16.2 Corporate objectives

In the context of larger businesses, we reached the conclusion that maximisation of shareholder wealth is a reasonable statement of the goal that most businesses are likely to pursue. How different is this likely to be for smaller ones?

Management goals versus shareholder goals

With larger businesses, where the managers are probably not very substantial shareholders, conflict can arise between the objectives of each group.

In the case of the small business, the managers and the shareholders are likely to be substantially the same people, or at least closely connected. Thus agency problems, and their potential associated costs, are likely to have little, or possibly no, impact on the typical small business. This might lead us to the conclusion that, as managers are likely to be substantial shareholders, they would make decisions following a pure wealth-maximising goal more determinedly than would be the case in the typical large business.

On the other hand, whereas the vast majority of investors who buy shares in large businesses do so with only an economic motive, those who involve themselves in smaller ones may well have other motives. These motives might include a desire to experience the satisfaction of building up a business, a desire to lead a particular way of life, or a desire to keep some (perhaps family) tradition alive. Since it is possible for managers to know the personal objectives of the shareholders of the smaller business, decisions can probably be made with these in mind.

Irrespective of what other goals may be pursued by a small business, decisions cannot be taken that consistently ignore the question of wealth. A business that makes a series of decisions, each causing wealth to diminish, will sooner or later fail.

We may probably come to the conclusion that the wealth maximisation goal is very important to small businesses and that, even where it is not necessarily the only objective, it cannot be ignored. This implies that the NPV investment appraisal technique is as relevant to small businesses as it should be to large ones. In fact, the evidence that we discussed in Chapter 4 suggests that NPV is not as widely used by smaller businesses, but this may reflect a lack of sophistication rather than the pursuit of other goals.

16.3 Organisation of small businesses

Typically, the small businesses that we are considering here will be organised as private limited companies. In essence these are identical to their public counterparts. The main differences are as follows:

- Private companies need be of no minimum size; public companies must issue at least £50 000 of nominal share capital, of which at least 25 per cent must be paid up. There is no upper limit on the size of a private company.

- Private companies are entitled to restrict the transfer of their shares, that is, it is possible for the company's Articles of Association to contain a clause giving the directors the power to refuse to register a transfer, at their discretion.

- Although private companies must publish annual accounts, the volume of detail is rather less than that which the law requires of public companies.

- Private companies must generally include the word 'limited' or its abbreviation 'Ltd' in their names; public limited companies must include 'plc' in theirs.

Probably, in practice, the only one of these distinctions that is of any great significance is the second, concerning the restriction on transfer of shares. To the small business, the effect of the right of restriction can be something of a two-edged sword.

- On the one hand, it enables the majority of the shareholders to stop the minority, be it one or more shareholders, from transferring their shares to a third party unacceptable to the majority. In this way control, and even just influence through voting power, may be kept in the hands of those acceptable to the majority. In a family-type business it may be important to the shareholders that ownership remains in the same hands, not necessarily for financial reasons.

- On the other hand, potential equity investors would be reluctant to buy shares in a business that effectively had the power to stop them selling the shares when they wished to. Not unnaturally, most established secondary capital markets, certainly the London Stock Exchange, will not allow dealings in shares where there is a restriction on transfer. For small businesses eager to expand, being a private limited company may be an impediment to growth.

It is not necessarily true that all small businesses will be private limited companies, but given the attractions of the lesser requirement to account publicly and the ability to control their membership through share transfer restrictions, many of them are.

Of the total of about 1.5 million UK limited companies, about 99 per cent are private and only 1 per cent public.

16.4 Taxation of small businesses

As far as tax on corporate profits is concerned, the only likely difference between large and small businesses is the corporation tax rate. The current rates are set out in Table 16.1.

Capital allowances tend to be applied at more generous rates for small businesses.

Note that 'large' and 'small' for tax purposes are defined entirely in terms of profit, and so individual businesses can, and do, move from being large to being small from one year to the next as their profits fluctuate.

Table 16.1 UK corporation tax rates

Profit range	Rate
≤ £10 000	0%
£10 001–£50 000	Sliding scale between 0% and 19%
£50 001–£300 000	19%
£300 001–£1 500 000	Sliding scale between 19% and 30%
≥ £1 500 001	30%

Tax avoidance

Perhaps where the distinction between small and large businesses is likely to be most profound, in the context of taxation, is in the extent to which they take actions purely for tax reasons.

Since small businesses typically can know the personal circumstances of the shareholders, actions can be taken that will maximise the net (after-tax) wealth of those individuals. For example, where all shareholders pay income tax at a high marginal rate, it might be to their net advantage for profits to be retained by the business instead of being distributed as a dividend. This would possibly lead, in the long term, to a capital gains tax liability on disposal of the shares, but this may be more tax efficient.

16.5 Risk and the discount rate

In the context of large businesses it seems that discounting expected cash flows using a discount rate derived from CAPM is a reasonable way for considerations of risk to be incorporated into investment decision making. With small businesses this would probably be invalid for two reasons:

- It is thought to be true that investors in large businesses typically hold a relatively small proportion of each business's total equity as a relatively small proportion of a reasonably well-diversified portfolio of equities. (Casual observation shows this broadly to be true: about 80 per cent of equities of businesses listed on the London Stock Exchange are owned by the investing institutions, which tend to hold large, well-diversified portfolios.) For this reason investors would be exposed to relatively little specific risk, so a CAPM-derived discount rate, that is, one that deals only with systematic risk, is logical. Typically, equity investors in small businesses will not be well diversified. For shareholders in the typical small business, it is likely that this investment will represent a large proportion (by value) of their total investment. If the small business were to fail, most of their wealth might be lost.

  Since shares of small businesses tend not to be held in efficient portfolios, the discount rate that should be applied to the small business's investment opportunities should take account of specific as well as systematic risk.

- Fama and French (1996), discussed in Chapter 7, showed that, owing to higher bankruptcy risk, small businesses are more risky investments than larger ones. The Fama and French three-factor model seems more relevant here than the basic CAPM.

The first reason means that there is no theoretically correct way of arriving at an appropriate discount rate, although CAPM can be used to discover a figure below which the rate should not lie. The second means that it is necessary to use the Fama and French three-factor version of CAPM when considering a small business. Probably, the impressionistic devices such as sensitivity analysis and attempts to assess the worst possible outcome, best estimate and the best possible outcome, that we discussed in Chapter 6, could be used to gauge the level of risk.

Risk diversification within the business

In our previous discussion of diversification and risk reduction, particularly in Chapters 6 and 14, the point emerged that, with large businesses, the shareholders are generally not advantaged by attempts by the business to diversify its operations internally. The evidence supports this point.

Shareholders are not advantaged by diversification within the business because they can, and do, diversify their security portfolios to achieve the same effect. For the reason mentioned above, shareholders in small businesses may not be able to do this for themselves so there may be some point in the business doing it for them, with the objective of reducing specific risk. Of course, because the business is small, the practicality of internal diversification may be much less than would be the case with a larger business. There is also the problem that diversification may take the business into areas of activity that it is not competent to manage.

16.6 Sources of finance

Over the years, there have been several UK government-sponsored enquiries that have dealt at least partly with the financing of small businesses (for example, the Wilson Committee (1980) to review the functioning of financial institutions). Each of these discovered, to a greater or lesser extent, that small businesses find it more difficult and more expensive to raise external finance than do larger ones. For this reason they are forced to rely on internally generated funds (retained profits) to a great extent.

It seems that large businesses also rely heavily on retained profits as a major source of finance, with capital issues perhaps averaging about 25 per cent of total new finance over recent years.

No doubt small businesses do experience some problems in raising external finance and, triggered by the publication of the reports of the various enquiries into small business financing, numerous schemes and agencies were established to make it easier for them. The more recent enquiries found not so much the absence of sources available to small businesses, as ignorance on the part of their management of the existence of those sources. Efforts to plug the 'information gap' are manifest in the UK.

According to evidence provided by NatWest/SBRT and cited in Bank of England (2003b), access to finance is not seen by small businesses themselves as a major problem: only about 1 per cent of respondents to a survey of small businesses regarded it as 'their most important problem'. This put access to finance as only the eleventh most important problem, well behind the problem of 'government regulations and paperwork' (about 14 per cent) and the 'general economic climate' (about 20 per cent), which respondents indicated as their most important problem.

No doubt it remains difficult and expensive for small businesses to raise external finance, but at least their managers and shareholders may take comfort from the fact that just about everyone with any influence in the matter, most particularly the UK government, seems eager to improve the situation.

Exit routes

A particular problem faced by small businesses in their quest for equity capital is the lack of an 'exit route'. Generally, investors require that there be some way of liquidating their investment before they are prepared to commit funds to it. With businesses listed on the Stock Exchange, or a similar market, this normally poses no great problem. However, small businesses find this a significant problem.

The three possibilities facing the potential equity investors are:

- The business will be able to buy back the shares from the shareholder. However, this requires that it has generated sufficient cash, and that it does not need that cash for further investment. This is not a very attractive option for the business. One of equity's key advantages to the business is the absence of the need to liquidate it.

- The business will obtain a listing on the Stock Exchange. This may be a possibility, particularly in view of the existence of the Alternative Investment Market and Ofex (see below), but it is still only businesses towards the larger end of the small business sector that will be able to follow this route.

- The business is sold to another one or to a management buyout or buy-in team.

Since none of these can be regarded as likely possibilities, particularly for very small businesses, finding equity backing is a real problem. In the end, for most small businesses, the personal savings of their founders and ploughed-back profits are the only significant sources of equity finance.

Venture capital

→ Venture capital is the name given to equity finance provided to support new, expanding and entrepreneurial businesses. Venture capitalists usually prefer to take a close interest in the business concerned. This could involve taking part in decisions made by the business. Much venture capital comes from funds contributed to by a number of smaller investors, in many cases taking advantage of the tax incentives available to providers of equity finance through such funds.

Venture capitalists tend to be attracted to fast-expanding, often high-tech, businesses. They look for high returns, perhaps 25 to 35 per cent p.a., a relatively short-term involvement (up to five years) and an exit route. They tend to take equity holdings of up to 40 per cent of the equity, typically involving investments of more than £1 million.

According to the British Venture Capital Association (see Relevant Websites at the end of the chapter), during 2003 just over £4bn of new finance was invested by venture capitalists in 1274 different small UK businesses. The average amount invested in each business was just over £3m. Despite the valuable role played by venture capital, only a small minority of small businesses use it. Nevertheless, venture capital is massively more prevalent in the UK than in the rest of the EU.

Business angels

→ Whereas venture capital is provided by organisations that specialise in such investments, business angels are typically individual investors who are prepared to make investments, usually equity investments, in small businesses. There are estimated to be about 40 000 business angels active in the UK. Most investments made by business angels seem to be of amounts between £10 000 and £1m. According to the Bank of England (2003a), three-quarters of the investments made are of amounts less than £50 000. Typically, business angels tend to take between 10 per cent and 40 per cent of the equity. They seek to take a close interest in the business. The National Business Angels Network (see Relevant Websites at the end of the chapter) has been established in the UK. It seeks to put potential angels in contact with businesses needing finance.

→ Equity finance provided by venture capitalists and business angels is often referred to as private capital.

Alternative Investment Market

The Alternative Investment Market (AIM) was established in June 1995 by the London Stock Exchange for small, young and growing businesses. Many of these are family-type businesses and/or those established as a result of management buyouts and buy-ins. AIM has proved to be a very successful means for businesses to establish a market in which new equity finance could be raised and its shares could be traded. As such, it can provide a means for equity investors, like venture capitalists and business angels, to 'exit' from their investments. Businesses listed on AIM tend to have market values in the range £1m to £300m, although most fall within the £3m to £30m range. Businesses currently listed on AIM include **Monsoon plc**, the high street fashion retailer, **Center Parcs plc**, the holiday business, and the football clubs **Millwall** and **Preston North End**.

AIM was intended to be cheap to enter, compared with the costs of obtaining a full Stock Exchange listing. Obtaining an AIM listing and raising funds costs about £500 000 for the typical business. According to Blackwell (1999), the costs of raising finance on AIM are almost as high as those associated with a full Stock Exchange listing.

Currently there are just over 300 businesses listed on AIM.

Ofex

As a result of the high costs of a full or AIM listing, a new market, Ofex, was established by stockbrokers J. P. Jenkins Ltd in 1997, but is now operated by PLUS-Markets Group plc – itself a business listed on AIM.

Ofex is entirely independent of the Stock Exchange, and the costs and rigours of obtaining a listing and raising finance are very low. There are currently about 400 businesses listed on Ofex, including such household names as **Arsenal** and **Rangers** football clubs, and brewers **Adnams plc** and **Shepherd Neame Ltd**.

Going public

For the typical small business, the size of the step that needs to be taken in 'going public' (obtaining a Stock Exchange listing, or even an AIM one) should not be underestimated. Obtaining a listing means moving into a 'higher league' in various ways. The following factors are likely to be important:

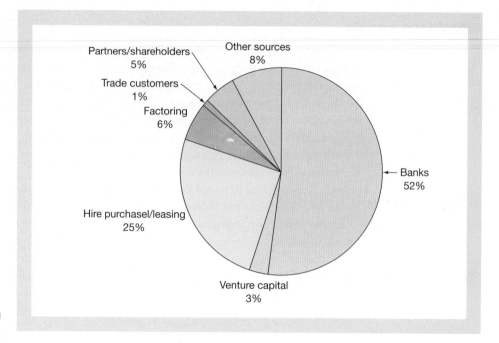

Figure 16.2
Sources of finance for small businesses, 2000–02

Source: Bank of England (2004).

- Strict rules are imposed on listed businesses, including requiring additional levels of financial disclosure to that already imposed by law and by International Accounting Standards (for example, the listing rules require that half-yearly financial reports must be published).

- Financial analysts, financial journalists and others closely monitor the activities of listed businesses. Such scrutiny may not be welcome, particularly if the business is dealing with sensitive issues or is experiencing operational problems.

- The costs of obtaining a listing are vast and this may be a real deterrent for some businesses.

Evidence on small business financing

Figure 16.2 shows the sources of finance for small UK businesses over recent years. It is striking how little of total funding comes from the owners (5 per cent). Bank financing accounts for the majority of finance. Of the bank finance, about three-quarters comes from term loans and the other one-quarter from overdrafts. Although venture capital is undoubtedly an important source of finance for some businesses, overall it is relatively insignificant (3 per cent).

16.7 Valuation of small businesses

The existence of an apparently efficient market for the securities of large businesses implies that, unless we have access to inside information, there is good reason to believe that the best estimate of the security's value available to us is the current market price. With small businesses, as we have defined them, this will not be true since there is no current market price. Nonetheless it is sometimes necessary to value the ordinary shares of small businesses, either to fix a price for a transfer for value (a sale) or where the transfer has been partly or fully a gift and a value is needed for capital gains or inheritance tax purposes.

There are basically four approaches that can be taken to such a valuation. We should bear in mind that we are seeking by each approach to value the equity of a business. Since each one has the same objective, in theory they should, if used correctly, give the same result. This they will not usually do, possibly reflecting inefficiencies or imperfections in the market for real assets. We shall now look at each approach in turn.

Dividend yield

The dividend yield approach is based on the notion that the ordinary shares of two different businesses should have a similar dividend yield provided that the businesses are roughly similar in size, activity, capital gearing and proportion of profit paid as dividend (dividend cover). If the shares of one of these businesses are listed and valued by an efficient market (such as the London Stock Exchange), this enables us to value the other one.

Example 16.1

A plc and B Ltd are two businesses similar in size, activity, gearing and dividend cover. A plc is Stock Exchange listed, B Ltd is not. The dividend yield (gross) for A plc is 10 per cent, and B Ltd has recently paid annual dividends of £0.15 per share. What is the value of each B Ltd share?

Solution

Bearing in mind that:

$$\text{Dividend yield} = \frac{\text{Dividend paid (grossed up)}}{\text{Current market price per share}}$$

then, assuming an income tax rate of 10 per cent:

$$10\% = \frac{0.15 \times 100/90}{p_B}$$

where p_B is the price of one share in B Ltd. This gives:

$$p_B = £1.67 \text{ per share}$$

The following points should be noted on using the dividend yield approach in practice:

- The difficulty of finding a listed business sufficiently like the unlisted one in the ways mentioned for the comparison to be valid.

- The doubts as to whether it is valid to assume that current dividend levels are the sole determinant of share values.

- The fact that prices are more likely to relate to future dividends. Past dividends will tend only to be useful as a guide to the future.

- The lack of marketability of unlisted shares: this will tend to make them less valuable than apparently identical listed ones.

In practice, this approach tends to be used where a minority holding is being valued. This is because the minority shareholder has little control over events, and simply receives a dividend.

Price/earnings

The price/earnings approach is similar to the dividend yield approach but concentrates on earnings rather than dividends, and takes the view that the shares of two similar businesses will have the same P/E ratio.

Example 16.2

C plc and D Ltd are two businesses similar in size, activity and gearing. C plc is listed, D Ltd is not. The P/E ratio for C plc is 12; the after-tax earnings per share for D Ltd have been £0.30 p.a. over recent years. What is the value of each D Ltd share?

Solution

Bearing in mind that:

$$P/E = \frac{\text{Current market price per share}}{\text{After-tax earnings per share}}$$

then the price of a share of D Ltd, p_D, is given by:

$$12 = \frac{p_D}{0.30}$$

$$p_D = £3.60 \text{ per share}$$

Clearly, most of the points that apply to the dividend yield approach also apply to this one. The P/E approach does overcome the question of dividend policy, which Modigliani and Miller (as we saw in Chapter 12) assert is irrelevant in any case.

In practice, this approach tends to be used to value a majority holding where the shareholder has some control over the business.

Net assets

Here the approach is to value the business by reference to the individual values of its assets.

Example 16.3

The balance sheet of E Ltd is as shown below. What is the value of each E Ltd share?

Balance sheet of E Ltd at 31 December

Sources of finance (claims)	£m	Uses of finance (investments)	£m
Ordinary shares of £1 each	8	Non-current assets	11
Retained profit	7	Working capital	10
Total equity	15		
Long-term loans	6		
	21		21

| **Solution** | If p_E is the price of an E Ltd share, then: |

$$p_E = \frac{11 + 10 - 6}{8}$$

$$= £1.875$$

The calculation in Example 16.3 was based on the book values of the assets and liabilities. It need not be done on this basis. Some current market value would be more logical, including a value for goodwill, if any. Since the assets concerned here are presumably purely economic ones, their value should be based on their ability to generate future benefits. Because of this, there is no reason why the net assets basis should give us a different value from that of the price/earnings approach.

Economic value (based on 'free' cash flows)

The economic value approach is the most logical. It bases the valuation on the discounted (present) value of the estimated future net free cash flows of the business. Logical it may be, but it is problematical. Cash flows will be difficult to estimate, certainly beyond the first year or two. A discount rate will need to be identified, which poses another problem. This might be able to be solved by using CAPM, or better still the Fama and French three-factor version of it, which we met in Chapter 7, with the average beta for the industry in which the business is engaged.

In practice, there tend to be differences between the values obtained from each approach. The dividend yield basis tends to be used to value minority shareholdings where the potential shareholder will not own sufficient shares to exercise any influence over dividend policy. Controlling shareholdings tend to be valued on the net assets, P/E or economic value bases.

Perhaps we should conclude this section by saying that valuing the shares of unquoted businesses is a highly inexact science – value is in the eye of the beholder. In practice, the price at which a transfer occurs, or (for tax purposes) is deemed to have occurred, is likely to be the result of negotiation and compromise between the concerned parties.

16.8 Gearing

In Chapter 11, we suggested that there might be some optimal level of gearing that balances the tax advantages of gearing against the increased bankruptcy risk that gearing engenders. Once again the small business is not in a fundamentally different position from that of the larger one. There are, however, differences that are likely to have a significant bearing on where the tax/risk balance lies.

The relatively low corporation tax rates that apply to small businesses mean that the effective relief for interest payments on borrowings is lower for them than it is for larger ones. This means that the greater tax efficiency of debt financing, relative to equity funding, does not apply quite so much to small businesses.

As we saw in Chapter 11, financial risk to which capital gearing gives rise tends to emphasise operating risk, which will be present with or without gearing. Business risk is part specific and part systematic. Since small businesses' shareholders may not be able to diversify sufficiently to eliminate most of the specific risk, they are likely to be more exposed to financial risk than would their typical large business counterparts. At the same time, it appears from Fama and French (1996) (see Chapter 7), and other sources, that bankruptcy risk tends to be higher for smaller businesses. These two risk points are not linked, except that they are both likely to make small businesses more cautious about taking on gearing than are their larger counterparts.

A combination of the tax and risk factors tends to mean that smaller businesses will reach their optimum gearing at a level significantly below that of a similar, but larger, business.

16.9 Dividends

Much of what is true concerning dividends in the context of large businesses also applies to small ones, although there are differences. Perhaps, most importantly, it is feasible for the directors of small businesses to know their shareholders' preferences as regards dividend policy and to make efforts to accommodate those preferences. This really is necessary, since typically it is not very practical for shareholders to sell their shares and replace them with those of another business whose dividend policy appeals rather more.

For a small business, it may be more practical than for a large one to treat individual shareholders differently. For example, it may be easier to offer cash dividends to some shareholders, while allowing others to take a **scrip dividend** (a bonus issue of shares, not available to all shareholders).

16.10 Working capital and small businesses

It seems likely that smaller businesses will not typically show the same working capital profile as their larger counterparts. The most obvious reasons for this are less bargaining power in the market and the inability to benefit from economies of scale.

Stock

Although there appears to be no available statistics to confirm the point, it seems likely that smaller businesses will hold larger stock levels (relative to, say, sales turnover) than their larger counterparts. There are several reasons for this, including:

- a general tendency for there to be economies of scale in stockholding: a business doubling its turnover would probably not have the need to double the level of stock held;

- the need to place orders of a minimum size to be able to gain bulk discounts on buying prices; and

- an inability to use techniques like just in time (JIT) because suppliers would not be prepared to apply this where the purchase quantities are small.

Trade debtors

It seems that small businesses have to finance proportionately higher levels of trade debtors than larger businesses. Wilson and Summers (2002) found that smaller businesses, when selling to larger ones, lack bargaining strength and this forces them to accept longer trade debtor payment periods. Morrison (2003) cites evidence compiled by the Credit Management Research Centre that shows that small businesses have to wait on average 19 days longer for their trade debtors to pay (60 days rather than 41 days). This means that the level of trade debtors for smaller businesses is 46 per cent higher, relative to sales revenue, than it is for larger ones.

Trade creditors

Again there appears to be no published statistics, but it seems likely that smaller businesses will tend to have lower average levels of creditors' payment period than larger ones. Similarly this is likely to be caused by relative bargaining power. Small businesses, typically buying in fairly small quantities, are likely to have to accept the payment conditions imposed by sellers or face the prospect of not being supplied at all.

The significantly higher levels of stock and trade debtors, combined with lower trade creditor levels, means that the average small business has a much higher working capital requirement for its size than does its larger counterpart. This factor alone is a likely contributor to the high failure rate of small businesses, mentioned earlier in this chapter. It is a failure of liquidity that leads to business failure.

Summary

Small businesses are important

- Provide a significant amount of employment, value added, sales turnover and capital investment in the UK.
- Tend to be innovative.
- Sector seems set to grow.

Small business failure

- High rate of failure.
- More than half do not survive the first four years of life.

Differences between small businesses and larger ones

- Can be more focused regarding pursuit of objectives.
- Tend to be private limited companies.
- Tend to be taxed at lower rates.
- Tend to be more risky, partly because shareholders tend not to be well diversified.
- Internal diversification more logical than with larger businesses.

- Lower tax rates and higher bankruptcy risk tend to make capital gearing less attractive.
- Directors can tailor dividend policy to shareholders more effectively.

Small business financing

- Tends to be difficult for small businesses to raise equity finance except from retained profit and their existing shareholders.
- Most potential equity investors will not invest where there is no exit route, that is, no way to liquidate their shares when they wish.
- Possible exit routes for an equity investor:
  - Business buys back the shares – requires that it has the cash available at some future point.
  - Business sold to another business.
  - Business obtains a listing on the Stock Exchange or Alternative Investment Market (AIM) – see below.
- A Stock Exchange or AIM listing is a major event for a small business, moving it into a different league, and it is very expensive.
- AIM is a market set up by the Stock Exchange for smaller businesses, but it is claimed that it is nearly as expensive to obtain a listing there as on the main Stock Exchange.
- Can be unrealistic to expect existing shareholders to take up new shares because:
  - they may not have the funds available;
  - they may be unwilling to commit additional funds to the business because of the lack of an exit route.
- Private capital might be provided by:
  - venture capitalists who support new, expanding, entrepreneurial businesses, often taking a fairly active role in the business's management. They are professional investors, in some cases using funds supplied by a number of small investors;
  - business angels, who are typically individuals who take equity stakes of up to about £50 000 and take a close interest in the business.

Valuing small businesses

- Cannot rely on a price for shares determined by an efficient market.
- Four approaches used in practice:
  1 Dividend yield (DY):
    - Based on the assumption that two businesses, similar in all respects except that one is listed and the other one not, should have the same DY.
    - Usually discount the calculated price to take account of non-marketability.
    - Difficult to find two such businesses.

2 Price/earnings (P/E):

- Based on the assumption that two businesses, similar in all respects except that one is listed and the other one not, should have the same P/E.
- Usually discount the calculated price to take account of non-marketability.
- Difficult to find two such businesses.

3 Net assets:

- Total the values of the various assets of the business, deduct the liabilities and divide by the number of shares to find the value per share.
- Balance sheet values can be misleading; market values of assets may be better than book values.
- Tends not to look at future earnings.

4 Economic value:

- Discounts future estimated cash flows to the shareholders.
- Theoretically the most sound approach.
- Difficult to estimate cash flows.
- Difficult to find the suitable discount rate.

Working capital

- Stock, likely to be proportionately higher than for a large business because:
  - limited access to economies of scale;
  - suppliers may require fairly large minimum order sizes;
  - limited opportunity to use just in time stock control.
- Trade debtors likely to be relatively high because:
  - evidence shows this to be true;
  - small businesses may lack sufficient market strength to push for prompt payment.
- Trade creditors likely to be relatively high because:
  - small businesses may lack sufficient market strength to be able to resist pressure from suppliers to pay promptly.

Further reading

Samuels, Wilkes and Brayshaw (1998) provide good coverage of small businesses generally. The further reading suggested at the end of previous chapters generally provide coverage of particular topics in the context of both large and small businesses. The various Bank of England reports, cited in the chapter, provide interesting insights into the features of small businesses, particularly in the context of financing.

Relevant websites

The Bank of England site provides access to the Bank's statistics and to various publications, including regular reports on the financing of small businesses, which can be downloaded.
www.bankofengland.co.uk

The British Venture Capital Association's website provides information about venture capital.
www.bvca.co.uk

The National Business Angels Network site is:
www.bestmatch.co.uk

Ofex's site provides details of the market that it operates.
www.ofex.com

The websites of businesses featured in this chapter are:

Adnams plc	www.adnams.co.uk
Arsenal Football Club plc	www.arsenal.com
Boots Group plc	www.boots-plc.com
Center Parcs (UK) Group plc	www.centerparcs.co.uk
Millwall Holdings plc	www.millwallfc.premiumtv.co.uk
Monsoon plc	www.monsoon.co.uk
Preston North End plc	www.pnefc.premiumtv.co.uk
Rangers Football Club plc	www.rangers.co.uk
Shepherd Neame Ltd	www.shepherd-neame.co.uk

REVIEW QUESTIONS

Suggested answers to review questions appear in Appendix 3.

16.1 What recent business trend is tending to promote the establishment and expansion of small, specialist businesses?

16.2 Why would it normally be appropriate for a small business to discount project cash flows at a higher rate than might be applied to a similar prospective project under consideration by a larger business?

16.3 When valuing unlisted shares, what problems arise when basing the valuation on the price/earnings ratio and/or dividend yield of a similar listed business?

16.4 What is wrong with using the balance sheet values of assets and claims when deducing the value of the shares of a small business?

16.5 What particular problem will face potential equity investors in small businesses, which may make the investors hesitant to buy shares and/or to seek higher expected returns than they would normally seek from a larger, stock market listed one?

16.6 Why would dividend policy tend to be easier to decide for the typical small business than for the typical large one?

PROBLEMS

Sample answers to problems marked with an asterisk appear in Appendix 4.

(Problems 16.1 and 16.2 are basic-level problems, whereas problems 16.3 to 16.6 are more advanced and may contain some practical complications.)

16.1* Tiny Tim Ltd, an unlisted business, is quite like Mega plc, a listed one, in terms of activities and gearing. Tiny Tim Ltd has steady after-tax profits of £350 000 a year. Mega plc's published price/earnings ratio is 16.

Estimate the total value of the shares in Tiny Tim Ltd, bearing in mind its unlisted and private company status.

16.2 XYZ Ltd, an unlisted business, is quite like ABC plc, a listed one, in term of activities, gearing and dividend policy. XYZ Ltd recently paid a dividend for the year of £0.20 per share. The effective income tax rate is 10 per cent. ABC plc's gross dividend yield is 12 per cent.

Estimate the value of a share in XYZ Ltd, bearing in mind its unlisted and private company status.

16.3* PR Industries plc, a major listed conglomerate, is considering acquiring an interest in Howard Pope Ltd, an unlisted business that has been trading for about 40 years as a manufacturer of domestic appliances.

The latest available summarised accounts of Howard Pope Ltd are as follows:

Profit and loss account for the year ended 31 December last year

	£m
Profit on ordinary activities after tax	15.30
Dividends	(5.00)
Profit retained	10.30

Balance sheet as at 31 December last year

	£m
Non-current assets	50.67
Net current assets	92.75
	143.42
Issued share capital (ordinary shares of 5p)	2.00
Share premium account	6.00
Revenue reserves	105.42
Floating rate term loan	30.00
	143.42

In recent years the directors of Howard Pope Ltd have adopted a policy of increasing dividends by approximately 10 per cent each year.

The cost of equity of listed businesses in the same industry as Howard Pope Ltd, which are similarly capital geared, is estimated at 13 per cent. The average price/earnings ratio of such businesses is 15.0.

The directors of PR Industries plc have not yet decided what proportion of the share capital of Howard Pope Ltd they wish their business to acquire, and you have

→

447

been asked to consider the possibility of acquiring either a minority or a majority stake.

Estimate the value of a share in Howard Pope Ltd. Would your view be different according to whether PR Industries plc was acquiring a controlling or a minority interest?

16.4 Alcantage Ltd owns a chain of dry-cleaning shops in South Wales. A UK-wide dry-cleaning business is considering making an offer to the shareholders of Alcantage Ltd with the idea of obtaining all the ordinary shares.

The draft accounts of Alcantage Ltd, for the year that has just ended, can be summarised as follows:

Profit and loss account for last year

	£m
Sales revenue	24.7
Profit before interest and tax	8.4
Interest	(0.5)
Profit before taxation	7.9
Corporation tax	(2.6)
Profit after taxation	5.3
Dividend	(1.5)
Retained profit for the year	3.8

Balance sheet as at the end of last year

	£m	£m
Non-current assets		
Freehold land and buildings at cost	5.9	
Less: Depreciation	1.0	4.9
Plant at cost	12.7	
Less: Depreciation	5.1	7.6
		12.5
Current assets		
Stock	4.3	
Debtors	0.7	
Cash at bank	4.1	
	9.1	
Less: Current liabilities		
Creditors	6.1	
Dividends	1.5	
Taxation	2.6	
	10.2	
Working capital		(1.1)
		11.4
Less: Non-current liabilities		
Debenture loan		4.7
		6.7
Equity		
Ordinary shares of £1 each		3.2
Retained profits		3.5
		6.7

Analysts estimate that the net cash flows of Alcantage Ltd, after taking account of tax and the need to replace non-current and current assets, will be:

	£m
Next year	6.7
Year 2	7.1
Year 3	7.5
Year 4	8.2
Year 5 and thereafter	8.5

The cost of equity of businesses in the industry, taking account of the level of capital gearing, is 12 per cent.

Professional valuers have recently assessed some of Alcantage Ltd's assets to have market values as follows:

	£m
Freehold land and buildings	12.3
Plant	6.2
Stock	4.8

The average of listed businesses in the industry for dividend yield is 7 per cent and for the price/earnings ratio it is 14. The effective basic rate of income tax is 10 per cent.

(a) Estimate the value of a share in Alcantage Ltd on the basis of as many methods as you can from the information provided.

(b) If you were a shareholder in Alcantage Ltd, how, in general terms, would you assess whatever offer you may receive from the national business?

16.5 Finn Engineering Ltd is an unlisted business. Ten members of the Finn family own most of the shares, but there are six senior managers who have very small holdings.

The most recent annual report contained accounting statements that can be outlined as follows:

**Profit and loss account for the year
ended 31 March this year**

	£000
Turnover	107 068
Operating profit	14 615
Interest payable	(1 300)
	13 315
Tax	(4 272)
	9 043
Dividends	(3 500)
Retained profit for the year	5 543

Balance sheet as at 31 March this year

	£000
Non-current assets	58 357
Current assets	37 241
Current liabilities	(34 215)
	3 026
Total assets less current liabilities	61 383
Non-current liabilities (10% loan repayable in full in nine years' time)	(13 000)
	48 383
Equity	
Ordinary shares of £1 each	10 000
Reserves	38 383
	48 383

This year's results are regarded as fairly typical of those over recent years, and they are in line with expectations for the foreseeable future.

Average figures for Stock Exchange listed businesses in the engineering sector are:

Gross dividend yield	3.30%
Dividend cover	2.45
Cost of equity	11.52%

(a) *Estimate the value of an ordinary share in Finn Engineering Ltd in* **three** *ways. Clearly explain the basis of your estimations, and justify any assumptions that you have made.*

(b) *Suggest a suitable price per share for each of the following possible transactions:*

   (i) *The purchase of 500 shares by one manager from another manager. The shares represent each manager's only holding of the shares.*

   (ii) *The purchase of the entire share capital by a conglomerate.*

   Your suggested prices should be **explained** *and justified.*

(c) (i) *Outline any additional information that would enable you to make a more informed valuation.*

   (ii) *Outline any alternative valuation methods that could have been used had more data been available.*

   (iii) *Outline the general problems of valuing shares in unlisted businesses.*

16.6 Opus Soft Drinks Ltd ('Opus'), an unlisted business, produces a range of mineral waters, mixers and fruit juices. Opus was formed in the 1980s by a consortium of listed brewery businesses to supply soft drinks for sale in their tied public houses and hotels. Opus makes about 20 per cent of its sales to customers other than members of the consortium.

At present Opus's ordinary shares are owned as follows:

	%
Great Northern Breweries plc ('GNB')	40
Peterstones Holdings plc	20
Heritage Ales plc ('Heritage')	15
Woodhall and Smith plc	15
Anchorage Brewery plc	10

Heritage wishes to sell its shares in Opus, and GNB has agreed to buy all of these, subject to a reasonable price being agreed.

Opus's latest annual report contained financial statements that can be summarised as follows:

Profit and loss account for the year ended 30 September last year

	£m
Turnover	52.3
Cost of sales	(30.9)
	21.4
Net operating expenses	(18.4)
	3.0
Interest	(0.5)
	2.5
Tax on profit from ordinary activities	(0.7)
	1.8
Dividends	(0.9)
Retained profit for the year	0.9

Depreciation of non-current assets for the year totalled £2.4m.

Balance sheet as at 30 September last year

	£m	£m
Tangible non-current assets		21.1
Current assets	15.2	
Current liabilities	(13.4)	
		1.8
Total assets less current liabilities		22.9
Non-current liabilities (see below)		(5.5)
		17.4
Equity		
Called up ordinary shares of £0.50 each		2.4
Reserves		15.0
		17.4

Cash flow statement for the year ended 30 September last year

	£m
Cash flows from operating activities	2.0
Cash flows from investing activities	(2.3)
Cash flows from financing activities	–
Net decrease in cash and cash equivalents	(0.3)

These results are fairly typical of Opus's performance over recent years, when adjusted for inflation.

The non-current liabilities consist of a debenture due for redemption in five years' time. This is owned as follows:

	£m
GNB	2.0
Heritage	1.5
Anchorage Brewery plc	2.0

The average figures for the Food Producers sector of the FTSE Actuaries Index are:

Price/earnings ratio	18.38
Dividend cover	1.84

(a) *Estimate a value per ordinary share in Opus using three methods. Explain your calculations, the logic of each method, and any assumptions that you have needed to make.*

(b) *Discuss the suitability of each of your estimations, in the context of the particular circumstances, as the basis of the price per share to be agreed between GNB and Heritage.*

(c) *Explain any factors that you believe will influence the final price to be agreed between GNB and Heritage.*

There are both a set of **multiple-choice questions** and **missing-word questions** available on the website. These specifically cover the material contained in this chapter. These can be attempted and graded (with feedback) online.

Go to **www.pearsoned.co.uk/atrillmclaney** and follow the links.

References

Adedeji, A. (1998). Does the pecking order hypothesis explain the dividend payout ratios of firms in the UK? *Journal of Business Finance and Accounting* (November/December).

Aharony, J. and Swary, I. (1980). Quarterly dividends and earnings announcements and stockholders' returns: an empirical analysis. *Journal of Finance* (March).

Al-Ali, J. and Arkwright, T. (2000). An investigation of UK companies practices in the determination, interpretation and usage of cost of capital. *Journal of Interdisciplinary Economics* (Vol. 11).

Alexander, S. (1961). Price movements in speculative markets: trends or random walks. *Industrial Management Review* (May).

Allen, F., Bernado, A. and Welch, I. (2000). A theory of dividends based on tax clienteles. *Journal of Finance* (December).

Andrade, G. and Kaplan, S. N. (1998). How costly is financial (not economic) distress? *Journal of Finance* (October).

Archer, S. H. and D'Ambrosio, C. A. (eds) (1983). *The Theory of Business Finance: A Book of Readings*, 3rd edn (Collier Macmillan).

Armitage, S. (2000). The direct costs of UK rights issues and open offers. *European Financial Management* (March).

Arnold, G. C. (2002). *Corporate Financial Management*, 2nd edn (Financial Times Pitman Publishing).

Arnold, G. C. and Hatzopoulos, P. D. (2000). The theory–practice gap in capital budgeting: evidence from the United Kingdom. *Journal of Business Finance and Accounting* (June/July).

Atrill, P. (2006). *Financial Management for Non-specialists*, 4th edn (Financial Times Prentice Hall).

Atrill, P. F. and McLaney, E. J. (2005). *Management Accounting for Decision Makers*, 4th edn (Financial Times Prentice Hall).

Atrill, P. F., McLaney, E. J. and Pointon, J. (1997). The effect of simplifying approximations on the investment decision. In Atrill, P. F. and Lindley, L. (eds), *Issues in Accounting and Finance* (Ashgate).

Baker, H., Powell, G. and Veit, E. (2002). Revisiting managerial perspectives on dividend policy. *Journal of Economics and Finance* (Fall).

Bancroft and O'Sullivan (2000). *Foundations of Quantitative Business Techniques* (McGraw-Hill).

Bank of England (2001). *Quarterly Report on Small Business Statistics* (Business Finance Division, Bank of England, October).

Bank of England (2003a). *Finance for Small Firms – A Tenth Report* (Bank of England, April).

Bank of England (2003b). *Quarterly Report on Small Business Statistics* (Business Finance Division, Bank of England, April).

Bank of England (2004). *Finance for Small Firms – An Eleventh Report* (Bank of England, March).

Barber, B. M. and Odean, T. (2000). Trading is hazardous to your wealth: the common stock investment performance of individual investors. *Journal of Finance* (April).

Barclay, M., Smith, C. and Watts, R. (1995). The determinants of corporate leverage and dividend policies. *Journal of Applied Corporate Finance* (Winter).

Beaver, W. H. (1998). *Financial Reporting: An Accounting Revolution*, 3rd edn (Prentice Hall).

Benito, A. and Young, G. (2003). Hard times or great expectations: dividend omissions and dividend cuts by UK firms. *Oxford Bulletin of Economics and Statistics* (December).

Beranek, W. (1963). *Analysis for Financial Decisions* (Irwin).

Black, F. and Scholes, M. (1974). The effect of dividend policy on common stock prices and returns. *Journal of Financial Economics* (May).

Blackwell, D. (1999). Ofex exerts a powerful pull. *Financial Times* (3 July).

Blake, D. and Timmermann, A. (1998). Mutual fund performance: evidence from the UK. *European Finance Review* (No. 2).

Boardman, C. M., Reinhart, W. J. and Celec, S. E. (1982). The role of the payback method in the theory and application of duration to capital budgeting. *Journal of Business Finance and Accounting* (Winter).

Bowman, C. and Asch, D. (1995). *Managing Strategy* (Macmillan).

Brealey, R. A. (1970). The distribution and independence of successive rates of return from the British equity market. *Journal of Business Finance*.

Brealey, R. A. and Myers, S. (2002). *The Principles of Corporate Finance*, 7th edn (McGraw-Hill International).

Bruner, R. (2004). Where M and A pays and where it strays: a survey of the research. *Journal of Applied Corporate Finance* (Fall).

Brusa, J., Liu, P. and Schulman, C. (2003). The weekend and reverse weekend effects: analysis by month of the year, week of the month and industry. *Journal of Business Finance and Accounting* (June).

Buckley, A. (2000). *Multinational Finance*, 4th edn (Prentice Hall Europe).

Bunn, P. and Young, G. (2004). Corporate capital structure in the UK: determinants and adjustment. *Bank of England Working Paper 226*. Available at www.bankofengland.co.uk/wp/index.html

Busse, J. and Green, T. (2002). Market efficiency in real-time. *Journal of Financial Economics* (September).

Carsberg, B. and Hope, A. (1976). *Business Investment Decisions Under Inflation* (Institute of Chartered Accountants in England and Wales).

Centre for Management Buy-out Research (2004). *CMBOR Quarterly Review* (Autumn).

Chen, S. (1995). An empirical examination of capital budgeting techniques: impact of investment types and firm characteristics. *The Engineering Economist* (Winter).

Chen, S. and Clark, R. L. (1994). Management compensation and payback period method in capital budgeting: a path analysis. *Journal of Accounting and Business Research* (Spring).

Chi-Cheng, H., Fuller, B. R. and Chen, B. Y. J. (2000). Is beta dead or alive? *Journal of Business Finance and Accounting* (April/May).

Chi-Hsiou Hung, D., Shackleton, M. and Xu, X. (2004). CAPM, higher co-moment and factor models of UK stock returns. *Journal of Business Finance and Accounting* (January).

Coggan, P. (2001). Equity markets: dividends dive as slowdown bites hard. *Financial Times* (20 October).

Coggan, P. (2003). Climbing aboard the flight from floatation. *Financial Times* (6 September).

Cooper, I. and Kaplanis, E. (1995). *Mastering Finance* (Financial Times).

Coopers and Lybrand (1993). *A Review of the Acquisitions Experience of Major UK Companies* (Coopers and Lybrand).

Copeland, T. E., Weston, J. F. and Shastri, K. (2004). *Financial Theory and Corporate Policy*, 4th edn (Addison-Wesley).

Corr, A. V. (1983). *The Capital Expenditure Decision* (National Association of Accountants and the Society of Management Accountants of Canada).

Crossland, M., Dempsey, M. and Moizer, P. (1991). The effect of cum- to ex-dividend charges on UK share prices. *Accounting and Business Research* (Vol. 22, No. 85).

Cunningham, S. W. (1973). The predictability of British stock market prices. *Applied Statistics* (Vol. 22).

Cyert, R. M. and March, J. G. (1963). *A Behavioural Theory of the Firm* (Prentice Hall).

Dann, L., Mayers, D. and Raab, R. (1977). Trading rules, large blocks and the speed of adjustment. *Journal of Financial Economics* (January).

Datta, S. and Iskandar-Datta, M. (1996). Who gains from corporate asset sales? *Journal of Financial Research* (Spring).

Davies, J. L., Fama, E. F. and French, K. R. (2000). Characteristics, covariances and average returns: 1929 to 1997. *Journal of Finance* (February).

Davies, R., Unni, S., Draper, P. and Paudyal, K. (1999). *The Cost of Equity Capital.* (Chartered Institute of Management Accountants).

Davis, E. and Pointon, J. (1994). *Finance and the Firm*, 2nd edn (Oxford University Press).

DeAngelo, H. and Masulis, R. (1980). Optimal capital structure under corporate and personal taxation. *Journal of Financial Economics* (March).

DeAngelo, H., DeAngelo, L. and Skinner, D. (2004). Are dividends disappearing? Dividend concentration and the consolidation of earnings. *Journal of Financial Economics* (July).

Demirag, I. (1998). Boards of directors' short-term perceptions and evidence of managerial short termism in the UK. *European Journal of Finance* (September).

Dempsey, M. J. (1991). Modigliani & Miller again revisited: the cost of capital with unequal borrowing and lending rates. *Accounting and Business Research* (Summer).

Dewenter, K. and Warther, V. (1998). Dividends, assymetric information and agency conflicts: evidence from a comparison of the dividend policies of Japanese and US firms. *Journal of Finance* (June).

Dhanani, A. (2003). Foreign exchange risk management: a case in the mining industry. *British Accounting Review* (March).

Dimson, E. and Mussavian, M. (1998). A brief history of market efficiency. *European Financial Management* (March).

Dimson, E., Marsh, P. and Staunton, M. (2002). Global evidence on the equity risk premium. Available at http://faculty.london.edu/edimson/Jacf1.pdf

Dissanaike, G. (1997). Do stock market investors overreact? *Journal of Business Finance and Accounting* (January).

Dissanaike, G. (1999). Long-term stock price reversals in the UK: evidence from regression tests. *British Accounting Review* (December).

Dixit, A. K. and Pindyck, R. S. (1995). The options approach to capital investment. *Harvard Business Review* (May/June). Reprinted in Rutterford (1998).

Draper, P. and Paudyal, K. (1999). Corporate takeovers: mode of payment, returns and trading activity. *Journal of Business Finance and Accounting* (June/July).

Drury, C. (2004). *Management and Cost Accounting*, 6th edn (Thomson Learning).

Drury, C. and Braund, S. (1990). The leasing decision: a comparison of theory and practice. *Accounting and Business Research* (Vol. 20, No. 79).

Drury, C., Braund, S., Osborne, P. and Tayles, M. (1993). *A Survey of Management Accounting Practices in UK Manufacturing Industries* (Chartered Association of Certified Accountants).

Dryden, M. M. (1970). A statistical study of UK share prices. *Scottish Journal of Political Economy* (November).

Elton, E. J. and Gruber, M. J. (1970). Marginal stockholders' tax rates and the clientele effect. *Review of Economics and Statistics* (February).

Emery, D. R. and Finnerty, J. D. (2004). *Corporate Financial Management*, 3rd edn (Prentice Hall).

Ernst and Young (2003). Survey of management accounting (Ernst and Young).

Ettridge, M. and Kim, J. (1994). Dividend behaviour surrounding LIFO adoption. *Review of Financial Economics* (Vol. 4, No. 2).

Evans, J. and Archer, S. H. (1968). Diversification and the reduction of dispersion: an empirical analysis. *Journal of Finance* (December).

Fama, E. F. (1965). The behaviour of stock market prices. *Journal of Business* (January).

Fama, E. F. (1998). Market efficiency, long-term returns and behavioural finance. *Journal of Financial Economics* (September).

Fama, E. F. and French, K. R. (1992). The cross-section of expected stock returns. *Journal of Finance* (June).

Fama, E. F. and French, K. R. (1996). Multifactor explanations of asset pricing anomalies. *Journal of Finance* (October).

Fama, E. and French, K. (1998). Taxes, financing decisions and firm value. *Journal of Finance* (June).

Fama, E. and French, K. (2001). Disappearing dividends: changing firm characteristics or lower propensity to pay. *Journal of Financial Economics* (April).

Fama, E. F., Fisher, L., Jensen, M. and Roll, R. (1969). The adjustment of stock prices to new information. *International Economic Review* (February).

Finnerty, J. (1976). Insiders and market efficiency. *Journal of Finance* (September).

Firth, M. (1977a). An empirical investigation of the impact of the announcement of capitalisation issues on share prices. *Journal of Business Finance and Accounting*.

Firth, M. (1977b). *The Valuation of Shares and the Efficient Markets Theory* (Macmillan).

Fletcher, R. (2002). Want to buy a football player? Get a mortgage. *Sunday Telegraph*, (14 July)

Frank, M. and Goyal, V. (2003). Testing the pecking order theory of capital structure. *Journal of Financial Economics* (February).

Franks, J. R. and Harris, P. (1989). Shareholder wealth effects of corporate takeovers: the UK experience (1955–1985). *Journal of Financial Economics* (Vol. 23).

Franks, J. R., Broyles, J. E. and Hecht, M. (1977). An industry study of mergers in the UK. *Journal of Finance* (December).

Friend, I. and Puckett, M. (1964). Dividends and stock prices. *American Economic Review* (September).

Fuller, K., Netter, J. and Stegemoller, M. (2002). What do returns to acquiring firms tell us? Evidence from firms that make many acquisitions. *Journal of Finance* (August).

Gordon, M. J. (1959). Dividends, earnings and stock prices. *Review of Economics and Statistics* (May).

Graham, J. R. and Harvey, C. R. (2001). The theory and practice of corporate finance; Evidence from the field. *Journal of Financial Economics* (Vol. 61).

Gregory, A. (1997). An examination of the long run performance of UK acquiring firms. *Journal of Business Finance and Accounting*.

Gregory, A., Rutterford, J. and Zaman, M. (1999). *The Cost of Capital in the UK* (Chartered Institute of Management Accountants).

Groenewald, N. and Fraser, P. (2000). Forecasting beta: how well does the 'five year rule of thumb' do? *Journal of Business Finance and Accounting*. (September/October).

Grullon, G. and Michaely, R. (2002). Dividends, repurchase and the substitution hypothesis. *Journal of Finance* (August).

Hamada, R. S. (1972). The effect of the firm's financial structure on the systematic risk of common stocks. *Journal of Finance* (May).

Hirshleifer, J. (1958). On the theory of optimal investment decisions. *Journal of Political Economy*. Reprinted in Archer and D'Ambrosio (1983).

Hodder, J. E. (1986). Evaluation of manufacturing investments: a comparison of US and Japanese practices. *Financial Management* (Spring).

Homaifar, G., Zeitz, J. and Benkato, O. (1994). An empirical model of capital structure, some new evidence. *Journal of Business Finance and Accounting* (January).

Horngren, C. T., Bhimani, A., Foster, G. and Datar, S. M. (2001). *Management and Cost Accounting*, 2nd edn (Prentice Hall Europe).

Ibbotson, R. C. and Sinquefield, R. (1979). *Stocks, Bonds and Inflation* (Financial Analysts Research Foundation).

Jaffe, J. (1974). Special information and insider trading. *Journal of Business* (July).

Jenkinson, T. J. (1990). New equity issues in the United Kingdom. *Bank of England Quarterly Bulletin* (May).

Jensen, M. (1986). Agency costs of free cash flow, corporate finance and takeovers. *American Economic Review* (Vol. 76).

Jensen, M. (2001). Value maximisation, stakeholder theory and the corporate objective function. *European Financial Management* (Vol. 7, No. 3).

Julio, B. and Ikenberry, D. L. (2004). Disappearing dividends. *Journal of Applied Corporate Finance* (Fall).

Keenan, D. and Riches, S. (2004). *Business Law*, 7th edn (Pitman).

Kendall, M. G. (1953). The analysis of economic time series. *Journal of the Royal Statistical Society* (Vol. 96, Part 1).

Kester, W. C. (1986). Capital and ownership structure. *Financial Management* (Spring).

Lamont, O. and Polk, C. (2002). Does diversification destroy value? Evidence from industry shocks. *Journal of Financial Economics* (January).

Lee, I., Lockhead, S., Ritter, J. and Zhao, Q. (1996). The costs of raising capital. *Journal of Financial Research* (Spring).

Leslie, K. and Michaels, M. (1998). The real power of real options. *Corporate Finance* (January). Reprinted in Rutterford (1998).

Levy, H. and Sarnat, M. (1988). *Principles of Financial Management* (Prentice Hall International).

Levy, H. and Sarnat, M. (1995). *Capital Investment and Financial Decisions*, 5th edn (Prentice Hall International).

Lewellen, W. G., Stanley, K. L., Lease, R. C. and Schlarbaum, G. G. (1978). Some direct evidence of the dividend clientele phenomenon. *Journal of Finance* (December).

Limmack, R. J. (1991). Corporate mergers and shareholder wealth effects (1977–1986). *Accounting and Business Research* (Vol. 21, No. 83).

Litzenberger, R. and Ramaswamy, K. (1982). The effects of dividends on common stock prices: tax effects or information effects? *Journal of Finance* (May).

Lumby, S. and Jones, C. (2003). *Investment Appraisal and Financial Decision Making*, 7th edn (International Thomson Business Press).

McClure, K. G., Clayton, R. and Hofler, R. A. (1999). International capital structure differences among the G7 nations: a current empirical view. *European Journal of Finance* (June).

McIntyre, A. D. and Coulthurst, N. J. (1985). Theory and practice in capital budgeting. *British Accounting Review* (Autumn).

McLaney, E. and Atrill, P. (2005). *Accounting: An Introduction*, 4th edn (Financial Times Prentice Hall).

McLaney, E., Pointon, J., Thomas, M. and Tucker, J. (2004). Practitioners' perspectives on the UK cost of capital. *European Journal of Finance* (April).

Madura, J. (2002). *International Financial Management*, 7th edn (West Publishing Company).

Mallin, C., Ow-yong, K. and Reynolds, M. (2001). Derivatives usage in UK non-finance listed companies. *European Journal of Finance* (March).

Marsh, P. (1982). The choice between equity and debt: an empirical study. *Journal of Finance* (March).

Marston, C. L. and Craven, B. M. (1998). A survey of corporate perceptions of short termism among analysts and fund managers. *European Journal of Finance* (September).

Masulis, R. (1980). The effect of capital structure changes on security prices. *Journal of Financial Economics* (June).

Mathur, I., Singh, M. and Gleason, K. (2004). Multinational diversification and corporate performance: evidence from European firms. *European Financial Management* (September).

Mehdian, S. and Perry, M. J. (2001). The reversal of the Monday effect: new evidence from US equity markets. *Journal of Business Finance and Accounting* (September/October).

Miller, M. H. (1977). Debt and taxes. *Journal of Finance* (Vol. 32, No. 2).

Miller, M. H. and Modigliani, F. (1961). Dividend policy, growth and the valuation of shares. *Journal of Business* (October).

Miller, M. H. and Modigliani, F. (1966). Some estimates of the cost of capital to the electrical utility industry 1954–57. *American Economic Review* (June).

Miller, M. H. and Orr, D. (1966). A model of the demand for money by firms. *Quarterly Journal of Economics* (August).

Modigliani, F. and Miller, M. H. (1958). The cost of capital, corporate finance and the theory of investment. *American Economic Review*. Reprinted in Archer and D'Ambrosio (1983).

Modigliani, F. and Miller, M. H. (1963). Corporate income taxes and the cost of capital. *American Economic Review* (June).

Moore, J. S. and Reichert, A. K. (1983). An analysis of the financial management techniques currently employed by large US corporations. *Journal of Business Finance and Accounting* (Vol. 10, No. 4).

Morris, R. (1975). Evidence of the impact of inflation accounting on share prices. *Accounting and Business Research* (Spring).

Morrison, D. (2003). Small firms still have to wait for their money. *Sunday Telegraph* (14 September).

Mougoue, M. and Rao, R. (2003). The information signalling hypothesis of dividends: evidence from cointegration and causality tests. *Journal of Business Finance and Accounting* (April).

Moyes, J. (1988). The dangers of JIT. *Management Accounting* (February).

Myers, S. (1984). The capital structure puzzle. *Journal of Finance* (July)

Newbould, A. (1970). *Management and Merger Activity* (Guthstead Press).

Nissim, D. and Ziv, A. (2001). Dividend changes and future profitability. *Journal of Finance* (December).

OECD (1998). Corporate governance: improving competitiveness and access to capital in global markets. *Organization for Economic Co-operation and Development.*

Osborne, A. (2004). Ryanair blunted by Buzz takeover. *Daily Telegraph* (6 August).

Oswald, D. and Young, S. (2002). Boom time for buybacks. *Accountancy* (October).

Ozkan, A. (2001). Determinants of capital structure and adjustment to long run target: evidence from UK company panel data. *Journal of Business Finance and Accounting* (January/March).

Pettit, R. R. (1972). Dividend announcements, security performance and capital market efficiency. *Journal of Finance* (December).

Pettit, R. R. (1977). Taxes, transactions costs and clientele effects of dividends. *Journal of Financial Economics* (December).

Petty, J. W. and Scott, D. F. (1981). Capital budgeting practices in large US firms. Reprinted in *Readings in Strategy for Corporate Investment*, ed. Derkinderin, F. G. J. and Crum, R. L. (1982) (Pitman Publishing).

Pike, R. H. (1982). *Capital Budgeting in the 1980s* (Institute of Cost and Management Accountants).

Pike, R. H. (1983). The capital budgeting behaviour and corporate characteristics of capital-constrained firms. *Journal of Business Finance and Accounting* (Summer).

Pike, R. H. (1985). Owner–manager conflict and the role of the payback method. *Accounting and Business Research* (Winter).

Pike, R. H. (1996). A longitudinal survey of capital budgeting practices. *Journal of Business Finance and Accounting* (January).

Pike, R. H. and Ooi, T. S. (1988). The impact of corporate investment objectives and constraints on capital budgeting practices. *British Accounting Review* (August).

Pike, R. H. and Wolfe, M. (1988). *Capital Budgeting in the 1990s* (Chartered Institute of Management Accountants).

Rappaport, A. (1986). *Creating Shareholder Value* (Free Press).

Ricci, C. and Di Nino, V. (2000). International working capital practices in the UK. *European Financial Management* (March).

Roberts, H. (1967). Statistical versus clinical predictions of the stock market. Unpublished paper, University of Chicago.

Ross, S. A. (1976). The arbitrage theory and capital asset pricing. *Journal of Economic Theory* (December).

Rutterford, J. (1998). *Financial Strategy* (Wiley).

Rutterford, J. and Montgomerie, R. (eds) (1993). *UK Corporate Finance Handbook*, 2nd edn (Butterworth).

Samuels, J. M., Wilkes, F. M. and Brayshaw, R. E. (1998). *Management of Company Finance*, 7th edn (International Thomson Business Press).

Scapens, R. W., Sale, J. T. and Tikkas, P. A. (1982). *Financial Control of Divisional Capital Investment* (Chartered Institute of Management Accountants).

Schooley, D. and Barney, L. (1994). Using dividend policy and managerial ownership to reduce agency costs. *Journal of Financial Research* (Fall).

Shapiro, A. C. and Balbirer, S. D. (2000). *Modern Corporate Finance*, 2nd edn (Macmillan).

Sharpe, W. (1963). A simplified model for portfolio analysis. *Management Science* (January).

Sharpe, W. (1998). *Investments*, 6th edn (Prentice Hall).

Siddiqi, M. (1995). An indirect test for dividend relevance. *Journal of Financial Research* (Spring).

Stiglitz, J. E. (1974). On the irrelevance of corporate financial policy. *American Economic Review* (Vol. 64, No. 6).

Stock Exchange Fact Book (annually) (The International Stock Exchange, London).

Storey, D. (1994). *Understanding the Small Business Sector* (Routledge).

Sun, Q. and Tong, W. (2002). Another new look at the Monday effect. *Journal of Business Finance and Accounting* (September/October).

Sunder, S. (1973). Relationship between accounting changes and stock prices: problems of measurement and some empirical evidence. *Journal of Accounting Research* (supplement).

Surowiecki, J. (2004) *The Wisdom of Crowds*. (Little, Brown).

Taffler, R. (1995). *The Use of the Z-Score Approach in Practice*. Available from the City University Business School, Barbican Centre, Frobisher Crescent, London EC2Y 8HB.

Walker, M. (2000). Corporate takeovers, strategic objectives and acquiring-firm shareholder wealth. *Financial Management* (Spring).

Welch, I. (2000). Herding among security analysts. *Journal of Financial Economics* (December).

Weston, J. F. (1963). A test of capital propositions. *Southern Economic Journal* (October).

Wilson Committee (1980). *Committee to Review the Functioning of Financial Institutions* (HMSO).

Wilson, N. and Summers, B. (2002). Trade credit terms offered by small firms: survey evidence and empirical analysis. *Journal of Business Finance and Accounting* (April/May).

Appendix 1

Present value table

Present value of £1 in _n_ years at discount rate _r_.

Years (n)					Discount rate (r)						Years (n)
	1%	2%	3%	4%	5%	6%	7%	8%	9%	10%	
1	0.990	0.980	0.971	0.962	0.952	0.943	0.935	0.926	0.917	0.909	1
2	0.980	0.961	0.943	0.925	0.907	0.890	0.873	0.857	0.842	0.826	2
3	0.971	0.942	0.915	0.889	0.864	0.840	0.816	0.794	0.772	0.751	3
4	0.961	0.924	0.888	0.855	0.823	0.792	0.763	0.735	0.708	0.683	4
5	0.951	0.906	0.863	0.822	0.784	0.747	0.713	0.681	0.650	0.621	5
6	0.942	0.888	0.837	0.790	0.746	0.705	0.666	0.630	0.596	0.564	6
7	0.933	0.871	0.813	0.760	0.711	0.665	0.623	0.583	0.547	0.513	7
8	0.923	0.853	0.789	0.731	0.677	0.627	0.582	0.540	0.502	0.467	8
9	0.914	0.837	0.766	0.703	0.645	0.592	0.544	0.500	0.460	0.424	9
10	0.905	0.820	0.744	0.676	0.614	0.558	0.508	0.463	0.422	0.386	10
11	0.896	0.804	0.722	0.650	0.585	0.527	0.475	0.429	0.388	0.350	11
12	0.887	0.788	0.701	0.625	0.557	0.497	0.444	0.397	0.356	0.319	12
13	0.879	0.773	0.681	0.601	0.530	0.469	0.415	0.368	0.326	0.290	13
14	0.870	0.758	0.661	0.577	0.505	0.442	0.388	0.340	0.299	0.263	14
15	0.861	0.743	0.642	0.555	0.481	0.417	0.362	0.315	0.275	0.239	15

	11%	12%	13%	14%	15%	16%	17%	18%	19%	20%	
1	0.901	0.893	0.885	0.877	0.870	0.862	0.855	0.847	0.840	0.833	1
2	0.812	0.797	0.783	0.769	0.756	0.743	0.731	0.718	0.706	0.694	2
3	0.731	0.712	0.693	0.675	0.658	0.641	0.624	0.609	0.593	0.579	3
4	0.659	0.636	0.613	0.592	0.572	0.552	0.534	0.516	0.499	0.482	4
5	0.593	0.567	0.543	0.519	0.497	0.476	0.456	0.437	0.419	0.402	5
6	0.535	0.507	0.480	0.456	0.432	0.410	0.390	0.370	0.352	0.335	6
7	0.482	0.452	0.425	0.400	0.376	0.354	0.333	0.314	0.296	0.279	7
8	0.434	0.404	0.376	0.351	0.327	0.305	0.285	0.266	0.249	0.233	8
9	0.391	0.361	0.333	0.308	0.284	0.263	0.243	0.225	0.209	0.194	9
10	0.352	0.322	0.295	0.270	0.247	0.227	0.208	0.191	0.176	0.162	10
11	0.317	0.287	0.261	0.237	0.215	0.195	0.178	0.162	0.148	0.135	11
12	0.286	0.257	0.231	0.208	0.187	0.168	0.152	0.137	0.124	0.112	12
13	0.258	0.229	0.204	0.182	0.163	0.145	0.130	0.116	0.104	0.093	13
14	0.232	0.205	0.181	0.160	0.141	0.125	0.111	0.099	0.088	0.078	14
15	0.209	0.183	0.160	0.140	0.123	0.108	0.095	0.084	0.074	0.065	15

Annuity table

Present value of £1 receivable at the end of each year for *n* years at discount rate *r*.

Years (n)	1%	2%	3%	4%	5%	6%	7%	8%	9%	10%	Years (n)
					Discount rate (r)						
1	0.990	0.980	0.971	0.962	0.952	0.943	0.935	0.926	0.917	0.909	1
2	1.970	1.942	1.913	1.886	1.859	1.833	1.808	1.783	1.759	1.736	2
3	2.941	2.884	2.829	2.775	2.723	2.673	2.624	2.577	2.531	2.487	3
4	3.902	3.808	3.717	3.630	3.546	3.465	3.387	3.312	3.240	3.170	4
5	4.853	4.713	4.580	4.452	4.329	4.212	4.100	3.993	3.890	3.791	5
6	5.795	5.601	5.417	5.242	5.076	4.917	4.767	4.623	4.486	4.355	6
7	6.728	6.472	6.230	6.002	5.786	5.582	5.389	5.206	5.033	4.868	7
8	7.652	7.325	7.020	6.733	6.463	6.210	5.971	5.747	5.535	5.335	8
9	8.566	8.162	7.786	7.435	7.108	6.802	6.515	6.247	5.995	5.759	9
10	9.471	8.983	8.530	8.111	7.722	7.360	7.024	6.710	6.418	6.145	10
11	10.37	9.787	9.253	8.760	8.306	7.887	7.499	7.139	6.805	6.495	11
12	11.26	10.58	9.954	9.385	8.863	8.384	7.943	7.536	7.161	6.814	12
13	12.13	11.35	10.63	9.986	9.394	8.853	8.358	7.904	7.487	7.103	13
14	13.00	12.11	11.30	10.56	9.899	9.295	8.745	8.244	7.786	7.367	14
15	13.87	12.85	11.94	11.12	10.38	9.712	9.108	8.559	8.061	7.606	15

	11%	12%	13%	14%	15%	16%	17%	18%	19%	20%	
1	0.901	0.893	0.885	0.877	0.870	0.862	0.855	0.847	0.840	0.833	1
2	1.713	1.690	1.668	1.647	1.626	1.605	1.585	1.566	1.547	1.528	2
3	2.444	2.402	2.361	2.322	2.283	2.246	2.210	2.174	2.140	2.106	3
4	3.102	3.037	2.974	2.914	2.855	2.798	2.743	2.690	2.639	2.589	4
5	3.696	3.605	3.517	3.433	3.352	3.274	3.199	3.127	3.058	2.991	5
6	4.231	4.111	3.998	3.889	3.784	3.685	3.589	3.498	3.410	3.326	6
7	4.712	4.564	4.423	4.288	4.160	4.039	3.922	3.812	3.706	3.605	7
8	5.146	4.968	4.799	4.639	4.487	4.344	4.207	4.078	3.954	3.837	8
9	5.537	5.328	5.132	4.946	4.772	4.607	4.451	4.303	4.163	4.031	9
10	5.889	5.650	5.426	5.216	5.019	4.833	4.659	4.494	4.339	4.192	10
11	6.207	5.938	5.687	5.453	5.234	5.029	4.836	4.656	4.486	4.327	11
12	6.492	6.194	5.918	5.660	5.421	5.197	4.988	4.793	4.611	4.439	12
13	6.750	6.424	6.122	5.842	5.583	5.342	5.118	4.910	4.715	4.533	13
14	6.982	6.628	6.302	6.002	5.724	5.468	5.229	5.008	4.802	4.611	14
15	7.191	6.811	6.462	6.142	5.847	5.575	5.324	5.092	4.876	4.675	15

Suggested answers to review questions

Chapter 1

1.1 Reasons for the popularity of the limited company include the following:

- *Number of participants.* The partnership, which is the only feasible alternative, is restricted to less than 20 participants in most cases. This limits the business that wishes to involve large numbers of participants providing equity finance to operating as a limited company.

- *Limited liability.* Potential equity investors are more likely to be prepared to invest where the liability for losses is limited. Thus limited companies are able to attract equity finance more easily than partnerships.

- *Perpetuity.* Limited companies continue to exist despite changes in their ownership. Thus if a shareholder transfers his or her shares, the company is strictly unaffected. When a partner leaves a partnership, the partnership comes to an end.

- *Transferability.* Linked to the previous point is the fact that shares can easily be transferred from one person to another. This means that one shareholder can sell shares to another, perhaps through the Stock Exchange.

- *Credibility.* Since most substantial businesses operate as limited companies, not to do so may imply some lack of substance or permanence about the business. This is not to say that operating as a limited company guarantees reliability, but this may, to some extent, accord with public perceptions.

1.2 In essence there is no difference between the position of a limited company and a human person in respect of its financial obligations to others. Both are fully liable to the extent to which they have assets to meet the obligation. In both cases, under normal circumstances the assets of third parties cannot be required to meet any shortfall between the obligation and the assets. Thus shareholders in limited companies cannot normally be asked to contribute assets to meet unsatisfied financial obligations of the company in which they own shares.

1.3 The position of the shareholders is that, so long as they have provided any funds that they have pledged to pay into the company, they cannot normally be required to make payments to cover any failure of the company to meet its financial obligations.

The owner of a sole proprietorship business (a sole trader) can be required to meet all of the debts of the business using what may be regarded as personal assets (for example, the sole trader's house) if necessary.

Thus owners/part-owners of different types of business find themselves in very different positions regarding the extent to which they risk their personal assets as a result of their participation in the business.

1.4 Preference shares are part of the equity or ownership of the business, usually entitling their owners to the first portion of any dividend paid, but there is no obligation for the business to pay a dividend, nor usually to redeem the preference shares.

Loan stocks represent loans made by people or investing institutions under a contract with the business concerned. The contract would normally specify the rate of interest to be paid, the date of payment of the interest, and the amount and date of repayment of the principal of the loan.

Preference shares and loan stock have a superficial resemblance in that they both tend to attract a fixed annual payment and are redeemed at some point. The essential difference is that such payments are contractual and can be enforced in the case of loan stocks, but not in the case of preference shares.

1.5 Many financing and investment decisions are vitally important to the business because they involve significant amounts of finance over long periods of time. Thus misjudgements can have far-reaching, possibly disastrous, effects.

Of course, not all such decisions are so significant, but many tend to be.

1.6 Both theory and practice indicate that investors seek higher returns to compensate them for bearing higher risk. The required return would be a risk-free rate, plus a risk premium. The risk-free rate would normally be equal to the rate that is available for very safe investments, like short-term deposits with very safe borrowers, such as a stable government. The risk premium would relate to the perceived level of risk.

Chapter 2

2.1 The two criteria are:

- The information must relate to the *objective(s) that is/are being pursued* by the decision maker. Thus if a decision needs to be made on whether to travel to a particular destination by car or by train, and the only objective being pursued is to spend the least possible time on the journey, only the time taken is relevant. The cost, level of comfort and convenience are all irrelevant, given the sole objective of least journey time.

- The information must be *different* between the two courses of action. Thus if the time taken is identical between car and train, the length of time is irrelevant, given the least journey time objective.

2.2 It is considered incomplete because it lacks a timescale. If the objective were to maximise accounting profit for next year, this might be easily achievable by taking short-term actions that could have adverse long-term effects. For example, all research and development could be abandoned, with resulting cost savings. This would be likely to have disastrous long-term effects since new products and methods would not be developed, making it likely the business would lose markets to rivals that had continued to innovate.

2.3 On the face of it, the higher the price that can be charged the better for the shareholders. However, in the medium and long term, such behaviour may be adverse to the interests of the shareholders. This may manifest itself in the following ways:

- The attentions of a regulatory body concerned with monopolies, such as the UK Competition Commission, may be attracted. This could lead to an order to reduce prices.

- Large profits could attract other suppliers to enter the market. Not only would this lead to price competition and lower prices, but the bad public sentiment of the market towards the exploiter could well cause the market to favour the newcomers, even where the price and quality were similar.

Thus there is nothing inconsistent between reasonable treatment of customers and the best interests of the shareholders.

2.4 The separation theorem says that the investment should be undertaken if it generates wealth for the business. Doing this will make the shareholders more wealthy.

How the investment is financed is a separate matter and, under the assumptions made by the separation theorem, unimportant. Either the dividend could be paid and money borrowed (or raised from a share issue) to make the investment, or the dividend not paid and the existing cash used to make the investment.

2.5 According to the assumptions made by the separation theorem, any dividends paid to a shareholder can be invested at the prevailing rate of interest. If the business has to pay that same rate to borrow cash to finance an investment, the shareholder gains an amount from lending that is equal to the shareholders' share of the interest paid on cash borrowed to make the investment.

2.6 The most obvious reasons for this are:

- The business, because it is better established in the financial market and because it would be borrowing a relatively large amount, may well be able to borrow at lower rates than could an individual shareholder borrowing a small amount.

- In the context of the UK tax system, the interest payable would be tax deductible to the business but not to an individual shareholder.

Chapter 3

3.1 A balance sheet is a list of assets and financial obligations of an organisation at a specified point in time. The assets are typically shown at how much they cost when they were acquired by the organisation (historic cost). Depreciating non-current assets are normally shown at cost, less some proportion of that cost depending on the anticipated useful life of the asset, and how much of that life has already expired.

Since assets are valued on the basis of their cost, the balance sheet does not provide any reliable indication as to how much the organisation is worth, in market value terms. Some assets may be overstated in the balance sheet, relative to their current economic value, some may be understated, and some assets (for example, goodwill), which have a current economic value, may not appear in the balance sheet at all because they have no cost.

3.2 The profit is the net increase in assets arising from trading activities. Net cash inflow from operating activities is the increase in cash. The difference between them arises from two broad factors:

- *Depreciation of non-current assets*, which is an expense deducted from profit but which has no effect on cash flow.

- *Increases and decreases in stocks, debtors and creditors*, which each have the effect of absorbing or releasing cash. Thus, for example, if stocks increase over the period under consideration, this additional investment means that the amount of increase in cash will be reduced.

3.3 A strong balance sheet normally means that the business is in a healthy position as regards the balance of assets and financial obligations. This usually refers to two areas:

- *Working capital*. Here the relationship between current assets, particularly the more liquid of them, and current liabilities is the issue. Thus ratios such as the current ratio and the quick assets (acid test) ratio would be fairly large in a strong balance sheet.

● *Long-term finance.* The relationship between equity capital and fixed return capital is the issue. A strong balance sheet would have a fairly modest capital gearing ratio and, probably, available assets to offer as security for further borrowings.

3.4 The matching convention says that expenses should be matched to the revenues that they helped to generate, within the same period as that in which those revenues were realised (recognised).

3.5 This is presumably because Taffler found that it added little or nothing to the reliability of the model. This is not to say that the ratio has no value, or even that it has little or no value in trying to identify problem businesses. It is probably the case that other ratios that are included in the model, and which are substantially correlated with the quick assets ratio, perform better in the context of the model.

3.6 A careful reading of the financial statements is certainly extremely valuable in drawing helpful conclusions about a business. It can provide insights that ratio analysis cannot provide. Ratio analysis can, however, by formally relating one figure to another, provide insights that a normal reading of the accounts cannot provide. A major reason for this is that ratios can correct for size differences between the businesses or time periods that are to be compared. Thus comparing the profit of Business A with that of Business B will not usually be very helpful, but comparing the profit per £1 of capital employed by Business A with that of Business B will usually be informative.

Chapter 4

4.1 Discounting is intended to take account of the effective cost of using the funds in the investment project under consideration. This cost is made up of three elements:

● a 'pure' rate of interest;
● an allowance for risk; and
● an allowance for inflation.

Inflation is a factor, but it is not the only reason for discounting. Discounting would need to be undertaken even where no inflation was expected over the lifetime of the project under consideration.

4.2 The opportunity cost of finance is the rate at which the business (or, more strictly, its shareholders) could invest the funds if they were not to be used in the investment project under review. Where relevant, this would take account of the risk involved in the project.

4.3 It is a fact that NPV is unique among the four methods that are found in practice, in relating directly to the presumed objective of private sector businesses to maximise the wealth of shareholders. Reliance on the other three methods will only, by coincidence, cause decisions to be taken that will work towards a wealth maximisation objective.

4.4 There seem to be two basic possibilities:

● Some users do not realise that it is flawed.
● Some users realise that it is flawed but feel that, nevertheless, it gives helpful information. Since it is easy to calculate, it is not expensive to produce, certainly not where the cash flows are to be estimated for use with, say, NPV.

4.5 IRR is flawed because it does not address the generally accepted objective of shareholder wealth maximisation. Following IRR would promote those projects that maximise the return on investment. Since this coincides, in most cases, with those projects that will maximise shareholder wealth, using IRR will tend to give the right signals, however.

IRR also has some anomalies, such as giving more than one IRR or no IRR, but these tend not to occur with typical projects.

4.6 Possibilities include:

● Using only one method per decision, but using different methods for each type of decision: for example, using NPV for projects involving an investment of more than £100 000, but using payback period for smaller decisions.

● Using more than one method for each decision so that a fuller picture of the decision data can be obtained.

Chapter 5

5.1 No, it is not illogical. Profit and NPV have two entirely different objectives. Profit is concerned with assessing trading effectiveness for a period of time that is shorter than the typical investment project's life. If some allowance for the cost of using non-current assets during that accounting period is to be made, depreciation must be calculated and charged. NPV has another objective, which is to look at the effectiveness of an asset (or set of assets) over its full life. In a sense, NPV assessments do take account of depreciation since the project is charged (cash outflow) with the capital cost of the asset, normally at the beginning of the project, and given credit (cash inflow) for any disposal proceeds, normally at the end of the project.

5.2 This is not logical as discounting takes account of the financing cost of the project.

5.3 It is slightly more complicated than this. The relationship is:

$$1 + \text{'Money' rate} = (1 + \text{'Real' rate}) \times (1 + \text{Inflation rate})$$

5.4 The two approaches are:

● Identify the *'money'* cash flow and discount this at the 'money' cost of capital.

● Identify the *'real'* cash flow and discount this at the 'real' cost of capital.

These two approaches are both equally valid and will give precisely the same NPV. In practice, the former tends to involve a more straightforward calculation, particularly where such complications as tax and working capital are involved.

5.5 Hard capital rationing arises where it is simply impossible to raise the funds to support all of the available projects. It can be argued that, in practice, funds can always be raised provided that a high enough rate of return is offered to the providers of the finance. This rate may well be too high to enable the project to be viable (that is, it leads to a negative NPV), but this simply means that the project should not be undertaken, not that capital rationing exists.

5.6 The profitability index is a measure of a project's NPV per £ of initial investment required. It can be useful for solving single-period capital rationing problems.

It is not normally a helpful approach to dealing with multi-period capital rationing problems. This is because the profitability index may suggest one project as being the most beneficial in the context of one year's capital shortage, but a different one in the context of that of another year.

Chapter 6

6.1 The two main limitations are:

- It assumes that only one of the variables will differ from its predicted value, in other words sensitivity analysis is too static. In reality the variables will probably all differ from prediction to some extent.

- It is difficult to interpret the results. This would be equally true even if the first limitation were overcome by using a scenario-building approach.

6.2 Approach (a) has the advantage in that all possible outcomes, and their probability of occurrence, can be identified. This will give you a feel for the distributions of possible outcomes, or it will enable you to calculate the standard deviation.

The number of possible outcomes could, in real life, be vast, which would make such an approach untenable.

Approach (b) is much more practical because it will be relatively easy to carry out the calculations. Since averages are used throughout, it is not possible to gain any feel, or deduce statistics, about the spread of possible outcomes and, therefore, of the risk involved.

6.3 *Specific risk* is peculiar to the project, but not necessarily to other projects. Combining projects in a portfolio will enable this risk to be eliminated.

Systematic risk is present in all projects, to some extent or another, and so cannot be diversified away by portfolio investment. This type of risk tends to be caused by macroeconomic factors.

It is helpful to distinguish between these two types of risk because the decision maker will be able to judge the extent to which total risk can be eliminated by investing in a portfolio of projects.

6.4 Utility is a measure of the degree of satisfaction that will be derived by an individual as a result of having a particular amount of something desirable, such as wealth.

6.5 In non-technical terms, a risk-averse person will only accept risk where this is rewarded. Because such people derive a decreasing utility from each additional £1 of wealth, they require an increased reward for each additional increment of risk undertaken.

It is fairly obvious that most human beings are risk averse, certainly where more than trivial amounts are involved.

6.6 The range of possible outcomes from the decision needs to be symmetrically distributed around their expected value (or mean), and the investor needs to be risk averse.

Chapter 7

7.1 It needs to be assumed that returns are symmetrically distributed around the expected value, and that investors are risk averse.

Evidence tends to suggest that investment returns from quoted securities are close to showing a normal distribution, which is a symmetrical distribution. Observation also tends to show that most people are risk averse.

7.2 The first statement is correct; the second one is not. The relationship is very much more complicated and depends, among other things, on the coefficient of correlation between the securities in the portfolio.

7.3 There is no other portfolio that will give a higher expected return for that portfolio's level of risk, and there is no other portfolio that will offer a lower level of risk for that portfolio's level of return.

7.4 It means that all rational, risk-averse investors will choose to invest their wealth in some combination of the market portfolio of risky investments and a risk-free deposit (at the risk-free rate). The risk-free investment might be a negative one, in other words, borrowing, for the less risk-averse investors.

7.5 The statement is not true. The beta relates only to the risk premium. Thus the risk premium of the former security will be expected to be twice that of the latter. In either case, the total return is the risk-free rate plus the risk premium.

7.6 This is justified on two grounds:

- The stock market is a free, efficient and observable market where risky investments are bought and sold. It thus provides us with the basis of price for risky investments not actually traded in that market.
- The returns from real investments made within businesses feed through to the investment returns of those businesses' shareholders. Thus there is a clear link between real investment returns and stock market returns.

Chapter 8

8.1 Loan finance is risky to the borrowing business because the business must meet contractual obligations (normally) to pay interest and repay the principal of the borrowing on the due date. Failure to meet these obligations could cause the business to be put into liquidation, with resulting losses to shareholders. By contrast, equity finance does not create these obligations.

8.2 If profits are paid out to shareholders as a dividend, the cash can be invested by the shareholders to generate an income. If profits are retained, there is an opportunity cost to shareholders for which they will require compensation from the business, equal to the value of that lost income.

8.3 The cost of 'raising' retained profits is zero. Unlike other forms of raising equity, no administrative or legal costs have to be paid. This makes it very cheap to raise finance by retaining profit. Also, provided that profits have been made, retained profits represent a pretty sure means of raising finance. Other ways of raising equity depend on decisions made by those to whom new shares are issued. Although the risk that investors will not buy new shares can be insured against through underwriters, the fees involved tend to be rather high.

8.4 Except where the loan stock has just been issued, it would be unusual for the coupon rate to equal the pre-tax cost of the loan to the business. Interest rates prevailing in the economy vary over relatively short periods of time. To cause the return from the loan stock (which is fixed as the coupon rate) to represent the market level of return, the market price of the loan stock will move away from its issue price. Also, some loan stocks are issued at a discount or redeemed at a premium on the value at which the coupon rate is calculated. In this case the 10 per cent does not represent the complete return from the loan stock.

8.5 A convertible loan stock is one that shows all of the characteristics of a pure loan stock until some predetermined date at which loan stockholders will be offered a number of ordinary shares in the business in exchange for their loan stock.

Factors that affect the value of loan stock include:

- the prevailing interest rates;
- the perceived riskiness of the loan stock;

- the rate of conversion (that is, how many shares per £100 of loan stock);
- the anticipated value of the shares at the date of conversion; and
- volatility of the share price.

8.6 A business that wishes to buy a particular non-current asset, and to use borrowed funds to do so, can borrow the cash from a bank, by issuing a loan stock (say), and buy the asset. It then pays interest on the loan and at the end of the loan period repays the loan. It may be the case that the loan will be repaid piecemeal.

In the case of leasing, the business arranges for a financier (for example, a bank) to buy the asset outright. The business then leases the asset from the financier for the duration of that asset's useful life. Each year the business pays the financier an equal leasing fee. From the financier's point of view, this fee must be sufficient to compensate for the cash tied up in the asset (interest) and to repay the loan. Thus a lease of this type closely resembles a loan that is repaid piecemeal over the period of the loan. If the latter is a source of finance, which undoubtedly it is, then the former must also be a source of finance.

Chapter 9

9.1 Members of the LSE, and most other of the world's stock markets, act as:

- *agents* for their clients who wish to buy securities through the LSE; and
- *market makers*, who buy and sell securities of particular types, much as any other trader does.

9.2 No. Shareholders can sell the shares as they wish. If a potential buyer can be identified, the shares can be transacted privately between the parties. The problem lies in finding a buyer. Since the LSE is the location where buyers and sellers, including LSE members in their market-making role, congregate (electronically, if not physically), this is a convenient place to sell the shares.

9.3 Price efficiency means that security prices always rationally reflect all information relevant to their value.

9.4 Yes. If the market reflects all information (public and private), it clearly reflects all public information.

9.5 Yes. Given the amount of research that is undertaken into individual businesses and their economic environment, by intelligent and skilled analysts, and that the results of the research feed into decisions to buy and sell securities, we should expect that, through the pressures of buyers and sellers, prices would rationally reflect all known, relevant information. The financial rewards to investors for getting the price right are such that the pressure and incentive to do so are enormous.

9.6 Not necessarily, but wherever there is a significant amount of valid research into the securities, and there is an orderly and fair market, we should expect price efficiency to exist, at least to some extent.

Chapter 10

10.1 The discounted value of all future cash flows that will be generated by the asset.

10.2 The approach (unless the loan stock would only generate returns for the next one or two years) would have to be to deduce the 'internal rate of return' of the loan stock by trial and error.

10.3 The level of capital gearing is such an important factor for businesses that it seems likely that the benefits (tax relief) and costs (potential bankruptcy and so forth) would be carefully weighed and a target established. Even if this is not always true for smaller businesses, it seems likely that larger ones will pay attention to establishing a target.

10.4 The reason is that the appropriate discount rate is the opportunity cost of capital for that particular project, which takes account of the risk involved in the project, and so forth. There is no reason why the cost of the particular finance just raised should bear any resemblance to the rate at which the project's cash flows need to be discounted. The suppliers of the finance will not see that they are specifically financing the project. They will see themselves as providing part of the finance for the business as a whole.

10.5 Market values should be used because WACC is meant to represent the opportunity cost of finance. Market values reflect the cost of any new capital that the business might raise, or the cost saving achieved by returning some finance to its providers.

10.6 No. These are both simplifying assumptions, one of which it is often expedient to make. Other assumptions could be made. Future dividends are difficult to predict, so a simple assumption is usually favoured.

Chapter 11

11.1 There are two main reasons:

- Because loan capital is the subject of a clear contractual relationship, regarding interest payments and repayment of capital, between the lender and the business, the risk borne by the loan stockholder is much less than that borne by the equity holder. Consequently loan stockholders do not expect such high returns.
- Loan stock interest is deductible for corporation tax purposes; returns to shareholders are not.

11.2 It increases, to reflect the higher level of risk associated with higher gearing.

11.3 It increases, to reflect the higher level of risk associated with higher gearing. Taxes do not really make any difference.

11.4 These include costs such as:

- any legal costs that might be involved with winding up the business;
- any losses arising from selling off assets at a lower value than they were worth to the business as a going concern; and
- any loss of profits involved in trying to keep a sinking business afloat.

11.5 We know because, in practice, nearly all businesses raise part, and in many cases a substantial part, of their total finance from borrowing.

11.6 The geared business is worth the same as the ungeared one *plus* $(T \times D)$, where T is the relevant rate of corporation tax and D is the market value of the borrowings.

Chapter 12

12.1 The future dividend must be equal to $D_0(1 + k)^n$, where D_0 is the present dividend, k is the shareholders' opportunity cost of finance and n is the number of years into the future that the dividend will be received.

12.2 All investments that yield a positive NPV, when discounted at the shareholders' opportunity cost of capital, should be made. If any funds remain in the business they should be paid out by way of a dividend.

12.3 A homemade dividend is a cash flow that arises from a shareholder's selling a part of his or her holding as a substitute for receiving a dividend from the business itself. A shareholder might create such a dividend where his or her individual preference for dividends does not match the business's dividend policy.

12.4 The traditional view of dividends seems to be that dividend levels are the key determinant of share prices, and that the payment of a steady dividend enhances the market value of shares, even if good investment opportunities must be forgone to pay dividends.

12.5 The tax position of many shareholders, and to some extent of the business itself, is affected by a decision as to whether to pay a dividend or to invest the funds. The MM 'dividend irrelevance' argument starts to weaken when taxes are taken into account.

12.6 Since creating or negating dividends by homemade methods (that is, selling or buying the business's shares) has costs, it is often better for shareholders to hold shares in businesses whose dividend policy suits their needs. The costs include dealing charges for buying and selling shares and, possibly, the tax effects of doing so.

Chapter 13

13.1 The large amounts of investment in stocks and debtors, the funds held in cash and the amount of finance provided by trade creditors make working capital a very important area for the average business.

13.2 'Overtrading' is the name given to a state of affairs where the amount of finance devoted to investment in working capital is insufficient to sustain the level of activity at which the business is operating. It can arise under any set of circumstances where this state of affairs exists, but it is often associated with a sudden and significant increase in activity.

13.3 Items of stock may lose value simply because they become less desirable. A simple case is fashion clothing, which can rapidly lose appeal as fashion changes. Another example is a bought-in component that was acquired for incorporation into a product that the business has decided not to make in the future. Note that, in both of these examples, there is no suggestion that the stock has physically deteriorated in any way.

13.4 Deficiencies include the following:

- A failure to allow for a safety level of stock, that is, it is assumed that stock will run down to zero just as the next delivery arrives.
- The assumption is made that stock is used on a constant rate per time period.

13.5 These would include:

- Establishing the creditworthiness of the potential credit customer. If this is not a new customer, this should already have been established and reviewed.
- Ensuring that the current sale will not take the customer's outstanding debt over the credit limit that has been established for that customer.

13.6 The advantages of using a bank overdraft include:

- It is relatively cheap.
- It is flexible.

The disadvantages include:

- The bank normally charges a fee for establishing the facility.
- The overdraft is usually repayable at very short notice.

Chapter 14

14.1 Corporate restructuring means businesses reorganising themselves in some way or another, in an attempt to meet their objectives more effectively. Thus, in principle, it is a good thing. Whether it is always such a good thing in practice is another matter.

14.2 As for any other investment, the shareholders should assess the present value of future cash flows from the existing shares with the equivalent for the shares in the 'bidder'. These cash flows may be difficult to predict, but this is true of all future events.

14.3 The general approach is that it is up to the private sector to organise itself as it sees fit, unless the public interest is threatened. This threat may arise where a particular merger creates an effective monopoly.

14.4 In the former case, the managers who are doing the buying are not existing managers in the business that is selling part of its operation. In the latter case, the managers work for the business, usually in the part that is the subject of the sale.

14.5 A *sell-off* involves a business selling part of its operation, perhaps to another business, perhaps to the managers. A *spin-off* involves dividing the existing business's operations into two (or, possibly, more) parts by creating a new business (or businesses) to take responsibility for the spun-off part. Shareholders are given shares in this new business (or businesses) in proportion to the shares that they already own in the original one. Thus the shareholders own the same assets, but through two (or more) separate shareholdings.

14.6 The evidence on takeovers suggests that they are not necessarily successful.

Chapter 15

15.1 It is claimed that internationalisation has the potential simultaneously to increase the quantity of profitable investments and lower the cost of finance.

15.2 The four key players in foreign exchange markets are:

- those who are involved in international trade who need to convert currencies;
- those who prefer to convert to and hold a foreign currency because higher interest rates are offered on deposits in that currency or because they expect the foreign currency to strengthen against their home currency;
- those who speculate in currencies; and
- governments in an attempt to manage the exchange rate between their own and other currencies.

15.3 The four rules are:

- purchasing power parity;
- Fisher effect;

- international Fisher effect; and
- interest rate parity.

15.4 The fact that governments with known or predictable exchange rate objectives are often major activists in the foreign exchange market means that the foreign exchange market is not always price efficient.

15.5 The three risks are:

- transaction risk;
- economic risk; and
- translation risk.

15.6 A money market hedge involves either:

- borrowing in a foreign currency, converting to the home currency and using a foreign currency receipt exactly to pay off the borrowings and interest thereon; or
- borrowing in the home currency, converting the borrowing to the foreign currency and lending this until a foreign debt becomes due for payment, by which time the loan and the interest will exactly pay off the foreign debt.

Chapter 16 **16.1** There is apparently an increasing trend towards larger businesses concentrating on their core activities and buying in ancillary services and products from outside. This tends to create opportunities for smaller businesses to establish and thrive.

16.2 Most larger businesses could assume that their shareholders hold efficient (well-diversified) portfolios of shares. Thus when such businesses assess projects, they can assume that shareholders do not need to be rewarded for bearing specific risk. The shareholders of smaller businesses are much less likely to hold efficient portfolios.

Also, the effect of capital gearing on the cost of capital is likely to be less beneficial for smaller businesses.

16.3 The real problem is finding the equivalent business. There are likely to be differences between the two businesses in the following areas:

- activities;
- size;
- capital gearing levels; and
- dividend policy (particularly relevant to the dividend yield basis of valuation).

16.4 The balance sheet provides a very unreliable basis for valuing shares. The reason is that, rightly or wrongly, the balance sheet is not intended to represent market values, either of individual assets or of the business as a whole. The balance sheet comprises a list of where funds came from (claims) and how those funds were deployed (assets). Current asset balance sheet values tend to bear some relation to current market values, albeit with a strong bias towards understatement relative to market values. With non-current assets, there is normally little resemblance between market and balance sheet values.

16.5 The principal problem is the lack of a reliable exit route for such investors when they wish to withdraw their funds. If there is no ready market for the shares (they are not capable of being sold through the stock market), it is often a question of selling the shares to an existing shareholder or to an outsider acceptable to the other shareholders. This means that it is unlikely that the would-be departing shareholder can obtain a fair value for the shares.

16.6 Ideally, dividend policy should be based partly on the position of the shareholders regarding matters such as need for a regular cash income and personal tax position. It is not practical to know the personal circumstances of all of the shareholders in the typical large business. With small businesses it *is* possible to know which dividend policy most shareholders would prefer, and, therefore, to tailor dividend policy to meet their needs.

Appendix 4

Suggested answers to selected problem questions

(Answers to the remaining problems are to be found in the Solutions Manual that accompanies this text.)

Chapter 2

2.1   Talco Ltd

Let the benefits of continuing with the research project be positive.

	£	
Sales proceeds	250 000	
Material – saving on disposal cost	8 000	(see Note 2)
Labour [2000 × (£25 – £12)]	(26 000)	(see Note 3)
Management (£10 000 – £8000)	(2 000)	(see Note 4)
Net benefit of completing the project	£230 000)	

Thus the overwhelming benefit lies with continuing with the project.

Notes

1 Costs already incurred, including the £200 000 incurred on the project and £40 000 for materials, are irrelevant to the present decision. What is not irrelevant, however, is the fact that the project has reached a stage where relatively little cost will bring it to completion. What it cost to bring it to that stage has no bearing on the present decision.

2 Talco will be £8000 better off as a result of continuing with the project since it will not have to pay to dispose of the material.

3 Since it appears that the skilled labour will be employed at a cost of £25 000, irrespective of the present decision, this amount is irrelevant. The difference between completing the project and abandoning it is that in the latter case it can make and sell 2000 units of a product, at a net benefit per product of £13 (that is, £25 – £12).

4 Abandoning the project will save £2000, the difference between the salary and the redundancy payment.

Chapter 3

3.1   Counterpoint plc

There has been a marked downturn in performance as measured both by RONA and by ROE. The proportional reduction is rather greater for ROE than it is for RONA. This difference between the reduction in RONA and ROE could be consistent with the increase in gearing, in that, all other things being equal, higher gearing implies higher interest costs.

The downturn in gross margin must have been caused by an increase in the cost of sales relative to revenue. (Note that this does not mean that cost of sales has increased; it may, for example, have reduced, but if so, revenue has reduced even more.)

The fact that net margin has declined by exactly the same percentage (10 per cent) as gross margin implies that the decline in the net margin was entirely due to the decline in gross profit.

The increase in debtors' collection period is something that needs investigating. It may be a deliberate strategy to encourage trade. It is often the result of a lack of control, however. The increase in the creditors' payment period is good, because the business is gaining more free credit than was the case last year. However, this may be at the cost of discounts for prompt payment and/or supplier goodwill.

The current ratio has declined although not necessarily to an alarming extent, given the nature of the business, which probably has a fairly fast stock turnover. The quick assets ratio has also declined. This may be of concern since it could indicate weakness to potential suppliers of credit.

By general standards the debt to equity ratio looks uncomfortably large and should probably be investigated.

Some comparison with other companies in the industry would probably be very helpful. 'Internal' time series analysis is very limited in this context.

3.3   Persona Ltd

	Last year	*This year*
Return on capital employed (net assets) $$\frac{\text{Net profit before long-term interest and tax}}{\text{Total assets less current liabilities}} \times 100\%$$ $$\frac{37}{185} \times 100\%$$ $$\frac{31}{190} \times 100\%$$	20.0%	16.3%
Return on equity (shareholders' funds) $$\frac{\text{Net profit after long-term interest and tax}}{\text{Share capital and reserves}} \times 100\%$$ $$\frac{16}{130} \times 100\%$$ $$\frac{6}{130} \times 100\%$$	12.3%	4.6%
Gross profit margin $$\frac{\text{Gross profit}}{\text{Sales revenue}} \times 100\%$$ $$\frac{164}{499} \times 100\%$$ $$\frac{179}{602} \times 100\%$$	32.9%	29.7%

	Last year	This year
Net profit margin $$\frac{\text{Net profit before long-term interest and tax}}{\text{Share revenue}} \times 100\%$$ $$\frac{37}{499} \times 100\%$$ $$\frac{31}{602} \times 100\%$$	7.4%	5.1%
Current ratio $$\frac{\text{Current assets}}{\text{Current liabilities}}$$ $$\frac{154}{79}$$ $$\frac{181}{116}$$	1.95 : 1	1.56 : 1
Quick assets (liquid or acid test) ratio $$\frac{\text{Liquid assets}}{\text{Current liabilities}}$$ $$\frac{154 - 68}{79}$$ $$\frac{181 - 83}{116}$$	1.09 : 1 0.84 : 1	
Stockholding period $$\frac{\text{Stock held}}{\text{Stock used}} \times 365$$ $$\frac{68}{335} \times 365$$ $$\frac{83}{423} \times 365$$	74 days	72 days

3.5   Prospect plc

	Last year	This year
Return on net assets (capital employed) $$\frac{\text{Net profit before long-term interest and tax}}{\text{Total assets less current liabilities}} \times 100\%$$ $$\frac{2100}{10\,474} \times 100\%$$ $$\frac{4618}{16\,600} \times 100\%$$	20.0%	27.8%

	Last year	This year
Return on equity (shareholders' funds)		
$\dfrac{\text{Net profit after long-term interest and tax}}{\text{Share capital and reserves}} \times 100\%$		
$\dfrac{1248}{6874} \times 100\%$	18.2%	
$\dfrac{2926}{9000} \times 100\%$		32.5%
Gross profit margin		
$\dfrac{\text{Gross profit}}{\text{Sales revenue}} \times 100\%$		
$\dfrac{6510}{14\,006} \times 100\%$	46.5%	
$\dfrac{10\,792}{22\,410} \times 100\%$		48.2%
Net profit margin		
$\dfrac{\text{Net profit before long-term interest and tax}}{\text{Sales revenue}} \times 100\%$		
$\dfrac{2100}{14\,006} \times 100\%$	15.0%	
$\dfrac{4618}{22\,410} \times 100\%$		20.6%
Stockholding period		
$\dfrac{\text{Stock held}}{\text{Stock used}} \times 365\text{ days}$		
$\dfrac{2418}{7496} \times 365$	118 days	
$\dfrac{4820}{11\,618} \times 365$		151 days
Debtor collection period (Days debtors)		
$\dfrac{\text{Trade debtors}}{\text{Credit sales revenue}} \times 365\text{ days}$		
$\dfrac{1614}{14\,006} \times 365$	42 days	
$\dfrac{2744}{22\,410} \times 365$		45 days

	Last year	This year
Current ratio		
$\dfrac{\text{Current assets}}{\text{Current liabilities}}$		
$\dfrac{4356}{2482}$	1.76 : 1	
$\dfrac{7974}{7844}$		1.02 : 1
Quick assets (liquid or acid test) ratio		
$\dfrac{\text{Liquid assets}}{\text{Current liabilities}}$		
$\dfrac{4356 - 2418}{2482}$	0.78 : 1	
$\dfrac{7974 - 4820}{7844}$		0.40 : 1
Debt to equity ratio		
$\dfrac{\text{Borrowings (long and short–term)}}{\text{Total equity}} \times 365$		
$\dfrac{3600}{6874} \times 100$	52.4%	
$\dfrac{7600 + 3250}{9000} \times 100$		120.6%

General comments

This business has experienced a major expansion in activities over the two years. This has led to an increase in the ROCE ratio, but a ROCE in excess of the interest rate caused a greater increase in ROE, an effective use of gearing. Despite the benefits of gearing, its level is now very high, and much of it is short term and represents a distinct risk to the business.

The gross profit ratio increased significantly. This was accompanied by an increase in the net profit margin.

The liquidity position has weakened considerably from a healthy position to one that looks distinctly unhealthy. The stockholding period is now rather long compared with last year. Attention needs to be paid to liquidity and gearing, which are linked since part of the gearing comes from the overdraft.

(a) An equity investor's perspective

This person will probably be pleased with the expansion in revenue and profit, also with the effective use of gearing. The high level of gearing and the significant deterioration in liquidity are major causes of concern.

(b) The bank's perspective

The bank will be concerned at the very weak liquidity position and the security for the overdraft. The latter should not pose a problem: there seem to be plenty of assets, though we do not know what quality they are as security, in terms of marketability.

Chapter 4 4.1

Barclay plc

Year	Cash flow £m	Factor	Present value £m
0	(10)	$1/(1 + 0.15)^0$	(10.00)
1	5	$1/(1 + 0.15)^1$	4.35
2	4	$1/(1 + 0.15)^2$	3.02
3	3	$1/(1 + 0.15)^3$	1.97
4	2	$1/(1 + 0.15)^4$	1.14
		Net present value	0.48

On the basis of NPV the project should be accepted since it is positive. On the basis of discounted PBP it should be rejected because it does not pay back until year 4. For a wealth-maximising business, the latter is not important.

4.3 Turners Ltd

(a) NPV

Year	Discount factor	Machine A		Machine B	
		Cash flows £000	PV £000	Cash flows £000	PV £000
0	1.000	(120)	(120.00)	(120)	(120.00)
1	0.909	40	36.36	20	18.18
2	0.826	40	33.04	30	24.78
3	0.751	40	30.04	50	37.55
4	0.683	20	13.66	70	47.81
5	0.621	40	24.84	50	31.05
		Net present value	17.94		39.37

Machine B shows itself to be significantly more desirable from an economic viewpoint than does Machine A. Since both machines have a positive NPV either would be worth buying.

(b) IRR

Clearly the IRR of both machines lies well above 10 per cent (the NPV at 10 per cent is fairly large relative to the initial outlay).

For our second trial, 10 per cent (above) being the first, let us try 20 per cent.

Year	Discount factor	Machine A		Machine B	
		Cash flows £000	PV £000	Cash flows £000	PV £000
0	1.000	(120)	(120.00)	(120)	(120.00)
1	0.833	40	33.32	20	16.66
2	0.694	40	27.76	30	20.82
3	0.579	40	23.16	50	28.95
4	0.482	20	9.64	70	33.74
5	0.402	40	16.08	50	20.10
			(10.04)		0.27

The IRR of Machine A lies below 20 per cent, but above 10 per cent. That of Machine B is just above 20 per cent. Further trials using other discount rates could be undertaken. Alternatively, a short cut can be made to a reasonable approximation, i.e. linear interpolation.

(c) ARR

	Machine A £000	Machine B £000
Outlay	120	120
Total return over years 1 to 5	180	220
Surplus for 5 years	60	100
ARR = Surplus/5	12	20
ARR = (as a % of outlay)	10%	16.7%

Machine B would be selected, as the ARR (accounting rate of return) is higher.

(d) PBP

	Machine A £000	Machine B £000
Outlay	120	120
Payback period	3 years	3 years, 104 days

Machine A would be selected, as the initial outlay is repaid in a shorter period.

4.5

Cantelevellers plc

	20X3 £000	20X4 £000	20X5 £000	20X6 £000	20X7 £000	20X8 £000
Capital cost and proceeds	(5000)					1000
Sales revenue		3000	3000	3000	3000	3000
Material cost (see workings)		(510)	(620)	(570)	(570)	(570)
Lease payments	(450)	(450)	(450)	(450)	(450)	
Redundancy payments	250					(300)
Staff costs		(200)	(200)	(200)	(200)	(200)
Overheads		(200)	(200)	(200)	(200)	(200)
	(5200)	1640	1530	1580	1580	2730
Discount factor	1.000	0.870	0.756	0.658	0.572	0.497
Present values	(5200)	1426.8	1156.7	1039.6	903.8	1356.8
Net present value	£683.70					

On the basis of the project's NPV, the project should be undertaken.

Workings

Annual material cash flows

	£
20X4	
First 500 units	
£380 − 120 = £260/unit	
500 × £260 =	£130 000
Other 1000 units	
1000 × £380 =	380 000
	£510 000
20X5	
Opportunity cost of C15s	
500 × £100 =	£50 000
Purchase of components	
1500 × £380 =	570 000
	£620 000
20X6	
1500 × £380 =	£570 000
20X7	
1500 × £380 =	£570 000
20X8	
1500 × £380 =	£570 000

Chapter 5   **5.1**   **Dodd Ltd**

	20X1 £000	20X2 £000	20X3 £000	20X4 £000
Investment and residual value*	(250)			58
Annual cash flows*		168	176	116
Tax on annual cash flows (30%)		(50)	(53)	(35)
	(250)	118	123	139
Discounted at 15.5% (see workings below)	(250)	102	92	90
NPV	34			

* Subject to inflation.

Workings

Discount rate:

$$(1 + r_m) = (1 + r_r)(1 + i)$$

where r_m is the 'money' discount rate, r_r is the 'real' discount rate and i is the rate of inflation. This gives us:

$$r_m = (1 + 0.05)(1 + 0.10) - 1$$

$$r_m = 0.155 \text{ or } 15.5\%$$

5.4

Livelong Ltd

Calculation of present cost of operating the machine for its expected life:

	Machine	
	Alpha £	*Beta* £
Initial cost	50 000	90 000
Salvage value:		
5000 × 0.683	(3 415)	
7000 × 0.513		(3 591)
Annual running costs:		
10 000 × 3.170	31 700	
8000 × 4.868		38 944
Present cost (a)	78 285	125 353
Annuity factor (b)	3.170	4.868
Equivalent annual value (a)/(b)	£24 696	£25 750

Where the equivalent annual cost of A is the same as B, then the present cost of operating A for four years would be £81 628 (that is, £25 750 × 3.170). Thus the initial cost would be £53 343 (that is, £81 628 − 31 700 + 3415), so the increase would be £3343.

5.5

Mega Builders plc

(a) 'Money' cost of salaries, wages and materials

'Real' cost (p.a.) = £1.3m + 2.5m + 0.25m = £4.05m

20X6   £4.05m × 1.03 = £4.172m

20X7   £4.05m × 1.03 × 1.04 = £4.338m

Plant

	£000	Tax effect
Cost (20X4)	6000	
20X4 WDA (25%)	(1500)	
	4500	
20X5 proceeds	(2500)	
Balancing allowance	2000	@ 30% = £600 000
	or	
WDV at 31 Dec. 20X4	4500	
Additions	100	
	4600	
20X5 WDA (25%)	(1150)	@ 30% = £345 000
	3450	
20X6 WDA (25%)	(862.5)	@ 30% = £258 750
	2587.5	
20X7 proceeds	zero	
Balancing allowance	2587.5	@ 30% = £776 250

Tax on incremental cash flows

Total incremental cost (excluding depreciation) = £4.172m + 4.338m = £8.510m

$\frac{1}{3}$ thereof = £2.837m

Tax charge (£4.500m − 2.837m) @ 30% = £0.499m

'Money' discount rate

20X6 = 1/(1.00 + 0.10) × (1.00 + 0.03) = 0.8826

20X7 = 0.8826 × 1/(1.00 + 0.10) × (1.00 + 0.04) = 0.7715

20X8 = 0.7715 × 1/(1.00 + 0.10) × (1.00 + 0.05) = 0.6680

Schedule of 'money' cash flows

31 December	20X5 £m	20X6 £m	20X7 £m	20X8 £m
Contract price	–	4.500	4.500	4.500
Incremental cost	–	(4.172)	(4.338)	–
Plant	(2.500)	–	–	–
Addition	(0.100)	–	–	–
Capital allowances	(0.600)	–	–	–
	0.345	0.259	0.776	–
Tax	–	(0.499)	(0.499)	(0.499)
	(2.855)	0.088	0.439	4.001
PV	(2.855)	0.078	0.339	2.673
NPV	0.235			

Thus the contract would be financially advantageous to BC at £13.5m.

(b) If the contract price were £12m, the differential 'money' cash flows would be as follows:

31 December	20X5	20X6 £m	20X7 £m	20X8 £m
Lower contract receipts	–	(0.500)	(0.500)	(0.500)
Lower tax charge	–	0.150	0.150	0.150
		(0.350)	(0.350)	(0.350)
PV		(0.309)	(0.270)	(0.234)
NPV	(0.813)			

NPV at a contract price of £12.0m = 0.235 − 0.813 = (0.578)

'Break-even' contract price = £13.5m − {(13.5m − 12.0m) × [0.578/(0.235 + 0.578)]}
= £12.434m or 3 instalments of £4.145m each

(c) Possible 'other factors' include:

- The small margin of safety means that the success of the contract will be sensitive to the accuracy of the input data.
- Civil engineering tends to be a fairly risky activity since outcomes are difficult to predict.
- In the long run, the contract price must bear head office costs.
- Precedent for future contracts.
- Level of competition in the market.
- The contract size, relative to the size of the business.

6.1 **Easton Ltd**

Different cash flows of Machine A

Year		2000 demand £	3000 demand £	5000 demand £
0		(15 000)	(15 000)	(15 000)
1	(£4−£1)/unit	6 000	9 000	15 000
2		6 000	9 000	15 000
3		6 000	9 000	15 000
Discounted: Factor		£	£	£
0	(1.00)	(15 000)	(15 000)	(15 000)
1	(0.94)	5 640	8 460	14 100
2	(0.89)	5 340	8 010	13 350
3	(0.84)	5 040	7 560	12 600
		1 020	9 030	25 050

Expected value = $(0.2 \times 1020) + (0.6 \times 9030) + (0.2 \times 25\ 050) = £10\ 632$

Different cash flows of Machine B

Year		2000 demand £	3000 demand £	5000 demand £
0		(20 000)	(20 000)	(20 000)
1	(£4−£0.5)/unit	7 000	10 500	17 500
2		7 000	10 500	17 500
3		7 000	10 500	17 500
Discounted: Factor		£	£	£
0	(1.00)	(20 000)	(20 000)	(20 000)
1	(0.94)	6 580	9 870	16 450
2	(0.89)	6 230	9 345	15 575
3	(0.84)	5 880	8 820	14 700
		(1 310)	8 035	26 725

Expected value = $(0.2 \times (1310)) + (0.6 \times 8035) + (0.2 \times 26\ 725) = £9904$

A more direct route to expected values would be to take the 'expected' demand $[(0.2 \times 2000) + (0.6 \times 3000) + (0.2 \times 5000) = 3200]$ and then find the NPV assuming that level of demand.

6.2 **Easton Ltd**

(a) NPV

The expression for the NPV may be put as follows:

$$NPV = D(S - V)A_n^r - I$$

where D is annual demand (in units), S is the selling price per unit, V is the variable cost per unit, A_n^r is the annuity factor at rate r over n years and I is the initial investment. Thus:

$$NPV = [2000(4 - 1)2.673] - 15\ 000 = £1038$$

Since the NPV is a significant positive figure the machine should be acquired.

(b) Sensitivity analysis

(i) *Annual demand*

This requires setting NPV at zero, putting in all inputs except annual demand, and solving for annual demand. That is:

$$[D(4-1)2.673] - 15\,000 = 0$$

$$D = \frac{15\,000}{3 \times 2.673} = \underline{1871} \text{ units}$$

(ii) *Selling price per unit*

$$2000(S-1)2.673 = 15\,000$$

$$S = \frac{15\,000}{2000 \times 2.673} + 1 = \underline{\underline{£3.806}}$$

(iii) *Variable cost per unit*

$$2000(4-V)2.673 = 15\,000$$

$$V = \frac{-15\,000}{2000 \times 2.673} + 4 = \underline{\underline{£1.194}}$$

(iv) *Discount rate*

$$2000(4-1)A_3^r = 15\,000$$

$$A_3^r = \frac{15\,000}{6000} = \underline{\underline{2.500}}$$

Looking at the annuity table for the 3 years row, 2.5 lies between 9 per cent and 10 per cent, nearer to 10 per cent, so say <u>10 per cent</u>.

(v) *Years of the project*

$$A_n^6 = 2.500 \text{ (from (iv) above)}$$

Looking down the 6 per cent column in the annuity table, 2.5 lies between 2 and 3 years, nearer to 3 years, so say 3 years.

(vi) *Initial investment*

$$I = 2000(4-1)2.673$$

$$= \underline{\underline{£16\,038}}$$

Table of sensitivities

Factor	Original estimate	Break-even point	Difference	Difference as % of original
D	2000 units	1871 units	129 units	6%
S	£4	£2.806	£1.194	30%
V	£1	£1.194	£0.194	19%
r	6%	10%	4%	67%
n	3 years	3 years	0 years	0%
I	£15 000	£16 038	£1038	7%

Note that r and n could be found with considerably more accuracy (if this were thought to be useful) by linear interpolation.

6.5

Hi Fido plc

(a) *Cash flows*

	20X0 £000	20X1 £000	20X2 £000	20X3 £000	20X4 £000
Plant	(1000)				
Tracker revenue		2160	2208	1104	
Materials cost		(756)	(773)	(386)	
Additional labour		(97)	(99)	(50)	
Lost Repro contributions		(432)	(442)	(221)	
Management	120	(48)	(48)	(188)	
Working capital	(243)	(5)	124	124	
Taxation		43	(211)	(233)	54
	(1123)	865	759	150	54
Discounted at 8%	(1123)	801	651	119	40

NPV = 488 (positive)

On the basis of this analysis, the project should go ahead.

Workings

Expected revenue

20X1	20X2	20X3
	8 000 (0.3)	4000 (1.0)
10 000 (0.6)		
	10 000 (0.7)	5000 (1.0)
	12 000 (0.5)	6000 (1.0)
12 000 (0.4)		
	15 000 (0.5)	7500 (0.1)

20X1

$$(10\ 000 \times 0.6) + (12\ 000 \times 0.4) = 10\ 800\ (\times £200)$$
$$= £2\ 160\ 000$$

20X2

$$(8000 \times 0.6 \times 0.3) + (10\ 000 \times 0.6 \times 0.7) + (12\ 000 \times 0.4 \times 0.5) + (15\ 000 \times 0.4 \times 0.5)$$
$$= 11\ 040\ (\times £200) = £2\ 208\ 000$$

20X3

$$11\ 040 \times 0.5\ (\times £200) = £1\ 104\ 000$$

Additional labour

Hours required per pair of Trackers = 3
Hours released per pair of Repros = 4
Additional hours required per pair of Repros = 3 − (4/2) = 1, paid at £6 × 150% = £9

Effective loss of contribution per Repro sale

For each unit lost = £100 − 20 = £80

Capital allowances

	£000
20X0	
Cost	1000
Capital allowance (25%)	(250)
20X1	
Brought down	750
Capital allowance (25%)	(188)
20X2	
Brought down	562
Capital allowance (25%)	(140)
20X3	
Brought down	422
Disposal proceeds	0*
Capital allowance (balancing allowance)	422

* This assumes that the project is abandoned after three years.

Taxation

	20X0 £000	20X1 £000	20X2 £000	20X3 £000
Tracker revenue		2160	2208	1104
Materials		(756)	(773)	(386)
Additional labour		(97)	(99)	(50)
Lost Repro revenue		(432)	(442)	(221)
Management	120	(48)	(48)	(188)
Capital allowances	(250)	(188)	(140)	(422)
	(130)	639	706	(163)
Tax at 33%	(43)*	211	233	(54)

* This assumes that there are sufficient taxable profits elsewhere in the business to set against the negative figure in 20X0.

Working capital

	20X1 £000	20X2 £000	20X3 £000
Tracker sales revenues	2160	2208	1104
Lost Repro revenue	(540)	(552)	(276)
Net increase in revenue	1620	1656	828
15% thereof	243	248	124

Chapter 7

7.1

(a) Specific risk factors might include:
- the possible loss of business to the Channel Tunnel;
- decline in trade between the UK and western Europe;
- a loss of interest in UK residents taking holidays in western Europe; and
- bad publicity arising from an accident involving one of the business's vessels.

(b) Systematic risk factors might include:
- levels of interest rates;
- fuel prices; and
- levels of demand in the economy.

7.5   **Court plc**

(a)

Year	r_m	$r_m - D_m$	$(r_m - D_m)^2$	r_i	$r_i - D_i$	$(r_i - D_m)(r_i - D_i)$
1	0.13	0.07	0.0049	0.19	0.12	0.0084
2	(0.07)	(0.13)	0.0169	(0.08)	(0.15)	0.0195
3	(0.13)	(0.19)	0.0361	(0.12)	(0.19)	0.0361
4	0.04	(0.02)	0.0004	0.03	(0.04)	0.0008
5	0.08	0.02	0.0004	0.08	0.01	0.0002
6	0.10	0.04	0.0016	0.17	0.10	0.0040
7	0.15	0.09	0.0081	0.14	0.07	0.0063
8	0.16	0.10	0.0100	0.14	0.07	0.0070
9	0.16	0.10	0.0100	0.14	0.07	0.0070
10	(0.02)	(0.08)	0.0064	0.01	(0.06)	0.0048
$\Sigma r_m =$	0.60	$\Sigma(r_m - D_m)$	0.0948	0.70 =	Σr_i	0.0941 =

$$D_m = \frac{0.60}{0.10} \qquad\qquad D = \frac{0.70}{0.10} \qquad\qquad \Sigma(r_m - D_m)(r_i - D_i)$$

$$= 0.06 \qquad\qquad\qquad = 0.07$$

$$\text{Var}(r_m) = \frac{0.0948}{10} = 0.0095$$

$$\text{Cov}(r_i, r_m) = \frac{\Sigma(r_m - D_m)(r_i - D_i)}{10} = \frac{0.0941}{10} = 0.0094$$

$$\beta = \frac{\text{Cov}(r_i, r_m)}{\text{Var}(r_m)} = \frac{0.0094}{0.0095} = 1.0$$

(b) Since Court's beta is 1.0, irrespective of the risk-free rate, if the expected return from equities generally is 12 per cent, then the expected return from Court will also be 12 per cent.

Chapter 8   **8.1**

The reasons for the relative popularity of convertible loan stocks include the following factors:

● They might be easier to issue than equity, in terms of acceptability to potential investors, because they are a loan stock as long as the stockholder wishes them to be, yet they can be converted to equity if it is beneficial to the stockholder to do so. Thus their value is underpinned by their value as a pure loan stock, yet they have 'upside' potential because, in effect, they bestow the right to buy equity at a predetermined price.

● The business may prefer to issue loan stocks to gain advantage from the tax relief on interest, but may find it hard to do so if investors seek investments with more potential for capital gains.

8.2

In essence financial claims fall into two types: *equity* and *debt*. As will be explored in some detail in Chapter 11, each one has its attractions from the business's (as represented by its existing shareholders) point of view. One of the reasons for having some claims that are, in essence, equity and some that are basically debt is that it enables the business to strike the appropriate balance. This does not really explain the wide diversity of equity and debt 'instruments' found in practice.

The major reason for businesses going beyond simple equity and debt is generally to try to meet the precise investment requirements of a variety of potential investors. This is much the same as a shoe shop stocking a range of different styles and sizes of footwear. By doing this it can appeal to the needs and tastes of a wide variety of customers. Businesses that limit their financial instruments to two will find it much more difficult to raise finance than those that can offer investors something that caters more precisely to their needs and tastes.

8.4 Memphis plc

Pre-contract announcement value of the business	20m × £1.20	£24m
NPV of the contract		4
Pre-rights value of the business		28
Rights issue (number of shares = £10m/£0.80)	12.5	10
Post-rights value of the business	32.5	38
Ex-rights price per share	£38m/32.5m =	£1.1692

The right to buy one of the new shares would theoretically cost £0.3692 each, because a buyer could pay this amount for the right to pay the business a further £0.80 and obtain a share worth £1.1692.

Chapter 9

9.1 XYZ plc

The statement implies that the person making it has superior knowledge compared with those who, by their actions (buying and selling) in the stock market, influence share prices. Evidence on the efficiency of the capital market, cited in Chapter 9, suggests that this is likely to be true only if the person making the statement has inside information. Otherwise the evidence shows that the market knows best, on average.

9.2

CME does not imply that all investors know all that there is to know about all securities traded in the market. It does not even imply that any individual investor knows all that there is to know about any particular security. CME simply implies that the current market price of a security at any given moment reflects a consensus view of the security and therefore reflects all information that is known by investors.

9.3

If the market is efficient in the semi-strong form, then all published information is impounded in the price of securities. The statement refers to unpublished information, and for it to be true that this is impounded in the share price would require the market to be strong-form efficient. Evidence shows the LSE to be semi-strong-form, but not strong-form, efficient. Thus the statement is incorrect.

Chapter 10

10.1 Gregoris plc

$$104 = \frac{8}{(1 + k_{\mathrm{L}})^1} + \frac{8}{(1 + k_{\mathrm{L}})^2} + \frac{8}{(1 + k_{\mathrm{L}})^3} + \frac{108}{(1 + k_{\mathrm{L}})^4}$$

This looks like a return of a little below 8 per cent because the stock with an 8 per cent 'coupon' is worth more than £100. Try 7 per cent:

$$104 = \frac{8}{(1 + 0.07)^1} + \frac{8}{(1 + 0.07)^2} + \frac{8}{(1 + 0.07)^3} + \frac{108}{(1 + 0.07)^4}$$

$$= 7.48 + 6.99 + 6.53 + 82.39$$

$$= 103.39$$

that is, k_{L} is very close to 7 per cent.

10.3   Fortunate plc

Summarised prospective profit and loss account for each future year

	£m
Profit before interest and tax	9.0
Less: Debenture interest	1.2
	7.8
Less: Taxation (50%)	3.9
Profit after interest and tax	3.9
Less: Preference dividend	0.5
Profit attributable to ordinary shareholders	3.4

Cost of debentures = 12% before tax

$$\text{Cost of preference shares} = \frac{£0.5m}{(5m \times £0.65)} \times 100\% = 15.4\%$$

$$\text{Cost of ordinary shares} = \frac{£3.4m}{(8m \times 2 \times £0.80)} \times 100\% = 26.6\%$$

$$\text{WACC} = \frac{[12\%(1 - 0.50) \times £10m] + (15.4\% \times 5m \times £0.65) + (26.6\% \times 8m \times 2 \times £0.80)}{£10m + (5m \times £0.65) + (8m \times 2 \times £0.80)}$$

$$= \frac{£0.6m + £500\,500 + £3\,404\,800}{£10m + £3.25m + £12.8m} = \frac{£4\,505\,300}{£26\,050\,000}$$

$$= \underline{\underline{17.3\%}}$$

10.5   Da Silva plc

(a)

Year	Growth
2	(0.0900 − 0.0800)/0.0800 = 0.125
3	(0.1050 − 0.0900)/0.0900 = 0.167
4	(0.1125 − 0.1050)/0.1050 = 0.071
5	(0.1250 − 0.1125)/0.1125 = 0.111
6	(0.1350 − 0.1250)/0.1250 = 0.080
7	(0.1450 − 0.1350)/0.1350 = 0.074
8	(0.1550 − 0.1450)/0.1450 = 0.069
	Sum 0.697

Arithmetic mean = 10%

(The mean could be calculated from the more recent data and/or a weighting used.)

$$k_E = [d_0(1 + g)/V_0] + g$$
$$= [£0.1550(1 + 0.1)/2.75] + 0.10$$
$$= 16.2\%$$

Hence:

$$\text{WACC} = \frac{(£5.5m \times 16.2\%) + [£1.5m \times 10\% \times (1 - 0.33)]}{£5.5m + £1.5m} = \underline{\underline{14.2\%}}$$

(b) The main assumption being made in the estimation of the WACC figure is that past experience is a good guide to the future. More specifically:

- that the risk of the proposed investment is similar to the average risk of the business's recent past activities;

- that past dividend growth is similar to future prospects. This seems a dubious assumption in this particular case since the dividend growth rate has been very erratic from one year to the next;

- that future interest and tax rates are likely to be similar to current ones.

Chapter 11

11.1   Shiraz plc

According to MM:

$$k_{EG} = k_{EE} + (k_{EE} - k_L) \frac{L_G}{S_G}$$

where k_{EG} is the cost of equity in the geared business, k_{EE} the cost of equity in the all-equity business, k_L the cost of loan finance, L_G the value of loan stock in the geared business and S_G the value of equity in the geared business.

Thus in the case of Shiraz plc:

$$20\% = k_{EE} + (k_{EE} - 10\%) \frac{£14m}{(10m \times £2.40)}$$

$$1.583 \, k_{EE} = 20\% + 5.833\%$$

$$k_{EE} = 16.3\%$$

The share price would be identical (£2.40) because the lower risk attaching to the returns in the all-equity business would be exactly compensated by lower returns as a result of the absence of the cheap loan finance.

11.3   Particulate plc

(a) According to Modigliani and Miller (MM) the value of a geared business (V_G) is equal to the value of the equivalent all-equity financed (V_U) one *plus* the value of the so-called, tax shield provided by the tax relief on loan interest (TD), that is:

$$V_G = V_U + TD$$

Thus, for Particulate plc:

$$V_G = £35m + (£8m \times 0.30) = \underline{£37.4m}$$

This is made up of £8m loan finance and £29.4m equity.

(b) Equity earnings are expected to be constant as follows:

	£m
Annual earnings after tax (£35m × 20%)	7.00
Add: Tax (£7.00m × 30/70)	3.00
Annual earnings before tax	10.00
Less: Interest (£8m × 10%)	0.80
	9.20
Less: Tax @ 30%	2.76
Available for shareholders	£6.44

The business's cost of equity is:

$$k_E = 6.44/29.4 \times 100\% = \underline{\underline{21.9\%}}$$

(c) The weighted average cost of capital (WACC)

$$= \frac{(21.9 \times 29.4) + [10 \times (1 - 0.30) \times 8]}{29.4 + 8} = \underline{\underline{18.7\%}}$$

Thus WACC has decreased from 20 per cent to 18.7 per cent as a result of introducing the debt finance. At the same time the cost of equity has increased from 20 per cent to 21.9 per cent as a result of the increased risk that shareholders will have to bear.

11.5   Ali plc

Return on equity earned by the business $= [12.80/(10 \times 4 \times 1.60)] \times 100\% = 20\%$.

Assuming that the same level of return is earned on the additional finance, after the rights issue, Lee's investment in the business would be:

Original investment (10 000 × £1.60)	£16 000
Rights issue [(10 000/4) × £1.20]	£3 000
	£19 000

After the expansion, by either means, the pre-interest profit would be $20\% \times [(10m \times 4 \times £1.60) + (2.5m \times 4 \times 1.20)] = £15.2m$. Therefore the dividend per share is $15.2/50 = £0.304$.

(a) Personal borrowing

Lee's dividend after the issue (12 500 × £0.304)	£3800
Less: Interest (10% × £3000)	£300
Lee's income	£3500

(b) The business borrowing

Profit (pre-interest)	£15.2m
Less: Interest (10% × £12.0m)	£1.2m
	£14.0m
Earnings and dividend per share (£14.0m/40m)	£0.35
Lee's income (10 000 × £0.35)	£3500

Thus Lee's income is identical for identical risk. Since homemade gearing is a perfect substitute for corporate gearing, logically investors will not pay a premium to invest in geared equities. Thus the cost of capital will be independent of the level of gearing, subject to the MM assumptions.

Chapter 12   12.1   Distributors plc

The dividend will need to be such that its present value, discounted at the shareholders' opportunity cost of capital, is £25m. That is:

$$£25m \times (1 + 0.20)^3 = £43.20m$$

Together with the normal dividend of £25m, this makes a total of £68.20m.

If the payoff were to be more than £43.20m the shareholders would, in theory, prefer the investment to be made. If the payoff were to be less than this amount the shareholders would prefer the immediate dividend of £25m.

12.3   HLM plc

The equity cost of capital is $(1.5/10) \times 100\% = 15\%$ p.a.

In effect, the investment amounts to two outlays of £1.0m, the first after one year and the second after two years, and an annual inflow of £0.4m in perpetuity starting after three years.

The NPV (in £m) of this investment is:

$$-\frac{1.0}{(1+0.15)} - \frac{1.0}{(1+0.15)^2} + \frac{0.4/0.15}{(1+0.15)^2} = -0.870 - 0.756 + 2.016$$

which is equivalent to a £0.39m increase in the value of the business or a 3.9p increase in the value of each share.

12.6   Images plc

The NPVs of the projects are:

I	$-2.00 + (0.75 \times 2.283) = -0.288$
II	$-2.00 + (0.65 \times 3.352) = +0.179$
III	$-3.00 + (0.80 \times 3.352) = -0.318$
IV	$-1.00 + (0.50 \times 2.283) = +0.142$

Thus, logically, the cash generated from profits should be invested in Projects II and IV, a total investment of £3m. This would leave £2m to be distributed as a dividend, since the shareholders can employ the cash more effectively than the business can. This assumes that shareholders are indifferent between receiving dividends and the business investing available cash at the relevant cost of capital.

Other factors

MM said that since the profits belong to the shareholders they would be indifferent as to whether they receive a dividend or whether the business retains the assets concerned, all other things being equal. Thus provided that the business can invest the funds at a rate above that which is available to the shareholders, the shareholders will prefer it to invest these funds rather than to pay dividends. If it can only achieve an investment return equal to the rate available to shareholders on other investments, shareholders will be indifferent as to whether they receive a dividend or whether the business invests the available funds. Only where the business cannot achieve investment returns as high as the shareholders can achieve, will the shareholders have a positive preference for dividends. This means that, in theory, the business should make all investments that yield a positive NPV when discounted at the opportunity cost of capital, up to a maximum of the funds available. Any funds that it cannot invest at the opportunity cost of capital should be returned to the shareholders as dividends, enabling them to make their own investments. Thus the level of dividends is a residual, that is, it is what is left after the business has made all of the beneficial investments available. In the case of Images plc, the dividend should be what is left after making the two advantageous investments (II and IV).

This assumes that the shareholders will always wish to invest all of their wealth. In fact they may wish to consume some of it, and may find the level of dividends insufficient for their consumption requirements. MM argued that any shareholder who wished to consume, could sell as many shares as necessary to provide the cash required for consumption. It can easily be shown that such shareholders will be better off if the business invests in Projects II and IV because the price of the shares will be enhanced by making these investments, meaning that shareholders will need to sell fewer shares to produce the amount of cash that they wish to consume.

The following points also need to be raised:

- *Availability of cash.* Profit does not equal cash. Given the business's steady level of profit, however, net cash inflows should exceed profit, unless there has been new investment in non-current or current assets or a net repayment of finance.

- *Clientele effect.* It is claimed by some that investors are attracted to buy the shares in one business rather than another because of its dividend policy. Thus many of the share-holders of Images plc may be attracted by the generous dividend policy. If this policy is now altered, they may feel disadvantaged. As MM pointed out, it is open to them to create 'dividends' by selling some of their shares. However, dealing charges are not trivial in amount, and a disposal of some shares could trigger a capital gains tax charge, which would otherwise be delayed or even avoided.

    This means that a change in the dividend policy of Images plc could be disadvantageous to its shareholders. This might outweigh the advantage to them of the business investing in Projects II and IV. The shareholders' best interests may lie with Images paying the usual level of dividend and investing the balance of available funds.

- *Taxation.* Dividends are subject to income tax, whereas retained profit, leading to higher share prices, attracts capital gains tax. Although the legislation has sought recently to equalise the effect of these two taxes in the UK, there are still significant differences between them. Perhaps the most important of these is the fact that capital gains only come within the scope of taxation when the shares are disposed of, whereas the tax on dividends bites when the dividend is paid.

- *Informational effect of dividends.* It is argued by some people that businesses use dividend payment levels as a device to signal information to the outside world. It is claimed that high dividend payments signal confidence in the future of the business whereas small payments signal a lack of confidence. If it is true that small dividends will be interpreted by the market as a sign of an uncertain future, then the fact that Images plc is paying a smaller than usual dividend could have an adverse effect on the wealth of its shareholders.

Chapter 13   13.1   **Dixon plc**

(a)
$$E = \sqrt{\frac{2AC}{H}}$$

where E is the economic order quantity, A is the annual usage, C is the cost of placing each order and H is the annual holding cost of one unit. This gives:

$$E = \sqrt{\frac{2 \times 23\,000 \times £50}{£1.50}}$$

$$= \sqrt{1\,533\,333}$$

$$= 1238.3 \text{ units}$$

Therefore, orders should be placed of 1238 or 1239 units, but since the round figure of 1250 is not too far away, orders of that size would probably be placed.

(b) During the one-week lead time $(1/52) \times 23\,000 = 442$ units would be used, so the order must be placed when the stock is no lower than 442 units if 'stockouts' are to be avoided.

13.3   Arcadia Ltd

Cash budget for six months to June

	January £	February £	March £	April £	May £	June £
Receipts from debtors	2 800	3 200	3 200	4 000	4 800	5 200
Receipts from cash sales	4 800	6 000	7 200	7 800	8 400	9 600
(A)	7 600	9 200	10 400	11 800	13 200	14 800
Outflows						
Payments to creditors	4 000	4 800	4 800	5 600	6 000	6 000
Wages etc.	3 000	3 600	3 600	4 200	4 500	4 500
Advertising	1 000	–	–	1 500	–	–
Salaries etc.: 80%	1 280	1 280	1 280	1 280	1 600	1 600
20%	280	320	320	320	320	400
Non-current assets acquired	–	–	2 000	2 000	2 000	–
Dividend	–	–	–	600	–	–
(B)	9 560	10 000	12 000	15 500	14 420	12 500
Surplus/deficit for the month (A – B)	(1 960)	(800)	(1 600)	(3 700)	(1 220)	2 300
(Cumulative surplus/deficit)	5 540	4 740	3 140	(560)	(1 780)	520

13.5   North Anglia Engineering Ltd

(a) Optimum level of stockholding

Businesses hold stocks to the extent that the financial benefits of holding stock are outweighed by those of not holding stock to the maximum extent.

The costs of holding stock include:

- *The cost of financing the stock.* Finance is tied up in stock.
- *Storage costs.* Storing stock costs money. If the stock is valuable or fragile, these costs could be considerable.
- *Insurance costs.* Stock would normally be insured against losses and damage.
- *Obsolescence costs.* Items of stock may become obsolescent during the stockholding period. This may seriously reduce their value.

The costs of holding insufficient stock include:

- *Loss of customer goodwill.* If a customer cannot be supplied from stock that customer may go elsewhere, never to return.
- *Production dislocation.* Running out of a stock line may mean that production has to cease, which can be very expensive in terms of lost production time and other production costs.
- *Loss of flexibility.* Holding very low stocks makes it difficult to respond rapidly to an opportunity to increase output to meet an unexpected demand or to engage in large production runs that could yield economies of scale.

(b) Reasons for large stock levels

The points that should be investigated in an attempt to identify the reason for large stock levels include the following:

- *Optimum order quantities.* Does the business use any technique for deducing the optimum size of order or manufacturing batch?
- *Stock reorder levels.* Are there established stock reorder levels for each stock line such that a new order is triggered when the reorder level is reached?

- *Budgets*. Are stock requirements carefully planned and budgeted?
- *Reliable stock records*. Is there reliable information available on a day-to-day basis that provides a basis for decisions relating to stock management?
- *Ratios*. Are ratios such as stock turnover systematically used to monitor stock levels, both generally and in respect of particular stock lines?
- *Security and authorisation*. Are there clear rules established surrounding the authority to order and issue stock?

Chapter 14

14.1 ABB plc and CDD Ltd

Pre-merger value of ABB plc = £12m/20% = £60m

Post-merger value of ABB plc = £60m + £27.5m = £87.5m

Estimated rate of return = £14m/£87.5m × 100% = 16%

14.3 Thruster plc and Relaxation plc

Pre-takeover price per share of Thruster plc	
EPS [48/(170 × 2)]	£0.1412
Price per share (£0.1412 × 18)	£2.5416
Pre-takeover price per share of Relaxation plc	
EPS [11/(90 × 2)]	£0.0611
Price per share (£0.0611 × 14)	£0.8556
Price for three shares (3 × £0.8556)	£2.5668

Combined after tax earnings of the post-takeover business:	£m
Pre-takeover earnings of Thruster plc	48
Pre-takeover earnings of Relaxation plc	11
Cost savings	8
Total earnings	67

Number of shares	Shares (m)
Pre-takeover shares of Thruster plc (170 × 2)	340
Shares issued to Relaxation plc shareholders [(90 × 2)/3]	60
Total shares	400

Earnings per share (£67m/400)	£0.1675
At new P/E ratio each share is worth £0.1675 × 16	£2.68

Thus, on the assumption that share price was the only criterion, both sets of shareholders would welcome the takeover since both will be better off.

Chapter 15

15.1

The note should make the following points:

- *Political risk*. The risk of war, civil unrest, unexpected increases in taxes, restrictions on remittances of cash, from sales, to the UK. This risk can be assessed in advance, and there are commercial services that provide an assessment. Countries with a high political risk could be avoided and/or the risk can be insured against.
- *Lack of local knowledge*. The problems that may arise from not being in touch with the cultural, commercial and legal environment of the country concerned. Probably the best approach here is to do as much research into these matters as possible before trying to trade in the market. It seems likely that a government agency will be able to help here. It might be worth considering employing someone who has a good understanding of the country and the market as a consultant.

- *Foreign currency risk.* This is the risk that currency markets may cause sterling to strengthen against the local currency during the period between making a sale and receiving the cash. There are several steps, none of them costless, that can be taken to cover this risk:

  - Buy a put option in the foreign currency: that is, buy the right to sell the foreign currency for a stated amount of sterling at a future time. If sterling holds its value against the foreign currency, the option need not be exercised.

  - Borrow immediately an amount of the foreign currency that, with interest, will grow to the value of the receipt by the scheduled receipt date. When the receipt occurs, the loan can be paid off from the proceeds.

  - Sell the foreign currency, at the close of the sale, for future delivery on the scheduled date of receipt.

15.2 Pavlov plc

Borrow A\$490 196 (that is, A\$500 000 × 100/102) and convert this to £188 537 (that is, A\$490 196/2.60). When the three months have elapsed, the borrowing, with interest, will exactly equal A\$500 000, which will be paid off from the receipt from the Australian customer.

Chapter 16

16.1 Tiny Tim Ltd and Mega plc

$$\text{Price/earnings ratio} = \frac{\text{Market price of a business (or single share)}}{\text{After-tax earnings of the business (or a single share)}}$$

or:

Market price of a business = Price/earnings ratio × After-tax earnings of the business

Market price of Tiny Tim Ltd = 16 × £350 000 = £5.6m

This needs to be adjusted to take account of the fact that Tiny Tim Ltd is less marketable than Mega plc. A discount of, say, 25 per cent should be applied, giving an estimated value of £4m to £4.5m for Tiny Tim Ltd.

16.3 PR Industries and Howard Pope Ltd

On the basis of the information provided, the following approaches can be taken to valuing the shares of Howard Pope Ltd (HP Ltd):

(i) *Price/earnings basis*

$$\text{Price/earnings ratio} = \frac{\text{Market price of a share}}{\text{After-tax earnings per share}}$$

Market price of a share = Price/earnings ratio × After-tax earnings per share

$$\text{Market price of a share of HP Ltd} = 15 \times \frac{£15.3m}{(2m \times 20)} = \underline{\underline{£5.74}}$$

(ii) *Dividend growth model basis*
According to the Gordon growth model:

$$\text{Cost of equity} = \frac{\text{Next year's dividend per share}}{\text{Current share price}} + \text{Growth rate of dividends}$$

or:

$$\text{Current share price} = \frac{\text{Next year's dividend per share}}{\text{Cost of equity} - \text{Growth rate of dividends}}$$

$$\text{Current price of an HP Ltd share } \frac{[\pounds5m/(2 \times 20)] \times 1.10}{0.13 - 0.10} = \underline{\underline{\pounds4.58}}$$

(iii) *Net (balance sheet) assets basis*

$$\text{Price per share} = \frac{\text{Net assets (from the balance sheet)}}{\text{Number of shares}}$$

$$\text{Price of an HP Ltd share} = \frac{(143.42 - 30.00)}{2 \times 20} = \underline{\underline{\pounds2.84}}$$

The figures resulting from the use of the first two methods would need to be fairly heavily discounted (say by 25 or 30 per cent) to take account of the fact that the HP Ltd shares are very unlikely to be easy to sell, HP Ltd being a private company.

There are many problems with these valuations, for example:

- The first two methods rely on finding a suitable business, or businesses, whose shares are traded in an 'efficient' market, to use as a basis for comparison. The principle of these two approaches is that the P/E ratio and cost of equity of listed businesses can be applied directly to the unlisted one. This makes all sorts of assumptions about the comparability of such factors as:

  - activities;
  - dividend policy;
  - operating risk; and
  - financial risk (gearing).

The use of the Gordon growth model also assumes constant dividend growth of HP Ltd into the future.

- The net assets basis assumes that the balance sheet represents a fair value of assets and claims, on a going concern basis. It also assumes that all assets and claims are included on the balance sheet. These assumptions are unlikely to be valid. The balance sheet is (and is intended to be) a historical record of the assets, still in existence, acquired by the business as a result of transactions and the sources of funds used to finance them. Thus the balance sheet has little to do with current values of assets and claims, and still less to do with assets such as goodwill which were not acquired as a result of a particular transaction but through a gradual process.

The P/E and net assets bases of valuation tend to be applied where the buyer is interested in acquiring the whole of, or at least a controlling interest in, the business, that is, a *majority stake*.

Dividend valuation methods tend to be used where a *minority stake* is involved. The logic of this is that, for the minority shareholders, their only economic interest in the business is related to dividends.

Other approaches that could have been used include:

- *Dividend yield*. Here, the valuation is obtained by taking the view that two similar businesses, one listed and the other not listed, will have a similar dividend yield. Normally a 25 to 30 per cent discount will be applied to the valuation obtained to allow for the lack of marketability of the unlisted one's shares.

- *Economic value*. This is, without doubt, the most theoretically correct approach. It is based on estimations of the amount and timing of the net cash flows that are likely to be generated by the shares and an appropriate discount rate. Estimating cash flows and discount rates is difficult, which may well explain the popularity of 'market' and balance sheet based methods. Nevertheless, an approach that has a sound base in logic has a head start on other approaches.

Glossary

Accounting rate of return An investment appraisal technique that assesses the average accounting profit as a percentage of the investment. Also known as unadjusted rate of return and return on investment.

Agency costs Costs incurred when using an agent to act on behalf of the principal. In the business finance context, they can be incurred by shareholders by using managers to run the business on the shareholders' behalf.

Annuity A fixed payment, or receipt, arising on a continual annual basis.

Arbitrage pricing model A formula for deriving the expected return from a risky asset/investment. It only takes account of the systematic risk of the asset/investment, but has several risk premium measures.

Balance sheet A statement that lists the assets of a business, or other organisation, at some specified point in time, together with the claims against those assets.

Bankruptcy The colloquial name given to the forced liquidation of a business.

Beta (β) A measure of the level of systematic risk relating to a particular asset/investment. It relates to assets and portfolios of assets that are not efficient (in other words, they are exposed to specific risk).

Bonds Long-term loans made by a business. This is the word used in the USA; in the UK such loans tend to be referred to as 'loan stocks'.

Bonus issue An issue, usually of ordinary shares, to existing shareholders without any payment being involved.

Business angels Financiers (usually private individuals) who provide finance for small businesses and, usually, commercial advice as well.

Business risk Risk that arises from the trading activities of the business. It excludes financial risk, which arises from financial (capital) gearing.

Buy-in A divestment device where a group of individuals not previously connected with a business, buys the business from the owners.

Capital allowances The equivalent to depreciation that is allowed by the UK tax authorities in computing the taxable profit.

Capital asset pricing model A formula for deriving the expected return from a risky asset/investment. It takes account only of the systematic risk of the asset/investment and has just one risk premium measure.

Capital gearing See Financial gearing.

Capital market line The straight line on a graph of return against risk (as measured by standard deviation) that runs from the risk-free rate tangentially to the efficient frontier and beyond.

Capital markets Markets in which new finance is raised by businesses and other organisations and in which 'second-hand' securities are traded.

Capital rationing A situation that exists when there are insufficient funds available to undertake all beneficial investment opportunities faced by a particular business.

Cash flow statement A financial statement that sets out the amount and sources of cash received by a business, or other organisation, for a period, and the cash payments made during that period.

Clientele effect A tendency for certain shareholders to be attracted to the shares of a particular business because of some feature of that business, for example its dividend policy.

Coefficient of correlation A statistical measure of the extent to which the value of one variable is linked to that of another variable.

Combined Code A code of practice for businesses listed on the London Stock Exchange that deals with corporate governance matters.

Consumption Spending funds on current needs and wants, as opposed to investment.

Convertible loan stock A loan stock that is convertible into ordinary shares at some stage.

Corporate governance Systems for directing and controlling a business.

Cost of capital The cost of servicing the various sources of finance. It serves as the appropriate discount rate for assessing investment decisions.

Coupon rate The rate of interest, based on the nominal or par value, that an organisation is contracted to pay on its loan stocks.

Covariance A statistical measure of the extent to which a change in the value of one variable is linked to that of another variable.

Covenants (on loans) Restrictions imposed by lenders, as part of the lending contract, on the freedom of action of borrowers: for example, restricting the total amount of dividend that may be paid each year.

Creative accounting Adopting accounting policies to achieve a particular view of performance and position that preparers of financial statements would like users of those statements to see rather than what is a true and fair view.

Cum dividend During the period (that is, most of the time) that a share is quoted as cum dividend, a buyer of the share will be entitled to receive all of any future dividends, for as long as that buyer holds the share.

Currency futures Forward contracts, made in standardised amounts for delivery on standardised dates, so that they may be bought and sold.

Currency options A right but not an obligation to buy or sell a stated quantity of foreign currency at a stated exchange rate, on a stated date.

Currency swaps An arrangement where two businesses, each with an obligation in a foreign currency, but in the opposite foreign currency, agree to take on the other business's obligation.

Debentures A type of long-term loan.

Derivatives Assets or obligations whose value is dependent on some asset from which they are derived; for example, an option.

Diversification Investing in more than one asset, real or financial, such that the assets' returns are not perfectly positively correlated, leading to risk reduction.

Divestment Selling off some asset or group of assets, the opposite of investment.

Economic risk (exchange rate) The risk to any business that arises from the fact that transactions are carried out, by that business and/or by others in foreign currencies.

Economic value added A measure of economic, as opposed to accounting, profit. It is said to be more useful than accounting profit as a measure of business performance because it overcomes some weaknesses of accounting in this context.

Efficiency (portfolio) A portfolio is said to be efficient when all of the specific risk has been diversified away.

Efficiency (pricing) A state of affairs that exists when security prices fully, rationally and at all times reflect all that is known about businesses and their environment.

Efficient frontier A curve on a graph of return against risk that shows the return/risk profiles of all of the various efficient portfolios that it is theoretically possible to create.

Equities See Ordinary shares.

Eurobonds Unsecured loan stocks denominated in a currency other than the home currency of the borrowing business.

Ex dividend During the period (usually only a small part of the time) that a share is quoted as ex dividend, a buyer of the share will not be entitled to receive the immediately forthcoming dividend from that share.

Exchange rate risk The risk that foreign exchange rates between currencies will shift to the disadvantage of a particular business.

Expected value A weighted average of the possible values of the outcomes, where the probabilities of each of the outcomes are used as weights.

Finance lease An arrangement where a financial institution buys an asset needed by a potential user and then leases that asset to the user for the whole of the asset's effective life.

Financial assets Shares, loan stocks and the like, as opposed to real productive assets.

Financial gearing The existence of loans and preference shares in the long-term financing of a business. Also known as capital gearing.

Financial risk That part of the total risk to shareholders' returns that arises from the method of financing the business. The more highly capital (financially) geared, the higher the level of financial risk.

Fisher effect A theoretical explanation of relative foreign currency exchange rates. It maintains that the exchange rate between two currencies will adjust in the light of different rates of interest on deposits, between the two currency areas, to ensure that there is the same equivalent rate of interest.

Fixed interest rate loans Loans, where the contract specifies a fixed interest rate throughout the period of the contract.

Floating interest rate loans Loans, where the contract specifies that the interest rate should vary, usually with the general level of interest rates in the economy.

Forward (foreign exchange) contract A contract to exchange two currencies where the contract (including the exchange rate being stated) takes immediate effect, but where the currencies are to be delivered at a later date.

Forward (foreign exchange) rate The rate of exchange between two currencies where the foreign exchange transaction is to be contracted immediately, but delivery of the currency will not take place until a later date.

Free cash flows The cash flows generated by the business that are available to the ordinary shareholders and long-term lenders. This is the net cash flow from operating activities, less tax and funds laid out on additional non-current (fixed) assets.

Hard capital rationing This arises where a business's capital rationing is caused by an inability to raise the necessary funds, that is, it is a market-imposed constraint.

Income statement See Profit and loss account

Inflation The tendency for a currency to lose value over time, so that commodities cost more in terms of a particular currency as time passes.

Initial public offering A business's first offer of shares to the public, usually following its first listing on a recognised stock market.

Integer programming A technique for identifying the optimum use of scarce resources that identifies whole numbers of units of output.

Interest rate parity A theoretical explanation of relative foreign currency exchange rates. It maintains that where nominal interest rates differ from one currency area to another, the 'spot' and 'future' exchange rates will not be the same, but they will be linked by the difference in the interest rates.

Interest rate risk The risk, to both borrower and lender, that during the period of the fixed-interest loan contract the general level of interest rates may alter, to the disadvantage of one of the parties.

Interest rate swaps Arrangements where two businesses, each with borrowings, one at a fixed rate and the other at a floating rate, agree to take on the other business's obligation to pay interest.

Internal rate of return An investment appraisal technique that identifies the return on the investment, taking precise account of the amount of funds that are devoted to the investment and for what length of time.

International Fisher effect A theoretical explanation of relative foreign currency exchange rates. It maintains that the exchange rate between two currencies will adjust in the light of different rates of inflation and different interest rates to ensure that real interest rates will be equivalent in both currency areas.

Junk bonds Loan stocks, usually issued by businesses, that are rated below investment grade and broadly represent a risky and speculative investment.

Law of one price A theoretical explanation of relative foreign currency exchange rates. It maintains that the exchange rate between two currencies will ensure that the same product or service will have the same equivalent cost in both currency areas.

Linear programming A technique for identifying the optimum use of scarce resources.

Liquidation Selling off the assets of a business, paying off the claimants and closing the business down.

Loan stocks Long-term loans made by businesses.

Management buyout A divestment device where a group of managers working in a business, buy that business from the owners.

Market portfolio A portfolio that contains part of all possible investments that can be made in the world.

Merger See Takeover.

Money market hedge A device to protect against transaction risk, where foreign currencies are exchanged immediately and funds are either borrowed or lent during the period between the transaction and the date of receipt or payment of the foreign currency.

Money terms A cash flow and/or cost of capital expressed in money terms is increased due to inflation. Also known as nominal terms.

Net present value An investment appraisal technique that is based on the cash receipts and payments associated with a project, discounted according to how long each cash flow will occur in the future.

Nominal terms See Money terms.

Nominal value The face value of shares and loan stocks. Also known as par value.

Objective probabilities Probabilities based on information from past experience.

Operating cash cycle A measure of the length of time that elapses between paying trade creditors and receiving cash from trade debtors. It is used to assess the amount invested in working capital.

Operating gearing The extent to which the total cost of a business operation is fixed irrespective of the volume of activity, as opposed to varying with the level of activity.

Opportunity cost The cost incurred when pursuing one course of action prevents an opportunity to derive some benefit from an alternative course of action.

Option The right, but not the obligation, to buy or sell an asset at a predetermined price on a predetermined date, or range of dates.

Ordinary shares Shares of a business owned by those who are due the benefits of the business's activities after all obligations to other stakeholders have been satisfied. Also known as equities.

Outsourcing Having some activity, that could be undertaken by the business, subcontracted to an outside supplier.

Overtrading Operating at a level of activity that is beyond the level that a particular business's working capital can sustain.

Par value See Nominal value.

Payback period An investment appraisal technique that assesses how long it takes for the initial cash investment to be repaid from the cash receipts from the investment.

Pecking order theory The notion that businesses tend to favour new sources of finance in a hierarchy of desirability, with retained profit at the top and public equity issues at the bottom.

Portfolio A set of assets, real or financial, held by an investor.

Portfolio theory A set of principles relating risk and return for a portfolio, based on the risk/return profiles of the constituent portfolio assets.

Position analysis A step in the strategic planning process in which the business assesses its present position in the light of the commercial and economic environment in which it operates.

Post audit A review of the performance of an investment project to see whether actual performance matched planned performance and whether any lessons can be drawn from the way in which the investment was originally assessed or carried out.

Preference shares Shares of a business owned by those who are entitled to the first part of any dividend that the business might pay.

Primary capital market A market in which new finance is raised by businesses and other organisations.

Private capital Capital provided to smaller businesses by financiers such as venture capitalists and business angels.

Profit and loss account A statement that sets the total revenues (sales) for a period against the expenses matched with those revenues to derive a profit or loss for the period. Also known as the income statement.

Profitability index The net present value of an investment divided by the initial investment required.

Purchasing power parity A theoretical explanation of relative foreign currency exchange rates. It maintains that the exchange rate between two currencies will adjust in the light of different rates of inflation to ensure that the same product or service will have the same equivalent cost in both currency areas.

Real assets Business productive assets, as opposed to financial assets.

Real options Options that are based on business choices and their anticipated cash flows, rather than on values of individual assets.

Real terms A cash flow and/or cost of capital expressed in real terms ignores inflation, that is, it treats the rate of inflation as zero.

Return on investment See Accounting rate of return.

Rights issues Issues, usually of ordinary shares issued for cash, to existing shareholders, such that each shareholder has a right to subscribe for a number of new shares, whose quantity depends on how many ordinary shares are already held.

Risk The possibility that what is projected to occur may not actually occur.

Risk averse Being prepared to take a risk only where the expected value of the payoff is greater than the cost of entry to the project.

Risk-free asset Lending at the risk-free rate.

Risk-free rate The rate of interest that is obtainable from the risk-free asset, that is, a rate that contains no element of risk premium.

Risk loving Being prepared to take a risk even where the expected value of the payoff is less than the cost of entry to the project, provided that at least one possible outcome has a value greater than the cost of entry.

Risk neutral Being prepared to take a risk where the expected value of the payoff is equal to the cost of entry to the project.

Sale and leaseback An arrangement where the owner and user of an asset sells it to a financial institution subsequently to lease it back for the remainder of its effective life. It is a means of raising finance.

Satisficing A business objective that seeks to provide all stakeholders with satisfactory returns, rather than promoting the interests of any single one of them.

Scenario building A decision-analysis tool where various feasible combinations of input data are combined in an attempt to assess possible outcomes. In effect, an extension of sensitivity analysis.

Scrip dividend The issue of bonus shares to certain shareholders as an alternative to a cash dividend. The expression usually applies only where there is a choice for the shareholders between the shares and cash.

Seasoned equity offering A public issue of shares by a business that has already made at least one previous offering of shares to the public.

Secondary capital market A market in which 'second-hand' securities issued by businesses (for example, shares) and other organisations are traded.

Secured creditors A person or organisation owed money under a contract that links the obligation with a particular asset of the borrower.

Securities Shares and loan stocks of businesses and other organisations.

Security market line The straight line on a graph of return against risk (as measured by beta).

Sell-offs Divestment devices where one business sells part of its undertaking to another business.

Semi-strong-form capital market efficiency A situation where security prices, at all times, rationally reflect all publicly known information about the securities concerned.

Sensitivity analysis An examination of the key variables affecting a project, to see how changes in each input might influence the outcome.

Separation theorem The notion that business financing and investment decisions are strictly separate.

Servicing (of finance) The cost of providing returns to suppliers of finance (for example, interest and dividends).

Share repurchase Where a business buys some of its own shares from existing shareholders, usually to cancel them.

Shareholder value analysis A method of measuring and managing business value based on the long-term cash flows generated. It identified various factors that are seen as the key 'value drivers'.

Short termism A tendency for managers to make decisions that will provide benefits in the short term, while possibly jeopardising the long-term future of the business.

Signalling A business indicating, through its behaviour (such as having a particular level of capital gearing or paying a particular level of dividend), something about itself to the outside world.

Soft capital rationing This arises where a business's capital rationing is caused by a self-imposed unwillingness to provide funds to meet all desirable potential investments.

Specific risk That aspect of total risk that arises from factors that are related to the particular investment concerned as opposed to general/macroeconomic factors. It can, in theory, be eliminated by diversification of investments.

Spin-off Where a business takes part of its operations and turns it into a separate business. Shareholders of the old business are issued with shares in the new business in proportion to the size of their investment in the old business.

Spot (foreign exchange) rate The rate of exchange between two currencies where the foreign exchange transaction is to be completed immediately.

Standard deviation A statistical measure of the dispersion of individual outcomes about their mean or expected value; it is the square root of the variance.

Strategic planning The act of establishing the best area of activity and style of approach for the business.

Strong-form capital market efficiency A situation where security prices, at all times, rationally reflect all publicly and privately known information about the securities concerned.

Subjective probabilities Probabilities based on opinion rather than past data.

SWOT analysis A framework in which many businesses set a position analysis. Here the business lists its strengths, weaknesses, opportunities and threats.

Synergy The name given to the phenomenon that when two or more businesses combine, the combined business is more effective and valuable than the sum of the constituent businesses.

Systematic risk That aspect of total risk that arises from general/macroeconomic factors as opposed to factors that are related to the particular investment concerned.

Takeover A business amalgamation where one business buys sufficient shares in another business to control it. Also known as merger.

Tax shield The value of the asset of the tax benefit of using loans in the long-term finance of the business.

Technical analysis The use of technical rules and charts of past security price movements to spot profitable investment opportunities.

Term loans Loans, typically from a bank or similar institution, usually for a specified period of time.

Trade-off theory A theory of capital/financial gearing that holds that determining the optimum level of gearing requires that a balance is struck between the value of the tax shield, on the one hand, and potential bankruptcy cost, on the other.

Transaction risk The risk that buying or selling a product or service, priced in a foreign currency, will lead to losses because of an adverse shift in exchange rates between the time of the transaction and the payment or receipt of the foreign currency.

Translation risk The risk that the value of assets held overseas may reduce, in terms of the home currency, as a result of an adverse shift in the exchange rate.

Two-fund separation The notion that all rational risk-averse investors will choose to invest only in a risk-free investment and the market portfolio.

Unadjusted rate of return See Accounting rate of return.

Unsecured creditors A person or organisation owed money under a contract that links the obligation with the general assets of the borrower, rather than with a particular one.

Utility Personal satisfaction from some desirable factor.

Value drivers The factors that are seen in shareholder value analysis as being key in generating shareholder value.

Variance A statistical measure of the dispersion of individual outcomes about their mean or expected value; it is the square of the standard deviation.

Venture capital Equity finance provided to support new, expanding and entrepreneurial businesses.

Warrants Options, granted by a business, that entitle the holder to subscribe for a specified quantity of (usually) ordinary shares, for a specified price, on or after a specified date.

Weak-form capital market efficiency A situation where security prices, at all times, reflect all information about the securities concerned implied by their past price movements.

Weighted average cost of capital The average cost of capital for a business, being the average of the costs of the various constituents of capital (such as shares and loan stocks), weighted by the market value of each constituent.

Working capital Short-term assets, net of short-term liabilities.

Z-score A measure of the potential for a business to survive rather than fail due to financial inadequacies.

Index